D0461835

UTAH

2nd Edition

**Where to Stay and Eat
for All Budgets**

**Must-See Sights
and Local Secrets**

Ratings You Can Trust

Fodor's Travel Publications   New York, Toronto, London, Sydney, Auckland
www.fodors.com

FODOR'S UTAH

Editor: Caroline Trefler

Editorial Production: David Downing
Editorial Contributors: John Blodgett, Kelley J.P. Lindberg, Denise Leto, Janet Lowe, Dana Doherty Menlove, Mark Menlove
Maps: David Lindroth, Inc. and Ed Jacobus, *cartographers*; Bob Blake and Rebecca Baer, *map editors*
Design: Fabrizio La Rocca, *creative director*; Guido Caroti, *art director*; Melanie Marin, *senior picture editor*
Production/Manufacturing: Robert B. Shields
Cover Photo (Queen's Garden Trail, Bryce Canyon N.P.): George H. H. Huey/Corbis

COPYRIGHT

Copyright © 2006 by Fodors Travel, a division of Random House, Inc.

Fodor's is a registered trademark of Random House, Inc.

All rights reserved under International and Pan-American Copyright Conventions. Published in the United States by Fodor's Travel, a division of Random House, Inc., and simultaneously in Canada by Random House of Canada Limited, Toronto. Distributed by Random House, Inc., New York.

No maps, illustrations, or other portions of this book may be reproduced in any form without written permission from the publisher.

Second Edition

ISBN: 1–4000–1653–3

ISBN–13: 978–1–4000–1653–2

ISSN: 1547–870X

SPECIAL SALES

This book is available at special discounts for bulk purchases for sales promotions or premiums. Special editions, including personalized covers, excerpts of existing guides, and corporate imprints, can be created in large quantities for special needs. For more information, write to Special Markets Premium Sales MD 6-2, 1745 Broadway, New York, NY 10019 or e-mail specialmarkets@randomhouse.com.

AN IMPORTANT TIP & AN INVITATION

Although all prices, opening times, and other details in this book are based on information supplied to us at press time, changes occur all the time in the travel world, and Fodor's cannot accept responsibility for facts that become outdated or for inadvertent errors or omissions. So **always confirm information when it matters,** especially if you're making a detour to visit a specific place. Your experiences—positive and negative—matter to us. If we have missed or misstated something, **please write to us.** We follow up on all suggestions. Contact the Utah editor at editors@fodors.com or c/o Fodor's at 1745 Broadway, New York, NY 10019.

PRINTED IN THE UNITED STATES OF AMERICA

10 9 8 7 6 5 4 3 2 1

Be a Fodor's Correspondent

Your opinion matters. It matters to us. It matters to your fellow Fodor's travelers, too. And we'd like to hear it. In fact, we *need* to hear it.

When you share your experiences and opinions, you become an active member of the Fodor's community. That means we'll not only use your feedback to make our books better, but we'll publish your names and comments whenever possible. Throughout our guides, look for "Word of Mouth," excerpts of your unvarnished feedback.

Here's how you can help improve Fodor's for all of us.

Tell us when we're right. We rely on local writers to give you an insider's perspective. But our writers and staff editors—who are the best in the business—depend on you. Your positive feedback is a vote to renew our recommendations for the next edition.

Tell us when we're wrong. We're proud that we update most of our guides every year. But we're not perfect. Things change. Hotels cut services. Museums change hours. Charming cafés lose charm. If our writer didn't quite capture the essence of a place, tell us how you'd do it differently. If any of our descriptions are inaccurate or inadequate, we'll incorporate your changes in the next edition and will correct factual errors at fodors.com *immediately.*

Tell us what to include. You probably have had fantastic travel experiences that aren't yet in Fodor's. Why not share them with a community of like-minded travelers? Maybe you chanced upon a beach or bistro or B&B that you don't want to keep to yourself. Tell us why we should include it. And share your discoveries and experiences with everyone directly at fodors.com. Your input may lead us to add a new listing or highlight a place we cover with a "Highly Recommended" star or with our highest rating, "Fodor's Choice."

Give us your opinion instantly at our feedback center at www.fodors.com/feedback. You may also e-mail editors@fodors.com with the subject line "Utah Editor." Or send your nominations, comments, and complaints by mail to Utah Editor, Fodor's, 1745 Broadway, New York, NY 10019.

You and travelers like you are the heart of the Fodor's community. Make our community richer by sharing your experiences. Be a Fodor's correspondent.

Happy traveling!

Tim Jarrell, Publisher

CONTENTS

MAPS AND CHARTS

CLOSEUPS

ABOUT THIS BOOK

Our Ratings

Sometimes you find terrific travel experiences and sometimes they just find you. But usually the burden is on you to select the right combination of experiences. That's where our ratings come in.

As travelers we've all discovered a place so wonderful that its worthiness is obvious. And sometimes that place is so unique that superlatives don't do it justice: you just have to be there to know. These sights, properties, and experiences get our highest rating, **Fodor's Choice,** indicated by orange stars throughout this book.

Black stars highlight sights and properties we deem **Highly Recommended,** places that our writers, editors, and readers praise again and again for consistency and excellence.

By default, there's another category: any place we include in this book is by definition worth your time, unless we say otherwise. And we will.

Disagree with any of our choices? Care to nominate a place or suggest that we rate one more highly? Visit our feedback center at www.fodors.com/feedback.

Budget Well

Hotel and restaurant price categories from ¢ to $$$$ are defined in the opening pages of each chapter. For attractions, we always give standard adult admission fees; reductions are usually available for children, students, and senior citizens. Want to pay with plastic? **AE, D, DC, MC, V** following restaurant and hotel listings indicate whether American Express, Discover, Diner's Club, MasterCard, and Visa are accepted.

Restaurants

Unless we state otherwise, restaurants are open for lunch and dinner daily. We mention dress only when there's a specific requirement and reservations only when they're essential or not accepted—it's always best to book ahead.

Hotels

Hotels have private bath, phone, TV, and air-conditioning and operate on the European Plan (aka EP, meaning without meals), unless we specify that they use the Continental Plan (CP, with a continental breakfast), Breakfast Plan (BP, with a full breakfast), or Modified American Plan (MAP, with breakfast and dinner) or are all-inclusive (including all meals and most activities). We always list facilities but not whether you'll be charged an extra fee to use them, so when pricing accommodations, find out what's included.

Many Listings

★ Fodor's Choice
★ Highly recommended
⊠ Physical address
✛ Directions
⌖ Mailing address
☎ Telephone
🖷 Fax
⊕ On the Web
✑ E-mail
💷 Admission fee
☉ Open/closed times
▶ Start of walk/itinerary
Ⓜ Metro stations
⊟ Credit cards

Hotels & Restaurants

🛏 Hotel
🛌 Number of rooms
♿ Facilities
🍽 Meal plans
✕ Restaurant
🕱 Reservations
🏛 Dress code
➘ Smoking
🍸 BYOB
✕🛏 Hotel with restaurant that warrants a visit

Outdoors

⛳ Golf
⛺ Camping

Other

☺ Family-friendly
🎦 Contact information
⇨ See also
⊠ Branch address
☞ Take note

WHAT'S WHERE

SALT LAKE CITY	Utah's capital city is cradled between the foothills of the Wasatch Range to the east and the Ochre Mountains and Great Salt Lake to the west. Since it's home to the state's only major airport, most visits to Utah begin here. Salt Lake City is in the middle of the Wasatch Front—Utah's urban corridor—which is home to about 80% of the state's population and stretches 175 mi from Brigham City in the north to Payson in the south. Interstate 15 runs north and south along the Wasatch Front and is the major route from Utah to Las Vegas and Los Angeles, encouraging commerce along its sweep. The world headquarters of the conservative Church of Jesus Christ of Latter-day Saints (you can hardly visit Salt Lake City without at least passing by Temple Square), Salt Lake City is surprisingly cosmopolitan, with the state's most diverse—and most politically liberal—population. Contrary to what you might have heard, Salt Lake City has a thriving nightlife scene and yes, you can get a drink. There's an active arts community and no dearth of good restaurants. And if you're a spectating sports enthusiast you'll have no problem finding a game: Salt Lake City is home to major basketball, hockey, baseball, and soccer clubs. Utah's largest newspapers and television stations originate here, and a significant feather in this city's cap was its terrific success as host to the world during the 2002 Winter Olympics.
PARK CITY & THE SOUTH WASATCH	The Wasatch Mountains form a rugged divider spanning the center of the state for 160 mi from north to south, providing spectacular staging ground for some of the finest ski resorts in the country, if not the world. With exceptional Wasatch Mountain terrain, the lightest, driest, deepest powder around, the ski resorts of the southern Wasatch in and around Park City please even the most discriminating skiers and snowboarders. And, surprise-surprise, it's not just about the snow: this part of Utah is home to world-class fly-fishing streams, a variety of challenging golf courses, and loads of high adventure in the backcountry. And after all that recreating, you can enjoy a drink in a chichi club, move on to a yummy supper, and then, if you don't feel like going home to the hot tub just yet, you can cut loose with some live music on Main Street. Park City's rep of being Utah's "Sin City" is inextricably tied to its past: it, along with the towns of Alta (where Alta and Snowbird are located) and Brighton (where Brighton and Solitude are located) were birthed by raucous mining camps and a significant vein

WHAT'S
WHERE

of that wild lifestyle continues to this day. In contrast the Heber City area is a classically Mormon pioneer-formed community, as is Provo, home to Brigham Young University. Recreation opportunities abound here, too, but the nightlife is decidedly toned-down.

NORTH OF SALT LAKE CITY

Northern Utah has striking scenery but far fewer tourists than the more popular regions to the south. Heading north from Salt Lake City along the Wasatch Front you pass a number of bedroom communities that fuse Odgen, the largest town in northern Utah, with the greater Salt Lake City area. North beyond Ogden, Utah is still rough and rugged country, not so unlike the way it was when the Transcontinental Railroad builders met in lonely Promontory to drive their celebratory golden spike and link the two coasts for the first time, in 1869. A large part of the region is within boundaries of the Wasatch-Cache National Forest, home to breathtaking landscapes and countless miles of mostly undiscovered trails. In the northeastern part of the state is Logan, home to both Utah State University and the Utah Festival Opera. Logan is also a reliable homebase for hiking, biking, boating, and skiing excursions. Northern Utah is not necessarily the place for urban culture, but if you want genuine small town charm you're likely to find a dose or two here. It doesn't get more down-home than the legendary fresh raspberry shakes made by locals in Bear Lake.

DINOSAURLAND & EASTERN UTAH

The Uinta Range of the Rocky Mountains is a land of craggy peaks whose foothills give way to the rural ranching country of the Uinta Basin, where fertile farm valleys and grazing lands mingle with red-rock deserts. The quickest access to the wild Uinta Mountains also happens to be highly scenic. Take the Mirror Lake Scenic Byway through canyons and over passes to Mirror Lake, an excellent base for hikes into the surrounding mountains. To the east, and named in 1869 by explorer John Wesley Powell for the way the sun reflects on the red rock, Flaming Gorge is indeed a sight to behold with the dramatic red rock mountains surrounding the reservoir. Visitors enjoy activities such as powerboating, waterskiing, camping, parasailing, rafting, swimming, and fishing from boat or shore for the lake's renowned trophy trout. Not unlike Powell, many folks today like to raft or canoe the Green River below the dam, famous also for its world-class trout fishing. And even if your children haven't already suggested a trip to the fascinating Dinosaur National Monument, consider it. You can't visit this neck of the woods without checking out the Dinosaur Quarry, where 1,500 dinosaur bones and replicas are on display. In addition to spending time at the exhibits and bookstore in the Dinosaur Quarry, many folks like to strike out on a self-guided walk or auto tour to orient themselves to the unique character of dinosaur habitat. Along the auto tour there are periodic stops for short nature trails that lead you to overlooks of this spectacular terrain. Another classic idea is to enjoy the area's scenic beauty from a boat on a one- to multiday river trip with one of the park's river concessionaires.

CAPITOL REEF NATIONAL PARK AND ENVIRONS

Formed by cataclysmic forces that have pushed and compressed the earth, Capitol Reef National Park is an otherworldly landscape with oversize, unique sandstone formations, some layered with plant and animal fossils. Though still pretty down-home by most standards, Loa, Teasdale, and Torrey have become hot spots for artists and a more progressive, cosmopolitan population. If there is a place outside of downtown Salt Lake City, Park City, and Moab where a traveler might find a hint of hip urban culture, this would be it. So, grab whatever suits you—espresso or a bottle of water—and head out to Cassidy Arch to watch the sun work shadows across the rocks. The quietude and sheer visual experience of Capitol Reef National Park will set to soothing even the weariest soul.

ZION, BRYCE & SOUTHWESTERN UTAH

St. George is a regional hub for shopping, dining, sporting, and cultural events, but the best reason to visit this part of the state is not related to anything man-made. If you want to get out of your car and venture onto one of the many and varied trails, and if 2,500-foot red-and-white sandstone cliffs and intensely narrow canyons impress you, this entire region could be your paradise. Hikes vary from easy saunters to strenuous treks, and the spectacular views and ecological diversity leave no one dissatisfied. But you don't have to be a hiker to get a good sense of why these places are so special: the roadways leading through Zion and Bryce National Parks provide ample viewing opportunities. This isn't the case with the mostly roadless, expansive Grand Staircase–Escalante National Monument. There are a few side roads off U.S. 89, the closest

WHAT'S WHERE

major road, that allow car travelers a peek into the stark, magnificent beauty of this landscape. Another way to view the high-layered cliffs and smooth, colorful formations is by boat from Lake Powell. It is no wonder natural beauty attracts artists, many of whose work you'll find for sale in galleries in Springville, the gateway community to Zion National Park.

MOAB & ARCHES AND CANYONLANDS NATIONAL PARKS

The vibrant red rock of the Colorado Plateau characterizes the southeastern part of Utah. With the discovery of Moab as a world-class mountain bike and river-running destination, the town has taken on something of a counter-culture feel. The people of southeastern Utah—whether or not they're native—are resilient and inventive, if not inherently artistic. They understand elemental aspects of water, wind, desert, and stone, and the need to carefully manage the landscape that sustains them, as evidenced in the region's two national parks, Arches and Canyonlands. On the state's southern edge, stretching into Arizona, Monument Valley's iconic spires and buttes enchant and energize. Mile after mile of sage-brush flats may suddenly drop away into deep and narrow slot canyons. Mesas stretch, level and unbroken, or stacked one next to the other like giant step stools. Snow-capped mountains rise like a verdant mirage above the desert. Whether you're hiking to Delicate Arch, driving through Canyonlands, boating the Colorado River, or testing your skills mountain biking the nearby slickrock trail system, this landscape will grab hold of you in ways that you won't want to forget.

IF YOU LIKE

Hiking

Hiking is easily the least expensive and most accessible recreational pursuit. Sure, you could spend a few hundred dollars on high-tech hiking boots, a so-called "personal hydration system," and a collapsible walking staff made of space-age materials, but there's no need for such expenditure. All that's really essential are sturdy athletic shoes, water, and the desire to see the landscape under your own power.

Hiking in the Rockies is a three-season sport that basically lasts so long as you're willing to tromp through snow, though in the arid desert regions of Southern Utah and Southwestern Colorado it is possible to hike year-round without the need to attach snowshoes to your boots. (You could look at snowshoeing as winter hiking, for the trails are often the same.) One of the greatest aspects of this region is the wide range of hiking terrain, from high-alpine scrambles that require stamina, to flowered meadows that invite a relaxed pace, to confining slot canyons where flash floods are a real danger and can be fatal to the unwary adventurer.

There are few real hazards to hiking, but a little preparedness goes a long way. Know your limits, and make sure the terrain you are about to embark on does not exceed your abilities. It's a good idea to check the elevation change on a trail before you set out—a 1-mi trail might sound easy, until you realize how steep it is—and be careful not to get caught on exposed trails at elevation during afternoon thunderstorms in the summer. Dress appropriately, bringing layers to address changing weather conditions, and always carry enough drinking water. Also, make sure someone knows where you are going and when to expect your return.

Some of our favorite Utah hikes include:

Angels Landing Trail, Zion National Park. One of the park's most popular hikes also happens to be one of the most spectacular. Stop at Scout's Lookout for a breathtaking view. This isn't the trail to take, though, if you are afraid of heights.

Hickman Bridge Trail, Capitol Reef National Park. Just 2 mi long, this trail is a perfect introduction to Capital Reef. You'll walk past a great natural bridge as well as Fremont Indian ruins.

Horseshoe Canyon Trail, Canyonlands National Park: Every weekend from April through October, a park ranger guides hikers on this trail through one of the wilder section of Canyonlands. The highlight is one of the largest rock-art panels in North America.

The Narrows Trail, Zion National Park: When you take the trail through this narrow desert canyon, you're actually walking in the riverbed—and you might have to wade or even swim for part of the way—but you get to see parts of the park that are visible nowhere else.

Paria Canyon–Vermilion Cliffs Wilderness, Paria: The "Wave" may be the most sought-after hiking permit in all of Utah. These waves near Paria, in southwestern Utah, are made of sandstone, though.

Mount Timpanogas: One hour south of Salt Lake Valley, "Timp" is one of the tallest and most striking of the Wasatch Mountains. Trails rate moderate to difficult.

IF YOU LIKE

Biking

The Rockies are a favorite destination for bikers. Wide-open roads with great gains and losses in elevation test (and form) the stamina for road cyclists, while riders who prefer pedaling fat tires have plenty of mountain and desert trails to test their skills. Unmatched views often make it difficult to keep your eyes on the road.

Thanks to the popularity of the sport here, it's usually easy to find a place that rents bicycles if you'd prefer to leave yours at home. Shops often rent a variety of bikes from entry-level to high-end, though the latter come at a premium, and if you're in the market for a used bike, good deals can often be found when shops unload one season's rentals to make room for next year's models. Bike shops are also a good bet for information on local rides and group tours.

The rules of the road are the same here as elsewhere, though some areas are less biker-friendly than others. On the road, watch for trucks and stay as close as possible to the side of the road, in single file. On the trail, ride within your limits and keep your eyes peeled for hikers and horses (both of which have the right of way), as well as dogs. Always wear a helmet and carry plenty of water.

Some of our favorite areas in Utah for moutain biking include:

Flaming Gorge National Recreation Area: Because it mixes high-desert vegetation—blooming sage, rabbit brush, cactus, and wildflowers—and red rock terrain with a cool climate, Flaming Gorge is an ideal destination for road and trail biking. The 3-mi round-trip Bear Canyon–Bootleg ride begins south of the dam off U.S. 191 at the Firefighters' Memorial Campground and runs west to an overview of the reservoir.

Bonneville Shoreline Trail: Partway up and along the Wasatch Front on the Northeast side of Salt Lake City, this trail offers expansive views of the entire Salt Lake Valley, plus points west and south. Easy to moderate in difficulty, with challenging stretches near the University of Utah Hospital.

Antelope Island State Park: It's cheaper to enter Antelope on two wheels, and much more enjoyable. After crossing the 7-mi causeway, there are miles of rolling and empty trails to choose from. Watch out for bison and people on horseback.

Klondike Bluffs Trail, Moab: Though the trailhead is about 15 miles north of Moab, this trail offers the less-experienced mountain biker a relatively easy introduction to why the Moab area is esteemed with off-road cyclists. The climb to Klondike Bluffs is not difficult, and the reward is a fantastic view into Arches National Park. And how many bike rides can boast dinosaur footprints?

Skiing/Snowboarding

Utah's Greatest Snow on Earth can be a revelation for skiers and snowboarders familiar only with the slopes of other regions. Forget treacherous sheets of rock-hard ice, single-note hills where the bottom can be seen from the top, and mountains that offer only one kind of terrain from every angle. In the Utah the snow builds up quickly, leaving a solid base at each resort that hangs tough all season, only to be layered upon by thick, fluffy powder that holds an edge, ready to be groomed into rippling corduroy or left in giddy stashes along the sides and through the trees. Moguls and half-pipe-studded terrain parks are the norm, not the special attractions, at Utah resorts.

Skiing Utah means preparing for all kinds of weather, sometimes in the same day, because the high altitudes can start a day off sunny and bright but kick in a blizzard by afternoon. Layers help, as well as plenty of polypropylene to wick away sweat in the sun and a water-resistant outer layer to keep off the powdery wetness that's sure to accumulate, especially if you're a beginner snowboarder certain to spend time on the ground. Must-haves: Plenty of sunscreen, because the sun is closer than you think, and a helmet, because so are the trees.

The added bonus of Utah terrain is that there's something for everyone—often in the same ski resort, since so many of the areas have a wide variety of beginner, intermediate, advanced and expert slopes. Turn yourself over to the rental shops, which are specialized enough at each resort to offer experts in helping you plan your day and the types of equipment you'll need.

Some of our favorite places in Utah to ski and snowboard include:

Alta Ski Resort/Snowbird Resort: These Little Cottonwood Canyon neighbors, within 40 minutes of downtown Salt Lake City, are regularly ranked the top ski resorts in the United States. Seasons with 500 to 600 and more inches of Utah's famous powder are at the root of the accolades. The AltaSnowbird pass lets you ski both mountains on one ticket, but snowboarders take heed: you're still not allowed at Alta.

Brian Head Ski Resort, Brian Head: The closest Utah ski resort to the Las Vegas airport, it's worth checking out for the novelty of skiing in Southern Utah. The red-orange rock formations of nearby Cedar Breaks National Monument form a backdrop to many trails, which tend to focus on beginner and intermediate skiers and snowboarders. Experts can ski off the 11,000 foot summit.

Utah Olympic Park, Park City: At the site of the 2002 Olympic bobsled, luge, and ski-jumping events, you can take recreational ski-jumping lessons or strap in behind a professional driver for a bobsled ride down the actual Olympic course.

Deer Valley, Park City: This posh resort is known for its groomers, fine dining, and accommodations: the skiing is excellent, but for many it's the whole experience—including the midday feast at Silver Lake Lodge and suntanning on the snow-covered meadow—that keeps them coming back.

IF YOU LIKE

Rafting

Rafting combines a sea of emotions ranging from the calming affects of flat waters surrounded by stunning scenery and backcountry beauty and wildlife to the thrill and excitement of charging a raging torrent of foam.

For the inexperienced, the young and the aged, dozens of tour companies throughout the West offer relatively mundane floats ranging from one hour to one day, starting at just $20, that are ideal for anyone from 4 years old to 90. Others fulfill the needs of adventure tourists content only with chills, potential spills and the occasional wall of water striking them smackdab in the chest.

Seasoned outfitters know their routes and their waters as well as you know the road between home and work. Beginners and novices are encouraged to use guides, while the more experienced rafters may rent watercraft. Many guides offer multi-day trips in which they do everything, including searing your steak in a beach barbecue, setting up your tent and rolling out your sleeping bag.

If you go, wear a swimsuit or shorts and sandals and bring along sunscreen and sunglasses. Outfitters are required to supply a life jacket for each passenger, although most states don't require that it be worn. Mid-summer is the ideal time to raft in the West, although many outfitters will stretch the season, particularly on calmer routes.

Select an outfitter based on recommendations from the local chamber, experience, websites and word of mouth. The International Scale of River Difficulty is a widely accepted rating system that ranges from Class I (the easiest) to Class VI (the most difficult—think Niagara Falls). When in doubt, ask your guide about the rating on your route before you book. Remember, ratings can vary greatly throughout the season due to run-off and weather events.

Numerous outfitters and guide services offer rafting trips in Utah, and the journey can vary from relaxing family outings to white-knuckled runs through raging waters. In all cases, you'll discover scenery, wildlife and an off-the-road experience that you'll never get looking through a windshield.

Some of our favorite spots for rafting in Utah include:

Colorado River, Moab: The Grand Poobah of river rafting in Utah. There are numerous outfitters in the Moab area with a wide assortment of half-, full-, and multi-day trips of the river. Even in periods of low water, such as recent drought years, the infamous Cataract Canyon section still provides plenty of thrills and spills.

Green River: Before it meets up with the Colorado River in Canyonlands National Park, the Green River offers plenty of stunning scenery and fast water through canyons such as Desolation and Gray. Sign on with an outfitter in the town of Green River, about 45 minutes north and west of Moab.

Horseback Riding

Horseback riding options in Utah run the gamut, from hour-long rides on a well-worn trail to multi-day excursions out into the wilderness. A short trek is a great way to get acquainted with landscape—and with horseback riding if you're a beginner. Longer horse-pack trips are great ways to visit the backcountry, since horses can travel distances and carry supplies that would be impossible for hikers. Although horsemanship isn't required for most trips, it is helpful, and even an experienced rider can expect to be a little sore for the first few days. June through August is the peak period for horse-packing trips; before signing up with an outfitter, inquire about the skills they expect.

Since this is the West, jeans and cowboy boots are still the preferred attire for horseback, although hiking boots and Gore-Tex have long since become fashionable, especially in colder months and at higher altitudes. Long pants are a must either way. And as with most Utah activies, layering is key; plan to have some kind of fleece or heavier outer layer no matter what time of year since the mountains will be cooler the higher you go. Generally, outfitters provide most or all of the gear you'll need for extended trips, including a pack animal to carry it all for you and plenty of food for the sometimes surprisingly lavish dinners that they whip up in the middle of nowhere.

You can also find ranch-like resorts in Utah, that offer a wide range of activities in addition to horseback riding, including fishing, four-wheeling, spa services, and cooking classes. For winter, many ranches also have added such snow-oriented amenities as sleigh rides, snowshoeing and cross-country skiing.

Some of our favorite places in Utah for horseback riding include:

Bryce Canyon National Park: The park's namesake claimed it was a "Hell of a place to lose a cow," but failed to say anything about how great a place it is to explore on horseback. Sign up for a guided tour at Ruby Red Canyon Horseback Rides near the park entrance. Orange-pink spires and hoodoos offer a ride unmatched anywhere else.

Capitol Reef National Park: Much of this park is accessible only by foot or horseback, which promises an experience of wide-open western spaces that harken back to the time of cowboys. Indeed, some of the trails may have been used by herdsman and Native Americans. Sandstone, canyons, mesa, buttes—they're all here. Sign up with Hondoo Rivers & Trails or Wild Hare Expeditions for an unforgettable experience.

Zion Ponderosa Ranch Resort: Located just east of Zion National Park at the site of a former pioneer logging camp, this multi-pursuit resort offers plenty of things to do after time spent in the saddle meandering along the multitude of pioneer-era trails. Horseback riding options run from beginner to experienced (and even include a cattle round-up), and when you're not in the saddle you can ride an ATV, rent a Harley Davidson motorcycle, or learn how to rappel and rock climb on the only man-made climbing wall in the Zion National Park area.

IF YOU LIKE

Fishing

Trout do not live in ugly places. And, so it is in the American West where you'll discover unbridled beauty, towering pines, rippling mountain streams and bottomless pools. It is here that blue-ribbon trout streams remain much as they were when Native American tribes, French fur trappers, and a few thousand faceless miners, muleskinners and sodbusters first placed a muddy footprint along their banks.

However, those early-day settlers had one advantage that you won't: time. If you're going to make best use of that limited vacation in which fishing is a preferred activity, you'll want to follow some basic observations.

Hire a guide. You could spend days locating a great fishing spot, learning the water currents and fish behavior, and determining what flies, lures or bait the fish are following. A good guide will cut through the clutter, get you into fish, and turn your excursion into an adventure complete with a full creel.

If you're comfortable with your fishing gear, bring it along, though most guides loan or rent equipment. Bring a rod and reel, waders, vest, hat, sunglasses, net, tackle, hemostats, and sunscreen. Always buy a fishing license.If you're not inclined to fork over the $250-plus that most quality guides charge per day for two fishermen and a boat, your best bet is a stop at a reputable fly shop. They'll shorten your learning curve, tell you where the fish are, what they're biting on, and whether you should be "skittering" your dry-fly on top of the water or "dead-drifting" a nymph.

Famed fisherman Lee Wolff wrote that "catching fish is a sport. Eating fish is not a sport." Consequently, you'll find most fishermen practicing "catch and release" in an effort to maintain productive fisheries and protect native species.

Seasonality is always a concern when fishing. Spring run-offs can cloud the waters. Summer droughts may reduce stream flows. Fall weather can be unpredictable in the West. But, as many fishing guides will attest, the best time to come and wet a line is whenever you can make it.

Some of our favorite places in Utah to fish include:

Provo River: One of Utah's world-class fly fishing rivers, the Provo is divided into three sections, starting in the High Uintas Wilderness about 90 minutes east of Salt Lake City and ending in Utah Lake in Provo. Brown and Rainbow trout are the big draw here, and Utah.com claims in some sections upward of 7,500 fish per square mile can be sought.

Lake Powell: Formed by the construction of Glen Canyon Dam, this popular recreational attraction in Southern Utah is home to a wide variety of fish, including striped, smallmouth and largemouth bass, bluegill and channel catfish. Ask the locals about night fishing for stripers.

Flaming Gorge: For some of the finest river fishing, try the Green River below Flaming Gorge Dam, where rainbow and brown trout are plentiful and big. Fed by cold water from the bottom of the lake, this stretch has been identified as one of the best trout fisheries in the world.

GREAT ITINERARY

HIGHLIGHTS OF UTAH

If you have a week to see Utah, this seven-day tour will show you much of what the state is best known for, including the site of a famous film festival, mountains 10,000 feet high and higher, wide-open desert plains, and three of the state's five national parks.

Most people use Salt Lake City as a starting-point for touring Utah due to the major airport here. If you have enough time, designate a day to look around at the beginning or end of your stay, but otherwise most people agree that the real sights are away from all things metropolitan.

Day 1: Salt Lake City & Park City

After a quick morning tour of downtown, stopping for beer-battered fish-and-chips at Squatters Pub Brewery or an authentic Italian sandwich at Tony Caputo's Deli, head toward Park City. Visit Olympic Park on the way into town, then check into one of Park City's hotels before exploring the shops of historic Main Street. Choosing from among the many fine restaurants here is a fun challenge, but we recommend the casual but elegant Italian-inspired dining at Grappa.

Day 2: Sundance

After a morning of golfing, skiing, or biking in Park City, drive to Robert Redford's Sundance Resort, visiting quaint and Swiss-scenic Midway along the way. The phenomenal views of 12,000-foot Mt. Timpanogas will fill your windshield for much of the drive. Dine at the resort's rustic but refined Tree Room restaurant, and stay for a very quiet and star-filled night in one of the cabins.

Note: dress warmly in the off-season; it gets chilly at these elevations.

Day 3: Capitol Reef National Park

Rise early for breakfast at Sundance so you can make Capital Reef National Park by lunch. The crowds are smaller here than at other national parks in the state, but the scenery is stunning and you went on vacation to get away from it all anyhow. Orchards in the small enclave of Fruita produce fruit in the late summer and early fall, and are close by ancient Indian rock art. Nearby Torrey is your best bet for lodging, and if it's open you must eat at the seasonal Cafe Diablo, one of Utah's finest Southwestern restaurants.

Note: buy a National Park pass for $50. It'll get you into all three national parks on your tour.

Day 4: Moab & Canyonlands NP

Drive northeast from Torrey back to I–70 eastbound, turning south on U.S. 191 for Moab, mecca to mountain bikers, river runners, and other outdoor enthusiasts. After checking into one of the many hotels along Main Street, grab a quick lunch then, drive back north along U.S. 191, and west on Route 313, to visit Dead Horse Point State Park and the Island in the Sky District of Canyonlands National Park. A good supper option is Eddie Mc-Stiff's.

Day 5: Moab

It's time to get active and outside. Choose from a half- or full-day tour of the Colorado River by raft, rent a mountain bike and ride the world-famous Slickrock Trail, or travel

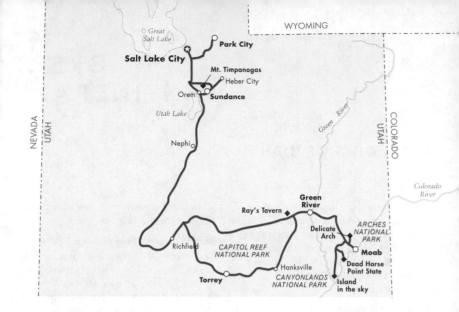

into the backcountry on a guided four-wheel-drive tour. Stay the night again in Moab.

Day 6: Arches National Park

After breakfast in the morning, drive the few minutes north to Arches National Park. There's enough to see here that you'll want to spend the day both driving and hiking. Make sure to hike to Delicate Arch, easily Utah's best-known natural attraction.

Day 7: Departure

In the morning, grab last-minute gifts along Main Street and then drive north along U.S. 191, turning east on the Colorado River Scenic Byway (Route 128), which takes you all the way to I–70. Head west to Green River and stop at Ray's Tavern for one of their famous burgers, and you won't need to stop to eat until you return to Salt Lake City in the evening.

TIPS

❶ U.S. 6, the most direct route from Southeastern Utah to Salt Lake City, is unfortunately one of the most accident-prone roads in the country, though improvements are being made. Drive with extreme caution and patience, especially through Price and Spanish Fork canyons.

❷ Don't despair if it starts to rain in Southern Utah; showers rarely last long, and they always seem to be followed by spectacular sunsets.

❸ Bring old sneakers or sandals to enjoy rafting or other water sports in the Moab area.

❹ Gas isn't difficult to find, but it's always smart to top off the tank whenever you can just in case.

GREAT ITINERARY

BRYCE & ZION NATIONAL PARKS

If you have just four days to visit Utah, this four-day tour packs a scenic wallop, offering up two of Utah's most popular national parks. Hint: fly into Las Vegas instead of Salt Lake City, and you'll save hours of driving.

Day 1: Arrival/Springdale

Arrival in Springdale, the bustling town right next to Zion National Park, is usually in the early afternoon or evening, depending on whether you fly into Las Vegas (smart move) or Salt Lake City. If you didn't make reservations ahead of time, the Best Western Zion Park Inn is your best bet for getting a room in the high season. Its Switchback Grille is excellent and open for breakfast, lunch, and dinner.

Day 2: Zion National Park

Ease into your exploration with a quick morning hike along the short and easy (read: family friendly) Canyon Overlook Trail, where you can gaze at the massive rock formations, such as East and West Temples, which define the park. It won't take very long, even if you linger with your camera, so follow it with a stroll along the Emerald Pools Trail in Zion Canyon itself, where you might come across tame wild turkeys and ravens looking for handouts. After lunch at the nearby Zion Lodge, the adventurous and fit (and fearless of exposed heights) can tackle the strenuous but stunning Angels Landing Trail; spend some time in the Zion Canyon Visitor Center and the Zion Human History Museum before eating Southwestern fare for dinner at the lively Bit & Spur.

Note: travel into Zion Canyon Scenic Drive is only allowed by National Park Service bus, which lets you watch the scenery instead of the road.

Day 3: Bryce Canyon National Park

Rise early and plan to spend some time in the car today, but at least the 90-minute drive to Bryce Canyon National Park area is beautiful. Central to your tour of the park is the 18-mi main park road, from which numerous scenic turnouts reveal vistas of bright red-orange rock (we recommend starting with the view at Sunrise Point). Trails most worth checking out include the Bristlecone Loop Trail and the Navajo Loop Trail, both of which you can easily fit into a day trip and will get you into the heart of the park with minimum effort. Listen for peregrine falcons deep in the side canyons, and keep an eye out for the species of prairie dog that only lives in these parts. Don't leave without checking out the sprawling Ruby's Inn complex, now owned by Best Western. The General Store has a post office, and across the street is a rodeo and helicopter flights.

Note: gas is not hard to find here, but fill up the rental car before you leave Springdale and buy snacks and water for the day.

Day 4: Zion National Park/Departure

Plan on an early-afternoon departure. After breakfast at the Switchback Grille, explore the shops and galleries of Springdale, and buy your souvenirs at Canyon Offerings. On the way out of town, check out the ghost town at Grafton before heading to the airport or your next destination.

WHEN TO GO

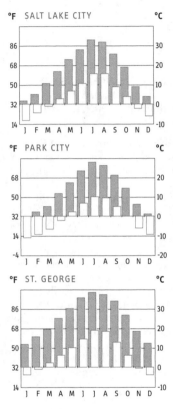

°F SALT LAKE CITY **°C**

°F PARK CITY **°C**

°F ST. GEORGE **°C**

Given the different elevations and climates in Utah, there's something to experience in Utah year-round, whether hiking the southern canyons in spring or fall, skiing in the mountains in winter, or golfing, biking, fishing, or swimming in summer. The national parks can become crowded in summer (and also hot). Early to mid-October is an ideal time to visit nearly any part of Utah, though the extreme high country can get chilly and even experience a surprise early snowstorm on occasion. Fall color displays can be found in nearly every canyon in the state. Cottonwood trees turning brilliant gold along river bottoms with a backdrop of red rock make particularly good photographs.

Climate

The Wasatch Front, including Salt Lake City, experiences four distinct seasons, and temperatures can vary wildly, reaching triple digits in summer and even falling below zero occasionally in winter. Valleys experience winter inversions, when hot air above traps fog and smog below for days. When this happens, head to the mountains where the skies will be blue and the temperatures warmer. Expect afternoon mountain thundershowers in the mountains, especially the High Uintas, in July and August.

Southern Utah's weather can be ideal any time of year, though heat in summer can be unpleasant. Spring break and Easter vacation bring some of the biggest crowds to places such as Moab, St. George, and Zion National Park. But always be prepared for the unpredictable. Be especially aware of the potential for flash floods in late summer in southern Utah parks, avoiding narrow canyons if there is any threat at all of a thunderstorm.

🔳 Forecasts **Weather Channel Connection** ⊕ www.weather. com.

ON THE CALENDAR

	Utah's top seasonal events are listed below, and any one of them provides the stuff of lasting memories. Contact local tourism authorities for exact dates and for more detailed information.
ONGOING June–Oct.	From late June through October, the **Utah Shakespearean Festival** ☎ 435/586–7880 ⊕ www.bard.org is held at Southern Utah University in Cedar City. Irish, English, and Scottish dancing, as well as puppet shows, lectures, and seminars, supplement the productions.
WINTER Dec.	Salt Lake City's biggest holiday show is the **Christmas Lights Ceremony** held at Temple Square on the Saturday before Thanksgiving. Lights remain on throughout the holidays.
Jan.	For 10 days each January, Park City morphs into a mountain version of Hollywood as movie stars and film executives gather for the internationally recognized **Sundance Film Festival** ⊕ www.sundance.org, hosted by Robert Redford's Sundance Institute. In addition to seminars, tributes, premieres, and screenings of independent films at various venues in Park City, Sundance, Ogden, and Salt Lake City, the festival's Music Café hosts daily and nightly performances by emerging and established feature musicians.
	Come to Deer Valley Ski Resort in Park City for the **Freestyle International World Cup** ☎ 800/424–3337 or 435/649–1000 ⊕ www.deervalley.com where aerial and mogul competitors fly, twist, jump, and bump on runs used in the Winter 2002 Olympics. Live music takes place on snow at the venue, but the real show is the final night's mogul competition under lights. A spectacular fireworks show rounds out the activities.
SPRING Mar.	Spring is an exceptional time of year to be in Moab, and the **Canyonlands Half Marathon** ☎ 435/259–4525 ⊕ www.moabhalfmarathon.org is one of the most popular races of its kind in the region, in large part due to the beauty of its rolling course along the Colorado River.
Apr.	Classic cars from all over the West descend on Hurricane in Southwestern Utah every March for the **Hurricane Rotary Easter Car Show** ☎ 435/635–3402 ⊕ www.hurricanevalley.org, which attracts about 7,000 people each year.
Apr.	Artisan booths, food, children's activities, and entertainment are all part of the **St. George Arts Festival** ☎ 435/634–5850 ⊕ www.ci.st-george.ut.us/artfestival, held Friday and Saturday of Easter weekend.

ON THE
CALENDAR

May	If you're lucky enough to be in Blanding in May, explore the world of Native American arts and crafts at the **Four Corners Indian Arts Festival** ☎ 435/678–2238 at Edge of the Cedars State Park. Traditional tribal music, dancing, and demonstrations of ancient Indian crafts such as flute making and katsina carving fill this two-day event. The festival draws the finest artists in the competition for the Native American Arts Awards.
	The Living Traditions Festival ☎ 801/596–5000 ⊕ www.slcgov.com/arts/livingtraditions in Salt Lake City celebrates traditional ethnic food, crafts, music, and dance in Washington Square during the third weekend in May.
	The **Moab Arts Festival** ☎ 435/259–2742 ⊕ www.moabartsfestival.org is held in May, when the Moab weather is at its finest. Artists from across the West gather at Swanny City Park to show their wares, including pottery, photography, and paintings. Live music and lots of food keep everyone happy.
	Thousands of marathon runners kick off the special events season the first weekend in May with the **Ogden Marathon** ☎ 801/816–2508 ⊕ www.ogdenmarathon.com, which starts in the Upper Ogden Valley and follows Ogden Canyon down to the center of Ogden City.
	Come to Logan in May for **Old Ephraim's Mountain Man Rendezvous** ☎ 435/770–2663 or 435/716–9123, a reenactment of an 1820s rendezvous. Held in the Left Hand Fork of Black Smith Fork Canyon, the celebration features participants dressed in period costumes, and lively games test hatchet, knife, and black-powder skills. It's one of the West's best mountain-man gatherings.
SUMMER June	Moab's **Butch Cassidy Days** ☎ 800/635–6622 ⊕ www.discovermoab.com in June offer traditional fun in honor of the Western outlaw tradition of southeastern Utah. There's a PRCA (Professional Rodeo Cowboys Association) rodeo, parade, shoot-outs, and other cowboy activities.
	Every June, Vernal celebrates its feisty past during the **Outlaw Trail Ride** ☎ 866/658–7433 ⊕ www.outlawtrailride.com. Guided horseback rides along outlaw trails, camping, cookouts, and Western-theme entertainment are among the main events.
	During each June's **Pony Express Re-Ride** ⊕ www.xphomestation.com, horseback riders in period costumes reenact the carrying of mail along Utah's section of the trail. The event is held at various places in the

	state along the old Utah Pony Express Trail, including Simpson Springs Station, 57 mi southwest of Tooele.
	During the bitter winter of 1864, Panguitch residents were freezing and starving. A group of men from the settlement set out over the mountains to fetch provisions from the town of Parowan, 40 mi away. When they hit waist-deep snow drifts they were forced to abandon their oxen. Legend says the men, frustrated and ready to turn back, laid a quilt on the snow and knelt to pray. Soon they realized the quilt had kept them from sinking into the snow. Spreading quilts before them as they walked, leapfrog style, the men traveled to Parowan and back, returning with lifesaving provisions. The three-day **Quilt Walk Festival** ☎ 866/590–4134 ⊕ www.panguitch.org commemorates the event with quilting classes, a tour of Panguitch's pioneer homes, crafts shows, and a dinner theater production in which the story is acted out.
June–July	The monthlong **Freedom Festival** ☎ 801/818–1776 ⊕ www.freedomfestival.org in Provo combines a series of patriotic activities and contests. The event peaks with a hot-air balloon festival and the state's biggest Independence Day parade. A gathering in 65,000-seat Cougar Stadium on the Brigham Young University campus closes the festival with live entertainment and a world-class fireworks display.
July	Don't get out your best black beret to attend the **Bicknell International Film Festival** ☎ 435/425–3123 ⊕ www.waynetheatre.com/biff.html in the small town of Bicknell near Capitol Reef National Park. It's a spoof on the serious film festivals that you read about—and for which you can't get tickets unless you live in Hollywood. This July festival centers around films of different genres each year. Past themes have included "Japanese Monster Movies," "Viva! Elvis," and "The B-er, The Better, The Best of BIFF." Each year's extravaganza begins with the world's fastest parade, a 60-mi-an-hour procession that starts in Torrey and ends in Bicknell. Included in the crazy events are a swap meet and mutton fry.
	The **Brian Head Bash Fat Tire Festival** ☎ 888/677–2810 celebrates mountain biking with guided bicycle tours, games for children, live entertainment, and nightly barbecues.
	Over July 4 weekend, the **Northern Ute Pow Wow** ☎ 435/722–8541 in Fort Duchesne has drumming, dancing, and singing competitions, a rodeo, golf and softball tournaments, and an arts-and-crafts fair. One of the biggest powwows in the West, it's free to the public, who are welcome to attend and camp on the grounds.

ON THE CALENDAR

		At the end of the month, the **Festival of the American West** ☎ 800/225–3378 ⊕ www.americanwestcenter.org is held at the American West Heritage Center in Cache Valley. The festival features Native American, mountain man, pioneer, and military reenactments and displays, historical lectures, and heritage workshops. Visitors also enjoy the Wild West Show as well as other performing and fine arts exhibits.
		Vernal plays host to what has been voted one of the top five PRCA rodeos in the world—the **PRCA Dinosaur Roundup Rodeo** ☎ 800/421–9635 ⊕ www.vernalrodeo.com at the Western Park Convention Arena. Four days of rodeo events, dances, and parades on Main Street heat up the summer and celebrate the real-life cowboys who wear cowboy boots because they're practical, not because they're fashionable.
	Aug.	The **Fidelity Investments Park City Jazz Festival** ☎ 435/940–1362 ⊕ www.parkcityjazz.com is a major summer event. Artists like George Benson, Stanley Clarke, Bela Fleck, and the Ramsey Lewis Trio have performed at this annual three-day festival dedicated to jazz. Daily workshops and clinics for jazz musicians are held, and the nightly performances feature various kinds of jazz groups and styles.
		Celebrating visual, culinary, and performance art, the **Park City Arts Festival** ☎ 435/649–8882 ⊕ www.kimball-art.org/artsfestival, held the first weekend in August, is the biggest summer event in the Wasatch region. More than 200 artists from all over North America exhibit and offer their work to 40,000 festival attendees. Live music, upscale food, and local microbrewery beers are featured.
		The **Railroaders Festival** ☎ 435/471–2209 takes place on the second Saturday in August at the Golden Spike National Historic Site in Promontory. Reenactments of the Transcontinental Railroad's completion ceremony, talks by railroad historians, and displays of functioning steam locomotives draw visitors to this festival.
		The great American county fair tradition is at its finest in Loa. Horse shows, turkey shoots, and the tilt-a-whirl are all standards at the August **Wayne County Fair** ☎ 435/836–2765, which also schedules a rodeo and a parade. Look at hand-made quilts and other crafts, see agricultural exhibits, play games, and eat plenty of good food while you spend a day at the fair.

		The nostalgic **Western Legends Roundup** ⊕ www.westernlegendsroundup.com is for anyone who loves authentic, old-time Western culture. For five days every August the small town of Kanab fills with cowboy poets and storytellers, musicians, Western arts-and-crafts vendors, and Native American dancers and weavers.
FALL Sept.		The **Dixie Roundup** ☎ 435/656–8998 rodeo has been a St. George tradition for decades. The novelty of the PRCA event is that it's held on the green grass of Sun Bowl stadium.
		Moab Music Festival ☎ 435/259–7003 ⊕ www.moabmusicfest.org welcomes classical musicians from all over the world to play music throughout canyon country. Concerts are staged in a dome set amid the red rock cliffs. The unique Colorado River Concert features a 45-minute boat ride downriver for a performance at the pristine natural grotto, carved over time by spring floods of the Colorado River. The acoustics have been compared to Carnegie Hall.
		Many of the Mormons who settled in Southwestern Utah in 1861 were converts from Switzerland, and the nearby small town of Santa Clara, northwest of St. George, celebrates this heritage the fourth weekend in September during the **Santa Clara Swiss Days** ☎ 435/673–6712 ⊕ www.santaclaracityutah.com, which includes crafts and food booths, games, a parade, and a tour of historic homes.
Oct.		One of the most popular marathons in the West, the **St. George Marathon** ☎ 435/634–5850 ⊕ www.stgeorgemarathon.com takes runners beneath extinct volcanoes and along the rim of Snow Canyon on the first Saturday of October.

FODOR'S CHOICE

The sights, restaurants, hotels, and other travel experiences on these pages are our editors' top picks—our Fodor's Choices. They're the best of their type in the area covered by the book—not to be missed and always worth your time. In the destination chapters that follow, you will find all the details.

LODGING	
$$$$	**Grand America,** Salt Lake City. Step into a world of Italian marble floors and walls, and pure old-world style. This is a great place to sit back with room service and revel in some pampering.
$$$$	**Green Valley Spa & Tennis Resort,** St. George. Small and luxurious, this is Utah's answer to Arizona's Canyon Ranch, a worthwhile stop whether you want a pampering spa trip or to improve your tennis game; it's also within easy striking distance of Zion National Park.
$$$$	**SkyRidge Bed and Breakfast,** Torrey. Once you've experienced the breakfast here, you'll need to explore some of the great scenery on view from every room of this first-rate B&B.
$$$$	**Sorrel River Ranch,** Moab. The most luxurious and comfortable spot to base yourself during a trip to Arches and Canyonlands is also a great outfitter for some adventurous trips in the region.
$$$$	**Stein Eriksen Lodge,** Deer Valley. Like the legendary Norwegian ski hero it's named after, this slope-side lodge is perfectly groomed, timelessly gracious, and incredibly charming.
$$$–$$$$	**Hotel Monaco Salt Lake City,** Salt Lake City. This swank hotel is sophisticated, eclectic, and upbeat. Rooms offer extras such as big fringed ottomans, oversize framed mirrors and beds, and lots of pillows.
$$$–$$$$	**Sundance Cottages,** Sundance Resort. The design and decor of the cottages reflect their woodland setting with rough-sawn beams, natural-wood trim, and richly textured, colorful fabrics.
$$$	**Falcon's Ledge Lodge,** Altamont. This little bit of luxury is in the far eastern part of the state, near Dinosaurland National Monument. It's also the top spot for dining in the region.
$–$$$	**Lodge at Red River Ranch,** Teasdale. A strong entry in the tradition of great Western lodges, this one will grab your attention with original Remington sculptures and a toy train around the top of the dining room.
$–$$	**Desert Pearl Inn,** Springdale. Just outside the entrance to Zion National Park, this contemporary inn is a delight to the senses. Tow-

	ering cliffs surround you and the Virgin River is only a few feet from your doorstep.
$–$$	**Dreamkeeper Inn**, Moab. Find serenity at this classy B&B that fills up fast with repeat visitors.
$–$$	**Old Town Guest House**, Park City. This country-style inn is warm and cozy, and an excellent place to make use of your hiking boots or ski boots.
$	**Sherwood Hills Resort**, Wellsville. This inexpensive mountain retreat comes with magnificent views and a first-rate restaurant.
¢–$	**Austin's Chuckwagon Lodge**, Torrey. If you're visiting Capitol Reef, this is your best bet. Even Zane Grey, who frequented the place, would have told you the same.
¢–$	**Desert Rose Inn & Cabins**, Bluff. This log-cabin motel is the biggest and best in Bluff, which is itself an overlooked gem in an isolated location.
¢	**Zanavoo**, Logan. The rooms at this nice but basic log-cabin lodge cost only around $50, but the views are worth a million. Plus, they bring breakfast to your door.
RESTAURANTS $$$–$$$$	**Cafe Diablo**, Torrey. You can't go wrong with the southwestern fare at this intimate restaurant, but if you're really adventurous, try the rattlesnake cakes.
$$$–$$$$	**Glitretind**, Deer Valley. Wood trim, crystal glasses, and fresh-cut flowers set the scene for creative dishes like tea-and Szechuan pepper-crusted duck breast. Every continent is represented among the 300-plus wine selections.
$$$–$$$$	**Tree Room**, Sundance Resort. With its rustic decor, exquisite collection of Native American art and Western memorabilia, the setting here is incredibly intimate.
$$$–$$$$	**Wahso**, Park City. Start your evening with a sake martini shaken tableside. Warmed finger towels, deep jade table settings, curtained booths, and attentive service recall the Jazz-era Orient.
$$–$$$$	**Log Haven**, Salt Lake City. Longtime chef David Jones put this elegant mountain retreat on the map with his inventive takes on American cuisine laced with everything from Asian ingredients to pure Rocky Mountain style.

FODOR'S
CHOICE

$$-$$$$	**Metropolitan,** Salt Lake City. From its inventive "handcrafted New American cuisine" to its minimalist design, this restaurant is chic in every way.
$$-$$$	**Bit & Spur Restaurant and Saloon,** Springdale. This Mexican restaurant has been a legend in Utah for 20 years, with a mix of old favorites like tacos and more contemporary and daring fare, too.
$-$$$	**Buck's Grill House,** Moab. Vegetarians and meat eaters alike will be licking their fingers at this popular dinner spot that features dishes from the American West as well as Southwestern options.
$-$$$	**Hell's Backbone Grill,** Boulder. The menu at the Boulder Mountain Lodge's great restaurant uses only organic, locally grown ingredients that are actually relevant to the area's history.
$	**Red Iguana,** Salt Lake City. It's a bit rough around the edges and located on a bleak thoroughfare, but this lively Mexican restaurant is staffed with a warm and accommodating crew, serving the best house-made moles and chili verde in town.
¢–$	**The Greek Streak,** Price. Who would have guessed that there's been a good Greek restaurant on this spot in Price since the turn of the 20th century? And it's cheap, too.
¢–$	**Idle Isle,** Brigham City. One of Utah's many great, hometown cafés has been in business since 1921 and has hardly changed—and we mean that in a good way.
¢	**Dairy Keen,** Heber City. A welcome respite from chain fast-food, this family-owned drive-in serves the best shakes and burgers for miles around.
HISTORY AND NATURE	**Bear River Migratory Bird Refuge,** Brigham City. This refuge north of the Great Salt Lake is one of the best places in the state to view migratory water birds.
	Bingham Canyon Copper Mine, Salt Lake City. This enormous open-pit mine measures nearly 2½ mi across and ¾ mi deep. You can view the mine from an overlook and visit exhibits and multimedia presentations that explain the site's history.
	Nine Mile Canyon, Price. The Fremont people have etched hundreds of petroglyphs into the cliff faces here, making it one of the most important archaeological sites in the eastern part of Utah.

	Salt Lake Temple, Salt Lake City. The Mormon Temple took 40 years to the day to complete. Though non-Mormon visitors are not allowed inside, the exterior is truly a sight to see.
	Union Station, Ogden. There's an abundance of diversions to be found in the five museums in this reconstruction of Ogden's original 1870s train depot. Whether your interest is firearms, railroads, antique cars, or natural history, this is a great place to spend a few hours.
	Western Mining and Railroad Museum, Helper. You'll learn a lot about how this particular corner of the West was won at this very good museum, perhaps the best local history museum in the state.
SUMMER SPORTS	**Boating,** Bear Lake. One of northern Utah's best boating destinations, Bear Lake and its turquoise waters can even get a bit chilly on a warm summer day. Be sure to have some of the famous Bear Lake raspberries when you're in the area.
	Fishing, Flaming Gorge National Recreation Area. The stretch of the Green River below Flaming Gorge Dam is one of your best bets if you want to do some fly-fishing in Utah; in fact, it's one of the best places in the West.
	Mountain Biking, Moab. Moab remains one of the best mountain-biking spots in the world. Better yet, dozens of top-notch outfitters are available to help you find the best tracks and even give instruction if you're a novice.
	River Expeditions, Moab. Southeastern Utah is one of the top white-water rafting destinations in the West, and the stretch through Cataract Canyon is among the best.
SCENIC DRIVES & VIEWS	**Colorado River Scenic Byway–Route 128,** Moab. One of the most scenic drives in the Southwest starts in Moab. You'll swear you've seen this landscape before—and you have. It's one of the most-photographed anywhere.
	Highway 12 Scenic Byway to Capitol Reef National, Escalante. From Escalante, a narrow hogback allows 360-degree views into the Grand Staircase–Escalante National Monument. Pine, spruce, and aspen line the climb toward Boulder Mountain that every now and then reveals a stunning vista across southern Utah.

FODOR'S CHOICE

Main Park Road, Bryce Canyon National Park. So much of the beauty of Bryce Canyon is visible even from a car, but the Martian-like landscape of the ruddy pinnacles and spires is especially beautiful when dusted with snow. The bristlecone pines along the amphitheaters' rims heighten the colors' effect.

Mirror Lake Scenic Byway, Eastern Utah. This road passes through the Wasatch National Forest in the heart of the Uinta Mountains, past meadows and small lakes, providing access for hikers and anglers in summer and cross-country skiers and snowmobilers in winter.

Utah Pony Express Trail, Fairfield. Utah has one of the best-preserved stretches of the original route of the Pony Express. On this drive across the barren Sevier Desert, you'll see old outposts and desert towns, left much as they were when the real riders saw them in the 19th century.

SMART TRAVEL TIPS

Finding out about your destination before you leave home means you won't spend time organizing everyday minutiae once you've arrived. You'll be more streetwise when you hit the ground as well, better prepared to explore the aspects of Utah that drew you here in the first place. The organizations in this section can provide information to supplement this guide; contact them for up-to-the-minute details, and consult the A to Z sections that end each chapter for facts on the various topics as they relate to the state's many regions. Happy landings!

ADDRESSES

Most Utah municipalities, including Salt Lake City, are based on a grid plan that was devised by Brigham Young in the 19th century. Most street names have a directional and a numerical designation, which describes their location in relation to one of two axes. Streets with "East" or "West" in their names are east or west of (and parallel to) Main Street, which runs north–south; while "North" and "South" streets run parallel to South Temple in Salt Lake City, and usually Center Street elsewhere. The numbers tell how far the streets are from the axes. (For example, 200 East Street is two blocks east of Main Street.) Addresses typically include two directional references and two numerical references—320 East 200 South Street, for instance, is in the east 300 block of 200 South Street.

AIR TRAVEL

Salt Lake City has a large international airport, so you'll be able to fly here from anywhere, though you may have to connect somewhere else first. The airport is a major hub for Delta Airlines and is also served by discount airlines, including Southwest and JetBlue, which often have incredibly good prices but not as many flights in and out. If you're flying in from somewhere other than the United States, you'll likely connect in Los Angeles or San Francisco if you're coming from Australia or New Zealand, or a major airport in the East, such as Detroit or New York, if you're traveling from Europe. Occasionally in winter you may be delayed by a major snowstorm, but those generally affect the mountain areas, not the airport. If you're heading to southern Utah, you will probably find it more convenient to fly into Las Vegas, which has more flights and is often a cheaper destination. Connecting flights to smaller airports throughout Utah are available most frequently from either Salt Lake or Las Vegas, though it's often just as easy (and cheaper) to drive. During ski season some of the major resort towns have increased service, and direct flights may be available.

BOOKING

When you book, look for nonstop flights and remember that "direct" flights stop at least once. Try to avoid connecting flights, which require a change of plane. Two airlines may operate a connecting flight jointly, so ask whether your airline operates every segment of the trip; you may find that the carrier you prefer flies you only part of the way. To find more booking tips and to check prices and make online flight reservations, log on to www. fodors.com.

CARRIERS

🔢 Major Airlines AeroMexico ☎ 800/237–6639 ⊕ www.aeromexico.com. American Airlines ☎ 800/433–7300 ⊕ www.aa.com. Continental ☎ 800/525–0280 ⊕ www.continental.com. Delta ☎ 800/221–1212 ⊕ www.delta.com. Northwest ☎ 800/225–2525 ⊕ www.nwa.com. United Airlines ☎ 800/241–6522 ⊕ www.united.com. 🔢 Smaller Airlines America West ☎ 800/235–9292 ⊕ www.americawest.com. Frontier ☎ 800/432–1359 ⊕ www.frontierairlines.com. JetBlue ☎ 800/538–2583 ⊕ www.jetblue.com. SkyWest ☎ 800/453–9417 ⊕ www.skywest.com. Southwest ☎ 800/435–9792 ⊕ www.southwest.com.

CHECK-IN AND BOARDING

Always **find out your carrier's check-in policy.** Plan to arrive at the airport about two hours before your scheduled departure time for domestic flights and 2½ to 3 hours before international flights. You may need to arrive earlier if you're flying from one of the busier airports or during peak air-traffic times.

If you're traveling during snow season, **allow extra time for the drive** to the airport, as weather conditions can slow you down. If you'll be checking skis, arrive even earlier. To avoid delays at airport-security checkpoints, try not to wear any metal. Jewelry, belt and other buckles, steel-toe shoes, barrettes, and underwire bras are among the items that can set off detectors.

Assuming that not everyone with a ticket will show up, airlines routinely overbook planes. When everyone does, airlines ask for volunteers to give up their seats. In return, these volunteers usually get a several-hundred-dollar flight voucher, which can be used toward the purchase of another ticket, and are rebooked on the next available flight out. If there are not enough volunteers, the airline must choose who will be denied boarding. The first to get bumped are passengers who checked in late and those flying on discounted tickets, so get to the gate and check in as early as possible, especially during peak periods.

Always **bring a government-issued photo ID** to the airport; even when it's not required, a passport is best.

CUTTING COSTS

The least expensive airfares to Utah are often priced for round-trip travel and must usually be purchased in advance. Airlines generally allow you to change your return date for a fee; most low-fare tickets, however, are nonrefundable. If you don't mind some driving, check into flying into Las Vegas rather than Salt Lake City, especially if you're traveling to southern Utah. Fares to Las Vegas are often cheaper. It's smart to call a number of airlines and check the Internet; when you are quoted a good price, book it on the spot—the same fare may not be available the next day, or even the next hour. Always check different routings and look into using alternate airports. Also, price off-peak flights and red-eye, which may be significantly less expensive than others. Travel agents, especially low-fare specialists (⇨ Discounts & Deals), are helpful.

Consolidators are another good source. They buy tickets for scheduled flights at reduced rates from the airlines, then sell them at prices that beat the best fare available directly from the airlines. (Many also offer reduced car-rental and hotel rates.) Sometimes you can even get your money back if you need to return the ticket. Carefully read the fine print detailing penalties for changes and cancellations, purchase the ticket with a credit card, and confirm your consolidator reservation with the airline.

When you fly as a courier, you trade your checked-luggage space for a ticket deeply subsidized by a courier service. There are restrictions on when you can book and how long you can stay. Some courier companies list with membership organizations, such as the Air Courier Association and the International Association of Air Travel Couriers; these require you to become a member before you can book a flight.

🛪 **Consolidators AirlineConsolidator.com** ☎ 888/468-5385 ⊕ www.airlineconsolidator.com, for international tickets. **Best Fares** ☎ 800/880-1234 ⊕ www.bestfares.com; $59.90 annual membership. **Cheap Tickets** ☎ 800/377-1000 or 800/652-4327 ⊕ www.cheaptickets.com. **Expedia** ☎ 800/397-3342 or 404/728-8787 ⊕ www.expedia.com. **Hotwire** ☎ 866/468-9473 or 920/330-9418 ⊕ www.hotwire.com. **Now Voyager Travel** ☎ 212/459-1616 ⊕ www.nowvoyager.com. **Onetravel.com** ⊕ www.onetravel.com. **Orbitz** ☎ 888/656-4546 ⊕ www.orbitz.com. **Priceline.com** ⊕ www.priceline.com. **Travelocity** ☎ 888/709-5983, 877/282-2925 in Canada, 0870/111-7061 in U.K. ⊕ www.travelocity.com.

ENJOYING THE FLIGHT

State your seat preference when purchasing your ticket, and then repeat it when you confirm and when you check in. For more legroom, you can request one of the few emergency-aisle seats at check-in, if you're capable of moving obstacles comparable in weight to an airplane exit door (usually between 35 pounds and 60 pounds)—a Federal Aviation Administration requirement of passengers in these seats. Seats behind a bulkhead also offer more legroom, but they don't have underseat storage. Don't sit in the row in front of the emergency aisle or in front of a bulkhead, where seats may not recline. SeatGuru.com has more information about specific seat configurations, which vary by aircraft.

Ask the airline whether a snack or meal is served on the flight. If you have dietary concerns, request special meals when booking. These can be vegetarian, low-cholesterol, or kosher, for example. It's a good idea to pack some healthful snacks and a small (plastic) bottle of water in your carry-on bag. On long flights, try to maintain a normal routine, to help fight jet lag. At night, get some sleep. By day, eat light meals, drink water (not alcohol), and **move around the cabin** to stretch your legs. For additional jet-lag tips consult *Fodor's FYI: Travel Fit & Healthy* (available at bookstores everywhere).

Smoking policies vary from carrier to carrier. Most airlines prohibit smoking on all of their flights; others allow smoking only on certain routes or certain departures. Ask your carrier about its policy. Smoking on airplane flights within the United States is prohibited.

FLYING TIMES

Salt Lake City is approximately 16 hours from Sydney, 12 hours from London, 3 hours from Dallas, 5 hours from New York, 4 hours from Chicago, and 3¾ hours from Los Angeles.

HOW TO COMPLAIN

If your baggage goes astray or your flight goes awry, complain right away. Most carriers require that you **file a claim immediately.** The Aviation Consumer Protection Division of the Department of Transportation publishes *Fly-Rights*, which discusses airlines and consumer issues and is available online. You can also find articles and information on mytravelrights.com, the Web site of the nonprofit Consumer Travel Rights Center.

🛪 **Airline Complaints Aviation Consumer Protection Division** ✉ U.S. Department of Transportation, Office of Aviation Enforcement and Proceedings, C-75, Room 4107, 400 7th St. SW, Washington, DC 20590 ☎ 202/366-2220 ⊕ www.airconsumer.ost.dot.gov.

Federal Aviation Administration Consumer Hotline ✉ For inquiries: FAA, 800 Independence Ave. SW, Washington, DC 20591 ☎ 800/322-7873 ⊕ www.faa.gov.

RECONFIRMING
Check the status of your flight before you leave for the airport. You can do this on your carrier's Web site, by linking to a flight-status checker (many Web booking services offer these), or by calling your carrier or travel agent.

AIRPORTS
The major gateway to Utah is Salt Lake City International Airport. Flights to smaller, regional, or resort-town airports generally connect through this hub. A convenient gateway to southern Utah, particularly Zion and Bryce Canyon national parks, is McCarran International Airport in Las Vegas.

🚩 Airport Information **McCarran International Airport (LAS)** ☎ 702/261-5733 ⊕ www.mccarran. com. **Salt Lake City International Airport (SLC)** ☎ 801/575-2400 ⊕ www.slcairport.com.

BICYCLE TRAVEL
Mountain biking is popular throughout Utah, and rental bikes (and helmets) are available just about everywhere. Popular spots to bike include Moab, Zion Canyon, and, during the summer season, major ski resorts, where you can hook your bike on the ski lift to go to the top then ride your bike down. You can ride up, too, but keep the altitude in mind and pace yourself accordingly.

Bikes can be rented by the day, for anywhere from $25 to $50 or more, depending on the quality of the bike. Multiday bike trips begin at around $500.

🚩 Tour Companies **Dreamride** ✉ 59 E. Center St., Moab 84532 ☎ 888/662-2882 ⊕ www. dreamride.com. **Escape Adventures** ✉ 391 S. Main St., Moab 84532 ☎ 800/596-2953 ⊕ www. escapeadventures.com. **Western Spirit Cycling** ✉ 478 Mill Creek Dr., Moab 84532 ☎ 800/845-2453 ⊕ www.westernspirit.com.

🚩 Bike Maps **Off Road Publications** ☎ 801/486-0698 ⊕ www.offroadpub.com. **REI** ☎ 800/426-4840 ⊕ www.rei.com. **Utah Travel Council** ☎ 800/200-1160 ⊕ www.utah.com/bike.

BIKES IN FLIGHT
Most airlines accommodate bikes as luggage, provided they are dismantled and boxed; check with individual airlines about packing requirements. Some airlines sell bike boxes, which are often free at bike shops, for about $20 (bike bags can be considerably more expensive). International travelers often can substitute a bike for a piece of checked luggage at no charge; otherwise, the cost is about $100. Most U.S. and Canadian airlines charge $40–$80 each way.

BUS TRAVEL
Greyhound Lines runs several buses each day to Salt Lake's terminal on South Temple. The company also serves Provo, Ogden, Tremonton, Green River, Logan, Price, Parowan, and St. George.

🚩 **Greyhound Lines** ✉ 160 W. South Temple, Salt Lake City ☎ 801/355-9579 or 800/231-2222 ⊕ www.greyhound.com.

BUSINESS HOURS
Most retail stores are open from 9 AM or 9:30 AM until 6 PM or 7 PM daily in downtown locations and until 9 or 10 in suburban shopping malls and in resort towns during high season. Downtown stores sometimes stay open later Thursday night. Normal banking hours are weekdays 9–5; some branches are also open on Saturday morning. In rural Utah you may occasionally run into some stores and/or restaurants closed on Sunday, but this is not generally the case, especially in the major tourist areas.

CAMERAS & PHOTOGRAPHY
Photographers love Utah—and with good reason. The scenery is among America's best, and every season offers a multitude of breathtaking images. When you're at Native American sites, be sure to ask if taking pictures is appropriate. The *Kodak Guide to Shooting Great Travel Pictures* (available at bookstores everywhere) is loaded with tips.

You can arrange a photo shoot tour of Utah with a major company that runs large, photo-oriented bus tours, such as Photo Travel or Photo Traveler, or create your own with a smaller, locally owned company, such as Sinbad Tours, which also arranges painting tours.

⚡ Photo Help Kodak Information Center ☎ 800/242-2424 ⊕ www.kodak.com.
⚡ Photo Tours Photo Travel ☎ 800/417-4680 ⊕ www.phototravel.com. **Photo Traveler** ☎ 800/417-4680 ⊕ www.phototraveler.com. **Sinbad Tours** ☎ 801/277-4515 ⊕ www.sinbadtours.com.

EQUIPMENT PRECAUTIONS

Utah is a land of extreme temperatures. Mountain winters have temperatures well below freezing, while desert summers are well into the 100s; the climate is also very dry. If you're doing any river activities, make sure you bring waterproof gear to keep your equipment dry. **Don't pack film or equipment in checked luggage,** where it is much more susceptible to damage. X-ray machines used to view checked luggage are extremely powerful and therefore are likely to ruin your film. Try to ask for hand inspection of film, which becomes clouded after repeated exposure to airport X-ray machines, and keep videotapes and computer disks away from metal detectors. Always keep film, tape, and computer disks out of the sun. Carry an extra supply of batteries, and be prepared to turn on your camera, camcorder, or laptop to prove to airport security personnel that the device is real.

CAR RENTAL

You can rent an economy car with air-conditioning, an automatic transmission, and unlimited mileage in Salt Lake City for about $30 a day and $150 a week. This does not include tax on car rentals, which is 16.1% in Salt Lake City. If you're planning to do any skiing, biking, four-wheeling, or towing, check into renting an SUV, van, or pickup from a local company like Rugged Rentals, which specializes in outdoor vehicles and provides supplemental insurance as part of the rental charge. For $60 per day or $300 per week, you can rent a relatively new vehicle with bike rack, ski rack, or towing equipment included.

⚡ Major Agencies Alamo ☎ 800/327-9633 ⊕ www.alamo.com. **Avis** ☎ 800/331-1212, 800/879-2847 or 800/272-5871 in Canada, 0870/606-0100 in U.K., 02/9353-9000 in Australia, 09/526-2847 in New Zealand ⊕ www.avis.com. **Budget** ☎ 800/527-0700 ⊕ www.budget.com. **Dollar** ☎ 800/800-4000, 0800/085-4578 in U.K. ⊕ www.dollar.com. **Hertz** ☎ 800/654-3131, 800/263-0600 in Canada, 0870/844-8844 in U.K., 02/9669-2444 in Australia, 09/256-8690 in New Zealand ⊕ www.hertz.com. **National Car Rental** ☎ 800/227-7368 ⊕ www.nationalcar.com.

CUTTING COSTS

Renting a car in Las Vegas can be less expensive than renting one in Salt Lake City, especially if you're visiting southern Utah. The driving time between Las Vegas and Salt Lake City is 7 to 9 hours, but it's only a 2- to 3-hour trip to Zion National Park.

For a good deal, book through a travel agent who will shop around. Also, price local car-rental companies—whose prices may be lower still, although their service and maintenance may not be as good as those of major rental agencies—and research rates on the Internet. Consolidators that specialize in air travel can offer good rates on cars as well (⇨ Air Travel). Remember to ask about required deposits, cancellation penalties, and drop-off charges if you're planning to pick up the car in one city and leave it in another. If you're traveling during a holiday period, also make sure that a confirmed reservation guarantees you a car.

⚡ Local Agencies Rugged Rentals ☎ 800/977-9111 ⊕ www.ruggedrental.com.

INSURANCE

When driving a rented car you are generally responsible for any damage to or loss of the vehicle. You also may be liable for any property damage or personal injury that you may cause while driving. Before you rent, see what coverage you already have under the terms of your personal auto-insurance policy and credit cards.

For about $9 to $25 a day, rental companies sell protection, known as a collision- or loss-damage waiver (CDW or LDW), which eliminates your liability for damage to the car; it's always optional and should never be automatically added to your bill. In most states you don't need a CDW if you have personal auto insurance or other liability insurance. Some states, including Nevada, have capped the price of the CDW and LDW. However, **make sure you have enough coverage to pay for the car.** If you do not have auto insurance or an umbrella policy that covers damage to third parties, purchasing liability insurance and a CDW or LDW is highly recommended.

REQUIREMENTS & RESTRICTIONS

Most agencies won't rent to you if you're under the age of 21.

In Utah you must be 21 and have a valid driver's license to rent a car; most companies also require a major credit card. If you're over 65, check the rental company's policy on overage drivers. You may pay extra for child seats (but shop around; some companies don't charge extra for this), which are compulsory for children under five, and for additional drivers. Non-U.S. residents will need a reservation voucher, a passport, a driver's license, and a travel policy that covers each driver, in order to pick up a car.

SURCHARGES

Before you pick up a car in one city and leave it in another, ask about drop-off charges or one-way service fees, which can be substantial. Also inquire about early-return policies; some rental agencies charge extra if you return the car before the time specified in your contract while others give you a refund for the days not used. Most agencies note the tank's fuel level on your contract; to avoid a hefty refueling fee, return the car with the same tank level. If the tank was full, refill it just before you turn in the car, but be aware that gas stations near the rental outlet may overcharge. It's almost never a deal to buy a tank of gas with the car when you rent it; the understanding is that you'll return it empty, but some fuel usually remains. Surcharges may apply if you're under 25 or if you take the car outside the area approved by the rental agency. You'll pay extra for child seats (about $8 a day), which are compulsory for children under five, and usually for additional drivers (up to $25 a day, depending on location).

CAR TRAVEL

You'll need a car in Utah. Public transportation exists, but caters to commuters, not tourists. You'll seldom be bored driving. Scenery ranges from snow-capped mountains to endless stretches of desert with strange rock formations and intense color. There are more national parks here than in any other state except Alaska and California, although their interiors are not always accessible by car.

Before setting out on any driving trip, it's important to **make sure your vehicle is in top condition.** It is best to have a complete tune-up. At the least, you should check the following: lights, including brake lights, backup lights, and emergency lights; tires, including the spare; oil; engine coolant; windshield-washer fluid; windshield-wiper blades; and brakes. For emergencies, take along flares or reflector triangles, jumper cables, an empty gas can, a fire extinguisher, a flashlight, a plastic tarp, blankets, water, and coins or a calling card for phone calls (cell phones don't always work in high mountain areas).

GASOLINE

In major cities throughout Utah, gas prices are roughly similar to the rest of the continental United States; in rural and resort towns, prices are considerably higher. In urban areas, stations are plentiful, and most stay open late (some are open 24 hours). In rural areas, stations are less frequent, and hours are more limited, particularly on Sunday; you can sometimes drive more than 100 mi on back roads without finding gas. It's best to always keep your tank at least half full.

ROAD CONDITIONS

Utah has some of the most spectacular vistas and challenging driving in the world. Roads range from multilane blacktop to narrow dirt roads; from twisting switchbacks bordered by guardrails to primitive backcountry paths so narrow that you must back up to the edge of a steep cliff to make a turn. Scenic routes and lookout points are clearly marked, enabling you to slow down and pull over to take in the views.

One of the more unpleasant sights along the highway are roadkills—animals struck by vehicles. Deer, elk, and even bears may try to get to the other side of a road just as you come along, so watch out for wildlife on the highways. Exercise caution, not only to save an animal's life, but also to avoid possible extensive damage to your car.

🚩 Road Conditions In Utah ☎ 800/492-2400.

RULES OF THE ROAD

You'll find highways and the national parks crowded in summer, and almost deserted (and occasionally impassable) in winter. Follow the posted speed limit, drive defensively, and **make sure your gas tank is full.** Utah law requires seat belts for drivers, front-seat passengers, and children under 16. Always **strap children under age 5 into approved child-safety seats.** Helmets are required for motorcyclists and passengers under the age of 18.

You may turn right at a red light after stopping if there is no sign stating otherwise and no oncoming traffic. Right turns on red are prohibited in some areas, but these are signed accordingly. When in doubt, wait for the green.

SPEED LIMITS

The speed limit on U.S. interstates is 75 mph in rural areas and 65 mph in urban zones. But watch out. "Rural areas" are determined by census boundaries and sometimes make little sense. Increased speeds are allowed only where clearly posted. Transition zones from one speed limit to the next are indicated with pavement markings and signs. Fines are doubled for speeding in work zones and school zones.

WINTER & DESERT DRIVING

Modern highways make mountain driving safe and generally trouble free even in cold weather. Although winter driving can occasionally present some real challenges, road maintenance is good and plowing is prompt. However, in mountain areas, tire chains, studs, or snow tires are essential. If you're planning to drive into high elevations, be sure to **check the weather forecast and call for road conditions** beforehand. Even main highways can close. Be prepared for stormy weather: **carry an emergency kit** containing warm clothes, a flashlight, some food and water, and blankets. It's also good to carry a cell

phone, but be aware that the mountains can disrupt service. If you do get stalled by deep snow, **do not leave your car.** Wait for help, running the engine only if needed, and remember that assistance is never far away. Winter weather isn't confined to winter in the high country (it's been know to snow on July 4), so be prepared year-round. Keep your tank full of gas and remember water, even in winter. **Always tell someone,** even if it's the hotel clerk or gas station attendant, where you're going and when you expect to return.

Desert driving can be dangerous winter or summer. Always carry water, even in winter. You'll encounter extreme conditions in remote areas with drifting snow and/or sand and little chance of anyone driving by to help. **Never leave children or pets in a car**—summer temperatures climb quickly into the 100s.

CHILDREN IN UTAH

Utah is tailor-made for family vacations, with guest ranches; old railroads; mining towns; national parks; large wildlife; white-water rivers; and plenty of places for fun outdoor activities. Visitor centers and lodgings are often good at recommending places to spend time with children. Local culture is very child-friendly, and many attractions have reduced family admission tickets.

If you are renting a car, don't forget to arrange for a car seat when you reserve. For general advice about traveling with children, consult *Fodor's FYI: Travel with Your Baby* (available in bookstores everywhere).

FLYING

If your children are two or older, ask about children's airfares. As a general rule, infants under two not occupying a seat fly at greatly reduced fares or even for free. But if you want to guarantee a seat for an infant, you have to pay full fare. Consider flying during off-peak days and times; most airlines will grant an infant a seat without a ticket if there are available seats.

Experts agree that it's a good idea to use safety seats aloft for children weighing less than 40 pounds. Airlines set their own policies: if you use a safety seat, U.S.

carriers usually require that the child be ticketed, even if he or she is young enough to ride free, because the seats must be strapped into regular seats. And even if you pay the full adult fare for the seat, it may be worth it, especially on longer trips. Do **check your airline's policy about using safety seats during takeoff and landing.** Safety seats are not allowed everywhere in the plane, so get your seat assignments as early as possible.

When reserving, request children's meals or a freestanding bassinet (not available at all airlines) if you need them. But note that bulkhead seats, where you must sit to use the bassinet, may lack an overhead bin or storage space on the floor.

LODGING

Most hotels in Utah allow children under a certain age to stay in their parents' room at no extra charge, but others charge for them as extra adults; be sure to find out the cutoff age for children's discounts.

Although most guest ranches are ideal for children of all ages, be sure you know not only the activities at a ranch but also which are emphasized before booking your vacation. A few ranches may have age restrictions excluding very young children or only limited activities for children of certain ages. When visiting ski areas (winter or summer), condos are an excellent choice for accomodating families. Chain motels are often good family bets, and they are located all over the state; especially recommended are Best Western and Holiday Inn.

ℐ Best Choices Best Western Hotels ☎ 800/528-1234 ⊕ www.bestwestern.com. **Holiday Inns** ☎ 800/465-4329 ⊕ www.holiday-inn.com. **Park City Accommodations** ⊕ www.condoparkcity.com. **Resort Quest** ⊕ www.resortquest.com. **Sheraton** ☎ 888/625-5144 ⊕ www.sheraton.com.

SIGHTS & ATTRACTIONS

Places that are especially appealing to children are indicated by a rubber-duckie icon (🐥) in the margin. All of Utah's national parks have a Junior Ranger program for kids from 6 to 12. Most ski areas have special kinder ski schools for children, and some have snowboarding lessons. Hogle

Zoo, Clark Planetarium, the Children's Museum, and Wheeler Farm are all in or near downtown Salt Lake City.

SPORTS & THE OUTDOORS

Altitude can be even more taxing on small lungs than on adult lungs, so **be conservative** when evaluating what level of activity your child will enjoy.

Some trip organizers arrange backpacking outings for families with small children, especially for family groups of eight or more. Short half-day or full-day bike trips with plenty of flat riding are possible in the vicinity of Park City. Ask at local bike shops for recommended rides for children.

Fishing can be difficult, as the nuances of the sport and the patience it requires are often lost on children. For family fishing trips, visit lakes and reservoirs rather than streams and rivers, because kids who are bored by fishing can go swimming, boating, or simply explore the shoreline. Don't take children under seven on extended rafting trips unless the trip is geared toward young children. Outfitters designate some trips as "adults only," with the cutoff usually 16 years old. You might want to test the waters with a half- or full-day excursion. Several outfitters run short trips out of Moab. For families with younger children, trips aboard larger, motorized rafts are probably safest.

CONSUMER PROTECTION

Whether you're shopping for gifts or purchasing travel services, **pay with a major credit card** whenever possible, so you can cancel payment or get reimbursed if there's a problem (and you can provide documentation). If you're doing business with a particular company for the first time, contact your local Better Business Bureau and the attorney general's offices in your state and (for U.S. businesses) the company's home state as well. Have any complaints been filed? Finally, if you're buying a package or tour, always consider travel insurance that includes default coverage (⇨ Insurance).

ℐ BBBs Council of Better Business Bureaus ✉ 4200 Wilson Blvd., Suite 800, Arlington, VA

22203 ☎ 703/276-0100 🖷 703/525-8277 ⊕ www. bbb.org. **Utah Better Business Bureau** ✉ 5673 S. Redwood Rd., Suite 22, Salt Lake City, UT 84123 ☎ 801/892-6009 ⊕ www.saltlakecity.bbb.org.

CUSTOMS & DUTIES

IN AUSTRALIA

Australian residents who are 18 or older may bring home A$900 worth of souvenirs and gifts (including jewelry), 250 cigarettes or 250 grams of cigars or other tobacco products, and 2.25 liters of alcohol (including wine, beer, and spirits). Residents under 18 may bring back A$450 worth of goods. If any of these individual allowances are exceeded, you must pay duty for the entire amount (of the group of products in which the allowance was exceeded). Members of the same family traveling together may pool their allowances. Prohibited items include meat products. Seeds, plants, and fruits need to be declared upon arrival.
🛈 **Australian Customs Service** ☖ Regional Director, Box 8, Sydney, NSW 2001 ☎ 02/9213-2000 or 1300/363263, 02/9364-7222 or 1800/803-006 quarantine-inquiry line 🖷 02/9213-4043 ⊕ www. customs.gov.au.

IN CANADA

Canadian residents who have been out of Canada for at least seven days may bring in C$750 worth of goods duty-free. If you've been away fewer than seven days but more than 48 hours, the duty-free allowance drops to C$200. If your trip lasts 24 to 48 hours, the allowance is C$50; if the goods are worth more than C$50, you must pay full duty on all of the goods. You may not pool allowances with family members. Goods claimed under the C$750 exemption may follow you by mail; those claimed under the lesser exemptions must accompany you. Alcohol and tobacco products may be included in the seven-day and 48-hour exemptions but not in the 24-hour exemption. If you meet the age requirements of the province or territory through which you reenter Canada, you may bring in, duty-free, 1.5 liters of wine *or* 1.14 liters (40 imperial ounces) of liquor *or* 24 12-ounce cans

or bottles of beer or ale. Also, if you meet the local age requirement for tobacco products, you may bring in, duty-free, 200 cigarettes, 50 cigars or cigarillos, and 200 grams of tobacco. You may have to pay a minimum duty on tobacco products, regardless of whether or not you exceed your personal exemption. Check ahead of time with the Canada Border Services Agency or the Department of Agriculture for policies regarding meat products, seeds, plants, and fruits.

You may send an unlimited number of gifts (only one gift per recipient, however) worth up to C$60 each duty-free to Canada. Label the package UNSOLICITED GIFT—VALUE UNDER $60. Alcohol and tobacco are excluded.
🛈 **Canada Border Services Agency** ✉ Customs Information Services, 191 Laurier Ave. W, 15th fl., Ottawa, Ontario K1A 0L5 ☎ 800/461-9999 in Canada, 204/983-3500, 506/636-5064 ⊕ www.cbsa.gc.ca.

IN NEW ZEALAND

All homeward-bound residents may bring back NZ$700 worth of souvenirs and gifts; passengers may not pool their allowances, and children can claim only the concession on goods intended for their own use. For those 17 or older, the duty-free allowance also includes 4.5 liters of wine or beer; one 1,125-ml bottle of spirits; and either 200 cigarettes, 250 grams of tobacco, 50 cigars, *or* a combination of the three up to 250 grams. Meat products, seeds, plants, and fruits must be declared upon arrival to the Agricultural Services Department.
🛈 **New Zealand Customs** ✉ Head office: The Customhouse, 17–21 Whitmore St., Box 2218, Wellington ☎ 09/300-5399 or 0800/428-786 ⊕ www.customs. govt.nz.

IN THE U.K.

From countries outside the European Union, including the United States, you may bring home, duty-free, 200 cigarettes, 50 cigars, 100 cigarillos, or 250 grams of tobacco; 1 liter of spirits or 2 liters of fortified or sparkling wine or liqueurs; 2 liters of still table wine; 60 ml of perfume; 250 ml of toilet water; plus £145 worth of other goods, including gifts and souvenirs.

Prohibited items include meat and dairy products, seeds, plants, and fruits.

⊞ HM Customs and Excise ⊠ Portcullis House, 21 Cowbridge Rd. E, Cardiff CF11 9SS ☎ 0845/010–9000 or 0208/929–0152 advice service, 0208/929–6731 or 0208/910–3602 complaints ⊕ www.hmce.gov.uk.

DISABILITIES & ACCESSIBILITY

Utah is all about getting outdoors and taking advantage of what nature has to offer, and travelers with disabilities should take advantage of all the state has to offer. Most ski areas have adaptive ski programs—Park City Mountain Resort, for example, has excellent lesson programs. Most of the U.S. Forest Service campgrounds have wheelchair-accessible sites, and many resort towns have created activities for all types of visitors. Salt Lake City is home to SPLORE, an organization dedicated to making outdoor adventures accessible to people with disabilities and special needs. SPLORE arranges rafting, skiing, rock climbing, and canoeing trips. A good source for information about accessible activities is the Utah Travel Council, which has a list of accessible activities and where you can perform them.

⊞ Local Resources SPLORE ⊠ 880 E. 3375 South St., Salt Lake City ☎ 801/484–4128 ⊕ www.splore.org. **Utah Travel Council** ☎ 801/538–1030 ⊕ www.utah.com.

LODGING

Despite the Americans with Disabilities Act, the definition of accessibility seems to differ from hotel to hotel. Some properties may be accessible by ADA standards for people with mobility problems but not for people with hearing or vision impairments, for example.

If you have mobility problems, ask for the lowest floor on which accessible services are offered. If you have a hearing impairment, check whether the hotel has devices to alert you visually to the ring of the telephone, a knock at the door, and a fire/emergency alarm. Some hotels provide these devices without charge. Discuss your needs with hotel personnel if this equipment isn't available, so that a staff member can personally alert you in the event of an emergency.

If you're bringing a guide dog, get authorization ahead of time and write down the name of the person with whom you spoke.

RESERVATIONS

When discussing accessibility with an operator or reservations agent, ask hard questions. Are there any stairs, inside *or* out? Are there grab bars next to the toilet *and* in the shower/tub? How wide is the doorway to the room? To the bathroom? For the most extensive facilities meeting the latest legal specifications, opt for newer accommodations. If you reserve through a toll-free number, consider also calling the hotel's local number to confirm the information from the central reservations office. Get confirmation in writing when you can.

SIGHTS & ATTRACTIONS

Major attractions in downtown Salt Lake City are all fully accessible. Temple Square is paved, with accessible restrooms and elevators. The Gateway shopping area, where you'll find the Clark Planetarium and the Children's Museum, is paved with cobblestones in some areas but is generally accessible. Accessibility in national parks varies widely. Zion has a wide, level paved trail to the Narrows area and a paved but steep trail to Weeping Rock. Canyonlands has a few accessible overlooks, but no accessible trails. The Capitol Reef campground is accessible, but trails are generally inaccessible. Arches has no easily accessible trails. The National Park Service is constantly working to improve access, so check before you go.

TRANSPORTATION

The U.S. Department of Transportation Aviation Consumer Protection Division's online publication *New Horizons: Information for the Air Traveler with a Disability* offers advice for travellers with a disability, and outlines basic rights. Visit DisabilityInfo.gov for general information.

Public transportation is not generally a good way to get around Utah, not even in Salt Lake City. However, the Utah Transit Authority provides paratransit, or flextrans, services; the authority's Web site has information on specific routes. You may want to rent a car through an agency that specializes in vehicles for those with special needs, such as Wheelers.

🚹 Utah Transit Authority ⊕ www.rideuta.com/paratransit/. **Wheelers** ☎ 800/456-1371 ⊕ www.wheelersvanrentals.com.

🚹 Information & Complaints Aviation Consumer Protection Division (⇨ Air Travel) for airline-related problems; ⊕ airconsumer.ost.dot.gov/publications/horizons.htm for airline travel advice and rights. **Departmental Office of Civil Rights** ✉ For general inquiries, U.S. Department of Transportation, S-30, 400 7th St. SW, Room 10215, Washington, DC 20590 ☎ 202/366-4648, 202/366-8538 TTY 🖷 202/366-9371 ⊕ www.dotcr.ost.dot.gov. **Disability Rights Section** ✉ NYAV, U.S. Department of Justice, Civil Rights Division, 950 Pennsylvania Ave. NW, Washington, DC 20530 ☎ ADA information line 202/514-0301, 800/514-0301, 202/514-0383 TTY, 800/514-0383 TTY ⊕ www.ada.gov. **U.S. Department of Transportation Hotline** ☎ For disability-related air-travel problems, 800/778-4838 or 800/455-9880 TTY.

TRAVEL AGENCIES

In the United States, the Americans with Disabilities Act requires that travel firms serve the needs of all travelers. Some agencies specialize in working with people with disabilities.

🚹 Travelers with Mobility Problems Access Adventures/B. Roberts Travel ✉ 1876 East Ave., Rochester, NY 14610 ☎ 800/444-6540 ⊕ www.brobertstravel.com, run by a former physical-rehabilitation counselor. **Accessible Vans of America** ✉ 37 Daniel Rd. W, Fairfield, NJ 07004 ☎ 877/282-8267, 888/282-8267, 973/808-9709 reservations 🖷 973/808-9713 ⊕ www.accessiblevans.com. **Flying Wheels Travel** ✉ 143 W. Bridge St., Box 382, Owatonna, MN 55060 ☎ 507/451-5005 🖷 507/451-1685 ⊕ www.flyingwheelstravel.com.

DISCOUNTS & DEALS

Salt Lake City Travel and Tourism has a free visitor guide and discount coupons for major attractions on its Web site.

Be a smart shopper and compare all your options before making decisions. A plane ticket bought with a promotional coupon from travel clubs, coupon books, and direct-mail offers or purchased on the Internet may not be cheaper than the least expensive fare from a discount ticket agency. And always keep in mind that what you get is just as important as what you save.

🚹 Salt Lake City Travel & Tourism ⊕ www.slctravel.com.

DISCOUNT RESERVATIONS

To save money, look into discount reservations services with Web sites and toll-free numbers, which use their buying power to get a better price on hotels, airline tickets (⇨ Air Travel), even car rentals. When booking a room, always **call the hotel's local toll-free number** (if one is available) rather than the central reservations number—you'll often get a better price. Always ask about special packages or corporate rates.

🚹 Hotel Rooms Accommodations Express ☎ 800/444-7666 or 800/277-1064. **Hotels.com** ☎ 800/246-8357 ⊕ www.hotels.com. **Quikbook** ☎ 800/789-9887 ⊕ www.quikbook.com. **Turbotrip.com** ☎ 800/473-7829 ⊕ w3.turbotrip.com.

PACKAGE DEALS

Don't confuse packages and guided tours. When you buy a package, you travel on your own, just as though you had planned the trip yourself. Fly/drive packages, which combine airfare and car rental, are often a good deal. In cities, ask the local visitor's bureau about hotel and local transportation packages that include tickets to major museum exhibits or other special events.

EATING & DRINKING

Dining in Utah is generally casual. Menus are becoming more varied, but you can nearly always order a hamburger or a steak. There are a growing number of fine restaurants in Salt Lake and Park City, and good places are cropping up in various other areas. Also look for good dining in Springdale, Moab, and Torrey. Seek out colorful diners along the secondary highways like U.S. 89; they usually serve up meat and potatoes along with the local flavor of each community. Authentic ethnic food is easy to find in Salt Lake City but generally not available elsewhere. Dinner hours are from 6 PM to 9 PM. Outside the large cities and resort towns in the high seasons, many restaurants close by 10 PM.

The restaurants we list are the cream of the crop in each price category. Properties indicated by an ✕▣ are lodging establishments whose restaurant warrants a special trip.

In general, when you order a regular coffee, you get coffee with milk and sugar.

MEALTIMES

Unless otherwise noted, the restaurants listed in this guide are open daily for lunch and dinner.

RESERVATIONS & DRESS

Reservations are always a good idea; we mention them only when they're essential or not accepted. Book as far ahead as you can, and reconfirm as soon as you arrive. (Large parties should always call ahead to check the reservations policy.) We mention dress only when men are required to wear a jacket or a jacket and tie—which is almost never in casual Utah. Even at nice resorts, dress is usually casual, and in summer you're welcome nearly everywhere in your shorts, T-shirt, and hiking shoes.

SPECIALTIES

Although you can find all types of cuisine in the major cities and resort towns, don't forget to try native dishes like trout, elk, and buffalo (the latter two have less fat than beef and are just as tasty); organic fruits and vegetables are also readily available. When in doubt, go for a steak, forever a Utah mainstay. Southwestern food is popular, and you'll find several restaurants that specialize in it or show Southwestern influences in menu selections.

WINE, BEER & SPIRITS

Despite what you've heard, it's not hard to get a drink in Utah, though you must be 21 to purchase or consume alcohol. The Utah legislature relaxed some laws just before the 2002 Olympics came to town, and now a server can offer you a drink rather than wait for you to ask for one. The key is knowing what kind of place you're in according to Utah liquor laws. There are three types of places you can get a drink: a private club, a restaurant with a liquor license, and a brewpub, beer bar, or tavern.

A private club is a bar that sells just about any kind of liquor you can imagine, usually along with at least appetizers if not a full menu. The trick here is that you must either buy a membership (usually $4 for a three-week membership) or get someone who's already a member to sponsor you. Usually, all you have to do is catch someone going in to a club, tell them you're from out of town, and ask them to sponsor you. There may be a cover charge if a popular band is in town.

Most restaurants have liquor licenses, which allow them to serve you liquor with a meal. You can simply sit down and order your food and drink from a server. Some restaurants—generally those that cater to families—have decided that it's too much trouble to deal with the State Liquor Commission and have opted not to carry a liquor license. If you're set on having a drink with your meal, check before you go.

At brewpubs, beer bars, and taverns, you can get beer, beer, more beer, and, generally, wine coolers. There are several brewpubs with their own beers on tap—try St. Provo Girl and Polygamy Porter to get a taste of the local drinking humor. You don't need a membership, and there's generally no cover charge unless a hot band is playing. Many brewpubs also have a liquor license that allows the sale of wine and spirits—only in the dining room, not at the bar.

If you're staying in a nicer hotel, your "membership" to the hotel bar will be included in your accommodation fees. Most hotel restaurants carry a liquor license, and you'll be able to get your own drinks from the minibar in your room.

To buy your own liquor (other than beer with 3.2% alcohol), you'll have to go to a state liquor store. There are 17 liquor stores throughout Salt Lake City and others throughout the state. They are closed on Sunday and holidays. It's best not to take your own wine or other liquor to a restaurant—lots of regulations cover brown bagging.

ECOTOURISM

Although neither the Bureau of Land Management (BLM) nor the National

Park Service has designated any particular parts of Utah to be endangered ecosystems, many areas are open only to hikers; vehicles, mountain bikes, and horses are banned. It's wise to respect these closures, as well as the old adages—"leave only footprints, take only pictures" and "pack it in, pack it out." Recycling is taken seriously throughout Utah, and you will find yourself very unpopular if you litter or fail to recycle your cans and bottles (locals can be strident about protecting their wilderness).

Much of Utah is public land. That doesn't mean it's yours to take home. All archaeological artifacts, including rock etchings and paintings, are protected by federal law and must be left untouched and undisturbed. The laws protecting artifacts have been strongly reinforced with "pothunter" lawsuits resulting in harsh punishments for those who have disturbed Native American items on public or private lands.

🔁 **U.S. Bureau of Land Management, Utah State Office** ☎ 801/539-4001 ⊕ www.blm.gov. **National Park Service** ⊕ www.nps.gov.

GAY & LESBIAN TRAVEL

The Gay and Lesbian Community Center of Utah is a resource center for gays and lesbians in Utah and posts a schedule of events. For details about the gay and lesbian scene, consult *Fodor's Gay Guide to the USA* (available in bookstores everywhere).

🔁 **Gay and Lesbian Community Center** ✉ 361 N. 300 West St., Salt Lake City ☎ 801/539-8800 or 888/874-2743 ⊕ www.glccu.com.

🔁 **Gay- & Lesbian-Friendly Travel Agencies Different Roads Travel** ✉ 1017 N. LaCienega Blvd., Suite 308, West Hollywood, CA 90069 ☎ 310/289-6000 or 800/429-8747 (Ext. 14 for both) 🖷 310/855-0323 ✍ lgernert@tzell.com. **Kennedy Travel** ✉ 130 W. 42nd St., Suite 401, New York, NY 10036 ☎ 800/237-7433 or 212/840-8659 🖷 212/730-2269 ⊕ www.kennedytravel.com. **Now, Voyager** ✉ 4406 18th St., San Francisco, CA 94114 ☎ 415/626-1169 or 800/255-6951 🖷 415/626-8626 ⊕ www.nowvoyager.com. **Skylink Travel and Tour/Flying Dutchmen Travel** ✉ 1455 N. Dutton Ave., Suite A, Santa Rosa, CA 95401 ☎ 707/546-9888 or 800/225-5759 🖷 707/636-0951, serving lesbian travelers.

HOLIDAYS

Major national holidays are New Year's Day (Jan. 1); Martin Luther King Day (3rd Mon. in Jan.); Presidents' Day (3rd Mon. in Feb.); Memorial Day (last Mon. in May); Independence Day (July 4); Labor Day (1st Mon. in Sept.); Columbus Day (2nd Mon. in Oct.); Thanksgiving Day (4th Thurs. in Nov.); Christmas Eve and Christmas Day (Dec. 24 and 25); and New Year's Eve (Dec. 31).

Utah celebrates Pioneer Day on July 24 to commemorate the day the original pioneers entered the Salt Lake Valley. Local businesses throughout the state may be closed, and downtown Salt Lake City is busy, with streets blocked off for the Days of '47 Parade (one of the largest in the United States) and a rodeo.

INSURANCE

The most useful travel-insurance plan is a comprehensive policy that includes coverage for trip cancellation and interruption, default, trip delay, and medical expenses (with a waiver for preexisting conditions).

Without insurance you'll lose all or most of your money if you cancel your trip, regardless of the reason. Default insurance covers you if your tour operator, airline, or cruise line goes out of business—the chances of which have been increasing. Trip-delay covers expenses that arise because of bad weather or mechanical delays. Study the fine print when comparing policies.

U.K. residents can buy a travel-insurance policy valid for most vacations taken during the year in which it's purchased (but check preexisting-condition coverage).

Always **buy travel policies directly from the insurance company**; if you buy them from a cruise line, airline, or tour operator that goes out of business you probably won't be covered for the agency or operator's default, a major risk. Before making any purchase, review your existing health and home-owner's policies to find what they cover away from home.

🔁 Travel Insurers In the U.S.: **Access America** ✉ 2805 N. Parham Rd., Richmond, VA 23294 ☎ 800/284-8300 🖷 804/673-1469 or 800/346-9265 ⊕ www.accessamerica.com. **Travel Guard**

International ✉ 1145 Clark St., Stevens Point, WI 54481 ☎ 800/826-1300 or 715/345-1041 🖷 800/ 955-8785 or 715/345-1990 ⊕ www.travelguard.com.

FOR INTERNATIONAL TRAVELERS
For information on customs restrictions, *see* Customs & Duties.

CAR RENTAL
When picking up a rental car, non-U.S. residents need a reservation voucher for any prepaid reservations that were made in the traveler's home country, a passport, a driver's license, and a travel policy that covers each driver.

CAR TRAVEL
In Utah gasoline costs $2.06–$2.59 a gallon. Stations are plentiful. Most stay open late (24 hours along large highways and in big cities), except in rural areas, where Sunday hours are limited and where you may drive long stretches without a refueling opportunity. Highways are well paved. Interstate highways—limited-access, multilane highways whose numbers are prefixed by "I–"—are the fastest routes. Interstates with three-digit numbers encircle urban areas, which may have other limited-access expressways, freeways, and parkways as well. Tolls may be levied on limited-access highways. So-called U.S. highways and state highways are not necessarily limited-access but may have several lanes.

Along larger highways, roadside stops with restrooms, fast-food restaurants, and sundries stores are well spaced. State police and tow trucks patrol major highways and lend assistance. If your car breaks down on an interstate, pull onto the shoulder and wait for help, or have your passengers wait while you walk to an emergency phone (available in most states). If you carry a cell phone, dial 911, noting your location on the small green roadside mileage markers.

Driving in the United States is on the right. Do obey speed limits posted along roads and highways. Watch for lower limits in small towns and on back roads. Utah requires front-seat passengers to wear seat belts. On weekdays between 6 and 10 AM and again between 4 and 7 PM expect heavy traffic in urban areas. To encourage carpooling, some freeways have special lanes for so-called high-occupancy vehicles (HOV)—cars carrying more than one passenger.

Bookstores, gas stations, convenience stores, and rest stops sell maps (about $3) and multiregion road atlases (about $10).

CONSULATES & EMBASSIES
🛂 **Australia** Australian Consulate General Los Angeles ✉ Century Plaza Towers, 19th fl., 2049 Century Park E, Los Angeles, CA 90067-3121 ☎ 310/ 229-4800.
🛂 **Canada** The Consulate General of Canada ✉ 10th fl., 300 S. Grand Ave., Los Angeles, CA 90071 ☎ 213/346-2700.
🛂 **New Zealand** Consulate of New Zealand ✉ 1379 N. Brookhurst Circle, Centerville, UT 84014 ☎ 801/296-2494.
🛂 **United Kingdom** British Consulate General ✉ 11766 Wilshire Blvd., Suite 400, Los Angeles, CA 90025 ☎ 310/477-3322.

CURRENCY
The dollar is the basic unit of U.S. currency. It has 100 cents. Coins are the copper penny (1¢); the silvery nickel (5¢), dime (10¢), quarter (25¢), and half-dollar (50¢); and the golden $1 coin, replacing a now-rare silver dollar. Bills are denominated $1, $5, $10, $20, $50, and $100, all mostly green and identical in size; designs and background tints vary. In addition, you may come across a $2 bill, but the chances are slim. The exchange rate at this writing is US$1.48 per British pound, US$0.64 per Canadian dollar, US$0.50 per Australian dollar, US$0.70 per New Zealand dollar, and US$0.91 per euro.

ELECTRICITY
The U.S. standard is AC, 110 volts/60 cycles. Plugs have two flat pins set parallel to each other.

EMERGENCIES
For police, fire, or ambulance, **dial 911** (0 in rural areas).

INSURANCE
Britons and Australians need extra medical coverage when traveling overseas.
🛂 **Insurance Information** In the U.K.: **Association of British Insurers** ✉ 51 Gresham St., London EC2V 7HQ ☎ 020/7600-3333 🖷 020/7696-8999 ⊕ www.

abi.org.uk. In Australia: **Insurance Council of Australia** ✉ Level 3, 56 Pitt St. Sydney, NSW 2000 ☎ 02/9253-5100 🖷 02/9253-5111 ⊕ www.ica.com. au. In Canada: **RBC Insurance** ✉ 6880 Financial Dr., Mississauga, Ontario L5N 7Y5 ☎ 800/387-4357 or 905/816-2559 🖷 888/298-6458 ⊕ www. rbcinsurance.com. In New Zealand: **Insurance Council of New Zealand** ✉ Level 7, 111-115 Customhouse Quay, Box 474, Wellington ☎ 04/472-5230 🖷 04/473-3011 ⊕ www.icnz.org.nz.

MAIL & SHIPPING

You can buy stamps and aerograms and send letters and parcels in post offices. Stamp-dispensing machines can occasionally be found in airports, bus and train stations, office buildings, drugstores, and the like. You can also deposit mail in the stout, dark blue, steel bins at strategic locations everywhere and in the mail chutes of large buildings; pickup schedules are posted. You can deposit packages at public collection boxes as long as the parcels are affixed with proper postage and weigh less than one pound. Packages weighing one or more pounds must be taken to a post office or handed to a postal carrier.

For mail sent within the United States, you need a 39¢ stamp, as of January 2006, for first-class letters weighing up to 1 ounce (23¢ for each additional ounce) and 23¢ for postcards. You pay 80¢ for 1-ounce airmail letters and 70¢ for airmail postcards to most other countries; to Canada and Mexico, you need a 60¢ stamp for a 1-ounce letter and 50¢ for a postcard. An aerogram—a single sheet of lightweight blue paper that folds into its own envelope, stamped for overseas airmail—costs 70¢.

To receive mail on the road, have it sent c/o General Delivery at your destination's main post office (use the correct five-digit ZIP code). You must pick up mail in person within 30 days and show a driver's license or passport.

PASSPORTS & VISAS

When traveling internationally, carry your passport even if you don't need one (it's always the best form of ID) and **make two photocopies of the data page** (one for someone at home and another

for you, carried separately from your passport). If you lose your passport, promptly call the nearest embassy or consulate and the local police.

Visitor visas aren't necessary for Canadian or European Union citizens, or for citizens of Australia who are staying fewer than 90 days.

🗗 Australian Citizens **Passports Australia** ☎ 131-232 ⊕ www.passports.gov.au. **United States Consulate General** ✉ MLC Centre, Level 59, 19-29 Martin Pl., Sydney, NSW 2000 ☎ 02/9373-9200, 1902/941-641 fee-based visa-inquiry line ⊕ usembassy-australia.state.gov/sydney. 🗗 Canadian Citizens **Passport Office** ✉ To mail in applications: 70 Cremazie St., Gatineau, Québec J8Y 3P2 ☎ 800/567-6868, 866/255-7655 TTY ⊕ www. ppt.gc.ca. 🗗 New Zealand Citizens **New Zealand Passports Office** ✉ For applications and information, Level 3, Boulcott House, 47 Boulcott St., Wellington ☎ 0800/22-5050 or 04/474-8100 ⊕ www.passports.govt.nz. **Embassy of the United States** ✉ 29 Fitzherbert Terr., Thorndon, Wellington ☎ 04/462-6000 ⊕ usembassy.org.nz. **U.S. Consulate General** ✉ Citibank Bldg., 3rd fl., 23 Customs St. E, Auckland ☎ 09/303-2724 ⊕ usembassy.org.nz. 🗗 U.K. Citizens **U.K. Passport Service** ☎ 0870/521-0410 ⊕ www.passport.gov.uk. **American Consulate General** ✉ Danesfort House, 223 Stranmillis Rd., Belfast, Northern Ireland BT9 5GR ☎ 028/9038-6100 🖷 028/9068-1301 ⊕ www.usembassy. org.uk. **American Embassy** ✉ For visa and immigration information or to submit a visa application via mail (enclose an SASE), Consular Information Unit, 24 Grosvenor Sq., London W1A 2LQ ☎ 090/5544-4546 or 090/6820-0290 for visa information (per-minute charges), 0207/499-9000 main switchboard ⊕ www.usembassy.org.uk.

TELEPHONES

All U.S. telephone numbers consist of a three-digit area code and a seven-digit local number. Within many local calling areas, you dial only the seven-digit number. Within some area codes, you must dial "1" first for calls outside the local area. To call between area-code regions, dial "1" then all 10 digits; the same goes for calls to numbers prefixed by "800," "888," "866," and "877"—all toll-free. For calls to numbers preceded by "900" you must pay—usually dearly.

For international calls, dial "011" followed by the country code and the local number. For help, dial "0" and ask for an overseas operator. The country code is 61 for Australia, 64 for New Zealand, 44 for the United Kingdom. Calling Canada is the same as calling within the United States, although you might not be able to get through on some toll free numbers. Most local phone books list country codes and U.S. area codes. The country code for the United States is 1.

For operator assistance, dial "0." To obtain someone's phone number, call directory assistance at 555–1212 or occasionally 411 (free at many public phones). To have the person you're calling foot the bill, phone collect; dial "0" instead of "1" before the 10-digit number.

At pay phones, instructions often are posted. Usually you insert coins in a slot (usually 25¢–50¢ for local calls) and wait for a steady tone before dialing. When you call long-distance, the operator tells you how much to insert; prepaid phone cards, widely available in various denominations, are easier. Call the number on the back, punch in the card's personal identification number when prompted, then dial your number.

LODGING

Chain motels are everywhere. Other than that, accommodations are varied. The resort towns along the Wasatch Front—especially Park City and Snowbird—cater to the wealthy jet set and there are posh resorts in Deer Valley and pampering spas at Green Valley or Red Mountain. Salt Lake City has hotels in every price range. National chains like Best Western, Super 8, and Motel 6 are dependable in Utah and are sometimes the best beds in town. The gateway towns to the national parks usually have a large range of accommodations. There are also more bed-and-breakfasts, as international tourists often prefer to meet the locals at such places. Independent motels can also be found all over the state. Look for guest ranches if you're trying to find an authentic cowboy experience. They often require a one-week stay, and the cost is all-inclusive. During the busy summer season from Memorial Day to Labor Day, it's a good idea to book hotels and bed-and-breakfasts in advance. Some motels and resorts have off-season rates. Take advantage of these since hiking is best in the south in cool weather and the mountains are beautiful even without snow.

The lodgings we list are the cream of the crop in each price category. We always list the facilities that are available—but we don't specify whether they cost extra: When pricing accommodations, always ask what's included and what costs extra. Properties indicated by an ✕⚏ are lodging establishments whose restaurant warrants a special trip.

Assume that hotels operate on the European Plan (EP, with no meals) unless we specify that they use the Continental Plan (CP, with a continental breakfast), Breakfast Plan (BP, with a full breakfast), Modified American Plan (MAP, with breakfast and dinner), or the Full American Plan (FAP, with all meals).

🚩 **General Information** Utah Hotel & Lodging Association ⊠ 9 Exchange Pl., Suite 115, Salt Lake City, UT 84114 ☎ 801/359-0104 ⊕ www.uhla.org.

APARTMENT & CONDO RENTALS

If you want a home base that's roomy enough for a family and comes with cooking facilities, consider a furnished rental. These can save you money, especially if you're traveling with a group. Home-exchange directories sometimes list rentals as well as exchanges.

Condo rentals are widely available in ski resort areas, often at great prices in the off-season.

🚩 **International Agents** Hideaways International ⊠ 767 Islington St., Portsmouth, NH 03801 ☎ 603/430-4433 or 800/843-4433 🖷 603/430-4444 ⊕ www.hideaways.com, annual membership $185. 🚩 **Local Agents** Utah Ski ☎ 877/719-2900 ⊕ www.utahski.com. About.com Salt Lake City ⊕ saltlakecity.about.com/cs/timeshare.

BED & BREAKFASTS

Charm is the long suit of these establishments, which generally occupy a restored older building with some historical or architectural significance. They're generally small, with fewer than 20 rooms. Breakfast is usually included in the rates.

Reservation Services BB Getaways ⊕ www.bbgetaways.com. **Bed and Breakfast Inns of Utah** ⌂ Box 3066, Park City 84060 ⊕ www.bbiu.org. **BNB Finder** ⊕ www.bnbfinder.com.

CAMPING

Camping is invigorating and inexpensive. Utah is full of state and national parks and forests with sites that range from rustic (pit toilets and cold running water), to campgrounds with bathhouses with hot showers, paved trailer pads that can accommodate even jumbo RVs, and full hookups. Fees vary, from $7 to $11 a night for tents and up to $21 for RVs, but are usually waived once the water is turned off for the winter.

Sometimes site reservations are accepted, and then only for up to seven days (early birds reserve up to a year in advance); more often, they're not. Campers who prefer a more remote setting may camp in the backcountry; it's free but you might need a permit, available from park visitor centers and ranger stations. If you're visiting in summer, **plan well ahead.**

The facilities and amenities at privately operated campgrounds are usually more extensive (swimming pools are common), reservations are more widely accepted, and nightly fees are higher: $7 and up for tents, $23 for RVs.

The National Parks: Camping Guide ⊠ Superintendent of Documents, U.S. Government Printing Office, Washington, DC 20402 ☎ 800/365-2267 ⌨ $3.50. **U.S. Forest Service** ☎ 800/280-2267 reservations. **Utah State Parks and Recreation** ⊠ 1594 W. North Temple, Suite 116, Salt Lake City 84114-6001 ☎ 801/538-7220 ⊕ www.stateparks.utah.gov.

GUEST RANCHES

If the thought of sitting around a campfire after a hard day on the range makes your heart beat faster, consider playing dude on a guest ranch. These range from wilderness-rimmed working ranches that accept guests and encourage them to pitch in with chores and other ranch activities to luxurious resorts on the fringes of a small city, with an upscale clientele, swimming pools,

tennis courts, and a lively roster of horse-related activities such as breakfast rides, moonlight rides, and all-day trail rides. Rafting, fishing, tubing, and other activities are usually available; at working ranches, you even may be able to participate in a cattle roundup. In winter, cross-country skiing and snowshoeing keep you busy. Lodgings can run the gamut from charmingly rustic cabins to the kind of deluxe quarters you expect at a first-class hotel. Meals may be fancy or plain but hearty. Many ranches have packages and children's and off-season rates. *See* Guest Ranches *in* Sports & the Outdoors.

Dude Ranchers' Association ⌂ Box 2307, Cody, WY 82414 ☎ 307/587-2339 ⊕ www.duderanch.org.

HOME EXCHANGES

If you would like to exchange your home for someone else's, join a home-exchange organization, which will send you its updated listings of available exchanges for a year and will include your own listing in at least one of them. It's up to you to make specific arrangements.

Exchange Clubs HomeLink USA ⊠ 2937 NW 9th Terrace, Wilton Manors, FL 33311 ☎ 954/566-2687 or 800/638-3841 ⌨ 954/566-2783 ⊕ www.homelink.org; $75 yearly for a listing and online access; $45 additional to receive directories. **Intervac U.S.** ⊠ 30 Corte San Fernando, Tiburon, CA 94920 ☎ 800/756-4663 ⌨ 415/435-7440 ⊕ www.intervacus.com; $128 yearly for a listing, online access, and a catalog; $68 without catalog.

HOSTELS

Hostelling through Utah is an inexpensive way to see the mountains and the desert. Utah has several, generally in Salt Lake City or around state or national parks.

No matter what your age, you can save on lodging costs by staying at hostels. In Utah, most hostels are geared to the student–backpacker crowd. Some have camping facilities with access to an indoor kitchen and bath. In some 4,500 locations in more than 70 countries around the world, Hostelling International (HI), the umbrella group for a number of national youth-hostel associations, offers single-sex, dorm-style beds and, at many hostels, rooms for couples and family accommodations. Membership in any HI national hostel association, open to travelers of all ages, allows you to stay in HI-affiliated hostels at member rates; one-year membership is about $28 for adults (C$35 for a two-year minimum membership in Canada, £15 in the U.K., A$52 in Australia, and NZ$40 in New Zealand); hostels charge about $10–$30 per night. Members have priority if the hostel is full; they're also eligible for discounts around the world, even on rail and bus travel in some countries.

HI is also an especially helpful organization for road cyclists.

7 Organizations Hostelling International–USA ✉ 8401 Colesville Rd., Suite 600, Silver Spring, MD 20910 ☎ 301/495-1240 ☐ 301/495-6697 ⊕ www.hiusa.org. **Hostelling International–Canada** ✉ 205 Catherine St., Suite 400, Ottawa, Ontario K2P 1C3 ☎ 613/237-7884 or 800/663-5777 ☐ 613/237-7868 ⊕ www.hihostels.ca. **YHA England and Wales** ✉ Trevelyan House, Dimple Rd., Matlock, Derbyshire DE4 3YH, U.K. ☎ 0870/870-8808, 0870/770-8868, 0162/959-2600 ☐ 0870/770-6127 ⊕ www.yha.org.uk. **YHA Australia** ✉ 422 Kent St., Sydney, NSW 2001 ☎ 02/9261-1111 ☐ 02/9261-1969 ⊕ www.yha.com.au. **YHA New Zealand** ✉ Level 1, Moorhouse City, 166 Moorhouse Ave., Box 436, Christchurch ☎ 03/379-9970 or 0800/278-299 ☐ 03/365-4476 ⊕ www.yha.org.nz.

HOTELS

Most Salt Lake City hotels cater to business travelers, with such facilities as restaurants, cocktail lounges, Internet, swimming pools, exercise equipment, and meeting rooms. Room rates usually reflect the range of amenities available. Most other Utah towns and cities also have less expensive hotels that are clean and comfortable but have fewer facilities. A popular accommodations trend is the all-suite hotel, which gives you more room for the money; examples include Courtyard by Marriott and Embassy Suites. In resort towns, hotels are decidedly more deluxe, with every imaginable amenity in every imaginable price range; rural areas generally have simple, and sometimes rustic, accommodations.

Many properties have special weekend rates, sometimes up to 50% off regular prices. However, these deals are usually not extended during peak summer months, when hotels are normally full. The same discounts generally hold true for resort town hotels in the off-seasons.

All hotels listed have private bath unless otherwise noted.

7 Toll-Free Numbers Best Western ☎ 800/528-1234 ⊕ www.bestwestern.com. **Choice** ☎ 800/424-6423 ⊕ www.choicehotels.com. **Comfort Inn** ☎ 800/424-6423 ⊕ www.choicehotels.com. **Days Inn** ☎ 800/325-2525 ⊕ www.daysinn.com. **Doubletree Hotels** ☎ 800/222-8733 ⊕ www.doubletree.com. **Embassy Suites** ☎ 800/362-2779 ⊕ www.embassysuites.com. **Fairfield Inn** ☎ 800/228-2800 ⊕ www.marriott.com. **Hilton** ☎ 800/445-8667 ⊕ www.hilton.com. **Holiday Inn** ☎ 800/465-4329 ⊕ www.ichotelsgroup.com. **Howard Johnson** ☎ 800/446-4656 ⊕ www.hojo.com. **Hyatt Hotels & Resorts** ☎ 800/233-1234 ⊕ www.hyatt.com. **La Quinta** ☎ 800/531-5900 ⊕ www.lq.com. **Marriott** ☎ 800/228-9290 ⊕ www.marriott.com. **Quality Inn** ☎ 800/424-6423 ⊕ www.choicehotels.com. **Radisson** ☎ 800/333-3333 ⊕ www.radisson.com. **Ramada** ☎ 800/228-2828, 800/854-7854 international reservations ⊕ www.ramada.com or www.ramadahotels.com. **Sheraton** ☎ 800/325-3535 ⊕ www.starwood.com/sheraton. **Sleep Inn** ☎ 800/424-6423 ⊕ www.choicehotels.com. **Westin Hotels & Resorts** ☎ 800/228-3000 ⊕ www.starwood.com/westin. **Wyndham Hotels & Resorts** ☎ 800/822-4200 ⊕ www.wyndham.com.

MOTELS

The once-familiar, locally owned roadside motel is fast disappearing from the American landscape. In its place are chain-run motor inns at highway intersections and in rural areas off-the-beaten path. Some of these establishments have very basic facilities; others provide restaurants, swimming pools, and other amenities.

7 Motel Chains Motel 6 ☎ 800/466-8356 ⊕ www.motel6.com. **Rodeway Inns** ☎ 800/228-2000 ⊕ www.choicehotels.com. **Shilo Inn** ☎ 800/222-2244 ⊕ www.shiloinns.com. **Super 8 Motels** ☎ 800/800-8000 ⊕ www.super8.com. **Travelodge** ☎ 800/578-7878 ⊕ www.travelodge.com.

RESORTS

Ski towns throughout Utah such as Deer Valley, Sundance, and Brian Head, are home to dozens of resorts in all price ranges; the activities lacking in any individual property are usually in the town itself—in summer as well as winter. Off the slopes, there are both wonderful rustic and luxurious resorts bordering the national parks: Zion Ponderosa Ranch Resort near Zion, Red Cliffs Lodge near Arches, and Hidden Falls Resort near Capitol Reef and Bryce Canyon.

MEDIA

NEWSPAPERS & MAGAZINES

The *Salt Lake Tribune* is Utah's leading newspaper, with listings of all current events, weather, and local news; it's also the most liberal voice in Utah. The *Deseret Morning News* is a more conservative newspaper and tends to be the local voice of the LDS Church. *Salt Lake Magazine* has a calendar of events and social news. *Utah Business* is a local magazine highlighting what's happening in the Utah business world and generally focuses on Salt Lake City.

▶ Newspaper Web Sites *The Salt Lake Tribune* ⊕ www.sltrib.com. *The Deseret Morning News* ⊕ www.deseretnews.com. *Utah Business* ⊕ www.utahbusiness.com. *Salt Lake Magazine* ⊕ www.saltlakemagazine.com.

RADIO & TELEVISION

Radio stations are plentiful throughout Utah. Remember that stations fade in and out in mountain areas. There are several radio stations in Salt Lake City: KALL (700 AM) is sports radio; KBZN (97.9 FM) plays smooth jazz; KKAT (101.9 FM) plays country; KRCL (90.9 FM) is community radio; KODJ (94.1 FM) plays oldies; KSFI (100.3 FM) plays adult contemporary; KUER (90.1 FM) is the local NPR station; and KBER (101.1 FM) plays rock.

Television also fades in and out because of the state's mountains, so affiliates may be broadcast on different channels in different areas. Salt Lake television stations include the following: KBYU, channel 11 (the BYU station); KSL, channel 5 (NBC); KSTU, channel 13 (Fox); KTVX, channel 4 (ABC); KUTV, channel 2 (CBS); KUWB, channel 30 (WB); KUED, channel 7 (PBS).

MONEY MATTERS

Hotel prices in Salt Lake City run the gamut, but on the average prices are a bit lower than in most major cities. You can pay $100–$350 a night for a room in a major business hotel, though some "value" hotel rooms go for $50–$75, and budget motels are also readily available. Weekend packages at city hotels can cut prices in half (but may not be available in peak winter or summer seasons). As a rule, costs outside cities are lower, except in the deluxe resorts, where costs can be double those anywhere else in the state. Look for senior and kids' discounts at many attractions. Prices throughout this guide are given for adults. Substantially reduced fees are almost always available for children, students, and senior citizens. For information on taxes, *see* Taxes.

ATMS

ATMs are widely available throughout Utah and are generally reliable. You'll often find them in grocery stores. If you're buying groceries, you may want to use your ATM card and get extra cash back to avoid ATM surcharges.

CREDIT CARDS

Throughout this guide, the following abbreviations are used: **AE,** American Express; **D,** Discover; **DC,** Diners Club; **MC,** MasterCard; and **V,** Visa.

▶ Reporting Lost Cards American Express ☎ 800/992-3404. **Diners Club** ☎ 800/234-6377. **Discover** ☎ 800/347-2683. **MasterCard** ☎ 800/622-7747. **Visa** ☎ 800/847-2911.

NATIONAL PARKS

Utah has five national parks—more than any other state except Alaska and California. Though Bryce and Zion are the best known, fascinating landscape can be seen at Arches, Canyonlands, and Capitol Reef, too. Utah's 41 state parks range from historic monuments to recreation areas, many of which have public lakes, often reservoirs, that are popular spots for camping as well as boating and other water sports. Officially, national and state parks are open 24 hours a day, but visitor centers are usually open 8 AM to sunset with shorter hours in the off-season.

Look into discount passes to save money on park entrance fees. For $50, the National Parks Pass admits you (and any passengers in your private vehicle) to all national parks, monuments, and recreation areas, as well as other sites run by the National Park Service, for a year. (In parks that charge per person, the pass admits you, your spouse and children, and your parents, when you arrive together.) Camping and parking are extra. The $15 Golden Eagle Pass, a hologram you affix to your National Parks Pass, functions as an upgrade, granting entry to all sites run by the NPS, the U.S. Fish and Wildlife Service, the U.S. Forest Service, and the Bureau of Land Management. The upgrade, which expires with the parks pass, is sold by most national-park, Fish-and-Wildlife, and BLM fee stations. A major percentage of the proceeds from pass sales funds National Parks projects.

Both the Golden Age Passport ($10), for U.S. citizens or permanent residents who are 62 and older, and the Golden Access Passport (free), for persons with disabilities, entitle holders (and any passengers in their private vehicles) to lifetime free entry to all national parks, plus 50% off fees for the use of many park facilities and services. (The discount doesn't always apply to companions.) To obtain them, you must show proof of age and of U.S. citizenship or permanent residency—such as a U.S. passport, driver's license, or birth certificate—and, if requesting Golden Access, proof of disability. The Golden Age and Golden Access passes are available only at NPS-run sites that charge an entrance fee. The National Parks Pass is also available by mail and phone and via the Internet.

National Park Foundation ✉ 11 Dupont Circle NW, Suite 600, Washington, DC 20036 ☎ 202/238-4200 ⊕ www.nationalparks.org. **National Park Service** ✉ National Park Service/Department of Interior, 1849 C St. NW, Washington, DC 20240 ☎ 202/208-6843 ⊕ www.nps.gov. **National Parks Conservation Association** ✉ 1300 19th St. NW, Suite 300, Washington, DC 20036 ☎ 202/223-6722 or 800/628-7275 ⊕ www.npca.org.

Passes by Mail & Online National Park Foundation ⊕ www.nationalparks.org. **National Parks Pass** National Park Foundation ✐ Box 34108, Washington, DC 20043 ☎ 888/467-2757 ⊕ www.nationalparks.org; include a check or money order payable to the National Park Service, plus $3.95 for shipping and handling (allow 8 to 13 business days from date of receipt for pass delivery), or call for passes.

PACKING

Informality reigns here; jeans, sport shirts, and T-shirts fit in almost everywhere, for both men and women. The few restaurants and performing-arts events where dressier outfits are required, usually in resorts and larger cities, are the exception.

If you plan to spend much time outdoors, and certainly if you go in winter, choose clothing appropriate for cold and wet weather. Cotton clothing, including denim—although fine on warm, dry days—can be uncomfortable when it gets wet and when the weather's cold. A better choice is clothing made of wool or any of a number of new synthetics that provide warmth without bulk and maintain their insulating properties even when wet.

In summer you'll want shorts during the day. But because early morning and night can be cold, and high passes windy, pack a sweater and a light jacket, and perhaps also a wool cap and gloves. Try layering—a T-shirt under another shirt under a jacket—and peel off layers as you go. For walks and hikes, you'll need sturdy footwear. To take you into the wilds, boots should have thick soles and plenty of ankle support; if your shoes are new and you plan to spend much time on the trail, break them in at home. Bring a day pack for short hikes, along with a canteen or water bottle, and don't forget rain gear, a hat, sunscreen, and insect repellent.

In winter, prepare for subfreezing temperatures with good boots, warm socks and liners, thermal underwear, a well-insulated jacket, and a warm hat and mittens. Dress in layers so you can add or remove clothes as the temperatures fluctuate.

If you attend dances and other events at Native American reservations, dress conservatively—skirts or long pants for women, long pants for men—or you may be asked to leave.

When traveling to mountain areas, **remember that sunglasses and a sun hat are essential at high altitudes,** even in winter; the thinner atmosphere requires sunscreen with a greater SPF than you might need at lower elevations. Bring moisturizer even if you don't normally use it. Utah's dry climate can be hard on your skin.

In your carry-on luggage, pack an extra pair of eyeglasses or contact lenses and enough of any medication you take to last a few days longer than the entire trip. You may also ask your doctor to write a spare prescription using the drug's generic name, as brand names may vary from country to country. In luggage to be checked, **never pack prescription drugs, valuables, or undeveloped film.** And don't forget to carry with you the addresses of offices that handle refunds of lost traveler's checks. Check *Fodor's How to Pack* (available at online retailers and bookstores everywhere) for more tips.

To avoid customs and security delays, carry medications in their original packaging. Don't pack any sharp objects in your carry-on luggage, including knives of any size or material, scissors, nail clippers, and corkscrews, or anything else that might arouse suspicion.

To avoid having your checked luggage chosen for hand inspection, don't cram bags full. The U.S. Transportation Security Administration suggests packing shoes on top and placing personal items you don't want touched in clear plastic bags.

CHECKING LUGGAGE

You're allowed to carry aboard one bag and one personal article, such as a purse or a laptop computer. Make sure what you carry on fits under your seat or in the overhead bin. Get to the gate early, so you can board as soon as possible, before the overhead bins fill up.

Baggage allowances vary by carrier, destination, and ticket class. On international flights, you're usually allowed to check two bags weighing up to 70 pounds (32 kilograms) each, although a few airlines allow checked bags of up to 88 pounds

(40 kilograms) in first class. Some international carriers don't allow more than 66 pounds (30 kilograms) per bag in business class and 44 pounds (20 kilograms) in economy. If you're flying to or through the United Kingdom, your luggage cannot exceed 70 pounds (32 kilograms) per bag. On domestic flights, the limit is usually 50 to 70 pounds (23 to 32 kilograms) per bag. In general, carry-on bags shouldn't exceed 40 pounds (18 kilograms). Most airlines won't accept bags that weigh more than 100 pounds (45 kilograms) on domestic or international flights. Expect to pay a fee for baggage that exceeds weight limits. Check baggage restrictions with your carrier before you pack.

Airline liability for baggage is limited to $2,500 per person on flights within the United States. On international flights it amounts to $9.07 per pound or $20 per kilogram for checked baggage (roughly $640 per 70-pound bag), with a maximum of $634.90 per piece, and $400 per passenger for unchecked baggage. You can buy additional coverage at check-in for about $10 per $1,000 of coverage, but it often excludes a rather extensive list of items, shown on your airline ticket.

Before departure, itemize your bags' contents and their worth, and label the bags with your name, address, and phone number. (If you use your home address, cover it so potential thieves can't see it readily.) Include a label inside each bag and **pack a copy of your itinerary.** At check-in, make sure each bag is correctly tagged with the destination airport's three-letter code. Because some checked bags will be opened for hand inspection, the U.S. Transportation Security Administration recommends that you leave luggage unlocked or use the plastic locks offered at check-in. TSA screeners place an inspection notice inside searched bags, which are re-sealed with a special lock.

If your bag has been searched and contents are missing or damaged, file a claim with the TSA Consumer Response Center as soon as possible. If your bags arrive damaged or fail to arrive at all, file a written report with the airline before leaving the airport.

F Complaints U.S. Transportation Security Administration Contact Center ☎ 866/289-9673 ⊕ www.tsa.gov.

SAFETY

All those strenuous activities in high altitudes can be fun but dangerous. Utah is full of wide open, lonely spaces. Though you may enjoy the freedom, openness, and solitude, it's always best to tell someone—the hotel desk clerk, the ski rental person—where you're going. Cell phones don't always work in the backcountry, and if you're stranded in temperatures below freezing or above 100°F, even a general idea of where you are can help rescuers find you quickly. Regardless of the outdoor activity or your level of skill, safety must come first. Remember: know your limits.

Many trails are at high altitudes, where oxygen is thinner. They're also frequently desolate. Hikers and bikers should **carry emergency supplies** in their backpacks. Proper equipment includes a flashlight, a compass, waterproof matches, a first-aid kit, a knife, and a light plastic tarp for shelter. Backcountry skiers should add a repair kit, a blanket, an avalanche beacon, and a lightweight shovel to their lists. Always **bring extra food and a canteen of water** as dehydration is a common occurrence at high altitudes. **Never drink from streams or lakes,** unless you boil the water first or purify it with tablets. Giardia, an intestinal parasite, may be present.

Always check the condition of roads and trails, and get the latest weather reports before setting out. In summer take precautions against heat stroke or exhaustion by resting frequently in shaded areas; in winter take precautions against hypothermia by layering clothing. Ultimately, proper planning, common sense, and good physical conditioning are the strongest guards against the elements.

ALTITUDE

You may feel dizzy and weak and find yourself breathing heavily—signs that the thin mountain air isn't giving you your accustomed dose of oxygen. Take it easy and **rest often for a few days until you're acclimatized.** Throughout your stay drink plenty of water and watch your alcohol consumption. If you experience severe headaches and nausea, see a doctor. It is easy—especially in Utah, where highways climb to 10,000 feet and higher—to go too high too fast. The remedy for altitude-related discomfort is to go down quickly, into heavier air. Other altitude-related problems include dehydration and overexposure to the sun due to the thin air.

FLASH FLOODS

Flash floods can strike at any time and any place with little or no warning. The danger in mountainous terrain intensifies when distant rains are channeled into gullies and ravines, turning a quiet streamside campsite or wash into a rampaging torrent in seconds; similarly, desert terrain can become dangerous when heavy rains falls on land that is unable to absorb the water and thus floods quickly. Check weather reports before heading into the backcountry and be prepared to head for higher ground if the weather turns severe.

WILD ANIMALS

One of the most wonderful parts of Utah is the abundant wildlife. And while a herd of grazing elk or a bighorn sheep high on a hillside is most certainly a Kodak moment, an encounter with a bear or mountain lion is not. To avoid such an unpleasant situation while hiking, make plenty of noise, keep dogs on a leash, and small children between adults. While camping, be sure to store all food, utensils, and clothing with food odors far away from your tent, preferably high in a tree (also far from your tent). If you do come across a bear or big cat, **do not run.** For bears, back away quietly; for lions, make yourself look as big as possible. In either case, be prepared to fend off the animal with loud noises, rocks, sticks, etc. And, like the saying goes, do not feed the bears—or any wild animals, whether they're dangerous or not.

When in any park, give all animals their space and never attempt to feed any of them. If you want to take a photograph, use a long lens and keep your distance.

This is particularly important for winter visitors. Approaching an animal can cause stress and affect its ability to survive the sometimes brutal climate. In all cases remember that the animals have the right-of-way; this is their home, you are the visitor.

SENIOR-CITIZEN TRAVEL

To qualify for age-related discounts, mention your senior-citizen status up front when booking hotel reservations (not when checking out) and before you're seated in restaurants (not when paying the bill). Be sure to have identification on hand. When renting a car, ask about promotional car-rental discounts, which can be cheaper than senior-citizen rates.

🄵 **Educational Programs Elderhostel** ⊠ 11 Ave. de Lafayette, Boston, MA 02111 ☎ 877/426-8056, 978/323-4141 international callers, 877/426-2167 TTY 🖷 877/426-2166 ⊕ www.elderhostel.org.

SHOPPING

While there are plenty of modern shopping malls in Utah, a trip through the West is a chance to buy authentic memorabilia and clothing—choose from cowboy boots, cowboy hats, bolero ties, and the like. It's also a great place to find Native American crafts, but be careful of shams. Small artisan colonies often neighbor ritzy resorts. These enclaves of creative souls produce some of the finest handcrafted wares anywhere; look for local galleries and boutiques that showcase their work.

KEY DESTINATIONS

Outlet malls are in both St. George and Park City. Park City's Main Street is lined with little shops, many specializing in Western items. In downtown Salt Lake City, Crossroads Mall and the ZCMI Center are across the street from Temple Square. The Gateway Center near downtown has upscale shops, the Clark Planetarium, and the Olympic Fountain. Trolley Square is an old trolley station converted to shops and restaurants.

SPORTS & THE OUTDOORS

Utah is one of America's greatest playgrounds, and many residents make exercise a high priority. Within 30 minutes of leaving their homes and offices, Utah jocks can do their thing in the midst of exquisite scenery—not boxed in at a gym watching ceiling-mounted televisions. The same companies that outfit skiers in winter can supply summer travelers with everything from golf equipment to bikes.

Regardless of the outdoor activity or your level of skill, safety must come first. Know your limits, and keep in mind that you're in high-altitude country. Respect area rules and closures, as well as the admonition to leave only footprints, take only pictures. Many areas are open only to hikers, with vehicles, mountain bikes, and horses banned. All archaeological artifacts, including rock etchings and paintings, are protected by federal law and must be left untouched and undisturbed. Locals can be strident about protecting their wilderness.

ADVENTURE TRIP OUTFITTERS

If you're looking for a place where you can do things you've never done before, here it is. You may need some help from an outfitter to have that adventure you've always imagined. Many trip organizers specialize in only one type of activity; however, a few companies guide different kinds of active trips. (In some cases, these larger companies also act essentially as a clearinghouse or agent for smaller trip outfitters.) Be sure to sign on with a reliable outfitter; getting stuck with a shoddy operator can be disappointing, uncomfortable, and even dangerous. Some sports—white-water rafting and mountaineering, for example—have organizations that license or certify guides, and you should be sure that the guide you're with is properly accredited.

🄵 **Outfitters America Outdoors** 🕮 Box 10847, Knoxville, TN 37939 ☎ 800/524-4814 ⊕ www.americaoutdoors.org. **REI** ⊠ 3285 E. 3300 South St., Salt Lake City 84109 ☎ 800/622-2236 ⊕ www.rei.com. **Sierra Club Outings** ⊠ 85 2nd St., San Francisco, CA 94105 ☎ 415/977-5500 ⊕ www.sierraclub.org. **The World Outdoors** ⊠ 2840 Wilderness Pl. F, Boulder, CO 80301 ☎ 303/413-0938 or 800/488-8483 ⊕ www.theworldoutdoors.com. **Utah Guides & Outfitters** ⊕ vpp.com/utah. **Utah Travel Council** ⊠ 300 N. State St., Salt Lake City, UT 84114 ☎ 801/538-1030 ⊕ www.utah.com.

BICYCLING

Some say mountain biking was invented in Moab—where the rugged terrain and slickrock is still one of the best environments in the world for the sport—and is a popular activity all over Utah, with trails nearly everywhere from well-groomed, easy rides to rugged, dangerous ones. If you have a particular trail in mind, check before you go—some trails are open to only bikers one day, only hikers the next. Ski resorts are open to bikers in summer; you can ride the lift up with your bike, then ride down the mountain. High, rugged country puts a premium on fitness. Even if you can ride 40 mi at home without breaking a sweat, you might find yourself struggling terribly on steep climbs and in elevations that often exceed 10,000 feet. If you have an extended tour in mind, you might want to come a couple of days early to acclimate yourself to the altitude and terrain. Pre-trip conditioning is likely to make your trip more enjoyable.

On tours where the elevation may vary 4,000 feet or more, the climate can change dramatically. Although the valleys may be scorching, high-mountain passes may still be lined with snow in summer. Pack clothing accordingly. (Bicycle racers often stuff newspaper inside their jerseys when descending from high passes to shield themselves from the chill.) Although you shouldn't have much problem renting a bike (trip organizers can usually arrange rentals), it's a good idea to bring your own pair of sturdy, stiff-bottom cycling shoes to make riding easier, and your own helmet. Some experienced riders bring not only their own shoes but their pedals if they use an interlocking shoe-and-pedal system. If you do decide to bring your own bike, be prepared to spend as much as $150 in special luggage handling. Summer and early fall are the best times to plan a trip; at other times, snow and ice may still obstruct high-terrain roads and trails.

Guided bike trips generally range in price between $80 and $150 a day, depending on lodging and meals. The Adventure Cycling Association is perhaps the best general source of information on biking in Utah—including detailed maps and information on trip organizers. They also guide trips stretching along the Continental Divide. Hostelling-International (HI; ⇨ Lodging) is a good connection for cycling tours as well. Remember that biking is not permitted in National Wilderness areas.

☑ **Adventure Cycling Association** ✑ Box 8308, Missoula, MT 59807 ☎ 406/721-1776 or 800/755-2453 ⊕ www.adventurecycling.org. **Moab Cyclery** ✑ Box 339, Moab, UT 84532 ☎ 800/559-1978 ⊕ www.moabcyclery.com. **Timberline Adventures** ✉ 7975 E. Harvard St., Suite J, Denver, CO 80231 ☎ 303/759-3804 or 800/417-2453. **Utah Mountain Biking** ⊕ www.utahmountainbiking. com. **Utah Travel Council** ☎ 800/200-1160 ⊕ www.utah.com/bike/.

FISHING

Utah is famous for its fly-fishing. *Field and Stream* magazine is a leading source of information on fishing travel, technique, and equipment. For lists of guides to rivers and lakes of Utah, contact the Utah Division of Wildlife Resources.

Fishing licenses, available at tackle shops and local stores as well as online, are required in Utah. The fishing season in Utah is year-round, but limits vary from species to species. A few streams are considered "private" streams, in that they are privately stocked by a local club, other rivers are fly-fishing or catch-and-release only, so be sure you **know the rules before making your first cast.** Tribal fishing licenses are necessary on reservation land.

Utah water can be cold, especially at higher elevations and especially in spring and fall (and winter, of course). You'd do well to **bring waterproof waders** or buy them when you arrive in the region. Outfitters and some tackle shops rent equipment, but you're best off bringing your own gear. Lures are another story, though: Whether you plan to fish with flies or other lures, local tackle shops can usually give you a pretty good idea of what works best in a particular region, and you can buy accordingly.

In the mid-1990s, whirling disease—a parasitic infection that afflicts trout and a few other types of fish—began to reduce fish populations in some Utah streams. Efforts to curb the spread of the disease have met with some success, but some waters may still suffer from a smaller fish population.

A guide will cost about $250 per day and can be shared by two anglers if they are fishing from a boat and possibly by three if they are wading. Lunch will probably be included and flies might be, although there may be an extra $15–$20 charge for these. **🇫 Utah Division of Wildlife Resources** ✉ 1596 W. North Temple, Salt Lake City 84116 ☎ 801/538-4700 ⊕ www.wildlife.utah.gov. **Utah Fish Finder** ⊕ www.utahfishfinder.com. **Utah Travel Council** ☎ 800/200-1160 ⊕ www.utah.com/fish. **🇫 Instruction Jan's Mountain Outfitters** ✉ 1600 Park Ave., Box 280, Park City 84060 ☎ 801/649-4949 or 800/745-1020 ⊕ www.jans.com.

GUEST RANCHES

Several dude ranches call Utah home; many specialize in certain activities or age levels, so check before you go to see that the ranch provides activities you like for the age ranges in your group. Most dude ranches don't require any previous experience with horses, although a few working ranches reserve weeks in spring and fall—when the chore of moving cattle is more intensive than in summer—for experienced riders. No special equipment is necessary, although if you plan to do much fishing, you're best off bringing your own tackle (some ranches have tackle to loan or rent). Be sure to check with the ranch for a list of items you might be expected to bring. If you plan to do much riding, a couple of pairs of sturdy pants, boots, a wide-brimmed hat to shield you from the sun, and outerwear as protection from the possibility of rain or chill should be packed. Expect to spend at least $125 per day. Depending on the activities you engage in, as well as accommodations, the price can exceed $250 a day. *See* Guest Ranches *in* Lodging, as well.

KAYAKING

The streams and rivers of Utah tend to be better suited to kayaking than canoeing. Steep mountains and narrow canyons usually mean fast-flowing water in which the maneuverability of kayaks is a great asset. Fast water also means you need to

have some experience. Don't assume that because you have lake or ocean experience you can kayak in white water. A means of transport for less experienced paddlers is the inflatable kayak. Dvorak Expeditions leads trips on the Green River in eastern Utah and conducts clinics, including certification courses, for kayakers of all abilities. Sheri Griffiths Expeditions focuses on family and women-only trips.

To minimize environmental impact as well as ensure a sense of wilderness privacy (riverside campgrounds are often limited to one party per night), a reservation policy is used for many rivers in Utah. Often, the reserved times—many of the *prime* times—are prebooked by licensed outfitters, limiting your possibilities if you're planning a self-guided trip. For those rivers with restricted-use policies, it's best to reserve through a guide company several months or more in advance. Also, try to be flexible about when and where to go; you might find that the time you want to go is unavailable, or you may find yourself closed out altogether from your river of choice. If you insist on running a specific river at a specific time, your best bet is to sign on with a guided trip (which will cost at least $100 a day).

Outfitters provide life jackets and, if necessary, paddles and helmets; they often throw in waterproof containers for cameras, clothing, and sleeping bags. Bring bug repellent as well as a good hat, sunblock, and warm clothing for overnight trips. The sun on the river can be intense, but once it disappears behind canyon walls, the temperature can drop 30 degrees or more. The best footwear is either a pair of water-resistant sandals or old sneakers. **🇫 Instruction & Trips Dvorak Expeditions** ✉ 17921 U.S. 285, Nathrop, CO 81236 ☎ 800/824-3795 ⊕ www.dvorakexpeditions.com. **Sheri Griffiths Expeditions** ✍ Box 1324, Moab 84532 ☎ 800/332-2439 ⊕ www.griffithexp.com.

MAPS

If you plan to do much traveling where trails might not be well marked or maintained, you'll need maps and a compass. Topographical maps are sold in well-equipped outdoor stores (REI or Eastern Mountain Sports, for example). Maps in several different scales are available from the U.S. Geological Survey. Before ordering, you will need to request the free index and catalog, from which you can order the specific maps you need. Many local camping, fishing, and hunting stores carry U.S.G.S. and other detailed maps of the surrounding region. The U.S. Forest Service and the BLM also publish useful maps.

🔄 Maps U.S. Geological Survey ⊕ Distribution Center, Box 25286, Federal Center, Denver, CO 80225 ☎ 303/202–4700 or 888/275–8747.

PACK TRIPS & HORSEBACK RIDING

Horsemanship is not a prerequisite for most trips, but it is helpful. If you aren't an experienced rider (and even if you are), you can expect to experience some saddle discomfort for the first day or two. If you're unsure of how much of this sort of thing you can put up with, sign up for a shorter trip (one to three days) before taking on an adventure of a week or longer. Another option is to spend a few days at a guest ranch to get used to life in the saddle, then try a shorter, overnight pack trip organized by the ranch. Pack trips in Utah often use llamas, peaceful sturdy animals bred for high altitudes.

Clothing requirements are minimal. A sturdy pair of pants, a wide-brim sun hat, and outerwear to protect against rain are about the only necessities. Ask your outfitter for a list of items you'll need. You might be limited in the gear (extra clothing) or luxuries (alcoholic beverages) an outfitter will let you bring along. Trip costs typically range between $120 and $180 per day.

Pack trips tend to be organized by local outfitters or ranches rather than national organizations. Local chambers of commerce can usually provide lists of outfitters who work in a particular area.

🔄 Outfitters Buckhorn Llama Company ⊕ Box 64, Masonville, CO 80541 ☎ 970/667–7411 ⊕ www.llamapack.com. **Hondoo Rivers and Trails** ⊕ Box 98, Torrey 84775 ☎ 800/332–2696 ⊕ www.hondoo.com. **Rosebud Llamas Utah** ⊕ Box 270090, Fruitland 84027 ☎ 435/548–2630 ⊕ www.rosebudllamasutah.com.

RAFTING

In addition to its central importance for mountain bikers, Moab is also the center of the rafting industry and a take-off point for several of the most popular float trips in the Southwest. A trip on Utah's stretch of the Colorado River, particularly the exhilarating stretch through Cataract Canyon, is an experience that is not easily forgotten. But Utah's white water can be cold and dangerous. The type of trip you'll have depends on the time of year you go and the weather conditions. Early in the year, spring thaws run fast and cold. As summer goes on, the water gets slower and warmer, though it's never truly warm. If it's a drought year, even spring waters can be slower.

Unless you're an expert, **pick a recognized outfitter** if you're going into white water. Even then, you should be a good swimmer and in solid general health. Different companies are licensed to run different rivers, although there may be several companies working the same river. Some organizers combine river rafting with other activities: pack trips, mountain-bike excursions, extended hikes, fishing.

"Raft" can mean any of a number of things: an inflated raft in which passengers do the paddling; an inflated raft, or wooden dory in which a licensed professional does the work; a motorized raft on which some oar work might be required. Be sure you know what kind of raft you'll be riding—or paddling—before booking a trip. Day trips typically run between $30 and $60 per person. Expect to pay between $80 and $120 per day for multiday trips. Raft Utah publishes a comprehensive directory with full descriptions of all of Utah's rivers, and the outfitters who run them.

🔄 Outfitters Adrift Adventures ⊕ Box 192, Jensen 84035 ☎ 800/824–0150 ⊕ www.adrift.com. **ARTA River Trips** ✉ 24000 Casa Loma Rd., Groveland, CA 95321 ☎ 800/323–2782 ⊕ www.arta.org. **OARS** ⊕ Box 67, Angels Camp, CA 95222 ☎ 800/346–6277 ⊕ www.oars.com. **World Wide River Expeditions** ☎ 800/231–2769 ⊕ www.worldwideriver.com.

ROCK CLIMBING & MOUNTAINEERING

Some of the most difficult climbing in the world is in Utah. You've seen the terrain in the movie *Mission Impossible II* and many television commercials. Keep in mind that along with tricky terrain, you're climbing at a very high high altitude.

Before you sign on with any trip, be sure to clarify to the trip organizer your climbing skills, experience, and physical condition. Climbing tends to be a team sport, and overestimating your capabilities can endanger not only yourself but other team members. A fair self-assessment of your abilities also helps a guide choose an appropriate climbing route; routes (not unlike ski trails) are rated according to their difficulty. The way to a summit may be relatively easy or brutally challenging, depending on the route selected. You may want to get some instruction at a climbing wall before a trip to Utah.

Guide services usually rent such technical gear as helmets, pitons, ropes, and axes, and be sure to ask what equipment and supplies you'll need to bring along. (Outfitters usually rent equipment on a per-item, per-day basis.) Some mountaineering stores rent climbing equipment. As for clothing, temperatures can fluctuate dramatically at higher elevations. Bringing several thin layers of clothing, including a sturdy, waterproof–breathable outer shell, is the best strategy for dealing with weather variations.

Organized trip costs can vary considerably, depending on group size, length of climb, instruction rendered, and equipment supplied. Count on spending at least $80 a day. However, the cost of a small-group multiday instructional climb can push $200 a day.

🔽 **Instructional Programs & Outfitters Exum Utah Mountain Adventures** ✉ 2070 E. 3900 South St. #B, Salt Lake City 84124 ☎ 801/550-3986 ⊕ www. exum.ofutah.com.

SKIING

Known all over the world for their powdery slopes, Utah's ski resorts are among the best in the United States. You might not get that at first view, when the state's resorts can seem quaint and rather small. But it's the snow that makes the difference. Utah's climate is dry, which makes the snow extremely light and powdery. Ski conditions are often such that you can ski in powder up to your waist. Runs used for the 2002 Olympics can now be used by any skier. Generally the ski season runs from late November through March or April, though in good snow years the season may open in late October and run into May. Each resort has trails of varying levels of difficulty, and most have ski schools, some specifically for kids. No matter which resort you choose, you'll find the "Greatest Snow on Earth", generally within 20 minutes of downtown Salt Lake City and 30–45 minutes from the Salt Lake International Airport.

Where you go depends on what type of amenities you like. Deer Valley is the poshest resort in the state. Park City, home of the Canyons, is the ultimate resort town along the lines of Jackson Hole and Sun Valley. Snowbird is another high-class resort with all the perks. Brighton is a favorite place for snowboarders and families (check out the "kids ski free" deal). Locals head to Alta, which doesn't allow snowboarders; Solitude is another place that tends not to advertise to tourists. Other major resorts in Utah include Brian Head, near Cedar City in southern Utah; Powder Mountain and Snow Basin, both near Ogden; and Sundance, near Provo.

If you're a cross-country skier, there are plenty of groomed trails. Try Solider Hollow, site of the 2002 Olympic biathlon, Mill Creek Canyon, or Solitude Nordic Center. Even southern Utah, which is known for relatively mild winters, can bring up enough snow for some first-rate cross-country skiing, particularly around Bryce Canyon.

If you don't ski, you can try snowshoeing. It's easy for kids to do, and snowshoe rentals are available at ski rental shops.

Avoid backcountry unless you've checked the avalanche warnings and **always tell someone where you're going.**

All resorts have rental equipment, but the prices are often one-quarter to one-half cheaper at outside rental companies, and the equipment is often better. You're sure to get exactly what you want if you rent in advance from a nonresort company.

Avalanche risks make backcountry skiing ill-advised for all but those with the proper safety equipment and considerable experience. The guided Ski Utah Interconnect Adventure Tour is a combination of lift-service and backcountry skiing in Utah's three major skiing regions: Big Cottonwood, Little Cottonwood, and Park City. Much of the trip is within resort boundaries, and it can be negotiated either on telemark skis or with regular alpine gear. The fee is $150, including lunch and transportation.

Strong intermediate and advanced skiers can also enjoy heli-skiing, whether in search of powder or the solitude of the backcountry. Wasatch Powderbird Guides has permits for several thousand acres of skiable terrain, mostly in the basins and drainages on the periphery of Alta and Snowbird. Tours cost $525–$770 per person per day, and reservations are required.

Ski Utah Interconnect Adventure Tour Ski Utah ✉ 150 W. 500 South St., Salt Lake City 84101 ☎ 801/534-1779 ⊕ www.skiutah.com. **Wasatch Powderbird Guides** ✍ Box 920057, Snowbird 84092 ☎ 801/742-2800 ⊕ www.powderbird.com.
Resort Web Sites Alta ⊕ www.alta.com. **Brian Head** ⊕ www.brianhead.com. **Brighton** ⊕ www.skibrighton.com. **The Canyons** ⊕ www.thecanyons.com. **Deer Valley** ⊕ www.deervalley.com. **Powder Mountain** ⊕ www.powdermountain.com. **Snow Basin** ⊕ www.snowbasin.com. **Snowbird** ⊕ www.snowbird.com. **Solitude** ⊕ www.skisolitude.com. **Sundance** ⊕ www.sundanceresort.com.

STUDENTS IN UTAH

Most ski resorts and attractions give discounts to students. Be prepared to show your current school identification to take advantage of the discounts.

IDs & Services STA Travel ✉ 10 Downing St., New York, NY 10014 ☎ 212/627-3111, 800/777-0112 24-hr service center 🖶 212/627-3387 ⊕ www.sta.com. **Travel Cuts** ✉ 187 College St., Toronto, Ontario M5T 1P7, Canada ☎ 800/592-2887 in the U.S., 416/979-2406 or 866/246-9762 in Canada 🖶 416/979-8167 ⊕ www.travelcuts.com.

TAXES

SALES TAX

Sales tax is 4.75% in Utah. Most areas have additional local sales and lodging taxes, which can be quite significant. For example, in Salt Lake City, the sales tax is 6.60%. Utah sales tax applies to everything, including food.

TIME

Utah is in the Mountain Time Zone. Mountain time is two hours earlier than Eastern time and one hour later than Pacific time. It is one hour earlier than Chicago, seven hours earlier than London, and 17 hours earlier than Sydney. In summer, Utah observes Daylight Savings Time.

TIPPING

It is customary to tip 15% at restaurants; 20% in resort towns is increasingly the norm. For coat checks and bellmen, $1 per coat or bag is the minimum. Taxi drivers expect 10% to 15%, depending on where you are. In resort towns, ski technicians, sandwich makers, coffee baristas, and the like also appreciate tips.

TOURS & PACKAGES

Because everything is prearranged on a prepackaged tour or independent vacation, you spend less time planning—and often get it all at a good price.

BOOKING WITH AN AGENT

Travel agents are excellent resources. But it's a good idea to collect brochures from several agencies, as some agents' suggestions may be influenced by relationships with tour and package firms that reward them for volume sales. If you have a special interest, find an agent with expertise in that area. The American Society of Travel Agents (ASTA) has a database of specialists worldwide; you can log on to the group's Web site to find one near you.

Make sure your travel agent knows the accommodations and other services of the place being recommended. Ask about the hotel's location, room size, beds, and whether it has a pool, room service, or programs for children, if you care about these. Has your agent been there in person or sent others whom you can contact?

Do some homework on your own, too: local tourism boards can provide information about lesser-known and small-niche operators, some of which may sell only direct.

BUYER BEWARE

Each year consumers are stranded or lose their money when tour operators—even large ones with excellent reputations—go out of business. So check out the operator. Ask several travel agents about its reputation, and try to **book with a company that has a consumer-protection program.** (Look for information in the company's brochure.) In the United States, members of the U.S. Tour Operators Association are required to set aside funds (up to $1 million) to help eligible customers cover payments and travel arrangements in the event that the company defaults. It's also a good idea to choose a company that participates in the American Society of Travel Agents' Tour Operator Program; ASTA will act as mediator in any disputes between you and your tour operator.

Remember that the more your package or tour includes, the better you can predict the ultimate cost of your vacation. Make sure you know exactly what is covered, and beware of hidden costs. Are taxes, tips, and transfers included? Entertainment and excursions? These can add up.

🎫 Tour-Operator Recommendations **American Society of Travel Agents** (⇨ Travel Agencies). **CrossSphere–The Global Association for Packaged Travel** ⊠ 546 E. Main St., Lexington, KY 40508 ☎ 859/226–4444 or 800/682–8886 🖷 859/226–4414 ⊕ www.CrossSphere.com. **United States Tour Operators Association** (USTOA) ⊠ 275 Madison Ave., Suite 2014, New York, NY 10016 ☎ 212/599–6599 🖷 212/599–6744 ⊕ www.ustoa.com.

TRAIN TRAVEL

Amtrak connects Utah to both coasts and many major American cities, with trains that stop in Salt Lake City, Ogden, Provo, Helper, Green River, and St. George.

🎫 Train Information **Amtrak** ☎ 800/872–7245 ⊕ www.amtrak.com.

SCENIC TRAIN TRIPS

On the Heber Valley Historic Railroad in Utah, you can catch the *Heber Creeper,* a turn-of-the-20th-century steam engine train that rides the rails from Heber City across Heber Valley, alongside Deer Creek Reservoir, down Provo Canyon to Vivian Park. Depending on the time of year, you can catch the Murder Mystery Train, the Old West Casino Train, the Movie Train, or special holiday rides.

🎫 **Heber Valley Historic Railroad** ⊠ 450 S. 600 West St., Heber City 84032 ☎ 435/654–5601 ⊕ www.hebervalleyrr.org.

TRAVEL AGENCIES

A good travel agent puts your needs first. Look for an agency that has been in business at least five years, emphasizes customer service, and has someone on staff who specializes in your destination. In addition, **make sure the agency belongs to a professional trade organization.** The American Society of Travel Agents (ASTA) has more than 10,000 members in some 140 countries, enforces a strict code of ethics, and will step in to mediate agent-client disputes involving ASTA members. ASTA also maintains a directory of agents on its Web site; ASTA's TravelSense.org, a trip planning and travel advice site, can also help to locate a travel agent who caters to your needs. (If a travel agency is also acting as your tour operator, *see* Buyer Beware *in* Tours & Packages.)

🎫 Local Agent Referrals **American Society of Travel Agents** (ASTA) ⊠ 1101 King St., Suite 200, Alexandria, VA 22314 ☎ 703/739–2782 or 800/965–2782 24-hr hotline 🖷 703/684–8319 ⊕ www.astanet.com and www.travelsense.org. **Association of British Travel Agents** ⊠ 68–71 Newman St., London W1T 3AH ☎ 020/7637–2444 🖷 020/7637–0713 ⊕ www.abta.com. **Association of Canadian Travel Agencies** ⊠ 130 Albert St., Suite 1705, Ottawa, Ontario K1P 5G4 ☎ 613/237–3657 🖷 613/237–7052 ⊕ www.acta.ca. **Australian Federation of Travel Agents** ⊠ Level 3, 309 Pitt St., Sydney, NSW 2000 ☎ 02/9264–3299 or 1300/363–416 🖷 02/9264–1085 ⊕ www.afta.com.au. **Travel Agents' Association of New Zealand** ⊠ Level 5, Tourism and Travel House, 79 Boulcott St., Box 1888, Wellington 6001 ☎ 04/499–0104 🖷 04/499–0786 ⊕ www.taanz.org.nz.

VISITOR INFORMATION

Learn more about foreign destinations by checking government-issued travel advisories and country information. For a broader picture, consider information from more than one country.

🚩 Tourist Information **Utah Travel Council** ✉ Council Hall, Capitol Hill, 300 N. State St., Salt Lake City 84114 ☎ 801/538-1030, 800/200-1160 brochures, 801/521-8102 ski reports ⛁ 801/538-1399 ⊕ www.utah.com.

🚩 Government Advisories **Consular Affairs Bureau of Canada** ☎ 800/267-6788 or 613/944-6788 ⊕ www.voyage.gc.ca. **U.K. Foreign and Commonwealth Office** ✉ Travel Advice Unit, Consular Directorate, Old Admiralty Bldg., London SW1A 2PA ☎ 0870/606-0290 or 020/7008-1500 ⊕ www.fco. gov.uk/travel. **Australian Department of Foreign Affairs and Trade** ☎ 300/139-281 travel advisories, 02/6261-1299 Consular Travel Advice ⊕ www. smartraveller.gov.au or www.dfat.gov.au. **New**

Zealand Ministry of Foreign Affairs and Trade ☎ 04/439-8000 ⊕ www.mft.govt.nz.

WEB SITES

Do check out the World Wide Web when planning your trip. You'll find everything from weather forecasts to virtual tours of famous cities. Be sure to visit Fodors.com (⊕ www.fodors.com), a complete travel-planning site. You can research prices and book plane tickets, hotel rooms, rental cars, vacation packages, and more. In addition, you can post your pressing questions in the Travel Talk section. Other planning tools include a currency converter and weather reports, and there are loads of links to travel resources.

Salt Lake City

WORD OF MOUTH

"Visit the Temple Square. You'll get a guided tour by one of the Mormon volunteers . . . Try to either go to a concert or a choir rehearsal of the Mormon Tabernacle choir. This is one of the best choirs in the whole world."

—torvarich

"Antelope Island, connected to SLC via a long causeway across the Great Salt Lake, is nearby and well worth a visit . . . especially toward evening for photo ops."

—FlyFish

Updated by
John Blodgett

SITTING AT THE FOOT of the rugged Wasatch Mountains and extending to the south shore of the Great Salt Lake, Salt Lake City has some of the best scenery in the country. The interface between city and nature draws residents and visitors alike to the Salt Lake Valley. There are few other places where you can enjoy urban pleasures and, within 20 minutes, hike a mountain trail or rest by a rushing stream.

The city is emerging as a prominent economic center in the Rocky Mountains. Since 2001 the number of people living in the Salt Lake Valley has climbed from 720,000 to more than 1 million. As a reflection of this growth, a dynamic skyline has sprouted, along with ever-widening rings of suburbia. Smog occasionally bedevils the town, and some crime exists, but Salt Lake is working hard to remain a small, personable city.

Brigham Young led the first party of Mormon pioneers to the Salt Lake Valley in 1847. The valley appealed to him because, at the time, it was under the control of Mexico rather than the U.S. government, which the Mormons blamed for much of their persecution. Also, the area had few permanent settlements and an adequate supply of water and building materials, and it offered a protected location, with the high Wasatch Mountains on the east side and a vast desert to the west. Still, on July 24, 1847, when Young gazed across the vast and somewhat desolate valley and reportedly announced "This is the right place," it would have been understandable if his followers had some mixed feelings. They saw no familiar green forests or lush grasslands, only a dry valley and a salty lake.

Within hours of arriving, Young and his followers began planting crops and diverting water for irrigation. They would build homes later; their existence depended on being able to harvest crops before winter. Within days Young drew up plans for Salt Lake City, which was to be the hub of the Mormon's promised land, a vast empire stretching from the Rocky Mountains to the southern California coast. Although the area that eventually became the state of Utah was much smaller than Young originally planned, Salt Lake City became much grander than anything he could have imagined. Missionaries throughout Scandinavia and the British Isles converted thousands who flocked to the city from around the world to live near their church president—who is also a living prophet according to Mormon doctrine—and to worship in their newly built temple.

In the 1860s, income from railroads and mines created a wealthy class of industrialists who built mansions near downtown and whose businesses brought thousands of workers—mainly from Europe and most of whom were not Mormon—to Utah Territory. By the time Utah became a state in 1896, Salt Lake had become a diverse and thriving city. Although the majority of the city was Mormon, it claimed a healthy mix of Protestant, Catholic, and Jewish citizens.

Today the city is an important western center for business, medicine, education, and culture; and the Church of Jesus Christ of Latter-day Saints

If you have

3 days

The best place to start in Salt Lake City is downtown. Spend your first day visiting **Temple Square** ❶–⓫, shopping **The Gateway** ⓰, and taking in a show at **Clark Planetarium** ⓱. On Day 2, visit **Red Butte Garden & Arboretum** ㉚ and **This Is the Place Heritage Park** ㉞ in the foothills of Salt Lake. Save Day 3 for experiencing the Great Salt Lake. A short 20 minutes away is **Great Salt Lake State Park Marina,** where you can see what it feels like to float in water three times heavier than freshwater. Finish your day with a visit to the **Bingham Canyon Copper Mine,** one of the largest man-made holes on earth.

1

If you have

5 days

Spend two full days in downtown Salt Lake City. Use your entire first day to visit the sites at Temple Square. On your second day, tour the **Kearns Mansion** ㉘ and the **Pioneer Memorial Museum** ㉔. Spend Day 3 at the **Utah Museum of Natural History** ㉝ and the **Utah Museum of Fine Arts** ㉜ on the University of Utah campus. Finish the day with a shopping trip to **Trolley Square** ㉟ and a meal at the Hard Rock Cafe or Green Street Social Club at Trolley Square. On your fourth day, tour **This Is the Place Heritage Park** ㉞ and **Utah's Hogle Zoo** ㉟. Spend the evening at the symphony, opera, or one of many theaters in the city. On Day 5 visit **Antelope Island State Park** in the Great Salt Lake.

If you have

7 days

Spend your first five days as outlined above. Take advantage of the city's great cultural offerings and restaurants at night. Depending on the season, take in a baseball or basketball game, or go to a play or concert in the evening. Make reservations for a dinner cruise on the Great Salt Lake on Day 5. On Day 6 start the morning with a walk or jog through **Liberty Park** ㉟ and visit **Tracy Aviary** ㊱. Then head to the **Bingham Canyon Copper Mine.** On Day 7 start the day walking in **Memory Grove** ㉒ or **Ensign Peak** ㉖, then visit any of the sights you didn't have time for the rest of the week. History buffs might opt to check out a portion of the **Pony Express Trail.**

(LDS), as the Mormon faith is officially called, still has its headquarters in Temple Square. Several high-rise hotels mark the skyline, restaurants serve up a whole world of tastes, fashionable retail enclaves are appearing all around town, and nightlife is hopping. Increased commitment to the arts from the public and private sectors has created a cultural scene as prodigious as you'd expect in a city twice Salt Lake's size. When it comes to sports, the community takes great pride in its NBA team, the Utah Jazz. And of course, no one can forget the hundreds of volunteers who gathered together to help Salt Lake City host the 2002 Olympic Winter Games.

Near Salt Lake City, Antelope Island has superb hiking, mountain biking, and wildlife watching. American history buffs might choose to travel one of the best-preserved sections of the original Pony Express Trail, the 133-mi section through the desert of west-central Utah.

EXPLORING SALT LAKE CITY

Despite its population of roughly 180,000, Salt Lake City feels like a small city. Wide streets and an efficient mass transit system make it easy to get around. The heart of Salt Lake's social, religious, and political institutions can be found within a few blocks of Temple Square downtown. Numerous museums and a state-of-the-art planetarium thrive here, and because many of the cultural institutions are supported by public funds you'll spend little money touring the city. In addition, the emphasis put on green spaces by past and present city planners means you won't experience the claustrophobic feeling found in many big cities.

Take time to stroll around the city center, shopping or visiting Temple Square. Choose a museum, theater, or historic building to explore, then branch out into the surrounding neighborhoods to capture more of the flavor of the city. Reminders of the 2002 Winter Olympics are scattered throughout.

Like most Utah municipalities, Salt Lake City is based on a grid plan that was devised by Brigham Young in the 19th century. Most street names have a directional and a numerical designation, which describes their location in relation to one of two axes. Streets with "East" or "West" in their names are east or west of (and parallel to) Main Street, which runs north–south; while "North" and "South" streets run parallel to South Temple street. The numbers tell how far the streets are from the axes. (For example, 200 East Street is two blocks east of Main Street.) Addresses typically include two directional references and two numerical references—320 East 200 South Street, for instance, is in the east 300 block of 200 South Street. Three of Salt Lake's most prominent streets are named after the Mormon Temple: North Temple, South Temple, and West Temple, indicating that the streets run parallel to the north, south, and west borders of Temple Square. Main Street borders the square's east side.

Temple Square

When Mormon pioneer leader Brigham Young first entered the Salt Lake Valley, he chose this spot at the mouth of City Creek Canyon for the headquarters of the Mormon Church, a role it maintains to this day. The buildings in Temple Square range in age from the Tabernacle constructed in the 1860s to the Conference Center constructed in 2000. Perhaps the most striking aspect of the square is the attention to landscaping, which makes the heart of downtown Salt Lake City into a year-round oasis.

a good walk

Numbers in the text correspond to numbers in the margin and on the Salt Lake City and Temple Square maps.

Temple Square is a good place to begin a walking tour of Salt Lake City. It covers only slightly more than three city blocks (be aware, however, that Salt Lake City blocks are larger than the average city block). For a loop tour, start at the foot of the Eagle Gate monument, at the corner of

1

On the Menu

Utah's traditional local cuisine was the brunt of many jokes during the 2002 Winter Olympics. The fact that Utahns consume more green Jell-O than any state in the union and love a dish called funeral potatoes (a casserole made from frozen hash browns and cream of mushroom soup covered with crushed cornflakes and butter) led to countless chuckles and a few souvenir pins. Although it's true these dishes are common at potluck family and church dinners, when it comes to eating out, Salt Lakers have a much broader palate and many more choices. Pre- and post-Olympics the city experienced a rush of chefs relocating here from all over the world. Now Salt Lake is home to nationally recognized bastions of New American cuisine, as well as original "Rocky Mountain" cuisine that embraces fresh fish and game along with locally grown organic produce, wild mushrooms, bumper crops of local fresh berries, cherries, peaches, heirloom tomatoes, and artisan products such as goat cheese. The city and resort areas boast some very savvy northern Italian restaurants, French bistros, countless sushi bars, delis, and at least one or two restaurants for every exotic cuisine—from Afghan to Peruvian. You'll also find creative wine lists and knowledgeable service. Bakers here are rivaling San Francisco's bread-makers with their own rustic sourdough and Tuscan loaves. The weekly summer farmers' market is thriving, and chefs are building more and more of a food community. All in all, Salt Lake's culinary scene has finally grown up and offers something for every taste, from simple to sophisticated.

The Performing Arts

Two years after the pioneers began constructing the city, its first cultural organization was formed. The Deseret Musical and Dramatic Society entertained the faithful with musicals, concerts, and pageants in the Old Bowery Building on Temple Square. This tradition of supporting a healthy arts community has continued to the present. Small choral, musical, and theatrical companies flourish. A wide variety of professional arts companies, many of which have national and international reputations, are supported by an arts and parks tax. Ballet West, Repertory Dance Theatre, and Ririe Woodbury Dance Company rank with the best in the country, as does the Utah Symphony and Opera. All have beautiful halls in which to perform. Check performance schedules in the local newspaper or the *City Weekly,* a news and entertainment publication available at most newsstands downtown.

The Great Outdoors

Salt Lake City's magic lies not in its skyline, but its backdrops. The Great Salt Lake and Wasatch Mountains are more than pretty pictures, however. Rich outdoors experiences await you within minutes of downtown, from a quiet stroll up City Creek Canyon to a peaceful cruise on the Great Salt Lake. The weather usually cooperates with these pursuits—the city's average 10 inches of precipitation comes mainly in the form of snow. Even on the hottest summer day you can find a shady canyon with a stream passing through.

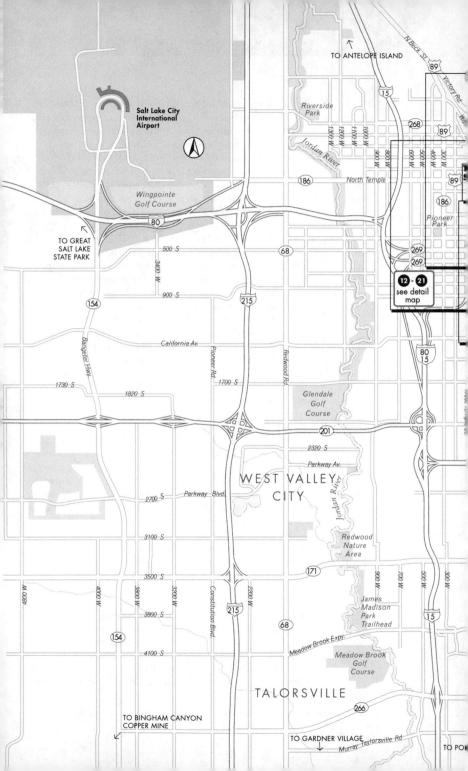

TO ANTELOPE ISLAND

N Beck St.

Victory Rd.

89

15

268

89

Riverside
Park

W 1000
W 1200
W 1100
W 1000

900 W
500 W
400 W
300 W

89

Jordan River

North Temple

186

186

Pioneer
Park

Salt Lake City
International
Airport

Wingpointe
Golf Course

80

269
269

TO GREAT
SALT LAKE
STATE PARK

500 S

3400 W

68

12 - 21
see detail
map

154

900 S

215

80
15

California Av.

Pioneer Rd.

Redwood Rd.

1730 S

1820 S

1700 S

Glendale
Golf
Course

Bangeter Hwy.

2320 S

Parkway Av.

WEST VALLEY
CITY

Jordan River

2700 S

Parkway Blvd.

201

3100 S

Redwood
Nature
Area

4000 W

3800 W

3200 W

3500 S

Constitution Blvd.

2900 W

215

171

900 W
700 W
500 W
300 W

James
Madison
Park
Trailhead

15

4800 W

3800 S

154

4100 S

68

Meadow Brook Expy.

Meadow Brook
Golf
Course

TALORSVILLE

266

TO BINGHAM CANYON
COPPER MINE

TO GARDNER VILLAGE

Murray Taylorsville Rd.

TO PO

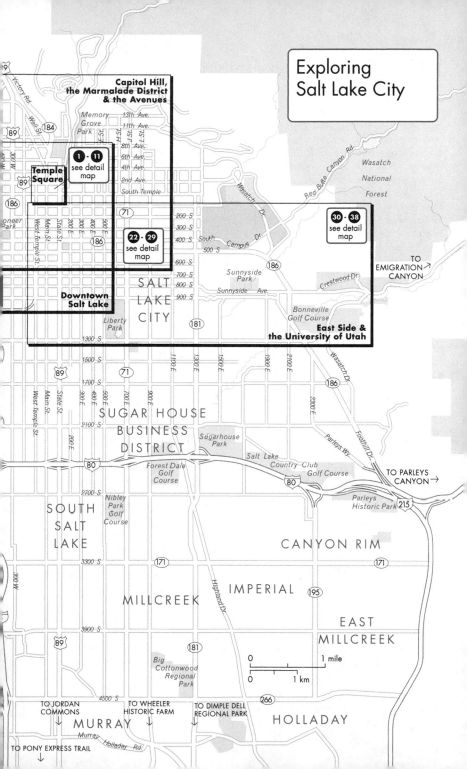

Exploring
Salt Lake City

CloseUp
THE MORMON INFLUENCE

FROM ITS BEGINNINGS IN 1830 with just six members, the Church of Jesus Christ of Latter-day Saints has evolved into one of the fastest growing religions in the world. There are more than 10 million members in more than 160 countries and territories. The church was conceived and founded in New York by Joseph Smith, who said God the Father and his son, Jesus Christ, came to him in a vision when he was a young boy. Smith said he also saw a resurrected entity named Moroni, who led him to metal plates that were engraved with the religious history of an ancient American civilization. In 1827 Smith translated this record into the Book of Mormon.

Not long after the Church's creation, religious persecution forced Smith and his followers to flee New York, and they traveled first to Ohio and then to Missouri before settling in Nauvoo, Illinois, in 1839. But even here the fledgling church was ostracized, and Smith was killed by a mob in June 1844 in Carthage, Illinois. To escape the mounting oppression, Brigham Young, who ascended to the Church's leadership following Smith's death, led a pilgrimage to Utah, then a territory, with the first group arriving in the Salt Lake Valley on July 24, 1847. Here, under Young's guidance, the Church quickly grew and flourished.

In keeping with the Church's emphasis on proselytizing, Young laid plans to both colonize Utah and spread the Church's word. This work led to the founding of small towns not only throughout the territory but from southern Canada to Mexico. Today the Church continues that work through its young people, with most taking time out from college or careers to spend two years on a mission at home or abroad.

Latter-day Saints believe that they are guided by divine revelations received from God by the Church president, who is viewed as a modern-day prophet in the same sense as other biblical leaders. The Book of Mormon is viewed as divinely inspired scripture and is used side-by-side with the Holy Bible. Families are highly valued in the Church, and marriages performed in the Church's temples are thought to continue through eternity. Though Mormons were originally polygamists, the Church ended the practice in order to gain statehood for the territory in the 1890s. Excommunication is the consequence for those continuing polygamy. In 2001, after publicizing his five-wife family on national talk shows, Tom Green learned that Utah authorities could in fact be moved to prosecute polygamy. Since the 1950s, Utah law enforcement had held a "don't ask, don't tell" policy regarding polygamy. Green's 2001 trial was the state's first polygamy trial since the 1950s.

Under the Church's guidance, Utah has evolved into a somewhat progressive, albeit conservative, state where the good of the Church is placed above most other concerns. Despite most states' belief that church and government should be separate, Utah legislative leaders regularly consult with Church officials on key legislation. And the Church's opposition to alcoholic products has led to the state's peculiar liquor laws. To enter a bar that sells liquor, you first must purchase a "membership," usually $4 for three weeks. Beer bars, however, do not require such memberships, nor do restaurants that serve food with liquor.

The population of Utah was 2,233,169 in 2000. About 50% of Salt Lake City residents belong to the Church, but statewide the number is closer to 70% of Utah's population.

State Street and South Temple. Brigham Young's city home is here, divided into the **Beehive House** ❶ ► and the **Lion House** ❷. These houses mark the historic center of the city. Walk west along South Temple to the **Joseph Smith Memorial Building** ❸, and if time allows, check out your family history at the Family Search Center inside. In front of the Joseph Smith Memorial Building is the newest addition to Temple Square, Main Street Plaza. Stroll along the plaza on your way to the center of the square and the **Salt Lake Temple** ❹. West of the Temple is the **Tabernacle** ❺, home to the famous Mormon Tabernacle Choir until 2000. South of the Tabernacle is **Assembly Hall**. From Assembly Hall, cross the street to the **Family History Library** ❻ and the **Museum of Church History and Art** ❼. For a more detailed history of the Church of Jesus Christ of Latter-day Saints, cross West Temple to the east to visit the **North Visitors' Center** ❽. Across North Temple from the North Visitors' Center, the **Church of Jesus Christ of Latter-day Saints Conference Center** ❾ covers the entire block north of the temple. Walk along North Temple in front of the Conference Center. The sidewalk here is buffered from the street by trees and a brook babbling along past boulders quarried from the same canyon as the center and the temple. Cross North Temple and head east past Main Street Plaza to the **Church Office Building** ❿. Church headquarters are housed in the Church Office Building. Finish the loop by crossing State Street to the east and walking through **City Creek Park and Brigham Young Historic Park** ⓫. These parks follow City Creek as it leaves the canyon.

TIMING   A walk around Temple Square can be completed in a half-hour if you don't visit any of the sights or take any of the tours. To get the most of your visit, however, it would be best to allow at least a half day. All guided tours at the sites around the square are free. Throw in lunch or dinner at the Pantry, the Roof, or the Lion House, and a stab at finding proof of distant relatives at the Family Search Center, and you could easily spend a day or two.

What to See

► ★ ❶ **Beehive House.** Brigham Young's home, a national historic landmark, was constructed in 1854 and is topped with a replica of a beehive, symbolizing industry. Inside are many original furnishings; a tour of the interior will give you a fascinating glimpse of upper-class, 19th-century polygamous life. ✉ *67 E. South Temple, Temple Square* ☎ *801/240–2671* ⊕ *www.placestovisit.org* 🎟 *Free* ☉ *Mon.–Sat. 9–9*.

❾ **Church of Jesus Christ of Latter-day Saints Conference Center.** The center features a 21,000-seat auditorium and a 900-seat theater. Equally impressive are the rooftop gardens landscaped with native plants and streams to mirror the surrounding mountains. Visitors must be accompanied by a guide. Tours are flexible but usually last 45 minutes. The Mormon Tabernacle Choir performs here regularly, and other concerts are scheduled on occasion. ✉ *60 W. North Temple, Temple Square* ☎ *801/240–0075* ⊕ *www.placestovisit.org* 🎟 *Free* ☉ *Daily 9–9*.

❿ **Church Office Building.** Get a 280-degree view of the Salt Lake Valley from the 26th-floor observation deck of the headquarters of the Church of Jesus Christ of Latter-day Saints. ✉ *50 E. North Temple, Temple Square*

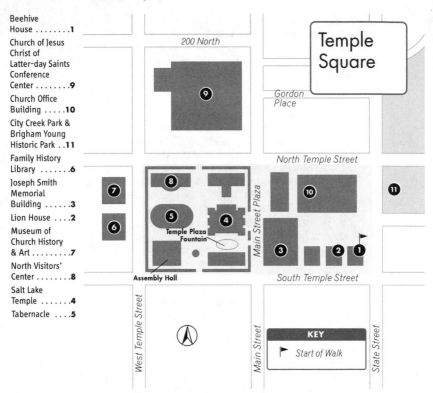

☎ *801/240–2190* ⊕ *www.placestovisit.org* ✉ *Free* ⊙ *Apr.–Sept., weekdays 9–5; Oct.–Mar., weekdays 9–4:30.*

🐾 ⓫ **City Creek Park and Brigham Young Historic Park.** These tiny twin parks
divided by 2nd Avenue are a natural diversion from the cityscape. Paths
are inlaid with the footprints and names of native animals and birds,
and a stone-lined stream drives a mill wheel. ⊠ *East side of State St. at
North Temple, Temple Square.*

❻ **Family History Library.** Genealogy is important to Mormons. This library
houses the world's largest collection of genealogical data. Mormons and
non-Mormons alike come here to do research. ⊠ *35 N. West Temple,
Temple Square* ☎ *801/240–2331 or 800/537–9703* ⊕ *www.familysearch.
org* ✉ *Free* ⊙ *Mon. 7:30–5, Tues.–Sat. 7:30 AM–10 PM.*

★ ❸ **Joseph Smith Memorial Building.** Once the Hotel Utah, this building on
the National Register of Historic Places is owned and operated by the
Mormon Church. You can use a computer program to learn how to do
genealogical research at the Family Search Center here or watch an hour-
long film about the Church's teaching of how Jesus Christ appeared in
the western hemisphere after his resurrection. The center also has two
restaurants and an elegantly restored lobby. The **Family Search Center,**

inside the Joseph Smith Memorial Building, has computers that allow you to search for ancestors using records compiled by the Mormon Church. Using the center costs nothing, and volunteers are on hand to help. Upstairs is the 1920 census and 70,000 volumes of personal histories of the faithful. ⊠ *15 E. South Temple, Temple Square* ☎ *801/ 240–1266 or 800/537–9703* ⊕ *www.placestovisit.org* ⊠ *Free* ⊗ *Mon.–Sat. 9–9.*

② **Lion House.** Built two years after the Beehive House, the Lion House was also home to Brigham Young's family. Today it houses a restaurant, the Pantry, which serves good and simple old-fashioned home cooking. ⊠ *63 E. South Temple, Temple Square* ☎ *801/363–5466* ⊕ *www.placestovisit.org* ⊠ *Free* ⊗ *Lunch Mon.–Sat. 11–2; dinner Thurs.–Sat. 5–8:30.*

⑦ **Museum of Church History and Art.** The museum houses a variety of artifacts and works of art relating to the history and doctrine of the Mormon faith, including personal belongings of church leaders Joseph Smith, Brigham Young, and others. There are also samples of Mormon coins and scrip used as standard currency in Utah during the 1800s, and beautiful examples of quilting, embroidery, and other handwork. Upstairs galleries exhibit religious and secular works by Mormon artists from all over the world. ⊠ *45 N. West Temple, Temple Square* ☎ *801/ 240–4615* ⊠ *Free* ⊗ *Weekdays 9–9, weekends 10–7.*

⑧ **North Visitors' Center.** The history of the Mormon Church and the Mormon pioneers' trek to Utah is outlined in displays and a 53-minute film here. ⊠ *50 W. North Temple, Temple Square* ☎ *801/240–4872* ⊕ *www. placestovisit.org* ⊠ *Free* ⊗ *Daily 9–9.*

④ **Salt Lake Temple.** Brigham Young chose this spot for a temple as soon as he arrived in the Salt Lake Valley in 1847, but work on the building didn't begin for another six years. Built of blocks of granite hauled by oxen and train from Little Cottonwood Canyon, the Mormon Temple took 40 years to the day to complete. Its walls are 16-feet thick at the base. Off-limits to all but faithful Mormons, the temple is used for marriages, baptisms, and other religious functions. ⊠ *South Temple and Main St., Temple Square* ☎ *No phone* ⊕ *www.placestovisit.org* ⊗ *Not open to public.*

Fodor'sChoice
★

⑤ **Tabernacle.** The Tabernacle is best known for the famous Mormon Choir that sang here, accompanied by the classic organ. The Tabernacle is currently being renovated and is closed to the public. When it reopens late in 2006, visitors will be able to tour the Tabernacle and hear organ recitals regularly. Until then, the daily organ recitals will be in the Conference Center. ⊠ *South Temple and Main St., Temple Square* ☎ *801/240–4872* ⊕ *www.placestovisit.org* ⊠ *Free.*

Downtown Salt Lake

Although businesses and homes stretch in all directions, downtown's core is a compact, six-block area that includes three large malls, numerous historic buildings, and several entertainment venues.

a good walk

Catch the mass transit train called TRAX at Salt Lake City's geographic center—the intersection of Main Street and South Temple. TRAX service is free in downtown. Get off at Symphony Hall and visit the **Salt Lake Arts Center** ⑫. Adjacent to the Arts Center is the **Salt Palace Convention & Visitor Center** ⑬, where you can find information about Salt Lake City and Utah. This is a good place to sign up for a tour of the Great Salt Lake or Bingham Copper Mine, located elsewhere in Salt Lake Valley. Return to TRAX. Take the train to the end of the line, the Delta stop, and get off to see the **Delta Center** ⑭ and the **Union Pacific Building** ⑮ (west of the Delta Center on South Temple). Walk through the Union Pacific Building into the **Gateway** ⑯, Salt Lake's newest shopping and entertainment center, with more than 90 shops and restaurants. At the south end of the Gateway, adjacent to the Megaplex 12, is **Clark Planetarium** ⑰, which houses a state-of-the-art IMAX theater. If history is your passion, walk south then west to the **Rio Grande Railroad Depot** ⑱, which houses the Utah State History Museum. Finish the loop by taking TRAX from the station outside back to visit the **Gallivan Center** ⑲, an outdoor gathering place with year-round activities. You can finish your tour with a snack at the wonderful **Salt Lake City Main Library** ⑳ by going east on 400 South Street to 200 East Street. Or rest on the beautiful grounds of the **City and County Building** ㉑, which is one block south of the library.

TIMING   You can easily spend a day enjoying downtown, not because it's a big area (it's not) but because it's historic, interesting, and pretty in any season. A horse-drawn carriage ride around downtown is especially inviting in spring when the blossoming trees and flower beds of Temple Square burst with color.

What to See

㉑ **City and County Building.** The seat of city government is on Washington Square, at the spot where the original Mormon settlers circled their wagons on their first night in the Salt Lake Valley. Said to be modeled after London's City Hall, the structure has details common to the Romanesque Revival style. Construction began in 1892 and continued for two years. After Utah achieved statehood in 1896, the building served as the capitol for 19 years until the current capitol could be built. Hundreds of trees, including species from around the world, and many winding paths and seating areas make the grounds a calm downtown oasis. ⊠ *451 S. State St., Downtown* ☎ *801/535–6321* ⊕ *www.slcgov.com/info/ccbuilding/default.htm* ⊡ *Free* ⊙ *Weekdays 8–5.*

★ ⟳ ⑰ **Clark Planetarium.** The Hansen Star Theatre and 3-D IMAX Theatre comprise this Salt Lake County facility completed in 2003. The Star Theatre uses state-of-the-art technology to simulate three-dimensional flights through space. Hands-on exhibits and science paraphernalia fill the "Wonders of the Universe" Science Store. ⊠ *110 S. 400 West St., Downtown* ☎ *801/456–7827* ⊕ *www.clarkplanetarium.org* ⊡ *Star Show $8, IMAX $8, combination tickets $12* ⊙ *Daily 11:30 AM–end of last show.*

⑭ **Delta Center.** This arena, the home court for the NBA Utah Jazz, seats 20,000. Concerts, rodeos, ice shows, and other events are also held here.

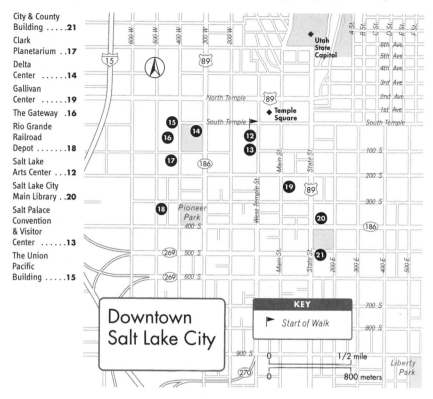

Downtown
Salt Lake City

KEY

▶ *Start of Walk*

An information desk and a gift shop—with the city's best assortment of Utah Jazz paraphernalia—are open daily 9–5. ✉ *300 W. South Temple, Downtown* ☎ *801/325–2000* ⊕ *www.deltacenter.com.*

🄳 **Gallivan Center.** This outdoor plaza hosts free lunchtime and evening concerts, farmers' markets, and unique arts-and-crafts activities for all ages. It also has an ice rink and a giant outdoor chessboard. ✉ *36 E. 200 South St., Downtown* ☎ *801/532–0459.*

★ ✪ 🄰 **The Gateway.** Thirty acres of shopping, entertainment, restaurants, offices, and housing cover the area called the Gateway. The Olympic Legacy Plaza stands in memory of the 2002 Winter Olympics, which were held in Salt Lake City. Entertainers perform regularly in the plaza and throughout the Gateway, which resembles shopping centers in Europe with its narrow streets and wide sidewalks. Two parking lots make access easy. Some of the stores and eateries here are part of national chains, but many are locally grown enterprises. The Clark Planetarium (*see* **Clark Planetarium**) and a large movie complex are also here. ✉ *Between 200 South and 50 North Sts., and 400 West and 500 West Sts., Downtown* ☎ *801/456–0000* ⊕ *www.shopthegateway.com* ☉ *Mon.–Sat. 10–9, Sun. noon–6.*

⑱ Rio Grande Railroad Depot. This 1910 depot was built to compete with the showy Union Pacific Railroad Depot three blocks north. It houses the **Utah State History Museum,** which has rotating exhibits on the history of Utah and the West. ⊠ *300 S. Rio Grande St., Downtown* ☎ *801/533–3500* ⊕ *www.history.utah.gov* ▭ *Free* ☉ *Weekdays 8–5, Sat. 9–1.*

⑫ Salt Lake Arts Center. You'll find art to challenge your senses and sensibilities at this art center where the mission is to explore contemporary issues through art. Recent exhibits have included "Scott Fife: Big Trouble, The Idaho Project," a series of 18 sculptures depicting the story of the 1905 assassination of Idaho Governor Frank Steunenberg. ⊠ *20 S. West Temple, Downtown* ☎ *801/328–4201* ⊕ *www.slartcenter.org* ▭ *Free* ☉ *Tues.–Thurs. and Sat. 10–5, Fri. 10–9.*

★ ♨ ⑳ Salt Lake City Main Library. The library, constructed in 2003, has become a cultural center for the city. Inspired by the Roman Coliseum, architect Moshe Safdie designed the six-story walkable wall as both sculpture and functioning building. A wide variety of art media is on display at the Gallery at Library Square. The Public Plaza creates yet another open space in downtown with water and garden features. Activities are scheduled here all year, in the 300-seat auditorium, the plaza, or the spacious atrium. From the rooftop garden, you get a 360-degree view of the valley and mountains. The on-site coffee shop and deli mean you can stay here all day; other shops sell comic books and gifts, and there's also a film center. ⊠ *210 E. 400 South St., Downtown* ☎ *801/ 524–8200* ⊕ *www.slcpl.lib.ut.us* ▭ *Free* ☉ *Mon.–Thurs. 9–9, Fri. and Sat. 9–6, Sun. 1–5.*

⑬ Salt Palace Convention & Visitor Center. The Convention Center is used for large conventions and trade shows. Volunteers are on hand at the visitor center to answer questions and dispense information on tourist sites in Salt Lake City and the state. A gift shop offers local books and gifts. ⊠ *90 S. West Temple, Downtown* ☎ *801/521–2822* ⊕ *www. visitsaltlake.com* ▭ *Free* ☉ *Weekdays 8–5, weekends 9–5.*

⑮ Union Pacific Building. This depot, built in 1909 at a cost of $300,000, is a striking monument to the importance of railroads in the settling of the West. The slate-shingle mansard roof sets a distinctive French Second Empire tone for the exterior. Inside, Western-theme murals and stained-glass windows create a setting rich with color and texture. The station has been restored and now functions as the entrance to the Gateway and as a special-event venue. ⊠ *400 W. 100 South St., Downtown* ☎ *801/456–2000* ⊕ *www.shopthegateway.com* ▭ *Free* ☉ *Mon.–Sat. 10–9, Sun. noon–6.*

Capitol Hill & the Avenues

The Capitol Hill and Avenues neighborhoods overlook the city from the foothills north of downtown. Two days after entering what would become Salt Lake City, Brigham Young brought his fellow religious leaders to the summit of the most prominent hill here, which he named Ensign Peak, to plan out their new home. After Temple Square was laid out, houses were constructed nearby. New arrivals built sod homes into the hillside of what is now known as the Avenues. Two-room log cabins and adobe houses dotted the area. With the coming of the railroad came Victorian homes.

The rich and prominent families of the city built mansions along South Temple. As the city has grown over the years, wealthy citizens have continued to live close to the city, but farther up the hill where the views of the valley are better. Since the early 1970s the lower Avenues have seen an influx of residents interested in restoring the older homes, making this area a diverse and evolving community.

The State Capitol, for which Capitol Hill is named, was completed in 1915. State offices surround the Capitol on three sides. City Creek Canyon forms its eastern boundary. The Avenues denotes the larger neighborhood along the foothills, north of South Temple, which extends from Capitol Hill on the west to the University of Utah to the east.

Getting around the Avenues is different than following the logic of the grid system of downtown. The Avenues start north of South Temple and increase in number as you head uphill, 1st Avenue being the beginning. From west to east, the streets are labeled alphabetically. Capitol Hill is a different story, obviously not planned by the master planner, Brigham Young.

a good tour

A tour of Capitol Hill and the Avenues is a logical extension of a tour of downtown Salt Lake City. To begin the tour of this area, head north along State Street from South Temple to North Temple and turn right. Turn left on Canyon Road to the beginning of **Memory Grove** 22 ⌐. The road is blocked by a gate at the entrance to the grove. Park your car here, and continue walking past the gate and up toward the **Utah State Capitol** 23. Visit the nearby **Pioneer Memorial Museum** 24 before returning east across East Capitol Boulevard to visit **Council Hall** 25, home of the Utah Travel Council, for information on tourist destinations in Salt Lake City and the state. From Council Hall, continue uphill on East Capitol Boulevard to Ensign Vista Drive. Turn left, and continue on to **Ensign Peak Nature Park** 26 to get a view of the Salt Lake Valley and the Great Salt Lake. From Ensign Peak, return on East Capitol Boulevard to South Temple. Turn left on South Temple and stop to visit the **Cathedral of the Madeleine** 27. Continue east on South Temple and finish your visit with a guided tour of the **Kearns Mansion** 28. If you have children who love to learn on their feet and with their hands, you may want to save time for the **Children's Museum of Utah** 29. To get there from the mansion, go west on South Temple, past Temple Square to 300 West Street. Turn right and continue north until you reach the museum.

TIMING You can spend a half day or more touring the Capitol, Kearns Mansion, and the Pioneer Memorial Museum. If you include a picnic in the canyon or Ensign Peak, your tour could take all day. The views from Capitol Hill are impressive any time of year. The Kearns Mansion, as the official residence of Utah's governor, is most festive during the Christmas season.

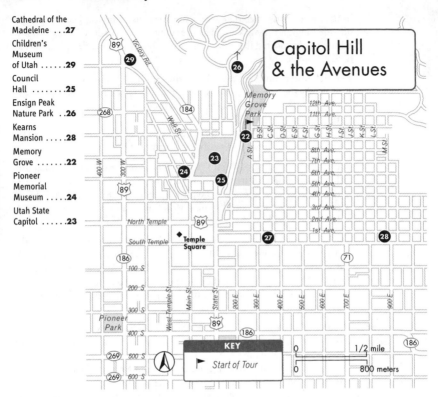

What to See

㉗ Cathedral of the Madeleine. Catholics have been the largest religious minority in the Salt Lake area since soldiers and miners entered the city. The cathedral was dedicated in 1906. Its Romanesque exterior bristles with gargoyles, while its Gothic interior showcases bright frescoes and a large organ. The Madeleine Choir gives concerts regularly. ✉ *331 E. South Temple, Temple Square* ☎ *801/328–8941* ⊕ *www. saltlakecathedral.org* 🎫 *Free* ⊙ *Mon.–Sat. 7 AM–9 PM, Sun. 7–7.*

need a
break?

It's always time for chocolate! For a sweet treat, stop at **Hatch Family Chocolates** (✉ 390 E. 4th Ave., Temple Square ☎ 801/532–4912), an old neighborhood grocery store that's been transformed into an immaculate candy and ice-cream shop. Jerry Hatch uses his mother's secret recipe for creamy caramel, and each piece of chocolate is hand-dipped. They also serve espresso, Italian soda, and ice-cream sundaes with homemade caramel sauce.

㉙ Children's Museum of Utah. The museum's goal is to "create the love of learning through hands-on experience," and that's exactly what it does. Children can pilot a jetliner, draw with computers, dig for mammoth bones, or lose themselves in the many other interactive exhibits. ✉ *840*

N. 300 West St., Capitol Hill ☎ *801/328–3383* ⊕ *www.childmuseum.
org* 🖃 *$5* ⊙ *Mon.–Thurs. and Sat. 10–5, Fri. 10–8.*

㉕ Council Hall. Once a meeting place for politicians in the Utah Territory,
Council Hall is now headquarters for the Utah Travel Council. You can
pick up brochures and books on tourist destinations throughout the city
and state, and ask questions of knowledgeable staff. A small gift store
carries Utah books and gifts. 🖃 *300 N. State St., Capitol Hill* ☎ *801/
538–1900* 🖃 *Free* ⊙ *Mon.–Sat. 8–5.*

> **need a
break?** Take a break from your tours with a picnic from **Cucina** (🖃 *1026 E.
2nd Ave., Temple Square* ☎ *801/322–3055*), an Italian deli
specializing in gourmet lunches to eat in or take out. Choose a
sandwich, like the Sicilian combo with capicolla ham, mortadella,
salami, provolone, and tomatoes, and a side dish of one of many
pasta salads. Bring your freshly packed lunch to Memory Grove, City
Creek Canyon, or Ensign Peak to relax and refuel amid beautiful
surroundings.

㉖ Ensign Peak Nature Park. This is the spot from which early settlers surveyed the valley and the Great Salt Lake. Markers on the plaza at the
nature park describe the history of this vantage spot. If you have time,
take the ½-mi walk to the top of Ensign Peak. Stations along the way
detail the geology, history, and natural history of the sights around you.

★ **㉘ Kearns Mansion.** Built by silver-mining tycoon Thomas Kearns in 1902,
this limestone structure—reminiscent of a French château with all its
turrets and balconies—is now the official residence of Utah's governor.
In its early days, the mansion was visited by President Theodore Roosevelt and other dignitaries from around the world. 🖃 *603 E. South Temple, Temple Square* ☎ *801/538–1005* ⊕ *www.utah.gov/governor/
mansion/index.html* 🖃 *Free* ⊙ *Tours June–Aug. and Dec. 1–15, Tues.
and Thurs. 2–4.*

▶ **㉒ Memory Grove.** Walk the quiet street, free from traffic, that runs through
the park or take one of many trails near City Creek. Monuments to vet-
erans of war are found throughout this grove. You can hike, jog, or bike
part or all of the paved road that is closed to cars on odd-numbered
days along **City Creek Canyon.** Additional trails take off from the road,
including the Bonneville Shoreline Trail, which takes you above the houses
at the top of the Avenues.

㉔ Pioneer Memorial Museum. The West's most extensive collection of set-
tlement-era relics, many of which relate to Mormon pioneers, fills 38
rooms—plus a carriage house—on four floors. Displays include clothing, furniture, tools, wagons, and carriages. 🖃 *300 N. Main St., Capitol Hill* ☎ *801/532–6479* 🖃 *Free, donations accepted* ⊙ *Mon.–Sat. 9–5.*

★ **㉓ Utah State Capitol.** In 1912, after the state reaped $800,000 in inheri-
tance taxes from the estate of Union Pacific Railroad president Edward
Harriman, work began on the Renaissance Revival structure that tops
Capitol Hill. From the exterior steps you get a marvelous view of the
entire Salt Lake Valley. In the rotunda beneath the 165-foot-high dome

a series of murals, commissioned as part of the WPA project during the Depression, depicts the state's history. The building is closed to tours due to renovations until 2008. ⊠ *400 N. State St., Capitol Hill* ☎ *801/ 538–1563.*

East Side & the University of Utah

Situated on one of the shorelines of ancient Lake Bonneville, the University of Utah is the state's largest higher-education institution and the oldest university west of the Mississippi. It contains a natural history museum, fine arts museum, football stadium that was the site of the opening and closing ceremonies during the 2002 Winter Olympics, and a 15,000-seat indoor stadium. The University Medical Center and its neighbor the Primary Children's Medical Center, east of the campus, are active in medical training and research. Research Park, south of the campus, houses scores of private companies and portions of 30 academic departments in a cooperative enterprise to combine research and technology in order to produce marketable products.

The University grew up around Fort Douglas, which houses limited facilities for the U.S. Army, but now is mostly campus housing. It's here that athletes stayed during the 2002 Winter Olympics. Other Olympic legacies are found around the campus.

As you leave the downtown and university area, there are opportunities to enjoy the outdoors. Hiking trails lead across the foothills above the university. Red Butte Garden and Arboretum is a treat for the eye and a great place to learn about plants that thrive in dry climates such as Utah's. Wander the boardwalks in This Is the Place Heritage Park, or explore Wheeler Historic Farm to relive Utah in the late 1800s. Shop at one of the smaller neighborhood centers like Foothill Village, Trolley Square, or Sugar House to find unique souvenirs of Utah.

a good tour

Start your tour at the **Red Butte Garden and Arboretum ㉚** ▶, east of the University of Utah. Salt Lake is a high desert, yet these gardens in the foothills are surprisingly lush. From here, head back west along 500 South Street where you will see the Hoberman Arch. The arch spanned the medals plaza and the Olympic torch in this small park in front of Rice-Eccles Stadium during the 2002 Winter Olympics. Stop in at one or more of the following while at the University: the **Fort Douglas Military Museum ㉛**, the **Utah Museum of Fine Arts ㉜**, or the **Utah Museum of Natural History ㉝**. When you've had your fill of museums, head south along the Lake Bonneville shoreline and spend an hour or two soaking up Utah's pioneer history at **This Is the Place Heritage Park ㉞**. The child in all of us will enjoy exploring **Utah's Hogle Zoo ㉟**, across the street from Heritage Park. If you're interested in a more detailed view of birds from around the world and specifically Utah, make your way to the **Tracy Aviary ㊱**, inside **Liberty Park ㊲**. To end your tour, return to 700 East Street and head north toward downtown. Take a break by shopping and dining at **Trolley Square ㊳**, one of the town's historic treasures, which has been converted from a 19th-century trolley garage into a high-end shopping, dining, and entertainment complex.

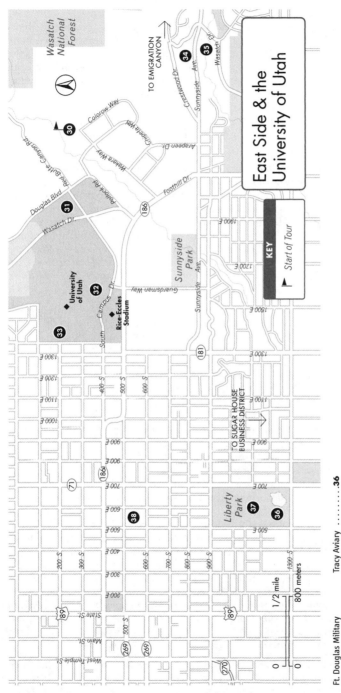

East Side & the University of Utah

KEY

▲ Start of Tour

Timing

This tour can take the whole day. Try to start early because the birds and butterflies are most active during the cool mornings in Red Butte Garden and Arboretum. Spend a large part of your day at This Is the Place Heritage Park, especially in summer when all of the living history takes place. If you only have half a day, start at This is the Place Heritage Park, then choose one or two of the destinations depending on your interest. In winter, with the heritage park on a limited schedule, the Utah Museum of Natural History will give you a good overview of Utah. Balance that with shopping and dining at Trolley Square.

What to See

③ Fort Douglas Military Museum. This former military post was established in 1862 because of strained relations between the U.S. government and the Mormon settlers. Acting on the assumption that Brigham Young might side with the Confederates during the Civil War, a brigade of California and Nevada Union volunteers was dispatched to this site to keep an eye on things. Today Fort Douglas showcases several examples of military architecture and contains a small military history museum near the old parade grounds. ✉ *Wasatch Dr. at 300 South St., University of Utah* ☎ *801/581–1251* ⊕ *www.fortdouglas.org* ☉ *Grounds daily until dusk; museum Tues.–Fri. noon–5, Sat. noon–4.*

★ ⟳ **③ Liberty Park.** Jog the outer path or stroll the inner sidewalk through Salt Lake's earliest and biggest city park. The Chase House, in the park's center, was built next to a mill and is now home to the Museum of Utah Folk Arts Council. Granite boulders from Little Cottonwood Canyon have been transported to the central sidewalk in Liberty Park to form a fountain that represents the major canyons of the Wasatch Front in Salt Lake City. Paddleboats ply the pond in summer, and there are playgrounds for children. ✉ *600 E. 900 South St., East Side.*

⎧ need a ⎫
⎩ break? ⎭
If you're getting hungry, make a pit stop at **Emigration Food Town** (✉ 1706 E. 1300 South St., East Side ☎ 801/581–0138), a small, beloved, and locally owned market that carries Utah products and food. Pack up your goodies and head to Red Butte Garden and Arboretum where you can eat in the shade, possibly next to the red sandstone grotto where there's a waterfall and pond.

★ ⟳ ⮞ **③ Red Butte Garden and Arboretum.** With 25 acres of gardens and 125 undeveloped acres, the grounds here provide many pleasurable hours of strolling. Of special interest are the Perennial, Fragrance, and Medicinal gardens, the Daylily Collection, the Water Pavilion, and the Children's Garden. Lectures on everything from bugs to gardening in arid climates, workshops, and concerts are presented regularly. The Botanic Gift Shop offers books, soaps, sculptures, and fine gifts. ✉ *300 Wakara Way, east of Foothill Dr., University of Utah* ☎ *801/581–4747* ⊕ *www. redbuttegarden.org* ⌘ *$5* ☉ *May–Aug., Mon.–Sat. 9–9, Sun. 9–5; Sept. and Apr., Mon.–Sat. 9–7:30, Sun. 9–5; Oct.–Mar., daily 10–5.*

Sugar House Business District. Utah pioneers tried to produce their own sugar at a mill here. Although sugar never made it to their tables, this shopping center is a sweet place to find funky little shops of all kinds. You'll find history all over the place from the historic Sprague Library to the row of 1920s businesses along 2100 South Street from 1300 East to 900 East streets. ⊠ *From 1700 South to 2700 South Sts. and 700 East to 1300 East Sts., East Side* ☎ *801/484–5259* ⊕ *www. yoursugarhouse.com.*

need a break?

Rolling grassy hills with a few scattered trees provide plenty of room to fly a kite or throw a Frisbee at **Sugarhouse Park** (⊠ At 1300 East and 2100 South Sts., East Side). The park was once a federal prison famous for incarcerating Utah polygamists. Stop in at **Rubio's Fresh Mexican Grill** (⊠ 1160 E. 2100 South St., East Side ☎ 801/466–1220), in the Sugar House Commons west, for a quick and healthy picnic to take with you to the park.

★ ☉ ❸❹ **This Is the Place Heritage Park.** Utah's premier historic park includes Old Deseret Village, a re-created 19th-century community, and This Is the Place Monument and visitor center. In summer almost 200 volunteers dressed in period clothing demonstrate what pioneer life was like. You can watch artisans at work in historic buildings, and take wagon rides around the compound. Watch a 20-minute movie depicting the pioneers' trek across America at the visitor center, or browse through the gift–book shop. ⊠ *2601 Sunnyside Ave., East Side* ☎ *801/582–1847* ⊕ *www. thisistheplace.org* ⊴ *$6* ☉ *This Is the Place Monument, Mon.–Sat. 10–6; Old Deseret Village, Memorial Day–Labor Day, Mon.–Sat. 10–6.*

☉ ❸❻ **Tracy Aviary.** Set on 7½ acres, this facility features some 135 species of birds from around the globe, including emus, bald eagles, flamingos, parrots, and several types of waterfowl. One of the aviary's missions is to educate the public about birds native to Utah and their corresponding ecosystems. There are two free-flight bird shows daily in summer. ⊠ *600 E. 900 South St., East Side* ☎ *801/596–8500* ⊕ *www.tracyaviary. org* ⊴ *$5* ☉ *Nov.–Mar., daily 9–4:30; Apr.–Oct., daily 9–6.*

❸❽ **Trolley Square.** From 1908 to 1945, this sprawling redbrick structure garaged nearly 150 trolleys and electric trains for the Utah Light and Railway Company. In the face of more contemporary modes of transport, however, the facility was closed. In the early 1970s the mission-style edifice was completely overhauled, and today it houses more than 90 boutiques and restaurants. ⊠ *600 S. 700 East St., East Side* ☎ *801/ 521–9877* ☉ *Mon.–Sat. 10–9, Sun. noon–5.*

★ ❸❷ **Utah Museum of Fine Arts.** Because it encompasses 74,000 square feet and more than 20 galleries, you'll be glad this facility has a café and a sculpture court—perfect places to rest. Special exhibits are mounted regularly, and the vast permanent collection includes Egyptian, Greek, and Roman relics; Italian Renaissance and other European paintings; Chinese ceramics and scrolls; Japanese screens; Thai and Cambodian sculptures; African and Latin American artworks; Navajo rugs; and American art from the 17th century to the present. ⊠ *1530 E. South Campus Dr., University of Utah* ☎ *801/581–7332* ⊕ *www.utah.edu/umfa* ⊴ *$4* ☉ *Tues.–Fri. 10–5, Wed. 10–8, weekends 11–5.*

ⓒ ㉝ **Utah Museum of Natural History.** Exhibits focus on the prehistoric inhabitants of the Colorado Plateau, the Great Basin, and other Southwestern locations. Utah's dry climate preserved for centuries not only the structures of these peoples, but also their clothing, foodstuffs, toys, weapons, and ceremonial objects. In the basement are thousands of dinosaur fossils, dominated by creatures from the late Jurassic period, many from the Cleveland-Lloyd quarry in central Utah. Collections of rocks, minerals, wildlife, and other fossils round out the museum. ⊠ *1340 E. 200 South St., on President's Circle, University of Utah* ☎ *801/581–6927* ⊕ *www.umnh.utah.edu* ✉ *$6* ⊙ *Mon.–Sat. 9:30–5:30, Sun. noon–5.*

ⓒ ㉟ **Utah's Hogle Zoo.** The zoo houses more than 1,400 animals from all over the world. Exhibits present animals in their representative habitats. A children's zoo, interactive exhibits, and special presentations make visits informative and engaging for both adults and children. In summer, youngsters can tour the zoo aboard a miniature train. ⊠ *2600 E. Sunnyside Ave., East Side* ☎ *801/582–1631* ⊕ *www.hoglezoo.org* ✉ *$8* ⊙ *Mar.–Oct., daily 9–5; Nov.–Feb., daily 9–4.*

★ ⓒ **BINGHAM CANYON COPPER MINE –** Depending on your point of view, the Bingham Copper Mine is either a marvel of human engineering or simply a great big eyesore. This enormous open-pit mine measures nearly 2½ mi across and ¾ mi deep—the result of removing 5 billion tons of rock. Since operations began nearly 90 years ago by the Kennecott Utah Copper company, more than 12 million tons of copper have been produced. At the visitor center, exhibits and multimedia presentations explain the history and present-day operation of the mine. Outside, trucks the size of dinosaurs and cranes as tall as apartment buildings continue to reshape the mountain. ⊠ *Rte. 48, Copperton* ☎ *801/252–3234* ⊕ *www.kennecott.com/SD_visitors_center.html* ✉ *$4 per vehicle* ⊙ *Apr.–Oct., daily 8–8.*

ⓒ **WHEELER HISTORIC FARM –** Come here to experience 1890s-era farm life by taking an "afternoon chores tour." Try your hand at milking a cow, or riding a draft horse–drawn wagon. ⊠ *6351 S. 900 East St., The Suburbs* ☎ *801/264–2241* ⊕ *www.wheelerfarm.com* ✉ *Free, $1 for special events* ⊙ *Mon.–Sat. 9–5.*

The Great Salt Lake

No visit to Utah is quite complete without a trip to the Great Salt Lake. This wonder of the world is actually more popular with tourists than locals. This was not always the case, but drastic changes in lake levels keep the state and private developers from cashing in on this unique site so close to a major city. Because the lake is so shallow, an inch or two of change in the lake's depth translates into yards of sticky mud between the sandy beach and water deep enough to float in. This shouldn't keep anyone from taking a cruise on the lake or visiting Antelope Island, where the shore dynamics are much different.

THE LEGENDARY GREAT SALT LAKE

LEGENDS OF AN ENORMOUS *body of water with an outlet to the Pacific Ocean drew explorers north from Mexico as early as the 1500s. By the 1700s, other legends—about piles of gold and mines full of jewels—had been proven false by Spanish explorers, but the lake legend endured. Following a source of water through the West's harsh desert, and traveling along a flat river bank instead of struggling over mountains, would make trade easier between New Mexico and the settlements springing up along California's coast. Perhaps goods could be shipped to the coast rather than hauled by mules, a trip the Spanish guessed (and they were right) would take months.*

Franciscan fathers Francisco Atanasio Dominguez and Francisco Silvestre Velez de Escalante came close to finding Great Salt Lake in 1776, but they cut through the Wasatch Mountains too far to the south. They did blaze a major trade route through Utah, but there is no record of any travelers wandering off the route to see the lake of legend. In 1804–05, Lewis and Clark searched for a water route to the west coast, but their focus on the Columbia River gave them no reason to travel south of Idaho. They, too, missed the lake.

Mountain men had heard of the lake. Legend has it that an argument about the lake broke out at the alcohol-soaked 1824 rendezvous in northern Utah—the trappers couldn't agree whether the nearby Bear River flowed into the lake. Jim Bridger was chosen to settle the argument, some say because he was the youngest. For whatever reason, he was set adrift on the Bear River in a rickety bull boat and told to report his findings at a future rendezvous—if he survived.

Jim Bridger did survive, and he was able to report that the Bear River did flow into the Great Salt Lake. However, his travels and those of fellow mountain man Jedediah Smith indicated that the lake was landlocked. Plus it was no good for drinking. (With no rivers to drain the lake, water that flows in has no way out but to evaporate, leaving behind a highly concentrated solution of salts and minerals.) Even worse, the explorers found that travel around the lake was hampered by vast expanses of marshland, a muddy shoreline, and hundreds of square miles of salt flats that looked solid but were often little more than a thin crust over layers of muck.

With dreams of a freshwater oasis and an easy route to the coast crushed, the legends of the lake changed. The lake became a place where monsters lurked in the water, giants rode elephantlike creatures on the islands, and the bottom periodically opened, swallowing everything nearby. The area became a place to avoid, or to pass by quickly, until 1847, when Brigham Young and the Mormon pioneers crossed the plains to settle on its shore.

What to See

Great Salt Lake State Park. The Great Salt Lake is eight times saltier than the ocean and second only to the Dead Sea in salinity. What makes it so briny? There's no outlet to the ocean, so salts and other minerals carried by rivers and streams become concentrated in this enormous evaporation pond. Ready access to this wonder is possible at Great Salt Lake State Park, 16 mi west of Salt Lake City, on the lake's south shore.

The fickle nature of the Great Salt Lake is evident here. From the marina you will see a large, Moorish-style pavilion to the north. This pavilion was built to re-create the former glory days of the lake from the 1890s to the 1950s when, first the train, then automobiles, brought thousands of people here for entertainment. Floating in the lake was the biggest draw, but ballroom dancing and an amusement park made for a day's recreation. Despite varying lake levels, three resorts made this a popular place. It was the decline of ballroom dancing together with a severe drop in the lake level that spelled the end of it in the 1960s. In 1981 the present pavilion, souvenir shop, and a dance floor were built. Two years later, record flooding made an island of the pavilion. It sits on dry land today, but its owners have been unable to reclaim their dream.

The state park used to manage the beaches north of the pavilion, but the lake is too shallow here for convenient floating. The picnic beaches on Antelope Island State Park are the best places to float. If you can't take the time to get to Antelope Island, however, you can walk down the boat ramp at the marina and stick your legs in the water to experience the unique sensation of floating on water that won't let you sink. Your feet will bob to the surface and you will see tiny orange brine shrimp floating with you. Shower off at the marina. At the marina, you can make arrangements for group or charter sails. Trips take from one to six hours, and there's a range of reasonable prices to match; some include meals. **Salt Island Adventures** (☎ 801/252–9336 ⊕ www.gslcruises. com) runs cruises between March and December. ✉ *Frontage Rd., 2 mi east of I–80 Exit 104, Salt Lake City* ☎ *801/250–1898* 🎫 *Free* ⊙ *Daily 7 AM–10 PM.*

WHERE TO EAT

Updated by
John Blodgett

Name your pleasure, and you can find it here: hot, hip destinations with worldly chefs and dazzling menus; sophisticated microbreweries known as much for their food as for their brew; superb sushi, and a range of ethnic options; neighborhood bistros that won't break the bank; dining in unique canyon settings; and of course most major chains. You can now find superb seafood in most restaurants, not just the few that specialize in seafood; it's easy to order a cocktail with dinner at almost any restaurant; and select wine lists and knowledgeable service are readily available. Chefs hail from all corners of the world, and many of them are avid fishermen, gardeners, foragers of local ingredients, and sticklers for quality. Be assured, your prospects for a good meal, in any price range, are excellent.

		WHAT IT COSTS			
	$$$$	$$$	$$	$	¢
AT DINNER	over $25	$19–$25	$13–$18	$8–$12	under $8

Restaurant prices are per person for a main course at dinner, excluding sales tax of 7.6%

Downtown Salt Lake

American

$–$$$ ✕ **Lamb's Grill Café.** With its long marble counter, deco-style trim, and cozy mahogany booths, one of the city's oldest dining establishments has aged well. It's a white-tablecloth kind of place where you can still indulge in an old-fashioned lamb shank, local fresh trout dinner, or a bowl of house-made lemon-and-rice soup at a reasonable price. The long-time Greek owners have added a few Mediterranean touches to the big menu. Newspaper, business, and political types often gather here for breakfast or lunch. ✉ *169 S. Main St., Downtown* ☎ *801/364–7166* ▭ *AE, D, DC, MC, V* ☺ *Closed Sun.*

$–$$ ✕ **Red Rock Brewing Company.** Head to this contemporary brewpub for creative whole-meal salads, an impossibly savory Reuben sandwich, thin-crust pizzas, and perfectly beer-battered fish-and-chips. An on-site brewery, house-brewed sodas, a full bar, wood-burning ovens, and an overall sense of style add up to a lively lunch and dinner spot near the Delta Center. ✉ *254 S. 200 West St., Downtown* ☎ *801/521–7446* ▭ *AE, D, DC, MC, V.*

★ **$–$$** ✕ **Squatter's Pub Brewery.** A glass wall separates gleaming fermentation tanks from the bar at this casual, high-energy brewpub in the 1906 Boston Hotel building. Locals convene here before or after pro sporting events at the nearby Delta Center. It's also a happening spot on summer days and nights when the patio with its cooling mist system is in full swing and the chef fires up the outdoor grill. The menu veers from locally made bratwurst to curry specials, fish tacos, and big, juicy buffalo burgers. ✉ *147 W. Broadway, Downtown* ☎ *801/363–2739* ⚲ *Reservations not accepted* ▭ *AE, D, DC, MC, V.*

¢–$$ ✕ **Stoneground.** On the top floor of a generic-looking building across the street from the city's architecturally spectacular main public library, this casual pizza, pasta, beer, and pool hangout is an easy ride from the University of Utah via TRAX. The menu offers basic pub food, including better than average pizzas at reasonable prices. Note the $10 "all you can eat" pizza-and-salad on Sunday. ✉ *249 E. 400 South St., Downtown* ☎ *801/364–1368* ▭ *AE, D, MC, V* ☺ *No lunch weekends.*

Chinese

$ ✕ **Hong Kong Tea House.** Lacquered wood and marble tables, comfortable chairs, and warm colors give the Tea House's three small dining rooms a welcoming look and feel. At lunch, ask for a dim sum menu and simply mark your choices, or wait until servers walk by with small dishes or bamboo baskets of all the Cantonese-style classics, from steamed pork buns to crunchy chicken feet. Don't miss the shrimp-stuffed

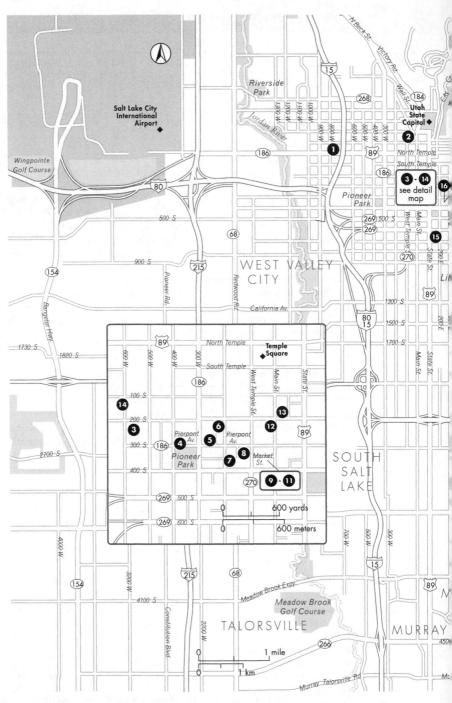

eggplant. Dinner menus are more formal, offering traditional Peking duck, whole stuffed fish, spicy Szechuan-style chicken with green beans, and other authentic, regional Chinese favorites. ⊠ *565 W. 200 South St., Downtown* ☎ *801/531–7010* ⊟ *D, DC, MC, V* ⊙ *Closed Mon.*

Contemporary

★ **$$–$$$$**   ✗ **Bambara.** Seasonal menus reflect regional American and international influences at this artfully designed destination restaurant. The setting, formerly an ornate bank lobby adjacent to the swank Hotel Monaco, is as much of a draw as the food. An open marble-fronted kitchen, big windows framed in fanciful hammered metal swirls, and a definite "buzz" make Bambara a popular gathering spot. You can also dine in the adjoining private club, or simply enjoy a cocktail while snuggled in a velvet-lined booth. ⊠ *202 S. Main St., Downtown* ☎ *801/ 363–5454* ⊟ *AE, D, DC, MC, V.*

$$–$$$$ ✗ **Metropolitan.** From its inventive cuisine to its minimalist design, owner
Fodor\$Choice   Karen Olson's restaurant is chic in every way. Chef Adam Findlay's menus
★   veer from Asian-fusion to regional Rocky Mountain fare. You can usually walk in and get a seat at the curved bar or a bar table and order from a small bistro menu. But for the full experience, reserve a table and put yourself in the chef's capable hands with the daily tasting menu. Service here borders on choreography—synchronized, yet unobtrusive. The wine list is excellent. ⊠ *173 W. Broadway, Downtown* ☎ *801/364– 3472* ⊟ *AE, D, MC, V* ⊙ *Closed Sun.*

Continental

$$–$$$$ ✗ **The New Yorker and the Café at the New Yorker.** This subterranean, clubby bar, café, and restaurant with its modern Continental menu, starched white tablecloths, stained-glass ceilings, and rounded banquette seating offers great people-watching potential. If you feel like indulging, try the filet mignon or the veal chop with morel mushrooms and brandy cream sauce. The café–bar area has a lower-price, more casual menu. You'll usually find a crowd of loyal locals, including power-lunchers mingling and having a good time. ⊠ *60 W. Market St., Downtown* ☎ *801/363– 0166* ⊟ *AE, D, DC, MC, V* ⊙ *Closed Sun. No lunch Sat.*

Delicatessens

★ **¢–$**   ✗ **Tony Caputo's Market and Deli.** The people who line up out the door at lunch hour are usually salivating in anticipation of a generous, authentic deli sandwich at this stocked-to-the-rafters Italian deli and market. Whether you fancy a juicy, sauce-drenched meatball concoction, buffalo mozzarella with basil and fresh tomatoes, salami with roasted red peppers, or a hot daily special such as lasagna, it's a great value and a convivial, casual place. Lunch and early dinner are available to eat in or take away. ⊠ *308 W. 300 South St., Downtown* ☎ *801/531–8669* ⊟ *AE, D, MC, V.*

Eclectic

★ **$–$$**   ✗ **The Bayou.** You'll find more than 200 microbrews, both bottled and on tap, at chef-owner Mark Alston's lively bar and restaurant. The menu offers everything from Cajun specialties such as jambalaya and étouffée to blackened seafood and a terrific, garlicky hamburger with sweet-potato fries. Live jazz, pool tables, and a clean, modern design create a casual, high-energy atmosphere. ⊠ *645 S. State St., Downtown* ☎ *801/ 961–8400* ▭ *AE, D, DC, MC, V* ☺ *Closed Sun. No lunch Sat.*

$-$$ ✕ **Oasis Cafe.** From morning to well into the evening, a selection of fine teas and espresso drinks, big breakfasts, and fresh, innovative entrées draw regulars to this café and its serene patio courtyard. The menu leans toward vegetarian and seafood selections, and there are plenty of rich, house-made pastries available, as well as a nice wine list. The café shares space with a book- and gift store, The Golden Braid, and is a popular gathering spot. ⊠ *151 S. 500 East St., Downtown* ☎ *801/322– 0404* ▭ *AE, D, DC, MC, V.*

¢-$$ ✕ **Spice.** Vegans, vegetarians, and meat-lovers enjoy this Bohemian café. Starters include roasted pepper hummus, a broiled-shrimp Caesar salad, and curried chickpea and tomato soup; wraps, hot pitas, and "healthy burgers" comprise the rest of the menu. Add chicken to the excellent portobello wrap (all wraps are tomato), or try the chicken and shrimp with brown rice. Wine and beer are served, as is breakfast on Saturday. On Friday and Saturday the café remains open until 3 AM, unheard-of in Salt Lake City. Monday is open mike, and live music plays other nights. ⊠ *123 S. W. Temple St., Downtown* ☎ *801/322–4796* ▭ *AE, MC, V* ☺ *Closed Sun.*

¢ ✕ **Caffè d'bolla.** It's more than a coffee and tea shop (no drip brew here, by the way). Choose from a variety of bagel sandwiches that can be served cold or hot, such as the Funky Clucker—chicken, provolone, tomato, and spices. There's also thick toast, and the daily selection of locally made desserts often includes cheesecake, praline pecan cake, baklava, and house-made gelato and brownies. The husband–wife owners are the only employees, and except for occasional holidays they remain open every day, often until 11 PM. ⊠ *249 E. 400 South St.* ☎ *801/355–1398* ⊕ *www. caffedbolla.com* ▭ *AE, D, DC, MC, V.*

Italian

★ **$-$$$** ✕ **Cucina Toscana.** One of the city's most bustling trattorias is tucked into the corner of a renovated brick Firestone Tire shop. Owner–host Valter Nassi takes great pride in his menus of house-made pastas, including ravioli with four cheeses and asparagus, or plump gnocchi with sage butter. Main courses include local trout grilled Tuscan style or osso buco with polenta. The deco-style pressed-tin ceiling, open kitchen, bas-relief trim, and banquette seating create an urban, artsy atmosphere, which complements the top-notch service, food, and wines. ⊠ *307 W. Pierpont Ave., Downtown* ☎ *801/328–3463* ▭ *AE, D, DC, MC, V* ☺ *Closed Sun.*

Japanese

★ **$-$$$** ✕ **Takashi.** One of Salt Lake's most popular Japanese restaurants is hip and lively and has the city's finest sushi, including *uni nigiri* (sea-urchin sushi) that defines melt-in-your-mouth. The calamari is a must-try, too, and many days owner–chef Takashi Gibo can be seen behind the sushi bar. The full-service bar serves up crisp sake and fine martinis. ⊠ *18 W. Market St., Downtown* ☎ *801/519–9595* ▭ *AE, D, DC, MC, V* ☺ *Closed Sun. No lunch Sat.*

$–$$ ✕ **Ichiban.** Three elements make this one of the most interesting dining destinations in town. One is its setting in an old church, complete with exquisite stained-glass windows and vaulted ceilings; the next is the modernized, feng-shui–inspired interior; third is the owner–sushi chef, Peggy Whiting. She and her crew specialize in classic sushi as well as multi-layered Americanized interpretations, some with hot chilis, or with esoteric, locally inspired combinations. You can order some fine cold sakes, and there's a full bar. ⊠ *336 S. 400 East St., Downtown* ☎ *801/ 532–7522* ⚘ *Reservations not accepted* ▤ *AE, MC, V.*

Mexican

$ ✕ **Red Iguana.** This lively Mexican restaurant is staffed with a warm and accommodating crew, serving the best house-made moles and chile verde in town. They pour premium margaritas and good Mexican beers, and always keep the salsa and chips coming. Expect a wait almost always. This is a great place to stop on your way to or from the airport if you don't want to take the freeway. ⊠ *736 W. North Temple, Downtown* ☎ *801/322–1489* ▤ *AE, D, DC, MC, V.*

Fodor's Choice
★

Seafood

★ **$$–$$$$** ✕ **Market Street Grill.** Seafood's the focus in this Salt Lake standby in a beautifully restored 1906 building. It's a popular breakfast, lunch, and dinner destination where the selections range from daily fresh seafood entrées to certified Angus beef. Portions are large and include all the side dishes. The atmosphere is usually lively. ⊠ *48 Market St., Downtown* ☎ *801/322–4668* ⚘ *Reservations not accepted* ▤ *AE, D, DC, MC, V.*

$–$$$ ✕ **Market Street Oyster Bar.** Some would call this popular bar–restaurant more of a "meet market," but it's a fun and upbeat place. Popular items include the clam chowder, crab and shrimp cocktails, and more expensive seafood entrées. The decor features original hand-painted pillars, rounded booths that face the action, and televisions on at all hours. The Market Street Oyster Bar is a private club (which means you have to buy a temporary membership for $4) adjoining the Market Street Grill. ⊠ *54 Market St., Downtown* ☎ *801/942–8860* ⚘ *Reservations not accepted* ▤ *AE, D, DC, MC, V.*

Capitol Hill & the Avenues

Eclectic

$–$$ ✕ **Em's.** Fresh, flavorful, creative, and artsy—chef Emily Gassmann's small café combines it all in a renovated brick storefront in the Marmalade District, west of the Capitol. The café has an urban feel with its modern art and polished wood floors. Sit at the counter, at wooden tables, or on the patio and enjoy the varied menu of salads, soups, special tamales, savory crepes, meat, and vegetarian entrées. ⊠ *271 N. Center St., Capitol Hill* ☎ *801/596–0566* ▤ *AE, MC, V* ⊙ *No dinner Mon.–Wed.*

$ ✕ **Cucina.** Locals flock to this neighborhood café and take-away food market for the creative salads and colorful entrées displayed like jewels in glass cases. Most people order a sampler of three or four salads, such as orzo with mint, feta, chicken, and artichoke hearts; or wild rice–based concoctions. Also on the menu are house-made soups, generous deli sandwiches, and hot entrées such as meat loaf and mashed

MORMON MUNCHIES

THE MORMON RELIGION HAS HELPED to shape the state's cuisine as well as its culture. The church advises followers to refrain from drinking beverages containing alcohol or caffeine. Some people theorize that this has led to the development of a collective sweet tooth. Sweet red punch is perhaps the state's most popular beverage; ice cream is consumed in great quantities (though the weight-conscious have switched to frozen yogurt); and pastries are all the rage.

Green Jell-O gelatin—topped with miniature marshmallows and mixed with grated carrots or cottage cheese and pineapple—appears at every Mormon social function. In 2001, when Salt Lake City lost its title as the number-one consumer of Jell-O to Des Moines, Iowa, the state legislature got into the act. During a visit by Jell-O Company spokesman and comedian Bill Cosby, lawmakers declared the wiggly stuff as

Utah's official state snack. The tide turned, and for the time being more of the stuff is consumed per capita here than in any other state.

At family functions such as potluck dinners, weddings, and funerals, you'll often see a dish that's dubbed "funeral potatoes" made from potatoes, cheddar cheese, canned soup, and sour cream—all baked and covered with buttered bread crumbs. One favorite that's readily available at restaurants is fry sauce. The originator of a local Salt Lake City hamburger chain, Arctic Circle, invented this combination of ketchup, mayonnaise, and spices. It caught on, and most Utahns demand the sauce for their french fries at all burger joints.

---

potatoes. Big windows and warm mustard and terra-cotta tones are reminiscent of a Tuscan-style café, with seating indoors and out. ☒ 1026 E. 2nd Ave., Temple Square ☎ 801/322–3055 ▤ AE, D, DC, MC, V ⊘ No dinner Sun.

Tibetan

¢–$ ✕ **Cafe Shambala.** Go for savory Tibetan food at bargain prices in this small, clean restaurant decorated with brightly colored Tibetan flags. You can indulge in hearty entrées such as spicy potatoes, chicken curry, and versions of chow mein, and specials such as beef chili, all washed down with pots of tea. The lunchtime buffet is the best deal. ☒ 382 4th Ave., Temple Square ☎ 801/364–8558 ▤ AE, MC, V ⊘ Closed Sun.

East Side & the University of Utah

Contemporary

$–$$ ✕ **Desert Edge Brewery.** This lively microbrewery has brass-top tables, loft seating, a sheltered patio, and lots of music and noise. It also offers a great view of the sunset through floor-to-ceiling windows. The menu offers basic pub food, but goes beyond with creative sandwiches such as salmon with pickled ginger-cucumber slaw, whole-meal salads, and

Mexican-inspired fare. ⊠ *273 Trolley Sq., East Side* ☎ *801/521–8917* ▤ *AE, D, MC, V.*

Indian

★ **$–$$** ╳ **Bombay House.** You're enveloped in exotic aromas the minute you step into this dark, intimate restaurant in a small strip mall above busy Foothill Boulevard. Enjoy good Indian standards, including the softest naan and spiciest of curries, tandoori dishes, and lots of vegetarian options. There's a selection of domestic and imported beers as well as traditional teas and tea-based drinks. Carved wood, print fabric, an aquarium, and the gracious Indian staff all combine to make you feel as though you've escaped to another little world for a while. ⊠ *1615 S. Foothill Dr., East Side* ☎ *801/581–0222* ▤ *AE, D, DC, MC, V* ☾ *Closed Sun. No lunch.*

Italian

$$–$$$ ╳ **Fresco Italian Cafe.** This intimate, modern restaurant is tucked back from the street in a clapboard house that adjoins an independent bookstore. Items like grilled wild salmon, the daily risotto, and peppered natural chicken take center stage as the season dictates. In summer seating is available on the small patio. ⊠ *1513 S. 1500 East St., East Side* ☎ *801/486–1300* ⚐ *Reservations essential* ▤ *AE, D, DC, MC, V* ☾ *Closed Mon. No lunch.*

Middle Eastern

¢–$ ╳ **Mazza.** Authentic and affordable Middle Eastern food in a casual order-at-the-counter setting is what Mazza is all about. The homemade falafel, stuffed grape leaves, lamb, chicken and beef kebabs, and an assortment of side dishes are all fresh and tasty. So are the sweets, such as the honey-drenched baklava. ⊠ *1515 S. 1500 East St., East Side* ☎ *801/484–9259* ▤ *AE, D, MC, V* ☾ *Closed Sun.*

Seafood

$$–$$$$ ╳ **Market Street Broiler.** Formerly a firehouse, circa 1930, this popular restaurant is casual, with a focus on seafood. You can sit at the counter, in the shaded sidewalk café area, or upstairs where the decor is nautical and made to feel like a luxury yacht. Menu highlights include crab cakes, daily fish specials, a great cobb salad, and some pricey steak and seafood combinations. There's also an on-site fish market. ⊠ *260 S. 1300 East St., University of Utah* ☎ *801/583–8808* ▤ *AE, D, DC, MC, V.*

Farther Afield

Contemporary

$$–$$$$ ╳ **Log Haven.** This elegant mountain retreat was put on the map with
Fodor'sChoice inventive takes on American cuisine laced with everything from Asian
★ ingredients to pure Rocky Mountain style. It excels with fresh fish, game, and seasonal local ingredients. The knowledgeable staff can help you pair wines with the menu's multilayered flavors. With its romantic setting in a beautifully renovated log home amid pine trees, waterfalls, and wildflowers, and its summertime patio seating, this is definitely a restaurant to remember. ⊠ *3800 South St., Millcreek Canyon, From I–15, take I–80 E to I–215 S; exit at 39th South; turn left at end of ramp, and*

left onto Wasatch Blvd., then turn right at 3800 South. Continue 4 mi up canyon ☎ *801/272–8255* ▤ *AE, D, DC, MC, V.*

Eclectic

$–$$$ ✕ **Porcupine Pub and Grille.** Above a ski and board rental shop at the mouth of Big and Little Cottonwood canyons sits one of the Valley's most lively pubs. Inside the A-frame chaletlike building you'll find polished wood floors and trim, and a friendly vibe. The menu offers more than 40 variations on standard pub food, including buffalo wings, Thai chicken pizza, burgers, ribs, filet mignon, and ahi tuna. The full-service bar features spirits, microbrews on tap, and a wine list. ⊠ *3698 E. Fort Union Blvd., Cottonwood* ☎ *801/942–5555* ▤ *AE, D, MC, V.*

Mexican

¢ ✕ **Lone Star Taqueria.** This place is hard to miss. Look for the lime-green building surrounded by a fence topped with old cowboy boots, and fronted by an old sticker-covered car that looks as though it crashed through the fence. Amid the concrete floors, metal tables, and bright umbrellas, there's some excellent, cheap Mexican food to be had—including house special fish tacos, handmade tamales, burritos of all types, and plenty of chilled Mexican beer. There's a drive-through window for takeout, too. ⊠ *2265 E. Fort Union Blvd., Cottonwood* ☎ *801/944–2300* ⌫ *Reservations not accepted* ▤ *No credit cards* ⊙ *Closed Sun.*

WHERE TO STAY

Luxury grand hotels, intimate bed-and-breakfasts, reliable national "all suites" chains—Salt Lake City has plenty of options when it comes to resting your head at night. Unlike in most cities, hotels, motels, and even bed-and-breakfasts here are all tuned into serving visiting skiers in winter months. Many offer ski packages, transportation, and equipment rental options, as well as knowledgeable staff who are probably on the slopes when they're not at work. Most of the hotels are concentrated in the downtown area and west of the airport, but there are also numerous options to the south of Salt Lake proper and closer to the canyon areas, where several high-tech companies and corporate headquarters are located.

WHAT IT COSTS				
$$$$	**$$$**	**$$**	**$**	**¢**
FOR 2 PEOPLE over $200	$151–$200	$111–$150	$70–$110	under $70

Hotel prices are for two people in a standard double room in high season, excluding taxes of 10.1% to 11.2%

Downtown Salt Lake

$$$$ 🏨 **Grand America Hotel.** With its white Bethel granite exterior, this 24-
Fodor'sChoice story luxury hotel dominates the skyline a few blocks south of down-
★ town. Inside the beveled-glass and brass doors, you step into a world of Italian marble floors and walls and pure old-world style—think En-

glish wool carpets, French furniture and tapestries, and colorful Murano-glass chandeliers. The posh guest rooms average 700 square feet. Most have views and small balconies. This is a great place to sit back with room service and revel in some pampering. The big outdoor pool and indoor spa are among the best in the city. ⊠ *555 S. Main St., Downtown 84111* ☎ *801/258–6000 or 800/621–4505* 🖷 *801/258–6911* ⊕ *www.grandamerica.com* ➩ *775 rooms* ⚘ *2 restaurants, room service, in-room safes, minibars, cable TV with movies and video games, in-room broadband, 2 pools (1 indoor), health club, hair salon, hot tub, outdoor hot tub, sauna, spa, lounge, shops, laundry service, concierge, concierge floor, business services, convention center, meeting rooms, airport shuttle, parking (fee)* ▤ *AE, D, DC, MC, V.*

$$$–$$$$
Fodor's Choice
★

🏨 **Hotel Monaco Salt Lake City.** This swank hotel is ensconced in a former bank, distinguished by an exterior decorated with classical cornices and cartouches. Inside, the look and feel are sophisticated, eclectic, and upbeat. Rooms offer extras such as big fringed ottomans, oversize framed mirrors and beds, and lots of pillows. And, there are special rooms for especially tall folks, with extra-long beds. Bambara Restaurant, on the ground level (under separate management), is one of the city's most celebrated dining spots. ⊠ *15 W. 200 South St., Downtown 84101* ☎ *801/595–0000 or 800/805–1801* 🖷 *801/532–8500* ⊕ *www. monaco-saltlakecity.com* ➩ *187 rooms, 38 suites* ⚘ *Restaurant, room service, in-room safes, minibars, cable TV with movies and video games, in-room broadband, Wi-Fi, health club, massage, ski storage, bar, babysitting, laundry service, concierge, meeting room, parking (fee)* ▤ *AE, D, DC, MC, V.*

$$$–$$$$

🏨 **Marriott City Center.** If you want to be in the heart of the city, this hotel's location is superb. It's right next to Gallivan Center, site of all kinds of concerts in summer and ice-skating in the winter. Inside, the lobby and public areas are clean and contemporary, with a fresh, upscale feeling. Rooms are furnished with king-size beds and comfortable seating. You have all the conveniences here, including a Starbucks, an indoor pool, and a fitness center. The hotel is relatively new, built just prior to the 2002 Winter Olympics. ⊠ *220 S. State St., Downtown 84111* ☎ *801/961–8700* 🖷 *801/961–8704* ⊕ *www.marriott.com* ➩ *342 rooms, 17 suites* ⚘ *Restaurant, coffee shop, room service, in-room safes, cable TV with movies and video games, in-room broadband, indoor pool, health club, hot tub, ski storage, lounge, dry cleaning, laundry service, concierge, concierge floor, business services, convention center, airport shuttle, car rental, parking (fee)* ▤ *AE, D, DC, MC, V.*

$$$

🏨 **Hilton–Salt Lake City Center.** This Hilton is one of the city's largest and best-appointed places to stay, and it's within walking distance of all downtown attractions and many great restaurants. Its on-site restaurants and bar are so good they're destinations for locals. Like many Salt Lake hotels, it also caters to skiers by offering complimentary ski storage. Knowledgeable staff can usually fill visitors in on the various ski resorts and rental shops. ⊠ *255 S. West Temple, Downtown 84101* ☎ *801/328–2000 or 800/445–8667* 🖷 *801/238–4888* ⊕ *www.hilton. com* ➩ *499 rooms* ⚘ *2 restaurants, in-room safes, cable TV with* *movies, in-room broadband, indoor pool, health club, massage, sauna, ski storage, bar, dry cleaning, laundry service, concierge, business services, convention center, meeting room, car rental, parking (fee)* ▭ *AE, D, DC, MC, V.*

$$$ ▦ **Red Lion Hotel.** Close to I–15, this downtown high-rise is within walking distance of the Salt Palace Convention Center and Delta Center, and there's a full ski-rental shop across the street. The lobby is intimate, with a fireplace and cushy furnishings. Rooms have a warm feeling, with dark colors and thick fabric, and some have chaise-type sofas. The downstairs bar and top-floor restaurant–bar (called the Sky Bar) are both popular among locals and airline crews. ⊠ *161 W. 600 South St., Downtown 84111* ☎ *801/521–7373 or 800/325–4000* 🖷 *801/524–0354* ⊕ *www.redlion.wchc.com* ↪ *392 rooms, 4 suites* ⚏ *Restaurant, coffee shop, room service, cable TV with movies and video games, in-room data ports, in-room broadband, pool, gym, hair salon, outdoor hot tub, business services, convention center, meeting room, airport shuttle, free parking, some pets allowed (fee)* ▭ *AE, D, DC, MC, V.*

★ $–$$$ ▦ **Little America Hotel.** Located on the TRAX light-rail line and inside the "free ride zone," this reliably comfortable hotel has a loyal following. You can choose between spacious "tower" rooms inside the 17-story building, or garden rooms with private entrances. There's a large indoor–outdoor pool, a lobby fireplace, and elegant details such as brass railings, chandeliers, and marble tubs. The spacious guest rooms are conservatively furnished, but with richly textured fabrics and plush seating. ⊠ *500 S. Main St., Downtown 84101* ☎ *801/363–6781 or 800/453–9450* 🖷 *801/596–5911* ⊕ *www.littleamerica.com* ↪ *850 rooms* ⚏ *Restaurant, coffee shop, room service, cable TV with movies and video games, in-room broadband, indoor-outdoor pool, health club, hair salon, hot tub, sauna, ski storage, piano bar, dry cleaning, laundry facilities, laundry service, concierge, business services, airport shuttle, free parking* ▭ *AE, D, DC, MC, V.*

$$ ▦ **Embassy Suites Hotel Salt Lake City.** The sunlit atrium with its soaring ceiling gives the entire hotel a light, airy feeling, and the cool terra-cotta tile floors are soothing in the summer heat. All the rooms are small suites, complete with two TVs and sofa sleepers. The hotel is immaculate and rooms are neat and tailored in style. The set-up makes it appealing for business travelers, skiers, and families. There's free underground parking, and easy freeway access to and from I–15. You can also walk two blocks east to the TRAX line. ⊠ *110 W. 600 South St., Downtown 84301* ☎ *801/359–7800* 🖷 *801/359–3753* ⊕ *www.embassysuites.com* ↪ *241 suites* ⚏ *Restaurant, room service, microwaves, refrigerators, cable TV with movies and video games, in-room broadband, Wi-Fi, indoor pool, health club, hot tub, ski storage, bar, lounge, dry cleaning, laundry facilities, business services, meeting room, airport shuttle, free parking* ▭ *AE, D, DC, MC, V* ❑ *BP.*

$$ ▦ **Sheraton City Centre Hotel.** One of the city's major full-service hotels and convention centers, the Sheraton has a huge lobby with its own Starbucks coffee shop, oversize chairs, and fireplace. There's a lounge-bar with two big-screen TVs on the main floor, and a courtyard with an inviting outdoor pool. Rooms are spacious and tailored, some have balconies

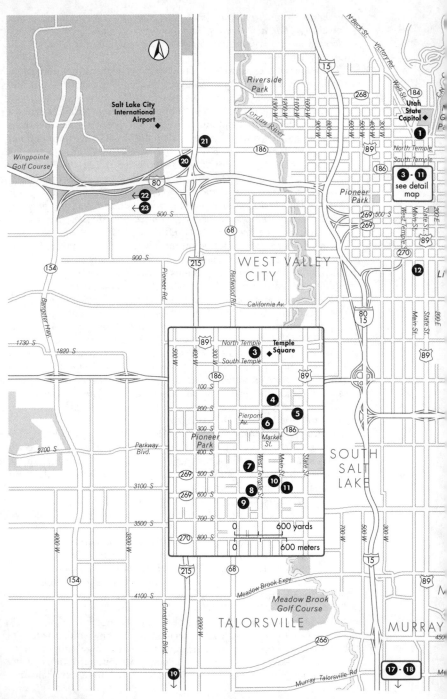

Where to
Stay in
Salt Lake City

and many offer mountain views. ⊠ *150 W. 500 South St., Downtown 84101* ☎ *801/401–2000 or 800/364–3295* 🖳 *801/531–0705* ⊕ *www. starwoodhotels.com* 🛏 *332 rooms, 30 suites* ⚒ *Restaurant, room service, cable TV with movies, in-room data ports, pool, gym, hair salon, hot tub, sauna, ski storage, bar, dry cleaning, laundry facilities, laundry service, business services, convention center, meeting rooms, airport shuttle, parking (fee)* ⊟ *AE, D, DC, MC, V.*

$–$$ 🏨 **Inn at Temple Square.** A nice alternative to the chains, this seven-story downtown brick hotel is across the street from the Salt Palace Convention Center, Temple Square, and the world-famous Genealogy Library, one of the city's biggest attractions for those interested in extensive research. The vibe here is very quiet and conservative, but it's an urban, upscale hotel with efficient service. Rooms have a 1930s style and floral wallpaper; some have chaise lounges. The high-ceiling lobby has a grand piano, chandelier, and fireplace. ⊠ *71 W. South Temple, Downtown 84101* ☎ *801/531–1000 or 800/843–4668* 🖳 *801/536–7272* ⊕ *www.theinn. com* 🛏 *80 rooms, 10 suites* ⚒ *Restaurant, room service, refrigerators, cable TV, in-room broadband, laundry service, concierge, business services, meeting room, airport shuttle, free parking; no smoking* ⊟ *AE, D, DC, MC, V* ◎ *CP.*

¢–$ 🏨 **Holiday Inn–Downtown.** South of the major business district, this full-service hotel is convenient to everything, including several nearby restaurants. You're right on the TRAX light-rail line, and can take it in either direction, north to downtown and the University of Utah, or to points south. The tennis courts are nice extras if you want to stay downtown but still be active, plus there's a basketball area and playground. ⊠ *999 S. Main St., Downtown 84111* ☎ *801/359–8600* 🖳 *801/359–7186* ⊕ *www.ichotelsgroup.com* 🛏 *161 rooms, 14 suites* ⚒ *Restaurant, cable TV with movies and video games, in-room broadband, 2 tennis courts, indoor pool, health club, hot tub, sauna, basketball, ski storage, bar, playground, dry cleaning, laundry facilities, business services, convention center, airport shuttle, free parking, some pets allowed* ⊟ *AE, D, DC, MC, V.*

Capitol Hill & the Avenues

★ $–$$$ 🏨 **Inn on the Hill.** This turn-of-the-20th-century Renaissance Revival mansion makes a striking impression with its red rock exterior and bold painted trim. Inside, it's like stepping into the just-polished parlor and living rooms of a private home, replete with stained-glass windows. Rooms are eclectic in style, with historic Utah themes. All are very cushy, with big bathtubs and fireplaces. ⊠ *225 N. State St., Capitol Hill 84103* ☎ *801/328–1466* 🖳 *801/328–0590* ⊕ *www.inn-on-the-hill.com* 🛏 *14 rooms* ⚒ *Cable TV, in-room VCRs, in-room data ports, Wi-Fi* ⊟ *AE, D, DC, MC, V* ◎ *BP.*

$$ 🏨 **Ellerbeck Mansion Bed and Breakfast.** Stay in this Victorian mansion to get a feel for why city residents flock to live in the historic Avenues district. Temple Square and other points downtown are a short 10-minute walk away. Each theme room is bright. Some feature a fireplace, private balcony, or hand-carved wood furniture and fixtures. ⊠ *140 B St., Capitol Hill 84103* ☎ *801/355–2500 or 800/966–8364* 🖳 *801/530–*

0938 ⊕ *www.ellerbeckbedandbreakfast.com* ⥽ *6 rooms* ⌂ *Cable TV, in-room data ports, free parking* ☰ *AE, D, DC, MC, V* ⑩ *BP.*

East Side & the University of Utah

$$ ⊞ **University Park Marriott.** This mid-size but spacious hotel is airy and inviting, with mountain views, and offers easy access to both downtown and nearby canyons. It's in Salt Lake's Research Park, home to biotech giants and University of Utah–affiliated research facilities. One of the city's major attractions, Red Butte Garden, is nearby. ⊠ *480 Wakara Way, University of Utah 84108* ☎ *801/581–1000* 🖷 *801/584–3321* ⊕ *www.marriott.com* ⥽ *218 rooms, 29 suites* ⌂ *Restaurant, room service, cable TV with movies, in-room broadband, indoor pool, health club, hot tub, bar, dry cleaning, laundry service, concierge, concierge floor, business services, convention center, airport shuttle, free parking, some pets allowed (fee)* ☰ *AE, D, DC, MC, V.*

$–$$ ⊞ **Wildflowers Bed & Breakfast.** An elegant "painted lady" with a private yard full of larkspur, columbine, and foxglove, this Victorian inn was built as a private home in 1891. The interior has been renovated to provide more light, but the rooms are furnished in keeping with the period. If you're traveling with a group, or just want more space, you can reserve the full-floor "bird's nest" suite with a full kitchen and dining room. A few blocks west of Westminster College, the inn frequently hosts visiting literary and National Public Radio figures. ⊠ *936 E. 1700 South St., East Side 84105* ☎ *801/466–0600, 800/569–0009 reservations* 🖷 *801/466–4728* ⊕ *www.wildflowersbb.com* ⥽ *4 rooms, 1 suite* ⌂ *Free parking; no smoking, no room TVs* ☰ *AE, D, MC, V* ⑩ *BP.*

¢–$$ ⊞ **Anton Boxrud Bed & Breakfast.** Quirky furnishings—some of them antiques—from all over the world fill the rooms of this eclectic Victorian manor a 15-minute stroll from the city center and around the corner from the stately Governor's mansion. The complimentary evening snacks and beverages served near the parlor's bay window are as delicious as the bountiful breakfasts served in the dining room. Ask the owners anything you need to know about Salt Lake—like most good B&B proprietors, they'll probably have the answers. ⊠ *57 S. 600 East St., East Side 84102* ☎ *801/363–8035 or 800/524–5511* 🖷 *801/596–1316* ⊕ *www.antonboxrud.com* ⥽ *6 rooms, 1 suite* ⌂ *Dining room, outdoor hot tub, free parking; no room TVs* ☰ *AE, D, DC, MC, V* ⑩ *BP.*

¢–$ ⊞ **Saltair Bed and Breakfast.** Sitting with a book before a roaring fire in the formal parlor of this 1903 Victorian home is the perfect way to end the day. Rooms have fine oak woodwork and period antiques, with cozy down comforters in winter. Suites with fireplaces and kitchens are available, and families or groups can stay in one of the small separate bungalows on the property. Breakfast in the dining room features hearty American fare. A stay here is one of the homiest experiences, at some of the best prices in the area. ⊠ *164 S. 900 East St., University of Utah 84102* ☎ *801/533–8184 or 800/733–8184* 🖷 *801/595–0332* ⊕ *www.saltlakebandb.com* ⥽ *7 rooms, 9 suites* ⌂ *Dining room, some kitchenettes, cable TV, outdoor hot tub, free parking* ☰ *AE, D, DC, MC, V* ⑩ *BP.*

West Side & the Airport

$–$$$ ⊞ **Hilton Salt Lake City Airport.** A self-contained world on a man-made lake, 2 mi from the airport, this big hotel meets business travelers' needs with plenty of business and personal services, shuttles, and proximity to the airport and downtown. ✉ *5151 Wiley Post Way, Airport 84116* ☎ *801/ 539–1515 or 800/999–3736* 🖷 *801/539–1113* ⊕ *www.hilton.com* ⇝ *276 rooms, 12 suites* ᗌ *Restaurant, cable TV with movies, in-room broadband, Wi-Fi, 2 pools (1 indoor), health club, hot tub, outdoor hot tub, basketball, bar, dry cleaning, laundry facilities, laundry service, concierge, concierge floor, business services, meeting rooms, airport shuttle, free parking, some pets allowed (fee)* ⊟ *AE, D, DC, MC, V.*

$$ ⊞ **Radisson Hotel Airport.** This very comfortable hotel is a good lodging bet near the airport. There's no need to leave the premises, as you have access to an on-site pool and gym, and you're literally five minutes from airport check in. Rooms include a wet bar and refrigerator, and there's a complimentary continental breakfast. ✉ *2177 W. North Temple, Airport 84116* ☎ *801/364–5800 or 800/333–3333* 🖷 *801/364–5823* ⊕ *www.radisson.com* ⇝ *126 rooms* ᗌ *Restaurant, room service, refrigerators, cable TV with movies, in-room broadband, pool, gym, hot tub, dry cleaning, laundry facilities, laundry service, business services, meeting rooms, airport shuttle, parking (fee)* ⊟ *AE, D, DC, MC, V* �🍽 *CP.*

$ ⊞ **Comfort Inn Airport.** Spacious, modern, and fully decked out with amenities, this is a good value for a stay near the airport, with easy access to downtown. The furnishings and separate work spaces in guest rooms make this facility a more upscale property than many in this chain. ✉ *200 N. Admiral Byrd Rd., Airport 84116* ☎ *801/746–5200* 🖷 *801/532–4721* ⊕ *www.comfortinn.com* ⇝ *155 rooms* ᗌ *Restaurant, microwaves, refrigerators, cable TV with movies and video games, in-room VCRs, in-room data ports, pool, gym, hot tub, dry cleaning, laundry facilities, laundry service, business services, meeting rooms, airport shuttle, free parking, some pets allowed (fee)* ⊟ *AE, D, MC, V* 🍽 *BP.*

¢–$ ⊞ **Days Inn Airport.** For the budget-conscious, this is a good choice, halfway between downtown and the airport. You'll find good amenities for both families and business travelers, including an indoor pool, hot tub, and meeting rooms. ✉ *1900 W. North Temple, Airport 84116* ☎ *801/539–8538* 🖷 *801/595–1041* ⊕ *www.daysinn.com* ⇝ *110 rooms* ᗌ *Cable TV with movies and video games, in-room data ports, indoor pool, gym, hot tub, laundry facilities, business services, meeting rooms, airport shuttle, some free parking, some pets allowed* ⊟ *AE, D, DC, MC, V* 🍽 *CP.*

Farther Afield

$–$$ ⊞ **Courtyard Salt Lake City Sandy.** Excellent for business travelers visiting Salt Lake's many south valley corporations, this full-service hotel offers large in-room desks with broadband and spacious work areas. The hotel is a standout in a cluster of properties set against a mountain backdrop, off I–15 and next to a factory outlet mall. There are also a few high-end chain steak houses nearby. ✉ *10701 S. Holiday Park Dr., Sandy 84070* ☎ *801/571–3600* 🖷 *801/572–1383* ⊕ *www.marriott.*

com ⬦ *124 rooms* ⬧ *Coffee shop, room service, cable TV with movies, in-room broadband, indoor pool, health club, hot tub, lounge, laundry facilities, laundry service, business services, meeting rooms, free parking* ⊟ *AE, D, DC, MC, V.*

¢ ▦ **Homestead Studio Suites Hotel/Mid Valley.** If you're thinking of a long-term stay, consider this option with deluxe and regular studios. Each studio is set up for efficient living with a fully equipped kitchen. The neighborhood doesn't offer a lot of amenities and you will probably want a car for getting around. ⊠ *5863 S. Redwood Rd., Mid Valley 84123* ☎ *801/269–9292* 🖷 *801/269–9994* ⊕ *www.homesteadhotels.com* ⬦ *136 suites* ⬧ *Kitchens, cable TV with movies, in-room broadband, Wi-Fi, outdoor hot tub, dry cleaning, business services, free parking* ⊟*AE, D, DC, MC, V.*

¢ ▦ **La Quinta Inn Salt Lake City Midvale.** Rooms are spacious, with large TVs and desks with broadband. You have easy access to the TRAX line (there's a stop a block from the hotel), which will take you downtown or to the University of Utah. ⊠ *7231 S. Catalpa St., Midvale 84047* ☎ *801/566–3291* 🖷 *801/562–5943* ⊕ *www.laquinta.com* ⬦ *122 rooms, 3 suites* ⬧ *Cable TV with movies and video games, in-room broadband, indoor pool, hot tub, laundry facilities, business services, free parking, some pets allowed* ⊟ *AE, D, DC, MC, V* ⦿ *CP.*

NIGHTLIFE & THE ARTS

For information on what's happening around town, pick up a *City Weekly* news and entertainment weekly, available at stands outside restaurants and stores in town.

The Arts

Salt Lake City's arts tradition officially started in 1847 with the Deseret Musical and Dramatic Society, founded by Brigham Young. The city has continued to give strong support, even voting for a special tax to support cultural organizations like the opera and symphony. Ballet West and the Utah Symphony have kept Utah on the nations' cultural map. The Capitol and Rose Wagner theaters host Broadway touring companies. The Pioneer Memorial Theatre Company ranks among the best in the country. Lesser known and locally written plays are presented in small theaters throughout the valley. Locals laugh at inside jokes on the community's religious and cultural idiosyncrasies in *Saturday's Voyeur,* a play produced each year and presented by the Salt Lake Acting Company.

FESTIVALS &   If you're in town in late June, check out the **Utah Arts Festival** (⊕ www.
EVENTS   uaf.org). Look for original art at the Marketplace, create your own at
★   the Art Yard, sample eclectic food, and swing to the beat of live music. Local artists and art galleries enjoy one evening each month (usually the third Friday of the month) sharing their artwork with the public in the **Gallery Stroll.** A possible starting point is Phillips Gallery (⊠ 444 E. 200 South St. ☎ 801/364–8284 ⊕ www.ourcommunityconnection.com/slga). Stop at any gallery on the stroll to obtain a self-guiding map. Artists and art lovers chat over wine and snacks at each stop.

Rub shoulders with the "beautiful people" in Park City during Robert Redford's **Sundance Film Festival** (⌂ Box 3630, Salt Lake City 84110 ☎801/328–3456 ⊕www.sundance.org) or come to three venues in downtown Salt Lake City. The festival has more than 100 screenings in Salt Lake City at the Tower Theatre, Broadway Center Theatre, and Trolley Corners Theatre. Buy tickets ahead online, or purchase day-of-show tickets, if available, at the theaters.

TICKETS   For tickets to cultural events, contact **ArtTix** (☎ 801/355–2787 or 888/ 451–2787 ⊕ www.arttix.org). **Smiths Tix** (☎ 801/467–8499 or 800/ 888–8499 ⊕ www.smithstix.com) sells tickets to sporting events and concerts. For tickets to events at the Delta Center, contact **Ticketmaster** (☎ 801/325–7328 ⊕ www.ticketmaster.com).

Major Performance Venues

There are three main performance spaces in Salt Lake City. Ballet West and the Utah Opera perform at the **Capitol Theatre** (✉ 50 W. 200 South St., Downtown ☎ 801/355–2787), which also hosts Broadway touring companies. The Utah Symphony plays at **Maurice Abravanel Hall** (✉ 123 W. South Temple St., Downtown ☎ 801/355–2787). **The Rose Wagner Center** (✉ 138 W. 300 South St., Downtown ☎ 801/355–2787) is comprised of the Black Box Theatre, the Jeanné Wagner Theatre, and the Studio Theatre. It's home to the Ririe-Woodbury Dance Company and the Repertory Dance Theatre, as well as providing performance space for many of the city's smaller theater and dance companies.

Dance

Ballet West (☎ 801/323–6900 ⊕ www.balletwest.org) is considered one of the nation's top ballet companies, performing both classic and original works. **Repertory Dance Theatre** (☎801/534–1000 ⊕www.xmission. com/~rdt/) presents modern-dance performances. **Ririe-Woodbury Dance Company** (☎ 801/297–4241 ⊕ www.ririewoodbury.com) is Salt Lake's premier modern-dance troupe, recognized for its innovation and commitment to community education.

Film

Art and independent films are shown at **Brewvies** (✉ 676 S. 200 West St., Downtown ☎ 801/355–5500 ⊕ www.brewvies.com) on their second run. You can have a beer and dinner with the show. The Salt Lake Film Society shows independent and foreign films at **Broadway Centre Theatre** (✉ 111 E. 300 South St., Downtown ☎ 801/321–0310). Independent, cult, and foreign films, often shown at midnight on weekends, are standard at **Tower Theatre** (✉ 876 E. 900 South St., East Side ☎ 801/ 321–0310), a historic art deco theater.

Music

The **Mormon Tabernacle Choir** (✉ Temple Sq. ☎ 801/240–4150 ⊕ www. mormontabernaclechoir.org), which includes men and women of all ages from around the Intermountain region, performs sacred music, with some secular—classical and patriotic—works.

The **Utah Symphony** (✉ Abravanel Hall, 123 W. South Temple, Downtown ☎ 801/533–6683 ⊕ www.utahsymphony.org) performs more

LIVING TRADITIONS

EACH YEAR ON THE THIRD WEEKEND in May, Salt Lake City celebrates its cultural diversity with the Living Traditions Festival. The Utah Humanities Council started the festival to spotlight traditional folk arts, to offer ethnic minorities a public opportunity to express pride in their heritages, and to educate the public about the richness of the city's many cultures.

In the heart of the city, at Washington Square, 20-odd food vendors, each representing a nonprofit community group, prepare different national specialties. Money raised goes toward funding each group's activities throughout the year. On the four stages set up around the square, musicians and dancers from more than 45 countries perform. Past festivals have showcased performing arts from Brazil, Tahiti, Bosnia, Japan, and Norway. Artisans conduct demonstrations under tents and answer questions about their work on everything from Hopi katsina dolls and Tibetan rugs to Tongan mats and Japanese origami. One tent is set up as a crafts market.

Living Traditions is just one of Salt Lake's many annual ethnic festivals. The second week of September sees a Greek Festival, with food, dancing, and music. The suburb of Murray hosts a Scottish Festival during the second week of June. The St. Patrick's Day Parade, held the Saturday closest to March 17, turns the streets green with colorful floats, bands, and good humor, and early May sees numerous Cinco de Mayo festivals in the area.

than 250 concerts annually, both at home in the acoustically acclaimed Maurice Abravanel Concert Hall and in cities across the nation and abroad.

Opera

The **Utah Opera Company** (✉ Abravanel Hall, 123 W. South Temple, Downtown ☎ 801/533–5626 ⊕ www.utahopera.org) produces five operas a year, often featuring nationally recognized stars.

Theater

Off Broadway Theatre (✉ 272 S. Main St., Downtown ☎ 801/355–4628 ⊕ www.theobt.com) puts on musicals, plays, and improvisational comedy events. **Pioneer Theatre Company** (✉ 300 S. 1400 East St., East Side ☎ 801/581–6961 ⊕ www.pioneertheatre.org) features classic and contemporary musicals and plays during its season, which runs from September through May. **Salt Lake Acting Company** (✉ 168 W. 500 North St., Downtown ☎ 801/363–7522 ⊕ www.saltlakeactingcompany.org) is recognized for its development of new regionally and locally written plays. Performances run year-round.

Nightlife

An increasingly cosmopolitan atmosphere is spreading through downtown Salt Lake City. Bars and clubs serve up cocktails and live music to meet diverse tastes. The state's quirky liquor laws make for a few surprises to newcomers, however. First of all, don't expect to spend the night barhopping along a single street. Only two private clubs, requiring a membership to be purchased for admission, are allowed per block. Last call is 1 AM, and some bars call it earlier. Cabs are not on hand at every bar or club, so you will probably have to call for one.

Bars & Lounges

Catch the game on the giant screen at **Cassadys** (⌧ 1037 E. 3300 South St., The Suburbs ☎ 801/486–3008), or take a turn at karaoke on Tuesday and Thursday nights. **Hard Rock Cafe** (⌧ 505 S. 600 East St., The Suburbs ☎ 801/532–7625) has pretty good burgers, rock and roll memories, and touring national bands. A good place for spotting Utah Jazz basketball players and their visiting competitors is **Port O' Call** (⌧ 78 W. 400 South St., Downtown ☎ 801/521–0589), a sports bar with 14 satellite dishes and 26 TVs. Expect to wait for a table here on weekends.

★ For beer brewed on the premises, head to **Squatters Pub Brewery** (⌧ 147 W. Broadway, Downtown ☎ 801/363–2739). Sandwiches and pasta dishes are on the menu. Try a martini at **The Red Door** (⌧ 57 W. 200 South St., Downtown ☎ 801/363–6030), a trendy bar with a cosmopolitan accent, where an eclectic crowd of T-shirt-and-jeans meets suit-and-tie hangs out. **The Tavernacle Social** (⌧ 201 E. Broadway, Downtown ☎ 801/519–8900) features dueling pianos and is smoke-free.

Nightclubs

★ **Green Street Social Club** (⌧ 602 E. 500 South St., East Side ☎ 801/532–4200) is a fine spot to meet or make friends while enjoying light food, live music, and dancing. Known as one of the city's premier pick-up joints, it's also a fine place for a game of pool with your friends. Jazz bands play on a draped circular stage at **Circle Lounge** (⌧ 328 S. State St., Downtown ☎ 801/531–5400), where you can also enjoy late-night sushi and cocktails. At **Kristauf's** (⌧ 16 W. Market St., Downtown ☎ 801/366–9490) you'll have a hard time choosing which martini to try. Service is sometimes slow, but the collegiate crowd doesn't seem to mind.

SPORTS & THE OUTDOORS

Salt Lake City is a gateway to the excellent ski resorts strung along the Wasatch Range. There are also a handful of nearby golf courses. In town you can readily bicycle or jog along the wide streets and through the many parks.

Smiths Tix (☎ 801/467–8499 or 800/888–8499 ⊕ www.smithstix.com) sells tickets to sporting events and concerts. For tickets to an NBA game or other events at the Delta Center, contact **Ticketmaster** (☎ 801/325–7328 ⊕ www.ticketmaster.com).

Basketball

★ The **Utah Jazz** (✉ Delta Center, 301 W. South Temple, Downtown ☎ 801/355–3865 ⊕ www.nba.com/jazz) is Salt Lake's NBA team and a real crowd-pleaser. Home games are played at the Delta Center.

Bicycling

Salt Lake City is a comparatively easy city to tour by bicycle, thanks to its extra-wide streets and not-so-frenetic traffic. Look for white striping on certain streets indicating a bike lane. An especially good route is

★ **City Creek Canyon,** east of the capitol. On odd-number days from mid-May through September the road is closed to motor vehicles. Liberty Park and Sugarhouse Park also have good cycling and running paths.

Golf

If you're near the east side of the city, try the **Bonneville Golf Course** (✉ 954 S. Connor St., East Side ☎ 801/583–9513). Less than five minutes from downtown you can tee off at the 18-hole **Rose Park Golf Course** (✉ 1386 N. Redwood Rd., West Side ☎ 801/596–5030). A championship course and spectacular scenery await you 20 minutes away at the **South Mountain Golf Club** (✉ 1247 E. Rambling Rd., Draper ☎ 801/495–0500). **Stonebridge Golf Club** (✉ 4415 Links Dr., West Valley City ☎ 801/957–9000) is a five-minute drive from Salt Lake International Airport, and it offers a Johnny Miller signature design course.

Ice-Skating

Classic Fun Center (✉ 9151 S. 255 West St., The Suburbs ☎ 801/561–1791) offers ice-skating along with roller-skating, a waterslide park, laser tag, and Rollerblade rentals. Choose to swim, jog, lift weights, play tennis, or ice skate at the **Cottonwood Heights Recreation Center** (✉ 7500 S. 2700 East St., The Suburbs ☎ 801/943–3160). The 2002 Winter Olympics started an ice-skating boom. Find time on the ice at **The Salt Lake County Sports Complex** (✉ 645 Guardsman Way, University of Utah ☎ 801/583–9713) near the University of Utah. Use the same ice as the 2002 Winter Olympians at the **Utah Olympic Oval** (✉ 5662 S. 4800 West St., The Suburbs ☎ 801/968–6825). The **West Valley Accord Ice Center** (✉ 5353 W. 3100 South St., The Suburbs ☎ 801/966–0223) was the 2002 Winter Olympics practice hockey and skating rink. Public ice-skating is available twice a day. Call the center for times.

Parks

Most neighborhoods have a small park, usually with a children's playground. **Salt Lake City Parks Division** (☎ 801/972–7800 ⊕ www.slcgov.com/publicservices/parks/) operates several pools and maintains many parks, including the Raging Waters Waterslide park. Parks not under the city's jurisdiction are operated by **Salt Lake County Parks & Recreation** (☎ 801/468–2603 ⊕ www.parks-recreation.org).

Take the kids to **Fairmont Park** (✉ 1044 Sugarmont Dr., East Side), a smaller park with a children's play area, duck pond, and large indoor swimming pool. **Liberty Park** (✉ 900 S. 700 East St., East Side) has a jogging path, tennis courts, picnic areas, and children's playgrounds, including a state-of-the-art playground for children with disabilities. **Sugarhouse**

Park (⊠ 2100 S. 1300 East St., East Side) is primarily open space where you can jog, bicycle, fly a kite, throw a Frisbee, or soak up some rays.

Skiing

If you are heading out to some of Utah's fine ski resorts, advance equipment and clothing rental reservations are available from **Utah Ski & Golf** (⊠ 134 W. 600 South St., Downtown ☎ 801/355–9088 or 801/539–8660 ⊕ www.utahskigolf.com). The company has locations downtown and at Salt Lake International Airport. It also offers free shuttle service from downtown hotels to their stores.

Soccer

Major League Soccer came to Utah when **Real Salt Lake** (⊠ 400 S. 1400 East St., Downtown ☎ 866/976–2237 ⊕ realsaltlake.com) started its first season in 2005. Home games are held at Rice-Eccles Stadium.

SHOPPING

Salt Lake's shopping is concentrated downtown as well as in several malls. Good bets for souvenirs include books, Mormon crafts, and Western collectibles. The vicinity of 300 South and 300 East streets has several shops that specialize in antique jewelry, furnishings, art, and knickknacks.

Plazas & Malls

Crossroads Plaza (⊠ 50 S. Main St., Downtown ☎ 801/531–1799) is an all-inclusive downtown shopping experience; among its 140 stores and restaurants are Nordstrom and Mervyn's.

Foothill Village (⊠ 1400 S. Foothill Dr., East Side ☎ 801/582–3646) has a wide range of shops—from apparel, gifts, and jewelry to health and wellness. Dining opportunities from fast food to fine dining are available at the village.

★ **The Gateway** (⊠ 90 S. 400 West St., Downtown ☎ 801/366–2160) is a combination shopping mall, restaurant district, and business and residential center, all accessible by TRAX, Salt Lake's mass transit.

★ The **Sugar House Business District** (⊠ Between 1700 South and 2700 South Sts., from 700 East to 1300 East Sts., East Side) is a funky mix of locally owned shops and restaurants, including a large thrift store.

The wares at **Trolley Square** (⊠ 600 S. 700 East St., East Side ☎ 801/521–9877) run the gamut from estate jewelry and designer clothes to bath products, baskets, and saltwater taffy. Stores include Laura Ashley, Gap, Williams-Sonoma, and Banana Republic.

Founded by Brigham Young in 1868, the Zion's Cooperative Mercantile Institution (ZCMI) was America's first department store. Although the ZCMI stores have now become part of the Meier & Frank chain, the name lives on at the **ZCMI Center Mall** (⊠ South Temple and Main St., Downtown ☎ 801/321–8745), which dates back to 1902. This modern shopping center features about 90 stores, including Eddie Bauer and Godiva. Note that it's closed on Sunday.

CRAFTS CULTURE

WHEN THE MORMONS *arrived in the Salt Lake Valley, the Church's women formed a group called the Relief Society. They gathered regularly to discuss religion and family, and their hands were never idle during these meetings. Many a quilt or other piece of handwork was created while chatting.*

Through the decades, the faces in Relief Society have changed but their focus on family and handicrafts has not. The Mormon Church encourages mothers to stay home, so producing and selling crafts is a great way for them to make extra cash. For more than 60 years a store called Mormon Handicraft, at 15 West South Temple, has provided crafts supplies and served as an outlet for finished work.

There are so many area craftspeople that the store's buyers have room for only the best quilts, porcelain dolls, baby clothes, wooden objects, and other crafts. You'll

also find honey (the state's symbol is a beehive) and saltwater taffy (in honor of the Great Salt Lake).

Although the Church no longer owns or operates the store, it retains a Mormon feel. You can see a re-created upscale Mormon pioneer home—all hardwoods and antiques—with a picture of Brigham Young over the mantel. Rolls, bread, and cookies made fresh daily at the Lion House, Young's historic home, are also for sale. Such baked goods go well with a traditional root beer or sarsaparilla.

Outdoor Markets

Farmers bring produce, flowers, and other goodies to Pioneer Park, at 300 West and 300 South streets, downtown, each Saturday from Memorial Day through Labor Day. Local bakeries and restaurants also sell tasty treats ranging from fresh salsa to cinnamon rolls.

Specialty Stores

ANTIQUES **Elementé** (✉ 353 W. Pierpont Ave., Downtown ☎ 801/355–7400) specializes in unique and unusual period pieces; look for bargains in the basement. Just a short walk from downtown is **Moriarty's Antiques & Curiosities** (✉ 959 S. West Temple, Downtown ☎ 801/521–7207), which specializes in furnishings for the home and garden. The staff will ship gifts nationwide. Visit **R. M. Kennard Antiques** (✉ 65 W. 300 South St., Downtown ☎ 801/328–9796) in the heart of downtown for fine American and European art, furniture, and dishes.

ART GALLERIES The **Glendinning Gallery** (✉ 617 E. South Temple, Downtown ☎ 801/533–3581) is housed in the historic Glendinning mansion that is also home to the Utah Arts Council. Find the best of Utah's artists' work at **Phillips Gallery** (✉ 444 E. 200 South St., Downtown ☎ 801/364–8284).

BOOKS **Deseret Book** (✉ 36 S. State St., Downtown ☎ 801/328–8191), purveyor of books and materials related to the Mormon church and its doctrine, has several Salt Lake locations, the largest of which is in the ZCMI Center. **Ken Sanders Rare Books** (✉ 268 S. 200 East St., Downtown ☎ 801/521–3819) specializes in literature about Utah, Mormons, and Western exploration. In a rambling house with room after

★ room packed with books, **The King's English** (✉ 1511 S. 1500 East St., East Side ☎ 801/484–9100) is a great place to browse. Ask about the owner's book on being an independent bookseller—it's a great read.

★ **Sam Weller's Zion Book Store** (✉ 254 S. Main St., Downtown ☎ 801/328–2586 or 800/333–7269) stocks more than half a million new and used books.

CRAFTS **Mormon Handicraft** (✉ 15 W. South Temple, Downtown ☎ 801/355–2141 or 800/843–1480) sells exquisite children's clothing as well as quilts and other crafts—all made by Utah residents. **The Quilted Bear** (✉ 145 W. 7200 South St., The Suburbs ☎ 801/566–5454) is a co-op with gifts, home accessories, and collectibles created by more than 600 craftspeople.

SPORTING GOODS Jack Kirkham, owner of **Kirkham's Outdoor Products** (✉ 2135 S. State St., The Suburbs ☎ 801/486–4161), sells tents that are easy to put up and take down and roomier than most. He has resisted offers to sell his design to others, insisting on keeping the quality up by making his products on-site. His store carries a wide spectrum of other outdoor gear.

SIDE TRIPS NEAR SALT LAKE CITY

Antelope Island State Park

25 mi north of Salt Lake City via I–15 and the Antelope Island Causeway.

In the 19th century, settlers grazed sheep and horses on Antelope Island, ferrying them back and forth from the mainland across the waters of

★ the Great Salt Lake. **Antelope Island State Park** is today the most developed and scenic spot in which to experience the Great Salt Lake. Hiking and biking trails crisscross the island, and the lack of cover—cottonwood trees provide some of the only shade—gives the place a wide-open feeling and makes for some blistering hot days. You can go saltwater bathing at several beach areas. Since the salinity level of the lake is always greater than that of the ocean, the water is extremely buoyant (and briny-smelling)—simply sit down in the water and bob to the surface like a rubber duck. Hot showers at the marina remove the chill and the salt afterward.

The island has historic sites, as well as desert wildlife and birds in their natural habitat. The island's most popular inhabitants are the members of a herd of more than 600 bison descended from 12 brought here in 1893. Each October at the **Buffalo Round-Up,** more than 250 volunteers on horseback round up the free-roaming animals and herd them to the island's north end to be counted. The island's **Fielding-Garr House,** built in 1848 and now owned by the state, was the oldest continuously inhabited home in Utah until the last resident moved out in 1981. Now owned by the state, the house displays assorted ranching artifacts, and guided horseback riding is available from the stables next to the house. Facilities and roads on the island have been upgraded in recent years. Be sure to check out the modern visitor center, and sample a bison burger at the stand that overlooks the lake to the north. If you're lucky, you'll hear coyotes howling in the distance. ⊠ *4528 W. 1700 South St., Syracuse* ☎ *801/773–2941* ⚏ *$8 per vehicle, $4 per bicycle including causeway toll* ⊙ *Daily 7 AM–10 PM.*

Sports & the Outdoors

HIKING Antelope Island State Park offers plenty of space for the avid hiker to explore, but keep a few things in mind. All trails are also shared by mountain bikers and horseback riders, so keep an eye out for your fellow recreationists—not to mention the occasional bison. Trees are few and far between on the island, making for high exposure to the elements, so bring (and drink) plenty of water and dress appropriately. In the spring, biting insects make bug repellent a must-have. Pick up a trail map at the visitor center.

Once prepared, hiking Antelope Island can be a very enjoyable experience. Trails are fairly level except for a few places, where the hot summer sun makes the climb even more strenuous. Mountain ranges, including the Wasatch Front to the east and the Stansbury Mountains directly to the west, provide beautiful background in every direction, though haze sometimes obscures the view. Aromatic sage plants offer shelter for a variety of wildlife, so don't be startled if your next step flushes a chukar partridge, horned lark, or jackrabbit. A bobcat is a rarely seen island resident that will likely keep its distance.

MOUNTAIN & Road bikers race along the causeway to Antelope Island then ride
ROAD BIKING through the park, which also offers superb mountain-bike trails. **Bountiful Bicycle Center** (⊠ 2482 S. Rte. 89, Woods Cross ☎ 801/295–6711) rents mountain and road bikes and offers great advice on trails.

Where to Camp

⚑ **Antelope Island State Park.** The abundant wildlife—it's not uncommon for free-roaming buffalo to wander through campsites—excellent bird-watching, and well-maintained facilities more than make up for lack of shade at this quiet state-run campground. The $11 camping fee is in addition to the $8 park entrance fee. ⚲ *Flush toilets, dump station, drinking water, showers, picnic tables, food service, public telephone, swimming (lake)* ⚐ *26 campsites without hookups* ⚑ *25 mi north of Salt Lake City via I-15, Exit 335 to Syracuse, then west 7½ mi on causeway across Great Salt Lake* ⊠ *4528 W. 1700 South St., Syracuse 84075* ☎ *801/773–2941, 800/322–3770 reservations* ⊕ *www.stateparks.utah. gov* ⚏ *$11* ⊟ *MC, V.*

CloseUp
RIDE ON THE PONY EXPRESS TRAIL

IMAGINE A YOUNG MAN RACING *over the dusty trail on the back of a foaming mustang. A cloud of dust rises to announce him to the station manager, who waits with a new mount, some beef jerky, and water. The rider has galloped 11 mi since breakfast and will cover another 49 before he sleeps. That was the daily life of a courier with the Pony Express.*

A rider had to weigh less than 120 pounds. He was allowed only 25 pounds in gear, which included four leather mail pouches, a light rifle, a pistol, and a Bible. The standard uniform consisted of a bright red shirt and blue pants. Hostile Indians, bandits, and rattlesnakes were handled with the guns. The blazing heat of the desert in the summer and blinding blizzards in the winter were his constant foes.

There are few places in the United States where the original trail and stations of the Pony Express exist in such pristine condition as they do in Utah. One of the best-preserved sections of the original Pony Express Trail, which was in operation for 19 months in the mid-19th century, is the 133-mi section through the desert of west-central Utah. You'll see territory that remains much as it was during the existence of the Pony Express, and many of the sights you'll see along the way haven't changed perceptibly since that time. The desert has preserved them.

If you want to traverse the route, the logical starting point is Camp Floyd–Stagecoach Inn State Park in Fairfield. The end is in Ibapah, 133 mi away on the Utah–Nevada border. Stone pillars with metal plaques mark the route that starts and ends on pavement, then becomes a dirt road for 126 mi that is passable when dry. The Bureau of Land Management maintains a campground at Simpson Springs, one of the area's most dependable water sources. Some interesting ruins are still visible at

Faust, Boyd, and Canyon stations. A brochure describing the major stops along the trail is available from the U.S. Bureau of Land Management's Salt Lake Field Office.

It takes a certain breed of romantic to appreciate the beauty of the land and life lived by those who kept the mail moving during the short time that the Pony Express existed. For those with a similar sense of adventure as the wiry young riders, who included "Buffalo Bill" Cody, traveling this trail is a chance to relive history. Historians say the enterprise enabled communications between Washington, D.C., and California, keeping the state in the union and helping to secure the North's eventual success in the Civil War.

Stagecoaches, freight wagons, the Transcontinental Railroad, and the Lincoln Highway all followed the route pioneered by the Pony Express. The labor-intensive system of communicating cross-country ended with the invention of the telegraph. But before the Pony Express, it took mail six to eight weeks to travel from Missouri to California. By Pony Express, the mail took 10 days to arrive. But by the time the telegraph was invented and put into wide use, messages went across the continent in a mere four hours.

SALT LAKE CITY A TO Z

To research prices, get advice from other travelers, and book travel arrangements, visit www.fodors.com.

AIRPORTS & TRANSFERS

Salt Lake City International Airport is 7 mi northwest of downtown Salt Lake City. It's served by American, America West, Continental, Delta, Northwest, Southwest, JetBlue, Frontier, Skywest, TWA, and United.

All the major car-rental agencies have desks at the airport. To drive downtown, take I–80 east to North Temple, which leads directly to the city center. A taxi ride from the airport into town will cost about $15. The Utah Transit Authority (UTA) runs buses between the airport and the city center. Most downtown hotels offer guests free shuttle service.

🛪 **Salt Lake City International Airport** 🕾 801/575–2400 ⊕ www.slcairport.com.
🛪 **Taxis & Shuttles City Cab Company** 🕾 801/363–8400. **Utah Transit Authority (UTA)** 🕾 801/743–3882 or 888/743–3882 ⊕ www.rideuta.com. **Ute Cab Company** 🕾 801/359–7788. **Yellow Cab** 🕾 801/521–2100, 801/521–5027, or 800/826–4746.

BUS TRAVEL TO & FROM SALT LAKE CITY

Greyhound Lines runs several buses each day to the terminal at 160 West South Temple.

🚌 **Bus Information Greyhound Lines** 🕾 801/355–9579 or 800/231–2222 ⊕ www. greyhound.com.

BUSINESS HOURS

Most retail stores are open daily 9 AM or 9:30 AM to 6 PM or 7 PM in downtown locations, and until 9 or 10 in suburban shopping malls. Downtown stores sometimes stay open later Thursday and Friday nights, and many shops close their doors on Sunday. Normal banking hours are weekdays 9–5; some branches are also open on Saturday morning. Museums are generally open weekdays and Saturday 10–6; some have shorter hours on weekends, and still others are closed Sunday and/or Monday.

CAR TRAVEL

Highway travel around Salt Lake is quick and easy. From I–80, take I–15 north to 600 South Street to reach the city center. Salt Lake City's streets are extra wide and typically not congested. Most are two-way. Expect heavy traffic weekdays between 6 AM and 10 AM and again between 4 PM and 7 PM. To encourage carpooling, some freeways have special lanes for so-called high-occupancy vehicles (HOV)—cars carrying more than one passenger.

EMERGENCIES

🏥 **Hospitals Columbia St. Mark's Hospital** ✉ 1200 E. 3900 South St., The Suburbs 🕾 801/268–7111. **LDS Hospital** ✉ 8th Ave. and C St., Temple Square 🕾 801/408–1100. **Primary Children's Medical Center** ✉ 100 N. Medical Dr., University of Utah 🕾 801/588–2000. **Salt Lake Regional Medical Center** ✉ 1050 E. South Temple, Downtown 🕾 801/350–4111. **University Hospital and Clinics** ✉ 50 N. Medical Dr., University of Utah 🕾 801/581–2121.

⨂ Pharmacies Rite Aid ⊠ 75 S. Main St., Downtown ☎ 801/531-0583. **Broadway Pharmacy** ⊠ 242 E. 300 South St., Downtown ☎ 801/363-3939, open until 9 PM. **Harmon's Supermarket** ⊠ 3270 S. 1300 East St., The Suburbs ☎ 801/487-5461 is open until midnight.

PUBLIC TRANSPORTATION

Finding your way around Salt Lake City is easy, largely because early Mormon settlers laid out the town in grids. However, the city blocks are longer than in many other cities, so distances can be deceiving. Salt Lake has a very workable public transportation system. A Free Fare Zone for travel by bus covers a 15-square-block area downtown and on Capitol Hill. A light rail system, called TRAX, moves passengers quickly around the city and to the suburbs south of Salt Lake. The north–south light-rail route begins at the Delta Center and ends at 10000 South Street; there are 16 stations along the way, and 11 have free park-and-ride lots. The east–west route begins at the University of Utah and ends at Main Street. For $3.50 you can buy an all-day ticket good for unlimited rides on buses and TRAX. For trips that begin on a bus, you must purchase the day pass at selected UTA Pass outlets. For trips beginning on TRAX, day passes must be purchased at a ticket vending machine.

⨂ Utah Transit Authority (UTA) ☎ 801/743-3882 or 888/743-3882 ⊕ www.rideuta.com.

TAXIS

Though taxi fares are low, cabs can be hard to find on the street. If walking and public transportation aren't your thing, it's best to rent a car or plan to call for taxis. Yellow Cab provides 24-hour service throughout the Salt Lake Valley; other reliable companies are Ute Cab and City Cab.

⨂ City Cab Company ☎ 801/363-8400. **Ute Cab Company** ☎ 801/359-7788. **Yellow Cab** ☎ 801/521-2100, 801/521-5027, or 800/826-4746.

TOURS

Gray Line provides tours of Salt Lake City; most tours include lunch at Brigham Young's historic living quarters. Utah Heritage Foundation offers the most authoritative tours of Salt Lake's historic sights.

⨂ Gray Line ⊠ 3359 S. Main St., Downtown ☎ 801/534-1001 ⊕ www.saltlakecitytours.org. **Utah Heritage Foundation** ⊠ 485 Canyon Rd., Temple Square ☎ 801/533-0858 ⊕ www.utahheritagefoundation.com.

TRAIN TRAVEL

Amtrak serves the area daily out of the Amtrak Passenger Station.

⨂ Amtrak Passenger Station ⊠ 340 S. 600 West St., Downtown ☎ 801/322-3510 ⊕ www.amtrak.com.

VISITOR INFORMATION

In downtown, the Salt Lake Convention and Visitors Bureau is open weekdays 8:30–5 and weekends 9–5. The Utah Travel Council on Capitol Hill has information as well as books on travel and related topics throughout the city and state.

⨂ Salt Lake Convention and Visitors Bureau ⊠ 90 S. West Temple, Downtown 84101 ☎ 801/521-2822 ⊕ www.saltlake.org. **Utah Travel Council** ⊠ 300 North State St. Capitol Hill 84114 ☎ 801/538-1030 or 800/200-1160 ⊕ www.utah.com.

Park City & Environs

WORD OF MOUTH

"Park City has ski resorts, the Utah Olympic Park (don't miss!) and lots of excellent restaurants and galleries. If you don't want to ski, you can go tubing, hot air ballooning, dog sledding, whatever! Snowbird is also very nice. If the weather is nice the tram ride to the top of Hidden Peak offers fantastic views and they have several great restaurants . . . Sundance is a bit further drive, but one of the most beautiful places in the world."
—Dayle

"A drive into Provo Canyon will give you some mountain sightseeing you'll remember a long time. Continue through Heber Valley to Park City for lunch or dinner and a visit to a mountain/ski town."

—dwooddon

By Mark and
Dana Doherty
Menlove

ALTHOUGH THE WASATCH RANGE shares the same desert climate as the Great Basin, which it rims, these craggy peaks rising to more than 11,000 feet cause storms moving in from the Pacific to stall and drop more than twice the precipitation they drop on the rest of the Great Basin. The result is a 160-mi stretch of verdure that is home to three-fourths of all Utahns. Although its landscape is crisscrossed by freeways and dappled by towns large and small, the vast Wasatch still beckons adventurers with its alpine forests and windswept canyons. Those who visit follow in the footsteps of Native Americans and in the wagon-wheel ruts of Mormon pioneers and miners.

As the meeting place of three geologically distinct regions—the Rocky Mountain Province, the Colorado Plateau Province, and the Basin and Range Province—the Wasatch Range combines characteristics of each. Within this one compact range you'll find broad glacial canyons with towering granite walls, stream-cut gorges through purple, tan, and green shale, and rounded red rock bluffs and valleys.

Uppermost in many people's minds is the legendary skiing found at resorts such as Snowbird, Alta, and Park City. But this region is truly a year-round destination. Bright-blue lakes afford fantastic boating, sailing, windsurfing, and waterskiing opportunities. Some of the West's best trout streams flow from the high country. Add to this picturesque mountain communities, miles of hiking and biking trails, and truly spectacular alpine scenery, and you have a vacation that's hard to beat.

The snow stops falling in April or May, and a month later the temperatures are in the 80s. (Locals joke that if you don't like the weather in spring, wait a minute and it will change.) Spring may be the shortest season, but it's one of the most interesting. You can ski in the morning, play 18 holes of golf or hike through fields of wildflowers in the afternoon, and take a dinner cruise on the Great Salt Lake at sunset.

In summer water-sports enthusiasts of all stripes flock to the region's reservoirs, alpine lakes, rivers, and streams to fish, waterski, windsurf, sail, and canoe. The Wasatch Mountains also draw people on foot, bike, and horseback seeking respite from the heat of the valley.

Fall's colors rival those of New England. On a walk through a forest or drive along a scenic route, you'll see the yellows, reds, oranges, and golds of aspens, maples, and oaks against the deep evergreen of fir and spruce. Fall drives along the Alpine Loop east of Provo or up Pine Canyon out of the Heber Valley are autumn traditions.

Regardless of the season, you can find cultural activities and entertainment at every turn. The Sundance Film Festival, hosted by actor–director Robert Redford, attracts movie stars and independent filmmakers from all over and seems to get bigger every January. Major recording artists of all types play both indoor and outdoor venues along the Wasatch Range. The number of nightclubs is increasing, featuring everything from blues and jazz to folk and rock; and Park City offers an ample variety of nightlife possibilities.

Numbers in the text correspond to numbers in the margin and on the Wasatch Front map.

If you have
3 days

In three days you'll be hard-pressed to see all of this region so your best bet is to stick to the central Wasatch. Start with a day and a night in ▣ **Park City ❶–❺ ▶**, skiing one of its three resorts in winter or taking advantage of lift-served mountain biking in summer, then enjoy a night out on Park City's historic Main Street. The next day drive west on I–80, south along Salt Lake City's eastern bench on I–215, and east again on Route 210 up ▣ **Little Cottonwood Canyon ❼**. In winter spend a day skiing at Alta or Snowbird. In summer hike the Catherine's Pass trail into neighboring **Big Cottonwood Canyon ❻**. On your final day head south again on I–15, then east on Route 92 on the Alpine Loop scenic drive to ▣ **Sundance Resort ⓫**, where you can pamper yourself with a massage at the Spa and a quiet meal at the Tree Room or the Foundry Grill. In winter the Alpine Loop will be closed to traffic, so instead of driving east on Route 92 continue south on I–15 and spend some time exploring **Provo ❿** before driving east on U.S. 189 to Sundance.

If you have
5 days

Start your five-day trip by following the suggested three-day itinerary above and then tack on the following: on Day 4 leave Sundance, heading east on Route 189 up Provo Canyon to the **Heber Valley ⓬ ▶**. In winter spend the day cross-country skiing or snowshoeing before your late-afternoon sleigh ride, and in summer spend the day hiking, golfing, or horseback riding in Wasatch Mountain State Park. The point is to take in the beauty of the Wasatch at a slower pace than is allowed while downhill skiing or snowboarding. Treat yourself to supper at Snake Creek Grill before retiring to the overnight comforts of the Homestead Resort. Strike out on Day 5 using River Road to connect to U.S. 40 and back to ▣ **Park City ❶–❺ ▶** where, even though you started your trip here, something new awaits. Ski and/or snowboard until you're worn out and then nestle into an après-ski lounge for a hot toddy before suppertime and your pre-sleep hot tub. In warmer months spend your day fly-fishing with one of the guides from Trout Bum 2 or hiking some of Park City's extensive trail system and cap it off with supper on the patio of one of Park City's fine restaurants.

If you have
7 days

In a week you can get a good feel for the diversity of the Wasatch. Follow the five-day itinerary above, adding a day and a night in ▣ **Big Cottonwood Canyon ❻** between Park City and Little Cottonwood Canyon. Then you can spend an extra day and night either exploring the **Heber Valley ⓬ ▶** or ▣ **Park City ❶– ❺ ▶**.

Exploring the Wasatch

Each canyon of the Wasatch is different in topography and scenery. The back side of the range is rural with high-mountain pastures, farms, and small towns while the front side is a long stretch of cosmopolitan metropolis. This is not an area that lends itself to linear exploration by checking off points along a straight line. You'll enjoy the area more if you let it unfold in a series of loops and meanders, using the larger canyons to move back and forth between the two sides of the range.

About the Restaurants

American cuisine dominates the Wasatch dining scene with great steaks, barbecue, and traditional Western fare. There's also an abundance of good seafood, which the busier eateries fly in daily from the West Coast. Resort towns like Park City cater to discriminating clientele with upscale Continental restaurants and ethnic food ranging from Chinese and Mexican to Afghan and Vietnamese. At most resort town restaurants, hours of operation vary due to seasonal change, so it's often a good idea to call ahead.

About the Hotels

Chain hotels and motels dot I–15 all along the Wasatch Front and nearly always have availability. Every small town on the back side of the range has at least one good bed-and-breakfast, and most towns have both independent and chain motels. The ski resorts of Big and Little Cottonwood offer hotels from quaint to ultramodern. Condominiums dominate Park City lodging, but you also find high-end hotels, luxurious lodges, and well-run bed-and-breakfast inns. All this luxury means prices here tend to be higher than other areas in the state. Make reservations well in advance for busy ski holidays like Christmas, Presidents' Day, and Martin Luther King Day. As the mountain country is often on the cool side, lodging facilities at higher elevations do not need air-conditioning.

WHAT IT COSTS					
	$$$$	$$$	$$	$	¢
RESTAURANTS	over $25	$19–$25	$13–$18	$8–$12	under $8
HOTELS	over $310	$241–$310	$171–$240	$100–$170	under $100

Restaurant prices are for a main course at dinner, excluding sales tax of 8.25%. Hotel prices are for two people in a standard double room in high season, excluding service charges and 10.35% tax.

Timing

One of the best reasons to vacation in the Wasatch is that a short drive from the valleys to the mountains will make you feel like you're getting two seasons in a single day. Winter is long in the mountains, but surprisingly short in the valleys. In March, when snow is still piling up at the ski resorts, you can golf, hike, bike, or fish in any of the Wasatch valleys or foothills. Hikers crowd the backcountry from June through Labor Day. Ski resorts buzz from December to early April. If you don't mind sometimes capricious weather, spring and fall are opportune seasons to visit. Rates drop and crowds are nonexistent. Spring is a good time for fishing, rafting on rivers swollen with snowmelt, birding, and wildlife-viewing. In fall, trees splash the mountainsides with golds and reds, the fish are spawning, and the angling is excellent.

Summer begins in the mountains in late June or early July. Fall begins in September, often with a week of unsettled weather around mid-month, followed by four to six gorgeous weeks of Indian summer—frosty nights

Fall Foliage

Few places in the world are as beautiful as the Wasatch Mountains in September and October. Seize the day to luxuriate in the bright colors and crisp temperatures. Pack a picnic lunch and head out on the Alpine Loop Scenic Byway, Route 92, from American Fork Canyon to Provo Canyon. Or take a ride on the Heber Valley Historic Railroad, which runs twice a day from Heber City. It snakes along the shore of Deer Creek Reservoir and parallels the Provo River as it plunges down narrow Provo Canyon. If you don't mind driving on a rough, sometimes washboard, dirt road, take the drive out of Midway up Pine Canyon through Wasatch Mountain State Park.

2

Summer Sports

Many transplanted locals in towns like Park City and Alta will tell you they first visited the Wasatch for the winters, but they moved here for the summers. It's hard to find a more comfortable climate than a Wasatch summer. The air is dry and temperatures range from 10 to 15 degrees cooler than in the Salt Lake Valley. Plus, the area becomes a summer recreation mecca. Well-maintained hiking and mountain biking trails lead between Big and Little Cottonwood canyons and the Park City area; local canyons offer excellent rock climbing; state parks on area reservoirs provide facilities for an array of water sports; and you'll find excellent trout fishing on Wasatch streams and lakes.

Winter Sports

There's more than local bragging behind the claim that Utah resorts have the best snow in the world. There's science behind it, too. The secret to Utah's famous powder is in the unique combination of atmospheric conditions and geography. Storms move from the Pacific across the Great Basin desert, pick up extra moisture over the Great Salt Lake, and then stall when they hit the high Wasatch Mountains. Large quantities of snowflakes called dendrites are formed under these conditions and fall to earth in layers with lots of air between them. Skiing through such light powder feels like floating through clouds. Although the area's downhill skiing receives most of the attention, snowmobiling, cross-country skiing, and snowshoeing are other popular powder-snow pursuits You can also head for the Utah Winter Sports Park to catch a U.S. Bobsled Team practice. Or, take a ride yourself while team members steer.

---

and warm days. Winter creeps in during November, and deep snows arrive in the mountains by December. Temperatures usually hover near freezing by day, thanks to the surprisingly warm mountain sun, dropping considerably overnight. Winter tapers off in March, though snow lingers into April on valley bottoms and into July on some mountain passes.

EAST OF SALT LAKE CITY

The best known areas of the Wasatch lie east of Salt Lake City. Up and over Parley's Canyon via I–80 you'll find the sophisticated mountain town of Park City with its three ski resorts and myriad summer attractions. The neighboring canyons of Big Cottonwood and Little Cottonwood are home to Brighton, Solitude, Alta, and Snowbird resorts. A network of hiking and mountain biking trails leads past pristine mountain lakes and connects all three canyons.

Park City

▶ *31 mi from Salt Lake City via I–80 east and Rte. 224 south*

Silver was discovered here in 1868, and in the years immediately following Park City became a rip-roaring mining town with more than two dozen saloons and a thriving red-light district. In the process it earned the nickname Sin City. A fire destroyed many of the town's buildings in 1898; this, combined with declining mining fortunes in the early 1900s, caused most of the residents to pack up and leave. It wasn't until 1946 that its current livelihood began to take shape in the form of the small Snow Park ski hill, which opened where Deer Valley Resort now sits.

Park City once again profited from the generosity of the mountains as skiing became popular. In 1963 Treasure Mountain Resort began operations with its skier's subway—an underground train and hoist system that ferried skiers to the mountain's top via old mining tunnels. Facilities were upgraded over time, and Treasure Mountain became the Park City Mountain Resort. Although it has a mind-numbing collection of condominiums, at Park City's heart is a historic downtown district that rings with authenticity and reminds you that this is a real town with real roots.

Park City and the surrounding area hosted the lion's share of skiing events during the 2002 Winter Olympic Games, and the excited spirit of the Games is still evident around town. Visitors often enjoy activities at the Utah Winter Olympic Park or simply taking candid photos at various memorable skiing venues.

Park City also serves as an excellent base camp for summer activities. Hiking trails are plentiful. A scenic drive over Guardsman Pass (via a gravel road that's passable for most vehicles) provides incredible mountain vistas. There are some acclaimed golf greens, hot-air ballooning is available, and mountain bikers find the ski slopes and old mining roads truly exceptional pedaling. With so much to offer summer and winter visitors, the town now has three resorts, each with its own special qualities.

The emphasis at the original Park City Mountain Resort is on skiing and socializing in town. In a somewhat secluded area on the edge of Park City you can revel in the peace and creature comforts of Deer Valley. The Canyons is a rapidly growing destination resort north of town; it ranks in the top five resorts in America in terms of overall ski area, and it combines luxury with a casual atmosphere. A free shuttle-bus system serves the town of Park City, the three resorts, and the many surrounding hotels. Although the shuttle is efficient, the region is fairly spread out, so a car can be helpful.

Small-town celebrations unofficially mark the beginning and end of summer in Park City. A traditional **Independence Day Celebration** (☎ 435/
649–6100 ⊕ www.parkcityinfo.com), complete with parade, fireworks,
and all-day activities in City Park, is a sure sign that summer has arrived. **Miner's Day** (☎ 435/649–6100 ⊕ www.parkcityinfo.com), Park
City's name for Labor Day, ends the summer season with a slightly campy
parade down Main Street, followed by miners' competitions of muck-
ing and drilling at City Park.

❶ Park City has several farmers' markets, but the biggest and longest running is the **Farmers' Market at the Canyons Resort**, held each Wednesday
from July through October. ⊠ *The Canyons Resort* ☎ *435/649–5400*
⊕ *www.thecanyons.com.*

❷ The **Park City Museum**, one of the best small museums in Utah, is housed
in Park City's old Territorial Jail. Life-size replicas of train cars that served
the area, displays that focus on the town's devastating 1898 fire, and
mining exhibits are highlights. The meticulous documentation accom-
panying all the exhibits makes mining history, and the history of mining towns, come alive.

The Park City Museum is the home of the **Park City Historical Society**,
which offers historian-led daylong hikes around Park City and the Wasatch

Mountains. Most of the tours, which focus on mining, railroad, or architectural history, begin in town; some include transportation to more distant locations. You must be a member to participate in the tours, but it's easy to join in advance over the Internet: membership is $25 for one person or $50 for a family. Each June the Park City Historical Society sponsors the **Historic Home Tour,** when many homeowners open their restored 19th-century homes in the historic section of Park City to the public. Food and drink receptions are provided by some of the best eateries in this resort area. The tour is self-guided, but advance registration is recommended. ⊠ *528 Main St., Box 555, 84060* ☎ *435/649–7457* ⊕ *www.parkcityhistory.org* ☞ *Free* ☉ *Mon.–Sat. 10–7, Sun. noon–6.*

❸ One of more than a dozen art galleries in Park City, the **Kimball Art Center** is the town's nonprofit community art center. It hosts national exhibitions as well as community art classes and workshops. ⊠ *638 Park Ave.* ☎ *435/649–8882* ⊕ *www.kimball-art.org* ☞ *Free, fees for classes* ☉ *Open Mon. and Wed.–Fri. 10–5, weekends noon–5.*

✋ ❹ In summer Park City Mountain Resort transforms itself to a mountain amusement park including attractions such as the **Alpine Slide, Zip Rider, and Little Miners' Park.** The Alpine Slide begins with a chairlift ride up the mountain, then special sleds carry sliders down 3,000 feet of winding concrete and fiberglass track at speeds controlled by each rider. The Zip Rider is 60 seconds of adrenaline rush as riders strap into a harness suspended from a cable for a 500-foot vertical drop spanning 3,000 feet of track. The Little Miners' Park has children's rides. There's also a miniature golf course, climbing wall, horseback riding, and lift-served mountain biking and hiking. ⊠ *1310 Lowell Ave.* ☎ *435/649–8111* ⊕ *www.parkcitymountain.com.*

❺ At the **Utah Olympic Park**—site of the 2002 Olympic bobsled, luge, and
Fodor'sChoice ski-jumping events—you can take recreational ski-jumping lessons or
★ strap in behind a professional driver for a bobsled ride down the actual Olympic course. The 389-acre park also serves as a year-round training site for members of the U.S. Ski Team and other athletes. In summer, check out the freestyle ski jumpers doing flips and spins into a splash pool and Nordic jumpers soaring to soft landings on a synthetic outrun. There's also an interactive ski museum and an exhibit on the 2002 Winter Olympics; guided tours are offered year-round, or you can take a self-guided tour. ⊠ *3000 Bear Hollow Dr., Park City* ☎ *435/658–4200* ⊕ *www.utaholympicpark.com* ☞ *$7; $35 Family Day Pass.*

Sports & the Outdoors

EQUIPMENT   Many shops in Park City rent equipment for skiing and other sports. You
RENTALS   can reserve your equipment in advance with **Breeze Winter Sports Rentals** (⊠ 1284 Lowell St., Park City, near Pay Day lift ☎ 435/649–2736 or 866/464–4430 ⊠ 1415 Lowell St., Park City, near ice rink ☎ 435/649–1902 ⊠ 4343 N. Rte. 224, The Canyons ☎ 435/655–7066 ⊕ www.breezeski.com ☉ Closed May–Nov.), which also rents clothing and helmets. For winter ski, snowboard, snowshoe, and clothing rental and summer bike rental, **Cole Sport** (⊠ 1615 Park Ave., Park City ☎ 435/649–4800 or 800/345–2938 ⊠ Park City Mountain Resort, Park City ☎ 435/

Park City

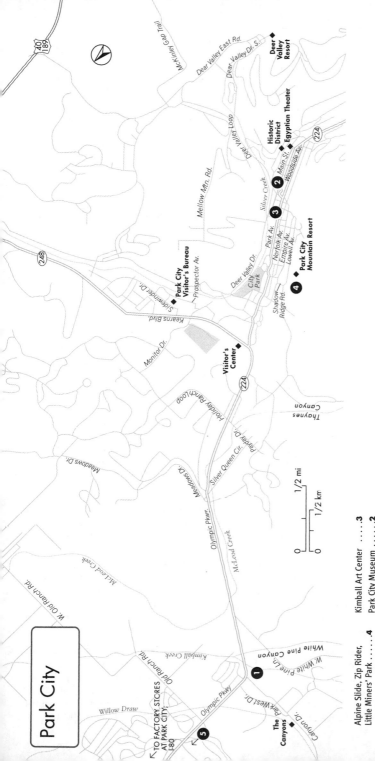

Alpine Slide, Zip Rider,
Little Miners' Park **4**

Farmers' Market at the
Canyons Resort **1**

Kimball Art Center **3**

Park City Museum **2**

Utah Olympic Park **5**

649–4600 ✉ Silver Lake Village at Deer Valley, Park City ☎ 435/649–4601 ⊕ www.colesport.com) offers expert fitting and advice with a broad range of equipment. **Jan's Mountain Outfitters** (✉ 1600 Park Ave., Park City ☎ 435/649–4949 or 800/745–1020 ⊕ www.jans.com ✉ Park City Resort Center ☎ 435/649–2500 ✉ The Lodges at Deer Valley ☎ 435/649–8770) rents ski and snowboard equipment packages and clothing in winter and bikes in summer. For a higher fee you can rent high-end demo packages and apply the rental fee toward equipment purchase. At the base of Park City Mountain Resort, **Park City Sport** (✉ 1335 Lowell Ave. ☎ 435/645–7777 or 800/523–3922 ⊙ Closed May–Oct.) is a convenient place to rent ski and snowboard equipment. You can drop off your personal gear at the end of a ski day and they'll have it tuned and ready for you the next morning. **Utah Ski & Golf** (✉ 698 Park Ave., Park City ☎ 435/649–3020 ⊕ www.utahskigolf.com ✉ 1255 Empire Ave., in Sweetwater Condo, Park City ☎ 435/655–8367) offers downhill and cross-country equipment, snowshoes, and clothing.

ROCK CLIMBING   If you're looking for some hang time on the local rocks but don't know the area, **White Pine Touring** (✉ 1790 Bonanza Dr. ☎ 435/649–8710 ⊕ www.whitepinetouring.com) offers guided climbing tours, equipment rental, and private and group lessons.

CROSS-COUNTRY   On the edge of town, **White Pine Touring** (✉ On Park City Golf Course,
SKIING   Rte. 224 ☎ 435/649–8710 or 435/649–6249 ⊕ www.whitepinetouring. com) offers 20 km (12 mi) of set track, cross-country ski instruction, equipment rentals, and a well-stocked cross-country ski shop. The fee to use the track is $18. Reservations are required for their guided backcountry ski and snowshoe tours in the surrounding mountains.

With an emphasis on harmony with nature, the **Norwegian Outdoor Exploration Center** (✉ 333 Main St. Mall, 1st fl. ☎ 435/649–5322 or 800/649–5322 ⊕ www.outdoorcenter.org) guides private and group cross-country and snowshoe tours as well as providing equipment rental. Reservations are recommended.

DOWNHILL   Strong intermediate and better skiers can hook up with the **Ski Utah In-**
SKIING &   **terconnect Adventure Tour** (☎ 801/534–1907 ⊕ www.skiutah.com) for
SNOWBOARDING   a guided alpine ski tour that takes you to as many as six resorts (Deer
Fodor's Choice   Valley, Park City, Brighton, Solitude, Alta, and Snowbird) in a single day,
★   all connected by backcountry ski routes with unparalleled views of the Wasatch Mountains. The tour includes guide service, lift tickets, lunch, and transportation back to the point of origin and costs $175. You'll even walk away with a finisher's pin. The Deer Valley Departure Tour operates Sunday, Monday, Wednesday, and Friday; the Snowbird Departure Tour operates Tuesday, Thursday, and Saturday. Reservations are required.

The Canyons has similar mountain terrain to that of neighboring Park City Mountain Resort, but intermediates will find somewhat longer cruising runs here. Above-tree-line bowls feed into some fine tree-skiing for experts, and first-time skiers and boarders have 7 acres designated just for them. Don't be deceived when you pull into the parking lot; most of the terrain is not visible from the base. The resort has 3,500 acres of

2002 WINTER OLYMPICS LEGACIES

THOUGH THE 2002 WINTER OLYMPICS *are a distant but pleasant memory, their legacy lives on. Thanks to the healthy profit the Games produced, main venues have been able to remain open to host world-class competitions and provide recreation and training.*

The best place to enjoy the legacy of 2002 is at the Utah Olympic Sports Park near Park City, the site of the bobsled, luge, skeleton and ski jumping. In addition to touring the facility, you can ride the bobsled—wheeled in summer and on ice in winter—or try freestyle skiing. The interactive Alf Engen Ski Museum offers a chance for a virtual reality trip down the Olympic ski courses.

At the nearby Soldier Hollow facility in Midway, site of the cross-country skiing and biathlon events, you can ski on groomed expert or beginner trails, snowshoe, tube, or use the trail system to hike or mountain bike in summer.

A tent-shape structure made of steel and glass covers the speed-skating oval in West Valley City. It provides year-round ice for speed skating, figure skating, hockey, and curling. To get a feel for how fast Olympic speed skaters go, just try to skate the 400-meter track. A running track goes around the outside of the skating oval.

The Olympic torch still stands at Rice-Eccles Stadium on the University of Utah campus. A park—including the Hoberman Arch used during the medal ceremonies, a fountain, and historical information— surrounds the torch.

On hot days kids of all ages gather at the Olympic Legacy Snowflake Fountain at the Gateway in downtown Salt Lake City where they dodge shooting sprays of water, often set to music. An Olympic Hall of Fame is east of the fountain.

skiable terrain with 144 runs and is building a year-round base. As the first Park City mountain to allow snowboarding, this resort is popular with younger crowds. The Perfect Turn program bills itself as a "coaching" program, rather than an instructional program, for skiers and snowboarders of all ages. In addition to the advanced terrain park, the Canyons has added a beginners terrain park for first-time terrain park skiers and riders. ⊠ *4000 The Canyons Resort Dr., Park City 84098* ☎ *435/649–5400, 866/604–4169 central lodging reservations, 435/ 615–3456 snow reports* 🖷 *435/649–7374* ⊕ *www.thecanyons.com* ☞ *3,190-ft vertical drop; 3,500 skiable acres; 14% beginner, 44% intermediate, 42% advanced; 1 8-passenger gondola, 1 open-air gondola, 5 high-speed quad chairs, 3 quad chairs, 2 triple chairs, 2 double chairs, 1 surface lift* 🎫 *Lift tickets $66.*

With 100 trails and 650 acres of open bowls, the **Park City Mountain Resort** is one of Utah's largest complexes. Roughly half the terrain is rated as intermediate, but the slopes that line Jupiter Peak are revered by experts. The east face of Jupiter has some particularly hairy, rock-lined chutes. Portuguese Gap is an elevator shaft lined by trees, and a "six-pack" (six-passenger) chair in McConkey's Bowl provides access to additional steeps. Snowmaking covers 475 acres, and night skiers will delight in Pay Day, the longest lighted run in the Rockies. Park City's main drawback is lack of length. Despite a vertical drop of 3,100 feet, it's hard putting together a run of more than about 1,400 vertical feet. The area is made up of a series of ridges and peaks rather than a single mountain face. That said, Park City probably has the best overall terrain mix of any area in Utah—enough to keep skiers of all abilities happy for days. The Eagle Superpipe, with 22-foot walls, is the largest in North America and, combined with the half-pipe and four terrain parks with state-of-the-art rails and funboxes, makes this resort an important destination for snowboarders too. Children's programs are available and there are also excellent programs for senior citizens and skiers with disabilities. ⊠ *1310 Lowell Ave., 84060* ☎ *435/649–8111, 800/222–7275 central lodging reservations and snow reports* 🖷 *435/647–5374* ⊕ *www. parkcitymountain.com* ⚲ *3,100-foot vertical drop; 3,300 skiable acres; 18% beginner, 44% intermediate, 38% advanced; 4 high-speed 6-passenger chairs, 2 high-speed quad chairs, 4 triple chairs, 4 double chairs* 🎫 *Lift tickets $63.*

🖑
Fodor'sChoice
★

One mile south of downtown Park City, **Deer Valley** set new standards in the ski industry by providing such amenities as ski valets, on-slope phones, grooming fit for a king, and slope-side dining of the highest caliber. For such pampering, the resort has drawn rave reviews from virtually every ski and travel magazine. The careful layout of runs—all taking advantage of the best possible fall line—and the quality of the grooming leads to skiing's version of ballroom dancing. With the addition of the Empire Canyon area in 2000, the resort also offers bona fide expert terrain. Skiers enjoy a fast ride to the top of Bald Mountain and, as of 2005, 75 new skiable acres. For many, part of the ski experience here includes a two- to three-hour midday interlude of feasting at the Silver Lake Lodge buffet and catching major rays on the snow-covered meadow in front of the lodge—an area known appropriately as McHenry's Beach. The ski experience, in other words, fits right in with the resort's overall image. Whether it's the Bambi or Adventure Club, Deer Valley's acclaimed children's ski school is sure to please both children and parents. ⊠ *2250 Deer Valley Dr., 84060* ☎ *435/649–1000, 800/558–3337 central lodging reservations, 435/649–2000 snow reports* 🖷 *435/645–6939* ⊕ *www.deervalley.com* ⚲ *3,000-ft vertical drop; 1,750 skiable acres; 15% beginner, 50% intermediate, 35% advanced; 1 high-speed gondola, 7 high-speed quad chairs, 2 quad chairs, 7 triple chairs, 2 double chairs* 🎫 *Lift tickets $74.*

FLY-FISHING   The mountain-fed waters of the Provo and Weber rivers and several smaller streams near Park City are prime trout habitat. See Chris Kunkel, owner of the **Park City Fly Shop** (⊠ 2065 Sidewinder Dr. ☎ 435/645–8382 or 800/324–6778 ⊕ www.pcflyshop.com), for good advice, guide service, and a modest selection of fly-fishing necessities. Jon "Harley" Jackson and the rest of the fly-fishing experts at **Trout Bum 2** (⊠ 4343 N. Rte. 224 ☎ 435/658–1166 or 877/878–2862 ⊕ www.troutbum2.com), Park City's full-service fly shop, can outfit you with everything you need, then guide you to where the fish are.

ALF ENGEN'S SKI DREAM

SKIERS RACING DOWN THE RUNS *at one of Utah's many resorts or enjoying a tram or chairlift ride to the top of the Wasatch Mountains might want to consider how much they take for granted. In 1930, when Norwegian Alf Engen came to Utah to compete for the world ski-jumping title, skiers hiked to the top.*

The eight-time ski-jumping champion liked Utah's mountains so much that he made his home here. He went on to scope out possible runs at what became the Alta ski resort. The Collins lift, the nation's second (the first was in Sun Valley, Idaho), was constructed at Alta in the late 1930s, and lift tickets cost 75 cents a day. Alf also had a hand in designing Brighton and Snowbasin. His legacy lives on at Snowbasin, site of the 2002 Winter Olympics alpine downhill events.

Although Alf left competition at age 55, sharing his love for winter sports was a life-long passion. He trained soldiers for

service in the Alps during World War II, coached the U.S. Olympic ski team in 1948, and spent five decades as an instructor at Alta's ski school. His enthusiasm for life and skiing infected everyone. One look at the smiling senior citizen inspired many skiers to keep in shape. When Alf died in 2001 at age 90, skiing had become a major industry in Utah with 14 resorts. Alta remains the most historic and the closest to his vision. Because of this vision, there's a ski museum named in his honor at the Utah Olympic Park near Park City.

GOLF Within 20 minutes of Park City are eight golf courses: four public and four private. The **Park City Municipal Golf Course** (✉ 1541 Thaynes Canyon Dr. ☎ 435/615–5800) has 18 holes right in the heart of town with views of the ski runs and surrounding peaks.

HIKING The Wasatch mountains surrounding Park City offer hundreds of miles of hiking trails, ranging from easy, meandering meadow strolls to strenuous climbs up wind-blown peaks. Many of the trails take off from the resort areas, but some of the trailheads are right near Main Street. For up-to-date information about trail conditions and answers to your trails questions, contact **Mountain Trails Foundation** (✉ Box 754, Park City 84060 ☎ 435/649–6839 ⊕ www.mountaintrails.org), whose mission is to promote, preserve, advocate, and maintain Park City's local trail system. Maps detailing trail locations are available at most local gear shops.

HORSEBACK RIDING **Red Pine Adventures** (✉ 2050 W. White Pine Canyon Rd. ☎ 435/649–9445 or 800/417–7669 ⊕ www.redpinetours.com) leads trail rides through thousands of acres of private land. Saddle up for a taste and feel of the Old West with **Rocky Mountain Recreation** (✉ Rte. 224, Deer Valley, Park City ☎ 435/645–7256 ⊕ www.rockymtnrec.com). Guided mountain trail rides are offered from several locations in the Park City area, complete with fantastic Wasatch scenery and good cowboy grub. **Wind In Your Hair Riding** (☎ 435/336–4795 ⊕ www.windinyourhair. com) is for folks with some riding experience who are looking for a get-up-and-go kind of mountain riding adventure on Paso Fino horses, noted for their smooth ride.

HOT-AIR　**Park City Balloon Adventures** (☎ 435/645–8787 or 800/396–8787 ⊕ www.
BALLOONING　pcballoonadventures.com) offers half-hour and one-hour scenic flights daily, weather permitting. Fliers meet at a local hotel and are shuttled to the take-off site, which varies from day to day. A continental breakfast is served prior to takeoff, and a champagne or nonalcoholic toast is offered on touchdown. Reservations are required.

MOUNTAIN &　With more than 200 mi of public trails and smooth blacktop roads stretch-
ROAD BIKING　ing in every direction, it's no wonder Park City is home to a number of internationally elite mountain and road bikers. You can join local road or mountain bikers three evenings a week for free group rides sponsored by Park City bike shops. Pick up a free map of area trails at any local bike shop or get details online from **Mountain Trails Foundation** (☎ 435/ 649–6839 ⊕ www.mountaintrails.org).

Road bikers can ride with a pack each Monday and Thursday evening from mid-May through mid-September with riders from **Cole Sport** (⊠ 1615 Park Ave. ☎ 435/649–4806 or 800/345–2938 ⊕ www. colesport.com). You can rent mountain and road bikes from Cole; be ready to ride from the shop at 6 PM. If you're looking to learn to mountain bike or improve your skills, **Deer Valley Mountain Bike School** (⊠ Silver Lake Village at Deer Valley ☎ 435/649–6648 or 888/754–8477 ⊕ www.deervalley.com) offers clinics and guided tours in myriad packages; a half-day group clinic is $35. For a little help getting uphill, **Deer Valley Resort** (⊠ Silver Lake Village at Deer Valley ☎ 435/649–1000 or 888/754–8477 ⊕ www.deervalley.com) offers lift-assisted mountain biking or hiking Wednesday–Sunday mid-June through mid-September; it's $20 for a lift ticket. Bike rentals are available. On Tuesday evenings from May through September, the bike experts at **Jans Mountain Outfitters** (⊠ 1600 Park Ave. ☎ 435/649–4949 or 800/745–1020 ⊕ www. jans.com) lead groups of mountain bikers up and down local trails. Meet at the shop at 6 PM for this free group ride, where you can also rent equipment. Mountain bikers and hikers can ride the chairs at **Park City Mountain Resort** (⊠ 1310 Lowell Ave. ☎ 435/649–8111 or 800/222–7275 ⊕ www.parkcitymountain.com) to access the on-mountain trail complex. An all-day lift pass is $18. Equipment rentals are available. Thursday evenings from May through September, mountain bikers of all levels get together for a free employee-led tour at **White Pine Touring** (⊠ 1790 Bonanza Dr. ☎ 435/649–8710 ⊕ www.whitepinetouring. com). Meet at the shop at 6 PM, and rent equipment there.

SNOWMOBILING　For a winter speed thrill of the machine-powered variety, hop on a snowmobile with **Red Pine Adventures** (⊠ 2050 W. White Pine Canyon Rd. ☎ 435/649–9445 or 800/417–7669 ⊕ www.redpinetours.com), and follow your guide along private groomed trails adjacent to the Canyons resort. **Thousand Peaks Snowmobile Adventures** (☎ 888/304–7669

⊕ www.thousandpeaks.com) operates backcountry snowmobile tours on one of Utah's largest private mountain ranches just minutes from Park City, where you can catch a free shuttle. Clothing, such as snowsuits, gloves, and boots, are available to rent.

SNOW TUBING · Park City Mountain Resort's **Gorgoza Park** (✉ 3863 W. Kilby Rd. ☎ 435/658–2648 ⊕ www.gorgozapark.com), off I–80 near Parley's Summit, offers lift-served snow tubing and mini-snowmobile rentals for kids ages 5–12.

Where to Eat

★ $$$–$$$$ · ✕ **Adolph's.** It's no wonder this longtime local favorite becomes the unofficial headquarters for the Swiss ski team during Park City's annual World Cup ski races. Chef Adolph Imboden's food is quintessentially Swiss. Start off with raclette or escargots, move to the chateaubriand, then finish with a flambé prepared table-side. Signed photos and posters of skiing greats through the years line the walls. ✉ *1500 Kearns Blvd.* ☎ *435/649–7177* ⌖ *Reservations essential* ▭ *AE, MC, V.*

$$$–$$$$ · ✕ **Glitretind.** Wood trim, cranberry tablecloths, crystal glasses, hand-Fodor'sChoice painted china, and fresh-cut flowers set the scene for executive chef Zane ★ Holmquist's creative dishes like tea-and-Szechuan pepper-crusted duck breast at this European-style restaurant. Every major region is represented among the 300-plus wine selections, and artistic desserts like mango-filled chocolate crepes provide a perfect finish. You'll be tempted to make an all-day affair out of the Jazz Sunday brunch. It's open for breakfast, lunch, and dinner daily. ✉ *7700 Stein Way, Deer Valley* ☎ *435/645–6455* ⌖ *Reservations essential* ▭ *AE, D, DC, MC, V.*

★ $$$–$$$$ · ✕ **Grappa.** At the top of Main Street, this restaurant specializes in northern Italian cuisine with impeccable presentation. Heavy floor tiles, bricks, and timbers lend a rustic, warm, farmhouse feel. Tables on the wraparound balcony overlook those on the first floor. The menus, which change seasonally, offer appetizers such as homemade duck prosciutto with a summer pear-and-balsamic vinegar salad. Innovative entrées include pancetta-wrapped chicken fricassee filled with spinach-and-mushroom risotto. ✉ *151 Main St.* ☎ *435/645–0636* ⌖ *Reservations essential* ▭*AE, D, MC, V* ⊙ *Open daily Nov.–May; call ahead June–Oct. No lunch.*

$$$–$$$$ · ✕ **Riverhorse Café.** Two upper-level warehouse loft rooms give this café an ultramodern big-city supper club feel, with exposed beams, polished hardwood floors, black-and-white furnishings, and walls adorned with original art. Piano or jazz entertainment adds to the metropolitan atmosphere. Choose from entrées such as ahi tuna, charred rack of lamb, or the signature macadamia-crusted Alaskan halibut, and don't miss out on the mashed potatoes—they're famous. ✉ *540 Main St.* ☎ *435/649–3536* ⌖ *Reservations essential* ▭ *AE, D, MC, V* ⊙ *No lunch.*

$$$–$$$$ · ✕ **Wahso.** Warm finger towels, deep jade table settings, curtained booths, Fodor'sChoice and attentive service call back the Jazz-era Orient. Start your evening ★ with a sake martini shaken table-side, then ask your server about the appetizer-and-soup sampler plate. Though it's not on the menu, if the kitchen isn't too slammed, the chef will prepare an artistic selection of appetizers such as crispy salt-and-pepper calamari, Malaysian curried-chicken pot stickers, and a couple of shot-glass-size soup tasters. The

Thai baby-back ribs and the soy-and-ginger-glaze sea bass are favorite entrées. ⊠ *577 Main St.* ☎ *435/615–0300* ⚞ *Reservations essential* ▤ *AE, D, MC, V* ⊘ *Closed May–Nov. No lunch.*

$$–$$$$ ✕ **Café Terigo.** This airy café serves several well-prepared pasta and seafood dishes using only fresh ingredients. Good picks include almond-crusted salmon or smoked chicken with sun-dried tomatoes over fettuccine. An order of bread pudding or mud pie perfectly tops off a meal. ⊠ *424 Main St.* ☎ *435/645–9555* ▤ *AE, D, MC, V* ⊘ *Closed Sun. May–Nov.*

$$–$$$$ ✕ **Easy Street Brasserie and Bar Bohéme.** On the corner of Main Street and Heber Avenue, this restaurant and bar probably has the best location in town. The menu tells you it's "French, without all the France," and indeed the attitude is a bit tongue-in-cheek, but the food is seriously good. In addition to entrées like paillard of veal with capers and lemon, or cassoulet with duck confit, parties of four or more can choose from the chef's special menu for a multicourse meal served family style. ⊠ *201 Heber Ave.* ☎ *435/658–2500* ▤ *AE, D, DC, MC, V* ⊘ *Closed Mon. and Tues. May–Nov.*

$$–$$$$ ✕ **Kampai.** This Main Street restaurant is classic Japanese with a lively sushi bar, private tables with sunken floors behind rice-paper doors, and a more informal dining area with tables and booths. Well-trained chefs carve and roll your sushi to order from a selection of fish flown in daily, and they're great at coming up with special rolls for children or uninitiated sushi eaters. During nonwinter months locals line up for half-price sushi and other great deals so be sure and ask about specials. ⊠ *586 Main St.* ☎ *435/649–0655* ▤ *AE, D, MC, V* ⊘ *No lunch weekends.*

★ $$–$$$$ ✕ **350 Main Brasserie.** Chef Michael LeClerc is known for innovative entrées like Pacific swordfish served with wasabi mashed potatoes, roasted red pepper coulis, asparagus, and orange eau-de-vie. This Old Town restaurant has verdigris-toned furniture and a rust-tint ceiling. It's warm and inviting after a day on the slopes. ⊠ *350 Main St.* ☎ *435/ 649–3140* ▤ *AE, D, MC, V* ⊘ *Closed May.*

$–$$$$ ✕ **Zoom.** Owned by Robert Redford, this "Western chic" eatery is housed in an old train depot and still sports the worn wooden plank floors and floor scale. When the weather is warm, the sunken patio surrounded by flower beds is a perfect place to enjoy cornmeal-crusted red trout fillet, mesquite smoked pork tenderloin, or the beefed-up, but totally meatless, portobello mushroom sandwich. Leave room for warm chocolate torte with cherry compote or homemade cherry-chip ice cream. ⊠ *660 Main St.* ☎ *435/649–9108* ▤ *AE, D, DC, MC, V.*

★ $$–$$$ ✕ **Windy Ridge Café & Bakery.** You'll think you're at one of Park City's high-end eateries—with all the fresh-cut flowers at every table, rustic wood furniture, attentive service, and creative menu selections—until you see the prices. It's well worth a short trip away from Main Street and the resorts for the healthy breakfasts, homemade soups and breads, and fresh sandwiches here. ⊠ *1250 Iron Horse Dr.* ☎ *435/647–0880* ▤ *AE, D, DC, MC, V.*

☾ $–$$ ✕ **Main Street Pizza & Noodle.** Huge windows, a bright dining area, good no-frills food, and reasonable prices make this a great family spot. The pizzas are made California style, and the pastas and calzones are filling. ⊠ *530 Main St.* ☎ *435/645–8878* ▤ *AE, D, DC, MC, V.*

⏱ $–$$ ✕ **Nacho Mama's.** In Prospector Square, a few minutes from Main Street, Nacho Mama's features Southwestern dishes that will test your taste buds' heat tolerance. The chiles rellenos, which come with chicken, beef, or shrimp, push the upper limits of spicy, while the beef chipotle, with its thinly sliced meat and tangy sauce, sates any carnivore's appetite. ⊠ *1821 Sidewinder Dr.* ☎ *435/645–8226* ▭ *AE, D, MC, V.*

$ ✕ **Morning Ray Café & Bakery.** An urban crowd favors this café for its specialty breads, bagels, and pastries, as well as its substantial omelets, pancakes, and quiches. Wooden chairs and tables and walls hung with local art make the space inviting. ⊠ *255 Main St.* ☎ *435/649–5686* ▭ *AE, D, MC, V.*

★ ¢ ✕ **El Chubasco.** For a quick and hearty meal of traditional Mexican food, this popular place is perfect. Favorites are shrimp fajitas, *posole* (a rich soup that combines pork and dried corn in a chili-laden tomato base), fish tacos, and warm empanadas. The low-key atmosphere is part of the charm. ⊠ *1890 Bonanza Dr.* ☎ *435/645–9114* ▭ *AE, D, DC, MC V.*

Where to Stay

★ $$$$ ▥ **The Chateaux at Silver Lake.** Just steps away from the Deer Valley lifts at Silver Lake Village, this modern interpretation of a luxury French château incorporates designer furnishings, heated towel racks, wet bars in hotel rooms, full kitchens in suites, gas fireplaces, and numerous windows to take advantage of the spectacular mountain views. The service is exemplary and the on-site restaurant, Bistro Toujours, and bar, Club Buvez, offer eclectic French food and drink in a warm and relaxing space. ⊠ *7815 Royal St. E, 84060* ☎ *435/658–9500 or 888/976–2732* ▤ *435/658–9513* ⊕ *www.chateaux-deervalley.com* ⬘ *109 rooms, 39 suites* △ *Restaurant, some kitchens, refrigerators, cable TV, in-room VCRs, in-room data ports, in-room broadband, Wi-Fi, pool, hot tub, bar, shops, laundry service, concierge, business services* ▭ *AE, D, DC, MC, V.*

$$$$ ▥ **Grand Summit Resort Hotel and Conference Center.** The Grand Summit hosted Katie and Matt and NBC's *Today* show during the 2002 Olympic Winter Games, so if you tuned into the games you've probably seen this luxury hotel at the base of the Canyons Resort. Nearly every room opens to a view of the mountains, and you can walk out of the lobby right onto the Flight of the Canyons Gondola. During ski season ask about the "ski free" package when you stay here. ⊠ *4000 The Canyons Resort Dr., 84098* ☎ *435/615–8040 or 866/604–4170* ▤ *435/615–8041* ⊕ *www.thecanyons.com* ⬘ *145 rooms, 207 suites* △ *Restaurant, room service, cable TV with movies and video games, in-room data ports, Wi-Fi, pool, gym, hot tub, massage, sauna, steam room, downhill skiing, bar, shops, babysitting, laundry service, concierge, business services, meeting rooms* ▭ *AE, D, DC, MC, V.*

★ $$$$ ▥ **Hotel Park City.** Completed in 2003 on the Park City golf course, this all-suites hotel is built in the tradition of the grand old lodges of the West and furnished with leather furniture, marble bathrooms, and rustic luxury in all the details. Each room has a private balcony or patio, fireplace, and jetted tub. The 8,500-square-foot spa includes everything you'd expect with extras like a yoga room and a candlelit couples treatment room. ⊠ *2001 Park Ave., 84060* ☎ *435/940–5000* ▤ *435/940–5001* ⊕ *www.hotelparkcity.com* ⬘ *54 suites* △ *Restaurant, room service, kitchens,* *cable TV with movies, in-room data ports, Wi-Fi, pool, gym, spa, bar, babysitting, laundry facilities, business services* ▤ *AE, D, DC, MC, V.*

$$$$ 🖭 **Stein Eriksen Lodge.** Like the legendary Norwegian ski hero it's named

Fodor'sChoice after, this slope-side lodge is perfectly groomed, timelessly gracious,

★ and uniquely charming. Massive stone fireplaces, vaulted ceilings, and natural woodwork in the main lodge combine with in-room fireplaces, imported European fabrics, and heavy wood furniture to create an old-world Norwegian atmosphere. The service and facilities are impeccable, right down to the heated sidewalks and bell staff who light your in-room fire for you. All rooms have oversize whirlpool baths and many have deck hot tubs and in-room steam showers. A full-service Norwegian spa will pamper you after a hard day on the slopes. ⊠ *7700 Stein Way, Deer Valley 84060* ☎ *435/649–3700 or 800/453–1302* 🖷 *435/ 649–5825* ⊕ *www.steinlodge.com* ⥲ *111 rooms, 59 suites* ⌂ *Restaurant, room service, kitchens, cable TV with movies and video games, in-room DVD/VCR, in-room data ports, Wi-Fi, pool, gym, hot tub, massage, sauna, mountain bikes, downhill skiing, sleigh rides, snowmobiling, bar, babysitting, dry cleaning, laundry service, concierge, business services, meeting rooms* ▤ *AE, D, DC, MC, V.*

$$$–$$$$ 🖭 **Marriott Mountainside Resort.** Gabled roofs, stonework, and heavy beams re-create the look of Park City's mining era buildings at this resort on the plaza at Park City Mountain Resort, steps away from the ski lifts. The rooms and indoor common areas have more traditional decor than the rustic exterior. This is a vacation ownership property, so be prepared for a sales pitch, but you can't beat the ski-in ski-out convenience to Park City Mountain Resort. ⊠ *1305 Lowell Ave., 84060* ☎ *435/940– 2000 or 800/845–5279* 🖷 *435/940–2010* ⊕ *www.mvci.com* ⥲ *182 rooms* ⌂ *Cable TV, in-room data ports, pool, gym, hot tub, sauna, laundry facilities, concierge* ▤ *AE, D, MC, V.*

★ **$$$** 🖭 **Washington School Inn.** Originally an 1880s schoolhouse, the inn has high, vaulted ceilings, cherry wainscoting, and a stunning center staircase leading to the bell tower. The large rooms and suites have Victorian-era furnishings with country-style wall coverings, handwoven area rugs, tile-and-stone flooring, claw-foot tubs, and, in some rooms, four-poster canopy beds. ⊠ *543 Park Ave., Box 536, 84060* ☎ *435/649– 3800 or 800/824–1672* 🖷 *435/649–3802* ⊕ *www.washingtonschoolinn. com* ⥲ *12 rooms, 3 suites* ⌂ *Dining room, cable TV, Wi-Fi, in-room data ports, hot tub, sauna* ▤ *AE, D, DC, MC, V* ⦿ *BP.*

$–$$ 🖭 **Holiday Inn Express Hotel and Suites.** With fireplaces and log furniture, this hotel near I–80 conveys the feel of a rustic cabin. Free shuttle service gets you to and from the Park City area resorts in winter. Continental breakfast is included. ⊠ *1501 W. Ute Blvd., 84098* ☎ *435/658– 1600 or 800/465–4329* 🖷 *435/658–1600* ⊕ *www.parkcityhie.com* ⥲ *76 rooms* ⌂ *Cable TV, Wi-Fi, in-room data ports, gym, indoor pool, hot tub, sauna, laundry facilities, some pets allowed* ▤ *AE, D, DC, MC, V* ⦿ *CP.*

$–$$ 🖭 **Old Town Guest House.** The country-style decor and lodgepole pine

Fodor'sChoice furniture make this inn, which is listed on the National Register of His-

★ toric Places, warm and cozy. Innkeeper Deb Lovci, a backcountry ski guide, triathlete, and mountain-bike racer, is an engaging host as well

as a wealth of information on outdoor activities in the area. ⊠ *1011 Empire Ave., 84060* ☎ *435/649–2642 or 800/290–6423 Ext. 3710* 🖷 *435/649–3320* ⊕ *www.oldtownguesthouse.com* ☜ *4 rooms* ⚭ *Dining room, cable TV, Wi-Fi, hot tub, some pets allowed; no a/c, no smoking* ☰ *AE, MC, V* ⊧◯⊧ *BP.*

¢–$$ ⊞ **Yarrow Resort Hotel & Conference Center.** Easy access to all three Park City resorts and the city golf course via shuttles are the principal attractions here. The high ceilings with exposed beams and flagstone entry to the lobby lend a mountain lodge feel to this otherwise standard hotel. Some rooms have fireplaces, jetted tubs, and kitchenettes. ⊠ *1800 Park Ave., 84060* ☎ *435/649–7000 or 800/927–7694* 🖷 *435/645–7007* ⊕ *www.yarrowresort.com* ☜ *173 rooms, 8 suites* ⚭ *Restaurant, room service, cable TV with movies, Wi-Fi, in-room data ports, pool, gym, hot tub, bar, laundry facilities, business services, meeting rooms* ☰ *AE, D, DC, MC, V.*

¢ ⊞ **Chateau Après.** Just 150 yards from Park City Mountain Resort, this classic skiers' lodge has been run by the Hosenfeld family since 1963. The rooms aren't fancy, but they're clean and the service is as friendly as you'll find anywhere. You can choose one queen or a double and a twin. Or, if privacy isn't a must, you can rent a bed in the dorm room for $30 a night, which also includes the continental breakfast. ⊠ *1299 Norfolk Ave., 84060* ☎ *435/649–9372 or 800/357–3556* 🖷 *435/649–5963* ⊕ *www.chateauapres.com* ☜ *32 rooms* ⚭ *Dining room, cable TV; no a/c, no smoking* ☰ *AE, DC, MC, V* ⊧◯⊧ *CP.*

CONDOS The reservationists at **Deer Valley Lodging** (⊠ 1375 Deer Valley Dr. S, 84060 ☎ 435/649–4040 or 800/453–3833 🖷 435/647–3318 ⊕ www.deervalleylodging.com) are knowledgeable and the service efficient at this high-end property-management company. They can book distinctive hotel rooms, condominiums, or private homes throughout Deer Valley and Park City.

WHERE TO CAMP ⚠ **Hailstone: Jordanelle State Park.** Shade is at a premium at this lakeside campground on the west side of Jordanelle Reservoir. The views of surrounding mountains are stunning and the facilities clean and modern. Reservations essential. ⚭ *Laundry facilities, flush toilets, full hookups, dump station, drinking water, showers, fire grates, picnic tables, food service, public telephone, swimming (lake)* ☜ *177 sites* ⊠ *U.S. 40 between Park City and Heber City, Rte. 319, 84032* ☎ *435/649–9148 or 800/322-3770* 🖷 *435/655–9058* ⊕ *www.stateparks.utah.gov* ⊡ *$14 tents, $17 full hookups* ☰ *MC, V* ☉ *Apr.–Sept.*

⚠ **Park City RV Resort.** Just off I-80, this RV and tent site has four acres of grassy sites from which to choose. ⚭ *Laundry facilities, flush toilets, full hookups, partial hookups, dump station, drinking water, gym, Wi-Fi, showers, fire pits, picnic tables, public telephone, general store, play area* ☜ *60 full hookups, 30 tent sites* ⊠ *2200 Rasmussen Rd., 84098* ☎ *435/649–2535* 🖷 *435/649–2536* ⊡ *$20 tents, $35 full hookups* ☰ *AE, D, MC, V.*

Nightlife & the Arts

NIGHTLIFE In a state where nearly every town was founded by Mormon pioneers who eschewed alcohol and anything associated with it, Park City has always been an exception. Founded by miners with healthy appetites for whiskey, gambling, and ladies of the night, Park City has been known since its mining heyday as the Sin City of Utah. The miners are gone, but their legacy lives on in this town that boasts far more bars per capita than any other place in Utah. **Cisero's** (⊠ 306 Main St. ☎ 435/649–5044) offers live music some evenings and also serves good Italian and American food. On lower Main, **Mulligan's** (⊠ 804 Main St. ☎ 435/658–0717) lives up to its name with Guinness on tap, occasional live music, and a congenial pub atmosphere with a couple of pool tables. The name has changed, or rather, disappeared, but the **No Name Saloon** (⊠ 447 Main St. ☎ 435/649–6667) is still the anchor of Main Street's nightlife: a classic wood-backed bar, lots of memorabilia, and a regular local clientele. If you're looking for a tasty garlic burger or

★ hot wings, a favorite of local ski bums is **O'Shucks** (⊠ 427 Main St. ☎ 435/645–3999). No frills, no attitude, just the saltiest peanuts—throw the shells on the floor—and the coldest beer around. Well worth the sleuthing it takes to find it (you walk through an alley next to 350 Main Restaurant), **The Spur** (⊠ 350 Main St. ☎ 435/615–1618) is an upscale, smoke-free club with good food—they share the kitchen with 350 Main restaurant—and live music nightly. Belly up to the bar on one of the leather bar stools and choose from eight different tequilas to order one of their famous margaritas. Six miles from Main Street at Kimball Junction, **Suede** (⊠ 1612 Ute Blvd. ☎ 435/658–2665) has lots of room for nationally prominent live music leaning toward the eclectic and draws crowds from the Salt Lake Valley as well as Park City. If quiet conversation and a good

★ single malt scotch in front of a fire is your idea of nightlife, try the **Troll Hallen Lounge** (⊠ 7700 Stein Way ☎ 435/649–3700), at Stein Eriksen Lodge.

THE ARTS Main Street is packed with great art galleries, and the best way to see them all is the **Arts and Eats Gallery Stroll** (⊠ 638 Park Ave. ☎ 435/649–8882 ⊕ www.kimball-art.org), presented by the Kimball Art Center, where you can pick up tickets and a map. You can sample fine art and hors d'oeuvres at more than 25 Old Town galleries and restaurants on the last Friday of each month.

★ The **Eccles Center for Performing Arts** (⊠ 1750 Kearns Blvd. ☎ 435/655–3114 ⊕ www.ecclescenter.org) hosts ballet, avant-garde theater, wide-ranging concerts, and other performances in a state-of-the-art auditorium that also hosts the biggest premieres during the Sundance Film Festival.

Theater has been a Park City tradition since its mining days in the 1880s. In 1922 the **Egyptian Theatre** (⊠ 328 Main St. ☎ 435/649–9371 ⊕ www.egyptiantheatrecompany.org) was constructed on the site of the original Dewey Theatre that collapsed under record-breaking snow. Patrons enjoy many different off Broadway–style plays by local groups as well as national touring companies.

🕭 **Mountain Town Stages** (☎ 435/901–7664 ⊕ www.mountaintownstages.com), a nonprofit organization fostering an internationally recognized musical community in the Park City area, uses five different venues from ski resort plazas to Main Street. No matter what show you go to, you're likely to see every age group represented and enjoying the music.

★ **Fidelity Investments Park City Jazz Festival** (☎ 435/940–1362 ⊕ www. parkcityjazz.com) is a major summer event. Each August, artists like George Benson, Stanley Clarke, Bela Fleck, and the Ramsey Lewis Trio have performed at this annual three-day festival dedicated to jazz. Daily workshops and clinics for jazz musicians are held, and the nightly performances feature various kinds of jazz groups and styles.

☾ Celebrating visual, culinary, and performance art, the **Park City Arts Festival** (✉ Main St. ☎ 435/649–8882 ⊕ www.kimball-art.org), held the first weekend in August, is the biggest summer event in town. More than 200 artists from all over North America exhibit and offer their work to 40,000 festival attendees. Live music, upscale food, and local microbrews are featured.

Deer Valley Resort's **Summer Concert Series** (☎ 435/649–1000 ⊕ www. deervalley.com) includes everything from Utah Symphony performances to country music.

For 10 days each January, Park City morphs into a mountain version of Hollywood as movie stars and film executives gather for the internationally recognized **Sundance Film Festival** (☎ 800/220–8333 ⊕ www. sundance.org), hosted by Robert Redford's Sundance Institute. In addition to seminars, tributes, premieres, and screenings of independent films at various venues in Park City, Sundance, Ogden, and Salt Lake City, the festival's Music Café hosts daily and nightly performances by emerging and established feature musicians.

Shopping

Within the colorful structures that line Park City's Main Street are a number of clothing boutiques, sporting-goods stores, and gift shops. **Bunny Bunny** (✉ 511 Main St. ☎ 435/649–1256) might be a small retail space, but it's neatly packed with unique and stylish women's clothing and accessories. **Chloe Lane** (✉ 558 Main St. ☎ 435/645–9888) has three different, but interconnected, store-fronts: one for high-fashion denim for women, one for high-quality, contemporary American and European clothing and accessories for women, and one combining all of the above for

★ ☾ men. For many returning visitors, the first stop in town is **Dolly's Bookstore** (✉ 510 Main St. ☎ 435/649–8062), to check on the cats, Dolly and Che Guevara, and to browse a great selection of Utah and regional books as well as national best-sellers. Dolly's also has a uniquely complete selection of children's books and toys. Classical music and the aroma of fresh-roasted coffee greet you at **La Niche** (✉ 401 Main St. ☎ 435/ 649–2372). Owner Jane Schaffner brings together a cozy collection of kitchen items, home decorations, quilts, cooking and decorating books,

★ and an intimate coffee and ice-cream bar in the back. **Mary Jane's** (✉ 613 Main St. ☎ 435/645–7463) has an eclectic selection of locally hand-made and independently designed shoes and accessories and handbags for women, men, and children. And then there are the items the owner–buyer just couldn't pass up. If you like shoes, this shop is a must.

☾ You'll find a quick fix for your sweet tooth at either location of **Rocky Mountain Chocolate Factory** (✉ 510 Main St. or 1385 Lowell Ave. ☎ 435/ 649–0997 or 435/649–2235), where you can watch them make homemade fudge, caramel apples, and other scrumptious treats. If you like Christmas, you'll love **Rocky Mountain Christmas Gifts** (⊠ 355 Main St. ☎ 435/649–9169), where Christmas ornaments, candles, and decorations crowd the tightly spaced shelves.

A few miles north of Park City, next to I–80, are the **Factory Stores at Park City** (⊠ 6699 N. Landmark Dr. ☎ 435/645–7078 or 888/746–7333). Represented in this collection of 47 outlets are Banana Republic, Nike, Gap, Ralph Lauren, Eddie Bauer, and Mikasa.

Big Cottonwood Canyon

⑥ *44 mi from Park City via I–80 west, I–215 west, and Rte. 190 south.*

The history of mining and skiing in Utah often go hand in hand, and that's certainly true of Big Cottonwood Canyon with its adjacent ski resorts of **Brighton** and **Solitude.** In the mid-1800s, 2,500 miners lived at the top of this canyon in a rowdy tent city. The old mining roads make great hiking, mountain biking, and backcountry ski trails. Rock climbers congregate in the lower canyon for excellent sport and traditional climbing.

Opened in 1936, Brighton is the second-oldest ski resort in Utah and one of the oldest in North America. Just down the canyon, Solitude has undergone several incarnations since it opened in 1957, and has invested heavily in overnight accommodations and new base facilities since the early 1990s. As an area, Big Cottonwood is quieter than Park City or neighboring Little Cottonwood Canyon, home of Alta and Snowbird resorts.

Sports & the Outdoors

CROSS-COUNTRY SKIING Just up the road from Solitude Village, the **Solitude Nordic Center** (⊠ Big Cottonwood Canyon Rd. ☎ 801/536–5774) has 20 km (12 mi) of groomed trails with a small shop offering rentals, lessons, food, and guided tours. For $12 you can use the trails all day; for $40 you receive an all-day trail pass and a one-hour private lesson.

DOWNHILL SKIING & SNOWBOARDING With the perfect combination of all the fluffy powder of Alta and Snowbird and all the quiet charm many large resorts have left behind, **Brighton Ski Resort** is a favorite among serious snowboarders and out-on-the-edge skiers. If you're looking for excitement, more than one-third of the runs are for advanced skiers, and lifts provide access to extensive backcountry areas for the real experts. Photos taken in the Brighton backcountry are regular fodder for the extreme skiing and snowboarding magazines. Its expert terrain and new renegade image notwithstanding, this is still a great place for families, with ideal beginner and intermediate terrain. It was the first in Utah to offer a kids-ski-free program, and it has received many awards for its service to children and parents. ⊠ *12601 Big Cottonwood Rd., Brighton 84121* ☎ *801/532–4731 or 800/873–5512, 800/873–5512 snow report* 🖷 *435/649–1787* ⊕ *www.brightonresort. com* ☞ *1,745-ft vertical drop; 850 skiable acres; 21% beginner, 40% intermediate, 39% advanced/expert; 3 high-speed quad chairs, 1 fixed grip quad, 1 triple chair, 2 double chairs* 🎟 *Lift tickets $44.*

Since the early 1990s the base of **Solitude Mountain Resort** has grown into a European-style village with lodges, condominiums, a luxury hotel, and award-winning restaurants, but downhill skiing and snowboarding are still the main attractions. Day guests will enjoy relaxing after a hard day on the slopes at the comfortable 12,000-square-foot Moonbeam Day Lodge, built in 2005. The Honeycomb quad chairlift accesses pristine expert terrain to go with a good mix of intermediate cruising runs and beginner-friendly slopes. Skiers and boarders can access the slopes directly from the parking lot on the fixed-grip quad lift, new in 2005. ⊠ *12000 Big Cottonwood Canyon, Solitude 84121* ☎ *801/534–1400 or 800/748–4754, 801/536–5774 Nordic Center, 801/536–5730 snow report* 🖶 *435/649–5276* ⊕ *www.skisolitude.com* ☞ *2,047-ft vertical drop; 1,200 skiable acres; 20% beginner, 50% intermediate, 30% advanced; 2 high-speed quad chairs, 1 quad chair, 2 triple chairs, 4 double chairs* ▣ *Lift tickets $50.*

HIKING The upper section of Big Cottonwood Canyon is a glacier-carved valley with many side drainages that lead to picturesque alpine lakes. In the Brighton area you can access beautiful mountain lakes just a short jaunt from the highway. The elevation at Brighton's parking lot is 8,700 feet, so take it easy, rest often, and drink plenty of water. A beautiful hike is along the **Brighton Lakes Trail** past four alpine lakes and then ascending to Catherine Pass. At Catherine Pass you have the option of continuing up to **Sunset Peak,** which, at 10,648 feet, is one of the most accessible summits in the Wasatch Range. It's another short grunt to the top but well worth the effort for the unsurpassed, nearly 360-degree views. The breathtaking vistas include the Heber Valley, Park City, Mt. Timpanogos, Big and Little Cottonwood Canyons, and even a portion of the Salt Lake Valley. From here you can choose to descend into Little Cottonwood's Albion Basin near Alta (but remember, you'll need a shuttle for the 45-minute ride back to Brighton), or back along the Brighton lakes trail to Brighton.

ICE-SKATING Open mid-December through April, from 3 PM to 8 PM, **Solitude Ice-Skating Rink** (⊠ Solitude Village ☎ 435/534–1400), in the heart of Solitude Village, provides skate rentals and a rink-side fire for family fun or a romantic outing.

MOUNTAIN BIKING There are great single track trails within Big Cottonwood Canyon as well as routes that connect neighboring canyons. **Solitude Mountain Resort** (⊠ 12000 Big Cottonwood Canyon Rd. ☎ 801/534–1400) offers lift-served mountain biking with rentals available at the Stone Haus general store in Solitude Village.

Where to Stay & Eat

$–$$$ ✕ **Creekside Restaurant.** Excellent pizzas and calzones from a wood-fired oven, creative pastas, and homey Italian side dishes like polenta make this Solitude Village restaurant a good choice for families. In summer the patio is a great outdoor retreat from the Salt Lake Valley heat, but bring a sweater because when the sun goes down you'll need it. It's open seven days a week, three meals a day during ski season; dinner and Sunday brunch only during summer. ⊠ *12000 Big Cottonwood Canyon Rd.* ☎ *801/536–5787* ▤ *AE, D, DC, MC, V* ☾ *Closed May; closed Mon.–Wed. June–Nov.*

★ **$–$$** ✕🍴 **Silver Fork Lodge.** Any day of the week, any time of the year, you'll find people driving up from the Salt Lake Valley for the consistently delicious food and friendly service in this rustic lodge a mile down the road from Solitude Mountain Resort. In warm months breakfast on the patio is delightful. Log furniture, wood paneling, and country decor make the rooms warm and inviting, and the views are unbeatable. Service is attentive, but not overbearing. ✉ *11332 Big Cottonwood Canyon Rd., 84121* ☎ *801/533–9977 or 888/649–9551* 🖨 *435/649–3428* ⊕ *www. silverforklodge.com* ⇌ *6 rooms, 1 suite* ☖ *Restaurant, gym, hot tub, sauna, bar, meeting rooms; no a/c, no room phones, no room TVs* ▭ *AE, D, MC, V* ⏐◯⏐ *BP.*

$$$ 🍴 **Powderhorn Lodge.** The clock tower on this Tyrolean-style lodge chimes hourly and is the centerpiece of Solitude Village. Many of these elegantly furnished studios and one- to four-bedroom condos have private balconies and all have fireplaces. ✉ *12000 Big Cottonwood Canyon Rd., 84121* ☎ *801/534–1400 or 800/748–4754* 🖨 *801/517–7705* ⊕ *www.skisolitude.com* ⇌ *60 units* ☖ *Kitchens, cable TV, in-room data ports, hot tub, laundry facilities; no a/c* ▭ *AE, D, DC, MC, V.*

$$–$$$ 🍴 **The Inn at Solitude.** You get ski-in ski-out luxury and VIP treatment at this well-appointed hotel with comfortable and spacious rooms. After a strenuous day on the slopes, enjoy a hot toddy at St. Bernard's bar, get a massage at the full-service spa, then relax under the stars in the outdoor heated pool or hot tub. ✉ *12000 Big Cottonwood Canyon Rd., 84121* ☎ *801/534–1400 or 800/748–4754* 🖨 *801/517–7705* ⊕ *www. skisolitude.com* ⇌ *42 hotel rooms, 4 suites* ☖ *Restaurant, cable TV, in-room VCR, pool, gym, hot tub, spa, laundry facilities; no a/c* ▭ *AE, D, DC, MC, V* ⊗ *Closed May–Nov.*

¢–$$ 🍴 **Brighton Lodge.** Brighton Ski Resort's emphasis on value extends to this lodge, which is quiet, comfortable, and so reasonably priced (keep in mind that children 10 and under stay free) that you might be able to stretch your ski weekend into a full week. Situated right on the slopes, the lodge has a tradition of friendliness. Rooms have few frills but are still comfortable. ✉ *12601 Big Cottonwood Canyon Rd., 84121* ☎ *435/ 649–7940 Ext. 236 or 800/873–5512 Ext. 236* 🖨 *435/649–1787* ⊕ *www.brightonresort.com* ⇌ *18 rooms, 2 suites* ☖ *Refrigerators, hot tub; no a/c, no room TVs* ▭ *AE, D, MC, V* ⏐◯⏐ *CP.*

WHERE TO CAMP △ **Spruces Campground.** As the name implies, this campground is in the middle of a grove of spruce pines which provide plenty of shade. This is the trailhead for several good hiking routes and Big Cottonwood Creek runs next to the campground. Reservations essential. ☖ *Flush toilets, drinking water, fire grates, picnic tables* ⇌ *100 sites* ✉ *10 mi up Big Cottonwood Canyon on Rte. 190* ☎ *801/733–2660 or 877/444–6777* ⊕ *www.reserveusa.com* 🎫 *$16* ▭ *AE, D, MC, V* ⊗ *June–Sept.*

Nightlife & the Arts

NIGHTLIFE Old-time ski bums and younger snowboarders come together to shoot pool and tip back a few at **Molly Green's** (✉ Brighton Ski Resort ☎ 435/ 649–7909 ⊗ Closed Mon.–Wed. May–Nov.), a smoky bar with a very laid-back attitude at the base of Brighton Ski Resort. A good place to

THIS LAKE IS FOR THE BIRDS

Although it's too salty for fish, the Great Salt Lake teems with algae and bacteria. These provide food for brine shrimp and brine flies, which seem like caviar to the millions of shore birds that stop here during their migrations. The following is a list of some of the more than 250 species that you can spot at natural saltwater marshes, man-made freshwater marshes, and wetland refuges around the lake: Avocet, Bald Eagle, Black-Necked Stilt, California Gull, Common Snipe, Cormorant, Egret (Great and Snowy varieties), Grebe (Eared and Western),

Heron (Great Blue and Black-Crowned Night), Killdeer, Long-Billed Curlew, Long-Billed Dowitcher, Marbled Godwit, Merganser, Northern Phalarope, Plover (Black-Bellied, Lesser, Golden, Snowy, Semipalmated), Red Knot, Sanderling, Sandpiper (Baird's, Least, Pectoral, Semipalmated, Solitary, Spotted, Stilt, Western), Tern (Caspian and Forster's), White-Faced Ibis, Willet, and the Yellowlegs (Greater and Lesser).

It's a bird-watchers paradise, so bring your binoculars!

---

unwind after skiing is the **Thirsty Squirrel** (✉ Powderhorn Bldg., Solitude Village ☎ 801/536–5797 ⊘ Hrs vary May–Nov.); it's pretty quiet once the après-ski crowd leaves.

Little Cottonwood Canyon

❼ *25 mi from Brighton and Solitude via Rte. 190 west, Rte. 210 south; 20 mi from Salt Lake City via I–15 south, I–215 east, Rte. 210 south.*

Skiers have been singing the praises of Little Cottonwood Canyon since 1938 when the Alta Lifts Company pieced together a ski lift using parts from an old mine tram to become the **Alta Ski Resort,** the second ski resort in North America. With its 500 inches per year of dry, light snow and unparalleled terrain, this canyon is legendary among diehard snow enthusiasts. A mile down the canyon from Alta, **Snowbird Ski and Summer Resort,** which opened in 1971, shares the same mythical snow and terrain quality. Since 2001 Alta and Snowbird have been connected via the Mineral Basin area. You can purchase an Alta Snowbird One Pass that allows you on the lifts at both areas, making this a huge skiing complex.

But skiing isn't all there is to do here. Many mountain biking and hiking trails access the higher reaches of the Wasatch–Cache National Forest, and the trails over Catherine Pass will put you at the head of Big Cottonwood Canyon at the Brighton Ski Area. The hike to Catherine Pass is relatively easy and quite scenic. Formed by the tireless path of an ancient glacier, Little Cottonwood Canyon cuts a swath through the Wasatch–Cache National Forest. Canyon walls are composed mostly of striated granite, and traditional climbing routes of varied difficulty abound. There are a few bolted routes as well. Down the canyon from Alta and Snowbird is the trailhead for the Red Pine Lake and White Pine Lake trails. Some 3½ mi and 5 mi in, respectively, these mountain lakes make for great day hikes.

"If it ain't broke, don't fix it," could be the motto at Alta Ski Resort. There's an old-world charm here that many regulars call magic. Most of the lodges have been here since the '40s or '50s, and the emphasis is on efficiency and quality rather than the latest fads.

At Snowbird's base area, modern structures house guest rooms, restaurants, and nightclubs. The largest of these buildings, the Cliff Lodge, is an entire ski village under one roof. The resort mounts a variety of entertainment throughout the year, including performances by the Utah Symphony, live jazz shows, food-and-wine festivals, and murder-mystery weekends. As a guest, you receive free membership to the Club at Snowbird and can enjoy a drink at any of several base area lounges.

From Memorial Day weekend to October, Snowbird fires up its tram to take sightseers and hikers to the top. Mountain bikers are discovering that the slopes make for some excellent, if strenuous, riding. The resort also has a competition-class outdoor climbing wall.

Sports & the Outdoors

HIKING The upper canyons provide a cool haven during the hot summer months. Wildflowers and wildlife are plentiful and most trails provide a good balance of shade and sun. Due to high altitude, even fit hikers often become fatigued and dehydrated faster than they would otherwise, so remember to take it easy, rest often, and drink plenty of water. **White Pine Trailhead**, 0.7 mi below Snowbird on the south side of the road, accesses some excellent easy hikes to overlooks. If you want to keep going on more intermediate trails, continue up the trail to the lakes in White Pine Canyon, Red Pine Canyon, and Maybird Gulch. All of these hikes share a common path for the first mile.

★ The trailhead for the 4-mi out-and-back hike to **Sunset Peak** starts high in Little Cottonwood Canyon, above Alta Ski Resort, in Albion Basin. This is a popular area for finding wildflowers in July and August. After an initial steep incline, the trail wanders through flat meadows before it climbs again to Catherine Pass at 10,240 feet. From here intermediate hikes continue along the ridge in both directions. Continue up the trail to the summit of Sunset Peak for breathtaking views of the Heber Valley, Park City, Mt. Timpanogos, Big and Little Cottonwood Canyons, and even a part of the Salt Lake Valley. You can alter your route by starting in Little Cottonwood Canyon and ending your hike in neighboring Big Cottonwood Canyon: from Catherine Pass descend into Big Cottonwood Canyon passing four lakes and finally ending up at Brighton Ski Resort.

CROSS-COUNTRY You'll find 5 km (3 mi) of groomed track for skating and classic skiing
SKIING plus a good selection of rental equipment and even an espresso bar at the **Alta Nordic Shop** (✉ Wildcat Ticket Office Bldg. ☎ 801/742–9722).

DOWNHILL When it comes to skiing, **Alta Ski Resort** is widely acclaimed for both what
SKIING & it has and what it doesn't have. What it has is perhaps the best snow any-
SNOWBOARDING where in the world—up to 500 inches a year, and terrain to match it.
Fodor'sChoice What it doesn't have is glitz and pomp. Neither does it have snow-
★ boarders. Alta is one of the few resorts left in the country that doesn't

allow snowboarding. Sprawling across two large basins, Albion and Wildcat, Alta has a good mixture of expert, intermediate, and beginner terrain. Much of the best skiing (for advanced or expert skiers) requires finding obscure traverses or some hiking: it takes some time to get to know this mountain so if you can find a local to show you around you'll be ahead of the game. Albion Basin's lower slopes have a terrific expanse of novice and lower-intermediate terrain. Rolling meadows, wide trails, and light dry snow create one of the best places in the country for less-skilled skiers to learn to ski powder. Two-hour lessons start at $42. Half-day group lessons for adults and children are available. *Box 8007, 84092* *801/359–1078, 801/572–3939 snow report* *www.alta.com* *2,020-ft vertical drop; 2,200 skiable acres; 25% novice, 40% intermediate, 35% advanced; 2 high speed quads, 3 triple chairs, 3 double chairs* *Lift tickets $49; Alta Snowbird One Pass $69.*

Like its up-canyon neighbor, **Snowbird Ski and Summer Resort** has plenty of powder-filled chutes, bowls, and meadow areas with an even longer vertical drop. Snowbird's signature 125-passenger tram takes you from the base all the way to the top in one fell swoop for a leg-burning top to bottom run of more than 3,000 vertical feet. The terrain here is weighted more toward experts—45% of Snowbird is rated black-diamond—and if there is a drawback to this resort it's a lack of beginner terrain. The open bowls, such as Little Cloud and Regulator Johnson, are challenging; the Upper Cirque and the Gad Chutes are hair-raising. On deep-powder days—not uncommon at the Bird—these chutes are exhilarating for skiers who like that sense of a cushioned free fall with every turn. If you're looking for intermediate cruising runs, there's the long, meandering Chips Run. After a day of powder turns, visitors can lounge on the 3,000-square-foot deck of Creekside Lodge, opened in 2005, at the base of Gad Valley. Of note is Snowbird's Mountain Experience Program, a combination of guidance and instruction for expert skiers or snowboarders in challenging, off-slope terrain and variable snow conditions. Full-day workshops for skiers and boarders of all levels start at $100. *9000 Little Cottonwood Canyon Rd., Box 929000, Snowbird 84092* *801/742–2222 or 800/385–2002, 800/232–9542 lodging reservations, 801/933–2110 special events, 801/933–2100 snow report* *801/947–8227* *www.snowbird.com* *3,240-ft vertical drop; 2,500 skiable acres; 27% novice, 38% intermediate, 35% advanced; 125-passenger tram, 3 quad lifts, 7 double chairs* *Lift tickets $62 tram and chairs, $51 chairlift only; Alta Snowbird One Pass $69.*

If you don't mind paying for it, the best way to find untracked Utah powder is with **Wasatch Powderbird Guides** (*Snowbird* *801/742–2800* *www.powderbird.com*). A helicopter drops you on the top of the mountain and a guide leads you back down. A full day costs $630 for low season and $770 for regular season.

Fodor's Choice ★ Strong intermediate and better skiers can hook up with the **Ski Utah Interconnect Adventure Tour** (*801/534–1907* *www.skiutah.com*) for a guided alpine ski tour that takes you to as many as six resorts (Deer Valley, Park City, Brighton, Solitude, Alta, and Snowbird) in a single day, all connected by backcountry ski routes with unparalleled views of the

Wasatch Mountains. The tour includes guide service, lift tickets, lunch, and transportation back to the point of origin and costs $175. You'll even walk away with a finisher's pin. The Deer Valley Departure Tour operates Sunday, Monday, Wednesday, and Friday; the Snowbird Departure Tour operates Tuesday, Thursday, and Saturday. Reservations are required.

MOUNTAIN BIKING   The steep, rocky terrain here is not recommended for beginners, but advanced mountain bikers can ride the tram at **Snowbird Ski and Summer Resort** (⊠ 9000 Little Cottonwood Canyon Rd. ☎ 801/742–2222 or 800/385–2002) to the top of the mountain and access a network of trails. Summer tram tickets are $14. Bike rentals are available.

ROCK CLIMBING   Whether you're an experienced climber or have never climbed but want to learn, **Snowbird Ski and Summer Resort** (⊠ 9000 Little Cottonwood Canyon Rd. ☎ 801/742–2222 or 800/385–2002) offers instruction and equipment rental with climbing on the man-made International Climbing Competition Wall on the Cliff Lodge. The fee of $10 per climb includes instruction and climbing shoes. Reservations are required.

Where to Stay & Eat

$$–$$$$ ✕ **The Aerie Restaurant, Lounge and Sushi Bar.** Spectacular panoramic views through 15-foot windows, white-linen tablecloths, and dark Oriental rugs set a romantic mood at Little Cottonwood's most elegant dining alternative on the 10th floor of the Cliff Lodge. Entrées like cardamom-cured ahi with sweet potatoes and braised greens are the fare in the restaurant, while the menu and mood are more casual at the sushi bar and lounge. ⊠ *Cliff Lodge, 10th fl., Snowbird Ski and Summer Resort, Snowbird* ☎ *801/933–2160* ▭ *AE, D, DC, MC, V* ۝ *Closed Sun. and Mon. No lunch May–Nov.*

★ $$–$$$$ ✕ **Shallow Shaft.** For fine Angus beef, wild game, seafood, poultry, and pasta dishes, Alta's only sit-down restaurant that's not part of a hotel is the place to go. The small interior is cozy and decorated in funky Southwestern style, with a sandy color scheme and walls adorned with 19th-century mining tools found on the mountain. The menu is also Southwestern, with specials like pork medallions braised in apple cider, balsamic vinegar, sun-dried cherries, and Fresno chilis. The restaurant makes its own ice cream daily. ⊠ *Rte. 210, across from Alta Lodge, Alta* ☎ *801/742–2177* ⌕ *Reservations essential* ▭ *AE, D, MC, V* ۝ *Closed May; closed Tues. and Wed. June–Nov. No lunch.*

$$–$$$$ ✕ **Steak Pit.** Views and food take precedence over interior design at Snowbird's oldest restaurant, where some of the original wait staff are still serving. The dining room is warm and unpretentious, with some wood paneling and an expanse of glass. The menu is full of well-prepared steak and seafood choices. Whether you opt for the oven-baked scallops or filet mignon, you can't go wrong. And be sure to save room for their famous mud pie. ⊠ *Snowbird Plaza Center, Rte. 210, Snowbird* ☎ *801/933–2260* ▭ *AE, D, DC, MC, V* ۝ *No lunch.*

★ $$$$ ▦ **Alta Lodge.** Built in 1939 this is the original lodge at Alta Ski Area. Wings were added later with wall-to-wall windows for excellent views. This is a homey place where many families have been booking the same week each year for several generations. Upstairs, the Sitzmark Club is a casual, quiet place for an après-ski cocktail. For price-conscientious guests, the Alta Lodge offers a bed in a dorm room for $135. The dining room is open to the public for lunch and summer Sunday brunch, but is for lodging guests only for breakfast and dinner (included in the lodging price, even for dorm room guests). ⊠ *Rte. 210, Alta, 84092* ☎ *801/742–3500 or 800/707–2582* 🖷 *801/742–3504* ⊕ *www.altalodge.com* ⫷ *57 rooms, 7 share bath* ♿ *Restaurant, 2 hot tubs, sauna, bar, laundry facilities, business services; no a/c, no room TVs* 🖃 *D, MC, V* ⏐◯⏐ *MAP.*

$$$$ 🏨 **Rustler Lodge.** Alta's fanciest lodge resembles a traditional full-service hotel. The interior is decidedly upscale; common areas have dark-wood paneling, burgundy chairs and couches, and handsome wooden backgammon tables. Guest quarters are warmly decorated with dark woods, white brick walls, and richly colored fabrics. Larger rooms have sofas and seating areas. All but three units have private baths. As at all of Alta's lodges, breakfast and dinner are included in the price. ⌂ *Box 8030, Alta 84092* ☎ *801/742–2200 or 888/532–2582* 🖷 *801/742–3832* ⊕ *www. rustlerlodge.com* ⫷ *85 rooms, 4 dorms* ♿ *Restaurant, outdoor pool, exercise equipment, indoor hot tub, steam room, spa, ski shop, bar, lobby lounge, laundry facilities; no a/c* 🖃 *AE, MC, V* ⏐◯⏐ *MAP.*

$$$–$$$$ 🏨 **Cliff Lodge.** The stark concrete walls of this 10-story structure are meant to complement the surrounding granite cliffs. Inside you'll find a self-contained village with restaurants, bars, shops, a high-end spa, and North America's foremost Oriental rug collection as decor. Every window has a scenic view, and rooms (upgraded in 2005) are decorated in hues matching the mountain landscape. Most spa-level rooms have flat-screen TVs and Tempur-Pedic beds. In addition to the two heated pools and four hot tubs, the luxurious Cliff Spa has a rooftop lap pool and 23 treatment rooms. Camp Snowbird offers summer activities for children. ⊠ *Little Cottonwood Canyon Rd., Snowbird Ski and Summer Resort, Snowbird 84092* ☎ *801/742–2222 or 800/453–3000* 🖷 *801/947–8227* ⊕ *www.snowbird.com* ⫷ *464 rooms, 47 suites* ♿ *4 restaurants, cable TV, 2 pools, health club, hair salon, spa, 6 bars, babysitting, children's programs (ages 3–12), dry cleaning, laundry facilities, laundry service, convention center, meeting room* 🖃 *AE, D, DC, MC, V.*

$$–$$$ 🏨 **Iron Blosam Lodge.** This Snowbird condominium lodging has accommodations and amenities to suit most any traveler's needs, including studios, bedrooms with lofts, and one-bedroom suites. Many have fireplaces and balconies. ⊠ *Rte. 210, Resort Entry 2, Snowbird 84092* ☎ *801/933–2222 or 800/453–3000* 🖷 *801/933–2148* ⊕ *www.snowbird. com* ⫷ *159 rooms* ♿ *Restaurant, some kitchenettes, 2 tennis courts, 2 pools, gym, hot tub, steam room, bar, laundry facilities, business services* 🖃 *AE, D, DC, MC, V* ◷ *Closed 1 wk Nov., 1 wk May.*

Nightlife & the Arts

NIGHTLIFE Almost all of the lodges in Little Cottonwood have their own bar or lounge and tend to be on the quiet side and center around the après-ski scene.

Lots of couches and a fireplace give the **Aerie Lounge** (⊠ Cliff Lodge, 10th fl., Snowbird ☎ 801/933–2222) a relaxed feel. You can hear live jazz here each Wednesday and Saturday night during ski season. Upstairs at the Alta Lodge, **The Sitzmark Club** (⊠ Alta Lodge, Alta ☎ 801/

742–3500) is a small, comfortable, retro bar that is a favorite with many of the free skiers who call Little Cottonwood home. Thick glass windows looking into the gears of the Snowbird tram give the **Tram Club** (✉ Snowbird Center, Snowbird ☎ 801/933–2222) an industrial feel. Live music most nights, pool, and video games draw a younger crowd.

THE ARTS When the snow melts, **Snowbird Ski and Summer Resort** (✉ 9000 Little Cottonwood Canyon Rd., Rte. 210, Snowbird ☎ 801/933–2110) hosts a number of events including a Jazz and Blues Festival in July, monthly Utah Symphony performances, and a murder mystery theater.

SOUTH OF SALT LAKE CITY

The Utah Valley was a busy place long before the Mormons settled here in 1851. With Utah Lake teeming with fish and game plentiful in the surrounding mountains, several bands of Native Americans lived in the area, and Spanish explorers passed through in 1775. Traders from several countries used the explorers' trail to bring goods here and to capture slaves to sell in Mexico, and fur trappers spent winter seasons in the surrounding mountains. With so many groups competing for the area's resources, conflicts were inevitable. The conflicts became more intense when Mormons settled Provo in 1851 and then began claiming land in other parts of the valley, land that had always been used by Native Americans. Several battles were fought here between Mormon settlers and Native American groups during the Walker and Black Hawk wars.

Between Salt Lake City and Provo you'll find chain motels and fast food off most of the I–80 exits. There are also a couple of great scenic and historic excursions, such as Timpanogos Cave and the Alpine Loop Scenic Byway, if you don't mind getting off the beaten path.

Timpanogos Cave National Monument

❽ *36 mi from Salt Lake City via I–15 south and Rte. 92 east.*

Soaring to 11,750 feet, Mount Timpanogos is the centerpiece of a wilderness area of the same name and towers over Timpanogos Cave National Monument along Route 92 within American Fork Canyon. After a strenuous hike up the paved 1½-mi trail to the entrance, you can explore three caves connected by two man-made tunnels. Stalactites, stalagmites, and other formations make the three-hour round-trip hike and tour worth the effort. No refreshments are available on the trail or at the cave, and the cave temperature is 45°F throughout the year, so bring water and warm clothes. Although there's some lighting inside the caves, a flashlight will make your explorations more interesting; it will also come in handy should you have to head back down the trail at dusk. These popular tours are often sold out; to guarantee your place, purchase tickets in advance. ✉ *Rte. 92, 3 mi from American Fork* ☎ *801/ 756–5239 cave information, 801/756–5238 advance tickets* ⊕ *www.nps. gov/tica* 🎫 *Tours $7* ☉ *Early May–Oct., daily 7–5:30.*

off the beaten path

ALPINE LOOP SCENIC BYWAY – Beyond Timpanogos Cave, Route 92 continues up American Fork Canyon before branching off to climb behind Mount Timpanogos itself. Designated the Alpine Loop Scenic Byway, this twisting road reveals stunning scenery before dropping into Provo Canyon to the south. The 9-mi Timpooneke Trail and the 8-mi Aspen Trail, both off the byway, reach the summit of Mount Timpanogos. Closed in winter, the Alpine Loop isn't recommended for motor homes and trucks pulling trailers. This is the roundabout way to get to scenic Provo Canyon from I–15; the more direct route is U.S. 189 east from Orem.

Lehi

9 *28 mi south of Salt Lake City via I–80.*

One of the first towns settled in the Utah Valley, Lehi is home to Thanksgiving Point, a great place for the whole family to unwind, as well as several historical museums and restored buildings.

Butch Cassidy's rifle is on display at the **John Hutchings Museum,** along with Native American and pioneer artifacts, paintings, and sculptures. You'll also find a good collection of guns and uniforms from the Revolutionary and Civil wars, as well as natural history displays of fossils, minerals, marine life, and birds. ⊠ *55 N. Center St.* ☎ *801/768–7180* ⊕ *www.hutchingsmuseum.org* ☞ *$3; free 1st Mon. 6–8* ⊗ *First Mon. 6–8; Tues.–Sat. 11–5.*

Initially purchased in 1995 by a local family as a small farm for their children, this piece of land is now home to an ever-evolving project for all visitors to enjoy. Wander through the world's largest dinosaur museum, the North American Museum of Ancient life; play golf on an 18-hole Johnny Miller–designed course; or take in a Western musical review

★ ⊙ at **Thanksgiving Point.** There are greenhouses, gardens, a hands-on barnyard animal park, two restaurants, and a movie theater. Two large gift shops sell home-decor items, jewelry, and unique children's learning toys. ⊠ *3003 N. Thanksgiving Way* ☎ *801/768–2300 or 888/672–6040* ⊕ *www.thanksgivingpoint.com* ☞ *$25 includes museum, theater, gardens, and farm; $9.50 museum only* ⊗ *Mon.–Sat. 10–8.*

Where to Eat

$–$$$$ ✕ **Porter's Place.** Belly up to the bar where the stools are made of old tractor seats, or sit down at one of the small tables and order a buffalo burger, or a 20-ounce porterhouse steak, followed by a bowl of providence pudding. The majority of entrée choices are economical. The atmosphere is friendly in a rough-around-the-edges way, just like the early Mormon purported hit man Porter Rockwell, after whom this place is named. ⊠ *24 W. Main St.* ☎ *801/768–8348* ▤ *AE, D, DC, V* ⊗ *Closed Sun.*

$–$$ ▦ **Best Western Timpanogos Inn.** Great views, convenient access, and clean updated rooms make this a good stopover. ⊠ *195 S. 850 East St., 84043* ☎ *801/768–1400 or 866/444–1218* ⊟ *801/768–1444* ⊕ *www.timpinn.com* ⚲ *57 rooms, 2 suites* ⚇ *Cable TV with movies, indoor*

pool, laundry facilities, business services, some pets allowed (fee) ▤ *AE, D, DC, MC, V* ⊘ *CP.*

¢–$ ⊞ **Lehi Historic Hotel.** Built in 1887, this hotel provided breakfast, supper, and a bed for travelers when the train made its overnight stop here. Part of the hotel was renovated in 1999, but the decor and service are still warm and friendly. ⊠ *394 W. Main St., 84043* ☎ *801/768–0307* ⇨ *11 rooms* ⚲ *Cable TV; no room phones* ▤ *MC, V* ⊘ *MAP.*

Provo

❿ *45 mi south of Salt Lake City via I–15; 14 mi south of Lehi via I–15.*

With Mount Timpanogos to the east and Utah Lake to the west, Provo and the adjacent city of Orem make up one of the prettiest communities in the West. With a combined population of 200,000, this two-city community is also one of the fastest-growing. Provo's historic downtown includes many small shops and family restaurants; in the newer sections you'll find malls, factory outlet stores, a variety of eateries, and the headquarters for several large corporations. The presence of Brigham Young University and the LDS Missionary Training Center imbue the community with a wholesome quality.

Each June, the monthlong **Freedom Festival** (☎ 801/818–1776 ⊕ www. freedomfestival.org) combines a series of patriotic activities and contests. The event peaks with a hot-air balloon festival and the state's biggest Independence Day parade. A gathering in 65,000-seat Cougar Stadium on the Brigham Young University campus closes the festival with live entertainment and an enormous fireworks display.

Provo and the entire region are probably best known as the home of **Brigham Young University.** The university was established by the Mormon church as the Brigham Young Academy in 1875, with a mandate to combine teaching about the sacred and the secular. It has grown into one of the world's largest church-affiliated universities, and still reflects the conservative nature of the Mormon Church. Students must adhere to a strict dress and honor code and refrain from alcohol, tobacco, and caffeine. BYU is known for its large variety of quality undergraduate and graduate programs, is a considerable force in regional athletics, and serves as a cultural center for the southern Wasatch area. Heading up BYU attractions is a quartet of museums. A free guided university tour is offered Monday through Friday on the hour by appointment. ⊠ *BYU visitor center, Campus Dr.* ☎ *801/422–4678* ⊕ *www.byu.edu.*

★ The permanent collection of more than 17,000 works at the **Museum of Art at Brigham Young University** includes primarily American artists such as Maynard Dixon, Dorothea Lange, Albert Bierstadt, and Robert Henri, and emphasizes the Hudson River School and the American impressionists. Utah artists are represented with works from the Mormon pioneer era to the present. Rembrandt, Monet, and Rubens also turn up, along with some fine Far Eastern pieces. The museum's café overlooks the sculpture garden. ⊠ *N. Campus Dr., southeast of Cougar Stadium* ☎ *801/422–2787* ⊕ *www.byu.edu* ▦ *Free* ☉ *Mon. and Thurs. 10–9, Tues., Wed., and Fri. 10–6, Sat. noon–5.*

Ⓒ BYU's **Monte L. Bean Life Science Museum** has extensive collections of birds, mammals, fish, reptiles, insects, plants, shells, and eggs from around the world as well as revolving nature-art exhibits. ⊠ *1430 North St., north of bell tower* ☎ *801/378–5051* ⊕ *www.byu.edu* ⊠ *Free* ⊙ *Weekdays 10–9, Sat. 10–5.*

Ⓒ The **BYU Earth Science Museum** features dinosaur bones, fossils, and tours for adults and children. Kids love the hands-on activities, which include a table of touchable artifacts. ⊠ *1683 N. Canyon Rd., across from Cougar Stadium* ☎ *801/378–3680* ⊕ *www.byu.edu* ⊠ *Free* ⊙ *Weekdays 9–5.*

The **BYU Museum of Peoples and Cultures** is an interesting student-curated collection of artifacts relating to cultures from all over the world. Clothing, pottery, rugs, weapons, and agricultural tools of Utah's Native American cultures are often on display. ⊠ *700 N. 100 East St.* ☎ *801/ 422–0020* ⊕ *www.byu.edu* ⊠ *Free* ⊙ *Weekdays 9–5.*

Re-created at **Pioneer Village and Museum** is a fort built by Mormon settlers in the mid-1800s to protect the community during conflicts with the several Native American tribes that had traditionally hunted and planted in this area. The cabins and shops have been furnished with period antiques, and costumed volunteers explain what life was like for those first settlers in the mid-19th century. ⊠ *500 W. 600 North St.* ☎ *801/ 852–6609* ⊕ *www.provo.org/parks.pioneer_main.html* ⊠ *Free* ⊙ *June–Aug., Tues. and Thurs.–Sat. noon–4.*

Ⓒ **Seven Peaks Resort Water Park** has 26 acres of waterborne fun with plenty of play areas and a wave pool. When you splash down from a waterslide or rope swing, there won't be a temperature shock because the water is heated. ⊠ *1330 E. 300 North St.* ☎ *801/373–8777* ⊕ *www.sevenpeaks.com* ⊠ *$18.50* ⊙ *Memorial Day–Labor Day, Mon.–Sat. 11–8.*

Fishing is popular at **Utah Lake State Park,** which, at 96,600 acres, is the state's largest freshwater lake. In spring and fall the lake gets some of the best wind in Utah for windsurfing and sailing. You can also come here for boating— power boats to canoes—and in winter skate at the Olympic-size ice rink. ⊠ *4400 W. Center St.* ☎ *801/375–0731 or 801/ 375–0733* ⊕ *www.stateparks.utah.gov* ⊠ *$9* ⊙ *Daily.*

off the beaten path

★

SPRINGVILLE MUSEUM OF ART – Springville, 10 mi south of Provo on I–15 or U.S. 89, is known for its support of the arts, and its museum is a must-stop for fine-arts fans. Beginning as a warehouse for works produced at the local high school, it later began to accept gifts from major artists. The present facility was built in 1937 and features mostly works by Utahns, among them Gary Lee Price, Richard Van Wagoner, and James T. Harwood. It also has a collection of Soviet working-class impressionism. ⊠ *126 E. 400 South St., Springville* ☎ *801/489–2727* ⊠ *Free* ⊙ *Tues., Thurs., Fri., and Sat. 10–5, Wed. 10–9, Sun. 3–6.*

Sports & the Outdoors

BICYCLING   In the Provo area, road cyclists may make a 100-mi circumnavigation of Utah Lake or tackle U.S. 189 through Provo Canyon or the Alpine Loop Scenic Byway. Mountain bikers can choose from a large selection of trails, varying in degrees of difficulty.

For information about biking in the area, bicycle sales, and world-class service, go to **Racer's Cycle Service** (⊠ 163 N. University Ave., Provo ☎ 801/375–5873 ⊕ www.racerscycleservice.com) and talk to owner "Racer" Jared Gibson.

GOLF   You'll find nine public courses within Utah Valley ranging from canyon or mountain settings to relatively flat and easy to walk. Tee times are usually easy to get and greens fees are reasonable.

★   The canyon setting at **Hobble Creek Golf Course** (⊠ Hobble Creek Canyon Rd. east of Springville ☎ 801/489–6297) makes for a beautiful day no matter how you play, particularly in fall when the hills explode with color. The 27 holes at the **Reserve at East Bay** (⊠ 1860 S. East Bay Blvd. ☎ 801/373–6262), near Utah Lake, give golfers a chance to meander along ponds and wetlands and to spot birds.

HIKING   Visitors to the southern part of the Wasatch find many trails from which to choose. The easy, paved **Provo Parkway** meanders along the Provo River from the mouth of Provo Canyon and provides a good mix of shade and sun. The trailhead to **Bridal Veil Falls** is 2½ mi up Provo Canyon; after the moderate climb, hikers are rewarded with a cold mountain waterfall shower. The 100-mi **Bonneville Shoreline Trail** from Brigham City to Nephi spans the foothills of the Wasatch Front following the eastern shoreline of ancient Lake Bonneville. The section near Provo begins at the Rock Creek trailhead and continues south along the foothills, past the Y trailhead, to the Hobble Creek Parkway trailhead.

ICE-SKATING   A 2002 Olympic Hockey venue, **Peaks Ice Arena** (⊠ 100 N. 7 Peaks Blvd. ☎ 801/370–0452 🖶 801/373–8711 ⊕ www.peaksarena.com 🖭 $4) includes two ice sheets and is open throughout the year for figure skating, hockey, and parties.

ROCK CLIMBING   **American Fork Canyon,** 10 mi north of Provo in the Uinta National Forest, has northern Utah's best sport climbing, with dozens of fixed routes. The steep walls also offer face, slab, and crack climbs.

WATER SPORTS   Although Utah Lake, the state's largest freshwater lake, is 11 mi wide and 24 mi long, it averages a scant 9 feet deep. Boating, sailing, windsurfing, and fishing are popular, but the cloudy water makes swimming questionable. On the east shore, **Utah Lake State Park** (⊠ 4400 W. Center St. ☎ 801/375–0731) is the best access point. In addition to three boat ramps, campgrounds, picnic areas, and a marina, the park has a wheelchair-accessible fishing area.

Where to Stay & Eat

$$–$$$$ ✗ **The Chef's Table.** Owner-Chef Kent Andersen serves freshly made pastas, meat dishes, and seafood. The macadamia nut–crusted halibut and duck in tart cherry reduction sauce are popular choices, and the large

wine list is impressive. An intimate atmosphere, and views of the Utah Valley and Wasatch Mountains through French windows, make this *the* place for a romantic meal in Orem. ☒ *2005 S. State St., Orem* ☎ *801/ 235–9111* ▤ *AE, D, DC, MC, V* ☽ *Closed Sun.*

$$ ✕ **Tucanos.** Servers in this festive Brazilian grill come to your table with skewers of shrimp, beef, poultry, pork, vegetables, and fruits and they keep coming back until you can't eat any more. The atmosphere is more conducive to a party than to quiet, intimate dining. ☒ *4801 N. University Ave.* ☎ *801/224–4774* ▤ *AE, D, MC, V* ☽ *Closed Sun.*

¢–$$ ✕ **Los Hermanos.** In an old downtown Provo building, this long-standing Utah Valley favorite serves great Mexican food in a mazelike space with separate rooms and cubby tables. Favorites are the halibut Vera Cruz, grilled with a secret blend of spices and extra-virgin olive oil, and the spicy fajitas. ☒ *16 W. Center St.* ☎ *801/375–5732* ▤ *AE, D, DC, MC, V* ☽ *Closed Sun.*

★ ¢ ✕ **Gandolfo's New York Deli.** In a basement location, just odd enough to be interesting, Gandolfo's serves a good variety of thick sandwiches like the Bronx Barbecue or Brooklyn Bridge, all named after New York City spots. Gandolfo's is now a franchise, but this location is the original. ☒ *18 N. University St.* ☎ *801/375–3354* ▤ *MC, V* ☽ *Closed Sun.*

$–$$ 🏨 **Hines Mansion Bed & Breakfast.** Much of the original woodwork, brick, and stained glass has been left intact in this 1896 mansion, originally owned by one of the wealthiest residents of Provo. The well-lit rooms are decorated with period furniture and antique household items, and have two-person Jacuzzis. A full breakfast is served in the dining room. ☒ *383 W. 100 South St., 84601* ☎ *801/374–8400 or 800/428–5636* 📠 *801/374– 0823* ⊕ *www.hinesmansion.com* ⇆ *9 rooms* ♨ *Dining room, cable TV, in-room VCRs, Wi-Fi; no smoking* ▤ *AE, D, DC, MC, V* ⋈ *BP.*

$–$$ 🏨 **Provo Marriott Hotel.** Close to downtown, this large hotel offers clean, upscale rooms and attentive service. Rooms and common areas have more sophisticated furnishings than many properties in this price range. The Seasons Lounge, one of Provo's few private clubs, is a great place to go for drinks and music. ☒ *101 W. 100 North St., 84601* ☎ *801/377–4700 or 800/777– 7144* 📠 *801/377–4708* ⊕ *www.marriott.com* ⇆ *331 rooms, 6 suites* ♨ *Restaurant, room service, cable TV, in-room data ports, Wi-Fi, 2 pools (1 indoor), gym, hot tub, sauna, bar, video game room, laundry facilities, concierge, business services, meeting rooms* ▤ *AE, D, DC, MC, V.*

★ ¢–$ 🏨 **Provo Courtyard by Marriott.** This hotel faces the Wasatch Range near BYU, so some of its rooms have mountain views. Friendly service, comfortable common areas, and touches like fresh fruit and warm cookies in the evening give this chain a personal feel. ☒ *1600 N. Freedom Blvd., 84604* ☎ *801/373–2222* 📠 *801/374–2207* ⊕ *www.marriott. com* ⇆ *94 rooms, 6 suites* ♨ *Restaurant, room service, cable TV, in-room data ports, Wi-Fi, indoor pool, gym, hot tub, lounge, laundry facilities, business services, meeting rooms* ▤ *AE, D, DC, MC, V.*

Nightlife & the Arts

NIGHTLIFE Although Provo isn't completely "dry," the standards of BYU are evident in the city's dearth of nightlife options. Local bands, DJs, and karaoke keep things hopping at **Atchafalaya** (☒ 210 W. Center St., off I–15 at the Center St. exit ☎ 801/373–9014). The **Seasons Lounge** (✉ 101 W. 100 North St. ☎ 801/377–4700), in the Provo Marriott Hotel, is a casual gathering spot. The music is generally soft, making this a good place for quiet conversation.

THE ARTS   Because **BYU** (☎ 801/378–4636) has a considerable interest in the arts, Provo is a great place to catch a play, dance performance, or musical production. BYU has a dozen performing groups in all. The BYU International Folk Dancers and Ballroom Dancers travel extensively, but also perform at home. The Deseret Chamber Music Festival takes place each May. Most performances are held in the **Harris Fine Arts Center,** which houses a concert hall, recital hall, and three theaters.

Shopping

Shopping in the Provo–Orem area centers around four primary areas. In addition to the malls, visitors find shopping opportunities at boutiques and galleries in downtown Provo, especially along Center Street.

★   The **Shops at Riverwoods** (✉ North University Ave. at the eastern extension of Orem's Center St. ☎ 801/802–8430) is home to upscale retailers like Ann Taylor, Banana Republic, Eddie Bauer, and Williams-Sonoma. On the south end of Provo, the **Towne Centre Mall** (✉ S. University Ave. ☎ 801/852–2400) has mainstream retailers like Dillard's and Sears Roebuck, and specialty shops like Hallmark and Victoria's Secret. **University Mall** (✉ 1300 S. State St., Orem ☎ 801/224–0694) caters to the needs of BYU students and departing missionaries with stores like Deseret Book and Missionary Emporium, as well as standard retailers like Nordstrom and Mervyn's.

Sundance Resort

⓫   *12 mi northeast of Provo (51 mi south of Salt Lake City), off Rte. 92.*

Fodor'sChoice
★   Sundance Resort, set on the eastern slopes of the breathtaking 11,750-foot Mount Timpanogos, came into being when Robert Redford purchased the land in 1969. In concept and practice, the 6,000-acre mountain community reflects Redford's commitment to the natural environment, outdoor exploration, and artistic expression. All resort facilities—constructed from local materials such as indigenous cedar, fir, and pine, and locally quarried stone—blend well with the natural landscape. No matter the season, you'll find plenty of recreational opportunities including hiking, biking, fly-fishing, horseback riding, alpine and cross-country skiing, snowboarding and snowshoeing. If you're looking for a more indulgent experience, relax with a body treatment in the Spa at Sundance or take one of many creative classes at the Art Center and Gallery. The Sundance Film Festival, based in nearby Park City each January, is an internationally recognized showcase for independent films. Festival screenings and workshops are held year-round at the resort. ✉ *N. Fork Provo Canyon, Sundance 84604* ☎ *801/225–4107 or 800/892–1600* 🖷 *801/223–4551* ⊕ *www.sundanceresort.com* ☞ *2150-ft vertical drop; 450 skiable acres; 20% novice, 40% intermediate, 40% advanced; 1 quad lift, 2 triple chairs, 1 surface lift* 🎟 *Lift tickets $44.*

Sports & the Outdoors

CROSS-COUNTRY SKIING
Enjoy terrain suitable for all skill levels while cross-country skiing Sundance Resort's 24 km (15 mi) of groomed trails. Ten km (6 mi) of dedicated snowshoeing trails wind through mature aspen groves and pines. Lessons and equipment rentals, including telemark gear, are available for all techniques of cross-country skiing and snowshoeing.

DOWNHILL SKIING & SNOWBOARDING
Skiers and snowboarders at Sundance Resort will find 450 acres of varied terrain. The mountain isn't big, but it does offer something for everyone and you'll almost never find a lift line here. The focus on a total experience, rather than just on skiing or snowboarding, makes this a delightful destination. Services include specialized ski workshops (including personal coaching), a PSIA-certified ski school, and a ski school just for children with programs that include all-day supervision, lunch, and ski instruction. Children younger than four may enroll in private lessons; children older than four are eligible for group lessons. Rentals are available for all skill levels.

FLY-FISHING
The Provo River, minutes from Sundance Resort, is a fly-fishing catch-and-release waterway. Access to the rainbow and German brown trout found in the river is year-round. You can purchase the required fishing license in the general store at the resort; if you opt for a tour, equipment is provided.

HIKING
Many of the hiking trails at Sundance Resort link with Uinta National Forest trails, making up a system of moderate to expert skill-level trails. Trail characteristics vary from the 1.5 mi easy Nature Trail to the Big Baldy Trail, 7.4 mi through a series of waterfalls up steep, rugged terrain. Select from three routes to summit the 11,000-foot Mount Timpanogos. Guided naturalist hikes are available.

MOUNTAIN BIKING
You'll find more than 25 mi of ski-lift accessed mountain biking trails at Sundance Resort, extending from the base of Mount Timpanogos to Arrowhead Summit at 8,250 feet. High-tech gear rentals are available for full or half days, as is individual or group instruction. **Sundance Mountain Outfitters** (☏ 801/223–4849) has answers to your mountain biking questions.

Where to Stay & Eat

★ $$$–$$$$ ✕ **Foundry Grill.** Wood-oven–baked pizzas, rotisserie rack of pork with mashed potatoes, and spit-roasted chicken are among the hearty staples served up at this restaurant. Like the rest of Sundance, everything here, from the food presentation to the decor to the staff, is natural, beautiful, and pleasant. If you're here on the weekend, don't miss Sunday brunch. ⊠ *Sundance Resort, N. Fork Provo Canyon* ☏ *801/223–4220* ▭ *AE, D, DC, MC, V.*

$$$–$$$$ FodorsChoice ★ ✕ **Tree Room.** With its rustic decor, exquisite collection of Native American art and Western memorabilia, and servers who look like they double as Sundance catalog models, the setting here is so intimate it's easy to imagine you're a personal guest of Robert Redford. Try the grilled elk short loin with black currant reduction or the braised red snapper with bell pepper, lemon, rosemary, and artichokes. Or, let executive chef

Colton Soelberg put together a tasting menu for your whole table. ⊠ *Sundance Resort, N. Fork Provo Canyon* ☎ *801/223–4200* ▤ *AE, D, DC, MC, V* ⊙ *No lunch.*

$$$–$$$$
Fodor'sChoice
★

▣ **Sundance Cottages.** All the cottages are connected by paths winding through old-growth pines, groves of aspen, and along clear mountain streams. Ranging in size from one to three bedrooms, the cottages reflect their woodland setting with rough-sawn beams, natural-wood trim, and richly textured, colorful fabrics; suites have a stone fireplace or woodstove, deck, and either full kitchen and dining area or kitchenette. There are also two- to five-bedroom mountain homes suitable for families or groups who want more space and privacy. Many rooms have large private baths, and some of the mountain homes have private hot tubs. All Sundance properties have the commercial-free Sundance Channel, showing award-winning feature films, documentaries, shorts, and international titles. ⊠ *Sundance Resort, N. Fork Provo Canyon, R.R. 3, Box A–1, 84604* ☎ *801/225–4107 or 800/892–1600* ▨ *801/ 226–1937* ⊕ *www.sundanceresort.com* ⤶ *95 units, 12 mountain homes* ⌂ *2 restaurants, some kitchens, some kitchenettes, in-room VCRs, fitness classes, spa, bar, theater, shops, babysitting, laundry service, concierge, meeting rooms; no a/c* ▤ *AE, D, DC, MC, V* �︗ *BP.*

Nightlife & the Arts

NIGHTLIFE
★

Whether you feel like a quiet midday chess game, or a more lively atmosphere at night, the **Owl Bar** (⊠ Sundance Resort, N. Fork Provo Canyon ☎ 801/225–4107) provides a good gathering space for guests and local clientele. Here you'll find live music nightly and a healthy selection of beers and spirits to accompany a limited but satisfying menu. Classic photographs of Paul Newman and Robert Redford as Butch Cassidy and the Sundance Kid hang on the walls, and with the worn plank floors, stone fireplace, and original 1890s rosewood bar (said to have been favored by Cassidy's Hole-in-the-Wall Gang) transported from Thermopolis, Wyoming, you might just feel like cutting loose.

THE ARTS

The **Sundance Art Center** (⊠ Sundance Resort, N. Fork Provo Canyon ☎ 801/225–4107 or 800/892–1600) offers workshops in photography, jewelry making, wheel-thrown pottery, watercolor painting, and charcoal or pencil drawing. The philosophy that everyone has creative talent is not lost here, and all ages are encouraged to participate. Mirroring the Sundance ethic, these classes blend the natural world with artistic process: you might begin a jewelry-making class with a jaunt to the nearby quarry for stone and mineral selection, or your photography workshop might be held on horseback or snowshoes. If you're interested in a more intensive artistic experience, inquire about three- and four-day Creative Retreats at the Artisan Center. All workshops and classes are open to resort guests as well as day visitors.

◷ The **Sundance Kids Camp** (⊠ Sundance Resort, N. Fork Provo Canyon ☎ 801/225–4107 or 800/892–1600), in operation for a couple of months in summer, offers unique adventures designed to cultivate environmental awareness as well as introduce children to the intersection of nature and art. Daily or weekly sessions are offered to children from ages 8 to 12.

In January the Sundance Institute, a nonprofit organization supporting independent filmmaking, screenwriters, playwrights, composers, and other film and theater artists, presents the **Sundance Film Festival** (☎ 801/328–3456 ⊕ www.sundance.org). A world-renowned showcase for independent film, the 10-day Festival is based in Park City, but has screenings and workshops at Sundance Resort, Salt Lake City, and Ogden.

From mid-July through August, the Utah Symphony teams with Sundance Resort for the **Sundance Concert Series** (☎ 801/355–2787 or 888/451–2787 ⊕ www.utahsymphonyopera.org), performed in a spectacular outdoor amphitheater. Performances include everything from Mozart to opera to Pops to unique-to-Sundance presentations. Lodging, preconcert dining in the Foundry Grill or Tree Room, and reserved seating packages are available. If you'd rather dine while you listen, Gourmet Baskets are also available. Concerts start at 8 PM and you should arrive 30 minutes in advance. The temperature will drop quickly after sundown, so you're encouraged to dress appropriately, in layers.

Shopping

The **General Store** (⊠ Sundance Resort, N. Fork Provo Canyon ☎ 801/223–4250) is home base for the award-winning Sundance catalog, with distinctive home furnishings, clothing, and jewelry reflecting the rustically elegant Sundance style.

Selling foods from American cottage farmers as well as homemade oils, soaps, and bath salts, the **Deli** (⊠ Sundance Resort, N. Fork Provo Canyon ☎ 801/223–4211) also has a juice bar and is a good place to get tea, coffee, shakes, pastries, deli meats, organic produce, and other tasty snacks. Stop here before your hike to pick up a fresh sandwich.

Heber Valley

⑫ *20 mi south of Park City via U.S. 40; 22 mi northeast of Sundance via Rte. 92 south and Rte. 189 east*

Bound by the Wasatch Mountains on the west and the rolling foothills of the Uinta Mountains on the east, the Heber Valley, including the towns of Heber, Midway, and Charleston, is well supplied with snow in winter for cross-country skiing, snowmobiling, and other snow sports. Summers are mostly cool and green. Events throughout the year entertain locals as well as visitors. A 60-car demolition derby is the popular kickoff for the weeklong **Wasatch County Fair** (☎ 435/654–3211) in August; a rodeo caps the action at the week's end. In September, Midway's **Swiss Days** (☎ 435/654–1271) honor the town's original Swiss settlers with entertainment and contests. More than 300 gallons of sauerkraut are consumed during the two-day event.

♻ Following a line that first ran in 1899, a train ride on the **Heber Valley Historic Railroad** takes you on a nostalgic trip through beautiful Provo Canyon. Each car has been restored, and two of the engines—Number 618 and Number 1907—are fully operational, steam-powered locomotives. The railroad offers special events, including murder mystery rides as well as the local favorite Christmas-time Polar Express ride. ⊠ *450*

CloseUp

THE FRONT & ITS FAULTS

THE GEOLOGY OF THE WASATCH *Mountains gives the Salt Lake Valley its character. Few places in the world can show off such distinct geologic features in an area as small as the 50 to 70 mi along the Wasatch Front. One section, from City Creek Canyon in the north to Bells Canyon in the south, has 10 distinct geologic zones. Each canyon has a different look, with rocks of varying ages and colors. Glaciers formed some; flowing water created others.*

The reddish rocks visible on a drive up Parley's Canyon come from the Jurassic period. Suicide Rock, at the canyon's mouth, dates from the earlier Triassic age. Lower portions of Big Cottonwood Canyon have billion-year-old Precambrian rock. To the south, Little Cottonwood Canyon has comparatively new formations: a molten igneous mass pushed its way almost to the surface a mere 32 million years ago.

Granite formed here was used to build the Mormon Temple in Salt Lake.

Tongues of the Wasatch Fault run along the front of the Wasatch Mountains. This fault is where the earth cracks as the Great Basin stretches by a couple of centimeters annually. For this to happen, the valleys from California through the Wasatch Range must fall slightly. Portions of Salt Lake Valley's Wasatch Boulevard and 1300 East Street are on fault lines. You can tell that you're near a fault when the east–west streets suddenly get steeper. Although geologists say that a quake could happen any time, the valley hasn't experienced a major one in recorded history. Where to grab some dinner should be a bigger concern than being shaken by an earthquake.

S. 600 West St., Heber ☎ 435/654–5601 ⊕ www.hebervalleyrr.org ✉ *Admission prices vary* ☉ *Tues.–Sun. 9–5.*

♨ **Wasatch Mountain State Park** (⊠ 1281 Warm Springs Rd. Midway ☎ 435/654–1791 or 800/322–3770, 435/654–0532 golf information ⊕ www.stateparks.utah.gov ✉ $5 per car at campground for day use), a 22,000-acre preserve, is 3 mi from Heber City. Visitors enjoy a number of activities ranging from serene hikes along winding mountain trails to golfing at one of the two 36-hole golf courses. Children have their own fishing pond near the visitor center, which also provides parking places. During winter, hiking turns to snowshoeing, cross-country or back-country skiing along Dutch Hollow, Snake Creek, or Pine Creek trails winding up through stands of gambel oak, aspen, and maple. Locals know the best time of year in the park is autumn when the mountainsides light up with deep crimson, ochre, and ruddy salmon-color leaves. On the south-

♨ ern end of the park is **Soldier Hollow** (⊠ 2002 Olympic Dr. Midway ☎ 435/654–2002 ⊕ www.soldierhollow.org), venue for the 2002 Winter Olympic biathlon and cross-country events. Soldier Hollow is open to the public year-round for hiking, horseback riding, cross-country skiing, tubing, snow-shoeing, biathlon, and other special events. A beautiful lodge has food concessions, equipment rentals, and a souvenir shop.

Sports & the Outdoors

CROSS-COUNTRY SKIING, SNOWSHOEING & TUBING
You can cross-country ski on the same trails as the 2002 Olympians at **Soldier Hollow** (✉ 2002 Olympic Dr., Midway ☎ 435/654–2002 ⊕ www. soldierhollow.org), which offers 31 km (19 mi) of groomed trails with cross-country ski lessons, lift-served tubing, and a dedicated trail system just for snowshoers. The **Homestead Resort** (✉ 700 N. Homestead Dr., Midway ☎ 435/654–1102 or 800/327–7220 ⊕ www. homesteadresort.com) has 12 km (7 mi) of groomed trails as well as cross-country ski and snowshoe rentals.

GOLF
The front nine at the **Homestead Resort** (✉ 700 N. Homestead Dr., Midway ☎ 435/654–1102 or 800/327–7220 ⊕ www.homesteadresort. com) gives you great views while the back nine winds through Snake Creek Canyon. With a challenging 18-hole mountain course as well as a gentler 18-hole lake course, **Wasatch Mountain State Park** (✉ 750 W. Snake Creek Rd., Midway ☎ 435/654–0532 ⊕ www.stateparks.utah. gov) is one of the most popular public courses in the state. Reflecting the Olympic Heritage of **Soldier Hollow Golf Course** (✉ 1371 W. Soldier Hollow La., Midway ☎ 435/654–7442), the names of the 18-hole courses are Gold and Silver. While on these greens, golfers enjoy the beauty of both the Heber Valley to the east and the stunning Mt. Timpanogos to the west. The Gold course is a typical mountain course with significant elevation changes; the Silver course is meadowland style with expanses of native grasslands separating the holes.

HIKING
The path connecting the towns of Heber and Midway is an easy walk with spectacular views of the Wasatch range at a distance and, up close, the Provo River. In **Wasatch Mountain State Park** (✉ 750 W. Snake Creek Rd., Midway ☎ 435/654–0532 ⊕ www.stateparks.utah.gov), hikers will find lots of foliage and wildlife on any number of trails in Dutch Hollow, Pine Canyon, and along Snake Creek. While the trail system at **Soldier Hollow** (✉ 2002 Olympic Dr., Midway ☎ 435/654–2002 ⊕ www. soldierhollow.org) is more exposed than that in the northern end of Wasatch Mountain State Park, hikers will enjoy the stunning view of the east side of Mt. Timpanogos as well as the vista of the Uinta Mountains to the east across the Heber Valley. For a quiet experience start your hike from the Rock Cliff Nature Center, tucked into tall cottonwoods at the east end of **Jordanelle State Park** (✉ Rte. 319, off U.S. 40, 10 mi north of Heber ☎ 435/783–3030 ⊕ www.stateparks.utah.gov). Hikers often report excellent wildlife viewing along this section of the upper Provo River.

HORSEBACK RIDING
Visitors can enjoy the spectacular setting of Wasatch Mountain State Park and surrounding areas on horseback year-round with **Rocky Mountain Outfitters** (✉ Box 344, Heber City ☎ 435/654–1655 ⊕ www. rockymountainoutfitters.com). Choose from a variety of ride durations and destinations: from one- to four-hour rides, from summiting the Crow's Nest—an original hunting camp of the Ute Indian tribe—to strolling through meadows to a pioneer cabin for lunch.

WATER SPORTS
Consistently good fishing, mild canyon winds, and water warmer than you'd expect are responsible for **Deer Creek State Park's** popularity with

windsurfers, sailboaters, swimmers, and those just kicking back in the mountain sunshine. ⊠ *U.S. 189, 5 mi south of Heber* ☎ *435/654–0171* ⊕ *www.stateparks.utah.gov* ⌷ *$9 day-use fee* ⊙ *Daily 6 AM–10 PM.*

Jordanelle State Park has two recreation areas on a large mountain reservoir. The Hailstone area, 10 mi north of Heber City via U.S. 40, offers tent and RV camping and day-use areas. There are also boat ramps, a children's playground, a visitor center, and a marina store where water toys (wave runners and the like) can be rented. To the east, across the reservoir on Route 32, the Rock Cliff area and facilities are near the Provo River. This is a quiet part of the park known for excellent wildlife watching, particularly along a series of elevated boardwalks winding through the aspen forest. The 50 campsites here are all walk-ins. The Rock Cliff Nature Center provides interpretation of the area's rich natural history. ⊠ *Rte. 319, off U.S. 40, 10 mi north of Heber* ☎ *435/649–9148 Hailstone, 435/783–3030 Rock Cliff* ⊕ *www.stateparks.utah.gov* ⌷ *$6 per vehicle* ⊙ *May–Sept., daily 6 AM–10 PM; Oct.–Apr., daily 8–5.*

Where to Stay & Eat

$$$–$$$$ ✕ **Simon's Restaurant.** Part of the Homestead Resort, this dining establishment overlooks the Heber Valley. The crisp linens and china place settings lend elegance. Two prix-fixe, five-course dinners are offered each evening, including such entrées as rack of lamb and salmon. Sunday brunch in the open-air patio is lovely in warm weather. Days and hours of operation vary seasonally. ⊠ *700 N. Homestead Dr., Midway* ☎ *435/654–1102* ⌔ *Reservations essential* ⊟ *AE, D, DC, MC, V.*

★ $$–$$$ ✕ **Snake Creek Grill.** In a refurbished train depot at the end of the Heber Valley Historic Railroad, Chef Barbara Hill serves comfort food with a twist. Blue cornmeal–crusted red trout, 10-spice salmon with red curry Japanese noodles, and "Belle Isle" baby back ribs with mopping sauce are local favorites. Whatever you do, leave room for dessert; the black-bottom banana cream pie is to die for. In addition to the great food, Chef Hill serves memorable ambience: during summer months the dining rooms are filled with fresh flowers from her own garden. ⊠ *650 W. 100 South St., Heber* ☎ *435/654–2133* ⌔ *Reservations essential* ⊟ *AE, MC, V* ⊙ *Closed Sun.–Tues. No lunch.*

☾ ¢ ✕ **Dairy Keen.** A welcome respite from chain fast-food, this family-**Fodor'sChoice** owned drive-in serves the best shakes and burgers for miles around. Train **★** artifacts line the walls, and an electric train draws children's attention as it passes over the booths in continuous loops around the inside perimeter of the restaurant. ⊠ *199 S. Main St., Heber* ☎ *435/654–5336* ⊟ *AE, MC, V* ⊙ *Closed Sun.*

★ $–$$$ ▦ **Johnson Mill Bed & Breakfast.** The waterfall that turned giant grinding stones in the 1800s still flows beside the old mill, which has been renovated as a cozy inn. Implements used at the mill decorate guest rooms and the dining room, where a full breakfast is served. All rooms have fireplaces and jetted tubs. The 26-acre grounds with pathways past ponds and streams offer excellent bird-watching. ⊠ *100 Johnson Mill Rd., Midway 84049* ☎ *435/654–4466 or 888/272–0030* ⊟ *435/657–1454* ⊕ *www.johnsonmill.com* ⇝ *9 rooms* ⌥ *Microwaves, refrigerators, cable TV, in-room VCRs, pond, boating, fishing, recreation room, meeting rooms; no smoking* ⊟ *AE, D, MC, V* ⏌⬤⏌ *BP.*

$–$$$ ⊞ **The Sundowner Inn Bed & Breakfast.** Private decks and fireplaces create a sense of intimacy in the rooms while high windows and a grand staircase make the common areas light and airy in this colonial-style bed-and-breakfast inn. The well-manicured grounds are a good place to unwind with lawn games or a stroll through floral gardens. Choose your own made-to-order preferences from the country custom breakfast menu. ⊠ *425 Moulton La., Heber 84032* ☎ *435/654–4200 or 866/455–4200* 🖷 *435/654–9646* ⊕ *www.thesundownerinn.com* ↝ *5 rooms, 2 suites* ⌂ *Cable TV, in-room VCRs, in-room data ports, tennis court, hot tub, laundry facilities, some pets allowed; no smoking* ▤ *AE, D, MC, V* �∣*BP.*

★ **$–$$** ⊞ **Homestead Resort.** Park City silver miners soaked in the hot springs of this resort, which has been in operation since 1886, and you can, too. Garden walkways lead between cottages and main buildings at this sprawling country retreat. Rooms and common areas are decorated in traditional period furnishings. ⊠ *700 N. Homestead Dr., Box 99, Midway 84049* ☎ *435/654–1102 or 800/327–7220* 🖷 *435/654–5087* ⊕ *www. homesteadresort.com* ↝ *147 rooms* ⌂ *2 restaurants, cable TV, some in-room VCRs, Wi-Fi, in-room data ports, 18-hole golf course, 2 tennis courts, 2 pools (1 indoor), gym, hot tub, sauna, horseback riding, cross-country skiing, snowmobiling, bar, lounge, recreation room, laundry service, business services, meeting rooms, no-smoking rooms* ▤ *AE, D, DC, MC, V.*

PARK CITY & ENVIRONS A TO Z

To research prices, get advice from other travelers, and book travel arrangements, visit www.fodors.com.

AIR TRAVEL

All commercial air traffic flies in and out of the Salt Lake International Airport, which is less than an hour from all destinations in the Wasatch and 7 mi northwest of downtown Salt Lake City. The airport is served by American, America West, Continental, Delta, Northwest, Southwest, JetBlue, Frontier, Skywest, TWA, and United. Provo and Heber have airports open to private planes only.

🛪 **Salt Lake City International Airport** ☎ 801/575–2400.

BUS TRAVEL

Greyhound Lines serves Provo. The Utah Transit Authority (UTA) has frequent service to all of Salt Lake Valley, Davis and Weber counties, and Utah Valley. UTA buses with ski racks make several runs a day from Salt Lake to ski areas in Little and Big Cottonwood canyons and from Provo to Sundance. UTA bus service from Salt Lake City to the ski resorts of Solitude, Brighton, Snowbird, or Alta, and from Provo to Sundance costs $2.75 each way; most other bus routes cost $1.40 per ride. In addition, several taxi and shuttle companies provide transportation between Salt Lake City and the ski resorts for about $65 round-trip. A free, efficient Park City shuttle bus will take you between all the area resorts and hotels.

🛪 **Bus Information All Resort Express** ☎435/649–3999 or 800/457–9547 ⊕www.allresort. com. **Canyon Transportation** ☎ 801/255–1841 or 800/255–1841 ⊕ www.canyontransport.

com. **Greyhound Lines** ☎ 801/355-9579 or 800/231-2222 ⊕ www.greyhound.com. **Lewis Bros. Stages** ☎ 801/359-8677 or 800/359-8677 ⊕ www.lewisbros.com. **Park City Transportation** ☎ 435/649-8567 or 800/637-3803 ⊕ www.parkcitytransportation.com. **UTA** ☎ 801/743-3882 or 888/743-3882 ⊕ www.rideuta.com.

CAR RENTAL

Most major car rental agencies have branches at the Salt Lake International Airport. Car rentals are also available in Provo and Park City. 🚗 **All Resort Car Rental** ☎ 435/649-3999 or 800/457-9457 ⊕ www.allresort.com. **Avis** ☎ 800/331-1212 ⊕ www.avis.com. **Dollar** ☎ 801/575-2580 or 800/800-4000 ⊕ www. dollar.com. **Enterprise** ☎ 801/537-7433 or 800/736-8322 ⊕ www.enterprise.com. **Hertz** ☎ 801/596-2670 or 800/654-7544 ⊕ www.hertz.com.

CAR TRAVEL

Highway travel around the region is quick and easy. The major routes in the area include I–80, which runs from Salt Lake City to Park City; and U.S. 40/189, which connects Park City to Heber City and Provo. Along larger highways, roadside stops with rest rooms, fast-food restaurants, and sundries stores are well spaced. Scenic routes and lookout points are clearly marked, enabling you to slow down and pull over to take in the views. Off the main highways, roads range from well-paved multilane blacktop routes to barely graveled backcountry trails. Watch out for wildlife on the highways. In rural and resort towns, expect gas prices to be considerably higher than in large cities. 🚗 Road Conditions **Utah Highway Patrol, Mirror Lake area** ☎ 435/655-3445. **Utah Road Condition Information** ☎ 511 Salt Lake City area, 800/492-2400 within Utah.

EMERGENCIES

🚗 Ambulance or Police **Emergencies** ☎ 911.
🚗 Hospitals **Heber Valley Medical Center** ✉ 1485 S. Hwy. 40, Heber City ☎ 435/654-2500. **Park City Family Health and Urgent Care Center** ✉ 1665 Bonanza Dr., Park City ☎ 435/649-7640. **Utah Valley Regional Medical Center** ✉ 1034 N. 500 West St., Provo ☎ 801/373-7850.

WHERE TO STAY

CAMPING There are a number of wonderful campgrounds across the Wasatch–Cache National Forest. Between Big and Little Cottonwood canyons there are four higher-elevation sites. In the vicinity of Provo, American Fork, Provo Canyon, and the Hobble Creek drainage there are dozens of possibilities. Additional campgrounds are at the region's state parks and national monuments.

Sites range from rustic (pit toilets and cold running water) to posh (hot showers, swimming pools, paved trailer pads, full hookups). Fees vary, from $6 to $10 a night for tents and up to $25 for RVs, but are usually waived once the water is turned off for the winter. Site reservations are accepted at most campgrounds, but are usually limited to seven days (early birds reserve up to a year in advance). Campers who prefer a more remote setting may camp in the backcountry. You might need a permit, which is available from park visitor centers and ranger stations. 🚗 **U.S. Forest Service** ☎ 877/444-6777 reservations ⊕ www.reserveusa.com. **Utah State Parks** ☎ 800/322-3770 reservations ⊕ www.stateparks.utah.gov.

VISITOR INFORMATION

Alta Resort Association (⌂ Box 8031, Alta 84092 ☎ 888/782–9258 ⊕ www.altaresortassociation.com). **Heber Valley County Chamber of Commerce** (✉ 475 N. Main St., Heber 84032 ☎ 435/654–3666 ⊕ www. hebervalleycc.org). **Mountainland Association of Governments** (✉ 586 E. 800 North St., Orem 84097 ☎ 801/229–3800 ⊕ www.mountainland. org/travel). **Park City Chamber of Commerce–Convention and Visitors Bureau** (⌂ Box 1630, Park City 84060 ☎ 435/649–6100 or 800/453–1360 ⊕ www.parkcityinfo.com). **Ski Utah** (✉ 150 W. 500 South St., Salt Lake City 84101 ☎ 801/534–1779 or 800/754–8824 ⊕ www. skiutah.com). **Utah County Convention and Visitors Bureau** (✉ 111 S. University Ave., Provo 84601 ☎ 801/851–2100 or 800/222–8824 ⊕ www.utahvalley.org/cvb).

North of Salt Lake City

3

WORD OF MOUTH

"Drive up to Bear Lake. It's a beautiful large lake on the Idaho/Utah border and down in a canyon . . . They grow raspberries there and after seeing thousands of billboards about raspberry shakes you'll have to have one."

—Connie

"Check out the Golden Spike Historic Site north of SLC. See what time they do the re-enactment to see the two trains in action. Very close by is the Thiokol rocket fuel plant. They have a display of rockets that you can visit in the parking lot. Especially interesting are the cross section of the shuttle booster and also a full scale model of the booster."

—bigtyke

WHEN MOST PEOPLE THINK OF UTAH, they picture the red rock crags and canyons of the south, but the north, with its cattail marshes and pasturelands framed by the grey cliffs of the Wellsville Mountains and the Bear River Range, has its own kind of beauty—without the throngs of tourists you'll encounter in the south.

Here the Shoshones (Sacagawea's tribe) made their summer camps, living on roots, berries, and the plentiful game of the lowlands. In the 1820s and '30s, mountain men came to trap beaver, fox, and muskrat, taking time out for their annual rendezvous on the shores of Bear Lake. Some, like the famous Jim Bridger, took Indian wives and settled here; to this day Cache, Rich, and Box Elder counties are collectively known as "Bridgerland." In the 1850s Mormon pioneers were sent by Brigham Young to settle here, and their descendants still populate this rugged land. In 1869 an event occurred here that would change the face of the West, and indeed the nation, forever: the Transcontinental Railroad was celebrated officially at Promontory Summit.

The region is characterized by alternating mountain ranges and valleys, typical of the Basin and Range geologic province that extends westward into Nevada and California. Much of the landscape has remained unspoiled, preserved for 100 years as part of the Wasatch-Cache National Forest. All four counties in this region—Weber, Cache, Rich, and Box Elder—offer outdoor activities of all types for all seasons: hiking, mountain biking, skiing, snowmobiling, and birding are popular activities among the locals. The miles of trails here are relatively undiscovered by tourists, who usually head to southern Utah or the Wasatch Mountains east of Salt Lake for such activities. The largest city north of Salt Lake City is Ogden, with more than 75,000 residents. In large part the draw to live here is lifestyle; Ogden offers many and diverse cultural and recreational activities and a good balance of urban life mixed with rural flavor. Farther north and roughly half the size of Ogden is the beautiful town of Logan, home to Utah State University and the Utah Festival Opera. Still, in the north of Utah as in the south, it's the landscape that steals the show. If you love a stroll through the backcountry, having breakfast with the locals at a small-town café, or exploring the legacy of the Old West, northern Utah may have a particularly strong appeal for you.

Exploring Northern Utah

Via two mountain ranges, Mother Nature has neatly divided northern Utah into three major sightseeing areas, each with its own attractions. Heading north up I–15 from Ogden (or, if you're in no hurry, up U.S. 89, where you'll find plenty of farm stands), you'll come upon the Golden Spike Empire. Pleasant farmlands in the shadow of the Wellsvilles give way to rolling sagebrush-covered hills and eventually the desolate salt flats of the Great Salt Lake. After a visit to the Bear River Migratory Bird Refuge and the Golden Spike National Historic Site, cut east through the Wellsvilles to Logan and the Cache Valley, soaking up the rural scenery along the way. You'll want to devote a day or two to the thriving college town of Logan, including a visit to the campus of Utah

State University where you'll find a student-run anthropology museum that will give you a feel for the area's earliest inhabitants, and a stop at the Daughters of Utah Pioneers Museum downtown. About an hour up winding U.S. 89 through spectacular Logan Canyon—a destination in itself—you'll get your first view of startlingly turquoise-color Bear Lake, where the mountain men used to rendezvous. Carefully descend the hairpin curves into the Bear Lake Valley, and plop yourself down for a raspberry shake at one of the local drive-ins as you ponder your next activity—most likely swimming, boating, or fishing the lake's cool waters, or perhaps biking its shoreline. From here, it's just a few hours— about 300 mi—to the Grand Tetons and Yellowstone National Park—but that's another guidebook. If you head back toward Salt Lake City, take at least a couple of hours to recharge yourself at Crystal Hot Springs at Honeyville.

About the Restaurants

A few fine restaurants are emerging around Logan, but in general, the fare in northern Utah is your basic Western-style grub. If your idea of a nice meal out is a big slab of meat that was on the hoof a few days ago and a giant Idaho potato, then you're in luck. If you can't look at another steak, there's at least one Mexican or Chinese place in every sizeable town, and most of them are pretty decent. Do sample the Aggie ice cream made at Utah State University and the Cache Valley Swiss cheese.

About the Hotels

Some reputable chains have made their way here, along with interesting family-owned hostelries and B&Bs in a full range of prices. At Bear Lake, you can rent a condo with kitchen facilities if you feel like putting down roots for a while. Reservations are recommended on summer weekends and holidays; otherwise, you should have no problem exploring your options once you get here.

WHAT IT COSTS				
$$$$	**$$$**	**$$**	**$**	**¢**
RESTAURANTS over $25	$19–$25	$13–$18	$8–$12	under $8
HOTELS over $200	$151–$200	$111–$150	$70–$110	under $70

Restaurant prices are for a main course at dinner, excluding sales tax of 6%–7%. Hotel prices are for two people in a standard double room in high season, excluding service charges and 6%–7% tax.

Timing

Unless you're an avid cross-country skier, snowshoer, or snowmobiler (in which case you'll find a frozen paradise of trails), you'll probably want to avoid northern Utah in winter, when the mercury can dip below zero for weeks at a time. The other three seasons are beautiful here: spring brings vistas of verdant pastures under the still snow-capped mountains; hot summer afternoons prepare you for a dip in Bear Lake followed by an evening at the Festival Opera; on crisp fall days breathtaking hues of red scrub oak, orange maple, and bright yellow aspen rub shoulders

Numbers in the text correspond to numbers in the margin and on the Northern Utah and Logan maps.

If you have
3 days

Make a quick tour of the attractions in **Ogden** ❶ ⌐ on the morning of Day 1 and then drive north on I–15 to Perry for lunch at the Maddox Ranch House. After lunch head west on Route 83 to **Golden Spike National Historic Site** ❹. When you've had your fill of railroad history, get back on Route 83 heading east and make your way to Honeyville for a cleanse at **Crystal Hot Springs.** Head back north to ▣ **Logan** ❺–❾, where you'll settle for the night. Day 2 finds you poking around the attractions in town or on the Utah State University campus, after which you'll pack a lunch for a leisurely drive up Logan Canyon to ▣ **Bear Lake State Park** ❿; get a motel or find a campsite and spend the next day boating, swimming, or lounging on Rendezvous Beach. If it's wintertime, three days is enough time to get a good sense of skiing in northern Utah. You have a day for each: Wolf Mountain, Powder Mountain, and Snowbasin. And if you find you have more than three days, just revisit your favorite resort and/or then drive up to Beaver Mountain Ski Resort for a taste of what skiing was like before it became a rich man's sport, or make a trip to Crystal Hot Springs to soak those tired muscles.

If you have
5 days

If you have five days in the area, you could skip Ogden and get to the really good stuff. Travel north from Ogden on I–15, exit onto U.S. 89 north and cruise the fruit stands for seasonal delicacies. Enjoy a buffalo steak at Maddox Ranch House on your way to relaxation at **Crystal Hot Springs** before settling in for a laid-back night in ▣ **Brigham City** ❸. Spend Day 2 exploring the **Bear River Migratory Game Bird Refuge** and the **Golden Spike National Historic Site** ❹; be sure to pack your lunch because food isn't available here. On Day 3 head northeast to ▣ **Logan** ❺–❾, to check out the sites and take in some museums and the **Stokes Nature Center.** Reserve most of Day 4 for the **American West Heritage Center,** southeast of Logan. After exploring the living history, you can cool off with a soda at the Bluebird's famous ice-cream counter, about the same vintage as the historic farm at the Heritage Center, before visiting the town's own historical attractions. Wake up early on Day 5 for a morning drive through Logan Canyon to **Bear Lake State Park** ❿, where you'll spend your final day in northern Utah picking your way along scenic hiking trails and picturesque beaches.

If you have
7 days

A week is enough time to see the sights and still have time to hang out and enjoy the trip back in time that is northern Utah. Follow the above five-day itinerary, but add a day or two for hikes in the **Upper Ogden Valley** ❷ or Logan Canyon, a visit to **Hardware Ranch** (in winter), a bike trip around **Bear Lake State Park** ❿ (in summer or fall), or a visit to one of the harvest festivals that always seem to be going on in fall. Browse the local newspapers for plays, concerts, or an interesting exhibit or lecture taking place at **Utah State University.** If you're interested in genealogy, you can easily while away a day researching your family tree in the excellent genealogical center in the basement of the **Logan Tabernacle.** No matter what your schedule, it's not a bad idea to try to make a show at the **Peery Egyptian Theater** in Ogden; the lineup is top-notch and the venue itself is always worth a visit.

with the blue-green firs. You'll never battle hordes of tourists in this less-discovered part of the state, but you might have to wait in a line of locals for a raspberry shake at Bear Lake on a hot summer weekend.

Ogden

▶ **❶** *35 mi from Salt Lake City via I–15 north.*

As the Wasatch Front population continues to swell, it's harder to tell where Salt Lake City ends and the next major city, Ogden, begins. In between are a string of towns that serve primarily as bedroom communities. The drive north, through and beyond these communities, bordered by the shores of the Great Salt Lake on the west and the Wasatch Mountains on the east, takes you through a world of recreational options. With a population of more than 75,000, Ogden combines a small-town feel with the infrastructure of a larger city. The oldest town in Utah, Ogden was founded by mountain man Miles Goodyear, who settled here with his family in the early 1840s. The Mormons arrived in the area in 1847 and in 1869 Ogden became a hub for the Transcontinental Railroad. The city quickly became a major Western crossroads. During World War II there was a considerable military presence here. This continues today, thanks to the proximity of Hill Air Force Base. Ogden is also a college town; Weber State University is within the city limits.

During the railroad heyday, 25th Street, directly east of the railroad depot, was infamous for its bars and bordellos. These days Ogden's city managers have moved forward by stepping back in time, turning 25th Street into a shopping, dining, and nightlife district. The buildings that once contained all the notorious businesses have been preserved and now house restaurants, clubs, crafts and antiques shops, and kitchen stores.

On the first Saturday after Memorial Day, **A Taste of Ogden** (☎ 801/479–6503 🖃 Free) presents Japanese, Greek, Tongan, and Thai food, among other cuisines, in a festival held at the amphitheater on the Ogden Municipal Building grounds. Diverse entertainment includes Thai, Native American, and Middle Eastern dancers, polka bands, Latin musicians, and African-American storytellers.

Incorporating elements of Ogden's original 1870s train depot, which was destroyed by fire in 1923, the impressive Spanish Revival **Union Station** (built in the early 1900s) houses five museums, an art gallery, restaurant, gift shop, and visitor center.

Fodor'sChoice ★

The **Browning Firearms Museum** showcases John M. Browning's gun inventions, many of which were built by Winchester, Colt, Remington, and others to become the firearms of choice in the Old West before Browning formed his own company. Original models and working prototypes of many of these weapons are displayed. Gun aficionados will feel like they're in a candy store.

At the **Browning-Kimball Car Museum,** almost 60 unique, restored cars are on display, including a single-cylinder 1901 Oldsmobile and a Cadillac that weighs 3 tons.

3

Small-Town Life

"Welcome to Utah; set your clocks back 50 years," the local kids say with a smirk, but in fact this is one of the charms of living here. With its friendly folk, low crime rate, and traditions dating back to the pioneers, Utah offers a glimpse of what the rest of the country was like during the Eisenhower years. Nowhere is this more evident than in the north, unjaded as it is by either the tourist throngs of the south or the big-city problems that are starting to plague Ogden and Salt Lake. Although there is plenty to see and do on the tourist beat, you'll enjoy your stay even more if you mingle with the natives at a Blue Sox baseball game, a Lions Club pancake breakfast, or one of the myriad town festivals that dot the calendar throughout the summer and fall, from Mendon's May Day to Paradise's Trout and Berry Days. Check the local newspapers and do a little time-traveling while you're here.

Viewing Wildlife

If you're willing to get out of your car and walk a bit, your chances of encountering wildlife in northern Utah are about 100%. Even from your car you're likely to spot mule deer, moose, elk, coyotes, or bobcats, especially around dawn or dusk (so drive vigilantly, especially in the mountains—many a visitor's trip has been ruined by a collision with an animal). Because of the varied topography—everything from marshes to deserts to mountains—northern Utah has an astounding variety of bird life, and birders come from all over the country to fill out their life lists. To learn about northern Utah wildlife, plan a visit to the Stokes Nature Center in Logan.

Learn about the Great Salt Lake and surrounding areas at the **Natural History Museum,** which displays a collection of Utah trilobites, fossilized wood and plants, and records of dinosaur and aquatic life forms.

The **Utah State Railroad Museum** has well-documented exhibits that explain all phases of Utah's railroad history through displays and interpretive signs. The high point of the museum is an outdoor exhibit of several dozen restored train cars, engines, and cabooses that date from the late 1800s to the mid-1900s.

Watch model trains run through depictions of famous features of the transcontinental railroad route at the **Wattis-Dumke Railroad Exhibit.** ⊠ *2501 Wall Ave.* ☎ *801/629–8444* ⊕ *www.theunionstation.org* ⊠ *Combined ticket to all 5 museums $5* ⊗ *Mon.–Sat. 10–5.*

★ In an impressive Victorian mansion, the **Eccles Community Art Center** has a permanent collection of works by such contemporary artists as LeConte Stewart, Henri Mosher, Pilar Pobil, David Jackson, and Richard Van Wagoner. There is also a sculpture garden; special exhibits change periodically, and there are monthly displays of works by emerging Utah artists. ⊠ *2580 Jefferson Ave.* ☎ *801/392–6935* ⊕ *www.ogden4arts. org* ⊠ *Free* ⊗ *Weekdays 9–5, Sat. 9–3.*

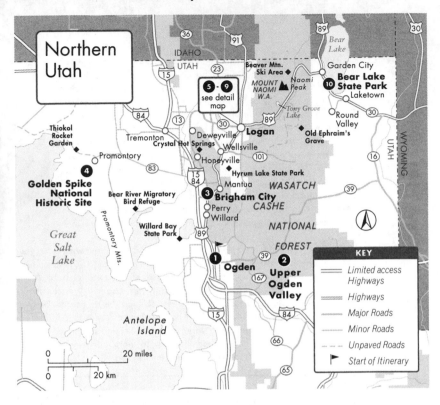

Northern Utah

KEY

═══	Limited access Highways
═══	Highways
━━━	Major Roads
────	Minor Roads
-----	Unpaved Roads
▶	Start of Itinerary

The Wasatch Mountains tower over **Weber State University** on the east side of the Ogden Valley. The university began as the Weber Academy in 1889 and is now a central part of the community, with a planetarium, an art gallery, and a museum of natural history. The **indoor ice sheet** (✉ 4390 Harrison Blvd. ☎ 801/399–8750) hosted the 2002 Olympic curling events and offers open skating daily. ✉ *3850 University Circle* ☎ *801/626–6000* ⊕ *www.weber.edu.*

🖑 The 5-acre **George S. Eccles Dinosaur Park,** near the mouth of Ogden Canyon, is the stomping grounds for about 100 dinosaur models and the delighted children who come to see them. But be prepared for realism in the form of the bloody teeth of a tyrannosaurus and the remains of its dinner on the ground. A playground with dinosaurs to crawl on is a lure for children. ✉ *1544 E. Park Blvd.* ☎ *801/393–3466* ⊕ *www. dinosaurpark.org* 🎫 *$6* ⊗ *Mon.–Sat. 10–6, Sun. noon–6.*

★ 🖑 If you like airplanes old or new you'll love the **Hill Aerospace Museum,** south of downtown Ogden near the Hill Air Force Base. Among the many planes housed here is a SR-71 Blackbird (a reconnaissance aircraft that made a transatlantic flight in less than two hours), a B-17 Flying Fortress, and a P-51 Mustang. ✉ *Hill Air Force Base, Exit 341 off I–15* ☎ *801/ 777–6868* ⊕ *www.hill.af.mil/museum* 🎫 *Free* ⊗ *Daily 9–4:30.*

Highlighting a chapter in history that unfolded decades prior to the railroad era, **Fort Buenaventura Park** is a 32-acre tract with replicas of the stockade and cabins that Miles Goodyear built in 1846. Guides in period costume interpret the ways of the early trappers. Camping and picnicking facilities are available. ✉ *2450 A Ave.* ☎ *801/399–8099* ⊕ *www. utah.com/stateparks/buenaventura.htm* ✉ *$4* ⊗ *Apr.–Nov.*

As one of very few wildlife sanctuaries set within a city, the 152-acre **Ogden Nature Center** is home to thousands of trees, marshlands, and ponds, with nature trails used for cross-country skiing in winter. You can see Canadian geese, great blue herons, red-tailed hawks, and snowy egrets, as well as red foxes, mule deer, porcupines, and more. The nature center museum has activities for children and the Nest gift shop sells nature-oriented items. ✉ *966 W. 12th St.* ☎ *801/621–7595* ⊕ *www. ogdennaturecenter.org* ✉ *$3* ⊗ *Weekdays 9–5, Sat. 10–4.*

In downtown Ogden the **Ogden River Parkway** runs for 3 mi to the mouth of Ogden Canyon. This urban greenway is perfect for fishing, biking, strolling, running, or playing tennis or baseball. The trail takes you past botanical gardens, pavilion facilities, a swimming pool, a skateboard park, the Eccles Dinosaur Park, and rodeo grounds. ✉ *1544 E. Park Blvd.* ✉ *Free.*

Sports & the Outdoors

More than 250 mi of trails for hiking, mountain biking, and horseback riding surround the Ogden area, and the scenic roads are perfect for road biking. The Weber and Ogden rivers provide high-adventure rafting and kayaking and even a free downtown white-water park. Eleven public courses await golfers, and Olympic-calibre skiing is just up the canyon.

GOLF The 18-hole **Ben Lomond Golf Course** (✉ 1800 N. Rte. 89, Harrisville ☎ 801/782–7754) has a serene setting with Wasatch Mountain views. While playing 18 holes at the **Mount Ogden Golf Course** (✉ 1787 Constitution Way ☎ 801/629–0699), try not to let the stunning view of Ogden Valley distract you. Just minutes from downtown Ogden, the 18 holes of the **Schneiter's Riverside Golf Course** (✉ 5460 S. Weber Dr. ☎ 801/ 399–4636) wind along the scenic Ogden River. For complete information about Ogden area golf courses, contact the **Ogden Convention Visitors Bureau** (☎ 866/867–8824 ⊕ www.ogdencvb.org).

HIKING From an urban stroll along the Ogden River Parkway to a challenging hike on the Bues Canyon Trail to the summit of Mount Ogden, hikes in the Ogden area provide something for everyone. Most of the trail system is connected in some way to the North–South Bonneville Shoreline Trail, a pathway following the high mark of the prehistoric Lake Bonneville along the Wasatch Front. An excellent resource for detailed trails information is **Weber Pathways** (☎ 801/393–2304 ⊕ www. weberpathways.org), a local nonprofit organization dedicated to preserving and maintaining nonmotorized pathways in Weber County.

RAFTING Located on the Weber River at Exchange Road and 24th Street, **Ogden's Kayak Rodeo Park** (⊕ www.ogdencvb.org/kayak.html ✉ Free) is a work in progress but offers great rides for kayakers and thrilling action for spectators. For a white-water adventure the whole family can enjoy, try rafting the Weber River on a tour with **Park City Rafting** (✉ 1105 N. Taggert La., Morgan ☎ 435/655–3800 ⊕ www.parkcityrafting.com). The relatively gentle two-hour trip is a great way to experience a rugged canyon, and there are several mild rapids (Class II–III) for excitement. All equipment is provided.

Where to Stay & Eat

$$–$$$$ ✕ **Gray Cliff Lodge Restaurant.** Set in scenic Ogden Canyon, this local favorite features Utah trout, prime rib, lamb, and seafood. Lace tablecloths, linen napkins, and a wall of windows offering views of mountains and forests create a quiet, romantic atmosphere. ✉ *508 Ogden Canyon* ☎ *801/392–6775* ⊕ *www.grayclifflodge.com* ▭ *AE, D, DC, MC, V.*

$–$$$$ ✕ **Prairie Schooner.** Desert sand covers the floor, and each table is enclosed in a covered wagon at this Western-style steak house. Although the setting may be a bit much for some, the steak and seafood specialties are top quality. The French dip and other sandwiches give the menu a lighter side. ✉ *445 Park Blvd.* ☎ *801/621–5511* ⊕ *www. prairieschoonerrestaurant.com* ▭ *AE, D, MC, V* ☻ *No lunch weekends.*

★ $–$$$ ✕ **Bistro 258.** The decor in this 25th Street hot spot wouldn't be out of place in Manhattan, though the attitude is decidedly laid-back. Owners Todd Ferrario and Michael Attento design and prepare upscale fare such as orange chili chicken, pan-seared tilapia, and pepper-seared filet mignon. For lunch try the curry chicken rice bowl or the creamy pesto tortellini. The outdoor patio and glassed-in back dining area are more casual than the front section accessed from 25th Street. Servers are friendly and offer smart suggestions from the brief but well-appointed wine list. ✉ *258 25th St.* ☎ *801/394–1595* ⊕ *www.bistro258.com* ▭ *AE, D, MC, V* ☻ *Closed Sun.*

★ $–$$$ ✕ **Rooster's.** On historic 25th Street, this brewpub is set in a 104-year-old building that was once a Chinese laundry. The pub offers excellent food and libations brewed on site. Pizzas, steak, and daily seafood specials are popular, as is the herb-crusted rack of lamb. Wash down your meal with a Polygamy Pale Ale or any of the brewmaster's specials, which vary by season. On a sunny day ask for a seat on the patio, which is partly glass-enclosed for year-round seating and makes for a lovely spot to enjoy Sunday brunch. ✉ *253 25th St.* ☎ *801/627–6171* ▭ *AE, D, DC, MC, V.*

$–$$$ ✕ **Union Grill.** Overlooking the train tracks, this is a great refueling spot when you're museum hopping at historic Union Station. The menu ranges from mozzarella sandwiches to steak; the service is friendly and casual if occasionally rushed. Save room for the caramel bread pudding. ✉ *2501 Wall Ave.* ☎ *801/621–2830* ▭ *AE, D, DC, MC, V* ☻ *Closed Sun.*

$–$$ ✕ **La Ferrovia Ristorante.** Owner Giuseppina Ashbridge brought her recipes with her when she left Naples. She and her husband Jeff serve authentic dishes with genuine Italian hospitality in this homey eatery. You can't go wrong with daily pasta specials. Pizza and calzones round out the menu and a well-chosen list of mostly Italian wines complements the food. ✉ *234 25th St.* ☎ *801/394–8628* ▭ *AE, D, DC, MC, V* ☻ *Closed Sun. and Mon.*

⚙ ¢–$ ✕ **The Greenery.** It's hard to tell if this green- and white-tile riverside restaurant is deliberately kitschy or trying to be one version of authentic Utah, but if a Mormon muffin, ham-it up sandwich, or homemade caramel apple pie suit your fancy, this is the place. After lunch or dinner browse the thousands of square feet of trinkets, souvenirs, and books at Rainbow Gardens next door for just the right piece of Utah to take with you. ✉ *1875 Valley Dr.* ☎ *801/392–1777* ⊟ *AE, D, MC, V.*

$–$$ ⌂ **Ogden Marriott.** Ogden's largest hotel downtown is close to government offices and corporate headquarters for the aerospace industry. It's also within walking distance of historic 25th Street shopping, dining, and nightlife. Relax in one of the spacious rooms, elegantly appointed with mahogany furniture and rich, classic fabrics in complementing florals and stripes. ✉ *247 24th St., 84401* ☎ *801/627–1190 or 800/421–7599* 🖶 *801/394–6312* ⊕ *www.ogdenmarriott.com* ⇔ *292 rooms, 5 suites* ⌂ *Restaurant, cable TV, Wi-Fi, in-room data ports, indoor pool, health club, hot tub, lounge, laundry facilities, concierge, business services, meeting rooms* ⊟ *AE, D, DC, MC, V.*

$ ⌂ **Comfort Suites of Ogden.** Decorated with a Southwestern motif, this is Ogden's only all-suites hotel. Built in 1995, clean well-maintained suites, easy freeway access, and a more-than-adequate list of amenities and services make this a good choice for business or vacation travelers. In warm weather you can unwind playing volleyball or basketball at the outdoor sports court. ✉ *2250 S. 1200 West St., 84401* ☎ *801/621–2545 or 800/462–9925* 🖶 *801/627–4782* ⊕ *www.ogdencomfortsuites.com* ⇔ *142 suites* ⌂ *Restaurant, microwaves, refrigerators, cable TV, Wi-Fi, indoor pool, gym, hot tub, lounge, video game room, playground, dry cleaning, laundry facilities, business services, meeting rooms, some pets allowed* ⊟ *AE, D, DC, MC, V* ¶⊙¶ *BP.*

★ $ ⌂ **Hampton Inn and Suites** Gray marble floors, deep-purple chairs, and ornate crown-molded ceilings greet you in the lobby of this art deco beauty. Designed in the Chicago style by architect Leslie S. Hodgson and completed in 1913 as an office center, the building sat vacant for years before it was restored and opened as a hotel in 2002. ✉ *2401 Washington Blvd., 84401* ☎ *801/394–9400 or 866/394–9400* 🖶 *801/394–9500* ⊕ *www.ogdensuites.hamptoninn.com* ⇔ *124 rooms, 21 suites* ⌂ *Cable TV, in-room data ports, gym, dry cleaning, laundry service* ⊟ *AE, D, DC, MC, V* ¶⊙¶ *CP.*

Nightlife & the Arts

NIGHTLIFE   At the height of the railroad era, Ogden's 25th Street housed a bawdy nightlife scene complete with saloons and gambling halls, opium dens, and a thriving red-light district. The area has gentrified since then, but it's still the center of one of Utah's most vibrant nightlife scenes. Beyond 25th Street you'll find good live music and dance clubs spread throughout the city.

★   At **Brewskies** (✉ 244 25th St. ☎ 801/394–1713), big-screen TVs, pool tables and arcade games, and pub fare such as Italian sandwiches and pizzas often draw a college crowd. Anyone (older than 21) who enjoys good music will love it here on Tuesday nights, when national blues acts play. And on weekends, bands ranging from country to punk rock take the stage. Filled with Beatles memorabilia, the **City Club** (✉ 264 25th St. ☎ 801/392–4447) caters to an upscale thirtysomething crowd. The John Lennon and Yoko Ono bathrooms are worth a visit. At **Kamikazes** (✉ 2404 Adams Ave. ☎ 801/621–9138), in an old church, you can dance to live music on one floor and to DJ tunes on another, or play pool. For two-stepping or line dancing, try the **Outlaw** (✉ 1206 W. 21st St. ☎ 801/334–9260). Stand-up comedians perform Thursday through Saturday at **Wiseguys Comedy Café** (✉ 269 25th St. ☎ 801/621–3700).

THE ARTS   Local and regional performing artists give free outdoor concerts each Wednesday night, June through August, at the **Ogden Amphitheater** (✉ Municipal Sq., 25th St. and Washington Blvd. ☎ 801/629–8253). The amphitheater also hosts free outdoor movies on Monday nights in July and August. Built in the 1920s then abandoned for years, the 🎬 **Peery Egyptian Theater** (✉ 2415 Washington Blvd. ☎ 801/395–3200) is a restored art deco jewel that hosts concerts ranging from world music to national blues, jazz, and country acts, as well as an ongoing film series. The theater also shows screenings and premieres during the Sundance Film Festival in January, and is home to Utah Musical Theatre performances in July and August. The first Friday of each month more than 20 downtown galleries and artists show off their wares at ★ the **Street Stroll** (✉ Downtown Ogden ☎ 801/393–3866), which begins at the Gallery at the Station, Union Station, and ends at the Eccles Community Art Center on the corner of 26th and Jefferson streets. Enjoy live music, art, and food stalls on Saturday, July through October, at the **25th Street Farmers' & Art Market** (✉ 25th St. and Municipal Sq. ☎ 801/ 629–8253). **Weber State University** (✉ 3750 Harrison Blvd. ☎ 801/626– 6000 ⊕ www.weber.edu) regularly offers theater, music, and dance performances by students and visiting artists at the Val A. Browning Center for the Performing Arts, home stage for the Ogden Symphony Ballet Association.

Shopping

As with nightlife and dining, you'll find the most interesting concentration of shops on historic 25th Street with a couple of don't-miss shopping stops scattered around the rest of town. Needlepointers from all over the West acclaim the **Needlepoint Joint** (✉ 241 25th St. ☎ 801/394–4355) as the best place around to find patterns, yarn, and thread. One-of-a-kind gifts and home decorations are the specialty at **Ruby & Begonia** (✉ 204 25th St. ☎ 801/334–7829), which also offers exceptional gift wrapping and delivery. The **Bookshelf** (✉ 2432 Washington Blvd. ☎ 801/621–4752) is a book lover's dream. Knowledgeable salespeople will point you to the latest titles or to dusty shelves stuffed with used and rare books. The **Newgate Mall** (✉ 36th St. and Wall Ave. ☎ 801/621–1161) houses contemporary shopping with popular retailers like Eddie Bauer, Dillard's, Gap, Sears Roebuck, and Victoria's Secret. If you're looking for a gift that says Utah, **Rainbow Gardens** (✉ 1851 Valley Dr. ☎ 801/621–1606), at the mouth of Ogden Canyon, is the place. More than 20 departments offer souvenirs, cowboy nostalgia, books, baskets, gadgets, and country accessories.

Upper Ogden Valley

❷ *8 mi east of Ogden City.*

Locals call it "the valley," as if it were the only valley in the world. It's sleepy and slow and if it had sidewalks they'd roll them up early, but once you see the valley, anchored by Pineview Reservoir, surrounded by the spectacular Wasatch Mountains, and inhabited by the quaint pioneer towns of Eden and Huntsville, you'll see why locals feel this way. With its world-class skiing, accessible water sports, great fishing, golf, climbing, hiking, biking, and camping, the Upper Ogden Valley is a recreation mecca still largely waiting to be discovered.

Thousands of marathon runners kick off the special events season in May with the **Ogden Marathon** (☎ 801/816–2577 or 888/913–9559 ⊕ www.ogdenmarathon.com), which starts in the Upper Ogden Valley and follows Ogden Canyon down to the center of Ogden City. Late August and fall colors bring the **Ogden Valley Balloon Festival** (✉ 3201 N. Wolf Creek Dr., Wolf Creek Resort Eden ☎ 800/413–8312 ⊕ www.ogdenvalleyballoonfestival.com), three days of hot-air balloon launches, music, homemade crafts, art, and food vendors.

Just beyond the mouth of Ogden Canyon, the mountains open up to make room for **Pineview Reservoir.** In summer this 2,000-acre lake is festooned with colorful sailboats and the graceful arcs of water-skiers. The fishing is good, and beaches, campgrounds, and marinas dot the shore. Anderson Cove, on the lake's southern end, is popular, as is Middle Inlet, on the eastern shore. ✉ *Rte. 39 east to Upper Ogden Valley* ☎ *801/625–5306* ⊕ *www.fs.fed.us/r4/wcnf* ✉ *$8* ☉ *Daily 7 AM–7 PM.*

Sports & the Outdoors

CROSS-COUNTRY SKIING **Wolf Creek Resort** (✉ 3900 N. Wolf Creek Dr., Eden ☎ 801/745–3737 or 877/492–1061 ⊕ www.wolfcreekresort.com) allows cross-country skiers to ski on its golf course in winter. Weber County Parks and Recreation grooms 5 mi of cross-country and snowshoe trails at **North Fork Park** (✉ North end of Ogden Valley off Rte. 39 ☎ 801/399–8491).

DOWNHILL SKIING & SNOWBOARDING Formerly named Nordic Valley and still Utah's smallest ski resort, **Wolf Mountain** is a good place to go if you're not quite ready for the high-powered resorts. A great place to learn, this resort also offers the most affordable skiing and riding in the state, and the whole mountain is lighted for night skiing. Opening days and hours can be sporadic so it's a good idea to call before you go. ✉ *3900 N. Wolf Creek Dr., Eden* ☎ *801/745–3511* ⊕ *www.wolfmountaineden.com* ☉ *Daily Dec.–Apr.* ☞ *1,000-ft vertical drop; 100 skiable acres; 30% beginner, 50% intermediate, 20% advanced; 2 double chairs* ✉ *Lift tickets $20.*

Rising north out of Ogden Canyon is **Powder Mountain.** As the name suggests, it receives a generous helping of the white stuff for which Utah is famous. This classic mom-and-pop ski resort offers huge terrain (more skiable acres than any other resort in the country) even though it doesn't have as many lifts as some of the destination resorts, and has two terrain parks and a half-pipe. You won't find fancy lodges or haute cuisine here, but crowds are nonexistent and four laid-back slope-side eateries serve everything from scones and hot soup to sandwiches or a flame-broiled Powder Burger at the Powder Keg. ⊠ *Rte. 158, Eden* ☎ *801/745–3772* ⊕ *www.powdermountain.com* ☞ *2,005-ft vertical drop; 5,500 skiable acres; 10% beginner, 50% intermediate, 40% advanced; 1 quad chair, 1 triple chair, 2 double chairs, 3 surface lifts* ⊠ *Lift tickets $45.*

A vertical drop of 2,959 feet and a dramatic start at the pinnacle of Mount Ogden made **Snowbasin** the perfect site for the downhill ski races during the 2002 Olympic Winter Games. With nine chairlifts accessing more than 2,600 acres of skiable terrain, this is one of Utah's largest resorts. The Holding family, who also own Sun Valley Resort in Idaho, has poured more than $100 million into improvements at Snowbasin since the mid-1990s. Snowbasin shares the same massive log lodges and state-of-the-art lifts and snowmaking as its more established sister resort, Sun Valley. There are no overnight accommodations. ⊠ *Rte. 226, Huntsville, 17 mi from Ogden* ☎ *801/399–1135 or 888/437–5488* ⊕ *www.snowbasin.com* ☞ *2,959-ft vertical drop; 2,650 skiable acres; 26% beginner, 38% intermediate, 36% advanced; 2 high-speed gondolas, 1 tram, 1 high-speed quad chair, 4 triple chairs, 1 double chair, 3 surface lifts* ⊠ *Lift tickets $58.*

GOLF On the upper end of the valley, cradled between mountains on both sides, the 18-hole **Wolf Creek Golf Course** (⊠ 3900 Wolf Creek Dr., Eden ☎ 801/745–3365 ⊕ www.wolfcreekresort.com) is known among Utah golfers as one of the most challenging in the state.

HIKING On many of the beautiful hikes in the Ogden Valley you discover ski terrain in the off season. Starting at 6,500 feet and ending at 9,600 feet, the moderate 2.5-mi trail (one-way) from the upper parking lot at **Snowbasin** leads to the saddle south of Mount Ogden. Hikers pass through bowls filled with colorful summer wildflowers. Several U.S. Forest Service trails branch off from trails at the resort. For detailed trail maps and information contact the Ogden Ranger District of the Wasatch-Cache National Forest at 801/236–3400, or if you're at Snowbasin you can get maps in the Grizzly Center.

HORSEBACK The view of these mountains is fine on horseback. **Red Rock Ranch and**
RIDING **Outfitters** (⊠ 13555 E. Rte. 39, Huntsville ☎ 801/745–4305 ⊕ www.redrockranchandoutfitters.com) will take you on a guided trail ride or a horse-drawn hayride to a Dutch-oven dinner.

SNOWMOBILING **Red Rock Ranch and Outfitters** (⊠ 13555 E. Rte. 39, Huntsville ☎ 801/745–4305 ⊕ www.redrockranchandoutfitters.com) puts you on a snowmobile and leads you to 200 mi of groomed trails in the Monte Cristo Mountains.

Where to Stay & Eat

$–$$$$ ✕ **The Grille at Wolf Creek.** Overlooking the golf course with a terrific view of the mountains and Upper Ogden Valley, this resort restaurant serves sandwiches and burgers to those looking for a quick bite, and dishes like caramelized king salmon or tenderloin of beef Oscar to those looking for a more relaxed meal. Save room for the cheesecake.

✉ *3900 Wolf Creek Dr.* ☎ *801/745–3737 Ext. 4* ▤ *AE, D, MC, V* ⊘ *No lunch.*

★ ¢–$ ✕ **Shooting Star Saloon.** Welcome to the oldest remaining saloon in Utah, in operation since the 1880s. From the dollar bills pinned to the ceiling to the stuffed head of a 300-pound Saint Bernard on the wall, there's something to look at in every corner of this tavern. The menu doesn't stray far from burgers—those served here are considered by many to be the best in the country—and beer, and you can't beat the frontier bar atmosphere. ✉ *7350 E. 200 South St., Huntsville, 17 mi from Ogden via Rte. 39* ☎ *801/745–2002* ▤ *No credit cards* ⊘ *Closed Mon. and Tues.*

$–$$ ✕▥ **Jackson Fork Inn.** In a restored dairy barn, this comfortable country inn and restaurant are warm and inviting. Antique decor adds to the country charm. Proprietor Vicki Petersen serves the most upscale dinner and Sunday brunch in the valley, with delicious soups and main courses like shrimp with marinated artichokes, boneless pork loin, or calamari steak. ✉ *Rte. 39, 7345 E. 900 South St., Huntsville 84317* ☎ *801/745–0051 or 800/609–9466* ⊕ *www.jacksonforkinn.com* ↪ *7 rooms* ⌂ *Restaurant, some pets allowed (fee); no room phones, no room TVs, no smoking* ▤ *AE, D, DC, MC, V* ▯◎▯ *CP.*

$$$$ ▥ **Moose Hollow Condominiums.** On the second fairway of Wolf Creek Golf Course, stone fireplaces, vaulted ceilings, moose antler chandeliers, and massive log beams provide rustic luxury lodging in the Upper Ogden Valley. ✉ *3605 N. Huntsman Path, Eden 84310* ☎ *801/745–0203 or 800/958–1311* ▦ *801/745–0224* ⊕ *www.moosehollowcondos.com* ↪ *119 units* ⌂ *Kitchens, cable TV, Wi-Fi, 18-hole golf course, pool, hot tub, sauna, laundry facilities* ▤ *AE, DC, MC, V.*

> **en route** The drive from the Upper Ogden Valley to Park City takes you through pastoral farmland along the back of the Wasatch. Take Trappers Loop, from Huntsville to the town of Mountain Green, skirting Mount Ogden. From there follow the Weber River on I–84, then I–80. In winter look for bald eagles roosting in the tall cottonwoods along the river. In summer great blue herons nest in the same trees. If you're hungry for a slice of Americana, at Wanship take Exit 156 and turn right to the big red café sign. The service at the **Spring Chicken Inn** (✉ *120 S. Wanship Rd.* ☎ *435/336–5334* ⊘ *Closed Mon.*) runs from down-home friendly to country surly depending on the day. The fried chicken is good and greasy and the pies are homemade.

THE GOLDEN SPIKE EMPIRE

Deserts, marshes, farmlands, mountains: there's enough landscape in the vast reaches of eastern Box Elder County to please any palate. The star attraction here, though, is history, specifically one day in history that changed the world: May 10, 1869. That's the date the Union Pacific and Central Pacific railroad officials met to drive their symbolic golden spike in celebration of the completion of the first transcontinental rail route. It happened at Promontory Summit, an ironically desolate spot about 15 mi north of the Great Salt Lake. The Wild West was about to be tamed.

The **Railroader's Festival** (✉ 32 mi west of Brigham City via Rte. 13/83 at the Golden Spike National Historic Site Promontory ☎ 435/471–2209 ⊕ www.nps.gov/gosp) takes place every second Saturday in August. Visitors of all ages enjoy reenactments of the celebration of the Transcontinental Railroad completion, talks by railroad historians, and games including a spike-driving contest, and handcar rides. Festival admission is free.

Brigham City

❸ *21 mi north of Ogden via I–15 or U.S. 89.*

Brigham City, first settled in 1851 by Mormon pioneers, reflects the best of both the old and the new. People passing through are charmed by its sycamore-lined Main Street and old-fashioned downtown, but they may not realize they are in one of Utah's most progressive towns. The Thiokol Corporation, which manufactures rocket motors about 45 minutes west of here, has brought a lot of highly paid, well-educated professionals who have settled here and, over the years, molded Brigham City to their liking. It's one of only three Utah municipalities that fluoridates its drinking water, and the local museum outclasses those in many of the state's larger cities.

★ ☾ In honor of the famous local crop, a **Peach Days Celebration** (☎ 435/723–3931) has been held each September since 1904—the longest continually celebrated harvest festival in Utah. There's a Peach Queen pageant, a parade, an art show, and freshly baked peach cobbler.Documents and artifacts from the city's early settlement and Mormon cooperative periods are the focus of the 3,300-square-foot **Brigham City Museum-Gallery,**
★ which also houses displays on the railroad and agricultural history of the Bear River valley. The large, open gallery is divided in half. The northern part houses pieces such as treasures brought across the plains by the Pioneers and furniture made in Brigham City around 1860. The south end of the gallery houses regional art collections and hosts monthly rotating regional and national touring shows such as Norman Rockwell lithographs and Oklahoma Memorial Art Quilts. ✉ *24 N. 300 West St.* ☎ *801/723–6769* 🖾 *Free* ☾ *Tues.–Fri. 11–6, Sat. 1–5.*

Willard Bay State Park, about 10,000 acres in size, is actually a freshwater arm of the Great Salt Lake. Fed by canals in spring, it's effectively protected from the saltwater of the Great Salt Lake by a series of dikes. Because it's freshwater, Willard Bay is a popular fishing, boating, and bird-watching area. Facilities include a marina, campground, concession stands, and shady picnic spots. Bald and golden eagles are spotted frequently in tall trees along the park's Eagle Beach. ✉ *Off I–15, 6 mi south of Brigham City* ☎ *435/734–9494* ⊕ *www.utah.com/stateparks/ willard_bay.htm* 🖾 *$9 per vehicle* ☾ *Daily 6 AM–10 PM.*

Established on the brackish marshes where the Bear River empties into
☾ the northern tip of the Great Salt Lake, **Bear River Migratory Bird Refuge**
Fodor'sChoice was originally a series of lagoons ideally suited for waterfowl. In 1983,
★ however, in the first of a series of flood years, Utah received an unusual amount of rainfall, and the 74,000-acre preserve was inundated by the

rising Great Salt Lake. By 1986 the lake had reached its historic high point, destroying all the refuge's facilities, including a just-completed visitor center. After a considerable amount of work, the U.S. Fish and Wildlife Service was able to resurrect a 12-mi driving tour that follows various dikes. The habitat has been reclaimed, and the refuge once again hosts seasonal influxes of ducks, geese, pelicans, swans, and shore birds. The 31,000 -square-foot James V. Hansen Wildlife Education Center is under construction with a scheduled grand opening of April 2006. ⊠ *Bird Refuge Rd. (Forest St.), 13 mi west of Brigham City* ☎ *435/ 723–5887* ⊕ *http://www.fws.gov/bearriver/* ⊠ *Free* ☉ *Daily dawn–dusk.*

★ ☾ Originally used as a winter camp by the Shoshones, **Crystal Hot Springs** is the world's largest natural hot and cold springs. Mixing water from the two springs allows for a variety of pools with temperatures ranging from 80°F to 105°F. The complex, which is in Honeyville, about 8 mi north of Brigham City, has its own campground, a series of three hot tubs, a large soaker pool, a cold freshwater swimming pool, two water slides, and a lap pool. The complex remains open year-round, but hours are variable so it's best to call ahead. ⊠ *8215 N. Rte. 38, Honeyville* ☎ *435/279–8104 or 801/547–0777* ⊠ *$5.50.*

Sports & the Outdoors

Box Elder County's long rural roads are great for road biking, but the dirt roads in the Wellsvilles are generally too steep for good mountain biking.

GOLF   On the campus of a former Indian school—that's what all the pink-and-green buildings are—**Eagle Mountain Golf Course** (⊠ 960 E. 700 South St. ☎ 435/723–3212), has a PGA pro, complete pro shop, and snack bar. It's a nice mix of challenging holes and straightforward greens, but rent a cart if you're not in shape because the switchbacks up the front nine will leave you puffing. Greens fees are $10 on weekends, $9.50 on weekdays.

Beginning golfers may prefer the straight, forgiving fairways of **Skyway Golf Course** (⊠ 432 N. 1320 West St., Tremonton ☎ 435/257–5706), a 9-hole course. Greens fees are $9.

HIKING   The pink-and-grey crags of the Wellsvilles beckon the adventurous, and you can practically hike out your back door in Brigham City because the mountains rise straight up from town. But the range is one of the steepest in the world, so you must pace yourself. Although the peaks are all federal wilderness, gaining access isn't always a straightforward proposition. North of Brigham City, the foothills encompass a string of private ranches. If you knock on a farmhouse door, however, the landowner will usually oblige and tell you the best place to cross his land.

Brigham City's 700 North Street dead-ends on the east at the head of a nice hiking trail. East of Honeyville, the only good public access to the Wellsvilles is from 7200 North Street, 9 mi north of Brigham City on Route 38; the road dead-ends at a gate, which you can open (don't forget to close it behind you) or just climb over. Beyond it are miles of hiking trails to explore.

In spite of all that irrigated farmland you see, you're still in the desert, so bring water on any trip, even if you only plan to be gone an hour.

Where to Stay & Eat

★ ☕ $–$$$ ✕ **Maddox Ranch House.** Down-home Western food—fried chicken, prime rib, or bison steak—and portions big enough to satisfy a ranch hand make this place, 2 mi south of Brigham City on U.S. 89, quite popular. Every dish is made from scratch, and people drive here from surrounding states just for a piece of the fresh peach pie in season. The restaurant has become such an attraction that it even has its own gift shop. The friendly service is a delight. Reservations are practically a must, even on weeknights. ⊠ *1900 S. U.S. 89, Perry 84302* ☎ *435/723–8545 or 800/544–5474* ♺ *Reservations essential* ▱ *AE, D, DC, MC, V* ⊘ *Closed Sun. and Mon.*

¢–$ ✕ **Idle Isle Café.** Built in 1921, this café maintains its antique atmosphere
Fodor'sChoice with original wooden booths and a player piano. The menu features home-
★ style dishes like beef pot roast and halibut steak, along with memorable desserts, which include its trademark "idleberry pie." Don't forget to grab a box of chocolates for the road at the Idle Isle's own candy factory across the street. ⊠ *24 S. Main St.* ☎ *435/734–2468* ▱ *AE, D, MC, V* ⊘ *Closed Sun.*

★ ¢ ✕ **Peach City Ice Cream Co.** Travel back in time to the 1950s at this drive-in, complete with carhops. Eat in your car or go inside to pick out a tune on the jukebox and enjoy your homemade ice cream out of a tulip bowl. ⊠ *306 N. Main St.* ☎ *435/723–3923* ▱ *AE, D, MC, V.*

$ ▦ **Crystal Inn.** The spacious rooms of this two-story motel have comfortable sitting areas with desks as well as such conveniences as microwaves, refrigerators, and VCRs; some rooms have Jacuzzi tubs. There are mountain views from the swimming pool. ⊠ *480 Westland Dr., 84302* ☎ *435/723–0440 or 800/408–0440* ▤ *435/723–0446* ⊕ *www.crystalinns.com* ⇆ *52 rooms* ⌂ *Some in-room hot tubs, cable TV, Wi-Fi, in-room VCRs, in-room data ports, indoor pool, hot tub, laundry facilities, business services, meeting rooms* ▱ *AE, D, DC, MC, V* ¶◉¶ *CP.*

¢–$ ▦ **Howard Johnson Inn.** Ask for an upstairs room with a balcony to enjoy the sunset view from this standard motel on the east bench. You're not far from the I–15/U.S. 89 split, and there are restaurants just through the parking lot and across the street. ⊠ *1167 S. Main St., 84307* ☎ *435/723–8511* ▤ *435/723–0957* ⊕ *www.hojobrighamcity.com* ⇆ *43 rooms, 1 suite* ⌂ *Cable TV, Wi-Fi, indoor pool, hot tub, business services, pets allowed* ▱ *AE, D, DC, MC, V* ¶◉¶ *CP.*

¢ ▦ **Galaxie Motel.** You won't believe what a clean, spacious room you can get for the low prices here. And for a few bucks more, six of the rooms add a microwave and refrigerator and four have full kitchenettes. Unless you grew up on a farm, ask for one of the newer rooms toward Main Street—otherwise you risk being awakened at dawn by the neighbor's roosters. ⊠ *740 S. Main St., 84302* ☎ *435/723–3439 or 800/577–4315* ▤ *435/734–2049* ⇆ *29 rooms, 1 suite* ⌂ *Some kitchenettes, some microwaves, some refrigerators, cable TV* ▱ *AE, D, DC, MC, V.*

Golden Spike National Historic Site

4 *32 mi west of Brigham City via Rte. 83.*

The Union Pacific and Central Pacific railroads met here at Promontory Summit on May 10, 1869, to celebrate the completion of the first transcontinental rail route. Under the auspices of the National Park Service, **Golden Spike National Historic Site** has a visitor center and two beautifully maintained locomotives that are replicas of the originals that met here for the "wedding of the rails." Every May 10 (and on Saturday and holidays in summer), a reenactment of the driving of the golden spike is held. In August, boiler stoking, rail walking, and handcar racing test participants' skills at the Railroader's Festival held here. Another festival around Christmas time gives steam buffs opportunities to photograph the locomotives in the cold, when the steam from the smokestacks forms billowing clouds. ⊠ *Rte. 83, 32 mi west of Brigham City, Promontory* ☎ *435/471–2209* ⊕ *www.nps.gov/gosp* ⊠ *$5 per vehicle Columbus Day–Apr., $7 per vehicle May–Columbus Day* ⊙ *Daily 9–5.*

The **Thiokol Rocket Garden** is an open-air display at the Thiokol Corporation's plant and testing facility 2 mi past the turnoff to Golden Spike. A casing for the space shuttle motor is here. You can also see motors for all the missiles and rockets Thiokol has been manufacturing for the U.S. government since the 1950s. ⊠ *9160 N. Rte. 83, Promontory* ☎ *435/863–3511* ⊠ *Free* ⊙ *Daily 9–5.*

CACHE VALLEY

East of Brigham City, U.S. 89/91 tops Sardine Summit in Wellsville Canyon before dropping into the highly scenic Cache Valley. Walled in on the west by the imposing Wellsville Mountains (often touted as having the steepest incline of any range in the country) and on the east by the Bear River Range (a subrange of the Wasatch), Cache Valley is 15 mi wide and 60 mi long.

The valley was originally home to bands of Northwestern Shoshone. During the 1820s it became a favorite haunt for Jim Bridger and other mountain men, who often stashed (or "cached") their furs and held rendezvous here. Mormon pioneers, led by Peter Maughan, arrived in 1856 and created permanent settlements. Today Cache Valley is one of Utah's most important agricultural regions. Topping the list of foods produced here is cheese. One of three cheese factories in the valley, Cache Valley Cheese is one of the nation's largest producers of Swiss cheese.

Logan

25 mi northeast of Brigham City via Rte. 89/91.

Mormon pioneers created the permanent settlement of Logan in 1859, but the town didn't become prominent until 1888, when it was chosen as the site for Utah's land-grant agricultural college, now called Utah State University (USU). Logan is now the hub of the Cache Valley.

Logan's historic Main Street is best explored on a walking tour; an illustrated brochure, available from the visitor information center, guides you along both sides and up a few cross streets. The more interesting buildings include St. John's Episcopal Church, representing Cache Valley's first non-Mormon denomination; the Ellen Eccles and Lyric theaters; and the Cache County Courthouse. Each Memorial Day weekend

★ in Blacksmith Fork Canyon is the **Old Ephraim's Mountain Man Rendezvous** (☎ 435/245–3778), a reenactment of an 1820s rendezvous. The celebration features participants dressed in period costumes. Lively games test hatchet, primitive archery, knife, black-powder, and Dutch-oven cooking skills. It's one of the West's largest mountain-man gath-

🌕 erings. At the Cache County Fairgrounds in August, the **Cache County Fair** (☎ 435/716–7150) is the scene of agricultural and culinary competitions and demonstrations, plus a nightly rodeo.

➎ In the same building as a well-stocked visitor information center, the **Daughters of Utah Pioneers Cache Museum** has mountain-man displays as well as musical instruments, furniture, clothing, and a large collection of personal journals from the 1850s to the early 1900s. ⊠ *160 N. Main St. ☎ 435/752–5139 or 435/753–1635 ◻ Free ☺ June–Aug., Tues.–Fri. 10–4; Sept.–May by appointment only.*

➏ Logan is home to **Utah State University,** a land-grant college established in 1888. Today USU has an enrollment of well over 20,000 and is a leader in such diverse fields as agriculture, natural resources, and space technology. East of downtown Logan, the USU campus is best toured by starting at the historic Old Main administration building—look for the bell tower.

★ Exhibits at the **Museum of Anthropology** (☎ 435/797–0219 ⊕ www. hass.usu.edu/~anthromuseum ☺ Weekdays 8–5 ◻ Free) in Old Main are entirely designed by students with faculty guidance. A large portion of the museum is devoted to the American West, but cultures from around the world are also represented. Exhibits change frequently, so it's a place you can go back to even if you've seen it before.

★ USU's Chase Fine Arts Center includes the **Nora Eccles Harrison Museum of Art** (⊠ 650 N. 1100 East St. ☎ 435/797–0163 ⊕ www. artmuseum.usu.edu). The free museum has revolving exhibits of works by locally, nationally, and internationally recognized artists. It's open weekdays from 10:30 to 4:30, with extended hours Wednesday until 8 PM.

Housed in a beautifully restored historic mansion, the **Alliance for the Varied Arts** (⊠ 35 W. 100 South St. ☎ 435/753–2970 ☺ Tues.–Sat. 11–4) offers classes in ceramics, weaving, and other media, and showcases artists from around northern Utah.

➐ It took Mormon settlers 27 years to build the **Logan Tabernacle,** which they completed in 1891. In Logan's early days, the tabernacle hosted church and community meetings; now it's a venue for concerts and lectures. You can search for information about your family history at the genealogical research facility or take a tour of the building in summer. ⊠ *50 N. Main St. ☎ 435/755–5598 ◻ Free ☺ June–Aug., hrs vary ☺ Closed Sun.*

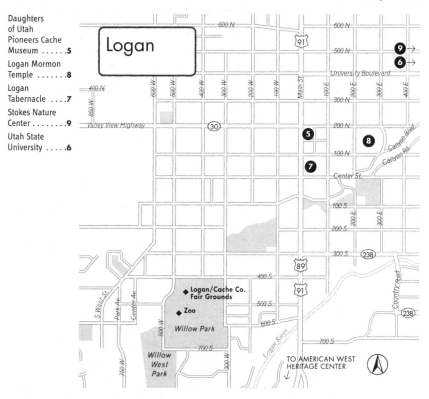

8 The twin towers of the **Logan Mormon Temple** (⊠ 175 North and 300 East Sts.) remind all that this college town is also a conservative community with Mormon roots. Built on a terrace of the ancient Lake Bonneville, this impressive limestone edifice took settlers seven years to complete. The site was chosen by Brigham Young himself in 1877, and the work was directed by architect Truman O. Angell, designer of the Salt Lake temple. As with all Mormon temples, it's open only to followers of the faith.

9 A visit to the **Stokes Nature Center,** about a mile up Logan Canyon, is a great way to get acquainted with the natural wonders of this area. There are special programs for adults and children on the second and fourth Saturday; visit the Web site for listings. ⊠ *2696 E. U.S. 89* ☎ *435/755–3239* ⊕ *www.logannature.org* ☞ *Free* ☺ *Tues., Wed., and Fri. 10–4, Thurs. noon–4, 2nd and 4th Sat. 9–5.*

Come to **Old Ephraim's Grave** to pay your respects to a northern Utah legend. Old Ephraim was the last grizzly bear known to roam and terrorize livestock around Garden City and Logan. His body was buried in 1923 at a site now designated by an 11-foot stone monument, which matches his height while standing on his hind legs; his huge skull is now exhibited in the Special Collections in Utah State University's Merrill

Library. You can also look for a wooden sign marking the actual burial place of Old Ephraim originally placed by scouts in 1923. Make sure you have a sturdy four-wheel-drive vehicle with lots of clearance before attempting this trip; do not even attempt it if it's been raining at all. Though it is only roughly 9 mi from the Logan Ranger District Station, the trip takes about 3 hours. Stop in at the ranger station for specific directions and road condition updates. ⊠ *1500 E. U.S. 89* ☎ *435/755–3620* ⊕ *www.fs.fed.us/r4/wcnf.*

off the
beaten
path

HARDWARE RANCH – If you pass through the Logan area in winter, it's worthwhile to take the drive up Blacksmith Fork Canyon to the Hardware Ranch, where the State Division of Wildlife Resources feeds several hundred head of elk through the snowy months. A 20-minute sleigh ride takes you up close to the majestic creatures. There's also a visitor center, gift shop, and a café. On Saturday night, there's an evening sleigh ride followed by dinner; reservations are required. Dress warmly in layers. ⊠ *Rte. 101, 24 mi southeast of Logan via U.S. 165 and Rte. 101, Hyrum* ☎ *435/753–6206 or 435/ 753–6168* ⊕ *www.hardwareranch.com* ⊙ *Mid-Dec.–mid-Mar., Thurs.–Mon. noon–5.*

★ ☾ **AMERICAN WEST HERITAGE CENTER –** To learn about Cache Valley's history from 1820 to 1920, drive 6 mi south of Logan to visit this living-history complex that spans 160 acres. At the farm, antique implements are on display, draft horses still pull their weight, docents dressed in period clothing demonstrate sheepshearing and quilting, and special events take place throughout the year. The Festival of the American West, held at the center in late July–early August, features additional displays and reenactments, along with food booths, cowboy poetry readings, and concerts. In addition to viewing, visitors can shop for authentic Western jewelry, clothing, and specialty items. ⊠ *4025 S. U.S. 89/91, Wellsville* ☎ *435/245–6050 or 800/225–3378* ⊕ *www.americanwestcenter.org* ☞ *$6* ⊙ *Memorial Day–Labor Day, Mon.–Sat. 10–5; Welcome Center year-round 9–5.*

Sports & the Outdoors

The outdoors are hard to ignore in the gorgeous Cache Valley, which is dominated east and west by mountains and by the lazy Bear River wending its way through the bottom lands. Birders love the marshes; hikers, skiers, picnickers, and mountain bikers head for the hills. Trails for all abilities are just minutes away from downtown Logan.

BICYCLING &
HIKING

Road cyclists pedal out to the long, flat country roads of scenic Cache Valley or venture up Logan and Blacksmith Fork canyons. Mountain bikers can spend an afternoon on the 9-mi round-trip from Wood Camp, in Logan Canyon, to the 1,500-year-old Jardine juniper tree that grows on a high ridge offering views of Wyoming and Idaho.

Just a few miles up Logan Canyon, hikers and bikers enjoy the wide passageway of the **Red Bridge–River Trail,** which continues 4.2 mi on the south side of the canyon along the Logan River. Mountain bikers and hikers alike can access a prime wilderness area via the 3-mi route from Tony

Grove Lake to the summit of Naomi Peak. In the Wellsville Mountains, a 2-mi trail climbs steeply from Maple Bench to Stewart Pass, a lofty ridge along the migration route of eagles and hawks; on a clear day the view from here extends for more than 80 mi. You can get maps and brochures for hiking trails in **Wasatch-Cache National Forest** (Logan Ranger District ⊠ 1500 E. U.S. 89, 84321 ☎ 435/755–3620 ⊕ www. fs.fed.us/r4/wcnf).

BOATING & **FISHING** Fishermen cast dry flies into the Logan River or angle for rare albino trout in the depths of Tony Grove Lake. Although you can paddle a canoe on virtually any body of water in the region, the best places include Tony Grove Lake in Logan Canyon and Bear River, northwest of Logan. Winding in serpentine fashion through Cache Valley, Bear River has several nice stretches, including a particularly satisfying one that runs 11 mi between Amalga and Tremonton. You pass a blue heron rookery along the way, so this is a good float for bird-watchers. Contact **The Trailhead** (⊠ 117 N. Main ☎ 435/753–1541 ⊙ Weekdays 10–5) for canoe rentals, which go for about $20 per day, including life vests, paddles, and the car top and straps you need for transport.

Bridgerland Audubon Society (⊕ www.bridgerlandaudubon.org) often sponsors boat trips on the Bear River. **Hyrum Lake State Park** (⊠ 405 W. 300 South St., Hyrum ☎ 435/245–6866 ⊕ www.stateparks.utah.gov) has a 450-acre reservoir that draws boaters in summer and fall. A campground, shady picnic areas, peaceful rural setting, and great views of the Wellsville Mountains and the Bear River Range make this a popular spot for family gatherings. In winter, ice fishing is the activity of choice. Day use is $5 per vehicle.

GOLF The **Logan River Golf Course** (⊠ 550 West 1000 S ☎ 435/750–0123 ⊕ www.loganutah.org) is also a wetlands preserve, as you'll discover when your ball plops irretrievably into one of the many cattail marshes. It's a very challenging course (par 71), particularly the back 9. For $12 you can play 9 holes walking; $21 for 18 holes. Riding, it's $18 and $32, respectively.

Considered by many to be one of the best golf courses in the U.S., **Birch Creek Golf Course** (⊠ 550 E. 100 North St., Smithfield ☎ 435/563–6825 ⊕ www.birchcreekgolf.com) is long and exceptionally well maintained. The clubhouse has one of the best views in Cache Valley. There's a full-service pro shop with custom club fitting and a PGA pro. Greens fees for the par-72 course are $20 on weekdays, $21 on weekends.

Roving herds of mule deer are the biggest hazard at the 9-hole **Sherwood Hills Golf Course** (⊠ U.S. 89/91, 14 mi southwest of Logan, Wellsville ☎ 435/245–6055 ⊕ www.sherwoodhills.com), but you can't beat the mountain setting. Greens fees for the par-36 course are $12 per person, $10 per cart.

Where to Stay & Eat

★ $–$$$ ✕ **Le Nonne.** Logan was lucky enough to produce a local lass who caught the eye of Italian chef Pierantonio Micheli, and after their marriage they opened this sophisticated storefront eatery where you can get an authentic four-course Italian meal with refreshingly brisk service. If your arteries can take it, the four-cheese gnocchi is ecstasy, and you can't go wrong with any of the appetizers. Whatever you do, leave room for a bite of homemade tiramisu. Combine dinner at Le Nonne with an opera at the Eccles Theatre across and down the street, and you might forget you're in the middle of the rural West. ⊠ *129 North 100 E* ☎ *435/752–9577* ⊟ *AE, D, MC, V* ☯ *Closed Sun.*

$–$$$ ✕ **The Painted Table.** Owner and chef Nelson Swett emphasizes cooking with as much local product as possible, and the result is splendid. The magical paintings of local artist Jerry Fuhriman adorn the walls of this intimate, upscale eatery with white tablecloths and a red-tile floor. The seasonal contemporary American fare includes grilled steak, tuna, salmon, and halibut; lunch is comprised mainly of sandwiches and salads. For a real treat and only $37, order "Whims of the Chef," a five-course meal prepared just for you. ⊠ *132 N. Main St.* ☎ *435/755–6811* ⊟ *AE, D, MC, V* ☯ *Closed Sun. No dinner Mon. No lunch Sat.*

★ ¢–$$ ✕ **Bluebird.** Stop by Utah's oldest continually operated restaurant to admire the early 1900s architectural details and enjoy an ice-cream treat at the original marble-counter soda fountain. Many of the photographs and decorative artifacts are from the 1800s; a multiwall mural in one dining area includes scenes from every period in Cache Valley history. You can buy chocolates, too. ⊠ *19 N. Main St.* ☎ *435/752–3155* ⊟ *AE, D, MC, V.*

¢   ✕ **Caffé Ibis.** People come here for Utah's best coffee (ground daily at the Ibis's own plant in Logan), but they soon discover the savory sandwiches and hearty breakfasts are the very thing to wash down with their double lattes. This hangout for Logan's small but colorful hipster set also displays work by area artists; local musicians perform for tips on Friday and Saturday nights. ⊠ *52 Federal Ave.* ☎ *435/753–4777* ⊟ *AE, MC, V.*

¢   ✕ **Crumb Brothers Artisan Bread.** The delicious artisan breads match the 1920s Arts and Crafts building and decor. Using simple, natural ingredients, including imported European butter, the Oblock brothers create outrageously tasty and delicate pastries, scones, fruit tarts, and coffee cakes, offered with fine tea, roasted coffee, or juice. Wednesday through Saturday gourmet sandwiches are also served. Get there early, though; hours are 7 AM–1 PM Monday through Saturday. ⊠ *291 South 300 W* ☎ *435/792–6063* ⊟ *No credit cards* ☯ *Closed Sun. No dinner.*

$ ✕🏠 **Sherwood Hills Resort.** You're a tad isolated at this mountain retreat
Fodor's Choice halfway between Logan and Brigham City, but who's complaining when
★ you've got hiking trails out your back door and a 9-hole golf course out your front? Local honeymooners often snap up the theme room, in which the bed is made from an actual 1950s-vintage pink Cadillac. There's a postcard view out every window. And then there's Sammy Scalise's Belle Monte Italian restaurant ($–$$$$), which has the best wine list on either side of the Wellsvilles. Sammy prides himself on fresh ingredients and grows his own herbs behind the lodge. His cheesecake is a don't-miss finale to the savory pasta and meat dishes. ⊠ *U.S. 89/91, 14 mi southwest of Logan, Wellsville 84339* ☎ *435/245–5054 or 800/532–5066* ⊕ *www.sherwoodhills.com* ⇆ *78 rooms, 1 theme room, 5 suites* ⚒ *Restaurant, some in-room hot tubs, Wi-Fi, microwaves, re-*

frigerators, cable TV, in-room VCRs, spa, golf, hiking, cross-country ski-
ing, meeting rooms ⊟ *AE, D, DC, MC, V* ☺ *No lunch in restaurant*
weekdays. No dinner Sun. |◎| *CP.*

¢ ✕🖃 **Zanavoo.** If you're on a tight budget but crave a million-dollar set-
Fodor'sChoice ting, check out this 1948 log cabin lodge 2½ mi up Logan Canyon. A
★ low rate of $55 gets you a basic room with satellite TV, breakfast
brought to your door (no kidding), and some of the country's prettiest
scenery out the window. Make sure you eat at least one night at the lodge's
rustic log Zanavoo Restaurant ($–$$), where they'll cook you up a per-
fect steak or whole fresh trout. The food is basic Western fare but very
fresh, snappily served, and beautifully presented. ⊠ *4880 E. U.S. 89,*
84321 ☎ *435/752–0085* ⊕ *www.zanavoo.com* ⇱ *10 rooms* ⚹ *Restau-*
rant, cable TV; no a/c ⊟ *AE, MC, V* ☺ *No lunch in restaurant* |◎| *CP.*

★ $$–$$$$ 🖃 **Anniversary Inn.** This inn actually consists of four buildings, includ-
ing a 22-room mansion and a carriage house. Rooms seem designed for
couples hoping to jump-start their love life. In the "Caribbean Sea
Cave," for example, your bed is a sunken ship, and walls and ceiling
are painted with murals of creatures from a coral reef. More importantly,
practically out your door is gorgeous Logan Canyon, which would hold
its own against any Caribbean isle for romantic inspiration. Guests are
welcomed by cheesecake and cider in each room and all rooms have giant
TVs and two-person jetted tubs. A continental breakfast of fruit and
fresh croissant sandwiches is delivered to your door. ⊠ *169 E. Center*
St., 84321 ☎ *435/752–3443 or 800/574–7605* ⊕ *www.anniversaryinn.*
com ⇱ *20 rooms* ⚹ *Hot tubs, cable TV* ⊟ *AE, D, MC, V* |◎| *CP.*

★ $–$$$ 🖃 **Providence Inn.** The stone part of the three-story stone and cream-brick
inn was once the Old Rock Church, built in 1889. Such architectural
embellishments as Palladian windows lend the structure considerable
elegance. Rooms are individually decorated—some colonial style, some
Georgian, and some Victorian. Breakfast is a refreshingly hearty affair
of omelets or French toast, brought to your room if you choose the higher-
end "king rooms" or suites; otherwise, it's served in a pleasant dining
room. ⊠ *10 S. Main St., Providence 84332* ☎ *435/752–3432 or 800/*
480–4943 🖷 *435/752–3482* ⊕ *www.providenceinn.com* ⇱ *17 rooms,*
6 suites ⚹ *Picnic area, in-room VCRs, Wi-Fi, in-room data ports, hot*
tubs, business services ⊟ *AE, D, DC, MC, V* |◎| *BP.*

¢–$ 🖃 **Comfort Inn.** In the newer, northern commercial district, this centrally
located motel is near several restaurants and grocery stores and right
on 400 North Street, which goes up Logan Canyon. The spacious, no-
nonsense rooms have two queen beds with floral bedding, a desk and
dresser; some have views of the mountains. ⊠ *447 N. Main St., 84321*
☎ *435/752–9141* 🖷 *435/752–9723* ⊕ *www.comfortinn.com* ⇱ *83*
rooms ⚹ *Some refrigerators, cable TV, Wi-Fi, in-room data ports, in-*
door pool, gym, hot tub, laundry facilities, business services ⊟ *AE, D,*
DC, MC, V |◎| *CP.*

Nightlife & the Arts

NIGHTLIFE The underage crowd gathers at **Club NVO** (⊠ 339 N. Main St. ☎ 435/
787–8848), an alcohol-free disco and pool hall, but it's also becoming
popular with older couples who like to dance but don't care for the bar

scene. Watch for theme nights (salsa, big band, etc.) and come early for dance lessons.

Rub shoulders with both townies and university types at **The White Owl** (✉ 36 W. Center St. ☎ 435/753–9165). This convivial downtown watering hole also happens to serve Logan's best burgers. If it's nice out, toast the sunset view of the Wellsvilles from the rooftop beer garden. There's live music on Thursday nights but no dance floor.

THE ARTS   Thanks to both the presence of Utah State University and the community's keen interest in the arts, Logan offers many fine theater productions. USU's theater and music departments present a variety of exciting performances. The **Ellen Eccles Theatre** (✉ 43 S. Main St. ☎ 435/752–0026 ⊕ www.ellenecclestheatre.com) presents Broadway musicals, Celtic music, and an annual series of performances appropriate for children. The **Caine Lyric Theatre** (✉ 28 W. Center St. ☎ 435/797–1500) features plays by the university's repertory company. Each Father's Day weekend in June, **Summerfest, an Art Faire and Music Festival** (✉ 400 South 500 W ☎ 435/716–9244) fill the fairgrounds with arts and crafts, music, folk dancing, and other cultural events. The **Utah Festival Opera Company** (☎ 435/750–0300 or 800/262–0074 ⊕ www.ufoc.org) performs a five-week season between July and August at the Ellen Eccles Theatre.

Shopping

★ **Maya's Corner** (✉ 1 N. Main St. ☎ 435/753–3497), an eclectic boutique, specializes in high-quality natural fiber clothing in great colors that flatter all ages and any figure; the store also sells an array of head-turning accessories, jewelry, unusual perfumes, natural cosmetics, and shoes. **Cox Honeyland and Gifts** (✉ 1780 S. U.S. 89/91 ☎ 435/752–3234) sells a wide variety of flavored, creamed honeys, as well as berry juices, candy, and Bear Lake raspberry jam. You can also get home decor items and gifts, and the store will create and ship lovely gift baskets to your family members who stayed at home. No one captures the essence of Cache Valley better than Jerry Fuhriman, who produces moody landscapes and his whimsical coyote paintings at **Coyote Arts** (✉ 28 Federal Ave. ☎ 435/753–9446). It's a feast for the nose at **Scentinel Candle Co.** (✉ 2788 S. U.S. 89/91 ☎ 435/755–6993), where shoppers find candles of every imaginable color, shape, size, and scent. The shop also stocks some cute decorative items. In summer or fall don't leave without visiting the **Cache Valley Gardeners' Market** (✉ Behind Tony Roma's, 130 S. Main St. ⊕ www.localharvest.org/farmers-markets/M3796), held every Saturday morning from 8 to noon. Buy fresh produce and locally made crafts while listening to music by local bands.

en route   From Logan, U.S. 89 continues for 30 mi up Logan Canyon before topping out at the crest of the Bear River Range. Within the canyon are a number of campgrounds and picnic areas administered by the Wasatch–Cache National Forest. For a particularly satisfying excursion, drive the 7-mi side road (marked) to **Tony Grove Lake.** At more than 8,000 feet, this subalpine jewel is surrounded by cliffs and meadows filled in summer with a stunning profusion of wildflowers. A short trail circles the lake, and other backcountry routes enter the Mount Naomi Wilderness Area to the west.

MOUNTAIN MEN

THE MEN WHO ONCE FORGED PATHS *through the wilderness in search of beaver, otter, and other furry creatures aren't needed to supply the wants of 21st-century fashion. Waterproof jackets, hiking boots with lug soles, and nylon backpacks have long since replaced beaver-pelt hats, buckskins, and moccasins. But the spirit of men like Jedediah Smith, Jim Bridger, Miles Goodyear, and Peter Skene Ogden lives on in the hearts of many.*

Fur traders were colorful characters—often they were loners, always they were adventurers. Some lived and trapped in small groups. Others saw other humans only at rendezvous to exchange goods and news. Native Americans often taught these trappers how to survive, and many mountain men had Native American wives.

One hapless trapper who unwittingly lent his name to Cache Valley's largest city. Ephraim Logan, the story goes, was

digging out one of his caches in the bank of a river when the bank collapsed on him and he drowned. Little else is known of him, but his name lives on in both the river and the city on its banks.

Mountain-men rendezvous still take place throughout Utah. Participants in buckskins or furs work on Indian beadwork or stir up Dutch-oven meals. There are skilled gunsmiths, tanners, leatherworkers, and hat makers. The crack of black-powder muskets echoes in the distance while Indian drums lure everyone into a circle dance.

The men and women who attend these rendezvous do so as a brief escape from the modern world. They come to barter, share ideas, and exchange stories. And though there's dancing, the meetings are seldom as uproarious as in times past.

BEAR LAKE COUNTRY

Home of the famed mountain man Jim Bridger, Rich County has only recently been discovered by tourists from outside the region, though residents of Utah and southern Idaho have vacationed here for a century. A few hardy ranchers live here year-round, but raspberries are the only crop besides hay that can stand the short growing season, and you'll see them everywhere in the form of syrup, jam, and the famous Bear Lake raspberry shakes. The deep Bear Lake Valley is generally 5 to 10 degrees cooler than the Cache Valley, so when the mercury hits 90°F in Logan, there's a mass migration over the Bear River Range.

Bear Lake State Park

⑩ *41 mi from Logan (to Garden City) via U.S. 89 north.*

Eight miles wide and 20 mi long, Bear Lake is an unusual shade of blue, thanks to limestone particles suspended in the water. It's home to five species of fish found nowhere else, including the Bonneville cisco, which draws anglers during its spawning season in January. Among the lake's more discreet inhabitants is the Bear Lake Monster, which according to local lore lurks somewhere in the depths like its Loch Ness counterpart.

Along the south shore of Bear Lake, Route 30 traces an old route used by Native Americans, mountain men, and settlers following the Oregon Trail. The lake was a popular gathering place for mountain men, who held two rendezvous here in the 1820s. Harsh winters persuaded most travelers to move on before the first snow flew, but hardy Mormon pioneers settled in the area and founded Garden City. You'll find several hotel and restaurant options in town, which sits at the junction of U.S. 89 and Route 30, on Bear Lake. The abundance of the berry is celebrated each year in early August at **Raspberry Days.** A parade, a craft fair, and entertainment are almost eclipsed by the main event: sampling myriad raspberry concoctions.

You can follow the ¼-mi **Garden City Boardwalk** (✉ 420 S. Bear Lake Blvd., Garden City) through a small wetlands preserve right to the shore of Bear Lake.

Bear Lake Marina (✉ U.S. 89, Garden City) has a beach, picnic area, campground, and visitor center with information on all the park's recreation areas. Boats can be rented from several local vendors around Garden City.

★ ☾ **Rendezvous Beach** (✉ Rte. 30, Laketown), which is on the south shore of Bear Lake, has more than a mile of sandy beaches, three campgrounds, and picnic areas. Mountain men gathered here for their annual rendezvous in 1827 and 1828. Their meeting place, Rendezvous Beach, now has interpretive signs about the gatherings. Each September a Mountain Man Rendezvous includes period cooking demonstrations, storytelling, cannon and rifle competitions, and a Native American encampment.

At **Eastside** (✉ 10 mi north of Laketown) the lake bottom drops off quickly, making this a favorite spot among anglers and scuba divers. Facilities include a primitive campground and a boat ramp.

☎ *435/946–3343 or 800/322–3770* ⊕ *www.stateparks.utah.gov* ✉ *$5 per vehicle* ☾ *Daily 8 AM–10 PM.*

At the south end of Bear Lake, **Round Valley,** now a ghost town, holds all that remains of a pioneer village, a small wood-frame schoolhouse and an old pioneer mansion. From Laketown, follow the signs to Round Valley.

Sports & the Outdoors

BICYCLING Cyclists of all abilities can enjoy all or any portion of the level 48-mi ride on the road circling Bear Lake. The paved Lakeside Bicycle Path curves from Bear Lake Marina south and east along the shore, with several rest stops. Interpretive signs contain stories about Bear Lake's history and local lore. **Bear Lake KOA** (✉ 485 N. Bear Lake Blvd., Garden City ☎ 435/946–3454), which is right on the trail, rents bikes, including a four-wheel, surrey-top bicycle-built-for-four that can actually carry a family of six.

OLD EPHRAIM

THERE'S A REASON FOR THE NAMES *"Bear Lake"* and *"Bear River."* In the old days these parts were swarming with bears, both grizzly and black. That was long before the Endangered Species Act and the environmental consciousness of people today. To protect their herds and livelihoods, sheep ranchers in the mid-1900s killed an average of a bear a day. One of the biggest grizzlies ever killed in North America—and maybe the smartest—was shot about 20 mi northeast of Logan.

By 1912 local sheep ranchers were well acquainted with the bear they came to know as "Old Ephraim." He could sneak into a herd without alarming the dogs until it was too late, and carry off a full-grown sheep. The old bear was so wily that the herders hardly ever got a look at him, unless he was ambling away out of gunshot range, a sheep under one arm. All they were left with were his tracks— bigger around than a man's outstretched hand and missing a toe on one front foot.

But the really spooky thing about Old Ephraim was the bear's uncanny intelligence. Eph knew how to spring a trap without getting caught in it.

By 1923 sheepman Frank Clark had had enough. On August 21, a fine, clear summer day, Clark set out to track down and kill Old Ephraim. Between Temple Fork and Right-Hand Fork he found a huge wallow he was sure was Eph's, and set a bear trap, attaching it with a logging chain to an aspen tree 6 inches in diameter.

That night Clark was awakened in his tent by a horrible groan, and went to wait out the night by the trap. Eph had chewed through the tree and the trap was gone, but it was apparent from his cries that he had been hurt and was still nearby. Here's what happened as Clark told it to historian Newell J. Crookston in the 1950s:

"Daylight came at last and now it was my turn. Eph was pretty well hidden in the creek bottom and willows so I threw sticks in to scare him out, but he slipped out and went down by the tent and crawled into the willows there. I got close to the tent. I could see a small patch of hide so I fired at it and grazed the shoulder. And now for the greatest thrill of my life: Ephraim raised up on his hind legs with his back to me and a 14-foot log chain wound around his right arm as carefully as a man would have done it and a 23-pound bear trap on his foot and standing 9 feet 11 inches high. I was paralyzed with fear and couldn't raise my gun and he was coming, still on his hind legs, holding that cussed trap above his head. He had a 4-foot bank to surmount before he could reach me. I was rooted to the earth and let him come within 6 feet of me before I stuck the gun out and pulled the trigger. He fell back but came again and received five of the remaining six bullets. He had now reached the trail, still on his hind legs. I only had one cartridge left in the gun and still that bear wouldn't go down so I started for Logan, 20 mi downhill. I went about 20 yards and turned. Eph was coming, still standing up, but my dog was snapping at his heels so he turned on the dog. I then turned back and as I got close he turned again on me, waddling along on his hind legs. I could see that he was badly hurt as at each breath the blood would spout from his nostrils so I gave him the last bullet in the brain. I think I felt sorry I had to do it."

BOATING Bear Lake's turquoise waters are a bit chilly for swimming on all but
Fodor's Choice the hottest summer days, but boating is a popular way to enjoy the lake,
★ which is one of the state's top boating destinations. Personal watercraft,
sailboats, and motorboats are available at the Bear Lake Marina, at Rendezvous Beach, and in the surrounding towns. Prices vary from about
$20 per hour for a catamaran to $60 an hour for a large motorboat capable of towing water-skiers. Be advised that the winds at this mountain lake can change 180 degrees within minutes (or go from 30 knots
to completely calm), so inexperienced sailors may want to stick to a motorboat.

At the Bear Lake Marina, **Cisco's Landing** (⊠ Bear Lake Marina, U.S.
89, Garden City ☎ 435/946–2717) offers everything from personal
watercraft to full-size ski boats. Don't neglect to pick owner Bryce Nielson's brain—he's a wildlife biologist and a former Garden City mayor,
and he can tell you everything you need to know about the lake and its
denizens, both above and below the water.

In addition to sailboats and motorized craft, **Bear Lake Sails** (⊠ Rte. 30,
Laketown ☎ 435/946–2900 or 866/867–5912) rents paddleboats, canoes, and kayaks that are great for poking around the lake's vast shoreline and marshes. You can also rent water skis, wet suits, tubes, and
wakeboards here.

GOLF **Bear Lake Golf Course** (⊠ 2180 S. Country Club Dr., Garden City ☎ 435/
946–8742) offers 9 holes in a lakeside setting when the weather permits (generally May–October). The 3,400-foot course has a par of 36,
and greens fees are $14 on weekdays, $16 on weekends ($20 and $22,
respectively, with a cart).

HIKING At 9,980 feet, Naomi Peak is the highest point of the Bear River Range
in Cache National Forest. The 3.2-mi **Naomi Peak Trail** starts in the
parking lot of the Tony Grove Campground and gains almost 2,000 feet
in elevation. You hike through conifer forests and open meadows and
along subalpine basins and rocky ledges. A shorter hike to **White Pine
Lake,** which begins on the same trail and splits after a quarter of a mile,
is also lovely. To reach the trailhead, take U.S. 89 southwest from Garden City approximately 15 mi to the Tony Grove turnoff, then follow
the signs. Closer to Garden City is the **Limber Pine Nature Trail,** a popular and easy hike (1 mi round-trip) at the summit between Logan
Canyon and Bear Lake and features interpretive information especially
designed for children.

SKIING & Owned and operated by the same family since 1939, **Beaver Mountain
SNOWBOARDING** **Ski Area** offers skiing as it was before it became a rich man's sport. A
★ terrain park invites aerial tricks. There aren't any trendy night spots at
the foot of this mountain, just an old-fashioned A-frame lodge with burgers and chili. In summer Beaver Mountain has Logan Canyon's only camping with RV hookups. ⊠ 1045½ N. Main St. ☎ 435/753–0921, 435/
753–4822, or 435/563–5677 ☎ 435/753–0975 ⊕ www.skithebeav.
com ☞ 1,600-ft vertical drop; 664 skiable acres; 45 runs; 35% beginner, 40% intermediate, 25% advanced; 3 double chairs, 1 triple chair,
1 surface lift ☎ Lift tickets $33.

Where to Stay & Eat

¢–$ ✕ **LaBeau's Drive-in.** Although there's no drive-up window, there's no microwave cuisine either—just old-fashioned fast food. The classic order would be a raspberry shake and a burger topped with ham, cheese, onions, and the homemade sauce. ⊠ *69 N. Bear Lake Blvd., Garden City* ☎ *435/946–8821* ⊟ *MC, V* ⊗ *Closed Sun. and mid-Oct.–late Apr.*

$$$–$$$$ ▦ **Ideal Beach Resort.** A private beach awaits you at this family-style resort. You can only rent by the week or "half-week," which is either three weekend nights or four weekday nights. The condos are all privately owned and vary in size and amenities, but all have private bedrooms and fully equipped kitchens. Restaurants are nearby in Garden City. ⊠ *2176 S. Bear Lake Blvd., Garden City 84028* ☎ *435/946–3364 or 800/634–1018* ▤ *435/946–8519* ⊕ *www.idealbeach.net* ⟿ *36 condos* ᗡ *Kitchens, cable TV, miniature golf, 6 tennis courts, 2 pools, hot tub, 2 saunas, beach, marina, shop, business services; no a/c* ⊟ *AE, DC, MC, V.*

WHERE TO CAMP

★ ⟳ △ **Bear Lake KOA.** The budget-minded get the best resort in town at Bear Lake. This spot, which has cute-as-a-button log cabins (some with bathrooms and kitchens) as well as campsites, is practically its own city, with a heated pool, miniature golf course, tennis courts, bicycle rentals, the biggest convenience store in Garden City, and programmed activities for kids. There's a pavilion for pancake breakfasts and the like. A shared outdoor kitchen allows tent campers the luxury of doing their own cooking. Service is snappier than at the area's luxury resorts. Reservations essential. ᗡ *Flush toilets, full hookups, drinking water, guest laundry, showers, picnic tables, electricity, public telephone, general store, service station, swimming (pool)* ⟿ *100 full hookups, 130 tent sites, 25 cabins* ⊠ *485 N. Bear Lake Blvd., 84028* ☎ *435/946–3454, 800/562–3442 reservations* ⊕ *www.koa.com* ▨ *$22–$35 tent sites, $39–$47 full hookups, $50–$150 cabins* ⊟ *AE, D, MC, V.*

★ ⟳ △ **Rendezvous Beach Campground.** You can camp at all three recreation areas on Bear Lake, but with 178 sites, the campground at Rendezvous Beach is by far the largest. It also has hot showers, which are a nice luxury after a cold plunge in Bear Lake. Plus, you can rent a boat on-site. ᗡ *Flush toilets, drinking water, showers, picnic tables, electricity, swimming (lake)* ⟿ *106 full hookups, 72 tent sites* ⊠ *Rte. 30, near Laketown, 84028* ☎ *801/538–7220 or 800/322–3770* ⊕ *www.stateparks.utah.gov* ▨ *$14–$20* ⊗ *Apr.–mid-Sept.*

Nightlife & the Arts

A lively local favorite since 1977, **Pickleville Playhouse,** which is open from June through Labor Day weekend, features musical-comedy performances and a huge Western cookout on Thursday, Friday, and Saturday nights. ⊠ *2049 S. Bear Lake Blvd., Pickleville* ☎ *435/946–2918* ⊕ *www.picklevilleplayhouse.com.*

Shopping

Along U.S. 89, just before you reach Garden City, you'll find a string of small gift shops—all virtually the same—where you can buy Bear Lake raspberry products, T-shirts, and other souvenirs.

NORTHERN UTAH A TO Z

To research prices, get advice from other travelers, and book travel arrangements, visit www.fodors.com.

AIR TRAVEL

CARRIERS The closest airport with regularly scheduled air service is Salt Lake International. Two charter airlines, Utah Jet Center and Leading Edge Aviation, operate out of the Logan-Cache Airport; one charter airline, Mountain Air Flying Service, operates out of Brigham City.

🛪 **Leading Edge Aviation** ☎ 435/752-5955 ⊕ www.leadingedgeaviation.net. **Mountain Air Flying Service** ☎ 435/723-1121. **Utah Jet Center** ☎ 435/753-2221 ⊕ www.utahjet.com.

AIRPORTS

Salt Lake International is 60 mi south of Brigham City on I–15. Ogden-Hinckley Airport is Utah's busiest general aviation airport. The Logan-Cache airport is capable of handling small charter jets, and Brigham City has an airport for propeller planes.

🛪 **Salt Lake International Airport** ☎ 801/575-2400. **Brigham City Airport** ⊠ 1780 N. 2000 West St., Brigham City ☎ 435/723-1121. **Logan-Cache Airport** ⊠ 120 N. 100 West St., Logan ☎ 435/716-7171. **Ogden-Hinckley Airport** ⊠ 3909 Airport Rd. Ogden ☎ 801/629-8251.

AIRPORT Cache Valley Limo shuttles between Logan and the Salt Lake Interna-
TRANSFERS tional Airport for $46 each way.

🛪 **Cache Valley Limo Airport Shuttle** ☎ 435/563-6400.

BUS TRAVEL

Greyhound Lines operates on a limited schedule between Tremonton, Logan, and Brigham City. You can also get to Salt Lake City, if you're willing to be at the Logan bus station at 3:35 AM, the only daily departure. A better option for getting to and from the Wasatch Front is the Utah Transit Authority, which runs buses more or less hourly between Brigham City and Ogden with stops in Willard and Perry. From Ogden there are many connections to Salt Lake City. The price is a steal: $1.40 for a two-hour ride (that should get you all the way to Salt Lake) or $3 for an all-day pass, which will also allow you to ride TRAX, Salt Lake City's light rail, once you get there. Within Cache Valley, catch the free blue-and-white Logan Transit District shuttles, which operate within Logan (with an express to Utah State University) or the Cache Valley Transit District between Richmond to the north and Hyrum to the south. The main station is within walking distance of most hotels at 500 North and 100 East streets.

🛪 **Greyhound Lines** ☎ 801/355-9579 or 800/231-2222 ⊕ www.greyhound.com. **Utah Transit Authority** ☎ 801/743-3882 or 888/743-3882 ⊕ www.rideuta.com. **Logan Transit District** ☎ 435/752-2877.

CAMPING

There are plenty of campgrounds in northern Utah, and sites vary from the primitive to the luxurious. Ten public campgrounds dot this neck of the Wasatch-Cache National Forest, one near Mantua (4 mi east of Brigham City on U.S. 89/91) and nine in Logan Canyon. National Forest campgrounds cost between $6 and $12 per night. Utah Parks and Recreation also runs campgrounds at the two state parks, Hyrum Reservoir ($12) and Bear Lake ($8–$20). If you want full hookups, showers, and all the amenities, your best bet is a private campground. There are several to choose from in Brigham City, Logan, and Garden City. If you prefer a mountain setting, Beaver Mountain Ski Area in Logan Canyon has RV hookups for rent in summer. Private campgrounds range from $14 to $25 per night. Reservations in the National Forest are handled through a concessionaire, the National Recreation Reservation Service. You can also backpack and camp on most of the public land in Utah; check at the ranger station at the mouth of Logan Canyon for suggestions. During drought years fires are prohibited in summer.

⛏ **Bridgerland Travel Region** ☎ 435/752-2161. **National Recreation Reservation Service** ☎ 877/444-6777 ⊕ www.reserveusa.com. **Utah State Parks and Recreation** ☎ 800/322-3770 reservations ⊕ www.stateparks.utah.gov.

CAR RENTAL

Ogden, Brigham City, and Logan have several car rental agencies. C&R Auto Sales and Rental is close to downtown in Brigham City and also has branches in Tremonton and Bear River City. Hertz and Enterprise have offices in Logan and Ogden.

⛏ **C&R Auto Sales and Rental** ☎ 435/723-3433. **Hertz** ☎ 435/752-2961 or 800/654-7544 ⊕ www.hertz.com. **Enterprise** ☎ 800/736-8322 or 435/755-6111 in Logan, 801/399-5555 in Ogden ⊕ www.enterprise.com.

CAR TRAVEL

Northern Utah has two main highways, I–15 running north–south and U.S. 89 running northeast–southwest. The latter is a national scenic byway, and the hour's drive between Logan and Bear Lake will reward you with breathtaking vistas and plenty of places to pull off for a picnic. Off the main highways, roads range from well-paved multilane blacktop routes to barely graveled backcountry trails. If you're going to venture off the beaten track at all, it's a good idea to have a four-wheel-drive vehicle or at least a truck with high clearance. Deer, elk, and even bobcats may try to get to the other side of a road just as you come along, so watch out for wildlife on the highways. In rural and resort towns, expect gas prices to be considerably higher than in large cities.

⛏ **Utah Highway Patrol Ogden Office** ☎ 801/476-7750. **Utah Highway Patrol Logan Office** ☎ 435/752-1110.

⛏ **Road Conditions Utah Road Condition Information** ☎ 511 in Salt Lake City area and 800/492-2400 within Utah.

EMERGENCIES

⛏ **Ambulance or Police Emergencies** ☎ 911.

⛏ **24-Hour Medical Care Brigham City Community Hospital** ✉ 950 S. Medical Dr., Brigham City ☎ 435/734-9471. **Cache Valley Specialty Hospital** ✉ 2380 N. 400 East St., North Logan ☎ 435/713-9700. **Logan Regional Hospital** ✉ 1400 N. 500 East St., Logan ☎ 435/716-1000. **Ogden Regional Medical Center** ✉ 5475 S. 500 East St. Ogden ☎ 801/479-2111.

MEDIA

NEWSPAPERS & MAGAZINES
The daily *Herald Journal* covers Cache Valley and Bear Lake (pick up a copy of Friday's edition, which includes the *Cache Magazine* insert, to find the arts and entertainment listings for that week; also check Fridays Outdoors page for free hiking and biking excursions into Logan Canyon). Brigham City has a weekly paper, the *News-Journal,* and Tremonton has a weekly called the *Leader.*

TELEVISION & RADIO
Channel 3 (17 on basic cable) is KVLY, the "Valley Channel." It has a regularly updated weather visual, local advertisements, some high school sporting events, and an interview show with area newsmakers. Channels 2, 4, 5, and 13 are the CBS, ABC, NBC, and Fox affiliates in Salt Lake City, respectively. Radio options, in addition to some of the Salt Lake and Ogden stations, include KVNZ (104.9 FM) and KKEX (96.7 FM) for country-western; KOOL (103.9 FM) and KLZX (95.9 FM) for oldies from the 1960s and '70s; KVFX (94.5) for modern rock; and KBLQ (92.9) for soft rock and local news. Utah State University has a particularly good NPR affiliate, KUSU at 89.5 and 91.5 FM; it airs the standard NPR fare plus local news and a local call-in show called "Access Utah," also a locally hosted folk music show. An AM station, KLGN (1390) plays hits from the 1940s, '50s and '60s and CBS news.

SPORTS & THE OUTDOORS

FISHING
The Logan River and Blacksmith Fork are blue-ribbon trout streams, and though trout have been hit by whirling disease as in most Western streams, the native fish are fairly resistant and haven't been decimated like in some areas. (Note: it is safe to eat a fish with whirling disease, although they become so disfigured they're not exactly appetizing.) You can pull indigenous Bear Lake cutthroat, which are found nowhere else in the world, out of Bear Lake, or join the locals in dip-netting Bear Lake cisco when they come to shore to spawn in January. Warm-water species are found in abundance in Mantua Reservoir, 4 mi east of Brigham City on U.S. 89. In the Bear River, it's mostly carp these days. For a novelty fishing experience, boat out to the middle of Tony Grove Lake and use a long line with plenty of sinkers to land one of the rare albino trout that frequent the depths of the lake. You can get a fishing license at most local sporting goods stores but if you want to obtain your license online, go to the **Logan City Website** (⊕ www.ci.logan.ut.us/services.html).
🗗 **Utah Division of Wildlife Resources Fishing Hotline** ☎ 877/592-5169.

HIKING
A great way to see northern Utah is on foot. All four counties here (Cache, Rich, Box Elder, and Weber) contain portions of national forest, and both the Wellsvilles and the Bear River Range have federal wilderness areas where no motor-vehicle traffic is allowed. For great hiking ideas in and around Weber County, contact Weber Pathways for detailed information. Your best source of trail information in the Logan area is the Logan Ranger District office at the mouth of Logan Canyon. It's closed on weekends, though. Most of the hiking trails are also great cross-country ski trails in winter.
🗗 **Weber Pathways** ☎ 801/393-2304 ⊕ www.weberpathways.org. **Logan Ranger District** ✉ 1500 E. U.S. 89, Logan 84321 ☎ 435/755-3620.

VISITOR INFORMATION

Bear Lake–Rendezvous Chamber of Commerce (📪 Box 55, Garden City 84028 ☎ 800/448–2327 ⊕ www.bearlake.dcdi.net). **Bear River Valley Chamber of Commerce** (📪 Box 311, Tremonton 84337 ☎ 435/257–7585 ⊕ www.bearriverchamber.com). **Brigham City Chamber of Commerce** (✉ 6 N. Main St., Brigham City 84302 ☎ 435/723–3931 ⊕ www.bcareachamber.com). **Cache Valley Tourist Council/Bridgerland Travel Region** (✉ 160 N. Main St., Logan 84321 ☎ 435/752–2161 or 800/882–4433 ⊕ www.tourcachevalley.com). **Golden Spike Empire** (✉ 2501 Wall Ave. Ogden 84401 ☎ 801/627–8288 or 800/255–8824 ⊕ www.ogdencvb.org). **Ogden Valley Business Association** (✉ 5460 East 2200 N, Eden 84310 ☎ 801/745–2550 ⊕ www.ovba.org).

Dinosaurland & Eastern Utah

4

By Kelley J. P. Lindberg

THE EASTERN CORNER OF UTAH, wedged neatly between Wyoming above and Colorado to the east, is the reward for those willing to take the road less traveled. Neither I–80 nor I–70 enter this part of the state, so most visitors who pass through the Western United States never even see it. That, of course, is part of its appeal. Small towns, rural attitudes, and a more casual and friendly approach to life are all part of the eastern Utah experience.

Eastern Utah is most spectacular when viewed out of doors. It's home to great boating and fishing at Flaming Gorge, Red Fleet, Steinaker, and Starvation reservoirs. Hundreds of miles of hiking and mountain-biking trails (often available to cross-country skiers, snowmobilers, or snowshoers in winter) crisscross the region. The Green and Yampa rivers entice white-water rafters as well as less ambitious float-trippers. The pine- and aspen-covered Uinta (pronounced *You-in-tah*) Mountains reveal hidden, pristine lakes and streams to campers and hikers.

This area of Utah was home to Native American cultures long before the first European fur trappers and explorers arrived. Cliff walls and boulders throughout the region are dotted with thousands of examples of rock art of the Fremont people (AD 300 to 1300), so called because they inhabited the region near the Fremont River. Some rock art is older—at least 2,000 years old—and some is more recent, created by early European explorers and homesteaders. Today the Uintah and Ouray Reservation covers a significant portion of eastern Utah (approximately 1.4 million acres), though much of the reservation's original land grant was reclaimed by the U.S. government for its mineral and timber resources. The Ute tribe, whose 3,000-some members inhabit the land, hold powwows and other cultural ceremonies, which help visitors understand their way of life.

Museums throughout the region are full of pioneer relics, and you'll find several restored homesteads in and near Vernal. You'll also be able to unearth the dinosaur legacy that's made eastern Utah one of the most important paleontological research areas in the world. You'll discover the rich mining history of the Price–Helper area. And, of course, you'll hear story after story of outlaws, robberies, mine disasters, and heroic deeds everywhere you go.

Exploring Eastern Utah

Helper and Price, towns rich in mining and railroad history as well as in dinosaur fossils, are only a couple of hours southeast of Salt Lake City. Price is the largest city on U.S. 6, the major route between the Wasatch Front and the southeastern portion of the state (and the quickest way to reach I–70 if you're headed east into Colorado). Vernal and Dinosaur National Monument (which spans the Utah–Colorado border) are four hours east of Salt Lake City on Route 40, or three hours northeast of Price via U.S. 191 and U.S. 40. Flaming Gorge is 40 mi north of Vernal via U.S. 191. The Uinta Mountains and the High Uintas Wilderness Area are about 1½ hours east of Salt Lake City, first via I–80 and U.S. 40 to Kamas and then via Route 150.

About the Restaurants

Because the towns in eastern Utah are small, dining options are generally more casual and less innovative than in more urban areas. Helper has the region's only brewpub (Grogg's Pinnacle Brewing Company); fortunately, it's a good one. Price has a mix of ethnic restaurants that represent its immigrant railroad and mining history. Vernal, a farming and ranching town, has good steak houses. The best dining in this part of the state can be found in upscale lodges—Falcon's Ledge Lodge, north of Duchesne, and Red Canyon Lodge and Flaming Gorge Lodge, both near Flaming Gorge—which pride themselves on having gourmet menus. Bear in mind that most locally owned restaurants are closed on Sunday, so motel restaurants and fast-food places are often the only places you can get food on Sunday.

About the Hotels

Most hotels and motels in eastern Utah are chains, and you can expect clean, comfortable rooms and the normal amenities. The area's lodges make for a nice change of pace, surrounding you with natural beauty and more individualized rooms and services.

WHAT IT COSTS				
$$$$	**$$$**	**$$**	**$**	**¢**
RESTAURANTS over $25	$19–$25	$13–$18	$8–$12	under $8
HOTELS over $200	$151–$200	$111–$150	$70–$110	under $70

Restaurant prices are for a main course at dinner, excluding sales tax of 7%–7.75% (depending on the city). Hotel prices are for two people in a standard double room in high season, excluding service charges and taxes of 9%–10.75% (depending on the city).

Timing

In eastern Utah, most museums, parks, and other sights extend their hours during the summer season, from Memorial Day to Labor Day. (Some museums and parks are only open in summer.) Summer also brings art festivals, rodeos, pioneer reenactments, and other celebrations. Of course, it's also the hottest period of the year, when temperatures can reach 100°F, so it's an ideal time for rafting trips down the Green River or boating on the region's reservoirs. Spring and autumn are cooler and less crowded, therefore nicer for hiking or biking, but you'll miss out on some of the festivities. Some campgrounds are open year-round, but the drinking water is usually turned off after Labor Day, so bring your own. In winter you can cross-country ski or snowshoe on many of the hiking trails; maps are available at local visitor centers.

EAST–CENTRAL UTAH (CASTLE COUNTRY)

Spanish explorers and traders crossed East-Central Utah as early as 1598 on a trail now followed by Route 10. In the 19th century fur trappers passed through the mountains in their search for beaver and other animals, and in the 1870s some of them decided to return to do some ranching. However, the area didn't thrive until a new kind of wealth was

Numbers in the text correspond to numbers in the margin and on Eastern Utah map.

If you have 3 days

Start your tour of eastern Utah in **Helper ❶** ▸. Orient yourself at the Western Mining and Railroad Museum, then spend some time browsing the Main Street galleries before heading off to the ghost towns in Spring Canyon and other areas around Helper. End your day in 🚉 **Price ❷**, where you will spend the next two nights. Spend the next morning at the College of Eastern Utah Prehistoric Museum, then head up Nine Mile Canyon. You might end your day with dinner at Grogg's Pinnacle Brewing Company in Helper. The next morning take in the Price Mural, shoot a round of golf at the Carbon Country Club, or do a little hiking or biking on local trails, then head to **Duchesne ❸** along the Indian Canyon Scenic Byway (U.S. 191). From there it's an easy 2½-hour trip back to Salt Lake City via U.S. 40 and I-80.

If you have 5 days

For the first two days, follow the itinerary above. On the third morning start off bright and early for **Duchesne ❸**. At Duchesne, turn east on U.S. 40 and go to 🚉 **Vernal ❺**, which will be your home for the next two nights. Once you've seen the sights in Vernal, drive out to **Dinosaur National Monument ❻** for a look at the fossils, the beautiful canyons, and the Josie Morris Cabin. Day 4 is perfect for a one-day river-rafting trip on the Green River, or you can visit Browns Park and the John Jarvie Ranch for some perspective on early ranching and the Outlaw Trail. That evening, see if the rodeo or the Outlaw Trail Theater in Vernal is in full swing. On Day 5, start early to give yourself time to explore **Flaming Gorge, ❼** making sure to stop at the Red Canyon visitor center to take in the view from atop 1,300-foot cliffs. From here, the fastest route back to Salt Lake City is through Wyoming (4½ hours).

---

discovered in the mountains—coal. Railroad tracks were laid in the valley in 1883 to bring miners from around the world to dig the black mineral and to carry the coal out to markets across the country. Coal continues to provide the economic base for many towns in Castle Country, so nicknamed for the impressive castlelike rock formations that grace many parts of the landscape.

Helper

▸ ❶ *50 mi south of Salt Lake City via I–15, then 60 mi southeast on U.S. 6.*

In the 1880s the Denver & Rio Grande Railroad established a terminal for the "helper" locomotives they used to get trains up the steep mountain. The town of Helper grew up around this terminal, populated with the most diverse set of immigrant railroad workers and coal miners in the state. Signs at the area coal mines were displayed in a half-dozen languages, and the town's history of growth and mining disasters is brimming with Greek, Italian, Japanese, Eastern European, and other ethnic names.

In the late 19th and early 20th centuries, canyons around Helper were crawling with mining operations and dotted with mining camps, whose inhabitants flocked to Helper on Saturday nights for movies, swimming, dancing, and sporting matches, as well as more illicit pleasures like gambling, bootleg liquor, and prostitution. Now the mining camps around Helper are ghost towns, and Helper's Main Street is an eclectic mix of historic buildings, empty storefronts, and art galleries. The railroad and remaining coal mines still keep the heart of Helper beating, although the pace is decidedly slower.

The **Western Mining & Railroad Museum,** which is in the Old Helper Hotel in the town's National Historic District, is a treasure and doubles as a visitor center. Model trains make their rounds and a simulated coal tunnel shows the history of mining tools. Rooms depict everyday activities of Helper's past and include a medical room, a children's toy room, a school room, a railroad office, and a beauty salon. One room is dedicated to the more illicit side of Helper, with a jail cell, stills, and early beer bottles. Incredible photographs and paintings throughout the museum put a face on the gamut of Helper history, and there's an outdoor exhibit of trains and mining equipment. ⊠ *296 S. Main St.* ☎ *435/ 472–3009* ⊕ *www.wmrrm.org* ✉ *$2 donation* ☉ *May–Sept., Mon.–Sat. 10–5; Oct.–Apr., Tues.–Sat. 11–4.*

FodorśChoice ★

The Helper area—in particular the area around **Spring Canyon**—probably holds the state's best concentration of ghost towns. Spring Canyon Road winds past the remnants of several ghost towns, including the town of Spring Canyon, Standardville, Latuda, and Mutual. While most of the buildings are slowly crumbling back into dust, you can still see some foundations, and if you're lucky, you might catch a glimpse of "The White Lady"—a ghostly figure rumored to haunt the Latuda mine office. You can get a map of all the ghost towns in the Helper area at the Western Mining and Railroad Museum's information desk. ⊠ *Spring Canyon Rd., 4 mi west of Helper.*

Kenilworth, 1½ mi south of Helper, then about 5 mi northeast on Kenilworth Road, is part mining ghost town, part living history. It was originally a company town built to support the Kenilworth Mine, but when the mine closed, residents bought up the houses and land and are still living there.

off the
beaten
path

SCOFIELD STATE PARK – High in the forests of the Manti–La Sal Mountains, Scofield Reservoir is a popular destination for boating and fishing in summer, and ice fishing, snowmobiling, and cross-country skiing in winter. Facilities close in late October. The town of Scofield at the southern end of the lake was once a thriving coal mining town, and the **Scofield Cemetery** is filled with headstones from the Winter Quarters mine explosion that killed 200 men and boys in 1900. ⊠ *17 mi north of Helper on U.S. 6, then 10 mi south on Rte. 96* ☎ *435/448–9449* ⊕ *www.stateparks.utah.gov* ✉ *$6* ☉ *May–Oct. daily, 6 AM–10 PM* ☉ *Facilities closed Nov.–Apr.*

4

The Outdoors

Towns in eastern Utah are small, and the population is sparse. Urban luxuries are an afterthought. The lure of this area is not indoors, air-conditioned, and antiseptic. It's all about being outside. This country is magnificent, whether you're perfecting that barely perceptible whisk of your hand-tied fly inches from the surface of a sun-dazzled creek in the High Uintas, listening to thousands of birds rising into the cool evening air over the Ouray National Wildlife Refuge, laughing out loud at the taste of cold river water drenching you as an experienced guide rafts you through the narrow walls of Dinosaur National Monument's sunset-color canyons, or savoring the smells of sage and wind-scoured sandstone as you pause during your hike along a high-ridge plateau over Price. Get outside. Take sunblock and water. And leave your walls at home.

History

America's Wild West grabs the imagination like few other time periods. There's something about pioneers, cowboys, Native Americans, mountain men, outlaws, miners, and intrepid explorers that keeps us fascinated. In eastern Utah, the Wild West wasn't really so long ago. Homesteaders were still staking out their claims in the 1900s, and ranchers still ride horses and use sheep dogs to round up their livestock. A good portion of eastern Utah is actually the sovereign land of the Uintah and Ouray Indian Reservation. Out here, the American West isn't some hokey Hollywood fiction—it's real, honest, and gritty. Experience the real West by searching for rock art, seeing a rodeo, watching the Northern Ute Pow Wow, touring the local history museums, visiting restored homesteads, or hiking or biking through landscapes that once sheltered outlaws and humbled pioneers.

Prehistory

Eastern Utah hasn't always been a place of carved canyons, dry plateaus, and rugged mountains. Throughout millions of years, this stretch of land has been alternately lush and verdant with giant ferns, flooded by seas, or frozen in ice. Now, all those layers of time have begun to reveal their secrets. Dinosaurs once trod footprints into mud, or lay down to die beside fast-moving rivers in the regions we now know as Vernal and Price. Since the 19th century, archaeologists have painstakingly excavated hundreds of tons of fossils from eastern Utah, puzzling together the intricate and elusive story of the Jurassic and Cretaceous eras. When you come to eastern Utah, you are entering one of the world's most important areas of dinosaur and fossil research. Let yourself be swept up in dino-mania, and visit the College of Eastern Utah Prehistoric Museum in Price, the Utah Field House of Natural History State Park in Vernal, and of course the astounding Dinosaur Quarry and scenic wonder of Dinosaur National Monument just outside Vernal. And keep your eyes peeled for fossils wherever you hike.

Where to Stay & Eat

★ ¢–$$ ✕ **Grogg's Pinnacle Brewing Company.** A surprising discovery on the road toward Price, this small microbrewery has a comfortable, modern feel to it. A stone fireplace welcomes you as warmly as the staff, and outdoor patio seating with umbrellas beckons in the warmer months. Try any of Grogg's own microbrewed beers with your pizza, steak, or sandwich. ✉ *1653 N. Carbonville Rd.* ☎ *435/637–2924* ▭ *AE, D, MC, V.*

¢–$ ✕ **Balance Rock Eatery & Pub.** Broad white walls, a white railing around the second-floor mezzanine, paddle fans, and open shelves of antiques give this combination restaurant and antiques store a light and airy feeling that it probably never had when it was a hardware store on historic Main Street. The sandwiches are popular, and the burgers are made with fresh ground beef that is never frozen. You can quaff domestic beers or Utah-made microbrews while you shoot a game of pool or browse the antiques. They also serve breakfast on weekends. ✉ *148 S. Main St.* ☎ *435/472–0403* ▭ *AE, MC, V.*

WHERE TO CAMP △ **Scofield State Park Campgrounds.** Both of the state park campgrounds (Mountain View and Madsen Bay) have boat ramps and swimming areas. Mountain View has scattered shade. ⚲ *Flush toilets, dump station, drinking water, showers (Mountain View only), fire pits, grills, picnic tables, ranger station, swimming (lake)* ⇲ *34 sites at Mountain View, 40 at Madsen Bay* ✉ *Rte. 96, 17 mi north and west of Helper* ☎ *435/ 448–9449 information, 801/322–3770, 800/322–3770 reservations* ⊕ *www.stateparks.utah.gov* ⌧ *$11 Madsen Bay, $14 Mountain View* ▭ *MC, V for phone reservations, no credit cards at the park* ☉ *May–Oct.*

The Arts

Much of Helper's Main Street is on the National Register of Historic Places, yet many of the buildings are empty. Artists are discovering Helper's quaint feel and rich history, and they are beginning to move into Helper and fill up some of the empty storefronts on Main Street with galleries, studios, and boutiques. It's worth a stroll to check out the latest artistic displays. The big event in town is the annual **Helper Arts Festival** (☎ 435/ 637–3009 or 800/842–0789 ⊕ www.helperartsfestival.com) in mid-August, which celebrates Helper's enthusiastic ambition to reinvent itself as an artists' colony.

Price

❷ *7 mi south of Helper via U.S. 6.*

Thousands of visitors annually come to Price to look at Utah's prehistoric past in the College of Eastern Utah Prehistoric Museum. Like many Utah towns, Price began as a Mormon farming settlement in the late 1800s. In 1883 the railroad arrived, bringing immigrants from around the world to mine coal reserves that had barely been acknowledged up until that point. Mining became the town's primary industry, which it remains to this day.

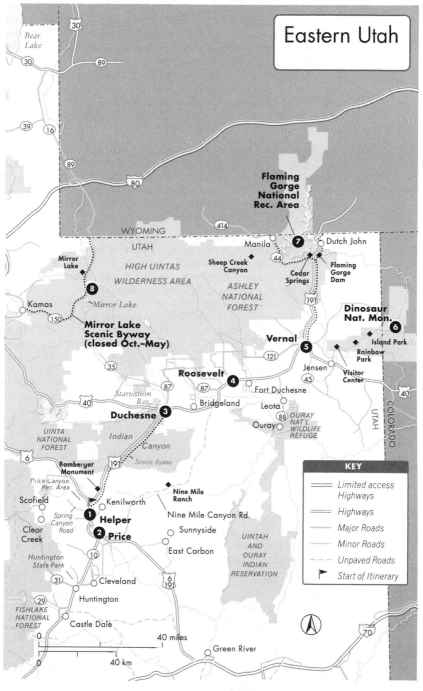

Miners working in the coal fields around Price in the late 1800s often saw and excavated rare treasures that most scientists could only dream of finding—dinosaur bones, eggs, skeletons, and fossilized tracks. These are all on view at the **College of Eastern Utah Prehistoric Museum.** A second hall is devoted to early humans, with displays of beadwork, clay figurines, and other area artifacts. In May the museum participates in the statewide Utah Prehistory Week, sponsoring children's activities, lectures, and field trips. ⊠ *155 E. Main St.* ☎ *435/613–5111 or 800/817–9949* ⊕ *http://museum.ceu.edu* ⊠ *$3* ☉ *Apr.–Sept., daily 9–6; Oct.–Mar., Mon.–Sat. 9–5.*

The 200-foot-long **Price Mural** in the Price Municipal Building is a visual narration of the history of the town as well as Carbon County, beginning with the first trappers and white settlers. The painting, which took artist Lynn Fausett almost four years to complete, was a Works Progress Administration project in the late 1930s. ⊠ *185 E. Main St.* ☎ *435/637–5010* ⊠ *Free* ☉ *Weekdays 9–5.*

Fodor's Choice **Nine Mile Canyon.** Hundreds of petroglyphs etched into the boulders and cliffs of Nine Mile Canyon are the handiwork of the Fremont Indians, who lived in much of what is now Utah from AD 300 to 1250. The canyon shelters the remnants of many early homesteads, stage stops, and ranches. However, the petroglyphs and pictographs are the main draw. It's important not to touch the fragile rock art because oils from your fingers can damage them. Most of this 80-mi round-trip is on a gravel road, so plan to take most of a day to complete it and bring water and a picnic, because there are no services. A brochure detailing significant sites is available at visitor centers in Price. Without it, many panels will go unnoticed. At the gas station where you turn off U.S. 6 in Wellington to head to the canyon, you can also buy a self-published book that contains far more sites, photos, and directions. To reach the canyon, go 7½ mi east of Price on U.S. 6 and then turn north on Nine Mile Canyon Rd. ⊠ *Nine Mile Canyon Rd., 7½ mi east of Price* ☎ *435/636–3600.*

Sports & the Outdoors
Carbon County covers a wide range of geography, from mountains to gorges to plateaus. Hundreds of miles of hiking and biking trails crisscross the region.

GOLF The 18-hole championship course at the **Carbon Country Club** (⊠ 3055 N. U.S. 6 ☎ 435/637–2388) is open to the public. Keep in mind that it may be hard to concentrate on your game when you're surrounded by sandstone cliffs, a waterfall, hidden Native American petroglyphs, and a pioneer burial ground.

MOUNTAIN BIKING The visitor center at the **College of Eastern Utah Prehistoric Museum** (⊠ 155 E. Main St. ☎ 435/613–5111 or 800/817–9949) has a mountain-biking guide that shows several trails you can tackle, including Nine Mile Canyon.

Where to Stay & Eat
¢–$$ ✗ **Farlaino's.** In a historic building on Main Street, this casual restaurant attracts the locals with its large menu of American fare for breakfast and lunch throughout the week, and its traditional Italian menu for

UTAH'S MINE DISASTERS

IN THE LATE 1800S, when coal mining began in earnest in the mountains around Helper, it was hard, dangerous work. On May 1, 1900, just days after a mine inspector had certified the Pleasant Valley Coal Company's Winter Quarters mine as being safe, the Number 4 shaft exploded. Two hundred men and boys were killed, some burned, some crushed, some asphyxiated by the deadly mix of post-explosion gases called afterdamp. Most of the families in the mining camps of Winter Quarters and Scofield were affected. Several families lost more than one member—one father and son were found dead together, arms entwined. More than one woman lost a husband and more than one son; at least one lost her father, two brothers, and newlywed husband.

On March 8, 1924, another disaster struck the same company, which had been renamed the Castle Gate Coal Company. Its mine exploded, killing over 150 men.

Today, the techniques of coal mining have changed. Machinery is far more high-tech, processes are safer, warning systems are incredibly sensitive, and miners are more educated about safety. Yet miners are still working deep underground, surrounded by potentially combustible material, so disasters still happen.

On December 19, 1984, a fire in the Wilberg mine in Emery county, south of Helper, claimed the lives of 27 miners, including the first woman miner ever killed in a Utah mining accident. And on June 2, 2003, a fire at the Willow Creek mine killed two men and injured eight others. Graves of victims from the 1924 Castle Gate mine explosion lie 150 yards from the entrance to the Willow Creek mine as silent reminders: coal mining is still difficult and dangerous work.

---

dinner Wednesday through Saturday. There's beer on draft. ⊠ 87 W. Main St. ☎ 435/637–9217 ⊟ AE, MC, V ☺ Closed Sun. No dinner Mon. and Tues.

¢–$$ ✕ **Ricardo's.** If everyone in the group is craving something different, the vast menu here will accommodate most any taste for breakfast, lunch, and dinner. This popular local diner-style restaurant at the Greenwell Inn serves enchiladas, burritos, and tacos, as well as sandwiches, steak, and seafood dishes. Alcohol is available from Wooly's Private Club downstairs. ⊠ 655 E. Main St. ☎ 435/637–2020 ⊟ AE, D, MC, V.

¢–$ ✕ **Greek Streak.** On the site of a Greek coffeehouse from the early
Fodor'sChoice 1900s, this café is a reminder of Price's strong Greek heritage. The menu
★ includes traditional recipes from Crete: gyros, dolmades, lemon-rice soup, and such. The baklava and other desserts made here are considered the best Greek pastries in the state. ⊠ 84 S. Carbon Ave. ☎ 435/637–1930 ⊟ MC, V ☺ Closed Sun.

¢ ✕ **El Salto Mexican Café.** Traditional Mexican specialities, such as tamales, chiles rellenos, and taquitos, make this one of the area's most popular restaurants. ⊠ 19 S. Carbon Ave. ☎ 435/637–6545 ⊟ MC, V ☺ Closed Sun. No lunch Sat.

¢ ✕ **Sherald's Burger Bar.** If you hanker for the nostalgia of an old-fashioned hamburger stand, where you order at the window and sit in your car, or sit outside at a picnic table where a carhop takes your order, you're in luck. Stop at Sherald's and see why locals stand in line here for their burgers, scones, malts, and shakes, ignoring the McDonald's across the street. ⊠ *434 E. Main St.* ☎ *435/637–1447* ⊙ *Closed Sun.*

$–$$ ⊞ **Holiday Inn Hotel and Suites.** This large, tastefully decorated hotel has a large atrium containing the pool, and the hotel's nightclub and restaurant have partial glass ceilings and walls for a sunroom effect. Rooms have irons, hair dryers, and coffeemakers, and suites have jetted tubs and kitchenettes. The restaurant is one of the few in Price open on Sunday; guests receive a complimentary membership to the nightclub, which serves alcohol. ⊠ *838 Westwood Blvd., 84501* ☎ *435/637–8880 or 800/465–4329* ⊟ *435/637–7707* ⊕ *www.ichotelsgroup.com* ⊃ *136 rooms, 15 suites* ⊂ *Restaurant, some in-room hot tubs, some kitchenettes, cable TV with movies and video games, Wi-Fi, in-room data ports, indoor pool, gym, nightclub, laundry facilities, business services, convention center, meeting rooms, airport shuttle, no-smoking rooms* ⊟ *AE, D, DC, MC, V.*

$ ⊞ **Greenwell Inn & Convention Center.** With more amenities than most local hotels, but still reasonably priced, the Greenwell is a good choice. Every room has a refrigerator, hair dryer, and coffeemaker, and a 15% discount to the restaurant and membership to the hotel's private club are included with the room. Luxury suites have waterfall tubs and remote-control fireplaces. ⊠ *655 E. Main St., 84501* ☎ *435/637–3520 or 800/666–3520* ⊟ *435/637–4858* ⊕ *www.greenwellinn.com* ⊃ *125 rooms, 3 suites* ⊂ *Restaurant, some kitchenettes, refrigerators, cable TV, Wi-Fi, in-room data ports, indoor pool, gym, hot tub, sports bar, video game room, laundry facilities, business services, convention center, no-smoking rooms* ⊟ *AE, D, DC, MC, V.*

¢ ⊞ **Best Western Carriage House Inn.** Behind a white, colonial-style facade, the motel-basic rooms all have irons, hair dryers, and coffeemakers; each day, you get a complimentary newspaper. Restaurants and shops are within reasonable walking distance. The roof over the pool retracts in summer to let the sun in. ⊠ *590 E. Main St., 84501* ☎ *435/637–5660* ⊟ *435/637–5157* ⊕ *www.bestwestern.com* ⊃ *41 rooms* ⊂ *Some microwaves, some refrigerators, cable TV, in-room data ports, indoor-outdoor pool, hot tub, airport shuttle, no-smoking rooms* ⊟ *AE, D, DC, MC, V* ⊠⧵ *CP.*

¢ ⊞ **Super 8 Motel.** Just off U.S. 6, this motel offers all manner of discounts. If you need a hair dryer or iron, ask for one at the desk. The indoor pool will please the kids during chillier months when outdoor pools at the other motels in town are closed. ⊠ *180 Hospital Dr., 84501* ☎ *435/637–8088* ⊟ *435/637–8483* ⊕ *www.super8.com* ⊃ *37 rooms, 3 suites* ⊂ *Some microwaves, some refrigerators, cable TV, Wi-Fi, indoor pool, hot tub, no-smoking rooms* ⊟ *AE, D, MC, V.*

WHERE TO CAMP ⚬ **Nine Mile Ranch.** Ben Mead grew up in beautiful Nine Mile Canyon and now runs a "bunk and breakfast" and campground here. If you camp or rent a sparsely furnished log cabin or teepee, arrange ahead of time for a cowboy breakfast or Dutch-oven dinner. If you rent a room in the Meads's house, breakfast is included. Play your cards right, and Ben may recite some of his cowboy poetry—he's the real deal, and there's nothing "dime-store" about him. There's no electricity in the cabins and no hookups for the campsites, but there is electricity in the restrooms. To reach the ranch, go 7½ mi east of Price on U.S. 6, then 25 mi north on Nine Mile Canyon Road. ⚅ *Flush toilets, dump station, drinking water, fire pits, picnic tables* ⚑ *20 sites, 2 cabins, 1 teepee, 2 rooms* ⊠ *Nine Mile Canyon Rd., Box 212, Wellington 84542* ☎ *435/637–2572* ⊕ *www. ninemilecanyon.com* ⚑ *$10 campsite, $50 cabin, $60 room.*

Nightlife & the Arts

THE ARTS   A sizable number of Greeks came to the Price area to work in the mines. At the **Greek Festival** (⊠ Assumption Greek Orthodox Church, 61 S. 200 Fast St. ☎ 435/637–3009 or 800/842–0789) in mid-July, traditional Greek food, dance, and music celebrate this heritage.

At the end of July, **International Days** (⊠ Washington Park, 150 E. 450 North St. ☎ 435/637–2788) uses music, dance, and food to celebrate the many nationalities that make up the Price community.

NIGHTLIFE   Inside the Holiday Inn, **Rockie's Lounge** (⊠ 838 Westwood Blvd. ☎ 435/ 637–8880 or 800/465–4329) is a private club for hotel guests, but nonguests can buy inexpensive memberships. Skylights give the club an atrium feel, and a pool table and big-screen TV keep patrons amused when there isn't a comedy act performing.

Tucked away downstairs from Ricardo's Restaurant at the Greenwell Inn, **Wooly's Private Club** (⊠ 655 E. Main St. ☎ 435/637–2020 or 800/ 666–3520) offers inexpensive memberships (free for hotel guests). You can watch the game on the big-screen TV or throw some darts.

en route   The **Indian Canyon Scenic Byway** is the section of U.S. 191 that climbs up out of the Helper vicinity, cresting at Indian Creek Pass at an elevation of 9,100 feet. Then it begins a long descent into the Uinta Basin area, ending at Duchesne. The 43-mi route takes you through canyons, over plateaus, and into the heart of the geology and natural beauty that make up this part of Utah.

THE UINTA BASIN (DINOSAURLAND)

The Uinta Basin is a vast area of gently rolling land bordered by the Uinta Mountains to the north, the Wasatch Mountains to the west, and a series of high plateaus and cliffs to the south. Originally home to the ancient Fremont people, the Uinta Basin was surveyed by Spanish explorers in 1775. Mountain men made frequent trips through the valley in the early 1800s. The Mormons thought about settling here in 1847 but decided the land was not fit for agriculture. When they checked the area again in the 1860s, they decided it was still no place to live. At their suggestion, President Abraham Lincoln set aside several million acres of the basin as an Indian reservation and moved members of Ute and other tribes here from their traditional lands in the Salt Lake and Utah Lake valleys. In the late 1800s and early 1900s, much of the Uinta Basin land that had been set aside as a reservation was taken back by the U.S. government and opened to settlers from the East.

In the early 1900s, an unbelievably rich trove of dinosaur fossils was discovered in the sandstone layers near the eastern Utah border. Since then, archaeologists have unearthed hundreds of tons of fossils, and the area encompassing Daggett, Duchesne, and Uintah counties has become known as Dinosaurland. An area particularly rich in fossils, straddling the Utah and Colorado borders, has been preserved as Dinosaur National Monument.

Duchesne

❸ *53 mi northeast of Price via U.S. 191, then 4 mi west on U.S. 40.*

The small town of Duchesne is probably best known for its proximity to **Starvation State Park,** most likely named for the early homesteaders and cattlemen who battled bitter winters, short growing seasons, and other hardships in the area. Now it's a playground for boaters and anglers, who come to cast for walleye, German brown trout, and bass in the reservoir. ☎ *435/738–2326* ⊕ *www.stateparks.utah.gov* ⌦ *$5* ☉ *Daily.*

Where to Stay & Eat

$$$ ✕⊞ **Falcon's Ledge Lodge.** Guest rooms are luxurious; all have vaulted
Fodor'sChoice ceilings and two have jetted tubs. The lodge also offers luxury sporting
★ packages, including fly-fishing and wing-shooting. With an emphasis on escaping the workaday world, there are no TVs in the rooms, but you can wheel a portable TV with games into your room or visit the central big-screen TV room if you must. The five- to seven-course meals ($$$$) are the best in the area, but bring your own wine or alcohol. Specialties include whiskey-grilled, glazed filet mignon, bacon-wrapped ahi tuna, and fresh home-baked bread. Guests and nonguests must make advance reservations for the restaurant. ⊠ *Rte. 87, Box 67, Altamont 84001, 15 mi north of Duchesne* ☎ *435/454–3737 or 877/879–3737* ⊕ *www.falconsledge.com* ⌦ *9 rooms* ⌂ *Restaurant, outdoor hot tub, fishing, hiking, meeting room, kennel; no room phones, no room TVs, no kids under 12, no smoking* ⊟ *AE, MC, V* ⎥◎⎥ *BP.*

WHERE TO CAMP ⚠ **Starvation State Park Campgrounds.** Swim at the beach, launch your fishing boat, or soak up the sun. The campgrounds are open year-round, but the water in the restrooms is only turned on from mid-May to mid-September. The Mountain View campground has some shade; the Beach campground doesn't. ⌂ *Flush toilets, pit toilets, dump station, drinking water, showers, grills, picnic tables, public telephone, ranger station, swimming (lake)* ⌦ *54 sites* ⊠ *River Rd., 4 mi west of Duchesne* ☎ *435/738–2326 information or 800/322–3770, 801/322–3770 reservations* ⊕ *www.stateparks.utah.gov* ⌦ *$14.*

Roosevelt

❹ *28 mi northeast of Duchesne via U.S. 40.*

Roosevelt, a small town named for President Theodore Roosevelt, lies between blocks of the sovereign land of the Uinta and Ouray Indian Reservation.

The 1.4 million acres of the **Uintah and Ouray Indian Reservation** spreads out in patchwork fashion across the Uinta Basin and northeastern Utah to the eastern edge of the state. Fort Duchesne is the tribal headquarters for the Ute Indians. Because it's sometimes difficult to tell whether you're on reservation land, public land, or private land, you are asked to stay on main roads unless you have permission to be on the reservation lands.

Each July 4 weekend, the **Northern Ute Pow Wow** (⊠ Fort Duchesne, 8 mi east of Roosevelt on U.S. 40, at Fort Duchesne turnoff ☎ 435/722–8541 Ute Bulletin and Tribal Public Relations ⊕ www.utetribe.com) has drumming, dancing, and singing competitions, a rodeo, golf and softball tournaments, and an arts-and-crafts fair. One of the biggest powwows in the West, it's free to the public, who are welcome to attend and camp on the powwow grounds. Another, smaller powwow is held over Thanksgiving weekend at the tribal gymnasium in Fort Duchesne. For information about the powwows and other tribal events, contact the *Ute Bulletin.*

Established in 1960, the **Ouray National Wildlife Refuge** consists of 12,467 acres of land along the Green River, where you can see more than 200 species of migratory birds in spring and fall, mule deer and golden eagles year-round, and bald eagles in early winter. An information kiosk at the refuge has an auto-tour guide and a bird checklist. To reach the refuge, go 15 mi east of Roosevelt on U.S. 40, then 13 mi south on Route 88. ⊠ *Rte. 88, Ouray* ☎ *435/789–0351* ⊕ *http://mountain-prairie. fws.gov/ouray* ▨ *Free* ☉ *Daily.*

Sports & the Outdoors

Information about camping, fishing, hunting, and photo safaris on the Uintah and Ouray Indian Reservation is available from the **Ute Tribe Fish & Wildlife Department** (☎ 435/722–5511 ⊕ www.utetribe.com).

PACK TRIPS **J/L Ranch Outfitters and Guides** (⊲ Box 129, Whiterocks 84085 ☎ 435/353–4049 ⊕ www.jlranch.com) leads fishing trips into the Uintas and the Ashley National Forest. Fishing the lakes, rivers, and mountain streams of the Ashley National Forest and High Uintas will give you an up-close perspective of their natural beauty.

Where to Stay & Eat

¢ ✕▦ **Frontier Grill & Motel.** Accommodations at this downtown motel are simple but adequate and inexpensive, and the location puts you close to shops. Hair dryers are in each room and irons are available at the front desk. A golf course is ½ mi away. The restaurant ($–$$) is the most popular in town and serves American fare like steak, fried chicken, burgers, and meat loaf. ⊠ *75 S. 200 East St., 84066* ☎ *435/722–2201* 🖷 *435/722–2212* ⤲ *54 rooms* ⚘ *Restaurant, some kitchenettes, some refrigerators, cable TV, in-room broadband, pool, hot tub, business services, meeting room, some pets allowed, no-smoking rooms* ▭ *AE, D, DC, MC, V.*

$$–$$$ ▦ **J/L Ranch.** The J/L Ranch is a place where you can sleep in cowboy-theme comfort and fish in numerous lakes, rivers, and mountain streams.

The Chepeta cabin sleeps four; the "bunkhouse suite" on the second floor of the log horse barn (yes, there really are horses down there) sleeps six. Both are surprisingly nice, furnished with handmade log furniture, full baths, and fully equipped kitchens so you can prepare your own meals. There is no air-conditioning, but there are fans in each room. The price you pay varies depending on the number of people in your party. ⌂ *Box 129, Whiterocks 84085* ☎ *435/353–4049* ⎙ *435/353–4181* ⊕ *www. jlranch.com* ⇨ *2 suites* ☖ *Picnic area, kitchens, fans, in-room VCRs, laundry facilities; no a/c, no smoking* ▤ *No credit cards.*

$ ▥ **Best Western Inn.** In small towns like this, lodging choices are limited, so chains are often comforting in their sheer familiarity. The pool and restaurant make this the place to stay in Roosevelt. Rooms have hair dryers, irons, and coffeemakers. ⊠ *2203 E. 200 North St., 84066* ☎ *435/722–4644 or 800/780–7234* ⎙ *435/722–0179* ⊕ *www. bestwestern.com* ⇨ *40 rooms* ☖ *Restaurant, refrigerators, microwaves, cable TV, in-room broadband, pool, hot tub, no-smoking rooms* ▤ *AE, D, DC, MC, V.*

Vernal

❺ *22 mi east of Fort Duchesne via U.S. 40.*

Vernal is the hub of "Dinosaurland," but dinosaurs aren't the only things they're proud of in Vernal. The town claims the ancient Fremont Indians, a rowdy ranching past, and more than a passing acquaintance with outlaws like Butch Cassidy, who frequented the area whenever he felt it was safe to be seen around town. Now the largest town (population 8,000) in the northeast corner of the state, the cattle-ranching community of Vernal is one of the few Utah towns founded by non-Mormons. However, it was the town's remote location—at the eastern edge of Utah, far from government authorities in Utah, Wyoming, and Colorado— not a lack of religion, that led to its early reputation as a wild and lawless place. Each June Vernal celebrates its feisty past during the **Outlaw Trail Ride** (☎ 866/658–7433 ⊕ www.outlawtrailride.com). Guided horseback rides along outlaw trails, camping, cookouts, and Western-theme entertainment are among the main events.

★ ☺ One hundred and fifty million years ago this land was the stomping ground of dinosaurs. At **Utah Field House of Natural History State Park** you can see rock samples, fossils, Fremont and Ute artifacts, and a large mural depicting the last 2.7 billion years of the Uinta Basin's geologic history. The biggest attraction for kids is undoubtedly the outdoor Dinosaur Garden with its 18 life-size dinosaur models. The Field House also doubles as a visitor center for all of Dinosaurland, so stop here for maps and guides for the entire area. ⊠ *496 E. Main St.* ☎ *435/789–3799* ⊕ *www. stateparks.utah.gov* ▨ *$5* ☽ *Memorial Day–Labor Day, daily 8–7; Labor Day–Memorial Day, daily 9–5.*

Inside the big, open **Western Heritage Museum** are collections of Fremont and Ute Indian artifacts, including baskets, water jugs, and beadwork pieces, as well as pioneer items like carriages, guns, saddles, and old-fashioned children's toys. Outside, you can see various horse-drawn farm

BUTCH CASSIDY, THE ROBIN HOOD OF UTAH

ONE OF THE WEST'S MOST NOTORIOUS OUTLAWS was born and raised in southern Utah by Mormon parents, and his footprints and legends are scattered over southern and eastern Utah like buckshot. Butch Cassidy (born Robert LeRoy Parker) started out as a migrant cowboy dabbling in rustling. A brief career as a butcher in Wyoming earned him the nickname "Butch," and "Cassidy" was likely the name of his old rustling mentor.

By 1896 he'd formed a gang of accomplices and had turned from rustling to the more lucrative pursuits of bank and train robberies. His Wild Bunch of loosely knit companions fancied themselves the "Robin Hoods" of the West. Outraged by large, wealthy cattle barons squeezing out the smaller ranchers, the outlaws justified their lifestyle choice by sharing their bounty with the local people, who often struggled in the harsh environment of the Utah desert. Of course, the fact that this generosity helped buy allies and protectors in the area didn't hurt. Butch Cassidy was well-known for being shrewd, quick-witted, and charming.

The only major heist he pulled in Utah was in Price Canyon, near Helper, with his friend Elza Lay. Butch and Elza stole $7,000 in gold coins from the Pleasant Valley Coal Mine office by shoving a gun in the paymaster's belly while 200 men stood nearby waiting for their pay. The steps from the Castle Gate store, where the robbery occurred, are still on display at the Western Mining and Railroad Museum in Helper.

The Wild Bunch often wintered near Vernal in Browns Park—a major hideout along the so-called Outlaw Trail, which stretched from Mexico to Montana. Browns Park residents were apparently content to have the outlaws among them. Recipients of occasional windfalls from Cassidy's exploits, they were quick to notify the Wild Bunch whenever the law approached. To show their gratitude, Cassidy and the Wild Bunch once cooked and served an extravagant Thanksgiving dinner to 35 of the area's inhabitants.

It was also in Browns Park that Butch met his girlfriend popularly known as Etta Place, most likely a woman named Ann Bassett, who was known as "Queen of the Rustlers." Ann's sister, Josie Morris, was also said to have entertained Butch Cassidy at her cabin in what is now Dinosaur National Monument.

After masterminding one of the longest string of successful bank and train robberies in America, Cassidy eventually escaped to Argentina with Etta Place and Harry Longabaugh (the Sundance Kid). What happened then is a source of continuing mystery. Some believe Cassidy and Longabaugh were killed there; others swear the two returned to the American West, living out their days in peaceful anonymity.

implements, and every month the museum hosts a different art show of local and national artists. ⊠ *328 E. 200 South St.* ☎ *435/789–7399* ⊕ *www.co.uintah.ut.us/museum/whmuseum.php* ✉ *Free* ⊙ *Memorial Day–Labor Day, weekdays 9–6, Sat. 10–5; Labor Day–Memorial Day, weekdays 9–5, Sat. 10–2.*

The Daughters of Utah Pioneers Museum provides a window into the daily lives of pioneers. The large collection of artifacts (most donated by descendents of the area's early settlers) range from a working loom to guns to a mortician's tools. Most everything is displayed in period rooms, including a shop, a house, and even a local doctor's office. Although the museum's regular hours are limited, the helpful and knowledgeable volunteers who keep the museum going are happy to provide tours anytime, year-round, by appointment. ⊠ *158 S. 500 West St.* ☎ *435/789–0352* ✉ *Free* ⊙ *June–Aug., Tues.–Sat. 10–4, or by appointment.*

Nicknamed the Parcel Post Bank, the **Zions First National Bank** building is probably the only bank ever mailed to its destination. At the time of its building in the early 20th century, U.S. parcel post was cheaper than freight, so the building's facade was mailed in—brick by brick. More than 5,000 bundles of bricks were shipped to Vernal during a six-year period. The building was finally finished in 1916. ⊠ *3 W. Main St.*

In 1879 the **Old Ashley Post Office and Store** was built of logs, wooden pegs, and square nails. Letter carriers on horseback and snowshoes brought mail in once a week to the post office in one room of the building, while patrons purchased necessities at the store in the other room. ⊠ *1335 W. 2000 North St.*

To leaf through the history of outlaws, pioneers, and other colorful characters, drop in at the **Uintah County Library,** which houses an excellent regional history research center. The library also displays a collection of First Ladies of the White House dolls dressed in replica Inaugural Ball gowns. ⊠ *155 E. Main St.* ☎ *435/789–0091* ⊕ *www.uintah.lib.ut.us* ⊙ *Mon.–Thurs. 10–9, Fri. and Sat. 10–6.*

An impressive array of easily accessible Native American petroglyphs adorn the 200-foot-high cliffs in **Dry Fork Canyon,** making the 32-mi round-trip drive from Vernal well worth your time. Next to the parking lot where you'll park to explore the petroglyphs is the Jean McConkie McKenzie house on the **Sadie McConkie Ranch.** You can see pioneer displays here, including a replica of a saloon. ⊠ *16 mi north of Vernal on 3500 West St. (Dry Fork Canyon Rd.)* ☎ *435/789–6733* ✉ *Free, donations requested* ⊙ *Daily.*

Forty miles northeast of Vernal, on the Utah-Colorado border, sits the **Jones Hole National Fish Hatchery,** where they breed nearly 2 million trout a year to stock nearby reservoirs. You can tour the operations and see thousands of baby trout in tanks or outdoor "raceways." ⊠ *1380 South 2350 W* ☎ *435/789–4481* ⊕ *http://joneshole.fws.gov* ✉ *Free* ⊙ *Daily 7–3:30.*

off the beaten path

BROWNS PARK – If you hanker for a glimpse of the Wild West, drive 65 mi northeast of Vernal to Browns Park. Lying along a quieter stretch of the Green River and extending into Colorado, this area features plenty of high-desert scenery, a national waterfowl refuge, and a history complete with notorious outlaws of the late 1800s. Inside the park, you can explore several buildings on the **John Jarvie Ranch.** Buildings date from 1880 to the early 1900s, and there's also a cemetery containing the graves of a few men who met violent ends in the area. In addition to his ranch, Jarvie ran a post office, store, and river ferry, and his spread was a major hideout on the so-called "Outlaw Trail." Each June (usually Father's Day weekend), the Jarvie Festival celebrates with mountain men, wagon rides, pioneer demonstrations, and live music. Reach the park and ranch by driving 65 mi north of Vernal on U.S. 191, then 22 mi east on a gravel road, following signs to the ranch. ⊠ *Browns Park* ☎ *435/885–3307 John Jarvie Ranch, 435/781–4400 Bureau of Land Management* ⊕ *www.blm.gov/utah/vernal* ☒ *Free* ⊙ *Jarvie Ranch tours May–Oct., daily 10–5.*

Sports & the Outdoors

BICYCLING Because Dinosaurland is less known than other parts of the state, bikers can often escape the crowds and enjoy some scenic solitude. Bring plenty of water and sunblock.

To talk to knowledgeable cyclists about local trails off the beaten path, stop in at **Altitude Cycle** (⊠ 580 E. Main St. ☎ 435/781–2595 or 877/ 781–2460 ⊕ www.altitudecycle.com), where they can set you up with trail guides, repairs, accessories, and war stories. You'll find good biking trails with great vistas and opportunities for seeing some of Utah's diverse wildlife in Browns Park, with trailheads near the **John Jarvie Ranch** (⊠ Browns Park ☎ 435/885–3307 John Jarvie Ranch, 435/781–4400 Bureau of Land Management).

BOATING **Red Fleet State Park** (⊠ 10 mi north of Vernal off U.S. 191 ☎ 435/789– 4432 ⊕ www.stateparks.utah.gov), like the other reservoirs in the region, is great for boat and bait. What really attracts visitors are the colorful sandstone formations surrounding the lake. In addition, a section of 200-million-year-old dinosaur tracks can be reached by a short hike or by boat, and camping is available. You'll pay $5 for day use. Boating and water-skiing enthusiasts love **Steinaker Lake State Park** (⊠ U.S. 191, 7 mi north of Vernal ☎ 435/789–4432 ⊕ www.stateparks.utah.gov). More than 2 mi long, Steinaker Reservoir relinquishes a fair number of largemouth bass and rainbow trout. Hiking and biking trails begin at the park, and wildlife viewing areas are nearby. A campground and covered group pavilions make this a popular park. You'll pay $5 for day use.

HIKING One of the most beautiful hikes in the area begins at the Jones Hole National Fish Hatchery and follows Jones Hole Creek through riparian woods and canyons, past petroglyphs and wildlife. The full trail is an 8-mi round trip to the Green River and back, but you can stop halfway at Ely Creek and return for an easier, but still lovely, 4-mi hike. There are numerous trails in this area that are unmarked and not maintained, but easy to follow if you use reasonable caution. Check with the rangers at the Dinosaur Quarry Visitor Center (☎ 435/781–7700 ⊕ www.nps.gov/dino) for more information about hiking trails.

RAFTING For a unique perspective of Dinosaur National Monument, take a white-water rafting trip on the Green or Yampa river. Joining forces near Echo Park in Colorado, the two waterways have each carved spectacular canyons through several eons' worth of rock, and they are still at it in rapids such as Whirlpool Canyon, SOB, Disaster Falls, and Hell's Half Mile.

Adrift Adventures (⌂ Box 192, Jensen 84035 ☎ 435/789–3600 or 800/824–0150 ⊕ www.adrift.com) offers one-day or multiday rafting trips as well as a package that includes rafting in the morning and a horseback ride in the afternoon. **Hatch River Expeditions** (⌂ Box 1150, Vernal 84078 ☎ 435/789–4316 or 800/342–8243 ⊕ www.hatchriver.com) lays claim to being the original river-running company; they've been at it since 1929. Their one-day and multiday rafting trips take you through both calm and white waters, and if fishing is your passion, they'll equip you for that, too.

Where to Stay & Eat

★ $–$$$ ✕ **Curry Manor.** Vernal's most elegant restaurant resides within the century-old home that once belonged to a state representative and is now on the National Register of Historic Places. In Victorian-era decorated rooms, indulge in steak, seafood, and pasta entrées, fresh-daily bread, and homemade desserts. And don't worry about a dress code—they'll welcome you right off the trail or river. Beer and wine are available. ⊠ 189 S. Vernal Ave. ☎ 435/789–0789 ▤ AE, D, MC, V ⊗ Closed Sun. and Mon. No lunch Sat.

¢–$$ ✕ **7–11 Ranch Restaurant.** No, this restaurant is not associated in any way with the convenience-store chain. Specialties are prime rib, steaks, and homemade soups and pies. It's open for breakfast, lunch, and dinner, and the down-home–style food is so good that locals have been crowding the place since it opened in 1965. A gift shop sells souvenirs from the area. ⊠ 77 E. Main St. ☎ 435/789–1170 ▤ AE, D, MC, V ⊗ Closed Sun.

¢–$$ ✕ **Cobble Rock Restaurant.** Craving mesquite-smoked ribs and a beer? Satisfy that craving at this family-style restaurant, where they smoke their own ribs and chicken, and serve steak, fajitas, burgers, and creative pasta dishes, too. Their outdoor seating area borders a city park. ⊠ 25 S. Vernal Ave. ☎ 435/789–8578 ▤ AE, D, MC, V.

¢–$ ✕ **Betty's Cafe.** Locals come here for breakfast, which is served from 6 AM until the busy little restaurant closes at 2 PM (noon on Sundays); you can get burgers, catfish, and sandwiches, too. Everything is homemade, including the jams, salsa, and pies. ⊠ 416 W. Main St. ☎ 435/781–2728 ▤ No credit cards ⊗ No dinner.

★ ¢–$$$ ▥ **Landmark Inn Bed & Breakfast.** Despite its history as a Baptist church building, this lovely inn has a homey feel. Rooms are decorated with quilts and Western Americana. Suites have gas fireplaces and jetted tubs. A breakfast of cereals, breads, yogurts, fruits, and juices is served in the dining room, and you're welcome to congregate around the living room fireplace in the evening. ⊠ *288 E. 100 South St., 84078* ☎ *435/781–1800 or 888/738–1800* ⊕ *www.landmark-inn.com* ➾ *7 rooms, 3 suites* ⚐ *Some in-room hot tubs, cable TV, Wi-Fi; no smoking* ⊟ *AE, D, DC, MC, V* ⦿⊙⦿ *CP.*

$ ⊞ **Best Western Antlers Motel.** Good-size rooms have coffeemakers, irons, and hair dryers. The pool, wading pool, and playground keep kids entertained. Your stay includes a coupon good for a Continental breakfast or a discount on other breakfast entrées at the neighboring JB's restaurant. ⊠ *423 W. Main St., 84078* ☎ *435/789–1202 or 888/791–2929* ▤ *435/789–4979* ⊕ *www.bestwestern.com* ➾ *31 rooms, 13 suites* ⚐ *Restaurant, some microwaves, refrigerators, cable TV, pool, wading pool, gym, hot tub, playground, no-smoking rooms* ⊟ *AE, D, DC, MC, V.*

$ ⊞ **Best Western Dinosaur Inn.** This basic one-story motel is a few blocks from downtown museums and restaurants. Most rooms have two queen beds, but two "family rooms" accommodate more sleepers. All rooms have hair dryers, irons and boards, and coffeemakers, and you might find a tiny plastic toy dinosaur or two in your room. The motel also has a gift shop with dinosaur toys, fossils, and Native American jewelry. ⊠ *251 E. Main St., 84078* ☎ *435/789–2660 or 800/780–7234* ▤ *435/789–2467* ⊕ *www.bestwestern.com* ➾ *60 rooms* ⚐ *Some refrigerators, some microwaves, cable TV, Wi-Fi, pool, hot tub, shop, playground, business services, no-smoking rooms* ⊟ *AE, D, DC, MC, V* ⦿⊙⦿ *CP.*

¢ ⊞ **Super 8 Motel.** Most rooms here have two queen beds, but a good number have one king-size bed. Rooms on the north side (away from the highway) are surprisingly quiet; avoid rooms on the west end, where you may hear noise from the swimming pool and the street. The indoor pool is ideal for letting kids burn off energy in cooler months, when other motels' outdoor pools are still closed. Irons and hair dryers are available at the front desk, and there's coffee in the lobby 24 hours a day. ⊠ *1624 W. U.S. 40, 84078* ☎ *435/789–4326 or 800/800–8000* ▤ *435/789–8844* ⊕ *www.Super8.com* ➾ *40 rooms, 3 suites* ⚐ *Some microwaves, some refrigerators, cable TV, Wi-Fi, indoor pool, hot tub, no-smoking rooms* ⊟ *AE, D, MC, V* ⦿⊙⦿ *CP.*

¢ ⊞ **Weston Lamplighter Inn.** The simply furnished rooms are larger than average. The half-dozen family suites can accommodate up to eight people (on two queen and two double beds). The motel is within a few blocks of area shops, theaters, restaurants, and attractions. ⊠ *120 E. Main St., 84078* ☎ *435/789–0312* ▤ *435/781–1480* ➾ *88 rooms, 6 suites* ⚐ *Restaurant, microwaves, refrigerators, cable TV, some in-room data ports, pool, some pets allowed, no-smoking rooms* ⊟ *AE, DC, MC, V.*

Nightlife & the Arts

NIGHTLIFE Each July, Vernal plays host to what has been voted one of the top five PRCA rodeos in the world—the **PRCA Dinosaur Roundup Rodeo** (⊠ Western Park Convention Center, 300 E. 200 South St. ☎ 435/789–1352 or 800/421–9635). Four days of rodeo events, dances, and parades on Main Street heat up the summer and celebrate the real-life cowboys that wear cowboy boots because they're practical, not because they're fashionable.

THE ARTS   In June and July, enjoy musicals, melodramas, or comedies under the stars during the **Outlaw Trail Theater** (✉ Western Park Outdoor Amphitheater, 302 E. 200 South St. ☎ 888/240–2080 ⊕ www.myartscouncil. org/outlawtr.html).

Shopping

Dinosaur memorabilia, rocks, fossils, and Native American jewelry and baskets are available at the **Ashley Trading Post** (✉ 236 E. Main St. ☎ 435/789–8447). If you prefer your rocks in stunning 14-karat gold settings, stop in at the **R. Fullbright Studio and Rock Shop** (✉ 216 E. Main St. ☎ 435/789–2451) to see what local artist Randy Fullbright has created lately. He often works bits of dinosaur fossils into his upscale jewelry or produces bronze or paper castings of petroglyphs.

Fourteen miles east of Vernal, on the road to the Dinosaur Quarry in Dinosaur National Monument, the **Silver Pick** (✉ 7750 E. 6000 South St., Jensen ☎ 435/789–5072) sells rocks, fossils, and Native American jewelry.

en route   Past Red Fleet Reservoir north of Vernal, U.S. 191 begins to ascend the eastern flank of the Uinta uplift as you head toward Flaming Gorge. The section of U.S. 191 and Route 44 between Vernal and Manila, Utah, is known as the **Flaming Gorge-Uintas National Scenic Byway.** Within a distance of 30 mi, the road passes through 18 uptilted geologic formations, including the billion-year-old exposed core of the Uinta Mountains, with signs identifying and describing them. The route also provides plenty of opportunity for wildlife watching. Before setting out, pick up a guide to the road at the Utah Field House of Natural History.

Dinosaur National Monument

🐚 ❻ *20 mi east of Vernal via Rte. 149.*

Dinomania rules at this 330-square-mi park that straddles the Utah–Colorado border. Although most of the park's acreage is in Colorado, its prime attraction is on the Utah side: the **Dinosaur Quarry and Visitor Center,** which houses some 2,000 dinosaur bones encased in a 200-foot-long sandstone wall. This collection of fossils resulted when floods deposited an astounding number of dinosaur carcasses on a sandbar; subsequent deposits covered the bodies where they lay, and they became part of the Morrison Formation. The cache of paleontological treasures was discovered by Earl Douglass in 1909, when he stumbled upon eight enormous dinosaur tailbones exposed on a sandstone ridge. During busy times of the year, use the parking lot down the road from the Utah visitor center; there is a shuttle bus to the quarry. ✉ *Rte. 149, 20 mi east of Vernal* ☎ *435/ 781–7700* ⊕ *www.nps.gov/dino* 💲 *$10 per vehicle* ☉ *Memorial Day–Labor Day, daily 9–6; Labor Day–Memorial Day, daily 8–4:30.*

Although most people visit Dinosaur National Monument to see dinosaur bones, the backcountry scenery itself is alluring. An especially scenic 22-mi round-trip drive, the **Tour of the Tilted Rocks,** runs from the Dinosaur

Quarry east to the **Josie Morris Cabin.** Josie was the sister of Ann Bassett, the "Etta Place" of Butch Cassidy legends. Ms. Morris lived alone for 50 years on her isolated homestead, keeping company with the likes of Butch Cassidy. Along the drive, watch for ancient rock art, geological formations, views of Split Mountain and rafters on the Green River, and hiking trails.

A scenic drive on the unpaved **Island Park Road,** along the northern edge of the park, not only passes some impressive Fremont petroglyph panels but also reaches a put-in point for rafters, who toss about on the white water of the Green and Yampa rivers.

The national monument **Headquarters Visitor Center** (✉ 4545 E. U.S. 40, Dinosaur, CO ☎ 970/374–3000), on the Colorado side of the park, is 37 mi east of Vernal. As far as fossils are concerned, this is the least interesting side of the park as there are no fossils to be found or seen, either at or near the headquarters building. **The Journey Through Time** self-guided auto tour begins at the national monument Headquarters Visitor Center in Colorado and winds along the Utah–Colorado border, providing overlooks of the spectacularly colored canyons and landscape that make up the park.

Sports & the Outdoors

BICYCLING Cycling is a pleasurable way to see Dinosaur National Monument, although you may have to contend with some car traffic in the summer months. The rangers can suggest biking routes but remember, you must stick to established roads. You'll have to bring your own bike or rent one in Vernal.

HIKING Four miles past the Dinosaur Quarry, the moderate 4-mi **Desert Voices Nature Trail** has interpretive signs (including some designed by children for children) that describe the arid environment you're hiking through. The more challenging 3-mi **Sounds of Silence Trail,** which begins 2 mi past the Dinosaur Quarry, tests (or boosts) your hiking knowledge by asking you to find your way using landmarks. To hike both trails without returning to your car, use the easy ¼ mi **Connector Trail,** which links the two.

Where to Camp

⚠ **Dinosaur National Monument Campgrounds.** You can camp alongside the Green River at two campgrounds inside the monument. Both campgrounds have a bit of shade and are surrounded by canyon scenery. Green River campground is only open when the water is turned on, from approximately April to October (exact dates vary due to weather and other factors), and it has a boat ramp for rafters. Split Mountain campground is open year-round, but only larger groups can camp there from approximately April to October. After the water is turned off in the fall, anyone can camp there, and vault toilets are available. Reservations are not accepted at either campground except for groups at Split Mountain in the summer. ♨ *Flush toilets, pit toilets, drinking water, fire grates, picnic tables* ◁ *92 sites, no hookups* ✉ *Rte. 149, 4 mi east of Dinosaur Quarry* ☎ *435/789–8277* ⊕ *www.nps.gov/dino* ◻ *Free Split Mountain (approx. Oct.–Apr.), $25 Split Mountain (approx May–Sept.), $12*

Green River ☉ *Green River campground approx. Apr.–Oct., Split Mountain year-round.*

Flaming Gorge National Recreation Area

❼ *40 mi north of Vernal (to Flaming Gorge Dam) via U.S. 191.*

In May 1869, during his mapping expedition on the Green and Colorado rivers, explorer John Wesley Powell named this canyon Flaming Gorge for its "flaming, brilliant red" color. Powell was not the first traveler to be in awe of the landscape. The first recorded white visitors were fur trappers who set up a long-term camp in 1825. By the late 1800s, scores of cattlemen and farmers, followed by rustlers and outlaws, had come to live in the area. The people came, but not the conveniences that generally follow. Flaming Gorge remained one of Utah's most remote and least-developed inhabited areas well into the 1950s. In 1964, Flaming Gorge Canyon and the Green River running through it were plugged with a 500-foot-high wall of concrete. The result is a 91-mi-long reservoir that twists and turns among canyon walls. Flaming Gorge Recreation Area is a part of the Ashley National Forest and administered by the U.S. Forest Service. Much of Flaming Gorge Reservoir, a major area destination for fishing and boating, stretches north into Wyoming; however, most facilities lie south of the state line in Utah.

The main information center for the Utah side is the **Flaming Gorge Dam Visitor Center** (✉ U.S. 191, 2 mi north of Greendale Junction ☎ 435/885–3135 ⊕ www.recreation.gov). Displays explain aspects of this engineering marvel, and depending on national terrorist alert levels and weather conditions, the dam may be open for free self-guided tours. The visitor center is open from Memorial Day to Labor Day, daily 8–6, and from Labor Day to Memorial Day, daily 10–4.

The **Swett Ranch** (✉ Off U.S. 191 ☎ 435/784–3445) was an isolated homestead that belonged to Oscar and Emma Swett and their nine children through most of the 1900s. The U.S. Forest Service has turned the ranch into a working historic site, complete with restored and decorated houses and buildings. At the Greendale Junction of U.S. 191 and Route 44, stay on U.S. 191; about ½ mi north of the junction there's a sign for the 1½-mi dirt road to the ranch, which is open from Memorial Day to Labor Day, Thursday–Monday 10–5.

The **Red Canyon Visitor Center** (✉ Rte. 44 ☎ 435/889–3713) explains the geology, flora and fauna, and human history of the Flaming Gorge area, but the most magnificent thing about the center is its location atop a cliff that towers 1,300 feet above the lake. The views here are outstanding, and you can enjoy them while having a picnic on the grounds. To reach the visitor center, turn left at the Greendale Junction of U.S. 191 and Route 44, and follow the signs. This visitor center is open only from Memorial Day to Labor Day, daily 10–5.

A scenic 13-mi drive traverses the **Sheep Creek Canyon Geological Area** (✉ Sheep Creek Canyon Loop Rd., 28 mi west of Greendale Junction off U.S. 191 and Rte. 44 ☎ 435/784–3445), which is full of upturned layers of rock. Watch for wild horses, bighorn sheep, and a bat cave alongside the road. In the fall salmon return to Sheep Creek to spawn; a viewing kiosk and several bridges provide unobtrusive locations from which to watch the spawning runs. **The Spirit Lake Scenic Backway** leads out from the Sheep Creek Canyon Loop road past the **Ute Lookout Fire Tower,** which was in use from the 1930s through the 1960s. Several newlywed couples spent their first summers together living in the tower watching for forest fires.

Sports & the Outdoors

BICYCLING Because it mixes high-desert vegetation—blooming sage, rabbit brush, cactus, and wildflowers—and red rock terrain with a cool climate, Flaming Gorge National Recreation Area is an ideal destination for road and trail biking. The 3-mi round-trip Bear Canyon–Bootleg ride begins south of the dam off U.S. 191 at the Firefighters' Memorial Campground and runs west to an overview of the reservoir. A free brochure, *Flaming Gorge Trails,* describes this and other cycling routes. The brochure is distributed at area visitor centers.

FISHING & Flaming Gorge Reservoir provides ample opportunities for boating and
BOATING water sports of all kinds, whether you prefer lounging on the deck of a
Fodor'sChoice rented houseboat or skiing behind a high-performance speedboat. Old-
★ timers maintain that Flaming Gorge provides the best lake fishing in the state, yielding rainbow and lake trout, smallmouth bass, and Kokanee salmon. Only artificial lures and fly-fishing are permitted; bait fishing isn't allowed. For the best river fishing, try the Green River below Flaming Gorge Dam, where rainbow and brown trout are plentiful and big. Fed by cold water from the bottom of the lake, this stretch has been identified as one of the best trout fisheries in the world. The Green River below Flaming Gorge dam is a calm, scenic stretch of water, ideal for risk-averse folk or for families who want to take smaller children (say, four or five years old) on rafting trips, but who don't want to worry about them falling into white water.

If you have your own boat, you can launch it, gas it up, or rent a slip from **Cedar Springs Marina** (✉ U.S. 191, approximately 2 mi southwest of Flaming Gorge Dam ✉ Box 337, Dutch John ☎ 435/889–3795 ⊕ www.cedarspringsmarina.com), where you can also rent a boat or hire a fishing guide. **Flaming Gorge Recreation Services** (✉ U.S. 191 at Dutch John Blvd., Box 326, Dutch John 84023 ☎ 435/885–3191 ⊕ www.fgrecservices.com) provides boat rentals, guided fishing trips, and daily float trips on the Green River. The **Lucerne Valley Marina** (✉ 1 Lucerne Valley Blvd., 7 mi east of Manila ✉ Box 10, Manila 84046 ☎ 435/784–3483 or 888/820–9225 ⊕ www.flaminggorge.com) has a boat launch, slips, mooring buoys, boat rentals, mechanical services, gas, dry storage, camping, and houseboat rentals.

HIKING Plenty of hiking opportunities exist in the Flaming Gorge area. Ask at any of the local visitor centers or lodges for recommended hikes. From the Red Canyon Visitor Center, you can take three different hikes along the **Canyon Rim Trail** through the pine forest: an easy ½-mi trek will take you to the Red Canyon Rim Overlook (above 1,300-foot cliffs); a 1½-

mi walk leads you to Red Canyon Lodge, and a moderate 3½-mi hike finds you at the Swett Ranch Overlook.

In the Sheep Creek Canyon Geological Area, the 4-mi **Ute Mountain Trail** leads from the Ute Lookout Fire Tower down through pine forests to Brownie Lake, then back the same way. The **Spirit Lake Trail** begins at Spirit Lake (on Rte. 44, go past the Ute Lookout Fire Tower turnoff and take F.S. Rd. 221 to Spirit Lake) and takes you to Tamarack Lake and back for a moderate 4-mi trek.

Where to Stay & Eat

$–$$ ✕🏠 **Flaming Gorge Lodge.** The lodge has motel rooms and condos, a good American-style restaurant ($–$$$), a store, and affiliation with Flaming Gorge Recreation Services, who rent rafts and boats and provide fishing-guide service. The one-bedroom condos have air-conditioning, a queen bed, twin bed, queen sofa bed, living room, dining room, and full kitchen. There is no air-conditioning in the motel rooms. ⊠ *155 Greendale U.S. 191, Dutch John 84023* ☎ *435/889–3773* 🖷 *435/889–3788* ⊕ *www.fglodge.com* ⬩ *21 rooms, 24 condos* ⚫ *Restaurant, some kitchens, cable TV, in-room VCRs, Wi-Fi in main lodge, business services, meeting rooms, travel services, a/c in condos only; no smoking* ▱ *AE, D, MC, V.*

★ $–$$ ✕🏠 **Red Canyon Lodge.** A pleasant surprise in the woods, this lodge is surrounded by well-built, handcrafted log cabins that face a private trout-stocked lake and have wood-burning stoves, bathrooms, and kitchenettes. The great restaurant ($–$$$) is open for breakfast, lunch, and dinner from April to October and for weekend dinners only from November to March; dinner specials are creative, often consisting of wild game or fish. The lodge provides recreation services like boat and bike rentals, horseback riding, and snowshoeing. ⊠ *790 Red Canyon Rd., Dutch John 84023* ☎ *435/889–3759* 🖷 *435/889–5106* ⊕ *www.redcanyonlodge.com* ⬩ *18 cabins* ⚫ *Restaurant, some kitchenettes, 2 lakes, pond, boating, fishing, mountain bikes, hiking, horseback riding, cross-country skiing, shop, business services, meeting room, some pets allowed; no a/c, no room phones, no room TVs* ▱ *AE, D, MC, V.*

WHERE TO CAMP � **Canyon Rim Campground.** This small campground sits along the Canyon Rim hiking trail atop 1,300-foot cliffs overlooking Flaming Gorge Reservoir. The location provides ample scenery, cool air, scattered shade, and close proximity to both the Red Canyon visitor center and the Red Canyon Lodge. The campground is 4 mi west of the Greendale Junction of U.S. 191 and Route 44, then 2½ mi down Red Canyon Road (look for the turnoff). ⚫ *Pit toilets, drinking water, fire pits, picnic tables* ⬩ *18 sites* ⊠ *Red Canyon Rd.* ☎ *435/784–3445 information, 877/444–6777 reservations* ⊕ *www.reserveusa.com* ▱ *$14* ☉ *Mid-May–mid-Sept.*

Mirror Lake Scenic Byway

⑧ *Kamas is 49 mi from Salt Lake City via I–80 and Rte. 32 south.*

Fodor'sChoice
★ Although the Wasatch may be Utah's best-known mountain range, the Uinta Mountains, the only major east–west mountain range in the

United States, are its tallest, topped by 13,528-foot Kings Peak. The Uinta Mountains area, particularly in the High Uintas Wilderness where no vehicles are allowed, is prime country for pack trips and horseback day rides between late June and September. The Uintas are ribboned with streams, and they have hundreds of small lakes set in rolling meadows. Access to the Uinta Mountains is either from Kamas (40 mi east of Salt Lake City on I–80) or from Route 150, 30 mi south of Evanston, Wyoming.

The quickest, easiest (read: paved) route to Uinta country is the **Mirror Lake Scenic Byway,** which begins in Kamas. The 65-mi drive follows Route 150 into the heavily wooded canyons of the Wasatch–Cache National Forest, cresting at 10,687-foot Bald Mountain Pass. Because of heavy winter snows, much of the road is closed from October to May. You can buy a guide to the byway from the Wasatch–Cache National Forest's Kamas Ranger District office in Kamas. ✉ *Wasatch–Cache National Forest, Kamas Ranger District, 50 E. Center St., Box 68, Kamas* ☎ *435/783–4338* ⊕ *www.fs.fed.us/r4/wcnf.*

Nearby **Mirror Lake** (1 mi north of the crest of Bald Mountain Pass on Route 150) is arguably the best-known lake in the High Uintas Wilderness. At an altitude of 9,000 feet, it offers a cool respite from summer heat, it's easy to reach by car, and families enjoy fishing, hiking, and camping along its rocky shores. Its campgrounds provide a base for hikes into the surrounding mountains, and Highline Trail accesses the 460,000-acre High Uintas Wilderness Area to the east. There's a $3 day-use fee for Mirror Lake.

Sports & the Outdoors

Bear River Lodge (✉ Mile marker 49 on Mirror Lake Rte. 150 ☎ 801/936–0780 or 800/559–1121) is 49 mi northeast of Kamas, or 30 mi south of Evanston, Wyoming, an ideal location for beginning your exploration of the Uinta Mountains. Employees at the lodge are intimately familiar with the area, and can tell you about any number of the hundreds of hiking trails you can try. The lodge also rents mountain bikes, fishing gear, ATVs, and snowmobiles, and they can arrange for guided fishing expeditions and snowmobiling tours.

Where to Stay & Eat

$$–$$$$ ✕▥ **Bear River Lodge.** Eleven log cabins in the forest let you reconnect with nature without giving up creature comforts. Simply appointed with log and wood furniture, the cabins are near the lodge where you can outfit yourself for a variety of outdoor adventures. The lodge's Burly Bear Grill serves up breakfast as well as burgers and sandwiches for lunch or dinner. Autumn rates (October to December) are often deeply discounted. From October to May, the route from Kamas on Route 150 is closed, so access is from Evanston, Wyoming. ✉ *Mile marker 49 on Mirror Lake Highway (Rte. 150), 49 mi northeast of Kamas, or 30 mi south of Evanston, WY* ☎ *801/936–0780 or 800/559–1121* ☏ *801/936–0798* ⊕ *www.bearriverlodge.com* ⇩ *11 cabins* ⚹ *Restaurant, some kitchens, microwaves, refrigerators, cable TV, in-room VCRs, hot tub,* *fishing, mountain bikes, hiking, snowmobiling; no a/c, no room phones, no smoking* ⊟ *AE, D, MC, V.*

WHERE TO CAMP ⚠ **Christmas Meadows Campground.** Escape the summer heat and surround yourself in a beautiful setting that just begs to be hiked or mountain biked. To reach the campground, go 45 mi northeast of Kamas on Route 150, then east 4 mi on Christmas Meadows Rd. ♿ *Pit toilets, drinking water, fire pits, picnic tables* ⛺ *11 sites* ✉ *Christmas Meadows Rd., 49 mi northeast of Kamas* ☎ *435/783–4338 information, 877/444–6777 reservations* ⊕ *www.reserveusa.com* 🍴 *$12* ☉ *June–Aug.*
⚠ **Mirror Lake Campground.** A popular destination in the summertime, this lovely campground borders Mirror Lake, in the thick Uinta forest. ♿ *Pit toilets, drinking water, fire pits, picnic tables* ⛺ *79 sites* ✉ *Rte. 150, 32 mi northeast of Kamas* ☎ *435/783–4338 information, 877/444–6777 reservations* ⊕ *www.reserveusa.com* 🍴 *$14* ☉ *July–Sept.*

EASTERN UTAH A TO Z

To research prices, get advice from other travelers, and book travel arrangements, visit www.fodors.com.

AIRPORTS
The closest major airport is Salt Lake International Airport—two hours from Price and four hours from Vernal; it's served by most major airlines. The Carbon County Airport in Price and the Vernal City–Uintah County Airport are open to the public, but neither has any regularly scheduled air service.
🛈 **Carbon County Airport** ✉ 3095 E. Airport Rd., Price ☎ 435/637-9556 ⊕ www. arrowwestair.com. **Vernal City–Uintah County Airport** ✉ 825 S. 500 East St., Vernal ☎ 435/789-3400.

BUS TRAVEL
Greyhound Lines has service to Price.
🛈 **Greyhound Lines** ☎ 801/355-9579 or 800/231-2222 ⊕ www.greyhound.com.

CAMPING
Campgrounds are scattered liberally throughout eastern Utah. Many are state-run campgrounds with no hookups, but you'll usually find flush toilets, drinking water, fire pits, barbecue grills, and picnic tables. The Ashley National Forest offers forested sites; areas around Price, Vernal, and the reservoirs tend to be more open. Many campsites can be reserved ahead of time through Reserve USA or through the Utah State Parks.
🛈 **Reserve USA** ☎ 877/444-6777 ⊕ www.reserveusa.com. **Utah State Parks** ☎ 800/ 322-3770 or 801/322-3770 ⊕ www.stateparks.utah.gov.

CAR RENTAL
Rental cars are available from most major car rental companies at Salt Lake International Airport. Vernal's local rental car agency, All Save Car Rental, will pick you up and take you back to the airport. In Price, you may be able to rent a car from the local car dealers.
🛈 **All Save Car Rental** ✉ Vernal ☎ 435/789-4777 or 800/440-5776.

CAR TRAVEL

Both U.S. 40 and U.S. 191 are well-maintained; however, there are some curvy, mountainous stretches. If you're headed away from major towns, be prepared for dirt roads. Keep your vehicle fueled up because gas stations can be far apart, and not all of them are open on Sunday.
🚗 Road Conditions ☎ 800/492-2400.

EMERGENCIES

For emergencies, call the local Utah Highway Patrol phone number or 911.
🚗 Ambulance or Police Emergencies ☎ 911. Utah Highway Patrol dispatch ☎ 435/789-4222 Vernal area, 435/637-0893 Price area, 435/615-3600 Mirror Lake area ⊕ www.highwaypatrol.utah.gov.
🚗 24-Hour Medical Care Ashley Valley Medical Center ✉ 151 W. 200 North St., Vernal ☎ 435/789-3342. Castleview Hospital ✉ 300 N. Hospital Dr., Price ☎ 435/637-4800. Uinta Basin Medical Center ✉ 250 W. 300 North St., Roosevelt ☎ 435/722-4691.

MEDIA

NEWSPAPERS & MAGAZINES
The *Vernal Express* (⊕ www.vernal.com), a weekly newspaper, keeps the residents of Vernal informed; the weekly *Uintah Basin Standard* (⊕ www.ubstandard.com) serves Roosevelt and Duchesne. The *Ute Bulletin* is the official newspaper of the Northern Ute Tribe on the Uintah and Ouray Indian Reservation. In Price, the *Sun Advocate* ⊕ www.sunadvocate.com is published on Tuesday and Thursday.

TELEVISION & RADIO
In Price, KWSA 100.9 FM and KSLL 1080 AM play adult contemporary music; KOAL 750 AM serves up talk, news, and sports; and KARB 98.3 FM plays country. In Vernal, KLCY 105.9 plays country and KVEL 920 AM does talk and oldies. In Roosevelt, KXRQ 94.3 FM plays classic rock, KIFX 98.5 FM plays adult contemporary, and KNEU 1250 AM plays country.

TOURS

In Vernal, Dinaland Aviation offers flights over Dinosaur National Monument, Flaming Gorge, and the canyons of the Green River. In Price, Redtail Aviation provides sightseeing flights over the Price area.
🚗 Tour Operators Dinaland Aviation ✉ 830 E. 500 South St., Vernal ☎ 435/789-4612. Redtail Aviation ✉ 3095 E. Airport Rd., Price ☎ 435/637-9556 ⊕ www.moab-utah.com/redtail.

TRAIN TRAVEL

Amtrak's daily *California Zephyr* stops in Helper.
🚗 Train Information Amtrak ☎ 800/872-7245 ⊕ www.amtrak.com.

VISITOR INFORMATION

🚗 Bureau of Land Management Price Area Office ✉ 125 S. 600 West St., Price 84501 ☎ 435/636-3600 ✉ Vernal Area Office ✉ 170 S. 500 East St., Vernal 84078 ☎ 435/781-4400 ⊕ www.blm.gov Carbon County Chamber of Commerce ✉ 90 N. 100 East St., #3, Price 84501 ☎ 435/637-2788 ⊕ www.carboncountychamber.com. Castle Country Travel Region-Carbon County Visitors Bureau ✉ 90 N. 100 East St., Price 84501

☎435/637-3009 or 800/842-0789 ⊕www.castlecountry.com. **Dinosaurland Travel Board** ✉ 25 E. Main St., Vernal 84078 ☎ 435/789-6932 or 800/477-5558 ⊕ www.dinoland. com. **Duchesne County Chamber of Commerce** ✉ 50 E. 200 South St., Duchesne 84066 ☎ 435/722-4598. **Flaming Gorge Chamber of Commerce** ⚓ General Delivery, Manila 84046 ☎ 435/784-3154 or 435/789-3445. **Northeastern Utah Visitor Center** ✉ Utah Field House of Natural History, 496 E. Main St., Vernal 84078 ☎ 435/789-7894. **Vernal Chamber of Commerce** ✉ 134 W. Main St., Vernal 84078 ☎ 435/789-1352 or 800/ 421-9635 ⊕ www.vernalchamber.com.

Capitol Reef
National Park
& Environs

5

WORD OF MOUTH

"I suggest Capitol Reef. I prefer it to Zion, although people will argue with me. I don't like to debate the issue unless a person has spent 3 days at both places and explored on foot for several hours. Same major rock formations, the Navajo Sandstone, and the same type of spectacular cliffs in a more varied geologic setting. Also some of the beautiful colors of the Chinle and Moenkopi formations are exposed at Capitol Reef."

—brookwood

Updated by
Janet Lowe

CAPITOL REEF NATIONAL PARK, and the sleepy little towns surrounding it, remains one of America's best-kept secrets. It's a place to reclaim quiet and solitude while exploring a region rich in history and geological wonders. In spite of being "in the middle of nowhere," there are a variety of approaches to Capitol Reef country. The main high-speed arteries through the region are I–70 and I–15, but any route will require travel of some secondary roads such as U.S. 50, U.S. 89, Route 24, or Route 72. All are well-maintained, safe roads that bisect rich agricultural communities steeped in Mormon history. The northern approach will take travelers through Fishlake National Forest—a cool respite in summer and a snowy mountain vision in winter. Whether approaching from the north or the south, U.S. 89 offers a look at idyllic pasturelands with a backdrop of mountains and foothills. This is a peaceful, unhurried drive through a part of America that remains little changed from the 19th century. Cattle and horses graze in pastures and crops grow green and lush in quiet valleys. The verdant valley eventually gives way to dramatic sandstone formations in a full palate of colors when traveling on Route 24 toward Capitol Reef National Park.

The more daring traveler (and one with plenty of time to spare) approaching the region from the south will veer off of U.S. 89 onto Route 12 at Panguitch. Route 12 is one of America's most scenic drives and should not be missed.

Travelers headed to Capitol Reef country from the east on I–70 will enjoy the jaw-dropping majesty of the San Rafael Swell before jumping off the Interstate at Route 24. The "Swell" as locals refer to it, is largely a roadless wilderness area that rises out of the earth at a crazy tilt. A good map is an absolute necessity for reaching Capitol Reef because all routes jig and jag, and sometimes twist back on themselves, before finally arriving in the colorful land of "the reef."

Exploring Capitol Reef and its Environs

Interstate 15 is the fastest way through central Utah, but U.S. 89 and the local roads that feed onto it will give you a more direct path into Utah's past and present-day character.

About the Restaurants

Traveling toward Capitol Reef National Park from Salt Lake or Las Vegas, you'll find the usual chains at almost any of the exits off I–15. The smaller towns away from the interstate often have only one or two mom-and-pop diners serving all-American comfort food. These locally owned restaurants are rich with local character, but the quality of the food can vary wildly. Finding a good hearty breakfast is relatively easy, however. The best food in the region by far is in the towns outside of Capitol Reef National Park. In Torrey you can find everything from restaurants serving high-end Southwestern cuisine to basic hamburger joints offering up consistently good food.

About the Hotels

Chains dominate the exits along I–15 and the western end of I–70, and you'll have no problem finding clean and comfortable accommoda-

5

Numbers in the text correspond to numbers in the margin and on Central Utah and Capitol Reef National Park maps.

If you have
3 days

If you have only three days, you'll have little trouble filling them at Capitol Reef National Park. Basing yourself in 🏨 **Torrey** ❸ ⚑, start your journey by exploring the popular, northern end of **Capitol Reef National Park** ❹–❸. On the first day, see the historical sights and take a short hike, perhaps the Hickman Bridge Trail, then have dinner in one of Torrey's excellent restaurants. Start your second morning with another hike, perhaps on the Fremont River Trail; in the afternoon, consider exploring some of the little towns surrounding the park, including **Teasdale** ❷ and **Loa** ❶. On your third day, explore either the more off-the-beaten-path locations of Waterpocket Fold area or Cathedral Valley, but be sure to check first at the visitor center for road conditions and recommendations since much of your driving will be on unpaved roads.

If you have
4 days

Spend your first three days in the vicinity of Capitol Reef National Park as in the itinerary above. On Day 4, head west out of Torrey on Route 24 toward Loa. Travel past Loa for 17 mi until you reach Route 25, which takes you to Fish Lake. Hike the perimeter of the lake or head up into the mountains on one of the Fishlake National Forest Trails.

tions no matter what your budget. Drive farther away from the interstate, into the region's towns, and you are more likely to find locally owned low- to moderate-price motels and even a few nice bed-and-breakfasts. The region around Capitol Reef National Park offers a mix of accommodations that will please any taste and pocketbook. Reservations are recommended in summer, the park's busy season.

WHAT IT COSTS					
	$$$$	$$$	$$	$	¢
RESTAURANTS	over $25	$19–$25	$13–$18	$8–$12	under $8
HOTELS	over $200	$151–$200	$111–$150	$70–$110	under $70

Restaurant prices are for a main course at dinner, excluding sales tax of 6% to 7% tax. Hotel prices are for two people in a standard double room in high season, excluding service charges and 6% to 7% tax.

Timing

Although summer days can be uncomfortably hot and winter storms potentially fierce, central Utah and Capitol Reef country has a generally moderate climate with four distinct seasons, so the best time to visit depends on what kinds of weather you tolerate best. In summer you might have to plan around either the late-day heat or thunderstorms that can roll in from the south in July and August. Winter will allow you to enjoy snow sports while avoiding the crowds that are drawn to the resorts in

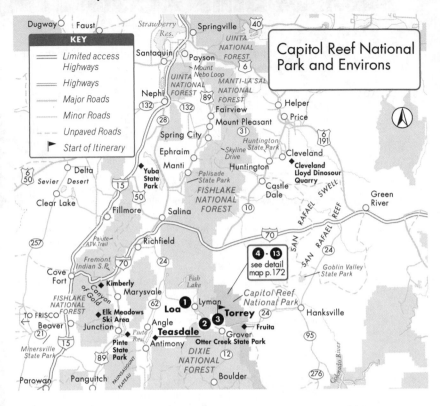

Capitol Reef National Park and Environs

KEY

━━━	Limited access Highways
━━	Highways
──	Major Roads
──	Minor Roads
---	Unpaved Roads
▶	Start of Itinerary

the north. Spring is undoubtedly one of the most beautiful times to visit this region, but weather can be unpredictable, and sudden, short-lived snow storms are not uncommon. Early fall is crisp and cool and offers generally reliable weather. Changing colors, freshly harvested fruit, and smaller crowds make this a particularly good time to visit. In general, festivals get cranked up in mid-May and run through September.

Loa

① *21 mi northwest of Capitol Reef via Rte. 24.*

Pioneers settled this little town at the northern end of the Fremont River Valley in the 1870s. A former Mormon missionary who had served in Hawaii named the town, and a rock from Mauna Loa rests at a historic marker. Because it is the county seat of Wayne County, Loa may be a bit more sophisticated than neighboring towns, but not too much. It remains charmingly quiet and serene.

The great American county fair tradition is at its finest in Loa. Horse shows, turkey shoots, and the Tilt-a-Whirl are all standards at the August **Wayne County Fair** (☎ 435/836–2662), which also schedules a rodeo and a parade. Look at hand-made quilts and other crafts, see agri-

Small-Town Tastes Every town here has a café that sustains more than just the palate. These places are gathering spots for locals, and they have names like El Bambi and the Satisfied Ewe. It can seem like these cafés all serve from the same menu, and to be honest, the quality of the food varies widely. But you don't go for just the food. Go for the conversation. You'll get a taste of local flavor and character that can't be beat.

Enjoying Capitol Reef Capitol Reef National Park isn't your usual national park. Far enough away from the beaten path, there's almost no congestion and nothing screams tourist trap. The small towns leading up to the park, from Loa to Torrey, have charming, locally owned motels and B&Bs. And the restaurants here, regardless of price, offer some of the best eating in central Utah. But a visit to Capitol Reef is all about soaking up the landscape. Just put on a pair of boots, rub in the sun block, grab a camera and a water bottle, and hit the trail. Almost any trail will do. You'll see a nearly constant change of color play across the red rock canyons as the sun rises and sets. During late summer and fall, you can pick a bounty of peaches, pears, and apples from the park's orchards. Here, being outside comes first, and everything else comes second.

5

---

cultural exhibits, play games, and eat plenty of good food while you spend a day at the fair.

Sports & the Outdoors

Fish Lake, which lies in the heart of its namesake, 1.4-million-acre **Fishlake National Forest** (Loa Ranger District Office ⊠ 138 S. Main St., Loa 84747 ☎ 435/836–2811 Loa Ranger District Office ⊕ www.fs.fed.us/r4/fishlake) lies at an elevation of 8,800 feet and is 1 mi wide and 6 mi long. It's known for its fishing, but you needn't have tackle box in hand to enjoy the beauty of the area. Mountain scenery and a quiet setting are the real draw. Some great hikes explore the higher reaches of the area; one good trail leads to the 11,633-foot summit of Fish Lake Hightop Plateau. There are several campgrounds as well as some wonderful lodges in the area. The lake's depth averages 85 feet. It's stocked annually with lake trout, rainbow trout, mackinaw, and splake. A large population of brown trout are native to the lake. The Loa Ranger District office can give you all the information you might need on camping, fishing, and hiking in the forest, which is north and east of town.

Where to Stay & Eat

¢–$ ✕ **Country Cafe.** Although the menu here is similar to those in other small-town Utah cafés, the food is better than most. Check out the wide variety of clocks lining the wood-panel walls. ⊠ *289 N. Main St.* ☎ *435/836–2047* ▤ *AE, D, MC, V.*

¢ ✕ **Wanda's.** This old-fashioned drive-through along Loa's main strip serves grilled burgers and has more than 40 flavors of shakes. ⊠ *193 E. 300 South St.* ☎ *435/836–2760* ▤ *No credit cards.*

$–$$$$ ✕▥ **Fish Lake Lodge.** This large, lakeside lodge built in 1932 exudes rustic charm and character and has great views. It houses the resort's restaurant, gift shop, game room, and even a dance hall. Guests stay in cabins that sleep 2 to 18 people. The larger houses are excellent for family reunions. Some of the lodgings are quite rustic. The larger cabins are the newest, but all focus on function rather than cute amenities. The lodge, general store, and restaurant are closed from early September to late May; cabins are available year-round. An RV park also has sites for $20 a night. ✉ *HC80, Rte. 25, 84701* ☎ *435/638–1000* 🖷 *435/638–1001* ⊕ *www.fishlake.com* 🛏 *45 cabins* ⌂ *Restaurant, grocery, kitchens, lake, boating, marina, fishing, recreation room, video game room, shop, meeting rooms; no TV in some rooms* ▤ *D, MC, V.*

¢–$$ ▥ **The Snuggle Inn.** On the second floor of a row of shops on Main Street, this hostelry has the feel of an old-time hotel with a name that's a little too cute. The rooms, however, are spacious, with modern decorations and touches like Internet access. Each room has a pillow-top queen bed. For families, there's a sofa bed in one room. The suite has two separate bedrooms, a living room, and a full kitchen. ✉ *55 S. Main St., 84747* ☎ *435/836–2898* 🖷 *435/836–2700* ⊕ *www.thesnuggleinn.com* 🛏 *4 rooms, 1 suite* ⌂ *Some kitchens, cable TV, in-room data ports* ▤ *AE, D, DC, MC, V.*

¢   ▥ **Aquarius Motel & Restaurant.** Large, comfortable rooms and recreational facilities that include basketball and volleyball courts as well as an indoor pool make this an attractive place for families. The restaurant next door serves decent comfort food. ✉ *240 W. Main St., Bicknell 84715* ☎ *435/425–3835 or 800/833–5379* 🖷 *435/425–3486* ⊕ *www. aquariusinn.com* 🛏 *27 rooms* ⌂ *Cable TV, in-room VCRs, pool, hot tub, basketball, volleyball* ▤ *AE, D, DC, MC, V.*

¢   ▥ **Sunglow Motel & Restaurant.** This well-maintained and inexpensive motel is right in the heart of Bicknell. Try the buttermilk and oatmeal pie at the restaurant next door. ✉ *63 E. Main St., Bicknell 84715* ☎ *435/425–3821* 🖷 *435/425–3821* 🛏 *15 rooms* ⌂ *Cable TV* ▤ *AE, D, MC, V.*

WHERE TO CAMP   🛆 **Fish Lake Campgrounds.** There are four Forest Service Campgrounds in the Fish Lake area. All are comfortable and well-maintained, if a bit on the basic side. Perhaps the two best are Doctor Creek and Mackinaw. Doctor Creek is a short drive from Fish Lake in a grove of aspen and pine. RVers will find a dump station here, too. Mackinaw sits on a hill overlooking Fish Lake, giving campers a good view of the surrounding basin. The showers here are a rarity in Forest Service campgrounds. ⌂ *Pit toilets, dump station (Doctor Creek), drinking water, showers (Mackinaw)* 🛏 *53 tent sites at Mackinaw, 29 tent sites at Doctor Creek* ✉ *About 20 mi northwest of Loa on Rte. 25* ☎ *435/836–2811* 🛢 *$12.*

The Arts

Don't get out your best black beret to attend the **Bicknell International Film Festival** (☎ 435/836–2632) in the small town of Bicknell, which is a few miles east of Loa on Route 24. It's a spoof on the serious film festivals that you read about—and for which you can't get tickets unless you live in Hollywood. This July festival centers around films of different genres each year. Past themes have included "UFO Flicks," "Japanese Monster Movies," and "Viva! Elvis." Each year's extravaganza begins with the world's fastest parade, a 60-mph procession that starts in Torrey and ends in Bicknell. Included in the crazy events is a swap meet and mutton fry.

en route **Route 24,** a Utah Scenic Byway, runs 62 mi between Loa and Hanksville, right through Capitol Reef National Park. Colorful rock formations in all their hues of red, cream, pink, gold, and deep purple extend from one end of the route to the other. The closer you get to the park the more colorful the landscape becomes. The vibrant rock finally gives way to lush green hills and the mountains west of Loa.

Teasdale

❷ *16 mi west of Capitol Reef National Park via Rte. 24; 14 mi east of Loa via Rte. 24*

Teasdale is a tiny, charming settlement cradled in a cove of the Aquarius Plateau. Many first-time visitors are so charmed by the bucolic setting that they quickly imagine how they might actually live here. The homes—many of which are well-preserved older structures—look out onto brilliantly colored cliffs and green fields. Although not as close to Capitol Reef as Torrey, it's still possible to base yourself here for a trip to the national park.

Where to Stay

$–$$$ 🏨 **Lodge at Red River Ranch.** You'll swear you've walked into one of the
Fodor'sChoice great lodges of Western legend when you walk through the doors at Red
★ River Ranch. The great room is decorated with wagon-wheel chandeliers, Native American rugs, leather furniture, and original Frederick Remington sculptures. Guest rooms are meticulously and individually decorated with fine antiques and art; each has a fireplace, and most have a patio or balcony overlooking the grounds. The dining area features a train that runs around the ceiling. ⊠ *2900 W. Rte. 24, Box 22, 84773* ☎ *435/425–3322 or 800/205 6313* 🖷 *435/425–3329* ⊕ *www. redriverranch.com* 🛏 *15 rooms* ⚐ *Restaurant; no a/c, no room TVs, no smoking* ⊟ *AE, DC, MC, V.*

$ 🏨 **Muley Twist Inn.** This gorgeous B&B sits on 30 acres of land, with expansive views of the colorful landscape that surrounds it. Sit in a rocking chair on the wraparound porch and watch the cliffs change color in the evening sun while classical music drifts through the air. The rooms are outfitted with contemporary furnishings. ⊠ *249 W. 125 South St., 84773* ☎ *435/425–3640 or 800/530–1038* 🖷 *435/425–3641* ⊕ *www.muleytwistinn.com* 🛏 *5 rooms* ⚐ *In-room data ports, library; no room TVs, no smoking* ⊟ *AE, MC, V* ⦿ *BP.*

$ 🏨 **Pine Shadows Cabins.** These housekeeping cabins are tucked against the pink-and-white cliffs and surrounded by pine trees. The cabins are large, clean, and have fully equipped kitchenettes, VCRs, one or two beds, and a futon. ⊠ *195 W. 125 South St., Box 25, 84773* ☎ *435/425–3939 or 800/708–1223* ⊕ *www.pineshadowcabins.net* 🛏 *6 cabins* ⚐ *Kitchenettes, in-room VCRs* ⊟ *MC, V.*

¢ 🏨 **Cactus Hill Motel.** One of the best-kept secrets in southern Utah, this small motel is on a working sheep ranch and farm. The setting amid the green alfalfa fields with red-and-white cliffs as a backdrop is stunning. It's a real bargain, too. ⊠ *830 S. 1000 East St., 84773* ☎ *435/425–3578 or 800/507–2624* ⊕ *www.cactushillmotel.com* ⇨ *5 rooms* ⚬ ⊟ *AE, D, MC, V.*

Torrey

▶ **3** *5 mi west of Capitol Reef National Park on Rte. 24; 5 mi east of Teasdale on Rte. 24*

Probably the best home base for exploring Capitol Reef National Park, Torrey, outside the park, is a pretty little town with lots of personality. Giant old cottonwood trees make it a shady, cool place to stay, and you'll find the townsfolk friendly and accommodating. At the junction of two of Utah's most scenic roads, Routes 12 and 24, is the town's rapidly growing commercial district. Scattered here and there are the small homes of longtime residents and newer vacation homes built by city-dwellers.

The **Robbers' Roost** is part coffee bar, part bookstore, and part performance space, all contained in the late Ward Roylance's practically pyramid-shape house. Roylance was a writer and naturalist who chronicled Utah's natural and cultural history in books and articles that were always methodically researched yet filled with emotion and a passion for Utah's landscapes. The Roost is an excellent place to stop to browse, talk about trails, or find out what's going on around town. The **Entrada Institute** (⊕ www.entradainstitute.org), a Torrey-based nonprofit organization committed to educating people about the Capitol Reef region, is headquartered at the store and sponsors the Art from the Land Workshop every September. Art exhibits, readings, and writing workshops are the highlight of this three-day celebration of creativity and culture. ⊠ *185 W. Main St. (Rte. 24)* ☎ *435/425–3265* ☉ *Apr.–Oct.*

There are no T-shirts, magnets, or postcards at the lovely **Torrey Gallery.** Several exhibits each summer fill two display areas. Art shown and sold here ranges from oil paintings, photographs, and Navajo rugs to eccentric batiks and barbed-wire sculptures. ⊠ *80 E. Main St. (Rte. 24)* ☎ *435/ 425–3909* ⊕ *www.torreygallery.com.*

Sports & the Outdoors

For highly personalized attention during guided fly-fishing trips into the high backcountry around Capitol Reef as well guided 4X4 and horseback tours, **Boulder Mountain Adventures & Alpine Angler's Flyshop** (⊠ 310 W. Main St., 84775 ☎ 435/425–3660 or 888/484–3331 ⊕ www.flyfishing-utah.net) has a stellar reputation.

Hondoo Rivers & Trails (⊠ Rte. 24, Box 98, 84775 ☎ 435/425–3519 or 800/332–2696 ⊕ www.hondoo.com) has a reputation for innovative adventures on horseback or via four-wheel-drive vehicle in the mountains and deserts surrounding Capitol Reef National Park, as well as within the park's boundaries, from May to October. Its trademark is the ability to take visitors' uninformed or uncertain ideas and turn them into specialty tours never to be forgotten.

For a real taste of the backcountry of Capitol Reef National Park, take a hiking, biking, or 4X4 expedition with **Wild Hare Expeditions** (✉ 2600 E. Rte. 24 ☎ 435/425–3999 ⊕ www.color-country.net/~thehare). Guides will teach you more in one day about geology, wildlife, and land ethics than you thought possible. You'll have fun, too.

Where to Stay & Eat

$$$–$$$$
Fodor'sChoice
★

✕ **Cafe Diablo.** Saltillo-tile floors and matte-plaster white walls are a perfect setting for the Southwestern art that lines the walls in this intimate restaurant. Innovative Southwestern entrées include fire-roasted pork tenderloin, artichoke and sundried tomato tamales, and local trout crusted with pumpkin seeds and served with a cilantro lime sauce. If you're really adventurous, try the rattlesnake cakes, made with free-range desert rattler and served with ancho-rosemary aïoli. ✉ *599 W. Main St.* ☎ *435/425–3070* ▤ *AE, D, MC, V* ⊘ *Closed mid-Oct.–mid-Apr. No lunch.*

$–$$$
✕ **Capitol Reef Café.** For standard fare that will please everyone in the family, visit this unpretentious restaurant. Favorites include the 10-vegetable salad and the flaky filet of locally caught rainbow trout. Numerous vegetarian offerings make for a refreshing break from beef and beans. ✉ *360 W. Main St. (Rte. 24)* ☎ *435/425–3271* ▤ *AE, D, MC, V* ⊘ *Closed Nov.–Apr.*

$–$$$
🏨 **Best Western Capitol Reef Resort.** Surrounded by red rock desert, this hilltop motel with some resortlike amenities also has great views of the colorful cliffs. The kitchenette units appeal especially to families. ✉ 2600 E. Rte. 24, 84775 ☎ 435/425–3761 or 888/610–9600 🖷 435/425–3300 ⊕ *www.bestwestern.com* ⇌ *80 rooms, 20 suites* ♨ *Restaurant, some in-room hot tubs, some minibars, some microwaves, some refrigerators, in-room VCRs, in-room data ports, tennis court, outdoor pool, outdoor hot tub, horseback riding, laundry facilities* ▤ *AE, D, DC, MC, V* ⊘ *Closed mid-Dec.–early Jan.*

$–$$$
Fodor'sChoice
★

🏨 **SkyRidge Bed & Breakfast.** Each of the inn's windows offers an exceptional view of the desert and mountains surrounding Capitol Reef National Park. The walls are hung with the works of local artists. Unusual furniture—each piece chosen for its special look and feel—makes the guest rooms and common areas both stimulating and comfortable. Breakfasts here, which might have you feasting on apple-stuffed croissants or homemade cinnamon rolls, are excellent, and you are served evening hors d'oeuvres as well. ✉ *950 E. Rte. 24, Box 750220, 84775* ☎ *435/425–3222* 🖷 *435/425–3222* ⊕ *www.skyridgeinn.com* ⇌ *6 rooms* ♨ *Dining room, some in-room hot tubs, cable TV, in-room VCRs, hot tub* ▤ *AE, MC, V* ⊗⧐ *BP.*

$
🏨 **Holiday Inn Express Hidden Falls Resort.** Comfortable, larger-than-average guest rooms are decorated with warm Southwestern tones and have views of the surrounding mountain country. You can hike the ½ mi to area trails. The friendly staff can help answer questions about area attractions, and a three-tier waterfall and pond with paddle boats are favorites with children. There's also a conference room here. ✉ 2424 E. Rte. 24 ☎ 435/425–3866 or 888/232–4082 ⇌ *36 rooms, 3 suites* ♨ *Microwaves, refrigerators, cable TV, in-room data ports, outdoor pool, gym, hot tub, laundry facilities* ▤ *AE, D, DC, MC, V.*

¢–$ 🏨 **Austin's Chuckwagon Lodge.** Foremost at this lodge are friendly service and immaculate rooms. The owner has taken great care to create comfortable accommodations with queen-size beds, satellite TV, and in-room movies. The especially nice outdoor pool is one of the largest around. You can choose between standard rooms at the motel-style lodge or stand-alone cabins. Zane Grey, the famous western novelist, used to rent an 1892 cabin on the grounds of this pleasant complex. ⊠ *12 W. Main St., 84775* ☎ *435/425–3335 or 800/863–3288* 📠 *435/425–3434* ⊕ *www. austinschuckwagonmotel.com* ⇌ *25 rooms, 3 cabins* ⚴ *Some kitchens, cable TV with movies, pool, hair salon, hot tub, shops, laundry facilities* ⊟ *AE, DC, MC, V* ⊙ *Closed Nov.–Feb.*

¢ 🏨 **Capitol Reef Inn.** Travelers on a tight budget can't beat the simple, well-lit rooms here. The walls are thin, but the rooms are big, and the grounds are nicely landscaped with desert plants. ⊠ *360 W. Main St., 84775* ☎ *435/425–3271* ⊕ *www.capitolreefinn.com* ⇌ *10 rooms* ⚴ *Restaurant, microwaves, refrigerators, cable TV with movies, outdoor hot tub, shops, playground, some pets allowed* ⊟ *AE, D, MC, V* ⊙ *Closed Nov.–Mar.*

¢ 🏨 **Cowboy Homestead Log Cabins.** These small but nicely appointed cabins practically ooze charm. On a working ranch a few minutes south of Torrey, the cabins have either two queen-size beds or a queen and a sofa bed; and although they aren't luxurious, the pine-panel cabins are carpeted and cozy. The owners also offer guided fly-fishing expeditions, pack trips, and horseback rides. ⊠ *2100 S. Rte. 12, 84775* ☎ *435/425–3414* 📠 *435/425–3414* ⊕ *www.cowboyhomesteadcabins.com* ⇌ *4 cabins* ⚴ *Cable TV, in-room VCRs, fishing, horseback riding* ⊟ *MC, V.*

¢ 🏨 **Wonderland Inn.** This hilltop motel has an incredible view as well as spacious rooms. The restaurant next door serves good Western-style comfort food. A nearby RV park is under the same management; it has full and partial hookups with plenty of grass and shade. ⊠ *Rte. 12 and Rte. 24, 84775* ☎ *435/425–3775 or 800/458–0216* 📠 *435/425–3212* ⊕ *www.capitolreefwonderland.com* ⇌ *50 rooms* ⚴ *Cable TV, pool, hot tub, hair salon* ⊟ *AE, D, MC, V.*

WHERE TO CAMP 🏕 **Thousand Lakes RV Park and Campground.** This is understandably one of the area's most popular RV parks. There's lots of grass and shade, and the level, 22-acre site provides good views of the surrounding red cliffs. The cabins come in either bare-bones or with bath, microwave, refrigerator, and TV. ⚴ *Flush toilets, full hookups, partial hookups, dump station, drinking water, guest laundry, showers, grills, fire pits, picnic tables, electricity, public telephone, general store, play area, swimming (pool)* ⇌ *46 full hookups, 12 partial hookups, 9 tent sites; 7 cabins* ⊠ *1050 W. Rte. 24, 84775* ☎ *435/425–3500 or 800/355–8995* 📠 *435/ 425–3510* ⊕ *www.thousandlakesrvpark.com* 🍽 *$14 tent sites, $19 partial hookups, $20full hookups, $30–$55 cabins* ⊟ *D, MC, V* ⊙ *Apr.–Oct.*

Shopping

The pleasing **Gallery 24** (⊠ 135 E. Main St. ☎ 435/425–2124) sells contemporary fine art from Utah-based artists that includes sculpture, hand-crafted furniture, folk art, photography, and ceramics.

en route One of Utah's—and America's—most spectacular drives is the 32-mi stretch of **Route 12,** a Utah Scenic Byway between Torrey and Boulder (⇨ *see* Chapter 7, "Zion, Bryce & Southwestern Utah"). You'll wind through alpine forests and see some of America's most remote and wild landscape along the way.

Capitol Reef National Park

224 mi south of Salt Lake City; 5 mi east of Torrey on Rte. 24.

Some of the most dramatic color in the West is found at Capitol Reef National Park, which gets its name from the dome-shape rocks that populate the area. The park is literally a reef in the desert—a giant fold in the earth that stretches for more than 100 mi. Your senses will be delighted by a visit to the park. Here you are saturated in colors that are almost indescribable—nowhere else in the West are the colors so dramatic. Deep blue-green juniper and pinyon stand out against the rich, red-chocolate hue of the dominant Moenkopi rock formation. Other sandstone layers are gold, ivory, and lavender. Sunset brings out the colors in an explosion of copper, platinum, and orange, then dusk turns the cliffs purple and blue. The texture of rock deposited in ancient inland seas and worn by subsequent erosion is pure art.

It's no wonder Native Americans called this part of the country the "land of sleeping rainbow." The golden rock and rainbow cliffs are at their finest at sunset, when it seems as if they are lit from within. That's also when mule deer wander through the orchards near the campground. Many of the park's animals move about only at night to escape the heat of the day, but pinyon blue jays flit around the park all day. Of course, the best place to see wildlife is near the Fremont River, where animals are drawn to drink. Ducks and small mammals such as the yellow-bellied marmot live nearby. Desert bighorn sheep also live in Capitol Reef, but they are elusive. Your best chance of spotting the sheep is during a long hike deep within the park. If you should encounter a sheep, do not approach it.

Northern Capitol Reef

Winding through the north part of the park is the Fremont River, which supports the valley's fruit orchards. Here the fragrance of pine and sage rises from the earth, and canyon wrens sing to you as you sit by the water. The narrow little creek can turn into a swollen, raging torrent during desert flash floods. The river sustains cottonwoods, wildlife, and verdant valleys rich with fruit that you can pick at harvest time. This area receives most of the park's visitors, and it's the location of the visitor center and campground.

a good tour Pack a picnic lunch, snacks, and cold drinks to take with you because there are no restaurants in the park. As you enter the park, look to your left for Chimney Rock; in a landscape of spires, cliffs, and knobs, this deep-red landmark is unmistakable. Start your journey at the **visitor center ❹** ⌐, where you can study a three-dimensional map of the area, watch the short slide show, and browse the many books and maps related to

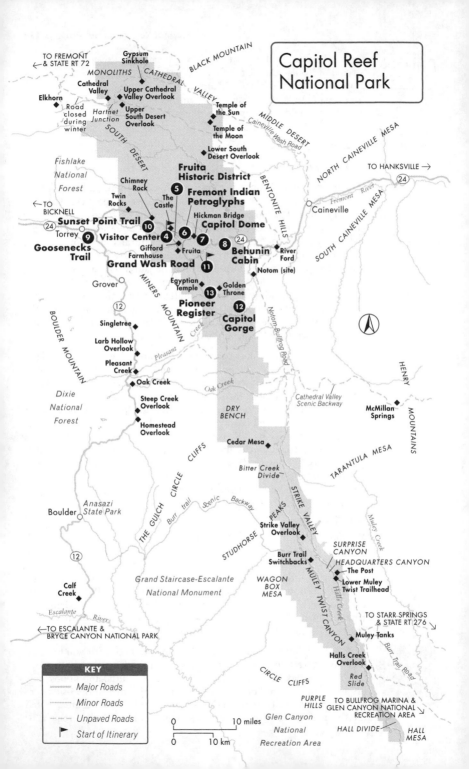

the park. Then head for the park's scenic drive, stopping at the **Fruita Historic District ❺** to see some of the sites associated with the park's Mormon history. As you continue on with your tour, stop to see the **Fremont Indian Petroglyphs ❻**, and if you feel like some exertion, take a hike on the Hickman Bridge Trail. From the trail (or if you skip the hike, from Route 24 about 2 mi east of the visitor center), you'll see **Capitol Dome ❼**. Continue on Route 24 to visit the **Behunin Cabin ❽**. Next you'll have to backtrack a few miles on Route 24 to find the **Goosenecks Trail ❾**. At the same parking lot you'll find the trailhead for **Sunset Point Trail ❿**; take this short hike in time to watch the setting sun hit the colorful cliffs.

TIMING   If you take the walks suggested, this tour should take a full day.

What to See

❽ **Behunin Cabin.** Elijah Cutlar Behunin used blocks of sandstone to build this cabin in 1882. Floods in the lowlands made life too difficult, and he moved on before the turn of the 20th century. The house is empty, but you can peep through a window. ⊠ *Rte. 24, 6⅕ mi east of visitor center.*

❼ **Capitol Dome.** One of the rock formations that gave the park its name, this giant, golden dome is visible in the vicinity of the Hickman Bridge trailhead. ⊠ *Rte. 24, about 2 mi east of visitor center.*

☾ ❻ **Fremont Indian Petroglyphs.** Nearly 1,000 years ago the Capitol Reef area was occupied by the Fremont Indians, whose culture was tied closely to the ancestral Puebloan (Anasazi) culture. Fremont rock art can be identified by the large trapezoidal figures often depicted wearing headdresses and ear baubles. Capitol Reef's petroglyphs are on a north-facing cliff wall. You can see more petroglyphs by walking along the cliff face, but stay on the boardwalk and do not climb the slope. ⊠ *Rte. 24, 1²/₁₀ mi east of visitor center.*

★ ☾ ❺ **Fruita Historic District.** In 1880 Nels Johnson became the first homesteader in the Fremont River Valley, building his home near the confluence of Sulphur Creek and the Fremont River. Other Mormon settlers followed and established small farms and orchards near the confluence, creating the village of Junction. The orchards thrived, and in 1902 the settlement's name was changed to Fruita. The orchards are preserved and protected as a Rural Historic Landscape.

An old **blacksmith shop** (⊠ Scenic Dr., less than 1 mi south of visitor center) exhibits tools, farm machinery, and harnesses dating from the late 1800s and Fruita's first tractor (which didn't arrive here until 1940). You can hear a recording in which a rancher talks about living and working in Fruita during the 1940s, '50s, and '60s.

Planted by Mormon pioneer settlers and their descendents, Capitol Reef's **fruit orchards** (⊠ Scenic Dr., less than 1 mi from visitor center) are still lovingly maintained by the park service. You can often see mule deer wandering here at dusk, making for great photographs. During harvest season, you can pick cherries, apricots, peaches, pears, and apples (the park charges for fruit you pick unless you eat it there, in which case it's free). A two-person crew maintains the orchards, which contain about 3,000 trees, with pruning and irrigation.

Mormon polygamist Calvin Pendleton built the primitive **historic Gifford Farmhouse** (✉ Scenic Dr., less than 1 mi from visitor center ☎ 435/425–3791) in 1908 and lived here with his family for eight years, followed by the Jorgen Jorgenson family, who resided here from 1916 to 1928. In 1928 Jorgenson's son-in-law, Dewey Gifford, bought the homestead and settled in with his family for 41 years. The last residents of Fruita, the Giffords sold their home to the National Park Service in 1969. The house has been faithfully restored, with several of the rooms furnished in period furniture and housewares. The former kitchen of the house has been converted to a gift shop. It's open daily from 11 to 5.

Mormon settlers built the one-room log **historic Fruita School** (✉ Rte. 24, 1 mi from visitor center) in 1896. In addition to classes, Mormon church meetings, dances, town meetings, and other community functions also took place in this building. The school closed in 1941 because there were no longer enough students to attend. You can peek inside the windows and listen to a recording of a former teacher recalling what it was like to teach here in the 1930s.

need a break?   There are no restaurants inside Capitol Reef National Park, but there's a nice shady **picnic area** at Gifford Farmhouse in the Fruita Historic District. In a grassy meadow with the Fremont River flowing by, this is an idyllic spot for a sack lunch. Picnic tables, drinking water, grills and a convenient rest room make it perfect.

⑨ Goosenecks Trail. This nice little walk gives you a good introduction to the land surrounding Capitol Reef. You'll no doubt enjoy the dizzying views from the overlook. It's only ²⁄₁₀ mi round-trip to the overlook and a very easy walk. ✉ *Rte. 24, about 3 mi west of visitor center.*

⑩ Sunset Point Trail. The trail starts from the same parking lot as the Goosenecks Trail. Benches along this easy, ⁷⁄₁₀-mi round-trip invite you to sit and meditate surrounded by the colorful desert. At the trail's end, you will be rewarded with broad vistas into the park; it's an even better treat at sunset. ✉ *Rte. 24, about 3 mi west of visitor center.*

▶ ❹ Visitor Center. Stop at the visitor center for an introduction to the park. Watch a film, talk with rangers, or peruse the many books, maps, and materials offered for sale in the bookstore. Towering over the center is the Castle, one of the park's most prominent rock formations. ✉ *Rte. 24, 11 mi east of Torrey* ☎ *435/425–3791* ☉ *May–Sept., daily 8–6; Oct. and mid-Apr.–May, daily 8–5; Nov.–mid-Apr., daily 8–4:30.*

The Waterpocket Fold

A giant wrinkle in the earth that extends 90 mi between Thousand Lake Mountain and Lake Powell, the Waterpocket Fold is a sight not be missed. You can glimpse the fold by driving south on Scenic Drive—after it branches off Route 24—past the Fruita Historic District, but for complete immersion enter the park via the 66-mi Burr Trail from the town of Boulder (⇨ *see* Chapter 7, Zion, Bryce & Southwestern Utah). Travel through the southernmost reaches of the park requires a substantial amount of driving on unpaved roads. It's accessible to most vehicles during dry weather; check at the visitor center for road conditions and recommendations before setting out. Most of the hikes in the area are strenuous.

Take Route 24 (Scenic Drive) through the Fruita Historic District to the **Grand Wash Road** ⓫ ▶ and drive into the canyon. Return to Scenic Drive and continue to the end of the pavement. Road conditions permitting, drive into **Capitol Gorge** ⓬. At the Capitol Gorge Trailhead, take the easy walk to see the **Pioneer Register** ⓭, and, if you don't mind a brief climb, take the Capitol Gorge Trail to the deep Waterpockets called the Tanks.

TIMING   You can see the main sights of the Waterpocket Fold portion of the park in a half day.

What to See

off the beaten path

BURR TRAIL SCENIC BACKWAY – Branching east off Route 12 in Boulder, Burr Trail travels through the Circle Cliffs area of Grand Staircase–Escalante National Monument into Capitol Reef. The views are of backcountry canyons and gulches. The road is paved between Boulder and the eastern boundary of Capitol Reef, then unpaved but well maintained inside the park. It leads into a hair-raising set of switchbacks that ascends 800 feet in ½ mi. The switchbacks are not suitable for RVs or vehicles towing trailers. Before attempting to drive this route from Boulder, check with the Capitol Reef visitor center for road conditions. From Boulder to its intersection with Notom-Bullfrog Road, the route is 36 mi long.

⓬ **Capitol Gorge.** At the entrance to this gorge Scenic Drive becomes unpaved. The narrow, twisting road on the floor of the gorge was a route for pioneer wagons traversing this part of Utah starting in the 1860s. After every flash flood, pioneers would laboriously clear the route so wagons could continue to go through. The gorge became the main automobile route in the area until 1962, when Route 24 was built. The short drive to the end of the road is an adventure in itself and leads to some interesting hiking trails. ⊠ *Scenic Dr., 9 mi south of visitor center.*

▶ ⓫ **Grand Wash Road.** A dirt road follows this twisting route down a canyon for about a mile. The unpaved, sometimes sandy, bumpy road winds between steep canyon walls. Allow a little more than a half hour for your adventure. Before taking this drive, check at the visitor center for flash flood warnings. ⊠ *Off Scenic Dr., about 5 mi from visitor center.*

⓭ **Pioneer Register.** Travelers passing through Capitol Gorge in the 19th and early 20th centuries etched the canyon wall with their names and the date they passed. Directly across the canyon from the Pioneer Register and about 50 feet up are signatures etched into the canyon wall by an early United States Geologic Survey crew. It's illegal to write or scratch on the canyon walls today; violations are taken very seriously. You can reach the register via an easy 1-mi hike from the end of the road. ⊠ *Off Scenic Dr., 9 mi south of visitor center.*

off the beaten path

NOTOM-BULLFROG ROAD – Although all of Capitol Reef is part of the 100-mi wrinkle in the earth known as the Waterpocket Fold, you can really only see the fold from the air or a higher elevation. The Notom-Bullfrog Road takes you right into the narrow fold. The road starts opposite the Orientation Pullout on Route 24 at the East Entrance to the park and is about 34 mi long, mostly unpaved and bumpy. ⊠ *Rte. 24, 10 mi east of visitor center.*

Sports & the Outdoors

BICYCLING   Bicycles are allowed only on established roads in the park. Since Route 24 is a state highway and receives a substantial amount of through traffic, it's not the best place to peddle. Scenic Drive is better, but the road is narrow, and you have to contend with drivers dazed by the beautiful surroundings. Four-wheel-drive roads are certainly less traveled, but they are often sandy, rocky, and steep. You cannot ride your bicycle in washes or on hiking trails. Wild Hare Expeditions offers guided bike tours in the park and also rents out bicycles (⇨ *see* Sports & the Outdoors *in* Torrey, above).

Cathedral Valley Scenic Backway. In the remote northern end of the park you can enjoy solitude and a true backcountry ride on this trail. You'll be riding on surfaces that include dirt, sand, bentonite clay, and rock, and you will also ford the Fremont River; you should be prepared to encounter steep hills and switchbacks, wash crossings, and stretches of deep sand. Summer is not a good time to try this ride, as water is very difficult to find and temperatures may exceed 100°F. The entire route is about 60 mi long; during a multiday trip you can camp at the primitive campground with five sites, about midway through the loop. ⊠ *Off Rte. 24 at Caineville, or at River Ford Rd., 5 mi west of Caineville on Rte. 24.*

Four-Wheeling

You can explore Capitol Reef in a 4X4 on a number of exciting backcountry routes. Drivers without high-clearance, four-wheel-drive vehicles should not attempt to make these drives. Road conditions can vary greatly depending on recent weather patterns. Spring and summer rains can leave the roads muddy, washed out, and impassable even to four-wheel-drive vehicles. Always check at the Capitol Reef visitor center for current conditions before you set out. Carry water, supplies, and preferably a cell phone on your trip. Outfitters in Torrey, including Hondoo Rivers & Trails and Wild Hare Expeditions, offer guided 4X4 tours in the park (⇨ *see* Sports & the Outdoors *in* Torrey, above), but ATVs are not allowed in the park.

Cathedral Valley Scenic Backway. The north end of Capitol Reef, along this backcountry road, is filled with towering monoliths, panoramic vistas, and a stark desert landscape. The area is remote and the road through it unpaved, so do not enter without a high-clearance vehicle, some planning, and a cell phone. The drive through the valley is a 58-mi loop that you can begin at River Ford on Route 24. From there the loop travels northwest, giving you access to Glass Mountain, South Desert, and Gypsum Sinkhole. Turning southeast at the sinkhole, the loop takes you past the side road that accesses the Temples of the Moon and Sun, then becomes Caineville Wash Road before ending at Route 24, 7 mi east of your starting point. Caineville Wash Road has two water crossings. Including stops, allow a half day for the drive on the unpaved road. If your time is limited, you may want to tour only the Caineville Wash Road. Starting from Route 24, the driving time on this route to lower Cathedral Valley is only about two hours. When you check at the visitor center for road conditions, you can pick up a self-guided auto tour brochure for $1. ⊠ *River Ford Rd., 11.7 mi east of visitor center on Rte. 24, or at Caineville, about 18 mi east of visitor center on Rte. 24.*

Hiking

Most of the trails in the park include steep climbs, but there are a few easy-to-moderate hikes. A short drive from the visitor center takes you to a dozen trails, and a park ranger can advise you on combining trails or locating additional routes. Hondoo Rivers & Trails and Wild Hare Expeditions in Torrey do guided hiking tours in the national park (⇨ *see* Sports & the Outdoors *in* Torrey, above).

★ **Capitol Gorge Trail and the Tanks.** Starting at the Pioneer Register, about a mile from the Capitol Gorge parking lot, is a trail that climbs to the Tanks. After a scramble up about ²⁄₁₀ mi of steep trail with cliff drop-offs you can look down into the Tanks and can also see a natural bridge below the lower tank. Including the walk to the Pioneer Register, allow an hour or two for this interesting little hike. ⊠ *At end of Scenic Dr., 9 mi south of visitor center.*

Chimney Rock Trail. You're almost sure to see ravens drifting on thermal winds around the deep red Mummy Cliff that rings the base of this trail. This loop trail begins with a steep climb to a rim above Chimney Rock. The trail is 3½ mi round-trip, with a 600-foot elevation change. You should allow three to four hours. ⊠ *Rte. 24, about 3 mi west of visitor center.*

☾ **Cohab Canyon Trail.** Children particularly love this trail for the geological features and native creatures, such as rock wrens and western pipistrels (canyon bats), that you see along the way. One end of the trail is directly across from the Fruita Campground on Scenic Drive, and the other is across from the Hickman Bridge parking lot. The first quarter-mile from Fruita is pretty strenuous, but then the walk becomes easy except for turnoffs to the overlooks, which are strenuous but short. Along the way you'll find miniature arches, skinny side canyons, and honeycombed patterns on canyon walls where the wrens make nests. The trail is 3.2 mi round-trip to the Hickman Bridge parking lot. The Overlook Trail adds 2 mi to the journey. Allow one to two hours to overlooks and back; allow two to three hours to Hickman Bridge parking lot and back. ⊠ *About 1 mi south of visitor center on Scenic Dr., or about 2 mi east of visitor center on Rte. 24.*

Fremont River Trail. What starts as a quiet little stroll beside the river turns into an adventure. The first half-mile of the trail is wheelchair accessible as you wander past the orchards next to the Fremont River. After you pass through a narrow gate, the trail changes personality and you're

CAPITOL REEF HIKING CHART

	Grade	Miles (one way)	Elevation Gain	Open Info	Shuttle Access	Toilet/ Restroom	Hiking Level	Trail Conditions
Capitol Gorge Trail and the Tanks	Level with one steep climb	1 mile		Year-round			Beginner	Maintained
Chimney Rock Trail	Steep	3.5-mile Loop		Year-round			Intermediate/ Advanced	Maintained
Cohab Canyon Trail	Steep first 1/4 mi	1.75 miles		Year-round			Beginner/ Intermediate	Maintained
Fremont River Trail	Level, then steep	1.25 miles		Year-round			Intermediate/ Advanced	Maintained
Golden Throne	Steep	2 miles		Year-round				Maintained
Grand Wash Trail	Level/sandy	2.25 miles		Year-round				Maintained
Hickman Bridge Trail	Moderately steep	1 mile		Year-round		Y (Trailhead)		Maintained

in for a steep climb on an exposed ledge with drop-offs. The views at the top of the 770-foot ascent are worth it as you look down into the Fruita Historic District. The trail is 2.5 mi round-trip; allow two hours. ✉ *Near amphitheater off Loop C of Fruita Campground, about 1 mi from visitor center.*

Golden Throne Trail. As you hike to the base of the Golden Throne, you may be fortunate enough to see one of the park's elusive desert bighorn sheep. You're more likely, however, to spot their small, split-hoof tracks in the sand. The trail itself is 2 mi of gradual elevation gain with some steps and drop-offs. The Golden Throne is hidden until you near the end of the trail, then suddenly you find yourself looking at a huge sandstone monolith. If you hike near sundown the throne burns gold, salmon, and platinum. The round-trip hike is 4 mi and you should allow two to three hours. ✉ *At end of Capitol Gorge Rd., at Capitol Gorge trailhead, 9 mi south of visitor center.*

Grand Wash Trail. At the end of unpaved Grand Wash Road you can continue on foot through the canyon to its end at the Fremont River. You are bound to love the trip. This flat hike takes you through a wide wash between canyon walls. It's an excellent place to study the geology up close. The round-trip hike is 4.5 mi, and you should allow two to three hours for your walk. It's a good idea to check at the ranger station for flash-flood warnings before entering the wash. ✉ *Rte. 24, east of Hickman Bridge parking lot, or at end of Grand Wash Rd., off Scenic Dr. about 5 mi from visitor center.*

Fodor'sChoice **Hickman Bridge Trail.** This trail is a perfect introduction to the park. It
★ leads to a natural bridge of Kayenta sandstone, which has a 135-foot opening carved by intermittent flash floods. Early on, the route climbs a set of steps along the Fremont River, and as the trail tops out onto a bench, you'll find a slight depression in the earth. This is what remains of an ancient Fremont pit house, a kind of home that was dug into the ground and covered with brush. The trail splits, leading along the right-hand branch to a strenuous uphill climb to the Rim Overlook and Navajo Knobs. Stay to your left to see the bridge, and you'll encounter a moderate up-and-down trail. As you continue up the wash on your way to the bridge, you'll notice a Fremont granary on the right side of the small canyon. Allow about 1½ hours to walk the 2-mi round-trip. The walk to the bridge is one of the most popular trails in the park, so expect lots of company along the way. ✉ *Rte. 24, 2 mi east of visitor center.*

HORSEBACK Many areas in the park are closed to horses and pack animals, so it's a
RIDING good idea to check with the visitor center before you set out with your animals. Day use does not require a permit, but you need to get one for overnight camping with horses and pack animals. Hondoo Rivers & Trails and Wild Hare Expeditions run horseback tours into the national park (⇨ *see* Sports & the Outdoors *in* Torrey, above). Unless you ride with a park-licensed outfitter, you have to bring your own horse, as no rentals are available.

Old Wagon Trail. For spectacular views of Waterpocket Fold, try this popular horse trail. It gradually climbs along the long rampart of

Miners Mountain, merging for a short distance with an old route that goes beyond into Boulder Mountain. There's very little shade on this trail. Allow two to three hours. ⊠ *About 6 mi south of visitor center on Scenic Dr.*

Where to Camp

★ ⚠ **Fruita Campground.** Near the orchards and the Fremont River, this shady campground is a great place to call home for a few days. The sites nearest the river or the orchards are the very best. Loop C is most appropriate for RVs, although the campground has no hookups. In summer, the campground fills up early in the day. ⚙ *Flush toilets, drinking water, grills, picnic tables* ⤙ *71 sites, 7 tent sites* ⊠ *Scenic Dr., about 1 mi south of visitor center* ☎ *435/425–3791* ⚑ *$10* ⚙ *Reservations not accepted.*

Nightlife & the Arts

In the amphitheater at the campground, you can attend a free lecture, slide show, or other ranger-led activity during the **Evening Program** (⊠ Amphitheater, Loop C, Fruita Campground, about 1 mi from visitor center on Scenic Dr. ☎ 435/425–3791). You'll learn about Capitol Reef's geology, Native American cultures, wildlife, or other features. A schedule of topics and times is posted at the visitor center. A regular schedule of programs is offered from May to September nightly, ½ hour after sunset.

Shopping

In the Fruita Historic District, **Gifford Homestead Gift Shop** (⊠ Scenic Dr. ☎ 435/425–3791), run by the Capitol Reef Natural History Association, sells jellies, soaps, looped rugs, and Roseville pottery. The **Visitor Center Bookstore** (⊠ In visitor center, Rte. 24 ☎ 435/425–3791) stocks a wide variety of books, maps, trail guides, posters, and postcards to help you make the most of your visit.

Capital Reef National Park Essentials

ADMISSION
There is a fee of $5 per vehicle for driving on the park's Scenic Drive beyond Fruita Campground; this fee is good for one week. Otherwise, there is no fee to enter the park.

EMERGENCIES
In the event of an emergency, call 911, report to a visitor center, or contact a park ranger. The nearest 24-hour medical center is the Beaver Valley Hospital in Beaver.

TOURS & CLASSES
From May to September, ranger programs, including guided walks and talks as well as evening programs in the Fruita campground amphitheater, are offered at no charge.

VISITOR INFORMATION
🚹 Capitol Reef National Park ⌂ HC70, Box 15, Torrey 84775 ☎ 435/425–3791 ⊕ www.nps.gov/care.

CAPITOL REEF & ENVIRONS A TO Z

To research prices, get advice from other travelers, and book travel arrangements, visit www.fodors.com.

AIR TRAVEL

CARRIERS Daily commuter service between Salt Lake City and Cedar City, the nearest city to Capitol Reef with an airport, is available through SkyWest.
🛪 **Airlines SkyWest** ☎ 801/575-2508 or 800/453-9417 ⊕ www.skywest.com.

AIRPORTS

Although small airports serving mainly charters and private planes dot the region, the vast majority of visitors coming by air to Capitol Reef National Park arrive at Salt Lake International Airport. The nearest regional airport is in Cedar City, 115 mi southwest of Richfield.
🛪 **Cedar City Regional Airport** ✉ 2281 Kitty Hawk Dr., Cedar City ☎ 435/867-9408 ⊕ www.cedarcity.org/city_government/airport.html.

BUS TRAVEL

Greyhound Lines runs buses along the I–15 corridor, making stops in various small towns. Check with Greyhound for current depots.
🛪 **Lines Greyhound Lines** ☎ 801/355-9579 or 800/231-2222 ⊕ www.greyhound.com.

CAMPING

In central Utah, campers have their choice from low-desert to high-mountain facilities. Campgrounds in Capitol Reef National Park fill up fast between Memorial Day and Labor Day. Most of the area's state parks have camping facilities, and the region's two national forests offer many wonderful sites. Fishlake National Forest and Fish Lake are good picks.
🛪 **Fishlake National Forest** ✉ 115 E. 900 North St., Richfield 84701 ☎ 435/896-9233 ⊕ www.fs.fed.us/r4/fishlake. **Utah State Parks and Recreation** ⬠ Box 146001 or 1594 W. North Temple, Salt Lake City ☎ 801/538-7220 ⊕ www.stateparks.utah.gov.

CAR RENTAL

Salt Lake City has a full range of major car rental agencies both at the airport and at in-town locations. Avis and National serve Cedar City Regional Airport. Some car dealerships in the region's larger towns, such as Richfield, rent cars as well.
🛪 **Avis** ✉ Cedar City Municipal Airport, 2281 W. Kittyhawk Dr., Cedar City ☎ 435/867-9898. **National** ✉ Cedar City Municipal Airport, 2281 W. Kittyhawk Dr., Cedar City ☎ 435/586-4004.

CAR TRAVEL

I–15 is the main route into the region, from Las Vegas to the southwest and Salt Lake City to the northeast. At Cove Fort I–70 heads east from I–15. Be aware that there are few exits and no gas stations along the 103-mi stretch of I–70 between Salina and Green River, so make sure your car is in good working order and the gas tank is topped off. U.S. 89 is a good, well-traveled road with interesting sights and plenty of gas stations and convenience stores. Other various well-maintained two-lane highways traverse central Utah. Some mountain curves can be expected, and winter months may see hazardous conditions, especially at higher elevations.

🚩 Road Conditions **Utah Highway Patrol** ☎ 801/965-4518 ⊕ www.highwaypatrol. utah.gov. **Utah Department of Transportation** ☎ 511 or 866/511-8824 ⊕ www.udot. utah.gov/public/road_conditions.htm.

EMERGENCIES
🚩 Ambulance or Police **Emergencies** ☎ 911.

MEDIA

NEWSPAPERS & MAGAZINES The largest newspaper for the region is the *Richfield Reaper.* The *Salt Lake Magazine* and *Deseret Morning News* cover central Utah regularly.

RADIO Once you get out of the range of radio stations along the Wasatch Front, local stations include KMTI 650 AM, KLGL 97.5 FM, and KSVC 93.7 FM, which play country music. KSVC 980 AM is talk.

SPORTS & THE OUTDOORS

BICYCLING Wild Hare Expeditions rents bikes, and offers guided bike tours.
🚩 **Wild Hare Expeditions** ⌖ P.O. Box 750194, Torrey 84775 ☎ 435/425-3999 or 888/304-4273 ⊕ www.color-country.net/~thehare.

🚩 VISITOR INFORMATION
Capitol Reef Country (⌖ Rte. 24, Box 7, Teasdale 84773 ☎ 800/858-7951 ⊕ www.capitolreef.org). **Capitol Reef National Park** (✉ Torrey, 84775 ☎ 435/425-3791 ⊕ www.nps.gov/care).

Zion, Bryce & Southwestern Utah

WORD OF MOUTH

"I loved Zion; we also went to Bryce Canyon and took a horseride into the canyon, which is not for the faint of heart, but something I will always remember. Bryce is spectacular at sunrise and sunset."

—suechef

"Went to Zion this year it was great, did the Narrows including the Riverside Walk, Angel's Landing, Emerald Pools, Weeping Rock, and Canyon Overlook. The Narrows and Angel's Landing were my favorite. Too hard to say one is better than the other. Because the Narrows you are walking in a depression or canyon in the water and Angel's Landing you walk up to the top of a narrow knife-edge ridge making them both unique."

—asdaven

By John
Blodgett

SOUTHWESTERN UTAH IS A LAND OF OPPOSITES. The state's lowest point, Beaver Dam Wash, is here, south and west of St. George, while the Pine Valley Mountains north of that growing city are among the tallest in Utah. The region is often perceived as a hot, dry place, yet from the desert depths you can see snowy peaks and evergreens and shiver.

Such contrasts have always attracted the curious. Famed explorer John Wesley Powell charted the uncharted; the young idealist and dreamer Everett Reuss left his well-to-do family and lost himself without a trace in the canyons; the author and curmudgeon Ed Abbey found himself, and has since been found either a voice crying in the wilderness or a pariah in Pareah. It depends on whom you ask. But that's the beauty of this place, the joy of choice in a land that confronts and challenges. We come, ostensibly, to escape; yet we really come to discover.

And come to Southwestern Utah we do in droves. The state can boast five national parks, and the two in this corner—Zion National Park and Bryce National Park—attract the most visitors every year. In fact, with more than 2.5 million visitors in 2004, Zion National Park is one of the most visited parks in the entire United States. The two are relatively close together, allowing a visit to each during a single trip, and yet they offer explorations and vistas quite different from one another. You won't repeat yourself by witnessing both parks.

Southwestern Utah is a land of adventure and contemplation, of adrenaline and retreat. It's not an either-or proposition; you rejuvenate whether soaking at a luxury spa or careening on a mountain bike down an alpine single-track headed straight for an aspen tree. The land settlers tamed for planting cotton and fruit is now a playground for golfers, bikers, and hikers. Arts festivals and concerts under canyon walls have smoothed the rough edges hewn by miners and the boomtowns that evaporated as quickly as they materialized. Ruins, petroglyphs, pioneer graffiti, and ghost towns—monuments to what once was—beckon new explorers. The region's secrets reveal themselves to seekers, yet some mysteries remain elusive—the paradox of the bustling world that lies hidden under the impression of spare, silent, and open space.

Some say that the desert reflects truth to those who pursue it. This is why we come here, and return: to discover the person staring back from a mirror of honest rock shining in the shimmering heat.

Exploring Southwestern Utah

Southwestern Utah is remarkable in the range of activities and terrain it has to offer. On one summer day you can explore an arid desert canyon at Snow Canyon State Park, the next you can camp in a high-alpine aspen grove in Dixie National Forest and bundle up for warmth. In winter you can sample mountain biking (at Gooseberry Mesa near Hurricane) and skiing (at Brian Head Resort) on the same trip.

Getting around is usually straightforward. The region's biggest cities, Cedar City and St. George, spring up alongside I–15, the major north–south travel corridor to the west. Farther east, U.S. 89 is a more

Numbers in the text correspond to numbers in the margin and on Southwestern Utah map.

If you have
3 days

Arrive at **Zion National Park** ⑪–⑳ ▶ via I–15. If you're traveling north on I–15, take the Route 9 exit. If you are southward bound, exit at Route 17, which will lead you to Route 9. Spend your afternoon getting oriented in the park and overnight in ▣ **Springdale** ⑩. After a morning hike in Zion, depart to the east via Route 9, the **Zion–Mt. Carmel Highway** ⑯, which passes through a 1¹⁄₁₀-mi-long tunnel that is so narrow, RVs and towed vehicles are required to pay to be escorted through. You emerge from the darkness into slickrock country, where huge, petrified sandstone dunes were etched by ancient waters. Stay on Route 9 for 23 mi and then turn north onto U.S. 89. After 42 mi you will reach Route 12, where you should turn east and drive 14 mi. Approaching the entrance of ▣ **Bryce Canyon National Park** ㉕–㉟, you may notice that the air is a little cooler here than it was at Zion, so get out and enjoy it. Overnight in or near the park and spend Day 3 enjoying the park's trails that skirt the rim of the amphitheater or drop down among the hoodoos.

If you have
5 days

Follow the suggested three-day itinerary above, adding a day to each of your national park visits—there's so much to see and do in each. If you would rather see a broader canvas of the southwestern corner of Utah, start your tour with a day in the Kolob Canyons section of **Zion National Park** ⑪–⑳ ▶, where you can take in views many never see because they focus on the more crowded Zion Canyon section of the park. Overnight in ▣ **St. George** ③–⑧ or ▣ **Cedar City** ①, where you can catch an evening play if the Shakespeare Festival is running. Depart for Zion Canyon the next morning and follow the three-day itinerary laid out above, adding a one-day detour to Cedar Breaks National Monument and ▣ **Brian Head** ② between your stops at Zion and Bryce Canyon.

If you have
7 days

After following either suggested five-day itinerary above, overnight in ▣ **Bryce Canyon National Park** ㉕–㉟ on your fifth night and take your sixth day to drive the spectacular and winding Route 12 scenic byway. Route 12 winds over and through an elevated hogback on the northern edge of Grand Staircase–Escalante National Monument. About 14 mi past the town of **Escalante** ㊱ on Route 12, stop at Calf Creek Recreation Area to stretch your legs on a 5¹⁄₂-mi round-trip hike to a gorgeous backcountry waterfall. Stop by Anasazi Indian Village State Park in ▣ **Boulder** ㊲ if you would prefer a less athletic break. Spend your sixth night in Boulder and on your final day, hike, bike, or drive into Grand Staircase–Escalante National Monument; the towns of Escalante and Boulder both have ranger stations and outfitters to inform and guide you.

---

scenic north–south route with access to Bryce Canyon National Park, the east side of Zion National Park, and the Kanab area. Routes 14 and 9 are the major east–west connectors between the two main highways, with Route 9 being the primary access to Springdale and Zion National Park. However, be warned: if you need to travel between I–15 and U.S.

89 via Route 9 during the day, you must pay the $20 admission fee to Zion National Park even if you do not plan to stop and visit. Access to the massive and remote Grand Staircase–Escalante National Monument is via Route 12 to the north and U.S. 89 to the south.

In winter the primary access roads to Brian Head and Cedar Breaks National Monument are either closed occasionally for snow removal (Route 143 from the north and east) or closed for the season (Route 148 from the south). Call the Cedar City office of the Utah Department of Transportation at ☎ 435/865–5500 for current road conditions.

About the Restaurants

Utah does not have a signature cuisine, per se; rather, restaurants borrow from a number of sources. In the southwestern corner of the state, reflecting the pioneer heritage of the region, traditional and contemporary American cuisines are most common, followed closely by those with Mexican and Southwestern influences. St. George and Springdale have the greatest number and diversity of dining options. Around St. George, there are a number of restaurants that serve seafood; keep in mind that at nicer restaurants, the fish is flown in daily from the West Coast; at the less expensive locales, the fish is usually frozen fresh. Because this is conservative Utah, don't presume a restaurant serves beer, much less wine or cocktails, especially in the smaller towns. Most restaurants are family friendly, and dress tends to be casual. Prices are reasonable, though they inch higher in and near Zion and Bryce Canyon national parks, and in comparatively remote Brian Head.

About the Hotels

Southwestern Utah is steeped in pioneer heritage, and you'll find many older homes that have been refurbished as bed-and-breakfast inns. Green Gate Village in St. George, a collection of pioneer homes gathered from around the state, is an excellent example. The area also has its share of older independent motels in some of the smaller towns. Moreover, with the increase in tourism brought about by Zion National Park, Bryce Canyon National Park, the Utah Shakespearean Festival, and other attractions, most of the major hotel and motel chains have opened up at least one facility in the region. With the exception of Brian Head, the high season is summer, and logic dictates that the closer you want to be to a major attraction, the further in advance you have to make reservations. If you are willing to find a room upward of an hour from your destination, perhaps with fewer amenities, you may be surprised not only by same-day reservations in some cases, but also much lower room rates. Panguitch has some particularly good options for budget and last-minute travelers.

WHAT IT COSTS				
	$$$$	$$$	$$	$	¢
RESTAURANTS	over $25	$19–$25	$13–$18	$8–$12	under $8
HOTELS	over $200	$151–$200	$111–$150	$70–$110	under $70

Restaurant prices are for a main course at dinner, excluding sales tax of 7½%–8½%. Hotel prices are for two people in a standard double room in high season, excluding service charges and 11%–12¼% tax.

6

Hiking & Backpacking

The horizon is the limit when it comes to exploring southwestern Utah by foot. There are hiking trails to fit all levels of experience and fitness. If you're short on time, make it a point to spend at least half a day out of the car and on the trail. For what seems like a small, parched, and desolate corner of the state, southwestern Utah offers an impressive diversity of hiking climates, from cool evergreen forests at alpine elevations near 10,000 feet to hot desert washes sprinkled with sandstone and sage. Zion National Park has trails that ascend steep switchbacks cut into orange cliffs, squeeze through narrow slot canyons, and meander alongside the cool currents of the Virgin River. Bryce Canyon National Park's paths tread the rim of the limestone amphitheater, descending in loops through the arches and hoodoos formed by erosion.

If you have the motivation and ability, consider a multiday backpacking trip into the region's wild backcountry. Time your trip right and you can experience true wilderness at comfortable temperatures and, most importantly, without the crowds of the Wasatch. Bryce Canyon and Zion have great overnight routes of their own—don't forget your required backcountry permit—but you might look beyond the national parks if you're looking to get farther off the beaten path. The peaks of the Pine Valley Wilderness warm to comfortable levels in spring, summer, and fall and are generally forsaken for the parks on the other side of I–15 during these seasons. Grand Staircase–Escalante National Monument contains nearly 2 million acres of desert plains, canyons, and badlands, though you will probably want to wait until the cooler fall and winter months to set out on your backcountry adventure here. Safety precautions are critical on any trip: travel in groups, prepare for all weather conditions in any season, and don't embark without notifying several people of your itinerary. If you don't feel comfortable leading your own trip, consider contacting a local outfitter about the availability of guided trips.

Utah's Tribute to the Bard

Recipient of the 2000 Tony Award for Outstanding Regional Theater, the Utah Shakespearean Festival has grown far from the humble first two-week season that attracted 3,300 patrons in 1962. Now more than 150,000 spectators enjoy the festival that lasts from June to October. Although the Bard lends his name to the festival and his famous Globe Theatre's design to the center stage at Southern Utah University, this festival is about more than just Shakespearean plays. Other playwrights' works are produced, and educational workshops and symposia are held for students and actors of all ages.

Timing

Year-round, far southwestern Utah is the warmest region in the state; St. George is usually the first city to break 100°F every year, and even the winters remain mild at lower desert elevations. Despite the heat, most people visit from June to September, making the off-season a pleasantly

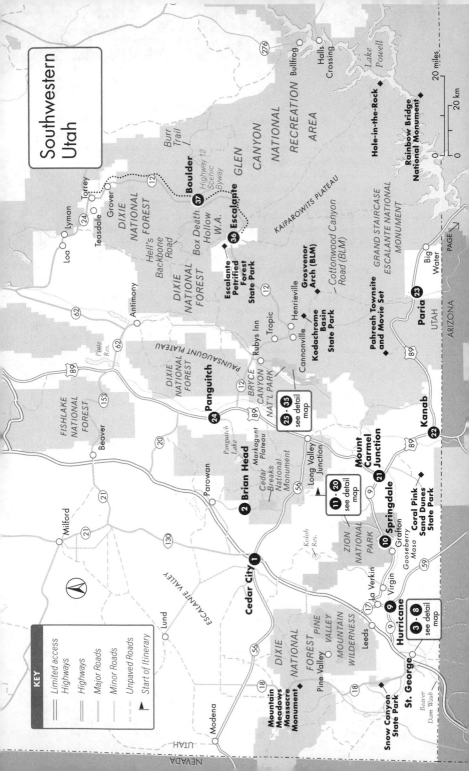

uncrowded experience for those willing and able to travel from fall to spring. Incidentally, Utahns from the north tend to stay away from the southern parts of the state during peak months for the very reasons—intense, dry heat and unyielding sun—that attract so many travelers from out of state. If you decide to brave the heat, wear sunscreen and drink lots of water, regardless of your activity level.

Farther east, around Bryce Canyon National Park and the Brian Head–Cedar Breaks National Monument area, elevations approach and surpass 9,000 feet, making for more temperamental weather, intermittent and seasonal road closures due to snow, and downright cold nights well into June. At this altitude, the warm summer sun is perfectly balanced by the coolness of the alpine forests during the day. While the peak season at Bryce Canyon is summer, it's a different story at Brian Head, where snow sports dominate; still, the resort has been pushing its summer recreation lineup of mountain biking and hiking, and the trails here are some of the finest in all of Utah.

Cedar City

❶ *250 mi southwest of Salt Lake City via I–15 south.*

Rich iron-ore deposits here grabbed Mormon leader Brigham Young's attention, and he ordered an LDS (Latter-day Saints) mission established. The first ironworks and foundry opened in 1851 and operated for only eight years; problems with the furnace, flooding, and hostility between settlers and Native Americans eventually put out the flame. Residents then turned to ranching and agriculture for their livelihood, and Cedar City thrived thereafter.

Cedar City calls itself "The Festival City." The Southern Utah University campus hosts the city's major event, the Utah Shakespearean Festival, which has been stretching its season longer and longer as its reputation has grown, a process that residents (and the city's lodging industry) have embraced wholeheartedly. Though better known for festivals than recreation, the city is well placed for exploring the Brian Head area.

Inside the Iron County Visitor Center, the **Daughters of the Utah Pioneers Museum** displays pioneer artifacts such as an old trundle sewing machine, an antique four-poster bed, and photographs of old Cedar City and its inhabitants. ⊠ *582 N. Main St.* ☏ *435/586–4484* 🖃 *Free* ☉ *Weekdays 1–4.*

The **Iron Mission State Park Museum** is a memorial to the county's iron-industry heritage. Explore the bullet-scarred stagecoach that ran in the days of Butch Cassidy, plus tools and other mining artifacts. A log cabin built in 1851—the oldest standing home in southern Utah—and a collection of wagon wheels and farm equipment are displayed outside. Local artisans demonstrate pioneer crafts. ⊠ *635 N. Main St.* ☏ *435/586–9290* ⊕ *www.stateparks.utah.gov* 🖃 *$2* ☉ *Daily 9–6.*

The large, beehive-shape charcoal kiln is the most complete and distinctive remnant of **Old Iron Town,** founded in the late 1860s and the site of southern Utah's second attempt to produce iron. A quick, self-guided walking tour passes the remains of a furnace, a foundry, and a mule-powered grinding stone called a "Spanish erastra," used to process ore. The town closed when the iron operations ceased in 1877. ⊠ *On Rte. 56, 25 mi west of Cedar City* ☎ *435/586–9290* 🎫 *Free.*

Sports & the Outdoors

Every June, more than 7,000 Utahns compete in everything from archery to horseshoes, arm wrestling, basketball, and gymnastics during the **Utah Summer Games** (☎ 435/865–8421 or 800/354–4849) at Southern Utah University.

The **Dixie National Forest headquarters** (⊠ 1789 Wedgewood La. ☎ 435/ 865–3700 ⊕ www.fs.fed.us/dxnf) administers an area encompassing almost 2 million acres, stretching 170 mi across southwestern Utah, and containing 26 designated campgrounds. The forest is popular for such activities as horseback riding, fishing, and hiking.

HIKING   Join **Southern Utah Scenic Tours** (☎ 435/867–8690 or 888/404–8687 ⊕ www.utahscenictours.com) for an all-day tour from Cedar City to either Zion National Park or Bryce National Park, including a short, easy-to-moderate hike. The price includes pick-up and drop-off at your hotel; snacks and lunch; and all applicable park fees.

Where to Stay & Eat

★ $$–$$$$ ✕ **Milt's Stage Stop.** This dinner spot in beautiful Cedar Canyon is known for its 12-ounce rib-eye steak, prime rib, fresh crab, lobster, and shrimp dishes. In winter, deer feed in front of the restaurant as a fireplace blazes away inside. A number of hunting trophies decorate the rustic building's interior, and splendid views of the surrounding mountains delight patrons year-round. ⊠ *Cedar Canyon, 5 mi east of town on Rte. 14* ☎ *435/586–9344* ☐ *AE, D, DC, MC, V* ☽ *No lunch.*

¢–$ ✕ **Market Grill.** A low-slung, ranch-style building next to the Cedar City stockyard, this place has vinyl-bench booths and a rutted dirt parking area well suited to the pickup trucks that usually park here, attesting to its popularity amongst locals. The fare is just as basic: burgers, barbecued ribs, and a salad bar. ⊠ *2290 W. 200 North St.* ☎ *435/586–9325* ☐ *MC, V* ☽ *Closed Sun.*

¢   ✕ **Bulloch Drug.** Swivel onto a stool in front of the circa-1942 soda fountain and cool off as the old timers did, with soda syrup hand-mixed with carbonated water right before you. Maybe your grandparents would remember Ironport, a soft drink from the '30s described here as a "spicy cream soda." There are shakes, malts, floats, and banana splits, too. ⊠ *91 N. Main St.* ☎ *435/586–9651* ☐ *AE, D, MC, V* ☽ *Closed Sun.*

¢   ✕ **The Pastry Pub.** Don't be fooled by the name—coffee and tea are the only brews on tap here, and sandwiches and salads join pastries on the chalkboard menu. (There is, nevertheless, prerecorded, pubby Irish folk music.) Build a sandwich of meat, egg, cheese, and more on a bagel, croissant, sliced bread, or one of five flavors of wraps. Caffeine-lovers, take note: they have the best java in Cedar City. ⊠ *86 W. Center St.* ☎ *435/ 867–1400* ☐ *MC, V* ☽ *Closed Sun.*

$$–$$$ ⊡ **Baker House Bed & Breakfast.** This three-story replica of a Queen Anne Victorian mansion was built in 1998, and each room is named after a writer; Lord Byron is the luxury room and occupies an entire floor. Breakfast might include quiche, fruit tarts, and muffins. Within 2 mi of the Globe Theatre, it's a perfect place to stay during the Shakespearean Festival. ⊠ *1800 Royal Hunte Dr., 84720* ☎ *435/867–5695 or 888/611–8181* 📠*435/867–5694* ⊕ *www.bakerhouse.net* ➳*4 rooms, 1 suite* ♨ *Cable TV, Internet room; no kids under 13, no smoking* ⊟ *AE, D, DC, MC, V* ❂ *BP.*

$–$$ ⊡ **Best Western Town & Country Inn.** Actually two buildings directly across the street from each other, this two-story motel has good amenities and a friendly staff. You can easily walk the few blocks to the Shakespearean Festival and the downtown shopping district. ⊠ *189 N. Main St., 84720* ☎ *435/586–9900 or 800/493–0062* 📠 *435/586–1664* ⊕ *www.bwtowncountry.com* ➳ *157 rooms* ♨ *Microwaves, refrigerators, cable TV, 2 indoor pools, hot tub, laundry facilities, business services, airport shuttle* ⊟ *AE, D, DC, MC, V* ❂ *CP.*

$ ⊡ **Abbey Inn.** This two-story property has somewhat dim but spacious rooms with balconies. Some suites have kitchens, and the elegant honeymoon suite has an in-room spa. Walk to nearby restaurants and the Utah Shakespearean Festival, all of which are a few blocks away. ⊠ *940 W. 200 North St., 84720* ☎ *435/586–9966 or 800/325–5411* 📠 *435/586–6522* ⊕ *www.abbeyinncedar.com* ➳ *80 rooms* ♨ *Microwaves, refrigerators, cable TV, in-room data ports, indoor pool, hot tub, laundry facilities, business services, airport shuttle; no-smoking rooms* ⊟ *AE, D, DC, MC, V* ❂ *CP.*

$ ⊡ **Bard's Inn Bed & Breakfast.** Rooms in this restored turn-of-the-20th-century house are named after heroines in Shakespeare's plays. There are antiques throughout and handcrafted quilts grace the beds. Enjoy a full breakfast that includes fresh home-baked breads such as nutmeg-blueberry muffins, plus fruit, juices, and shirred eggs. ⊠ *150 S. 100 West St., 84720* ☎ *435/586–6612* ⊕ *www.bardsandb.com* ➳ *7 rooms* ♨ *Cable TV; no room phones, no smoking, no pets* ⊟ *AE, MC, V* ⊗ *Closed mid-Oct.–mid-June* ❂ *BP.*

¢–$ ⊡ **Willow Glen Inn.** Staying on this 20-acre farm is like staying at grandma's. Three buildings (including the converted pony barn) contain rooms, no two alike, which have details like flowered quilts and aspen wood trim. ⊠ *3308 N. Bulldog Rd., 84720* ☎ *435/586–3275* 📠 *435/586–8422* ⊕ *www.willowgleninn.com* ➳ *10 rooms* ♨ *Microwaves, meeting room; no room phones, no smoking* ⊟*AE, D, DC, MC, V* ❂*BP.*

Nightlife & the Arts

NIGHTLIFE Dance to soft rock or country music at the **Playhouse** (⊠ 1027 N. Main St. ☎ 435/586–9010), a private club for members (temporary memberships are $4) that attracts an older crowd. Cedar City's college students gather at the **Sportsmen's Lounge** (⊠ 900 S. Main St. ☎ 435/586–6552), a beer-only bar with live music, dancing, and billiards.

THE ARTS From June to October, the **Utah Shakespearean Festival** (☎ 435/586–7880
Fodor'sChoice or 800/752–9849 ⊕ www.bard.org) puts on plays by the Bard and
★ others, drawing tens of thousands over the course of the season. The

outdoor theater at Southern Utah University is a replica of the Old Globe Theatre from Shakespeare's time, showcasing Shakespearean costumes and sets during the season. The Royal Feaste, a popular dinner event, requires reservations. Call ahead for a schedule of performances. The **Canyon Country Western Arts Festival** (☎ 800/354–4849 ⊕ www. westernartsfestival.org) brings the heritage of the Old West to life on the campus of Southern Utah University every March. Leather-working, blacksmithing, and other Western crafts demonstrations mix with traditional cowboy poetry and music. Traditional Paiute music and a parade are part of the **Paiute Restoration Gathering and Powwow** (☎ 435/ 586–1112), held in June at different locations on Paiute tribal lands.

Brian Head

❷ *29 mi northeast of Cedar City via Rte. 14 east and Rte. 143 and Rte. 148 north.*

Brian Head made a name for itself as a ski town (Brian Head Resort is Utah's southernmost and highest ski area at well over 9,000 feet), but the area's summer recreation, especially mountain biking, has been developed and promoted energetically. There are now more than 200 mi of trails for mountain bikers, many of which are served by chairlift or shuttle services. The bright red-orange rock formations of Cedar Breaks Monument are several miles south of town.

The snow season is still the high season in Brian Head, so book your winter lodging reservation in advance and don't be surprised by the high room rates. Food prices are high year-round. The fall "mud season" (October to November) and spring "slush season" (April to May) shut down many area businesses. You can celebrate the onset of fall with beer and bratwurst at Brian Head Resort's **Oktoberfest** (☎ 435/677–2810) in late September.

★ At **Cedar Breaks National Monument** a natural amphitheater similar to Bryce Canyon plunges 2,000 feet into the Markagunt Plateau. Short alpine hiking trails along the rim and thin crowds make this a wonderful summer stop. Although its roads may be closed in winter due to heavy snow, the monument stays open for cross-country skiing and snowmobiling. ✉ *Rte. 148, 9 mi south of Brian Head* ☎ *435/586–9451* ⊕ *www.nps. gov/cebr* ✐ *$4* ⊙ *Visitor center June–Oct., daily 8–6.*

Sports & the Outdoors

Brian Head Ski Resort is a favorite among California skiers weary of the crowded megaresorts of their own state. Eight lifts service 50 trails covering almost 500 acres of terrain starting at a base elevation of 9,600 feet. The Peak Express snowcat takes expert skiers to the 11,300-foot summit of Brian Head Peak for access to ungroomed runs. A half-pipe, rails, and terrain park attract hordes of snowboarders. From the top you can see the red rock cliffs of Cedar Breaks National Monument to the southwest. ✉ *329 S. Rte. 143* ☎ *435/677–2035* ⊕ *www.brianhead.com* ⊙ *Late Nov.–late Apr., daily 9:30–4:30.*

The largest outfitter in town, **Brianhead Sports** (✉ 269 S. Rte. 143 ☎ 435/677–2014) caters to cyclists, skiers, and snowboarders with equipment and accessories for rent or purchase. The store runs a mountain-bike shuttle that's handy for riding area trails that end far from where they start. Down the road from Brian Head Resort, **Georg's Ski Shop and Bikes** (✉ 612 S. Rte. 143 ☎ 435/677–2013) has new and rental skis, snowboards, and bikes.

BICYCLING Brian Head is a good place to base mountain-biking excursions. The area's most popular ride is the 12-mi Bunker Creek Trail, which winds its way through forests and meadows to Panguitch Lake. Brian Head Resort runs one of its ski lifts in summer, providing access to several mountain-bike trails, and Brianhead Sports, among others, shuttles riders to other trails on the resort property. Five miles south of Brian Head, road cyclists can explore Cedar Breaks National Monument and vicinity.

Only fat-tire fanatics with legs, lungs, and wills of steel need sign up for the **Epic 100** (☎ 909/866–4565 ⊕ www.brianheadepic.com), a National Championship of Endurance race held in July. The course stretches for 100 mi and gains 10,500 feet in elevation.

Where to Stay & Eat

★ **$$–$$$$** ✗ **Double Black Diamond Steak House.** The fire-roasted pork loin with mango chutney and homemade barbecue sauce is a perennial favorite. Steak and salmon dominate the remainder of the menu. Low lights, a crackling fire, and the clink of wine glasses set an upscale mood, but there's no need to dress up for the occasion. The restaurant, in Cedar Breaks Lodge, is open Friday and Saturday evenings only. ✉ *223 Hunter Ridge Rd. (Rte. 143)* ☎ *435/677–4242* ▭ *AE, D, MC, V* ⊘ *Closed Sun.–Thurs. No lunch.*

$ ✗ **The Bump and Grind.** Eat here or grab takeout—the service is quick if you can't wait to hit the trails. Classic American deli sandwiches and burgers offer no surprises, just good quality for hearty appetites. ✉ *259 S. Rte. 143* ☎ *435/677–3111* ▭ *AE, MC, V.*

$$–$$$$ ▦ **Brian Head Reservation Center.** The studio and condominium units rented out by central reservations are privately owned and individually decorated, so facilities and layout vary; ask about fireplaces and whirlpool baths. All kitchens are equipped, and linens provided. Reservations well in advance are recommended in winter. ✉ *356 S. Brian Head Blvd., 84719* ☎ *435/677–2042 or 800/845–9781* 🖷 *435/677–2827* ⊕ *www.brianheadtown.com/bhrc* ⇱ *40 units* ⚘ *Cable TV, sauna, laundry facilities; no a/c, no smoking* ▭ *AE, D, MC, V.*

★ **$–$$** ▦ **Cedar Breaks Lodge.** On the north end of town, this casual but upscale resort sits among aspen and pine trees. Large studio rooms have kitchenettes and suites have sleeper sofas in the sitting areas. ✉ *223 Hunter Ridge Rd. (Rte. 143), 84719* ☎ *888/282–3327* 🖷 *435/677–2211* ⊕ *www. cedarbreakslodge.com* ⇱ *120 units* ⚘ *2 restaurants, some kitchenettes, microwaves, cable TV, in-room data ports, pool, gym, hot tub, sauna, cross-country skiing, video game room, in-room data ports, Internet room, business services, no-smoking rooms; no a/c* ▭ *AE, MC, V* ▯◎▮ *BP.*

Nightlife & the Arts

NIGHTLIFE When night falls in Brian Head, so do most people—right into bed after a day of activity. Those with the stamina to go out have one choice in town, the **Cedar Breaks Club** (✉ 223 Hunter Ridge Rd. [Rte. 143], Cedar Breaks Lodge ☎ 888/282–3327), which is a private club for members. Membership is included for guests of Cedar Breaks Lodge; others must buy a temporary pass. Appetizers are served.

St. George

50 mi southwest of Cedar City via I–15.

Believing the mild year-round climate ideal for growing cotton, Brigham Young dispatched 309 LDS families in 1861 to found St. George. They were to raise cotton and silkworms and to establish a textile industry, to make up for textile shortages resulting from the Civil War. The area was subsequently dubbed "Utah's Dixie," a name that stuck even after the war ended and the "other" South could once again provide cotton to Utah. The settlers—many of them originally from southern states—found the desert climate preferable to northern Utah's snow, and they remained as farmers and ranchers. Crops included fruit, molasses, and grapes for wine that the pioneers sold to mining communities in Nevada and nearby Leeds, Utah. St. Georgians now number more than 50,000, many of whom are retirees attracted by the hot, dry climate and the numerous golf courses. But historic Ancestor Square, the city's many well-preserved, original pioneer and Mormon structures, and a growing shopping district make St. George a popular destination for families, as well.

Many of the Mormons who settled in southwestern Utah in 1861 were converts from Switzerland, and the nearby small town of Santa Clara, northwest of St. George, celebrates this heritage every September during the **Santa Clara Swiss Festival** (☎ 435/673–6712), which includes crafts and food booths, games, a parade, and a tour of historic homes.

❸ Mormon leader Brigham Young spent the last five winters of his life in the warm, sunny climate of St. George. Built of adobe on a sandstone-and-basalt foundation, **Brigham Young's Winter Home** has been restored to its original condition. A portrait of Young hangs over one fireplace, and furnishings authentic to the late-19th-century time period have been donated by supporters. Guided tours are available. ✉ *67 W. 200 North St.* ☎ *435/673–2517 or 435/628–1658* 🎫 *Free* ⊙ *Daily 9–7.*

❹ The red-sandstone **St. George Temple**, plastered over with white stucco, was completed in 1877 and served as a meeting place for both Mormons and other congregations. It's still in use today, and though only Mormons can enter the temple, a visitor center next door offers guided tours for everyone. ✉ *250 E. 400 South St.* ☎ *435/673–5181* 🎫 *Free* ⊙ *Visitor center daily 9–9.*

❺ Mormon settlers began work on the **St. George Tabernacle** in June 1863, a few months after the city of St. George was established. Upon completion of the sandstone building's 140-foot clock tower 13 years later, Brigham Young formally dedicated the site. This is one of the best-preserved pioneer buildings in the entire state, and is still used for public meetings and programs for the entire community. ✉ *18 S. Main St.* ☎ *435/628–4072* ⊙ *Daily 9–6.*

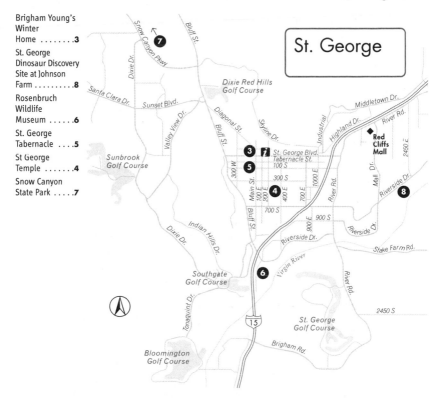

★ �％ ❻ Chances are the **Rosenbruch Wildlife Museum** in St. George is unlike any
museum you've ever seen. This modern 25,000-square-foot facility displays more than 200 species of wildlife (stuffed) from around the globe,
displayed in an uncanny representation of their native habitat—the
plains of Africa, the forests of North America, and the mountains of
Asia. A wheelchair-accessible pathway of almost ¼ mi winds through
the different environments. Two waterfalls cascade from a two-story
mountain, and more than 50 hidden speakers provide ambient wildlife
and nature sounds. Before your tour, check out the video presentation
in the 200-seat theater, and be sure not to miss the massive bug collection. ☒ *1835 Convention Center Dr.* ☏ *435/656–0033* ⊕ *www.
rosenbruch.org* ☒ *$8* ⊗ *Mon. noon–9, Tues.–Sat. 10–6.*

★ ❼ Red Navajo sandstone mesas and formations are crowned with black
lava rock, creating high-contrast vistas from either end of **Snow Canyon
State Park.** From the campground you can scramble up huge sandstone
mounds and overlook the entire valley. ☒ *1002 Snow Canyon Dr.,
Ivins, 8 mi northwest of St. George* ☏ *435/628–2255* ⊕ *www.stateparks.
utah.gov* ☒ *$5* ⊗ *Mar.–Nov., daily 6 AM–10 PM; Dec.–Feb., daily 8–5.*

☼ ❽ Follow footsteps cast in stone millions of years ago at **St. George Dinosaur
Discovery Site at Johnson Farm,** where property development came to a

halt when the ancient prints from the Jurassic period were unearthed in 2000. To reach the tracks, take 700 South Street east to Foremaster Drive and continue past the sod farm. ⊠ *2180 E. Riverside Dr.* ☎ *435/574–3466* ⊕ *www.dinotrax.com* ☎ *$2* ⊙ *Mon.–Sat. 10–6.*

off the beaten path

BEAVER DAM WASH – Utah's lowest point happens to mark the convergence of the Colorado Plateau, the Great Basin, and the Mojave Desert. In this overlapping of ecosystems, you'll find a great diversity of plants and animals, especially birds. In the southern part of the wash stands the greatest concentration of Joshua trees in the area. To get here, take Route 18 north of St. George and turn west onto Route 8, the paved road that runs 12 mi through Santa Clara. ⊠ *12 mi southwest of Shivwits on Old Hwy. 91* ☎ *801/539–4001* ☎ *Free.*

Sports & the Outdoors

BICYCLING   The folks at **Bicycles Unlimited** (⊠ 90 S. 100 East St. ☎ 435/673–4492 or 888/673–4492) are a font of information on mountain biking in southern Utah. They rent bikes and sell parts, accessories, and guidebooks.

GOLF   **Bloomington** (⊠ 3174 E. Bloomington Dr. ☎ 435/673–4687) offers a striking combination of manicured fairways and greens beneath sandstone cliffs. **Dixie Red Hills** (⊠ 645 W. 1250 North St. ☎ 435/634–5852) has 9 holes. The 18-hole **Entrada at Snow Canyon** (⊠ 2511 W. Entrada Trail ☎ 435/674–7500) is Utah's first Johnny Miller Signature Course. **St. George Golf Club** (⊠ 2190 S. 1400 East St. ☎ 435/634–5854) is a popular 18-hole course with challenging par-3 holes.

Water provides challenges at **Southgate Golf Club** (⊠ 1975 S. Tonaquint Dr. ☎ 435/628–0000), with several holes bordering ponds or crossing the Santa Clara River. Designed by Ted Robinson, fairway features at **Sunbrook** (⊠ 2240 W. Sunbrook Dr. ☎ 435/634–5866) include rock walls, lakes, and waterfalls.

HIKING   **Snow Canyon State Park** (⊠ 11 mi northwest of St. George on Rte. 18 ★   ☎ 435/628–2255 ⊕ www.stateparks.utah.gov) has several short trails and lots of small desert canyons to explore.

HORSE RACING &   For more than 25 years the St. George Lions Club has hosted the **Dixie** RODEO   **Downs Horse Races** (☎ 435/652–9067) on two April weekends to prepare horses for the larger tracks in summer. The September **Dixie Roundup** (☎ 435/628–1658) rodeo has been a tradition for decades. The novelty of the PRCA event is that it's held on the green grass of Sun Bowl stadium.

RUNNING   Fast becoming one of the most popular marathons in the West, the **St. George Marathon** (☎ 435/634–5850 ⊕ www.stgeorgemarathon.com) takes runners beneath extinct volcanoes and along the rim of Snow Canyon on the first Saturday of October.

Where to Stay & Eat

$–$$$$ ✕ **Rococo Steak House.** Specializing in beef and seafood, this restaurant is known for its prime rib. Because it sits atop a hill overlooking town, you can enjoy spectacular views from your table. ⊠ *511 S. Airport Rd.* ☎ *435/628–3671* ⊕ *www.rococo.net* ☐ *AE, D, DC, MC, V.*

★ **$$–$$$** ✕ **Scaldoni's Grill.** This charming and casual eatery is one of the best Italian restaurants in St. George. Try the penne with Gorgonzola and wild mushrooms, followed by fresh tiramisu for dessert. If you're not in the mood for Italian, don't despair; the kitchen also prepares standard American fare like steak and seafood. ⊠ *929 Sunset Blvd.* ☎ *435/674–1300* ▭ *AE, D, MC, V* ⊗ *Closed Sun.*

$–$$$ ✕ **Painted Pony.** Patio dining and local art hanging on the walls provide suave accompaniment to the creative meals served in this downtown restaurant. Be sure to try the cilantro-ginger escolar or the pan-roasted rack of lamb. ⊠ *2 W. St. George Blvd., Ancestor Sq.* ☎ *435/634–1700* ⊕ *www.painted-pony.com* ▭ *AE, D, MC, V* ⊗ *Closed Sun.*

¢–$$ ✕ **Pancho & Lefty's.** Locals come to this lively restaurant hung with sombreros and colorful blankets for the *flautas* (rolled, fried tortillas stuffed with meats and vegetables), chimichangas, sizzling fajitas, and ice-cold margaritas. ⊠ *1050 S. Bluff St.* ☎ *435/628–4772* ▭ *AE, D, MC, V.*

★ **¢–$** ✕ **Bear Paw Coffee Company.** There's so much on Bear Paw's menu that the restaurant suffers an identity crisis, with Southwestern, Tex-Mex, American, and Italian cuisines all represented. But no matter—the coffee is hot, the teas loose, the juice fresh, the servers smiling, and breakfast is served all day, every day. Home brewers (of coffee and tea, that is) can get their fresh beans and leaves here, too. There's no other place like it in southwestern Utah. ⊠ *75 N. Main St.* ☎ *435/634–0126* ▭ *AE, D, MC, V* ⊗ *No dinner.*

¢–$ ✕ **Panama Grill.** This restaurant serves New Mexican–style cuisine and one of the best fish tacos in town. There's open-air dining on the patio, and you can temper the St. George summer heat with an excellent margarita. ⊠ *2 W. St. George Blvd., Ancestor Sq.* ☎ *435/673–7671* ▭ *AE, D, DC, MC, V* ⊗ *Closed Sun.*

¢ ✕ **Irmita's Mexican Food.** Locals recommend this fruit-stand-turned-diner for its inexpensive Mexican fare. The selection is simple and no-nonsense—three items, three fillings, beans, and rice—but three temperatures of salsa (try the spicy "ooh la la") plus cabbage and lime round out a fine meal that proves cheap can be satisfying. The tiny dining room fills quickly, and the open kitchen's grill brings the St. George heat inside, but you can also sit outside at tables beneath palm-frond umbrellas. ⊠ *515 S. Bluff St.* ☎ *435/652–0161* ▭ *No credit cards* ⊗ *Closed Sun. No dinner Mon.*

$$$$ ▥ **Green Valley Spa & Tennis Resort.** Minutes from downtown but in a world of its own, this serene, luxurious resort and inn ranks among the

Fodor'sChoice ★ best in the world—*Travel and Leisure* magazine ranked it no. 3 in 2005. Here you can arrange your days around morning hikes, golf or tennis lessons, exercise classes, massage therapy, facials, and delicious low-calorie meals. All meals, and some spa services, are included in the weekly rate. Dozens of fitness classes are offered, as well as guided treks into the red rock canyon country surrounding the resort. A three-day minimum stay is required. ⊠ *1871 W. Canyon View Dr., 84770* ☎ *435/628–8060 or 800/237–1068* ▤ *435/673–4084* ⊕ *www.greenvalleyspa.com* ↵ *35 rooms* ⌂ *Dining room, cable TV, in-room safes, refrigerators, 19 tennis courts, 4 pools (3 indoor), 2 gyms, spa, hiking, laundry service, airport shuttle; no smoking* ▭ *AE, D, MC, V* ⋈ *FAP.*

★ **$–$$$**   ⊞ **Green Gate Village Historic Inn.** Step back in time in these restored pioneer homes dating to the 1860s. The inn takes its name from the green gates and fences that surrounded the homes of St. George's LDS leaders in the late 1800s. The last remaining original gate is displayed in the inn's garden and served as a model for those now surrounding Green Gate Village. Behind the gates is a village of nine fully restored pioneer homes filled with antique furnishings and modern amenities. Guests with children need to get prior approval from the management. ☒ *76 W. Tabernacle St., 84770* ☎ *435/628–6999 or 800/350–6999* ☒ *435/628–6989* ⊕ *www.greengatevillage.com* ⇥ *8 houses* ⚙ *Restaurant, snack bar, microwaves, cable TV, in-room VCRs, in-room data ports, pool, meeting rooms; no smoking* ▭ *AE, D, MC, V* ⊧⊙⊩ *BP.*

$–$$ ⊞ **Seven Wives Inn.** It's said that Brigham Young slept here, and that one of the buildings may have been a hiding place for polygamists after the practice was outlawed in the 1880s. In fact, the inn is named for an ancestor of the owner who indeed had seven wives. Not surprisingly the rooms are named after those wives. Antiques are liberally placed throughout the rooms, which are elaborately decorated with flowers and pastels. One room has a Jacuzzi tub installed in a Model T Ford. ☒ *217 N. 100 West St., 84770* ☎ *800/600–3737* ☒ *435/628–5646* ⊕ *www.sevenwivesinn.com* ⇥ *9 rooms, 3 suites, 1 cottage* ⚙ *Cable TV, Wi-Fi, in-room VCRs, pool, some pets allowed (fee); no smoking* ▭ *AE, D, MC, V* ⊧⊙⊩ *BP.*

$ ⊞ **Best Western Coral Hills.** The town's walking tour of historic pioneer buildings begins a block from this motel, which is next to the old courthouse and close to many restaurants. You can spend a hot afternoon relaxing in the shade of palm trees next to the outdoor pool. ☒ *125 E. St. George Blvd., 84770* ☎ *435/673–4844 or 800/542–7733* ☒ *435/673–5352* ⊕ *www.coralhills.com* ⇥ *98 rooms* ⚙ *Restaurant, microwaves, refrigerators, cable TV, in-room broadband, 2 pools (1 indoor), wading pool, gym, hot tub, laundry facilities, business services, airport shuttle, no-smoking rooms* ▭ *AE, D, DC, MC, V* ⊧⊙⊩ *CP.*

$ ⊞ **Ramada Inn.** On St. George's major thoroughfare and within a mile of restaurants, shopping, and the historic district, this is one of the city's most convenient properties. The rooms and furnishings are up-to-date and comfortable. ☒ *1440 E. St. George Blvd., 84790* ☎ *435/628–2828 or 888/704–8476* ☒ *435/628–0505* ⊕ *www.ramadainn.net* ⇥ *136 rooms* ⚙ *Some microwaves, cable TV, pool, hot tub, meeting rooms, no-smoking rooms* ▭ *AE, D, DC, MC, V* ⊧⊙⊩ *CP.*

¢**–$**   ⊞ **Comfort Suites.** Two blocks from the Dixie Convention Center, this hotel's "minisuites" have comfortable sitting areas and large TVs. The shaded outdoor common areas offer additional space in good weather. All rooms were refurbished in 2004. ☒ *1239 S. Main St., 84770* ☎ *435/673–7000* ☒ *435/628–4340* ⊕ *www.comfortsuite.com* ⇥ *125 suites* ⚙ *Microwaves, refrigerators, cable TV, in-room data ports, Wi-Fi, pool, gym, hot tub, business services* ▭ *AE, D, DC, MC, V* ⊧⊙⊩ *CP.*

¢**–$**   ⊞ **Travelodge Motel.** This modest-size chain motel has red rock views from most rooms and is within easy driving distance to St. George's many golf courses. ☒ *175 N. 1000 East St., 84770* ☎ *435/673–4621* ☒ *435/674–2635* ⊕ *www.travelodge.com* ⇥ *40 rooms* ⚙ *Some refrigerators,*

MORMON PROPHECY & THE CIVIL WAR

NO BATTLES WERE FOUGHT in Mormon-controlled Utah during the Civil War, but members of the new religion felt they would be deeply affected by the conflict—and in a most surprising way.

As tensions rose between the North and South, the position that Utah Territory would take in any resulting conflict was unclear. The most powerful man in the territory—Mormon leader Brigham Young—had neither condemned nor condoned slavery, although he had allowed Southern converts who emigrated to Utah to keep their slaves. Also, Utahns had fought to keep intruders out of the territory, acting as if their lands were separate from the rest of the United States, and Mormon leaders had made speeches about how "godless" and corrupt the federal government had become. These seemed like the words and actions of Southern sympathizers, or even secessionists, and the federal government sent troops to Utah Territory to keep the Mormons in line and to show the restless Southern states what would happen to them if they broke with the Union. Yet Brigham Young professed a love for the United States Constitution and for a whole America. His patriotism made the South nervous.

Young refused to take a stand for the North or for the South because he felt no great attachment to either side. In fact, he believed he knew the outcome of the Civil War long before the first shot was fired. Joseph Smith, founder of the Mormon Church and a prophet in the eyes of his followers, had preached that God would tear apart the United States because it had become wicked. After the destruction of the nation, Smith claimed, the newly humbled people would give up their sinful ways and become Mormons, and then God would make the nation whole again. When the Civil War began, Young was sure Smith's prophesy was coming true. All he had to do was wait until the war ended to take his place as the leader of a re-created America, which would be founded on the Constitution and on Mormon beliefs.

As the Civil War began to wind down and the North began to triumph, speeches condemning the federal government became less frequent in Utah Territory. A new spin was put on the Mormon stance: the nation had been torn apart, just as Joseph Smith had prophesied, and now, Mormons thought, it would surely be more humble and more in tune with God's will. Hopes rose that a less arrogant America would be more tolerant of Mormons. Thus Utahns reacted to the end of the Civil War in the same way people across much of the country reacted—with hope that peace would herald the beginning of a better and more tolerant age.

cable TV, pool, business services, some pets allowed, no-smoking rooms ☒ *AE, D, DC, MC, V* ⊙I *CP.*

Nightlife & the Arts

NIGHTLIFE   Ask locals where to go for nightlife in this conservative city and they'll say, with a straight face, Mesquite, Nevada (almost 40 mi away). Then they'll remember the aptly named **The One & Only Watering Hole** (☒ 800 E. St. George Blvd. ☎ 435/673–9191), a beer-only joint in a strip mall with billiards, televised sports, and live music on most weekends. The lively and predominantly working-class crowd prefers Willie Nelson on the jukebox.

THE ARTS   Artisan booths, food, children's activities, and entertainment, including cowboy poets, are all part of the **St. George Arts Festival** (☎ 435/634–5850), held the Friday and Saturday of Easter weekend. Spend a few quiet hours out of the Dixie sun at the **St. George Art Museum** (☒ 47 E. 200 North St. ☎ 435/634–5942). The permanent collection celebrates local potters, photographers, painters, and more. Special exhibits highlight local history. A rotating series of musicals such as *Joseph and the Amazing Technicolor Dream Coat* and *Seven Brides for Seven Brothers* entertain at **Tuacahn** (☒ 1100 Tuacahn Dr., Ivins ☎ 435/652–3200 or 800/746–9882 ⊕ www.tuacahn.org), an outdoor amphitheater nestled in a natural sandstone cove.

Shopping

★   Historic **Ancestor Square** (☒ St. George Blvd. and Main St. ☎ 435/628–1658) is the shopping and dining centerpiece of downtown St. George. Occupants of the tiny old jailhouse here now serve coffee instead of time, providing a pick-me-up from browsing the many galleries, shops, and restaurants. Pick up recreational items that made the packing list but not the pack at the **Outdoor Outlet** (☒ 1062 E. Tabernacle St. ☎ 435/628–3611 or 800/726–8106 ⊕ www.outdooroutlet.com). Shop for bargains at their frequent clearance sales. The **Red Cliffs Mall** (☒ 1770 E. Red Cliffs Dr. ☎ 435/673–0099 ⊕ www.redcliffsmall.com) is a retail mall with more than 40 stores. **Zion Factory Stores** (☒ 245 N. Red Cliffs Dr., I–15 Exit 8 ☎ 435/674–9800 or 800/269–8687 ⊕ www. promenadeatredcliff.com) is southern Utah's only factory-outlet center.

Hurricane

❾ *17 mi northeast of St. George via I–15 north and Rte. 9 east.*

An increasing number of lodging establishments makes Hurricane a less expensive and less crowded base for exploring Zion National Park and the rest of Dixie; the restaurants have been slow to catch up, however. Nearby Gooseberry Mesa is one of the best places to mountain bike in Utah.

Sports & the Outdoors

BICYCLING   The mountain biking trails on **Gooseberry Mesa,** off Route 59 south of
★   Hurricane, rival those of world-famous Moab on the other side of southern Utah, yet don't have the hordes of fat-tire fanatics. Come here for solitary and technical single-track challenges.

GOLF Hurricane has **Sky Mountain** (✉ 1030 N. 2600 West St. ☎ 435/635–7888), one of the state's most scenic 18-hole golf courses. Many fairways are framed by red-rock outcroppings; the course has a front-tee view of the nearby 10,000-foot Pine Valley Mountains.

Where to Stay & Eat

★ ¢ ✕ **Main Street Café.** One of the best cups of coffee in Dixie is poured right here in Hurricane. A full espresso bar will satisfy "caffeinds," while vegetarians and others can choose from salads, sandwiches, breakfast burritos, homemade breads, and desserts. Sit inside to admire the works of local artists, or share the patio with the hummingbirds. ✉ *138 S. Main St.* ☎ *435/635–9080* ▭ *No credit cards* ☉ *Closed Mon. No dinner.*

$ ▥ **Travelodge.** This is a pretty basic motel on the outskirts of town and will provide you with a comfortable night's rest if you want few other amenities, though there is a pool. With Zion National Park a 35-mi drive, it's a comfortable distance from the park if you can't find something a bit nearer. ✉ *280 W. State St., 84737* ☎ *435/635–4647 or 800/578–7878* ▤ *435/635–0848* ⊕ *www.travelodge.com* ➱ *63 rooms* ♨ *Some microwaves, some refrigerators, cable TV, pool, some pets allowed (fee), no-smoking rooms* ▭ *AE, D, DC, MC, V* ◎ *CP.*

¢–$ ▥ **Comfort Inn Zion.** Golfers will appreciate the package deals available with nearby courses, and everyone benefits from being fairly close to Zion National Park, which is a 35-mi drive away. If the hot southern Utah sun has sapped your energy, a dip in the pool will wake you for your next adventure. ✉ *43 N. Sky Mountain Blvd., 84737* ☎ *435/635–3500 or 800/635–3577* ▤ *435/635–7224* ⊕ *www.comfortinnzion.com* ➱ *53 rooms* ♨ *Cable TV, pool, laundry facilities, Wi-Fi, meeting room, no-smoking rooms* ▭ *AE, D, DC, MC, V* ◎ *CP.*

¢ ▥ **Dixie Hostel.** Few hostels can boast of being listed on the National Register of Historic Places and having such proximity to a national park, with a Zion shuttle service to boot for the 35-mi trip. Built in 1929, this bright and clean facility was first a hotel and then a boarding home before becoming a hostel. Reservations are a good idea, especially if you want one of the two private rooms. Prices include tax, linens, and a continental breakfast. ✉ *73 S. Main St., 84737* ☎ *435/635–8202* ▤ *435/635–9320* ➱ *2 private rooms, 28 dorm beds* ♨ *Kitchen, laundry facilities, Internet room; no room TVs* ▭ *No credit cards* ◎ *CP.*

WHERE TO CAMP ## Springdale

🔟 *21 mi east of Hurricane via Rte. 9.*

Springdale's growth has followed that of next-door neighbor Zion National Park, the most popular park destination in Utah and one of the most popular in the United States. Hotels, restaurants, and shops keep popping up, yet the town still manages to maintain its small-town charm. And oh, that view! Many businesses along Zion Park Boulevard, the main drag, double as shuttle stops for the bus system that carts tourists into the jaw-dropping sandstone confines of Zion Canyon, the town's main attraction.

A stone school, dusty cemetery, and a few wooden structures are all that remain of the nearby town of **Grafton,** a ghost town that has starred in films such as *Butch Cassidy and the Sundance Kid.* Indian attacks drove the original settlers from the site. ✉ *On Bridge La., 2 mi west of Rockville.*

Sports & the Outdoors

The folks at **Springdale Cycles** (✉ 1458 Zion Park Blvd. ☎ 435/772–0575 or 800/776–2099 ⊕ www.springdalecycles.com) rent bicycles, car racks, and trailers, and they can give you helpful tips on the local trails.

Where to Stay & Eat

★ **$$–$$$$** ✕ **The Switchback Grille.** Crowded with locals and tourists alike, this restaurant is known for its wood-fired pizzas, ribs, and vegetarian dishes. Try the excellent portobello sandwich for lunch. The vaulted ceilings make the dining room feel open and comfortable. ✉ *1149 S. Zion Park Blvd.* ☎ *435/772–3700* ⊕ *www.switchbacktrading.com* ▭ *AE, D, MC, V.*

$$–$$$ ✕ **Bit & Spur Restaurant and Saloon.** This restaurant has been a legend
Fodor'sChoice in Utah for 20 years. The seasonal menu lists familiar Mexican dishes
★ like burritos, tacos, and tostadas, but the kitchen also gets creative. Try the sweet potato tamale with tomatillo salsa, or the *puerco relleno,* grilled pork tenderloin filled with walnuts, apples, Gorgonzola, and raisins. Arrive early so you can eat outside and enjoy the lovely grounds and great views. ✉ *1212 Zion Park Blvd.* ☎ *435/772–3498* ⊕ *www.bitandspur. com* ▭ *AE, D, MC, V* ☙ *No lunch.*

$$–$$$ ✕ **Spotted Dog Cafe at Flanigan's Inn.** Named in honor of the family dog of Springdale's original settlers, the restaurant offers dinner entrées such as lamb, chicken, steak, and locally grown trout, which is sometimes encrusted in pumpkin seed and pan-seared. The kitchen really demonstrates its abilities through the pork tenderloin with apple-almond sauce and mango chutney. You can also get breakfast here. ✉ *428 Zion Park Blvd.* ☎ *435/772–3244* ▭ *AE, DC, MC, V* ☙ *No lunch.*

$–$$ ✕ **Zion Pizza and Noodle Co.** Creative Thai chicken or hot-and-spicy burrito pizzas put some pizzazz into the menu; you can also order pasta dishes like linguine with peanuts and spaghetti with homemade marinara sauce. A selection of microbrews is also served. You can dine indoors or in the beer garden at this restaurant, which occupies part of a former church building. ✉ *868 Zion Park Blvd.* ☎ *435/772–3815* ⊕ *www.zionpizzanoodle.com* ▭ *No credit cards* ☙ *Closed Dec.–Feb.*

¢–$ ✕ **Sol Foods.** For a quick, healthful meal any time of day, stop here. Daily specials include spanakopita, quiche, lasagna, and salads. They can also prepare picnic baskets or box lunches for your day in the park. Nearby is Sol's ice cream parlor, with hand-dipped ice cream cones, banana splits, and espresso. The patio seating is near the Virgin River, with views into the park. ✉ *95 Zion Park Blvd.* ☎ *435/772–0277* ⊕ *www.solfoods. com* ▭ *MC, V.*

★ **$$** 🏠 **Cliffrose Lodge and Gardens.** Flowers adorn the 5-acre grounds of this friendly, charming lodge. Comfortable rooms will keep you happy after a long hike, and from your balcony you can continue to enjoy views of the towering, colorful cliffs. The Virgin River runs right along the property, so you can have a picnic or barbecue out back to the sound of rushing water. The Cliffrose is within walking distance of the Zion Canyon visitor center and shuttle stop. ⊠ *281 Zion Park Blvd., 84767* ☎ *435/772–3234 or 800/243–8824* 🖷 *435/772–3900* ⊕ *www.cliffroselodge.com* 🖙 *40 rooms* ⚷ *Cable TV, in-room data ports, pool, outdoor hot tub; no smoking* ▤ *AE, D, MC, V.*

$–$$
Fodor'sChoice
★
🏨 **Desert Pearl Inn.** Every room is a suite, with vaulted ceilings and thick carpets, plus cushy throw pillows, Roman shades, oversize windows, bidets, sleeper sofas, and tiled showers with deep tubs. The pool area is exceptionally well landscaped and fully equipped, with a double-size hot tub and a shower–and–rest room block. Each room has a large balcony or patio, which overlooks either the Virgin River or the pool. ⊠ *707 Zion Park Blvd., 84767* ☎ *435/772–8888 or 888/828–0898* 🖷 *435/772–8889* ⊕ *www.desertpearl.com* 🖙 *61 rooms* ⚷ *In-room safes, kitchenettes, microwaves, refrigerators, cable TV, in-room VCRs, in-room data ports, Wi-Fi, pool, outdoor hot tub, shop; no smoking* ▤ *AE, D, MC, V.*

$–$$
🏨 **Flanigan's Inn.** Close to the park with canyon views, this rustic country inn has contemporary furnishings. The pool area is small but scenic. You can walk to the Zion visitor center from here (it's a few blocks), though the shuttle to the canyon stops on the property. ⊠ *428 Zion Park Blvd.* ☎ *435/772–3244 or 800/765–7787* 🖷 *435/772–3396* ⊕ *www.flanigans.com* 🖙 *34 rooms, 5 suites* ⚷ *Restaurant, cable TV, pool, business services; no smoking* ▤ *AE, D, MC, V.*

$
🏨 **Best Western Zion Park Inn.** This spacious and modern facility has large rooms. The Switchback Grille will get you going in the morning with a hearty breakfast, and since the inn is a stop on the park shuttle route, take one step out the door and you're on your way to Zion Canyon. ⊠ *1215 Zion Park Blvd., 84767* ☎ *435/772–3200 or 800/934–7275* 🖷 *435/772–2449* ⊕ *www.zionparkinn.com* 🖙 *114 rooms, 6 suites* ⚷ *Restaurant, cable TV, in-room data ports, pool, outdoor hot tub, shops, playground, laundry facilities, some pets allowed (fee), no-smoking rooms* ▤ *AE, D, DC, MC, V.*

Nightlife & the Arts

NIGHTLIFE As good as their Mexican food is, the **Bit & Spur Restaurant and Saloon** (⊠ 1212 Zion Park Blvd. ☎ 435/772–3498) is best known as the premier place to see live music in southern Utah. Many touring rock, blues, and reggae bands go out of their way to play here.

THE ARTS The **O. C. Tanner Amphitheater** (⊠ Lion Blvd. ☎ 435/652–7994 ⊕ www.dixie.edu/tanner) is set amid huge sandstone boulders at the base of the enormous red cliffs spilling south from Zion National Park. Here, the *Grand Circle,* a multimedia presentation on the Southwest, shows nightly at dusk from Memorial Day to Labor Day. Also, in summer live concerts are held each weekend, and everything from local country-music bands to the Utah Symphony Orchestra take to the stage. If it's too hot for you outside, escape to the cool confines of the ☾ **Zion Giant Screen Theater** (⊠ 145 Zion Park Blvd. ☎ 435/772–2400 or 888/256–3456 ⊕ www.zioncanyontheatre.com), where the six-story-high screen earns its superlative name. The 40-minute *Zion Canyon: Treasure of the Gods* takes you on an adventure through Zion and other points in canyon country. Two other films, including a Hollywood feature, are regularly shown here.

Shopping

Come to **Canyon Offerings** (✉ 933 Zion Park Blvd. ☎ 435/772–3456 or 800/788–2443) for some of Zion's snazziest souvenirs. The store is packed with gifts for mom, grandma, and the kids, and has one of the best selections of handcrafted jewelry in the region.

The **Happy Camper Market** (✉ 95 Zion Park Blvd. ☎ 435/772–3402) is right next to the park's south entrance. If you can't find your groceries, camping supplies, or forgotten items here, you probably don't really need them. Surrounded by apple orchards, **Springdale Fruit Company** (✉ 2491 Zion Park Blvd. ☎ 435/772–3222) makes an interesting and healthful stop. The store carries fresh-squeezed juices, organic fruit and vegetables, a great selection of trail mix concoctions, and bakery items. Its wood interior is refreshingly old-fashioned, and there's a picnic area in the back.

ZION NATIONAL PARK

The walls of Zion Canyon soar more than 2,500 feet above the valley below, but it's the character, not the size, of the sandstone forms that defines the park's splendor. The domes, fins, and blocky massifs bear the names and likenesses of cathedrals and temples, prophets and angels. You can spend a whole visit to Zion taking in views from the valley floor, marveling at every exhibit in this gallery of immense natural statuary.

For all Zion's grandeur, trails that lead deep into side canyons and up narrow ledges on the sheer canyon walls reveal a subtler beauty. Tucked among the monoliths are delicate hanging gardens, serene spring-fed pools, and shaded spots of solitude. So diverse is this place that 85% of Utah's flora and fauna species are found here. Some, like the tiny Zion snail, appear nowhere else in the world.

At the heart of Zion is the Virgin River, a tributary of the Colorado River. It's hard to believe that this muddy little stream is responsible for carving the great canyon you see, until you witness it transformed into a rumbling red torrent during spring runoff and summer thunderstorms. Cascades pour from the cliff tops, clouds float through the canyon, and then the sun comes out and you know you are walking in one of the West's most loved and sacred places. If you're lucky, you may catch such a spectacle, but when the noisy waters run thick with debris, make sure that you keep a safe distance—these "flash floods" can and do kill.

The elegance of Zion Canyon is most apparent as the morning sun alights upon the canyon walls or when the sunset draws out the brilliant colors of the rock. During the rains of March and September, you're likely to see waterfalls and fog. In fall, the canyon's trees explode into jarring hues of yellow and orange that mimic the sandstone backdrop. Winter is also dramatic, with a dusting of snow and storm clouds hugging the peaks. You are more likely to see wildlife on far-flung trails or in the off-season when there's less human and vehicular traffic. However, even in high season you may spot mule deer wandering in sheltered glens,

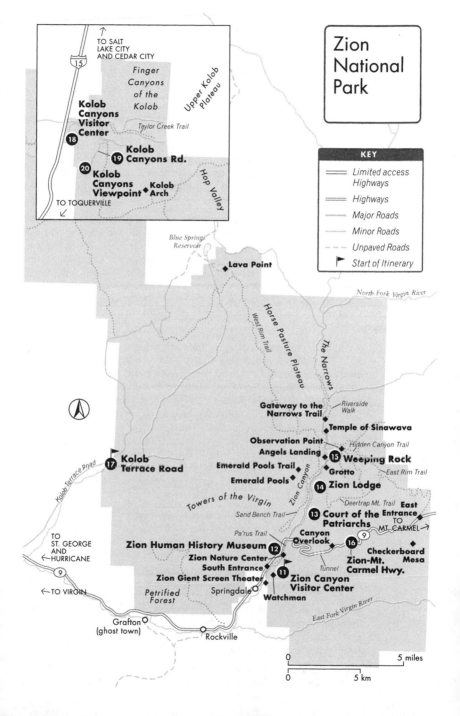

Zion
National
Park

KEY

═══	Limited access Highways
═══	Highways
⋯⋯	Major Roads
⋯⋯	Minor Roads
- - -	Unpaved Roads
▶	Start of Itinerary

especially early in the morning and at dusk. The park's many species of lizard come out to sun themselves on rocks during the heat of the day, and you may be surprised to come across a rattlesnake or, more benignly, a Gambel's quail. Mountain lion and ringtail cats prowl, but you're more likely to spot their tracks than catch a glimpse of the elusive animals themselves.

Zion is the most heavily visited national park in Utah, welcoming more than 2½ million visitors each year. Most come between April and October, when Zion Canyon is accessible only by free shuttle bus—a program instituted to eliminate traffic congestion. Summer in the park is hot and dry except for sudden cloudbursts; expect afternoon thunderstorms between July and September. Because it never gets bitterly cold in this part of the state, consider planning your visit for some time other than peak season.

The park comprises two distinct sections—Zion Canyon, and the Kolob Plateau and Canyons. Most people restrict their visit to the better-known Zion Canyon, especially if they have only one day to explore, but the Kolob area has much to offer and should not be missed if time allows. Due to geography—no roads connect Zion Canyon with Kolob Canyon—and to access points that are far apart, it is not feasible to explore both sections in one day.

Zion Canyon

If you have only one day to visit the park, stick with an exploration of Zion Canyon and save Kolob Canyon for another trip. You won't be disappointed, but keep in mind that there is much to see and you won't see it all in a single day. Sheer, vividly colored cliffs tower 2,500 feet above the Zion Canyon Scenic Drive that meanders along the floor of Zion Canyon. As you roll through the narrow, steep canyon you'll pass the Court of the Patriarchs, the Sentinel, and the Great White Throne, among other imposing rock formations. Zion Canyon Scenic Drive is accessed only by park shuttle April through October, but you can drive it yourself the rest of the year. To learn about the geology, ecology, and history of Zion Canyon, join a park ranger for a two-hour narrated shuttle tour that departs from the visitor center.

a good tour

Begin your visit at the **Zion Canyon Visitor Center** ⑪ ↦, where outdoor exhibits inform you about the park's geology, wildlife, history, and trails, as well as how to best enjoy the park. Catch the shuttle or drive—depending on the season—into Zion Canyon. On your way in make a quick stop at the **Zion Human History Museum** ⑫. You can watch a 22-minute orientation program on the park and visit exhibits chronicling the human history of the area. Board the shuttle and travel to the **Court of the Patriarchs** ⑬ viewpoint to take photos and walk the short path. Then pick up the next bus headed into the canyon. Stop at Zion Lodge and cross the road to the Emerald Pools trailhead, and take the short hike up to the pools themselves.

Before reboarding the shuttle, grab lunch in the snack shop or dining room at **Zion Lodge** ⑭ and browse the gift shop. Take the shuttle as far as **Weeping Rock** ⓯ trailhead for a brief, cool walk up to the dripping, spring-fed cascade. Ride the next shuttle to the end of the road, where you can walk to the gateway of the canyon's narrows on the paved, accessible Riverside Walk. Follow with a relaxing dinner in Springdale after a stroll to the downtown galleries and shops.

If you have another day, take a drive along the beautiful **Zion–Mt. Carmel Highway** ⓰, with its long, curving tunnels, making sure your camera is loaded and ready for stops at viewpoints along the road. Once you reach the park's east entrance, turn around, and stop on the return trip to take the short hike up to Canyon Overlook. Afterward, rest your feet at a screening of *Zion Canyon: Treasure of the Gods* at the Zion Giant Screen Theater in Springdale. In the evening, you might want to attend a ranger program at one of the campground amphitheaters or at Zion Lodge.

6

TIMING The two options here would each fill a day, with time for lingering at the sights along the way, or for making a couple of short hikes along the way.

What to See

⓭ **Court of the Patriarchs.** This trio of peaks bears the names of, from left to right, Abraham, Isaac, and Jacob. Mount Moroni is the reddish peak on the far right, which partially blocks your view of Jacob. You can see the Patriarchs better by hiking a half mile up Sand Bench Trail. ✉ *Zion Canyon Scenic Dr., 1½ mi north of Canyon Junction.*

need a break? In the shade of Zion Canyon, a picnic can be a relaxing break in a busy day of exploring. **The Grotto** (✉ Zion Canyon Scenic Dr., 3½ mi north of Canyon Junction), a cool lunch retreat, has drinking water, fire grates, picnic tables, and restrooms. The amenities make the Grotto ideal for families. A short walk takes you to Zion Lodge, where you can pick up fast food. On your way to or from the Junior Ranger Program, feed your kids at the **Zion Nature Center** (✉ Near the South Campground, ½ mi north of south entrance ☎ 435/772-3256) picnic area. When the nature center is closed, you can use the restrooms in South Campground.

★ ⓯ **Weeping Rock.** Once you take the short, paved walk up to this flowing rock face, you'll understand why this is one of the most popular stops in the park. Wildflowers and delicate ferns thrive near a spring-fed waterfall that seeps out of a cliff. The light "rain" that constantly falls from Weeping Rock feels great on a hot day. In fall, this area bursts with color. The ²⁄₁₀ mi trail to the west alcove takes about 25 minutes round-trip. It is paved, but it's too steep for wheelchairs. ✉ *Zion Canyon Scenic Dr., about 4 mi north of Canyon Junction.*

⚑ ⓫ **Zion Canyon Visitor Center.** Unlike most national park visitor centers, which are filled with indoor displays, Zion's presents most of its information in an appealing outdoor exhibit. Beneath shade trees beside a gurgling brook, displays help you plan your stay and introduce you to the geology, flora, and fauna of the area. Inside, a large bookstore operated by the Zion Natural History Association sells field guides and other publications. **Ranger-guided shuttle tours** of Zion Canyon depart from the parking lot and travel to the Temple of Sinawava. You'll make several stops along the way to take photographs and hear interpretation from the ranger. Free tickets are available at the visitor center, where a schedule of tour times is also posted. Backcountry permits, which are required for overnight hiking and climbing excursions, are available here. ⊠ *At south entrance, Springdale, 84767* ☎ *435/772–3256* ⊕ *www.nps.gov/zion* ☉ *Apr.–Oct., daily 8–7; Nov.–Mar., daily 8–5.*

⓬ **Zion Human History Museum.** Giving a complete overview of the park with special attention to human history, a stop here enriches your visit. Exhibits explain how settlers interacted with the geology, wildlife, plants, and unpredictable weather in the canyon from prehistory to the present. A 22-minute film plays throughout the day and provides a good start to a visit in the park. ⊠ *Zion Canyon Scenic Dr., 1 mi north of south entrance* ☎ *435/772–3256* ⊕ *www.nps.gov/zion/HHMuseum.htm* ☉ *Late May–early Sept., daily 8–7; Sept. and mid-Apr.–late May, daily 8–6; Oct.–mid-Apr., daily 8–5.*

⓮ **Zion Lodge.** The Union Pacific Railroad constructed the first Zion National Park lodge in 1925, with buildings designed by architect Stanley Gilbert Underwood. A fire destroyed the original building, but it was rebuilt to recapture some of the look and feel of the first building. The original Western-style cabins are still in use today. Among giant cottonwoods across the road from the Emerald Pools trailhead, the lodge houses a restaurant, snack bar, and gift shop. ⊠ *Zion Canyon Scenic Dr., about 3 mi north of Canyon Junction* ☎ *435/772–3213* ⊕ *www.zionlodge.com.*

⓰ **Zion–Mt. Carmel Highway.** If you enter or exit Zion via the east entrance you will have the privilege of driving a gorgeous, twisting 24-mi stretch of the Zion–Mt. Carmel Highway (Route 9). Two tunnels lie between the east park entrance and Zion Canyon. As you travel from one end of the longest (1¹⁄₁₀ mi) tunnel to the other, portals along one side provide a few glimpses of cliffs and canyons, and when you emerge on the other side you find that the landscape has changed dramatically. The tunnels are so narrow that vehicles more than 7 feet, 10 inches wide or 11 feet, 4 inches high require traffic control while passing through. Vehicles that exceed these size limits must pay an escort fee of $10 at either park entrance, and rangers, stationed at the tunnels daily (8–8) from April through October, stop oncoming traffic so you can drive down the middle of the tunnels. ⊠ *Zion–Mt. Carmel Rte. 9, about 5 mi, and 7½ mi east of Canyon Junction.*

The Kolob Plateau & Canyons

It's a pity that most people who come to Zion confine their visit to the main canyon. The Kolob area, in the northwestern section of the park, is considered by some to be superior in beauty, and you aren't likely to run into any crowds here. There are two ways to access the northern Kolob section of the park; the best choice depends on your starting point and time frame.

a good tour

If you want to visit the Kolob Canyons section of the park and you're starting in Springdale, you'll have to take the long route around the periphery for Zion—many people prefer to visit Kolob Canyons from Cedar City. From Springdale, take Route 9 west to I–15, follow the interstate north to Exit 40. Stop by the **Kolob Canyons Visitor Center ⓲** for trail and road conditions and the weather forecast before you start east up **Kolob Canyons Road ⓳**. After the first switchback, views will begin to unfold in front of you. Follow the road all the way to spectacular **Kolob Canyons Viewpoint ⓴**. If you feel up to it, embark here on the long, arduous hike to Kolob Arch or the shorter but still difficult route up Taylor Creek Trail.

From Route 9 in Virgin, 22 mi west of Springdale, the **Kolob Terrace Road ⓱** climbs steeply into the park's high country, from 3,500 feet along the Virgin River to more than 8,000 feet at Kolob Reservoir. Along the way you pass through a number of different ecosystems on the Lower Kolob and Upper Kolob plateaus. Trails that start along the road lead through Hop Valley, to Lava Point, and up to the Northgate Peak Viewpoint. You can spend the day hiking and exploring, or you can ascend the road as the late afternoon shadows fall and spend the night at Lava Point Campground. If you're just spending a half day, have your fill of exploring and turn around at Kolob Reservoir (or when you exit the national park boundaries and the pavement gives way to dirt) and backtrack to Route 9 and return to Zion Canyon.

TIMING Allow two to three hours to take either of the two tours highlighted above at a relaxed pace. Spring and summer tend to be warm to hot, but it's chilly in the fall and can get quite cold in the winter. The Kolob is easily accessible year-round from the paved Kolob Canyons Road, but beware Kolob Terraces Road in winter or during inclement weather; the road turns to dirt near Kolob Reservoir and can get rough. Call the visitor center for conditions.

What to See

★ ⓳ **Kolob Canyons Road.** From I–15 you get no hint of the beauty that awaits you on this 5-mi road. Most visitors gasp audibly when they get their first glimpse of the red canyon walls that rise suddenly and spectacularly out of the earth. The scenic drive winds amid these towers as it rises in elevation, until you reach a viewpoint that overlooks the whole Kolob region of Zion National Park. The shortest hike in this section of the park is the Middle Fork of Taylor Creek Trail, which is 2⁷⁄₁₀ mi one-way to Double Arch Alcove, and gets fairly rugged toward the end. During heavy snowfall Kolob Canyons Road may be closed. ⌧ *Kolob Canyons Rd. east of I–15, Exit 40.*

★ ⓴ **Kolob Canyons Viewpoint.** You can enjoy the magnificent views over the Timber Creek drainage to deep red sandstone monoliths while you munch on lunch at a picnic table. ⌧ *Kolob Canyons Rd., 5 mi east of visitor center.*

⓲ **Kolob Canyons Visitor Center.** At the origin of Kolob Canyons Road, this park office has a small bookstore plus exhibits on park geology and helpful rangers to answer questions. ⌧ *Exit 40 off I–15* ☎ *435/586-9548* ◷ *Oct.–Apr., daily 8–4:30; May–Sept., daily 7–7.*

⑰ Kolob Terrace Road. A 44-mi round-trip drive takes you from Route 9 in Virgin to Lava Point for another perspective on the park. The winding drive overlooks the cliffs of the Left and Right forks of North Creek. From the road, those experienced in canyon hiking and canyoneering can access a popular but rough route up the Left Fork of North Creek, which leads all the way to the Subway, a stretch of the stream where the walls of the slot canyon close in so tightly as to form a near-tunnel. Farther along the road, you reach the Northgate Peaks trailhead, where a path leads to a panorama of the Lower Kolob Plateau's crumpled and multihued topography. After passing near Lava Point, the road ends at the blue waters of Kolob Reservoir outside park boundaries. ⊠ *Starting from 14 mi west of Springdale in Virgin.*

Sports & the Outdoors

Bicycling

Although April through October cyclists no longer share Zion Canyon Scenic Drive with thousands of cars, be advised that there are several large buses plying the park road at any given time. Within the park proper, bicycles are only allowed on established park roads and on the 3½-mi Pa'rus Trail, which winds along the Virgin River in Zion Canyon. You cannot ride your bicycle through the the Zion–Mt. Carmel tunnels; the only way to get your bike past this stretch of the highway is to transport it by motor vehicle.

There are several bike rental shops and tour outfitters in Springdale, at the mouth of Zion Canyon. **Springdale Cycle Tours** (⊠ 1458 Zion Park Blvd. ☎ 800/776–2099) offers rentals and sales, as well as day- and multiday tours for both mountain bikers and road biking enthusiasts. Ask them about the best area trails if you prefer to explore on your own.

Hiking

The best way to experience Zion Canyon is to walk beneath, between and, if you can bear it, along its towering cliffs. You can buy a detailed guide to the trails of Zion at the visitor center bookstore. Whether you're heading out for a day of rock-hopping or an hour of strolling, you should carry—and drink—plenty of water to counteract the effects of southern Utah's arid climate. Wear a hat and sunscreen, and sturdy shoes or boots; make sure to bring a map.

Fodor's Choice **Angels Landing Trail.** This is one of the most spectacular hikes in the park
★ and a perfect adventure as long as you're not afraid of heights. On your ascent you must negotiate Walter's Wiggles, a series of 21 switchbacks built out of sandstone blocks, and traverse a narrow ridgeline between sheer cliffs, using chains bolted into the rock as handrails. In spite of its hair-raising nature, this is a popular route that attracts many people. However, be cautious; small children should skip this trail, and all other children should be carefully supervised the whole way. Allow 2½ hours round-trip if you stop at Scout's Lookout, and four hours if you keep going to where the angels (and birds of prey) play. ⊠ *Zion Canyon Scenic Dr., 4½ mi north of Canyon Junction.*

Canyon Overlook Trail. This trailhead is at the parking area east of Zion–Mt. Carmel Tunnel. The trail is moderately steep but only 1 mi round-trip; allow an hour to hike it. The overlook at trail's end gives you views of the West and East Temples, Towers of the Virgin, the Streaked Wall, and other Zion Canyon cliffs and peaks. ⊠ *Rte. 9, east of Zion–Mt. Carmel Tunnel.*

Emerald Pools Trail. Two small waterfalls cascade (or drip, in dry weather) into pools at the top of this relatively easy, popular trail. The way is paved up to the lower pool and is suitable for baby strollers and wheelchairs with assistance. Beyond the lower pool, the trail becomes rocky and steep as you progress toward the middle and upper pools. A less crowded and exceptionally enjoyable return route follows the Kayenta Trail connecting on to the Grotto Trail. Allow 50 minutes round-trip to the lower pool and 2½ hours round-trip to the middle and upper pools. ⊠ *Zion Canyon Scenic Dr., about 3 mi north of Canyon Junction.*

Grotto Trail. This flat and easy trail takes you from Zion Lodge to the Grotto picnic area, traveling for the most part near the park road. Allow 20 minutes or less for the walk. If you are up for a longer hike, meet the Kayenta Trail after you cross the footbridge, and head for the Emerald Pools. This detour gains elevation during a steady, steep climb to the pools. Give yourself two to three hours if you're going to hike to the upper Emerald Pools and back. ⊠ *Zion Canyon Scenic Dr., about 3 mi north of Canyon Junction.*

Hidden Canyon Trail. Not too crowded, the path to Hidden Canyon climbs 850 feet in elevation over its mile of ascent. The trail is paved all the way to the canyon, and you should allow about three hours for the round-trip hike. ⊠ *Zion Canyon Scenic Dr., 3¼ mi north of Canyon Junction.*

Fodor's Choice ★ The Narrows Trail. The route through the Narrows does not follow a trail or path; rather, you are walking on the riverbed and in however much water happens to be running through it. The gateway to the canyon admits adventurous souls deeper into Zion Canyon than most visitors go. As beautiful as it is, this hike is not for everyone. To see the Narrows you have to wade upstream through chilly water and over uneven, slippery rocks. You must walk deliberately and slowly using a walking stick. Be prepared to swim, as chest-deep holes may occur even when water levels are low. And like any narrow desert canyon, this one is famous for sudden flash flooding—even when skies are clear. Before attempting to hike in the Narrows always check with park rangers about the likelihood of flash floods. A day trip up the lower section of the Narrows is 6 mi one-way to the turnaround point. Allow at least five hours round-trip. ⊠ *At end of Riverside Walk, from end of Zion Canyon Scenic Dr., 5 mi north of Canyon Junction.*

Pa'rus Trail. This 2-mi walking and biking path parallels and occasionally crosses the Virgin River, starting at South Campground and proceeding north along the river to the beginning of Zion Canyon Scenic Drive. It's paved and gives you great views of the Watchman, the Sen-

ZION NATIONAL PARK TOP PICK HIKING TRAILS

	Grade	Miles (one way)	Elevation Gain	Open Info	Shuttle Access	Toilet/ Restroom	Hiking Level	Trail Conditions
Angels Landing Trail	Very Steep	2.5 miles	1,488 ft	Year-round	Shuttle Access	Y (Trailhead)	Intermediate–Experienced	Unmaintained
Canyon Overlook Trail	Level	.5 miles	163 ft	Year-round		Y (Trailhead)	Beginner–Intermediate	Maintained
Emerald Pools Trail	Level/Moderate	1 mile	150 ft	Year-round	Shuttle Access	Y (Trailhead)	Beginner	Maintained
Grotto Trail	Level	.5 miles		Year-round	Shuttle Access	Y (Trailhead)	Beginner	Maintained
Hidden Canyon Trail	Steep	1 mile	850 ft	Year-round	Shuttle Access	Y (Trailhead)	Intermediate–Experienced	Maintained
The Narrows Trail	Level	16 miles		seasonally (Call for conditions)			Experienced	Unmaintained
Pa'rus Trail	Level	1.75 miles	50 ft	Year-round	Shuttle Access	Y (Trailhead)	Beginner–Intermediate	Maintained
Riverside Walk	Level	1.5 miles	57 ft	Year-round	Shuttle Access	Y (Trailhead)	Beginner	Maintained
Taylor Creek Trail	Moderate	2.5 miles	450 ft	Year-round	Shuttle Access	Y (Trailhead)	Intermediate–Experienced	Maintained
Watchman Trail	Moderate	1 mile	368 ft	Year-round	Shuttle Access	Y (Trailhead)	Beginner–Intermediate	Maintained

tinel, the East and West Temples, and Towers of the Virgin. Dogs are allowed on this trail as long as they are leashed. Cyclists must follow traffic rules on this heavily used trail. ⊠ *Canyon Junction, ½ mi north of south entrance.*

☺ **Riverside Walk.** Beginning at the Temple of Sinawava shuttle stop at the end of Zion Canyon Scenic Drive, this easily enjoyed 1-mi round-trip stroll shadows the Virgin River. The river gurgles by on one side of the trail; on the other, wildflowers bloom out of the canyon wall in fascinating hanging gardens. This is the park's most popular trail; it is paved and suitable for baby strollers and for wheelchairs with assistance. A round-trip walk takes between one and two hours. The end of the trail marks the beginning of the Narrows Trail. ⊠ *Zion Canyon Scenic Dr., 5 mi north of Canyon Junction.*

Taylor Creek Trail. In the Kolob Canyons area of the park, this trail immediately descends parallel to Taylor Creek, sometimes crossing it, sometimes shortcutting benches beside it. The historic Larsen Cabin precedes the entrance to the canyon of the Middle Fork, where the trail becomes rougher. After the old Fife Cabin, the canyon bends to the right and delivers you into Double Arch Alcove, a large, colorful grotto with a high arch towering above. The distance one-way to Double Arch is 2¾ mi. Allow about four hours round-trip for this hike. ⊠ *Kolob Canyons Rd., about 1½ mi east of Kolob Canyons visitor center.*

Watchman Trail. For a view of the town of Springdale and a look at lower Zion Creek Canyon and the Towers of the Virgin, take the moderately strenuous hike that begins on a service road east of Watchman Campground. Some spring-fed seeps nourish hanging gardens and attract wildlife here. There are a few sheer cliff edges on this route, so children should be supervised carefully. Allow two hours for this 3-mi hike. ⊠ *East of Rte. 9 (main park road), on access road inside south entrance.*

Nightlife & the Arts

Held each night in campground amphitheaters and in Zion Lodge, entertaining 45-minute ranger-led **evening programs** (☎ 435/772–3256) inform you on subjects such as geology and history. You may learn about the bats that swoop through the canyons at night, the surreptitious ways of the mountain lion, or how plants and animals adapt to life in the desert. Programs may include a slide show or audience participation.

Horseback Riding

Grab your hat and boots and see Zion Canyon the way the pioneers did—on the back of a horse or mule. This is a sure way to make your trip to Zion National Park memorable. The friendly folks at **Canyon Trail Rides** (⊠ Across from Zion Lodge ☎ 435/679–8665) have been around for years, and they are the only outfitter for trail rides inside the park. Anyone over age five can participate in guided rides along the Sand Bench Trail. The horses work from late March through October; you may want to make reservations ahead of time.

Where to Stay & Eat

There is only one full-service restaurant in Zion National Park, and only one lodging option, so over the years places to stay and eat have sprouted up nearby. The best and most-established restaurants are in Springdale, but lodging fills up quickly and is more expensive in the high season. Many people get a room in Hurricane or Panguitch to the west, or Mount Carmel Junction to the east, and use these locales as bases for day trips into the park.

$-$$$ ✕ **Red Rock Grill at Zion Lodge.** This is the only full-service restaurant inside the park. A rustic reproduction of the original lodge dining room, the restaurant is hung with historic photos. You can dine on the patio overlooking the front lawn of the lodge. A good selection of steak, fish, and poultry is offered for dinner, and lunch includes sandwiches and salads. Breakfast is also served. ⊠ *Zion Canyon Scenic Dr., 3¼ mi north of Canyon Junction* ☎ *435/772–7760* ⊕ *www.zionlodge.com* ⚘ *Reservations essential* ▭ *AE, D, DC, MC, V.*

¢ ✕ **Castle Dome Café.** Right next to the Zion Lodge shuttle stop and adjoining the gift shop, this small fast-food restaurant defines convenience. Hikers on the go can grab a banana or a sandwich here, or you can while away an hour with ice cream on the sunny patio. ⊠ *Zion Canyon Scenic Dr., 3¼ mi north of Canyon Junction* ☎ *435/772–7700* ⊕ *www.zionlodge.com* ▭ *AE, D, DC, MC, V.*

$$-$$$$ ▦ **Zion Ponderosa Ranch Resort.** This multi-pursuit resort on an 8,000-acre ranch just east of Zion National Park, at the site of a former logging camp, offers activities from horseback riding to spa treatments, and just about everything in between. Lodging options include suites that sleep 6 and luxurious mountain homes for up to 13. Hearty meals are included. ⊠ *5 mi. north of route marker 46 on North Fork County Rd.* ☎ *800/293–5444* ⊕ *www.zionponderosa.com* ➬ *6 suites, 5 cabins, 8 houses* ♨ *restaurant, some microwaves, some in-room DVDs, 2 tennis courts, outdoor pool, spa, basketball, hiking, horseback riding, volleyball* ▭ *AE, D, MC, V* ⦿⃓ *AP* ⊗ *Closed Dec.-Feb.*

$$ ▦ **Zion Lodge.** Although the original lodge burned down in 1966, the rebuilt structure convincingly re-creates the classic look of the old inn. Knotty pine woodwork and log and wicker furnishings accent the lobby. Lodge rooms are modern but not fancy, and the historic Western-style cabins have gas-log fireplaces. This is a place of quiet retreat, so there are no TVs—kids can amuse themselves outdoors on the abundant grassy lawns. The lodge is within easy walking distance of trailheads, horseback riding, and, of course, the shuttle stop, all of which are less than ½ mi away. This popular hotel requires reservations at least six months in advance. ⊠ *Zion Canyon Scenic Dr., 3¼ mi north of Canyon Junction* ☎ *435/772–3213 or 888/297–2757* ⊟ *303/297–3175* ⊕ *www.zionlodge.com* ➬ *75 rooms, 6 suites, 40 cabins* ♨ *Restaurant; no room TVs* ▭ *AE, D, DC, MC, V.*

Where to Camp

⚕ **South Campground.** All the sites here are under big cottonwood trees, granting campers some relief from the summer sun. The campground operates on a first-come, first-served basis, and sites are usually filled before noon each day during high season. Many of the sites are suitable for either tents or RVs, although there are no hookups. Reservations not accepted. ⚭ *Flush toilets, dump station, drinking water, fire grates, picnic tables* ⊃ *126 sites* ⊠ *Rte. 9, ½ mi north of south entrance* ☎ *435/772–3256* ⊠ *$16* ⊟ *No credit cards* ☉ *Mid-Mar.–Oct.*

Shopping

At the **Fred Harvey Trading Company Gift Shop** (⊠ Zion Canyon Scenic Dr., 3¼ mi north of Canyon Junction ☎ 435/772–3213), in Zion Lodge, discover many local treasures, including Native American jewelry, handmade gifts, books, and other souvenirs. The **Zion Canyon Visitor Center Bookstore** (⊠ Visitor center at south entrance ☎ 435/772–3264) sells books, maps, puzzles, posters, postcards, videos, and even water bottles.

Zion National Park Essentials

ADMISSION

Entrance to Zion National Park is $20 per vehicle for a seven-day pass. People entering on foot or by bicycle or motorcycle pay $10 per person (not to exceed $20 per family) for a seven-day pass. Entrance to the Kolob Canyons section of the park costs only $10, and you receive credit for this entrance fee when you pay to enter Zion Canyon.

BUS & CAR TRAVEL WITHIN ZION CANYON

Zion's main park road, Zion Canyon Scenic Drive, is closed to private vehicles from April through October. During this time, the park's easy-to-use shuttle system ferries people into the canyon from the visitor center, where the parking lot is typically full between 10 and 3 daily from May through September. To avoid parking hassles, leave your car in the town of Springdale and ride the town shuttle to the park entrance and connect with the park shuttle. Town shuttle stops are at Eagles Nest, Driftwood Motel, Bit & Spur Restaurant, Zion Park Inn, Bumbleberry Inn, Pizza and Noodle Company, Watchman Cafe, Flanigan's Inn, and Zion Giant Screen Theater. From the theater you can walk across a small foot bridge to the visitor center and transfer to the park shuttle. The town and park shuttles are free, but you must pay the park entrance fee. From mid-May to mid-September the shuttles operate daily 5:30 AM to 11:15 PM; from April to mid-May and early September through October, 6:30 AM to 10:15 PM daily. From November through March, private vehicles are allowed on Zion Canyon Scenic Drive. For more information, contact the Zion Canyon visitor center.

CHILDREN IN ZION NATIONAL PARK

Kids ages 6 to 12 can learn about plants, animals, geology, and archaeology through hands-on activities and hikes in the Junior Ranger Program. Children five or younger can earn a Junior Ranger decal by completing an activity sheet available at the Zion Canyon Visitor Center. Sign up for Junior Ranger programs at the Zion Nature Center a half hour before they begin.

⚐ **Zion Junior Ranger Program** ⊠ Zion Nature Center, near South Campground entrance, ½ mi north of south entrance ☎ 435/772-3256 ⊠ One-time $2 fee ☉ Junior Ranger program late May–late Aug., daily 9–11:30 and 1:30–4; nature center daily 8–5.

EMERGENCIES

In the event of an emergency, call 911, report to a visitor center, or contact a park ranger. The nearest hospitals are in St. George, Cedar City, and Kanab.

🛈 Emergencies **Zion Park Ranger** ☎ 435/772-3322.

🛈 Medical Services **Zion Canyon Medical Clinic** ✉120 Zion Blvd., Springdale ☎ 435/772-3226 ☉ June–late Sept., Mon.–Sat. 9–5.

TOURS & CLASSES

Turn Zion Canyon into a classroom by participating in a seminar on edible plants, geology, photography, adobe-brick making, or any number of other educational programs provided by the Zion Canyon Field Institute, in the nature center. Classes cost from $25 to $200 and are limited to small groups; reserve ahead to assure placement.

🛈 **Zion Canyon Field Institute** ⌂ Zion National Park, Springdale 84767 ☎ 800/635-3959 or 435/772-3265 ⊕ www.zionpark.org.

VISITOR INFORMATION

🛈 **Kolob Canyons Visitor Center** ✉ Exit 40 off I-15 ☎ 435/586-9548. **Zion Canyon Visitor Center** ✉ At south entrance, Springdale 84767-1099 ☎ 435/772-3256 ⊕ www.nps.gov/zion.

ALONG U.S. 89—UTAH'S HERITAGE HIGHWAY

Winding north from the Arizona border all the way to Spanish Fork Canyon an hour south of Salt Lake City, U.S. 89 is known as the Heritage Highway for its role in shaping Utah history. At its southern end, Kanab is known as "Little Hollywood," having provided the backdrop for many famous Western movies and television commercials. The town has since grown considerably to accommodate tourists who flock here to see where Ronald Reagan once slept and Clint Eastwood drew his guns. Other towns north along this famous road may not have the same notoriety in these parts, but they do provide a quiet, uncrowded, and inexpensive place to stay near Zion and Bryce Canyon National Parks. East of Kanab, U.S. 89 runs along the southern edge of the Grand Staircase–Escalante National Monument, providing access to one of the most remote areas of Utah via the area near the old townsite of Paria.

Mt. Carmel Junction

㉑ *13 mi east of Zion National Park via Rte. 9 east.*

Little more than where Route 9 meets U.S. 89, Mt. Carmel Junction does offer some funky small-town lodging for those willing to stay about 15 minutes east of Zion National Park's east entrance. But don't miss the studio of Maynard Dixon, the artist many consider the finest painter of the American West.

The **Maynard Dixon Studio and Home** was the final residence of the best-known painter of the American West, who died here in 1946. The property and log cabin structure is now maintained by the nonprofit Thunderbird Foundation for the Arts, which gives tours and schedules artist workshops and retreats. ⊠ *2 mi north of Mt. Carmel Junction on U.S. 89, mile marker 84, Mt. Carmel* ☎ *435/648–2653 or 801/533–5330* ⊕ *www.maynarddixon.com* ⊠ *$20* ⊙ *Tours by appointment only May–Oct., Mon.–Sat.*

Where to Stay & Eat

¢ ✕⊞ **Golden Hills Motel.** This clean and simple establishment right at Mt. Carmel Junction is an inexpensive and no-frills lodging option. The funky pink-and-blue roadside diner serves good, basic country-style fare like country-fried steak, liver and onions, and homemade breads and pies. It's quieter and less crowded than many other Zion-area establishments. ⊠ *Junction of U.S. 89 and Rte. 9, 84755* ☎ *435/648–2268 or 800/648–2268* 🖶 *435/648–2558* ⊕ *www.goldenhillsmotel.com* ⇆ *30 rooms* ⌂ *Restaurant, cable TV, pool, laundry facilities, Internet room, some pets allowed (fee), no-smoking rooms* ☰ *AE, D, MC, V.*

$ 🖫 **Best Western Thunderbird Resort.** A quick 13 mi east of Zion National Park, this red-adobe motel is a good option if lodging in Springdale has filled, or if you want to be within an hour's drive of Bryce Canyon National Park as well. Surrounded by the Zion Mountains and bordered by a scenic golf course, the rooms are spacious and bright. ⊠ *Junction of U.S. 89 and Rte. 9, 84755* ☎ *435/648–2203 or 888/848–6358* 🖶 *435/648–2239* ⊕ *www.bestwestern.com* ⇆ *60 rooms, 1 suite* ⌂ *Restaurant, grocery, cable TV, in-room data ports, in-room broadband, Wi-Fi, 9-hole golf course, pool, hot tub, laundry facilities, no-smoking rooms* ☰ *AE, D, DC, MC, V.*

Kanab

㉒ *17 mi southeast of Mt. Carmel Junction via U.S. 89 south.*

Kanab is Hollywood's vision of the American West. Soaring vermilion sandstone cliffs and sagebrush flats with endless vistas have lured filmmakers to this area for more than 75 years. The welcoming sign at city limits reads "Greatest Earth on Show"; Kanab has been used as a setting in more than 100 movies and television shows. Abandoned film sets have become tourist attractions, and old movie posters or still photographs are a decorating staple at local businesses. In addition to a movie-star past, Kanab is ideally positioned as a base for exploration. With major roads radiating in four directions, it offers easy access to three national parks, three national monuments (including Grand Staircase–Escalante), two state parks, and several historic sites.

Dog lovers from around the world descend upon Kanab for the **Greyhound Gathering** (☎ 435/644–2903 ⊕ www.greyhoundgang.com) every May. Sponsored by the Greyhound Gang, a local home that rehabilitates former racing dogs and finds them loving homes, the event attracts hundreds of people and canines. The nostalgic **Western Legends Roundup** (☎ 800/733–5263 ⊕ www.westernlegendsroundup.com) is for anyone who loves cowboys, pioneer life, or Native American culture. For five days every August the small town of Kanab fills with cowboy poets and storytellers, musicians, Western arts-and-crafts vendors, and Native American dancers and weavers.

Old West movie memorabilia jam-pack **Frontier Movie Town.** Some of the buildings in this replica of a frontier town were actually used in movie sets, and photos on the walls inside reveal many familiar actor faces. Eat all you can at a cowboy-style buffet using tin plates and cups, or grab a beer and a light lunch at the Hole in the Wall Saloon. ✉ *297 W. Center St.* ☎ *800/551–1714* ⊕ *www.onlinepages.net/frontier_movie town/* ⌑ *Free* ☉ *Open daily 9 AM–11 PM.*

Formerly homeless dogs, cats, burros, horses, and other animals find refuge at **Best Friends Animal Sanctuary** in aptly named Angel Canyon. Best Friends is the largest no-kill animal shelter in the United States, with no fewer than 1,500 animals living here at any time. The 3,000-acre sanctuary gives unwanted pets, farm animals, and other creatures a permanent home or makes them available for adoption. ✉ *5001 Angel Canyon Rd.* ☎ *435/644–2001* ⊕ *www.bestfriends.org* ⌑ *Donations encouraged* ☉ *Daily tours by reservation only.*

Eroding sandstone formed the sweeping expanse of pink sand at **Coral Pink Sand Dunes State Park.** Funneled through a notch between two mountain ranges, the prevailing winds pick up speed and carry grains of sand into the area. When the wind subsides in the valley, the sand is deposited, creating this giant playground for dune buggies, ATVs, and dirt bikes. A small area is fenced off for walking, but the sound of the recreational vehicles is always with you. Children love to play in the sand, but before you let them loose, check the surface temperature, which can become very hot. ✉ *Yellowjacket and Hancock Rds., 12 mi west of U.S. 89 from turnoff 15 mi north of Kanab* ☎ *435/648–2800* ⊕ *www. stateparks.utah.gov* ⌑ *$5* ☉ *Daily dawn–dusk.*

Housed in a replica of an ancient Native American cliff dwelling, **Moqui Cave** offers a little bit of everything. Native American artifacts are displayed alongside dinosaur footprints, a fluorescent mineral display, and pre-Columbian artifacts from Mexico, as well as a gift shop selling Indian jewelry. The inside temperature of the cave never exceeds 70°F, even on hot summer days. ✉ *5½ mi north of Kanab on Utah U.S. 89* ☎ *435/ 644–8525* ⊕ *www.moquicave.com* ☉ *May–Sept., Mon.–Sat. 9–7; Oct.–Apr., Mon.–Sat. 10–4.*

Sports & the Outdoors

Want to get deep into Grand Staircase–Escalante National Monument and see slot canyons in person rather than on postcards? Let **Canyon Country Out-Back Tours** (✉ 1475 S. Lee Dr. ☎ 435/644–3807 or 888/783–3807 ⊕ www.ccobtours.com) guide you. Air-conditioned four-wheel-drive vehicles take you to and from your destination, but once there you're under your own power so take plenty of water and sunscreen. Canine companions are welcome, too.

Where to Stay & Eat

★ **$–$$$$** ✗ **Rocking V Cafe.** Fresh fish, including mahimahi when available, arrives four times a week at this respected café started by two former journalists with no prior restaurant experience. Filet mignon and rib-eye steaks are other menu favorites, but vegetarians and vegans have plenty of choice, as well. Save room for dessert—the crème brûlée is perfectly prepared.

Lunch offers a more casual selection of wraps, sandwiches, burgers, and salads. A full liquor license supports a decent wine and beer list, but cocktails are limited to standards such as margaritas. ⊠ *97 W. Center St.* ☎ *435/644–8001* ⊕ *www.rockingvcafe.com* ☰ *MC, V* ☽ *Closed Mon. and Tues. in Nov. and Dec.*

$–$$ ✕ **Nedra's, Too.** The first Nedra's restaurant was in Fredonia, Arizona, hence the name of this branch. Booths and tables, friendly service, and authentic Mexican specialties all come at a reasonable price. The menu also has sandwiches, soups, and desserts, and you can get breakfast here, too. ⊠ *310 S. 100 East St.* ☎ *435/644–2030* ☰ *AE, D, MC, V.*

¢–$ ✕ **Escobar's Mexican Restaurant.** Brown vinyl booths line the turquoise-and-pink walls of this family-owned diner, which hums with the conversation of locals who flock here for the chili verde and steak ranchero. Cool the warm flavors with a cold bottle of beer, but don't touch the plates—they arrive piping hot. Breakfast is served from 11 AM to noon. ⊠ *373 E. 300 South St.* ☎ *435/644–3739* ☰ *MC, V* ☽ *Closed Sat.*

¢–$ ✕ **Fernando's Hideaway.** Fernando's mixes the best margarita for miles— it's mighty fine with a quesadilla as a warm-up for dinner. The house salsa is chunky and fresh-tasting, and menu items are available as dinner platters or à la carte. Steaks and seafood will please those with a hankering for American food. Accommodations are made for vegetarians. Colorful Mexican folk art adorns the bright dining room, and the patio may encourage you to linger with another margarita. ⊠ *332 N. 300 West St.* ☎ *435/644–3222* ☰ *AE, MC, V.*

¢ ✕ **Vermillion Espresso Bar & Café.** If you like Internet access with your cup of coffee and pastry—or sandwich prepared on a croissant, bagel, or demi-baguette—this is the place for you. You can also relax on the sofa and choose from a selection of books and magazines littering the coffee table. The owner has been known to open early to accommodate tourists' schedules. ⊠ *4 E. Center St.* ☎ *435/644–3886* ☰ *MC, V.*

$ ⌂ **Best Western Red Hills.** One of Kanab's larger motels has a hearty dose of cowboy flavor accenting its city-style amenities. The downtown shopping and dining district is only a few blocks away. ⊠ *125 W. Center St., 84741* ☎ *435/644–2675 or 800/830–2675* ⊟ *435/644–5919* ⊕ *www.bestwesternredhills.com* ⟿ *75 rooms* ⚲ *Refrigerators, cable TV, in-room VCRs, pool, hot tub, business services, some pets allowed (fee), no-smoking rooms* ☰ *AE, D, MC, V* ⦿ *CP.*

$ ⌂ **Holiday Inn Express.** The spacious rooms have views of the coral cliffs right behind the inn. Ironing boards, curling irons, and work desks with lamps are included in the rooms. ⊠ *815 E. U.S. 89, 84741* ☎ *435/644–8888 or 800/574–4061* ⊟ *435/644–8880* ⊕ *www.hikanabutah. com* ⟿ *71 rooms* ⚲ *Cable TV, 9-hole golf course, pool, hot tub, laundry facilities, some pets allowed (fee)* ☰ *AE, D, DC, MC, V* ⦿ *CP.*

★ **¢–$** ⌂ **Parry Lodge.** The lobby of this colonial-style building, constructed in 1929, is lined with photos of movie stars, including Ronald Reagan and Barbara Stanwyk, who stayed here while filming in the area. Some of the spacious rooms have plaques over the doors to tell you who stayed here before you. The lodge barn, which housed Victor Mature's camels during the making of *Timbuktu*, is now a playhouse, where old-time Western melodramas are performed in summer. The dining room in front is open only for breakfast. ⊠ *89 E. Center St., 84741* ☎ *435/644–2601 or 888/289–1722* 🖷 *435/644–2605* ⊕ *www.parrylodge.com* 🖙 *89 rooms* ⚭ *Restaurant, cable TV, pool, hot tub, laundry facilities, some pets allowed (fee), no-smoking rooms* ⊟ *AE, D, DC, MC, V* ⊗ *Reservations required Nov.–Mar.* ⦿ *CP.*

Paria

㉓ *43 mi east of Kanab on U.S. 89.*

The town once known as Paria—or, historically, Pahreah—is long gone, but the name remains to describe the area around the intermittently flowing Paria River. Pahreah, incidentally, was Ute for "dirty water." Hike the world-famous rock expanse known as "The Wave" in the remote **Fodor'sChoice** and rugged **Paria Canyon–Vermilion Cliffs Wilderness,** beyond the southern boundary of the Grand Staircase–Escalante National Monument and along the Arizona border. Permits to hike the Wave—envision ocean waves frozen in striated red, orange, and yellow sandstone—and some of the other trails here are available online and usually fill many months in advance. However, if you arrive before 9 AM, you may be one of the 10 lucky walk-ins who can score a permit to hike the *following* day. It's not first-come, first-served; if more than 10 people show up, names are placed in a hat and drawn at random. By limiting the number of people who access the backcountry, the Bureau of Land Management hopes to preserve this area for years to come. From November 16 to March 14, apply for walk-in permits at 318 North 100 East Street in Kanab; the rest of the year visit the Paria Information Station at the turnoff for the monument. ⊠ *43 mi east of Kanab on U.S. 89, mile marker 21* ☎ *801/ 539–4001* 🖃 *$5 fee, reservations and permits required for some hikes* ⊗ *Information station open mid-Mar.–mid-Nov. daily 8–5.*

⟳ Visit two ghost towns at once at the **Pahreah Townsite and Movie Set,** one settled by hardy pioneers and one built by Hollywood (and then rebuilt by locals when the famous movie set was damaged by floods in 1999). In fact, floods also caused the demise of the original settlements along the Pahreah River. The last movie filmed here was Clint Eastwood's *The Outlaw Josey Wales* in 1976. The set is 35 mi east of Kanab. First stop by the **Kanab field office** (⊠ 318 N. 100 East St. ☎ 801/539–4001) for Grand Staircase–Escalante National Monument to get maps and an update on road conditions. ⊠ *35 mi east of Kanab via U.S. 89; turn north at monument onto Paria River Valley Rd.*

Panguitch

㉔ *67 mi north of Kanab via U.S. 89.*

An elevation of 6,650 feet helps this town of 1,500 residents keep its cool. Main Street is lined with late-19th-century buildings, and its early homes and outbuildings are noted for their distinctive brick architecture. Decent amenities, inexpensive lodging (mainly strip motels), and an excellent location 24 mi northwest of Bryce Canyon National Park make Panguitch a comfortable launching pad for recreation in the area.

EDWARD ABBEY: A PARIAH IN PAHREAH

MOST PEOPLE who are aware of Edward Abbey (1927–89) in passing are probably familiar with his landmark book Desert Solitaire, written while he was a park ranger at Arches National Park in southeastern Utah. Though he was born in Pennsylvania's Appalachian region, he went west at the age of 17 and never really left again—at least in his heart. Those familiar with his work and his radical environmentalist ideas also know that he spent many days and nights wandering and writing about the entire western United States, and this included southwestern Utah. One of his more memorable essays devoted to this part of the state is "Days and Nights in Old Pariah," which documents a hiking trip down Buckskin Gulch in what is now the Paria Canyon–Vermilion Cliffs Wilderness Area, not far from The Wave. Abbey's self-mocking sense of humor is evident in his essay's title. The Ute Indians named the area Pahreah, or "muddy water," after the river running through the region. Later settlers simplified it to Paria, but as Abbey put it in the first paragraph: "I like Pariah." (No doubt his detractors found that term suitable, too.) Among the adventures he documents in the essay are the rescue of a cow that had become stuck in quicksand and a swim in a 150-foot-wide pothole filled by recent rains.

During late June, you can watch hot-air balloons float over canyon country during the **Chariots in the Sky Balloon Festival** (☎ 866/590–4134).

During the bitter winter of 1864, Panguitch residents were on the verge of starvation. A group of men from the settlement set out over the mountains to fetch provisions from the town of Parowan, 40 mi away. When they hit waist-deep snow drifts they were forced to abandon their oxen. Legend says the men, frustrated and ready to turn back, laid a quilt on the snow and knelt to pray. Soon they realized the quilt had kept them from sinking into the snow. Spreading quilts before them as they walked, leapfrog style, the men traveled to Parowan and back, returning with life-saving provisions. Every June, the three-day **Quilt Walk Festival** (☎ 435/676–8585 or 866/590–4134) commemorates the event with quilting classes, a tour of Panguitch's pioneer homes, crafts shows, and a dinner theater production in which the story is acted out.

The old Panguitch High School, built in 1936, is still a place of learning. The taxidermic collection at the **Paunsagaunt Wildlife Museum** includes stuffed animals in tableaus mimicking actual terrain and animal behavior. The animals and birds come from all parts of the food chain. An African room has baboons, bush pigs, cape buffalo, and a lion. ✉ 205

E. Center St. ☎ *435/676–2500* ⊕ *www.brycecanyonwildlifemuseum. com* 🖃 *$2* ⊙ *May–Nov., daily 9* AM*–10* PM.

Sports & the Outdoors

FISHING Reportedly, **Panguitch Lake** takes its name from a Paiute Indian word meaning "big fish." They may not all be big, but several types of trout are plentiful, and ice fishing is popular in winter. Watch out that a bald eagle doesn't take your catch. ✉ *17 mi south of Panguitch on Rte. 143* ☎ *435/676–2649* ⊕ *www.panguitchlake.com.*

Where to Stay & Eat

★ ¢–$$ ✕ **Cowboy's Smokehouse Café.** Stuffed animal trophies and hundreds of business cards and photographs from customers line the walls at this barbecue joint run by two transplanted Texans and a rancher's son from southern Colorado. Specialties include mesquite-smoked beef, pork, turkey, and chicken, and a sauce with no fewer than 15 secret ingredients. Try homemade peach, apricot, or cherry cobbler if you have room for dessert. Breakfast is served, too. ✉ *95 N. Main St.* ☎ *435/676–8030* 🖃 *MC, V* ⊙ *Closed Sun.*

¢–$$ ✕ **Grandma Tina's Italian and Vegetarian.** A rare treat in meat-and-potatoes country, this family-run eatery serves such dishes as spaghetti with a vegetable sauce containing mushrooms, olives, green peppers, onions, garlic, and wine. Tina's seasonal strawberry pie and homemade cannolis are famously popular with the locals. Wine and beer are available. ✉ *523 N. Main St.* ☎ *435/676–2377* 🖃 *MC, V* ⊙ *Closed Nov.–Mar.*

¢–$ 🏨 **Marianna Inn.** Choose from one-, two-, three-, and four-bed rooms at this clean one-story motel; those with whirlpool baths are $25 extra. You can barbecue your own supper on one of the grills and eat your meal on the covered patio. Relax afterward on a hammock or in the covered outdoor spa, which is open in summer only. ✉ *699 N. Main St., 84759* ☎ *435/676–8844* 🖨 *435/676–8340* ⊕ *www.mariannainn. com* ⤙ *34 rooms* ⚬ *Hot tub, cable TV, some pets allowed (fee), no-smoking rooms* 🖃 *AE, D, DC, MC, V.*

¢–$ 🏨 **Panguitch Inn.** This quiet inn occupies a 100-year-old, two-story building a few blocks from downtown restaurants and shops. Rooms are simple and no-frills, but clean. ✉ *50 N. Main St., 84759* ☎ *435/ 676–8871* ⊕ *www.panguitchinn.com* 🖨 *435/676–8340* ⤙ *25 rooms* ⚬ *Cable TV, some pets allowed (fee), no-smoking rooms; no a/c* 🖃 *AE, D, DC, MC, V.*

¢ 🏨 **Blue Pine Motel.** The rooms are clean, bright, and no-frills—and the owners, friendly—at this budget-rate motel near downtown. You're on your own for breakfast, however, as none is served. ✉ *130 N. Main St., 84759* ☎ *435/676–8197 or 800/299–6115* 🖨 *435/676–2128* ⤙ *20 rooms* ⚬ *Cable TV, no-smoking rooms* 🖃 *AE, D, MC, V.*

Shopping

Dusty old boots in need of a cowhand sit ready to walk and ride again at **Cowboy Collectibles** (✉ 21 N. Main St. ☎ 435/676–8060). The owners travel all over the country to find saddles, chaps, and other antiques from the days when men on horseback roamed the ranges. There are also toys and other products that celebrate the Old West. Why not pick up a 19th-century buffalo fur coat for $750?

BRYCE CANYON NATIONAL PARK

Looking at Bryce Canyon is much like gazing at the clouds: in the colorful rock formations you can pick out the shapes of animals, ships, castles, or carriages. This astonishing landscape was named for Ebenezer Bryce, a pioneer cattleman and the first permanent settler in the area. His description of the landscape, oft repeated today, was more succinct: "It's a hell of a place to lose a cow."

The rock formations you see at Bryce Canyon began forming about 60 million years ago. At that time, freshwater lakes filled the shallow basins in southern Utah. When they receded, about 2,000 feet of lime-rich sediment was deposited, and the lack of fossils in that layer suggests that the lakes were inhospitable environments for most organisms. Some 16 million years ago, the earth in the Colorado Plateau—of which Bryce is a part—broke up and tilted, creating great blocks of rock-faulted uplands, which were then exposed to weathering and erosion. Water seeped into cracks in the rock, froze, expanded, and shattered the surrounding rock. Runoff from rain or melting snow created gullies that carried away soft layers of rock. In the process, Bryce Canyon was formed. Because of its origins and shape Bryce is actually an amphitheater, not a canyon, in geological terms. The hoodoos (vertical columns of rock) that populate the amphitheater took on their unusual shapes because the top layer of rock (caprock) is harder than the layers below it. Once erosion undercuts the soft rock beneath the cap too much, the hoodoo tumbles. But Bryce will not soon lose its hoodoos, because as the amphitheater's rim recedes further, new hoodoos will form to replace their fallen brethren.

The rim of Bryce Canyon is up to 9,000 feet in elevation, so the wildflower season arrives in late summer. Fall color in the park is stupendous as aspen, bigtooth maple, and other hardwoods turn golden. In winter, snow provides a good canvas on which to look for the footprints of mountain lions, mule deer, elk, and coyote, as well as plastering a brilliant white contrast on the pink rock of the amphitheater.

Exploring Bryce Canyon National Park

a good tour

Bryce Canyon can easily be experienced in a day, as long as you don't spend much time on the trail. Start at **Fairyland Point** ㉕ ┠, 1 mi north of the fee station and visitor center, to get a preview of the many amphitheater views that lie ahead. Proceed to the **Bryce Canyon Visitor Center** ㉖ to get an overview of the park and purchase any books or maps that might enhance your visit. Watch the video presentation on the park and peruse exhibits about the natural and cultural history of Bryce Canyon. Thus informed, drive to **Bryce Canyon Lodge** ㉗ to see the historic property. From the lodge, you can walk out to the Rim Trail and stroll along the half-mile stretch between **Sunset Point** ㉘ and **Sunrise Point** ㉙.

Drive the 18-mi **main park road** ㉚ and stop at several of the overlooks along the way. Before you take the road to Rainbow and Yovimpa points, take a 2-mi detour to **Bryce Point** ㉛, which provides the south-

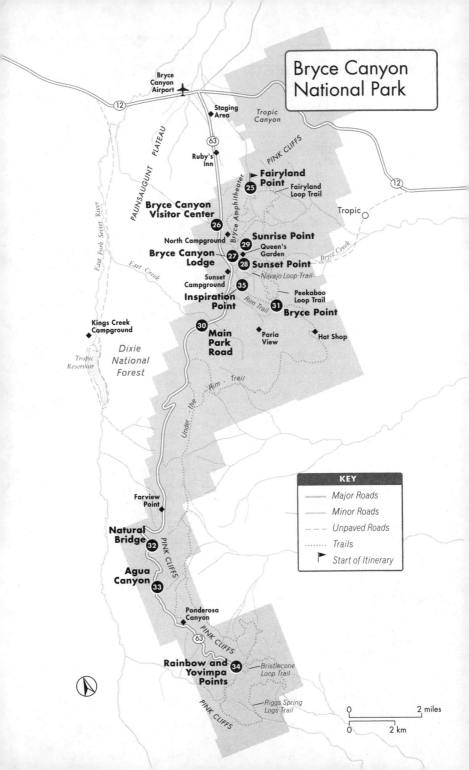

ernmost view looking back on the main amphitheater. Return to the main road and continue south past Fairview Point to the **Natural Bridge** ㉜, an arch that stands just off the edge of the rim. Another mile or so south is a narrow drainage called **Agua Canyon** ㉝, which contains several unique hoodoo formations, including the Hunter. Finally, continue another 4 mi or so to the end of the road, where you can linger at **Rainbow and Yovimpa Points** ㉞. From here the short rolling hike along the Bristlecone Loop Trail rewards you with spectacular views and a cool walk through a forest of bristlecone pines.

Consider ending your day with sunset at **Inspiration Point** ㉟. Have your camera ready to catch the dramatic play of light on the colorful hoodoos.

If you have the time and energy for a hike after checking out Sunrise Point, the Navajo Loop and Queen's Garden trails descend into the amphitheater. Although these are the least strenuous routes into the amphitheater, they still involve steep descents and return climbs to the rim. Before you hit the road again, unpack your picnic lunch on one of the benches along this part of the Rim Trail. From Bryce Point, you can access the Peekaboo Loop and Under-the-Rim trails, which lead to the unique hoodoo formations of the Wall of Windows and the Hat Shop, respectively.

TIMING This tour will take you the bulk of a day (10 to 12 hours), though you may have some extra time in the late afternoon for some rest or a short hike. Allowing for traffic, if you stop at all 13 overlooks, this drive to Rainbow Point and back will take you between two and three hours. If you cut out all of the stops except Rainbow Point, you can reduce the tour by 45 minutes to an hour. If you're really pressed for time, stick to the lodge area of the main amphitheater, where you can see quite a bit without having to retreat to your car.

What to See

㉝ **Agua Canyon.** When you stop at this overlook in the southern section of the park, pick out among the hoodoos the formation known as the Hunter, which actually has a few small hardy trees growing on its cap. The play of light and colorful contrasts are especially noticeable here. ⊠ *12 mi south of park entrance.*

㉗ **Bryce Canyon Lodge.** Gilbert Stanley Underwood designed this lodge, built in 1924, for the Union Pacific Railroad. The National Historic Landmark has been faithfully restored, right down to the lobby's huge limestone fireplace and log and wrought-iron chandelier, plus bark-covered hickory furniture made by the same company that created the originals. Inside the historic building are a restaurant and a gift shop, as well as plenty of information on park activities. Guests of the lodge stay in the numerous log cabins on the wooded grounds. ⊠ *2 mi south of park entrance* ☎ *435/834–5361.*

㉖ **Bryce Canyon Visitor Center.** You can visit with park rangers, watch a video about Bryce Canyon, study exhibits, or shop for informative books, maps, and other materials at this spacious visitor center. The rangers here dole out backcountry permits, and for first aid, emergency, or lost-and-found services, this is your place. ⊠ *1 mi south of park entrance*

☎ 435/834–5322 ⊕ www.nps.gov/brca ⊙ Oct.–June, daily 8–4:30; July–Sept., daily 8–8.

③① Bryce Point. After absorbing views of the Black Mountains and Navajo Mountain, you can follow the trailhead for the Under-the-Rim-Trail and go exploring down in the amphitheater to the cluster of top-heavy hoodoos known collectively as the Hat Shop. Along the Peekaboo Loop Trail, which also descends from this point, is the **Wall of Windows.** Openings carved into a wall of rock illustrate the drama of erosion that formed Bryce Canyon. ✉ 5½ mi south of park entrance on Inspiration Point Rd.

★ ↦ ㉕ Fairyland Point. At the scenic overlook closest to the park entrance (look for the sign marking the route off the main park road), there are splendid views of Fairyland Amphitheater and its delicate, fanciful forms. The Sinking Ship and other formations stand before the grand backdrop of the Aquarius Plateau and distant Navajo Mountain. Because it's not on the main park road, many people miss the worthwhile detour to this mini-amphitheater. ✉ 1 mi off main park road, 1 mi north of visitor center.

㉟ Inspiration Point. Not far at all (³⁄₁₀ mi) east along the Rim Trail from Bryce Point is Inspiration Point, site of a wonderful panorama and one of the best places in the park to see the sunset. ✉ 5½ mi south of park entrance on Inspiration Point Rd.

㉚ Main Park Road. One of the delights of Bryce Canyon National Park is
Fodor'sChoice that much of the park's grandeur can be experienced from scenic over-
★ looks along its main thoroughfare, which meanders 18 mi from the park entrance south to Rainbow Point. Allow two to three hours to travel the entire 36 mi round-trip. The road is open year-round, but may be closed temporarily after heavy snowfalls to allow for clearing. Major overlooks are rarely more than a few minutes' walk from the parking areas, and many let you see more than 100 mi on clear days. All overlooks lie east of the road—to keep things simple (and left turns to a minimum), you can proceed to the southern end of the park and stop at the overlooks on your northbound return. Trailers are not allowed beyond Sunset Campground. Day users may park trailers at the visitor center or other designated sites; check with park staff for parking options. RVs can drive throughout the park, but vehicles longer than 25 feet are not allowed at Paria View.

★ ㉜ Natural Bridge. Despite its name, this formation is actually an arch carved in the rock by rain and frost erosion; true natural bridges must be bored out by streams and rivers. Pine forests are visible through the span of the arch and down the debris chute below. ✉ 11 mi south of park entrance.

need a break? The best lunch option in Bryce is to pack your own lunch and break it out at noon at one of the park's picnic spots. The area near **North Campground** (✉ About ¼ mi south of the visitor center) has picnic tables and grills in the shade among ponderosa pine trees. A small (and undeveloped) picnic area lies north of Farview Point near a place locals call **Piracy Point** (⊠ 8 mi south of park entrance). This spot offers little other than a picnic table a short jaunt off the main road.

㉞ Rainbow and Yovimpa Points. While Rainbow Point's orientation allows a view north along the southern rim of the amphitheater and east into Grand Staircase–Escalante National Monument, the panorama from Yovimpa Point spreads out to the south and on a clear day you can see as far as 100 mi to Arizona. Yovimpa Point also has a shady and quiet picnic area with tables and rest rooms. The Bristlecone Loop Trail connects the two viewpoints and leads through a grove of bristlecone pine trees. There are informative displays on flora, fauna, and geological history at Rainbow Point. *⊠ 18 mi south of park entrance.*

★ ㉙ Sunrise Point. Named for its stunning views at dawn, this overlook is a popular stop for the summer crowds that come to Bryce Canyon and is the starting point for the Queen's Garden Trail and the Fairyland Loop Trail. You have to descend the Queen's Garden Trail to get a regal glimpse of **Queen Victoria,** a hoodoo that appears to sport a crown and glorious full skirt. The trail is popular and marked clearly, but moderately strenuous. *⊠ 2 mi south of park entrance near Bryce Canyon Lodge.*

㉘ Sunset Point. Bring your camera and plenty of film to watch the late-day sun paint its magic on the hoodoos here. You can only see **Thor's Hammer,** a delicate formation similar to a balanced rock and one of the park's most-photographed hoodoos, if you hike 521 feet down into the amphitheater on the Navajo Loop Trail. *⊠ 2 mi south of park entrance near Bryce Canyon Lodge.*

Sports & the Outdoors

Bird-Watching

More than 170 bird species have been identified in Bryce. Violet green swallows and white-throated swifts are common, as are Steller's jays, American coots, Rufous hummingbirds, and mountain bluebirds. Lucky bird-watchers will see golden eagles floating across the skies above the pink rocks of the amphitheater. The best time in the park for avian variety is from May through July, during the migration season. Get a birder's checklist at the visitor center.

Hiking

To get up close and personal with the park's hoodoos, set aside a half day to hike into the amphitheater. Just about any hike that descends below the rim is moderately strenuous, and in summer you should consider hiking in the morning to avoid the day's warmest temperatures and strongest sun. Always remember that you are hiking at elevations of up to 9,100 feet, where you can fall victim to altitude sickness—headaches, light-headedness, nausea, and stomach cramps—if you're not used to exercising at elevation. Uneven terrain calls for sturdy hiking boots and summer heat demands a hat and sunscreen; don't leave the trailhead without extra water. For trail maps, information, and ranger recommendations, stop at the visitor center.

BRYCE CANYON NATIONAL PARK TOP PICK HIKING TRAILS

	Grade	Miles (one way)	Elevation Gain	Open Info	Shuttle Access	Toilet/ Restroom	Hiking Level	Trail Conditions
Bristlecone Loop Trail	Level/Inclines	.5 miles	195 ft	Year-round	Shuttle Access	Y (Trailhead)	Beginner–Intermediate	Maintained
Fairyland Loop Trail	Steep	8 miles	2,309 ft	Year-round	Shuttle Access	Y (Trailhead)	Intermediate–Experienced	Maintained
Navajo Loop Trail	Level/Moderate	1.5 miles	550 ft	Year-round	Shuttle Access	Y (Trailhead)	Beginner–Intermediate	Maintained
Navajo/Queen's Combination Loop	Level/Moderate	3 miles	580 ft	Year-round	Shuttle Access	Y (Trailhead)	Beginner–Intermediate	Maintained
Peekaboo Loop	Moderate/Steep	5.5 miles	1,555 ft	Year-round	Shuttle Access	Y (Trailhead)	Intermediate–Experienced	Maintained
Riggs Spring Loop Trail	Moderate/Steep	6.5 miles	2,248 ft	Year-round	Shuttle Access	Y (Trailhead)	Intermediate–Experienced	Maintained
Trail to the Hat Shop	Steep	2 miles	1,436 ft	Year-round	Shuttle Access	Y (Trailhead)	Intermediate–Experienced	Maintained
Under-the-Rim Trail	Strenuous	23 miles	1,500 ft	Year-round		Y (Trailhead)	Experienced	Maintained

A $5 backcountry permit, available from the visitor center, is required for camping in the park's interior. Camping is allowed only on the Under-the-Rim Trail and Rigg's Spring Loop, both south of Bryce Point. Campfires are not permitted and camping is only allowed at designated sites.

Bristlecone Loop Trail. Hike through dense spruce and fir forest to exposed cliffs where ancient bristlecone pines somehow manage to survive the elements; some of the trees here are more than 1,700 years old. You might see yellow-bellied marmots and blue grouse, critters not found at lower elevations in the park. The popular 1-mi trail takes about an hour to hike. ⊠ *Rainbow Point, 18 mi south of park entrance.*

Fairyland Loop Trail. Hike into whimsical Fairyland Canyon on this strenuous but uncrowded 8-mi trail. The trail winds around hoodoos, across trickles of water, and finally to a natural window in the rock at Tower Bridge, 1½ mi from Sunrise Point and 4 mi from Fairyland Point. The pink-and-white badlands and hoodoos surround you the whole way. Allow four to five hours for the complete trip. You can pick up the loop at Fairyland Point or north of Sunrise Point. ⊠ *Fairyland Point, 1 mi off main park road, 1 mi south of park entrance; Sunrise Point, 2 mi south of park entrance.*

Navajo Loop Trail. A steep descent via a series of switchbacks leads to Wall Street, a narrow canyon with high rock walls and towering fir trees. The northern end of the trail brings Thor's Hammer into close view. Allow one to two hours on this 1½-mi trail. ⊠ *Sunset Point, 2 mi south of park entrance.*

★ **Navajo/Queen's Garden Combination Loop.** By walking this extended loop, you can see some of the best of Bryce on a 3-mi hike that takes two to three hours. The route passes fantastic formations and an open forest of pine and juniper on the amphitheater floor. Descend into the amphitheater from Sunset Point on the Navajo Trail and ascend via the less demanding Queen's Garden Trail; then return to your starting point via the Rim Trail. ⊠ *Sunset and Sunrise points, 2 mi south of park entrance.*

Peekaboo Loop. For a good workout, hike this steep trail past the Wall of Windows and the Three Wise Men. Horses use this trail in spring, summer, and fall and have the right-of-way. Start at Bryce, Sunrise, or Sunset Point and allow three to four hours to hike either the 5-mi or 7-mi loop. ⊠ *Bryce Point, 2 mi off main park road, 5½ mi south of park entrance; Sunrise and Sunset points, 2 mi south of park entrance.*

Queen's Garden Trail. This hike is the easiest into the amphitheater and therefore the most crowded. Allow two to three hours to hike the 2 mi down and back. ⊠ *Sunrise Point, 2 mi south of park entrance.*

Riggs Spring Loop Trail. One of the park's more rigorous day hikes, or a relaxed overnighter (backcountry camping permits are dispensed at the visitor center), this 9-mi trail between Yovimpa and Rainbow points takes about four to five hours to hike. ⊠ *Yovimpa and Rainbow points, 18 mi south of park entrance.*

Rim Trail. If you prefer your exercise in short, slow doses, you will find any part of the 11-mi trail along the rim of the main amphitheater suitable for strolling, especially the paved area between Sunrise and Sunset points. Every section of the trail from Bryce Point to Fairyland Point has outstanding views of hoodoos from above, as well as vistas that stretch over 100 mi on a clear day. Allow five to six hours for the entire 11-mi one-way journey. ⊠ *Access from Fairyland, Sunrise, Sunset, Inspiration, and Bryce points.*

Trail to the Hat Shop. Once you reach the end you understand how the trail got its name. Hard gray caps balance precariously atop narrow pedestals of softer, rust-colored rock. Allow three to four hours to travel this strenuous 4-mi round-trip trail. ⊠ *Bryce Point, 2 mi off main park road, 5½ mi south of park entrance.*

Under-the-Rim Trail. This is how serious backpackers immerse themselves in the landscape of Bryce. Starting at Bryce Point, the trail travels 22½ mi to Rainbow Point, passing through the Pink Cliffs, traversing Agua Canyon and Ponderosa Canyon, and taking you by several springs. Most of the hike is on the amphitheater floor, characterized by up-and-down terrain among stands of ponderosa pine; the elevation change totals about 1,500 feet. Four trailheads along the main park road allow you to connect to the Under-the-Rim Trail and cover its length as a series of day hikes. Allow at least two days to hike the route in its entirety. Obtain a backcountry permit at the visitor center if you intend to stay in the amphitheater overnight. Also inquire about the current availability of water along the trail. ⊠ *Access from Bryce Point, Swamp Canyon, Ponderosa Canyon, and Rainbow Point.*

Horseback Riding

Make the most of your visit to the West by saddling up a horse or mule with **Canyon Trail Rides** (⊠ Bryce Canyon Lodge ☎ 435/679–8665 or 435/834–5500) and descending to the floor of the Bryce Canyon amphitheater. Most who take this expedition have no riding experience, so don't hesitate to join in. Mules will give you the smoothest, most sure-footed ride. A two-hour ride ambles along the amphitheater floor to the Fairy Castle before returning to Sunrise Point. The half-day expedition follows Peekaboo Trail, winds past the Fairy Castle and the Alligator, and passes the Wall of Windows before returning to Sunrise Point. To arrange for a trail ride (reservations are suggested), call or stop by their desk in the lodge. Based in Best Western Ruby's Inn, **Ruby's Red Canyon Horseback Rides** (☎ 800/468–8660) retraces trails taken by outlaw Butch Cassidy in Red Canyon.

Skiing

Unlike Utah's other national parks, Bryce Canyon usually receives plenty of snow, making it a popular cross-country ski area. The park's 2½-mi Fairyland Ski Loop is marked but ungroomed, as is the 5-mi Paria Loop, which runs through ponderosa forests into long, open meadows. Rent skis from **Best Western Ruby's Inn** (⊠ Rte. 63, 1 mi north of park entrance ☎ 435/834–5341), which grooms a 31-mi private trail that connects to an ungroomed trail in the park.

Snowshoeing

The **National Park Service** (☎ 435/834–5322) lends out snowshoes for free at the visitor center; just leave your driver's license or a major credit card with a ranger. You can snowshoe on the rim trails, but the park service discourages their use below the rim.

Where to Stay & Eat

Like Zion National Park, Bryce National Park itself contains but a single lodging and a single dining option, but fortunately a host of dining and lodging options are within a mile or so of the park entrance. A smattering of choices exist within 10 miles to the east and west.

★ $$ ✕⊡ **Bryce Canyon Lodge.** A few feet from the amphitheater's rim and trailheads is this rugged stone-and-wood lodge. You have your choice of suites on the lodge's second level, motel-style rooms in separate buildings (with balconies or porches), and cozy lodgepole-pine cabins, some with cathedral ceilings and gas fireplaces. Reservations are hard to come by, so call several months ahead. Horseback rides into the park's interior can be arranged in the lobby. The lodge restaurant is also the only place to dine within the park. Reservations are essential at dinner. ✉ *2 mi south of park entrance, 84717* ☎ *435/834–5361 or 303/297–2757* 🖨 *435/834–5464* ⊕ *www.brycecanyonlodge.com* ➶ *70 rooms, 3 suites, 40 cabins* ⚖ *Restaurant; no a/c, no room TVs, no smoking* ☰ *AE, D, DC, MC, V* ☿ *Closed late Nov.–Mar.*

$ ✕⊡ **Bryce Canyon Pines.** This quiet, no-surprises motel complex is tucked into the woods 6 mi from the park entrance. Most of the rooms have excellent mountain views. There's a campground on the premises. Known for homemade soups like tomato-broccoli and corn chowder, the homey, antiques-filled restaurant here dishes out quality comfort food. ✉ *6 mi northwest of park entrance on Rte. 12, 84764* ☎ *435/834–5441 or 800/892–7923* 🖨 *435/834–5330* ⊕ *www.brycecanyonmotel.com* ➶ *51 rooms* ⚖ *Restaurant, cable TV, indoor pool* ☰ *AE, D, DC, MC, V.*

★ $–$$ ⊡ **Best Western Ruby's Inn.** This is "Grand Central Station" for visitors to Bryce. All of the guest rooms are consistently comfortable and attractive. Centered between the gift shop and restaurant, the lobby of rough-hewn log beams and poles sets a Southwestern mood. There's even a liquor store on-site. ✉ *Rte. 63, 1 mi south of Rte. 12, 84764* ☎ *866/866–6616* 🖨 *435/834–5265* ⊕ *www.bestwestern.com* ➶ *383 rooms, 2 suites* ⚖ *2 restaurants, cable TV, 2 pools, laundry facilities, in-room dataports* ☰ *AE, D, DC, MC, V.*

¢–$ ⊡ **Bryce Canyon Resort.** This rustic lodge stands across from the local airport and 3 mi from the park entrance. Cabins and cottages are also available if you're seeking a tad more privacy. ✉ *13500 E. Rte. 12, 84764* ☎ *866/834–0043* ⊕ *www.brycecanyonresort.com* 🖨 *435/834–5256* ➶ *62 rooms, 2 suites, 2 cabins* ⚖ *Restaurant, cable TV, in-room data ports, indoor pool, laundry facilities, some pets allowed (fee)* ☰ *MC, V.*

¢–$ ⊡ **Bryce Valley Inn.** Rest your head in this down-to-earth motel in the tiny town of Tropic. The accommodations are clean, and a small gift shop sells Native American crafts. ✉ *199 N. Main St. (Rte. 12), Tropic 84776* ☎ *435/679–8811 or 866/679–8811* 🖨 *435/679–8846* ⊕ *www.*

brycevalleyinn.com ᕕ *65 rooms* ᗬ *Restaurant, laundry facilities, some pets allowed (fee), no-smoking rooms* ▤ *AE, D, MC, V.*

$ 🏨 **Bryce View Lodge.** Next to the park entrance and across from the Best Western Ruby's Inn complex, this motel has reasonable rates. The rooms are pretty basic but comfortable nonetheless, and the lodge is operated by Ruby's Inn, so you can use the pool and other amenities across the way. ⊠ *Rte. 63, 1 mi south of Rte. 12, 84764* 🕾 *435/834–5180 or 888/ 279–2304* 🖷 *435/834–5181* ⊕ *www.bryceviewlodge.com* ᕕ *160 rooms* ᗬ *Cable TV, some pets allowed (fee)* ▤ *AE, D, DC, MC, V.*

Where to Camp

⚠ **North Campground.** A cool, shady retreat in a forest of ponderosa pines, this is a great home base for your exploration of Bryce Canyon. You're near the general store, Bryce Canyon Lodge, trailheads, and the visitor center. Sites are available on a first-come, first-served basis and the campground usually fills by early afternoon in July, August, and September. One loop of the campground remains open throughout winter. ᗬ *Flush toilets, dump station, drinking water, fire grates, picnic tables, public telephone, general store* ᕕ *107 sites, 47 for RVs* ⊠ *Main park road, ½ mi south of visitor center* 🕾 *435/834–5322* ⊕ *www.nps.gov/ brca* 🛏 *$10* ☉ *May–Oct.; some sites open year-round.*

⚠ **Best Western Ruby's Inn Campground and RV Park.** North of the entrance to Bryce Canyon National Park, this campground sits amid pine and fir trees. It's part of the Ruby's Inn complex. ᗬ *Flush toilets, full hookups, dump station, drinking water, guest laundry, showers, grills, picnic tables, electricity, public telephone, general store, swimming (pool)* ᕕ *200 sites; 5 cabins, 6 tepees* ⊠ *Rte. 63, 1 mi off Rte. 12, Bryce* 🕾 *435/834–5341* ⊕ *www.bestwestern.com* 🛏 *$16–$40* ▤ *AE, D, DC, MC, V* ☉ *Apr.–Oct.*

⚠ **Sunset Campground.** This serene alpine campground is within walking distance of Bryce Canyon Lodge and many trailheads. All sites are filled on a first-come, first-served basis. The campground fills by early afternoon in July, August, and September, so get your campsite before you sightsee. Reservations not accepted. ᗬ *Flush toilets, dump station, drinking water, fire grates, picnic tables, public telephone, general store* ᕕ *101 sites, 49 for RVs* ⊠ *Main park road, 2 mi south of visitor center* 🕾 *435/834–5322* ⊕ *www.nps.gov/brca* 🛏 *$10* ☉ *May–Oct.*

Nightlife & the Arts

Bryce Canyon's natural diversity comes alive during **Campfire and Auditorium Programs** (🕾 435/834–5322) in the park's two campgrounds or at Bryce Canyon Lodge. Lectures, slide programs, and audience participation introduce you to geology, astronomy, wildlife adaptations to the climate, wildfires, social and cultural history, and many other topics related to Bryce Canyon and the West.

Imagine how the hoodoos look by the light of a full moon. Three times each month, at or near full moon, you can take a two-hour **moonlight hike** (🕾 435/834–5322) with a park ranger. You must make reservations in person on the day of the hike at the visitor center. Once a month, an astronomer from Salt Lake City's Hansen Planetarium leads an evening **star party** (☎ 435/834–5322) complete with telescopes.

Shopping

The smallish **Bryce Canyon Lodge Gift Shop** (⊠ Bryce Canyon Lodge, off main park road, 2 mi south of park entrance ☎ 435/834–5361) carries Native American and Southwestern crafts, T-shirts, dolls, books, souvenirs, and sundries. Buy groceries, T-shirts, hats, books, film, postcards, and camping items that you might have left behind at the **Bryce Canyon Pines General Store** (⊠ Rte. 12, 6 mi northwest of park entrance ☎ 435/834–5441). Shopping at **Ruby's General Store** (⊠ Rte. 63, 1 mi off Rte. 12 ☎ 435/834–5341) is an integral part of the Bryce Canyon experience. The large, lively, souvenir-laden halls are packed with everything imaginable emblazoned with the park's name, from thimbles to sweatshirts. Native American arts and crafts, Western wear, camping gear, groceries, and sundries are plentiful. There's a large selection of children's toys and trinkets. The Bryce Canyon National History Association runs a bookstore inside the **visitor center** (⊠ 1 mi south of park entrance ☎ 435/834–5322 or 888/362–2642), where you can find maps, trail guides, videos, and postcards.

Bryce Canyon National Park Essentials

ADMISSION

The entrance fee is $20 per vehicle for a seven-day pass and $5 for pedestrians or bicyclists. An annual Bryce Canyon park pass, good for one year from the date of purchase, costs $30. This pass can also be used on the park shuttle. If you leave your private vehicle outside the park, the one-time entrance fee, including transportation on the shuttle, is $15.

BUS & CAR TRAVEL WITHIN BRYCE CANYON NATIONAL PARK

You can see the highlights of the park by driving along the well-maintained road that runs the length of main scenic area. There's a shuttle bus service, but unlike Zion, Bryce has no restrictions on automobile traffic in any season. However, in summer you may encounter heavy traffic and parking areas filled to capacity.

The shuttle bus system operates from mid-May through September and offers a good alternative if you would rather not drive. The shuttle departs from the staging area on the left side of Route 12 about 3 mi north of the park entrance every 10 to 15 minutes. The first stop is Best Western Ruby's Inn, followed by the North Campground and visitor center. The shuttle makes stops at all the major overlooks in the northern portion of the park, but does not go beyond Bryce Point. The shuttle is free, though you are still required to pay the park entrance fee. For more information on the Bryce Canyon shuttle, contact the visitor center.

🚌 Bryce Canyon shuttle ☎ 435/834–5322

CHILDREN IN BRYCE CANYON NATIONAL PARK

The Junior Ranger Program runs from Memorial Day to Labor Day; children ages 6 to 12 can sign up at the park visitor center. Activities vary depending on the park ranger, but a session might involve learning about geology and wildlife using arts and crafts and games. Schedules of events and topics are posted at the visitor center, Bryce Canyon Lodge, and on North and Sunset campground bulletin boards.

EMERGENCIES

In an emergency, dial 911. To contact park police, go to the visitor center or find a park ranger.

TOURS

Knowledgeable guides from Bryce Canyon Scenic Tours lead two-hour tours of Bryce Canyon and describe the area's history, geology, and flora and fauna. Choose from a sunrise tour, sunset tour, or general tour of the park; private tours can be arranged.

▪ Bryce Canyon Scenic Tours ☎ 435/834–5200 or 800/432–5383 ⊕ www.brycetours. com.

VISITOR INFORMATION

▪ Bryce Canyon National Park ⊠ 1 mi south of park entrance ✉ Box 170001, Bryce Canyon 84717 ☎ 435/834–5322 or 888/362–2642 📠 435/834–4102 ⊕ www.nps.gov/brca.

GRAND STAIRCASE–ESCALANTE NATIONAL MONUMENT

In September 1996, President Bill Clinton designated 1.7 million acres in south-central Utah as the Grand Staircase–Escalante National Monument, the first monument to be administered by the Bureau of Land Management instead of the National Park Service. Its three distinct sections—the Grand Staircase, the Kaiparowits Plateau, and the Canyons of the Escalante—offer remote backcountry experiences hard to find elsewhere in the lower 48. Waterfalls, Native American ruins and petroglyphs, shoulder-width slot canyons, and improbable colors all characterize this wilderness. Straddling the northern border of the monument, the small towns of Escalante and Boulder offer access, information, outfitters, lodging, and dining to adventurers. The highway that connects them, Route 12, is one of the most scenic stretches of road in the Southwest.

Escalante

❸❻ *47 mi east of Bryce Canyon National Park entrance via Rte. 12 east.*

Though the Dominguez and Escalante expedition of 1776 came nowhere near this area, the town's name does honor the Spanish explorer. It was bestowed nearly a century later by a member of a survey party led by John Wesley Powell, charged with mapping this remote area. These days Escalante has modern amenities and a state park like nothing else in the state, and is a western gateway to the Grand Staircase–Escalante National Monument.

Created to protect a huge repository of fossilized wood and dinosaur bones, **Escalante State Park** has two short interpretive trails to educate visitors. There's an attractive swimming beach at the park's Wide Hol-

THE HOLE-IN-THE-ROCK EXPEDITION

IN NOVEMBER 1879 *a group of 250 men, women, and children with 83 wagons and more than 1,000 head of livestock embarked on one of the most arduous journeys in the history of the Mormon colonization of Utah. Along the way, they spent six weeks in the freezing heart of winter blasting a road through a canyon wall to reach the Colorado River, 1,200 feet below. This "hole in the rock" would allow them to shorten the west–east emigration route and supply trail by hundreds of miles.*

Called by church leaders to settle the eastern part of the state, the Hole-in-the-Rock Expedition, as it came to be known, gathered at Forty-Mile Spring south of the ranching town of Escalante. Expedition leaders were determined to blaze a new, shorter trail across the Colorado River, and early scouting groups had reported the discovery of a "hole in the rock," a narrow crevice in the west rim of Glen Canyon above the banks of the Colorado.

Two weeks into their journey, the group reached the mesa overlooking the Colorado River Gorge. While the women and children struggled through winter in camp at a nearby spring, the men spent six weeks opening up a narrow slit at the top of a sheer sandstone canyon wall. Equipped with pickaxes, shovels, and a small supply of blasting powder, they widened the crevice to permit the passage of wagons and leveled the descent through the crevice as much as possible, cutting away a 40-foot drop-off and removing huge boulders. Near the bottom of the graded crevice, they had to devise a way to traverse the rest of the sheer drop to the canyon floor. They drilled holes into the north wall of the crack at 2-foot intervals, drove in oak stakes, and constructed a pathway atop the stakes using logs, brush, fill dirt, and rocks. This "crib" road would support the outside wagon wheels while the inside wheels hugged the rock along a treacherous decline.

On January 26, 1880, the wagons clattered through the "hole in the rock." Anxious animals pulled them one at a time to the brink of the crevice. The wagons' rear wheels were rough-locked with large chains, ropes were attached to the rear axles, and the wagons were pushed against the backsides of the animals, inching them slowly forward until the weight of the wagon physically forced them over the edge of the precipice and onto the makeshift trail. Men, women, boys, and animals pulled against the ropes tied to the wagons to slow the descent. The scene was repeated all day long and into evening until all the wagons reached the canyon floor, and the livestock and pioneer families then picked their way down on foot. A crude ferry was built to take the party across the river to the eastern bank. Young cattle drivers guided the livestock through the river to safety.

After another three months of grueling struggle through dense pinyon forests and across rock so slippery that they had to carve footholds for their horses, the pioneers arrived at what is now the town of Bluff. Amazingly, none in the group died, and two babies were born along the way. Much of the trail they blazed is still visible today, mostly across rough four-wheel-drive terrain. The Hole-in-the-Rock Trail is listed on the National Register of Historic Places.

low Reservoir, which is also good for boating, fishing, and birding. ✉ *710 N. Reservoir Rd.* ☎ *435/826–4466* ⊕ *www.stateparks.utah.gov* 🗐 *$5.*

A fine place to stop along the way for the view (and a brew) is **Kiva Koffeehouse** (✉ Near mile marker 74 on Rte. 12, 13 mi east of Escalante ☎ 435/826–4550), constructed by a local artist and inventor when in his 80s. He quarried the sandstone for the walls and floors on this very site and spent two years finding and transporting the 13 Douglas-fir logs surrounding the structure. It's open from April to October, and there are two rooms for rent in a cabin below.

While en route to southeastern Utah in 1879, Mormon pioneers chipped and blasted a narrow passageway in solid rock, through which they lowered their wagons. The **Hole-in-the-Rock Trail,** now a 60-mi gravel road, leads south from Route 12, east of Escalante, to the actual hole-in-the-rock site in Glen Canyon Recreation Area. Much of the original passageway has been flooded by the waters of Lake Powell.

Fodor'sChoice Keep your camera handy and steering wheel steady along **Highway 12**
★ **Scenic Byway** between Escalante and Loa, near Capitol Reef National Park. Though the highway starts at the intersection of U.S. 89, west of Bryce Canyon National Park, the stretch that begins in Escalante is one of the most spectacular. The road passes through Grand Staircase–Escalante National Monument and on to Capitol Reef along one of the most scenic stretches of highway in the United States. Be sure to stop at the scenic overlooks; almost every one will give you an eye-popping view. Don't get distracted, though; the paved road is twisting and steep, and at times climbs over a hogback with sheer drop-offs on both sides.

Sports & the Outdoors

Larger than most national parks at 1.7 million acres, the Grand Staircase–Escalante National Monument is popular with backpackers and hard-core mountain bike enthusiasts. You can explore the rocky landscape, which represents some of America's last wilderness, via dirt roads with a four-wheel-drive vehicle; most roads depart from Route 12. Roadside views into the monument are most impressive from Route 12 between Escalante and Boulder. It costs nothing to enter the park, but fees apply for camping and backcountry permits. Contact the **Escalante Interagency Visitor Center** (✉ 755 W. Main St. ☎ 435/826–5499 ⊙ Late Mar.–Oct., daily 7:30–5:30) for permits and detailed information.

Hikers, bikers, anglers, and photographers are all served by **Excursions of Escalante,** where tours are custom-fit to your schedule and needs. You can arrange tours lasting from four hours to eight days, and all necessary gear is provided. ✉ *125 E. Main St.* ☎ *800/839–7567* ⊕ *www. excursions-escalante.com* ⊙ *Mid-Apr.–mid-Nov. or by appointment.*

BICYCLING A good long-distance mountain-bike ride in the isolated Escalante region follows the 44-mi **Hell's Backbone Road** from Escalante to Boulder. The grade is steep and, if you're driving, a four-wheel-drive vehicle is recommended, but the views of Box Death Hollow make it all worthwhile. The road leaves from the center of town. Inquire about road conditions before departing.

HIKING Some of the best backcountry hiking in the area lies 15 mi east of Escalante on Route 12, where the **Lower Escalante River** carves through striking sandstone canyons and gulches. You can camp at numerous sites along the river for extended trips, or you can spend a little time in the small park where the highway crosses the river. With a guided tour from **Escalante Outback Adventures** (⊠ 325 W. Main St. ☎ 435/826–4967 ⊕ www.escalante-utah.com), you can slip into the slot canyons with confidence or end a day of adventure by watching a sunset from the rim of a canyon while eating hors d'oeuvres.

Where to Stay & Eat

$ ✕ **Trail Head Café & Grill.** This spot serves classic American hot coffee and fresh baked goods for breakfast, and burgers and deli sandwiches for lunch and early dinners (they close at 7 PM in spring and summer, and at 6 PM in winter. Ask the staff for the skinny on local hikes. ⊠ *125 E. Main St.* ☎ *800/839–7567* ▤ *No credit cards* ⊘ *Closed Tues. and Dec.–Mar.*

¢ ✕ **Esca-Latte Coffee Shop & Pizza Parlor.** Fuel up for your hike with the best coffee in town. When you're hot and spent after your day of exploration, there's no better place to sit back and relax with friends. Try a turkey sub or pizza with a cold draft microbrew, or opt for the salad bar. Watch hummingbirds fight the wind at the feeders while dining on the patio. ⊠ *310 W. Main St.* ☎ *435/826–4266* ▤ *D, MC, V.*

★ $ 🖭 **Escalante's Grand Staircase Bed & Breakfast Inn.** Rooms in this inn have skylights, tile floors, log furniture, and murals reproducing area petroglyphs. You can relax on the outdoor porches or in the library, or make use of the bike rentals to explore the adjacent national monument. ⊠ *280 W. Main St., 84726* ☎ *435/826–4890 or 866/826–4890* ⊕ *www.escalantebnb.com* 🛏 *5 rooms* ⌂ *Cable TV, in-room data ports, hot tub bicycles; no kids under 10, no smoking* ▤ *D, MC, V* ⦿ *BP.*

¢ 🖭 **Circle D Motel.** Basic but clean and comfortable, this motel will accommodate those traveling solo in a single room for as little as $30 a night. ⊠ *475 W. Main St., 84726* ☎ *435/826–4297* 🖷 *435/826–4402* ⊕ *www.utahcanyons.com/circled.htm* 🛏 *29 rooms* ⌂ *Some microwaves, refrigerators, cable TV, some pets allowed (fee)* ▤ *AE, D, MC, V.*

¢ 🖭 **Prospector Inn Motel.** A large, square, three-story brick building on Main Street, this is the largest motel in town, and the rates are reasonable. ⊠ *380 W. Main St., 84726* ☎ *435/826–4653* 🖷 *435/826–4285* ⊕ *www.prospectorinn.com* 🛏 *50 rooms* ⌂ *Restaurant, cable TV, some in-room data ports, business services* ▤ *AE, MC, V.*

Boulder

㊲ *29 mi northeast of Escalante via Rte. 12 north.*

That mail was delivered to Boulder by horse and mule until 1940 should give you an idea of how remote it is. The town was founded by cattle ranchers, and ranching continues to occupy many residents. The town of Escalante is larger with more services, but Boulder has one of the finest lodges and restaurants in the state.

Believed to be one of the largest ancestral Puebloan sites west of the Colorado River, the village at **Anasazi Village State Park** is largely unexcavated. A paved outdoor trail leads to the protected ruins of a surface pueblo pit house that predates AD 1200. Within a reproduction of an ancient dwelling is a museum featuring interactive exhibits and views into the climate-controlled environment where artifacts are stored. ⊠ *460 N. Rte. 12* ☎ *435/335–7308* ⊕ *www.stateparks.utah.gov* 🎫 *$2* ☉ *Daily 8–6.*

Sports & the Outdoors

BICYCLING Mountain bikers may want to pedal a portion of the **Burr Trail,** a 66-mi backcountry route (also passable by most vehicles when dry) that crosses east through the monument into the southern portion of Capitol Reef National Park.

HIKING **Calf Creek Falls** (⊠ 8 mi south of Boulder on Rte. 12) is an easy 6-mi
★ round-trip hike from the trailhead at Calf Creek Recreation Area. At the end of the trail, a large waterfall explodes over a cliff hundreds of feet above.

If you want to take a few days to hike and backpack in Grand Staircase–Escalante National Monument, let the professionals at **Escalante Canyon Outfitters** (⊠ 842 W. Rte. 12 ☎ 888/326–4453 ⊕ www.ecohike. com) guide you. Founded in 1991 by a husband-and-wife team with extensive knowledge of the area, the service provides some gear and all of your meals. Explore the slot canyons in the Boulder vicinity during the spring and fall on three to six individual day trips with **Earth Tours** (☎ 435/691–1241 ⊕ www.earth-tours.com).

Where to Stay & Eat

$–$$$ ✕ **Hell's Backbone Grill.** The owners use only local organic foods that
Fodor$Choice are historically relevant to the area, so you might find buffalo and corn-
★ meal-molasses and pecan skillet trout on the menu. Native American, Western range, Southwestern, and Mormon pioneer recipes inspire the chef. Salads might contain strawberries, jicama, pine nuts, and dried corn. ⊠ *20 N. Rte. 12, in Boulder Mountain Lodge* ☎ *435/335–7464* ⊕ *www. hellsbackbonegrill.com* ➡ *DC, MC, V* ☉ *Closed mid-Nov.–Feb. No lunch.*

$–$$$ 🏨 **Boulder Mountain Lodge.** A 15-acre pond serves as sanctuary to ducks,
Fodor$Choice coots, and other waterfowl at this pastoral lodge. Large, modern rooms
★ with either balconies or patios have gorgeous views of the wetlands. The main lodge contains a great sitting room with a fireplace and a library. There's also a fine-art gallery and outstanding restaurant nearby. ⊠ *20 N. Rte. 12, 84716* ☎ *435/335–7460 or 800/556–3446* 🖷 *435/335–7461* ⊕ *www.boulder-utah.com* ➡ *20 rooms* ♿ *Some kitchenettes, cable TV, hot tub, library, Internet room, meeting room, some pets allowed (fee); no smoking* ➡ *AE, D, MC, V* ⧫ *BP.*

¢ 🏨 **Boulder Mountain Ranch.** Consider this rustic out-of-the-way ranch if you'd like to get away from it all. There's no TV to distract, and don't be put off by the lack of air-conditioning—Boulder is at a high enough elevation that days are only warm and nights are cool. A ranch-style breakfast buffet is available for an extra fee. Hardy horseback riders can try the six-day trip into the backcountry, while novices can opt for half-day, full-day, or three-day jaunts. ⊠ *7 mi southwest of Boulder on Hell's Backbone Rd., 84716* ☎ *435/335–7480* 🖷 *435/335–7352*

⊕ *www.boulderutah.com/bmr/* ⇥ *5 rooms, 3 cabins* ⌂ *Some microwaves, gym, fishing, horseback riding, meeting room, some pets allowed (fee); no a/c, no room phones, no room TVs, no smoking* ⊟ No *credit cards.*

SOUTHWESTERN UTAH A TO Z

To research prices, get advice from other travelers, and book travel arrangements, visit www.fodors.com.

AIR TRAVEL

SkyWest flies to Cedar City and St. George municipal airports, and operates as a carrier for both United Express and Delta Connection flights. Las Vegas's McCarran International Airport is 116 mi from St. George, Utah; the St. George Shuttle makes nine trips a day between it and St. George.

🛪 Airport Information **Cedar City Regional Airport** ⊠ 2281 W. Kittyhawk Dr., Cedar City 🕾 435/867–9408. **McCarran International Airport** ⊠ 5757 Wayne Newton Blvd., Las Vegas, NV 🕾 702/261–5211 ⊕ www.mccarran.com. **St. George Municipal Airport** ⊠ 444 S. River Rd., St. George 🕾 435/634–5822.

🛪 Carriers **Delta Connections** 🕾 800/221–1212 ⊕ www.delta.com. **SkyWest Airlines** 🕾 435/634–3000 ⊕ www.skywest.com. **United Express** 🕾 877/228–1327 ⊕ www. united.com.

🛪 Shuttle Van **St. George Shuttle** ⊠ 1245 S. Main St. 🕾 435/628–8320 or 800/933–8320 ⊕ www.stgshuttle.com.

BUS TRAVEL

Greyhound Bus Lines serves the I–15 corridor, making stops in Parowan and St. George.

🛪 **Greyhound Bus Lines** 🕾 800/229–9424 ⊕ www.greyhound.com.

CAR RENTAL

St. George and Cedar City have major car rental agencies at their airports and within town.

🛪 **Avis** ⊠ 2281 W. Kittyhawk Dr., Cedar City Airport, Cedar City 🕾 435/867–9898 ⊕ www.avis.com ⊠ 330 W. 200 North St., Cedar City 🕾 435/586–2084. **Enterprise** ⊠ 987 N. Main St., Suite 3, Cedar City 🕾 435/865–7636 ⊕ www.enterprise.com ⊠ 652 E. St. George Blvd., St. George 🕾 435/634–1556. **National** ⊠ 2281 W. Kitty Hawk Dr., Cedar City Airport, Cedar City 🕾 435/586–4004 ⊕ www.nationalcar.com ⊠ 620 S.W. Airport Rd., St. George Airport, St. George 🕾 435/673–5098.

CAR TRAVEL

I–15 is the main route into southwestern Utah, from Las Vegas to the southwest and Salt Lake City to the northeast. U.S. 89, which leads to Bryce Canyon and beyond to Kanab and the east side of Zion National Park, is a good, well-traveled road with interesting sights, as well as gas stations and convenience stores. Routes 143 and 14 are the main east–west connecting routes. Some mountain curves can be expected on these roads, and winter months may see hazardous conditions and occasional closures in the higher elevations around Brian Head, Cedar Breaks, and Bryce Canyon. Keep the gas tank topped off, especially if you start to venture along any of the region's old Jeep roads. Contact the Utah Department of Transportation for construction delays and road conditions.

St. George AAA Office ☎ 800/541-9902 ⊕ www.aaa.com. **Utah Department of Transportation** ☎ 801/887-3710 ⊕ www.dot.state.ut.us/public/traveler_info.htm.

EMERGENCIES

In most towns, call ☎ 911 for police, fire, and ambulance service. In rural areas, the Utah Highway Patrol has jurisdiction, as do county sheriff departments.

Ambulance or Police Emergencies ☎ 911. **Utah Highway Patrol** ☎ 435/867-7540.

Hospitals Dixie Regional Medical Center ✉ 544 S. 400 East St., St. George ☎ 435/634-4000. **Kane County Hospital** ✉ 355 N. Main St., Kanab ☎ 435/644-5811. **Valley View Medical Center** ✉ 595 S. 75 East St., Cedar City ☎ 435/586-6587.

LODGING

The official travel site of the State of Utah is your single best bet for information on lodging and amenities in the southwestern part of the state. St. George, Hurricane, Springdale, Zion National Park, and other locations are also covered in the Washington County Travel Information Web site.

St. George Area Convention & Visitors Bureau ☎ 800/869-6635 ⊕ www.utahsdixie.com. **Utah Division of Travel Development** ✉ 300 N. State St., Salt Lake City 84114 ☎ 800/200-1160 ⊕ www.utah.com.

CAMPING In this region of Utah, campers can choose from low-desert to high-mountain facilities and more than 100 commercial campgrounds. Campgrounds in Bryce Canyon and Zion national parks fill up fast. Most of the area's state parks have camping facilities, and Dixie National Forest contains many wonderful sites. The Utah Bureau of Land Management also runs campgrounds in the area.

Dixie National Forest ✉ 82 N. 100 East St., Cedar City 84720 ☎ 435/865-3700. **Utah Bureau of Land Management** ✉ 345 East Riverside Dr., St. George 84720 ☎ 435/688-3200. **Utah State Parks and Recreation** ✉ 1594 W. North Temple, Salt Lake City 84114 ☎ 801/538-7220 ⊕ www.stateparks.utah.gov.

MEDIA

NEWSPAPERS & Utah's two largest daily newspapers, the *Salt Lake Tribune* and *Deseret*
MAGAZINES *Morning News,* both publish statewide editions available at stores and hotels throughout southwestern Utah. The *Spectrum,* published daily out of St. George, covers local news throughout the region and also publishes the glossy *St. George* magazine, covering area arts and living.

TELEVISION & Utah's major television networks—KSL (NBC), KUTV (CBS), and KSTU
RADIO (FOX)—all broadcast in this part of the state. Cedar City's KSUU 91.1 FM is run by Southern Utah University students.

Sports & the Outdoors

You should not visit southwestern Utah without exploring some of its wide-open and remote spaces using a mode of transportation other than a car or bus. In many instances, four wheels will not take you to the best sights. Consider a half- or full-day tour by bike, foot, or horse-back—or spend a few nights out on the range. The following outfitters offer tours that cover a wide geographical area with many different types of terrain; check the Sports & the Outdoors section of each town or park in this chapter for listings of outfitters which target a specific area.

BICYCLING The "other" southern corner of the state tends to grab the cycling spot-light, but southwestern Utah is making a name for itself as a destina-tion for the discriminating road or mountain biker. The higher elevations of Brian Head and Bryce Canyon National Park are popular in sum-mer, when temperatures are relatively cool; the winter climate at lower desert elevations is mild enough for off-season riding. The outfitters listed here are a great source of information on trails and conditions, but con-sider signing on for a professionally guided tour.

Escape Adventures ✉ 8221 W. Charleston, Suite 101, Las Vegas 89117 ☎ 800/596-2953 ⊕ www.escapeadventures.com. **Rim Tours** ✉ 1233 S. U.S. 191, Moab 84532 ☎ 800/626-7335 ⊕ www.rimtours.com. **Springdale Cycle Tours** ✉ 1458 Zion Park Blvd., Springdale 84767 ☎ 800/776-2099 ⊕ www.springdalecycles.com.

HORSEBACK RIDING TOURS The only thing more quintessentially "Old West" than the landscape it-self is the animal that helped conquer it—the horse. Ranchers and ex-plorers on horseback mapped the lands of southwestern Utah, and in many cases the trails they blazed are still used today. Ride the range for a half day, or consider a longer horse-packing route that takes four, five, or even six or more days. Blue Pine Tours guides trips on the Marka-gunt Plateau near Cedar Breaks National Monument. Mecham Outfit-ters covers more territory in the Bryce Canyon area. Canyon Trail Rides operates mule and horseback riding tours in Bryce Canyon and Zion national parks as well as on the North Rim of the Grand Canyon.

Blue Pine Tours ✉ 121 Duck Creek Village, Duck Creek Village 84762 ☎ 800/848-2525 ⊕ www.bluepinetours.com. **Canyon Trail Rides** ✉ Box 128, Tropic 84776 ☎ 435/679-8665 ⊕ www.canyonrides.com. **Mecham Outfitters** ✉ Box 71, Tropic 84776 ☎ 435/679-8823 ⊕ www.mechamoutfitters.com.

TOURS

Hondoo River & Trails arranges full-day four-wheel-drive vehicle tours into portions of the Grand Staircase–Escalante National Monument. Ar-chaeology Plus organizes half-day hikes and van drives through red rock canyons near Zion National Park, as well as multiday van tours through-out southwestern Utah. The theme of the multiday tours can be customized to meet your interests, and all tours are led by an archaeologist who is also a expert in local history.

Archaeology Plus ☎ 435/688-7325 ⊕ www.angelfire.com/trek/archaeology. **Hondoo River & Trails** ✉ 95 E. Main St., Box 98, Torrey 84775 ☎ 435/425-3519 or 800/332-2696 ⊕ www.hondoo.com.

VISITOR INFORMATION

Bryce Canyon National Park ✉ Box 170001, Bryce Canyon 84717 ☎ 435/834-5322 🖷 435/834-4102 ⊕ www.nps.gov/brca. **St. George Area Convention & Visitors Bu-reau** ✉ 1835 Convention Center Dr., St. George 84790 ☎ 800/869-6635 ⊕ www.utahsdixie.com. **Garfield County Travel Council** ✉ 55 S. Main St., Panguitch 84759

☎ 800/444-6689 ⊕ www.brycecanyoncountry.com. **Iron County Tourism and Convention Bureau** ⬦ 581 N. Main St., Cedar City 84720 ☎ 435/586-5124 or 800/354-4849 ⊕ www.scenicsouthernutah.com. **Kane County Travel Council** ⬦ 78 S. 100 East St., Kanab 84741 ☎ 800/733-5263 ⊕ www.visitsouthernutah.com. **Utah Division of Travel Development** ✉ 300 N. State St., Salt Lake City 84114 ☎ 800/200-1160 ⊕ www.utah. com. **Zion Canyon Visitors Bureau** ⬦ Box 331, Springdale 84767 ☎ 888/518-7070 ⊕ www.zionpark.com. **Zion Canyon Visitor Center** ⬦ Rte. 9, Springdale 84767-1099 ☎ 435/772-3256 ⊕ www.nps.gov/zion.

Moab & Arches & Canyonlands National Parks

7

WORD OF MOUTH

"If you want to do the Fiery Furnace, in Arches NP, sign up early. The nice thing about the hike is that it's mostly in the shade and will be about 15 to 20 degrees cooler than the rest of Arches. Good for the afternoon."

—Dayle

"In Canyonlands Island in the Sky you will want to do Mesa Arch. I also really liked the easy hike to Grand View Point . . . Upheaval Dome Overlook Trail didn't do that much for me, but maybe cause it was so hot. Other people really like this trail. Whale Rock trail was fun. In the Needles District make sure you stop at Newspaper Rock State Park on your way in. Cave Spring Trail is interesting and so is the Pothole Point Trail."

—utahtea

By Janet Lowe   **THE FIRST THING TRAVELERS TO SOUTHEASTERN UTAH** notice is the color. Red, orange, purple, pink, creamy ivory, deep chocolate, and even shades of turquoise paint the landscape. Rocks jut and tilt first one way, then another. There's no flat canvas of color in this country, and near-vertical walls stand in the way of easy route-finding. Deep canyons, carved by wild Western rivers, crisscross the area. Rocks teeter on slim columns or burst like mushrooms from the ground. Snowcapped mountains stand in the distant horizon no matter which direction you look. The sky is more often than not blue in a region that receives only about eight inches of rain a year. When thunderstorms do build, the sky turns a dramatic gunmetal gray, bringing deep orange cliffs into sharp relief.

Embroidered through the region is evidence of the people who came before rock climbers and Mormons. Rock art as old as 4,000 years is etched or painted on canyon walls. The most familiar of these ancient dwellers are the ancestral Puebloans, popularly known as Anasazi, who occupied the area between 700 and 2,000 years ago.

There is surprise around every corner, whether you explore the region by car, by raft, by foot, by bicycle, or in a rugged 4X4. On the trail you'll discover cactus or a lush garden of ferns created by precious springs or seeps. On the river, hawks float overhead. On the road, you'll encounter trading posts that have been selling Native American art for decades or, nearer Navajo land, you can purchase art directly from its makers. Enter these lands with a mind as open as the skies. Be a curious, willing traveler in one of the wildest regions left in America. Also be a prepared traveler. This is the area that invented the term "you can't get there from here," so plan your journey by using all or part of our suggested route. Whatever you do, don't forget your camera and lots of film; you're sure to use twice what you think you will.

Exploring Southeastern Utah

I–70 is the speedway that gets you across Utah, but to dip into southeastern Utah, you'll need to use the main artery, U.S. 191, which runs from the Arizona border to I–70 and beyond. The only road that stretches any distance westward across the region is Route 95, which dead ends at Lake Powell. No matter which of the state roads you use to explore the area, you're in for a treat. Here the earth is red, purple, and orange. The Manti–La Sal Mountains rise out of the desertlike ships. Mesas, buttes, and pinnacles interrupt the horizon in a most surprising way. But this is some of the most remote country in the United States, so services are sometimes far apart.

About the Restaurants

Since most people come to southeastern Utah to play on the rocks and rivers, casual is the *modus operandi* for dining. Whether you select an award-winning Continental restaurant or an outdoor patio grill, you can dress comfortably in shorts or jeans. Although you're in the middle of nowhere, there are some wonderful culinary surprises waiting for you, often with spectacular views as a bonus.

Numbers in the text correspond to numbers in the margin and on Southeastern Utah map.

If you have
3 days

On a short trip to Southeastern Utah, you'll be happier if you base yourself in ⊞ **Moab ❷** ↦, a central spot for visiting both of the region's national parks, and it's nice to have a comfortable place to come back to at the end of the day. Start your whirlwind tour with a day in **Arches National Park ❸–❾**. You can drive the park's main road and see a few of the top sights in day; be sure to save time for at least one short hike, but at least stop at the Delicate Arch trailhead to see Wolfe Ranch and then drive to the viewpoint trail for a glimpse of the state icon. On Day 2, pack a picnic lunch and head for **Canyonlands National Park**'s Island in the Sky District ⓫–⓯. On the way, stop at Dead Horse Point State Park. Make sure you have plenty of film for this day's tour. Make time for a morning hike and drive all the way to the tip of the "island" to Grandview Point. Spend Day 3 on the Colorado River with one of Moab's many river-rafting companies. Select either a playful daily raft trip or a scenic tour via a sturdy jet boat.

If you have
5 days

Spend your first and second days as above in the three-day tour, basing yourself in ⊞ **Moab ❷** ↦. On the third day choose between a river expedition or traveling south to the Needles District of **Canyonlands National Park ⓰–⓳**. Upon leaving Canyonlands continue your journey south on U.S. 191 to **Blanding ㉓**, where you should make a stop at **Edge of the Cedars State Park** to learn about the ancient Native Americans who inhabited this country. Continue south to Route 95, and stop at **Natural Bridges National Monument ㉖**. If you can, make arrangements to spent the night at ⊞ Fry Canyon Lodge in the heart of Cedar Mesa. On Day 4, continue on Route 95 and cross **Lake Powell ㉗** at Hite before continuing north. Camp that night at Goblin Valley State Park near ⊞ **Hanksville ㉘**, or continue on to ⊞ **Green River ❶** for less rustic accommodation.

If you have
7 days

Anyone can spend a week hiking in Arches or Canyonlands national parks, but if your goal is to cover more territory, follow the five-day itinerary selecting both the river trip and the Needles District. Instead of turning onto Route 95, however, continue south on Route 163 into ⊞ **Mexican Hat ㉕**, taking as much time as you can afford in Monument Valley; consider staying at Goulding's Lodge there. You'll have to backtrack a bit on Route 163 to reach Route 261. Stop briefly at Goosenecks State Park, Muley Point Overlook, and Moki Dugway Overlook; you'll pass the Valley of the Gods on this route, too. Continue north back to Route 95 and head to **Natural Bridges National Monument ㉖**, and follow the rest of the five-day itinerary.

About the Hotels

Travelers to southeastern Utah benefit by the explosion of overnight accommodations during the past decade. Every type of lodging is available, from economy chain motels to B&Bs and high-end–high-adventure resorts. It's important to know when popular events are held, however, as motels and resorts can fill up weeks ahead of time during the busiest periods.

WHAT IT COSTS					
	$$$$	**$$$**	**$$**	**$**	**¢**
RESTAURANTS	over $25	$19–$25	$13–$18	$8–$12	under $8
HOTELS	over $200	$151–$200	$111–$150	$70–$110	under $70

Restaurant prices are for a main course at dinner, excluding sales tax of 7½%–8½%. Hotel prices are for two people in a standard double room in high season, excluding service charges and 11%–12¼% tax.

Timing

There's no place like a desert in spring, and southeastern Utah is no exception. The weather is still a bit unsettled in March, but April brings cool, clear days perfect for hiking, biking, and sightseeing. May is wildflower season with cactus, Indian paintbrush, globemallow, and cliffrose painting the landscape lime-green, pink, orange, and fire-engine red. Daytime temperatures generally stay in the low 80s until late May or June. After June, the only way to describe the weather is hot. River-rafting trips are the best way to visit this part of the country in summer, when June and July churn up the biggest rapids. By October the desert has cooled again, and mountain bikers return to challenge their skills on the slickrock domes. Winters are mild, and repeat visitors know this is the best time to beat the crowds. There is seldom need to worry about rain as the area receives only eight inches per year. If you don't like crowds, avoid holidays, especially Easter week and the weeks before, when the annual Jeep Safari and college spring-breakers fill the area with extra vehicles and parties.

BOOK CLIFFS COUNTRY

The Book Cliffs, part of an escarpment that forms a 200-mi semicircle from Green River, Utah, across the state border into Colorado, are so named because they resemble the leaves of a partially opened book. Buried in the rocks are vast deposits of coal, oil shale, and rock asphalt. Compared to other parts of Utah, this area is desolate and monochromatic, but the implacable wall is testimony to the building up and tearing down of the earth's surface. The area remains remote, with only a few dirt roads making it accessible to hunters and four-wheel-drive recreationists.

Hiking

A visit to southeastern Utah is not complete without getting out and walking some of the many trails. You'll take the fragrance of sage and pine back home with you and be forever hooked on the desert. Trails range from pastoral creek-side paths shaded by towering red rock cliffs to sun-drenched stretches of slickrock. Many combine the best of both. Getting out on the trails allows you to watch lizards skitter under rocks or to gaze on gorgeous wildflowers and cactus. Hiking is also a good way to come upon some well-hidden ancient Native American rock art, which decorates canyon walls all over the region.

Rafting or River Expeditions

To truly get a taste of the Wild West, you have to get wet. Don't miss the opportunity to get out on the Colorado River while in southeastern Utah. Any of the outfitters we recommend can take you safely through the rapids. Some tour companies offer scenic flatwater tours that are relaxing but take you to places you'll never see otherwise. Look for an outfitter that offers a combination jet-boat and four-wheel-drive tour that gives you the very best of both in canyon country.

Scenic Drives

Some days are just meant for a quiet drive in the country, and a drive along the Colorado River makes for a great afternoon of sightseeing. You can spot rafts negotiating the rapids or, looking skyward, the red-tailed hawks and bald eagles that follow the river corridor. Look close and you might even see a coyote getting a drink from the river. Drives in the national parks allow you to stop at spectacular overlooks, which give you a sense of this vast, wild region. Other drives take you to ancient Native American carvings that have graced canyon walls for more than 1,000 years. While it's best to keep your eyes on the winding roads, you're likely to spot mule deer grazing along the road. If you are exceptionally lucky, you'll also see bighorn sheep or pronghorn on your driving tour as well. Always keep an eye out for "open range" signs, which indicate that cattle may be wandering across the roadway.

Green River

❶ *70 mi west of the Colorado state line via I–70.*

Named for the river that runs through town, Green River, Utah, and its namesake are historically important. Early Indians used the river for centuries. The Old Spanish Trail also crossed the river, and the Denver and Rio Grande Railroad bridged the river here in 1883. Some say "the green" refers to the color of the water; others claim it's the vegetation along the river bank. Another story reports that it was named after a mysterious trapper named Mr. Green. Whatever the etymology, Green River remains a sleepy little town and a nice break from some of the more "hip" tourist towns in southern Utah. In September the fragrance of fresh canteloupe, watermelon, and honeydew fills the air in Green River.

They celebrate the harvest with **Melon Days** (☎ 435/564–3526 or 888/
564–3600 ⊕ www.greenriver-utah.com) the third weekend of September. This small-town event features a parade and fair, plenty of music,
square dancing, a canoe race, and thousands of pounds of melons,
which are famous in the region.

The riverfront **John Wesley Powell River History Museum** gives visitors the
opportunity to see what it was like to travel down the Green and Colorado rivers in the 1800s. A series of interactive displays tracks the Powell party's arduous and dangerous 1869 journey. The center also houses
the River Runner's Hall of Fame, a tribute to those who have followed
in Powell's wake. An art gallery reserved for works thematically linked
to river exploration is also on-site. ⊠ *885 E. Main St.* ☎ *435/564–3427*
⊠ *$2* ⊙ *June–Sept., daily 8–8; Oct.–May, daily 9–5.*

The **Sego Canyon Rock Art Panels** are a treat for even the most jaded traveler. Alongside ancient petroglyphs, 19th-century Ute drawings cover
large rock panels in this spectacular canyon setting. Distinctive for their
large anthropomorphic figures, and for horses, buffalo, and shields
painted with red-and-white pigment, these rare drawings are some of
the finest Ute pictographs in the region. The panels are 3½ mi off I–70
on a maintained gravel road. The Moab Field Office of the Bureau of
Land Management can answer questions about the site. ⊠ *I–70, Exit
185, 25 mi east of Green River* ☎ *435/259–6111 Bureau of Land Management Office in Moab.*

**off the
beaten
path**

CRYSTAL GEYSER – The geyser erupts every 14 to 16 hours for about
30 minutes. The water shoots 80 to 100 feet high. On the banks of
the Green River, 10 mi south of town, you'll get a good taste of
backcountry on good, graded road. Mineral deposits have created a
dramatic orange terrace surrounding the eruption site. The staff at
the Green River Information Center, which is in the John Wesley
Powell River History Museum, can provide detailed directions and
updated road conditions.

Sports & the Outdoors

RIVER FLOAT
TRIPS

Bearing little resemblance to its name, Desolation Canyon acquaints
those who venture down the Green River with some of the last true
American wilderness. This journey takes you through a lush, verdant
canyon where the rapids promise more laughter than fear and trem-
bling. It's a favorite destination of canoe paddlers, kayakers, and beginning rafters. May through September raft trips through
Gray-Desolation Canyon are popular and can be arranged by outfitters in Green River. South of town the river drifts at a lazier pace
through Labyrinth and Stillwater canyons, and the 68-mi stretch of river
that runs south to Mineral Bottom in Canyonlands National Park is
best suited to canoes and motorized boats.

Holiday River Expeditions (⊠ 1055 E. Main St. ☎ 800/624–6323 🖶 801/
266–1448 ⊕ www.bikeraft.com) has been introducing people to the Green
River for decades. You can rent a canoe or book a raft trip on the Green
and Colorado rivers at this reliable company. **Moki Mac River Expeditions**

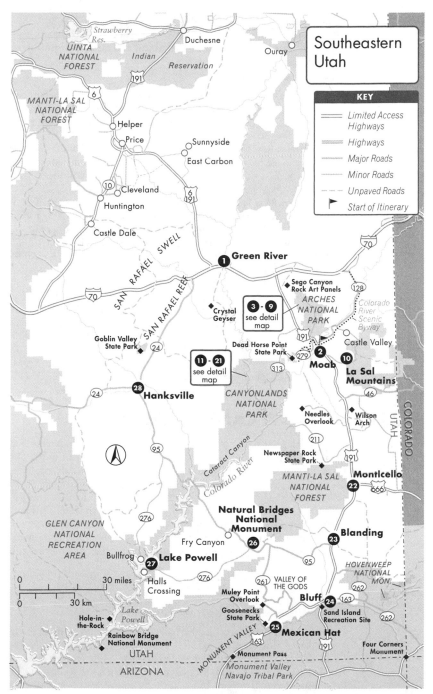

Southeastern Utah

Strawberry Res.

UINTA NATIONAL FOREST

Duchesne

Indian Reservation

Ouray

MANTI-LA SAL NATIONAL FOREST

191

6

Helper

Price

Sunnyside

East Carbon

10

Cleveland

6
191

Huntington

Castle Dale

SAN RAFAEL SWELL

SAN RAFAEL REEF

70

Green River ①

Sego Canyon Rock Art Panels

128

Crystal Geyser

③ - ⑨ see detail map

ARCHES NATIONAL PARK

Colorado River Scenic Byway

Goblin Valley State Park

24

Dead Horse Point State Park

191

279

Moab ②

Castle Valley

313

La Sal Mountains ⑩

⑪ - ㉑ see detail map

CANYONLANDS NATIONAL PARK

46

24

㉘ **Hanksville**

Needles Overlook

Wilson Arch

211

95

Cataract Canyon

Colorado River

Newspaper Rock State Park

191

MANTI-LA SAL NATIONAL FOREST

Monticello ㉒

666

276

GLEN CANYON NATIONAL RECREATION AREA

Natural Bridges National Monument ㉖

Fry Canyon

Blanding ㉓

95

HOVENWEEP NATIONAL MON.

Bullfrog

㉗ **Lake Powell**

Halls Crossing

276

261

VALLEY OF THE GODS

262

Muley Point Overlook

Goosenecks State Park

Bluff ㉔

163

Sand Island Recreation Site

262

0 ———— 30 miles

0 ———— 30 km

Lake Powell

Hole-in-the-Rock

Rainbow Bridge National Monument

UTAH

ARIZONA

㉕ **Mexican Hat**

163

MONUMENT VALLEY

Monument Pass

Four Corners Monument

191

Monument Valley Navajo Tribal Park

UTAH ▏ COLORADO

(⌂ Box 71242, Salt Lake City 84171 ☎ 801/268–6667 or 800/284–7280 ⊕ www.mokimac.com) is a well-regarded river company specializing in Desolation, Stillwater, Labyrinth, and other canyons on the Green River.

Where to Stay & Eat

¢–$$ ✕ **Ben's Cafe.** At the local hot spot for homemade enchiladas you can also get a good porterhouse steak. This unpretentious restaurant on Green River's main thoroughfare offers plenty of choices at reasonable prices. ⊠ *115 W. Main St.* ☎ *435/564–3352* ▤ *AE, D, DC, MC, V.*

★ ¢–$ ✕ **Ray's Tavern.** Ray's is something of a Western legend and a favorite hangout for river runners. Stop here for great tales about working on the river as well as the best all-beef hamburger in two counties. ⊠ *25 S. Broadway* ☎ *435/564–3511* ▤ *AE, D, MC, V.*

$ ▥ **Best Western River Terrace Hotel.** The setting, on the bank of the Green River, is conducive to a good night's rest. Comfortable, no-smoking rooms are furnished with large beds, and the premises are clean. Be sure to ask for a river-view room to take best advantage of this hotel's location. ⊠ *880 E. Main St., 84525* ☎ *435/564–3401 or 800/528–1234* 🖷 *435/564–3403* ⊕ *www.bestwestern.com* ⟿ *50 rooms* ⚿ *Cable TV, in-room data ports, pool, hot tub; no smoking* ▤ *AE, D, DC, MC, V.*

¢–$ ▥ **Green River Comfort Inn.** Right off I–70, this reliable motel is convenient if you're only stopping for the night. There's a restaurant directly across street. Rooms were renovated in 2000, giving them a contemporary look, but the decor is strictly modern-motel. ⊠ *1065 E. Main St.* ☎ *435/564–3300* 🖷 *435/564–3299* ⊕ *www.choicehotels.com* ⟿ *55 rooms, 3 suites* ⚿ *Some microwaves, some refrigerators, cable TV, in-room data ports, pool, gym, hot tub, laundry facilities* ▤ *AE, D, DC, MC, V* ⏸ *CP.*

MOAB, ARCHES & CANYONLANDS

Two of Utah's five national parks are in southeastern Utah. Arches National Park is 5 mi from its hub city Moab, and the Island in the Sky district of Canyonlands National Park is 32 mi from Moab (the Needles and Maze districts are a bit more of a drive). The Colorado River runs through the heart of Canyonlands, and you have to cross this legendary river to get in or out of Moab and southeastern Utah. This area offers an abundance of activities and services and some of the most unforgettable landscapes in the world. Arches is home to Delicate Arch, the red sandstone, free-standing rock formation that has become the symbol of Utah.

Moab

▶ ❷ *52 mi southeast of Green River via I–70 and U.S. 191.*

Although Spanish explorers led by Juan Maria Antonio de Rivera ventured through this area in 1765, few Europeans appear to have visited the Moab region before the 1850s. In the early 1800s, travelers along the Old Spanish Trail passed through, following the same route that U.S. 191 follows today. Then, in 1855, at the behest of Mormon leaders, a

OLD DOC WILLIAMS

DR. JOHN WILLIAMS, THE FIRST DOCTOR EVER TO VISIT MOAB, *arrived in town in 1896. He stayed a week and said it was the busiest of his life since the townsfolk of Moab had never had any medical care. So popular was his presence that the county health commissioners named him county health officer, paying him $150 a year to serve the community. Doc Williams set up an office and drug store in downtown Moab, and his place became especially popular with the area's Native Americans, who would receive some sort of treat—a bit of hard candy or sugar— when they visited the drug store. If it was closed, they would cluster around his house and watch through the windows until Mrs. Williams brought out a loaf of home-baked bread.*

Practicing medicine in such a remote region could be challenging. Although Williams could visit patients in the valley with his buggy, those in remote areas

required him to saddle up his horse and ride across the rugged country. But day or night, in the biting winter cold, or in the scorching summer heat, he would mount his horse and load his saddlebags. He would take along his small dog who rode on the back of his horse.

Doc Williams loved the rugged landscape of canyon country and spent as much time as he could exploring and hiking in the desert. He loved to hike in what is now Arches National Park, and you'll find a commemorative site named for him there. The doctor, who lived to be 103 years old, said his longevity was due to the fact that he rose every day at 5 AM to chop wood.

group of 41 men set out to establish the Elk Mountain Mission, where the city of Moab now stands. They were driven out by Indian attacks six months later, and permanent settlers did not return to the valley until the late 1870s. At first a ranching and farming community, Moab became a mining center and garnered a rich history as a boom-and-bust town. In the 1800s, Moab was a hangout for Butch Cassidy's Wild Bunch and other outlaw gangs.

A number of theories about how Moab got its name float around the local bookstores and coffee shops. The most accepted is the Biblical derivation. In the Bible the name Moab occurs frequently, referring to a dry, mountainous area east of the Dead Sea and southeast of Jerusalem. This explanation seems to fit Moab's geographical relationship to Salt Lake City and the Great Salt Lake as well as the geologic characteristics of the area.

Mining has historically been the major local economic activity, with vanadium being discovered nearby in 1912. The first of a boom-and-bust cycle began in 1920 with the discovery of uranium, but it was not until Charlie Steen, a down-on-his-luck prospector, wandered into town in the 1950s and made a dramatic uranium strike that Moab's character changed forever. For about a decade after that, Moab was known as a wild, rough-and-tumble town filled with hard-working and hard-playing miners. It was overflowing with people living in tents and other makeshift homes, and bars were plentiful as were barroom brawls. But in 1964, when the demand for uranium decreased, the largest mine closed and thousands of workers lost their jobs. The wealth and freewheeling ways of Moab disappeared as the town entered into almost two decades of economic downturn.

Moab is still one of the more lively small towns in Utah, but tourism has replaced mining as the economic resource. Arches and Canyonlands national parks lure nearly a million people to the area every year. The unique and colorful geology of the area also calls out to mountain bikers, who love to ride over the humps of slickrock that act like natural highways in the wilderness. Thousands more take four-wheel-drive vehicles into the backcountry to drive the challenging network of roads left from mining days. Still others flock to the shores of the Colorado River, where they set out in rafts to tackle some of the largest whitewater rapids in the country. The city has learned to accommodate guests by building many new motels, restaurants, and other visitor services. What was a sleepy, depressed town in the 1970s and '80s has become the hub of activity and a major tourist destination in the Southwest.

Moab's diverse population makes it a culturally fascinating place to visit. Environmentalists must learn to coexist with ranchers; prodevelopment factions come up against antigrowth forces; and Mormon church leaders struggle with values issues in a predominantly non-Mormon community. Whatever their viewpoint, differences between residents fade briefly in early December at the festive **Electric Light Parade** (☎ 435/259–7814). Merchants, clubs, and other organizations build whimsical floats with Christmas lights for a nighttime parade down Main Street. **Butch Cassidy Days** (☎ 435/259–6226) in June offer traditional fun in honor of the Western outlaw tradition of southeastern Utah. There's a PRCA rodeo, parade, shoot-outs, and other cowboy activities. Each year during Easter week **Jeep Safari** (☎ 435/259–7625) marks the beginning of the tourist season in Moab. More than 2,000 four-wheel-drive vehicles arrive to test their skills on Moab's rugged backcountry roads.

The **Moab Information Center,** right in the heart of town, is the best place to find information on Arches and Canyonlands national parks as well as other destinations in the Four Corners region. It has a wonderful book store operated by Canyonlands Natural History Association. The hours always vary, but during the busiest part of the tourist season it's open until at least 7 PM, and sometimes later; in winter the center is open a few hours each morning and afternoon. ⊠ *Center and Main Sts.* ☎ *435/ 259–8825* ☉ *Mar.–Oct., daily 8–7; Nov.–Feb. hrs vary.*

For a small taste of history in the Moab area, stop by the **Dan O'Laurie Museum.** Ancient and historic Native Americans are remembered in exhibits of sandals, baskets, pottery, and other artifacts. Other displays chronicle the early Spanish expeditions into the area and the history of uranium discovery and exploration. ⊠ *118 E. Center St.* ☎ *435/259–*

7985 ☞ *$2 per person, $5 per family* ☉ *Apr.–Oct., Mon.–Sat. 1–8; Nov.–Mar., Mon.–Thurs. 3–7, Fri. and Sat. 1–7.*

Scott M. Matheson Wetlands Preserve is the best place in the Moab area for bird-watching. This desert oasis is home to hundreds of species, including such treasures as the pied-billed grebe, the cinnamon teal, and the northern flicker. It's also a great place to spot beaver and muskrat playing in the water. A boardwalk winds through the preserve to a viewing shelter. Free nature walks are offered Saturday at 8 AM from March to May and from September to November. To reach the preserve, turn northwest off U.S. 191 at Kane Creek Boulevard and continue northwest approximately 2 mi. ☒ *Off Kane Creek Blvd.* ☎ *435/259–4629* ☞ *Free* ☉ *Daily.*

One of the finest state parks in Utah, **Dead Horse Point State Park** overlooks a sweeping oxbow of the Colorado River, some 2,000 feet below, as well as the upside-down landscapes of Canyonlands National Park. Dead Horse Point itself is a small peninsula connected to the main mesa by a narrow neck of land. As the story goes, cowboys used to drive wild horses onto the point and pen them there with a brush fence. Some were accidentally forgotten and left to perish. There's a modern visitor center and museum as well as a 21-site campground with drinking water and an overlook. ☒ *34 mi from Moab at end of Rte. 313* ☎ *435/259–2614, 800/322–3770 campground reservations* ⊕ *www.stateparks.utah.gov* ☞ *$7 per vehicle* ☉ *Daily 8–6.*

The start of one of the most scenic drives in the country is found 2 mi north of Moab off U.S. 191. The **Colorado River Scenic Byway—Route 128** runs along the Colorado River northeast to I–70. First passing through a high-walled corridor, the drive eventually breaks out into Professor Valley, home of the monoliths of Fisher Towers and Castle Rock, which you may recognize from various car commercials. The byway also passes the single-lane Dewey Bridge, which was in use from 1916 to 1986. Near the end of the 44-mi drive is the tiny town of Cisco. ☒ *Rte. 128, from Moab to Cisco.*

Fodor's Choice
★

If you're interested in Native American rock art, the **Colorado River Scenic Byway—Route 279** is a perfect place to spend a couple of hours. Along the first part of the route you'll see signs reading "Indian Writings." Park only in designated areas to view the petroglyphs on the cliff side of the road. After driving about 18 mi you'll see Jug Handle Arch on the cliff side of the road. After only a few more miles, the road turns into a four-wheel-drive road that takes you into the Island in the Sky District of Canyonlands. Do not continue on this road unless you are in a high-clearance four-wheel-drive vehicle with a full gas tank and plenty of water. Allow about two hours round-trip for this Scenic Byway drive. ☒ *Rte. 279, southwest of Moab.*

Sports & the Outdoors

Moab's towering cliffs and deep canyons can be intimidating and unreachable without the help of a guide. Fortunately, guide services are abundant in Moab. Whether you are interested in a 4X4 expedition into the rugged backcountry, a river-rafting trip, a jet-boat tour on calm water, bicycle tours, rock-art tours, or a scenic air flight, outfitters are ready to accommodate your needs. It's always best to make reservations, but don't hesitate to call if you make a last-minute decision to join an expedition. Cancellations or unfilled trips sometimes make it possible to jump on a tour with short notice.

FOUR-WHEELING There are thousands of miles of four-wheel-drive roads in and around Moab. The rugged terrain, with its hair-raising ledges, steep climbs, and smooth expanses of slickrock is the perfect place for drivers to test their mettle. There are abundant trails suitable for all levels of drivers. Seasoned 4X4 drivers might tackle the daunting **Moab Rim, Elephant Hill,** or **Poison Spider Mesa.** Novice drivers will be happier touring **Long Canyon, Hurrah Pass,** or, for those not afraid of precipitous cliff edges, the famous **Shafer Trail.** All of the routes offer spectacular scenery in the vast desert lands surrounding Moab. Expect to pay around $60 for a half-day tour, $100 for a full-day trip; multiday safaris usually start at around $500. Almost all of Moab's river-running companies also offer four-wheeling excursions. In addition to the companies listed here, *see* River Expeditions *below.*

Coyote Land Tours (⊠ 731 Mulberry La. ☎ 435/259–6649 ⊕ www. coyoteshuttle.com) gives you a big adventure in a Mercedes Unimog, which resembles a Hummer but sits higher off the ground. A half-day tour with this company will leave you begging for more. **Highpoint Hummer Tours** (⊠ 281 N. Main St. ☎ 435/259–2972 or 877/486–6833 ⊕ www.highpointhummer.com) does the driving while you gawk at the scenery as you travel off-road routes in an open-air Hummer.

GOLF **Moab Golf Course** (⊠ 2705 S. East Bench Rd. ☎ 435/259–6488) is undoubtedly one of the most beautiful in the world. The 18-hole course has lush greens set against a red rock sandstone backdrop, a lovely visual combination that's been know to distract even the most focused golfer. Greens fees are $37 for 18 holes, including cart rental.

HIKING Ramble through the desert near a year-round stream or get your muscles pumping with a hike up the side of a steep slickrock slope. Hiking is a sure way to fall in love with the high desert country and there are plenty of hiking trails for all fitness levels. For a great view of the Moab valley and surrounding red rock country, hike up the steep **Moab Rim Trail.** Better yet, ride the chairlift up at the Moab Adventure Park and hike down the trail. For something a little less taxing, hike the shady, cool path of **Negro Bill Canyon,** which is off Route 129. At the end of the trail you'll find giant Morning Glory Arch towering over a cool pool created by a natural spring. If you want to take a stroll through the heart of Moab, hop on the **Mill Creek Parkway,** which winds along the creek from one side of town to the other. It's paved and perfect for bicycles, strollers, or joggers. For a taste of slickrock trails that feels like the backcountry but is easy to access, hike the **Corona Arch Trail,** off Route 279. You'll be rewarded with two large arches hidden from view of the highway. The Moab Information Center carries a free hiking trail guide to these and other trails. The two nearby national parks can get your boots moving in the right direction as well.

MOUNTAIN
BIKING
Fodor'sChoice
★

Moab has earned a well-deserved reputation as the mountain-biking capital of the world, drawing riders of all ages off the pavement and onto rugged four-wheel-drive roads and trails. It's where the whole sport started and draws bikers from all over the world. One of the many popular routes is the **Slickrock Trail**, a stunning area of steep slickrock dunes a few miles east of Moab. Beginners should master the 2½-mi practice loop before attempting the longer, and very challenging, 10⅓-mi loop. More moderate rides can be found on the **Gemini Bridges** or **Monitor and Merrimac** trails, both off U.S. 191 north of Moab. Klondike Bluffs, just north of Moab, is an excellent for novices. The Moab Information Center carries a free biking trail guide. Mountain bike rentals range from $38 for a good bike to $50 for a top-of-the-line workhorse. If you want to go on a guided ride, expect to pay between $120 to $135 per person for a half day, $155 to $190 for a full day, including the bike rental; you can save money by banding together with a larger group to keep the per-person rates down. Several companies, including **Roadrunner Shuttle** (☎ 435/259–9402 ⊕ www.roadrunnershuttle.com), offer shuttles to and from trailheads.

Poison Spider Bicycles (⊠ 497 N. Main St. ☎ 435/259–7882 or 800/635–1792 ⊕ www.poisonspiderbicycles.com) is a fully loaded rental, repair, and gear shop staffed by young, friendly bike experts. **Rim Cyclery** (⊠ 94 W. 100 South St. ☎ 435/259–5333 or 888/304–8219 ⊕ www.rimcyclery.com) practically invented mountain biking. For full-suspension bike rentals and sales, solid advice on trails, and parts, equipment, and gear, this is the oldest bike shop in town.

Nichols Expeditions (⊠ 497 N. Main St., Moab ☎ 435/259–3999 or 800/648–8488 🖷 435/259–2312 ⊕ www.nicholsexpeditions.com), a professionally run company, takes about a dozen multiday bike trips a year into the backcountry of Canyonlands National Park. Departure dates and routes are predetermined, so contact them for a schedule. **Rim Tours** (⊠ 1233 S. U.S. 191 ☎ 435/259–5223 or 800/626–7335 🖷 435/259–3349 ⊕ www.rimtours.com) will take you into the backcountry of the red rock wilderness by bicycle. Destinations include Gemini Bridges, the Slickrock Trail, Klondike Bluffs, and many other locations—including the White Rim Trail in Canyonlands. **Western Spirit Cycling** (⊠ 478 Mill Creek Dr. ☎ 435/259–8732 or 800/845–2453 🖷 435/259–2736 ⊕ www.westernspirit.com) offers fully supported, go-at-your-own-pace multiday bike tours throughout the region.

RIVER
EXPEDITIONS
Fodor'sChoice
★

On the Colorado River northeast of Arches and very near Moab, you can take one of America's most scenic—yet unintimidating—river raft rides. This is the perfect place to take the family or to learn to kayak with the help of an outfitter. The river rolls by the red Fisher Towers as they rise into the sky in front of La Sal Mountains. A day trip on this stretch of the river will take you about 15 mi. Outfitters offer full- or half-day adventures here.

White-water adventures await more adventuresome rafters both upstream and down. Upriver, in narrow, winding Westwater Canyon near the Utah–Colorado border, the Colorado River cuts through the oldest exposed geologic layer on Earth. The result is craggy black granite jutting out of the water with red sandstone walls towering above. This section of the river is rocky and considered highly technical for rafters and kayakers, but it dishes out a great white-water experience in a short period of time. Most outfitters offer this trip as a one-day getaway, but you may also linger in the canyon as long as three days to complete the journey. A permit is required from the BLM in Moab to run Westwater Canyon. Heart-stopping multiday trips through Cataract Canyon are for folks ready for a real adventure.

Adrift Adventures (⊠ 378 N. Main St. ☎ 435/259–8594 or 800/874–4483 ⊕ www.adrift.net) gets you floating the Colorado or Green rivers for either day-long or multiday raft trips. Adrift also offers a unique combination of horse-packing and river trip, as well as motorcoach tours into Arches and 4X4 excursions into Canyonlands. **Canyon Voyages Adventure Company** (⊠ 211 N. Main St. ☎ 435/259–6007 or 800/733–6007 ⊕ www.canyonvoyages.com) is an excellent choice for a day trip on the Colorado River. This friendly, professional company is also the only company that operates a kayaking school for those who want to learn how to run the rapids on their own. You can rent rafts and kayaks here for your own use. Inside the booking office is a great shop that sells river gear, outdoor clothes, hats, sandals, and backpacks. **Moab Adventure Center–Western River Expeditions** (⊠ 225 S. Main St. ☎ 888/622–4097 ⊕ www.westernriver.com) heads out into the backcountry in Hummers or in rafts on the Colorado River. **NAVTEC** (⊠ 321 N. Main St. ☎ 435/259–7983 or 800/833–1278 ⊕ www.navtec.com) has engineered a fast little boat that gets you down the Colorado River and through Cataract Canyon in one day. The company also offers trips lasting up to five days, as well as 4X4 trips into the backcountry of Canyonlands. True, you don't use oars on a four-wheeling adventure, but **OARS** (⊠ 543 N. Main St. ☎ 435/259–5865 or 800/342–5938 ⊕ www.oarsutah.com), a reputable river company, also holds permits to take you into the backcountry of Canyonlands National Park via a comfortable four-wheel-drive vehicle. **Sheri Griffith Expeditions** (⊠ 2231 S. U.S. 191 ☎ 435/259–8229 or 800/332–2439 ⊕ www.griffithexp.com) specializes in big trips in the great canyons of the Colorado and Green rivers. Trips through the white water of Cataract Canyon, Westwater Canyon, and Desolation Canyon on the Green River will leave you knowing you've truly seen the wilderness of canyonlands. You might also enjoy one of their more luxurious expeditions, which make roughing it a little more comfortable. **Tag-A-Long Expeditions** (⊠ 452 N. Main St. ☎ 435/259–8946 or 800/453–3292 ⊕ www.tagalong.com) holds more permits with the National Park Service and has been taking people into Cataract Canyon and Canyonlands longer than any other outfitter in Moab. The company also runs four-wheel-drive expeditions into the backcountry of the park and calm-water excursions on the Colorado River. This is the only outfitter allowed to take you into the park via both water and 4X4—and the good news is that you can do both in one day. Ask about their jet-boat and 4X4 combination trip so you can experience the best of what canyon country has to offer.

Where to Stay & Eat

★ **$$–$$$$** ✕ **Center Café.** This little desert oasis is a fine spot for Mediterranean-inspired cuisine with a contemporary edge. The mood inside is Spanish, complete with a courtyard and made even more lovely by a roaring fireplace when it's cool outside. From grilled black Angus beef tenderloin with caramelized onion and Gorgonzola, to roasted eggplant lasagna with feta cheese and Moroccan olive marinara, there's always something here to make your taste buds go "ah." Be sure to ask for the impressive wine list. ✉ *60 N. 100 West St.* ☎ *435/259–4295* 🖪 *D, MC, V* ⊘ *Closed Dec. 15–Jan. 15. No lunch.*

$–$$$ ✕ **Buck's Grill House.** For a taste of the American West, try the buffalo
Fodor'sChoice meat loaf or elk stew served at this popular dinner spot. The steaks are
★ thick and tender, and the gravies will have you licking your fingers. A selection of Southwestern entrées including duck tamales and buffalo chorizo tacos round out the menu. Vegetarian diners shouldn't despair; there are some tasty choices for them, too. A surprisingly good wine list will complement your meal. Outdoor patio dining with the trickle of a waterfall will end your day perfectly. ✉ *1393 N. Rte. 191* ☎ *435/259–5201* 🖪 *D, MC, V* ⊘ *Closed Sat., Thanksgiving–mid-Feb. No lunch.*

$–$$ ✕ **Jail House Café.** Breakfast here will keep you going long into the afternoon, and since that's all that's offered, it will just have to do. From eggs Benedict to waffles, the menu is guaranteed to fill you up. Housed in what was once the county courthouse, the building held prisoners in the past. Plan your time carefully if you dine here; this is not fast food. ✉ *101 N. Main St.* ☎ *435/259–3900* 🖪 *MC, V* ⊘ *Closed Nov.–Mar. No lunch or dinner.*

¢–$$ ✕ **Eddie McStiff's.** This casual restaurant and microbrewery serves pizzas and zesty Italian specialties to go with the 13 freshly brewed concoctions such as raspberry and blueberry wheat beer and a smooth cream ale. ✉ *57 S. Main St.* ☎ *435/259–2337* 🖪 *MC, V.*

¢–$$ ✕ **La Hacienda.** This locally owned restaurant serves good south-of-the-border meals at an equally good price. The helpings are generous and the service is friendly. And yes, you can order a margarita, too. ✉ *574 N. Main St.* ☎ *435/259–6319* 🖪 *AE, D, MC, V.*

¢–$$ ✕ **Moab Brewery.** This is the restaurant where you'll always find someone to talk to about canyon country adventure: river runners, rock climbers, and locals all hang out here. A huge menu with lots of variety and locally brewed beer makes this a favorite with tourists, too. ✉ *686 S. Main* ☎ *435/259–6333* 🖪 *AE, D, MC, V.*

¢–$ ✕ **Eklecticafe.** This small place is easy to miss but worth searching out for one of the more creative menus in Moab. Breakfast and lunch items include a variety of burritos and wraps, scrambled tofu, Polish sausage, Indonesian satay kebabs, and many fresh, organic salads. On nice days you can take your meal outside to the large covered patio. In winter you'll want to stay inside by the wood-burning stove. ✉ *352 N. Main St.* ☎ *435/259–6896* 🖪 *MC, V* ⊘ *No dinner. No lunch weekends.*

$$$$ 🏨 **Sorrel River Ranch.** This luxury ranch 17 mi from Moab is the ulti-
Fodor'sChoice mate getaway. From its location on the banks of the Colorado River,
★ vistas are spectacular. Rooms are furnished with hefty log beds, tables, and chairs, along with Western art and Native American rugs. You can

choose to relax in the spa and have aromatherapy and a pedicure or go river rafting, mountain biking, or four-wheeling. If you want, you can even bring and board your own horse. ⊠ *Rte. 128, Box K, mile marker 17.5, 84532* ☎ *435/259–4642 or 877/359–2715* 📠 *435/259–3016* ⊕ *www.sorrelriver.com* ⤴ *32 rooms, 27 suites* ⚐ *Restaurant, some in-room hot tubs, kitchenettes, cable TV, some in-room VCRs, pool, gym, outdoor hot tub, spa, boating, mountain bikes, basketball, horseback riding, babysitting, playground, laundry facilities, Internet, meeting rooms; no smoking* ▤ *AE, MC, V.*

★ $$$ 🏨 **Red Cliffs Adventure Lodge.** You can have it all at this gorgeous, classically Western lodge. The Colorado River rolls by right outside your door, and canyon walls reach for the sky in all their red glory; you can gaze at it all from your private river-front patio. Rooms are decidedly Western in flavor, with log furniture, lots of wood, and Saltillo tile. Added attractions include an on-site winery, a movie memorabilia museum, a clay-pigeon shooting range, and horseshoes, as well as guided rafting, hiking, biking, and horseback riding adventures into the desert. ⊠ *Rte. 128, mile marker 14, 84532* ☎ *435/259–2002 or 800/325–6171* ⊕ *www.redcliffslodge.com* ⤴ *89 rooms, 1 suite* ⚐ *Restaurant, room service, kitchenettes, cable TV, in-room VCRs, in-room data ports, pool, gym, outdoor hot tub, horseback riding, horseshoes, hiking, volleyball, shops, laundry facilities* ▤ *AE, D, MC, V* ⧉ *CP.*

$–$$$ 🏨 **Sunflower Hill Bed and Breakfast.** This turn-of-the-20th-century dwelling is tucked away on a quiet neighborhood street and managed by a family that truly values its guests. A charming country feel is accomplished with antiques and farmhouse treasures, as well as well-tended gardens and pathways. ⊠ *185 N. 3rd East St., 84532* ☎ *435/259–2974* 📠 *435/259–3065* ⊕ *www.sunflowerhill.com* ⤴ *10 rooms, 2 suites* ⚐ *In-room hot tubs, cable TV, in-room VCRs, outdoor hot tub, shop, laundry facilities* ▤ *AE, D, MC, V* ⧉ *BP.*

$–$$ 🏨 **Cali Cochita Bed and Breakfast.** One of the first homes built in Moab—and a rare example of the construction that proliferated in 19th-century Moab—this late 1800s adobe has been restored to its classic Victorian style by owners David and Kim Boger. It's in the heart of town, two blocks from Main Street shops and restaurants. Down comforters, plush robes, and hair dryers lend a touch of luxury to smallish rooms decorated with country style. ⊠ *110 S. 200 East St., 84532* ☎ *435/259–4961 or 888/429–8112* 📠 *435/259–4964* ⊕ *www.moabdreaminn.com* ⤴ *3 rooms, 1 suite, 1 cottage* ⚐ *Cable TV, in-room VCRs, some in-room data ports, hot tub; no smoking* ▤ *AE, MC, V* ⧉ *BP.*

$–$$ 🏨 **Dreamkeeper Inn.** Serenity is just a few breaths away at this classy B&B
Fodor'sChoice   in a quiet Moab neighborhood. The home was originally built during
★   the uranium boom days and is a one-level ranch house. The large, shady grounds are filled with flower and vegetable gardens. Each room is uniquely decorated with antiques or Southwestern-style log furnishings. Two cottages off the main house offer a bit more privacy. ⊠ *191 S. 200 East St., 84532* ☎ *435/259–5998* 📠 *435/259–3912* ⊕ *www.dreamkeeperinn.com* ⤴ *6 rooms, 2 cottages* ⚐ *Some in-room hot tubs, some refrigerators, cable TV, some in-room VCRs, pool, hot tub* ▤ *AE, D, MC, V* ⧉ *BP.*

⊙ ¢–$ ⊞ **Red Rock Lodge and Suites.** This affordable, eclectic motel has lots of charm. One building is half of an old motel that was floated down the Colorado River to Moab on a barge. It has been gorgeously renovated with oak stairs, railings, and lots of amenities. Other units are bright and fun, with front porches and Old West appeal. The 12 suites are big enough for families or groups traveling together. The Red Rock building has basic motel rooms but is quiet, safe, and comfortable. All are within a few blocks of downtown restaurants and shops. ⊠ *51 N. 100 West St., 84532* ☎ *435/259–5431 or 877/207–9708* 📠 *435/259–3823* ⊕ *www.red-rocklodge.com* ⇆ *47 rooms, 4 suites* ⚇ *Some kitchenettes, cable TV, some in-room VCRs, in-room data ports, pool, hot tub, some pets allowed; no smoking* ⊟ *AE, D, MC, V.*

WHERE TO CAMP ⚐ **Dead Horse Point State Park Campground.** A favorite of almost every-
⚑ one who has ever camped here, either in RVs or tents, this mesa-top camp-
ground fills up a little later in the day than the national park campgrounds. It is impressively set near the edge of a 2,000-foot cliff above the Colorado River. If you want to pay for your stay with a credit card you must do so during business hours (8–6 daily); otherwise you must pay in cash in the after-hours drop box. ⚇ *Flush toilets, dump station, drinking water, picnic tables, public telephone, ranger station* ⇆ *21 sites* ⊠ *Dead Horse Point State Park, Rte. 313, 18 mi off U.S. 191* ☎ *435/259–2614, 800/322–3770 reservations* ⊕ *www.stateparks.utah.gov* ⊡ *$9* ⊟ *MC, V.*

⊙ ⚐ **Moab Valley RV and Campark.** Near the Colorado River, with a 360-
degree view, this campground seems to get bigger and better every year. There's even a hot tub for relaxing. Just 2 mi from Arches National Park, it's convenient for sightseeing, river rafting, and other area attractions. Plus, it's spotlessly clean. ⚇ *Flush toilets, full hookups, dump station, drinking water, guest laundry, showers, grills, picnic tables, electricity, public telephone, general store, play area, swimming (pool)* ⇆ *62 full hookups, 68 tent sites; 33 cabins* ⊠ *1773 N. U.S. 191, 84532* ☎ *435/259–4469* ⊕ *www.moabvalleyrv.com* ⊡ *$17 tent sites, $26 full hookups, $34–$65 cabins* ⊟ *MC, V.*

Nightlife & the Arts

NIGHTLIFE There's not much in the way of nightlife in Moab, but when there is, it's at the **Moab Brewery** (⊠ 686 S. Main St. ☎ 435/259–6333). Several TVs draw a crowd to the separate barroom and occasionally there's impromptu music. It's definitely a favorite of locals and tourists alike for an evening get-together. On weekends there's live music, dancing, and karaoke at the **Rio Colorado** ⊠ *2 S. 100 West St.* ☎ *435/259–6666.*

⊙ Operating from April to October, **Canyonlands by Night** (⊠ U.S. 191, north of Colorado River bridge ☎ 435/259–5261 ⊕ www.canyonlandsbynight. com) offers an unusual two-hour boat ride on the Colorado River after dark. While illuminating the canyon walls with 40,000 watts, the boat trip includes music and narration highlighting Moab's history, Native American legends, and geologic formations along the river. You can combine the boat trip with a barbecue dinner, too.

THE ARTS **The Moab Arts and Recreation Center** (☎ 435/259–6272) hosts art exhibits featuring local artists every other month as well as concerts, yoga classes, tai chi, Pilates, and dance classes. This historic building, which is right downtown, is the hub of arts activities in Moab.

The **Moab Arts Festival** (☎ 435/259–2742 ⊕ www.moabartsfestival. org/) happens in May, when the area's weather is at its finest. Artists from across the West gather at the Swanny City Park to show their wares, including pottery, photography, and paintings. Live music and lots of food keep everyone happy.

Fodor'sChoice September brings world-class music to red rock country with the **Moab**
★ **Music Festival** (☎435/259–7003 ⊕www.moabmusicfest.org/). Musicians from all over the globe perform primarily classical, jazz, and traditional music in the canyons, desert, and local performance halls. Try the Colorado River Benefit Concert for a once-in-a-lifetime experience. This September event is truly inspiring and truly worth driving great distances to attend.

The music continues to drift across the desert in November when the **Moab Folk Music Festival** (☎ 435/260–2488 ⊕ www.moabfolkfestival. com/) brings favorite folksinger–songwriters to downtown venues.

Shopping

In Moab, shopping opportunities are plentiful and there are art galleries, jewelry stores, and shops carrying T-shirts and souvenirs on every block. If your book shopping goes better with an espresso in your hand, try **Arches Book Company** (⊠ 78 N. Main St. ☎435/259–0782), a warm and lively store where a full coffee bar adds to the friendly ambience, and where you can find a wide selection of titles ranging from best sellers to local authors, as well as maps and guidebooks to the area. **Back of Beyond Books** (⊠ 83 N. Main St. ☎435/259–5154) is anything but mainstream; it carries many alternative titles, an excellent selection of environmental and Native American studies books, and art by local artists. If you forgot anything for your camping, climbing, hiking, or other outdoor adventure, you can get it at **Gearheads** (⊠ 471 S. Main St. ☎ 435/ 259–4327), which is packed not only with essentials, but with hard-to-find things like booties and packs for your dog. **Lema Kokopelli Gallery** (⊠70 N. Main St. ☎435/259–5055) has built a reputation for fair prices on a giant selection of Native American jewelry and other art; everything you buy here will be authentic. For irresistible photographic images of the landscape you'll be seeing, visit **Tom Till Gallery** (⊠ 61 N. Main St. ☎ 435/259–9808).

Arches National Park

3 mi north of Moab via U.S. 191.

In Arches National Park, 5 mi north of Moab, some of the most unimaginable rock formations in the world stand in testimony to the power of the Earth's movement and erosional forces. Giant pinnacles and balanced rocks teeter throughout the red-hue "rockscape" that makes you feel like you've landed on Mars. The park has the largest collection of natural arches in the world—more than 2,000. Although the process by which these spans of red rock were formed is complex, geologists do

HOODOOS & BRIDGES & ARCHES

AFTER A WHILE, the fantastically eroded landscapes and formations found in southern Utah can all begin to look the same. Don't worry. It happens to everyone. A brief course in the geology of the Colorado Plateau can get your vacation back on track and clear up any confusion while you're busy making memories.

An **arch** is an opening created primarily by the ceaseless erosional powers of wind and weather. Airborne sand constantly scours cliff faces; tiny and huge chunks of stone are pried away by minuscule pockets of water as it freezes, expands, and thaws, again and again over the course of thousands or millions of years. Arches are found in all stages, from cavelike openings that don't go all the way through a stone fin to gigantic stone ribbons shaped by an erosional persistence that defies imagination.

Bridges are the product of stream or river erosion. They span what at some time was a water source powerful enough to wear away softer layers of sedimentary stone through constant force and motion. As softer stone is washed away, the harder capstone layers remain in the form of natural bridges.

The most bizarrely shaped formations have the strangest name. **Hoodoos** are chunks of rock chiseled through time into columns or pinnacles. Like all rock formations, hoodoos are constructed of layers and layers of horizontal bands. Each band or stratum has its own composition. When wind or water, particularly in the form of heavy, sporadic rainstorms, goes to work on these pillars, the eventual result is a hoodoo—an eccentric and grotesque formation usually found in the company of other hoodoos.

point to an underlying bed of salt as the main impetus. As this material shifted, fissures formed in the overlying layer of sandstone. Wind and water then eroded this rock into freestanding fins, which were in turn sculpted into the arches and formations seen today. Many of the park's premier sights, including the Courthouse Towers, Balanced Rock, the Windows, and Skyline Arch, are found along the park's paved roads. The main park road runs 18 mi from the entrance to Devils Garden. Branching off the main road are two spurs: one (2½ mi) takes you to the Windows section; the other (1½ mi) leads to the Delicate Arch trailhead and viewpoint, though the arch itself is accessible only on the trail. A few other park highlights, including the Fiery Furnace and Devils Garden, are accessible only by foot as well, though Fiery Furnace can be seen from an overlook.

Exploring Arches National Park

a good tour

You can see the highlights of Arches in a day if you rise early. You'll need to pack plenty of water as there's no food service in the park. Start your tour with a stop at the **Arches Visitor Center** ❸ ▶ to get some information and look around the exhibits. Drive to **Balanced Rock** ❹ for photos and then on to the **Windows Section** ❺, one of the more popular areas.

If you only have one day, you're best off choosing between the 3-mi round-trip hike to famous **Delicate Arch ⑥**, a guided tour into the **Fiery Furnace ⑦**, or a hike into **Devils Garden ⑨** to see Landscape Arch, the park's second most famous arch. If the hike up to Delicate Arch sounds a little too arduous (there is no shade and it is quite steep), then opt for the Delicate Arch Viewpoint instead.

If you have two days, follow the itinerary above, but select two out of the last three options above. If you have three days, you'll have time to see all of the park's most famous features and hikes. You'll also have time to take the kids to **Sand Dune Arch ⑧**, where they can play in the huge sand dunes that surround the hidden arch—but don't let them climb up the arch or jump off its span; many people end up injured here because the sand looks like a soft landing.

What to See

▶ ❸ **Arches Visitor Center.** A stop at the park's visitor center before you drive the switchbacks into the park will do much to make your sightseeing more meaningful. Take time to view the park video, and shop the bookstore for trail guides, books, and maps to enhance to your visit. There's also an audio tour, which illuminates the geologic and human history of the park. Exhibits inform you about geology, natural history, and ancestral Puebloan presence in the Arches area. ⊠ *U.S. 191, at park entrance* ☎ *435/719–2299* ⊙ *Daily 8–4:30; extended hrs Apr.–Oct.*

➍ **Balanced Rock.** This amazing formation is always a favorite stop for visitors to Arches. The formation's total height is 128 feet, with the huge balanced rock rising 55 feet, or nearly six stories, above the pedestal. The balanced rock is estimated to weigh 3,577 tons—the equivalent of about 1,600 full-size automobiles. A short loop (³⁄₁₀ mi) around the base gives you an opportunity to stretch your legs and take photographs. ⊠ *Main Park Rd., 9 mi from entrance.*

➏ **Delicate Arch.** Some more adventurous visitors hike the strenuous, but highly rewarding, 3-mi round-trip route to the park's—and the state's— most famous landmark. The free-standing, red sandstone arch has come to symbolize the magnificent beauty of the state. Plan your walk in the early morning before desert temperatures soar, as there's no shade, and the hike is uphill all the way to the arch. Sunset is also a popular time for this destination as the arch glows brilliant red in the slanting sun. With La Sal Mountains lit by salmon-hue alpenglow and framed by Delicate Arch, postcard perfect photos are almost guaranteed.

Even if you don't plan on hiking up to Delicate Arch, a trip to this trailhead is worth it to see **Wolfe Ranch.** Built in 1906 out of Fremont cottonwoods, this rustic one-room cabin housed the Wolfe family after their first cabin was lost to a flash flood. The family lived in what is now Arches National Park from 1898 to 1910. In addition to the cabin, you'll also see remains of a root cellar and a corral. Even older than these structures is the **Ute rock art panel,** near the Delicate Arch trailhead. About 150 feet past the footbridge and before the trail starts to climb, you can see images of bighorn sheep as well as some smaller images believed to be dogs. To reach the panel, follow the narrow dirt trail along the rock escarpment until you see the interpretive sign. ⊠ *12⁹⁄₁₀ mi from park entrance, 1²⁄₁₀ mi off Main Park Rd.*

➒ **Devils Garden.** At the end of Main Park Road, Devils Garden is ideal for exploring as little or as much as you like. You can choose the level of your adventure by stopping after **Tunnel, Pine Tree** or **Landscape** arches, or you can "get primitive" by heading out on the more rugged, rocky trail to **Partition, Navajo, Wall** and **Double O** arches. On this trail you will get the chance to scale some of the park's famous "fins," towering walls of sandstone that you must travel across in order to get to hidden arches. Dark Angel is the end of the line in Arches National Park. ⊠ *Main Park Rd., 18 mi from park entrance.*

➐ **Fiery Furnace.** If you're up for a grand adventure, sign up for a ranger-guided hike through this section of the park. This expedition into a maze of rock walls and fins is not for the timid walker nor for those afraid of heights, but it does take you into some of the most mysterious and hidden areas of Arches National Park. Walks into the Fiery Furnace are usually offered twice a day (hours vary) and leave from Fiery Furnace viewpoint. Tickets may be purchased for this popular activity up to seven days in advance at the Arches Visitor Center. ⊠ *Fiery Furnace Trailhead,* *off Main Park Rd., about 15 mi from park entrance* 🏷 *$8* ⊙ *Mid-Mar.–Oct., daily.*

❽ Sand Dune Arch Trailhead. Between Fiery Furnace and Devils Garden, this trailhead makes a popular stop for three easy walks into the desert, each with a stunning arch as a reward at the end. Sand Dune Arch is particularly popular with the kids as it's home to a giant sand pile. ⊠ *Main Park Rd., 16 mi from park entrance.*

❺ Windows Section. Many visitors with limited time choose to go only as far as the Windows. It's often the most crowded area of the park as you can easily walk and stand beneath some of the park's most spectacular arches. Here you'll see **North and South Windows, Turrett Arch,** and **Double Arch.** ⊠ *Off Main Park Rd., 11⁷⁄₁₀ mi from entrance.*

Sports & the Outdoors

Getting out into the park will surely cause you to fall in love with this Martian landscape. But remember: you are in a desert environment. Many people succumb to heat and dehydration because they do not drink enough water. Park rangers recommend a gallon of water per day per person. It's also not the place to work on your suntan. Wear long-sleeve shirts, brimmed hats, and sunscreen. To ensure you do not become one of the park's many search and rescue missions, always stay on the trail. This also protects the fragile desert ecosystem. Keep children with you on the trail, away from edges off rock faces, which may be easy to scale but impossible to get down. Check with the Arches visitor center for special ranger-guided hikes or talks.

HIKING There are over half a dozen easy hikes in Arches National Park suitable for almost everyone, as well as some longer ones that require a bit more effort. Park Avenue is a spectacular 1-mi walk that takes you between towering walls of sandstone. Balanced Rock Trail is a quick little 0.3-mi loop around the famous landmark. It's wheelchair accessible to a viewing platform but crosses a rock outcropping for the return. Broken Arch and Sand Dune Arch are reached via an easy 2-mi round-trip walk across open grassland, with the Broken Arch trail turning into deep sand. The Windows Section also offers easy walking to some of the park's largest arches via a well-maintained 1-mi loop.

★ ❻ Delicate Arch Trail. The hike to see the park's most famous freestanding arch up close takes some effort. The 3-mi round-trip trail ascends a steep slickrock slope that offers no shade and is very hot in summer. Allow anywhere from one to three hours for this hike, depending on your fitness level and how long you plan to linger at the arch. For a view of the arch from a distance (but requiring far less work) take the Delicate Arch Viewpoint Trail. It's even possible to see the arch from a wheelchair-accessible route here. ⊠ *13 mi from park entrance, 2²⁄₁₀ mi off main park Rd.*

★ ❾ Devils Garden Trail. This is a longer hike where you can see a number of arches. You will reach Tunnel and Pine Tree arches after only ⁴⁄₁₀ mi on the gravel trail, and Landscape Arch is ⁸⁄₁₀ mi from the trailhead. Past Landscape Arch the trail changes dramatically, increasing in difficulty with many short, steep climbs. ⊠ *18 mi from park entrance on main park Rd.*

★ ❼ **Fiery Furnace Trail.** This challenging trail is best encountered during the ranger-guided walk (⇨ see Fiery Furnace, *above*). There's no marked trail, and the mazelike area can quickly disorient rookies. Ranger-led walks into the Fiery Furnace are usually offered twice daily (hours vary) and leave from Fiery Furnace viewpoint. A hike here is a challenging but fascinating trip through rugged terrain into the heart of Arches. The trail occasionally requires the use of hands and feet to scramble up and through narrow cracks and along narrow ledges above drop-offs. To hike this area on your own you must get a permit at the Arches visitor center ($2). ⊠ *About 15 mi from visitor center, off main park Rd.*

ROCK CLIMBING   Rock climbers travel from across the country to scale the sheer red rock walls of Arches National Park and the surrounding areas. Most climbing routes in the park require advanced techniques. Permits are not required, but you are responsible for knowing park regulations and restricted routes. One popular route in the park is Owl Rock in the Garden of Eden (about 10 mi from the park entrance), which ranges in difficulty from 5.8 to 5.11 on a scale that goes up to 5.13-plus. Many climbing routes are available in the Park Avenue area, a little over 2 mi from the visitor center. These routes are also extremely difficult climbs. Before climbing, stop at the Arches visitor center and talk with a ranger.

Where to Camp

🔺 **Devils Garden Campground.** Arches National Park offers one of the most gorgeous campgrounds in the West. The site makes the most of its natural setting with sites tucked away in red rock outcroppings. From March through October, when the campground is always full, you are required to preregister for your site at the visitor center between 7:30 and 8 AM or at the entrance station after 8 AM. Up to 28 of the sites may be reserved through a national reservation system. Reservations must be made no less than four days and no more than 240 days in advance. An additional $9 booking fee will be charged (⊕ www.reserveusa.com ☎ 877/444–6777 or 518/885–3639). Off-season, sites are available on a first-come, first-served basis. A few sites will accommodate an RV. ♿ *Flush toilets, pit toilets, drinking water, fire grates, fire pits, grills, picnic tables* 🛏 *52 sites* ⊠ *Main Park Rd., 18 mi from park entrance* ☎ *435/719–2299* ⊕ *www.nps.gov/arch* 🛏 *$10.*

Shopping

Arches Visitor Center Bookstore (⊠ Off U.S. 191, at park entrance ☎ 435/259–8161 or 435/259–6003, 800/840–8978 to order books) is operated by Canyonlands Natural History Association and is the place to buy maps, guidebooks, and material about the natural and cultural history of Arches National Park.

Arches National Park Essentials

ADMISSION

Admission to the park is $10 per vehicle and $5 per person on foot, motorcycle, or bicycle, good for seven days.

EMERGENCIES

In the event of an emergency, call 911, report to a visitor center, or contact a park ranger. The nearest hospital is in Moab.

TOURS & CLASSES
Every evening mid-March through October, a park ranger presents a Campfire Program at Devils Garden Campground. It's a great way to learn about subjects such as mountain lions, the Colorado River, human history in Arches National Park, or the night life of animals. Stargazing is a favorite activity, too. A Junior Ranger program is available for kids 6–12 years old.

VISITOR INFORMATION
🛈 Arches National Park Headquarters ⊠ N. U.S. 191, Moab 84532 ☎ 435/719–2299 or 435/259–2200 ⊕ www.nps.gov/arch

La Sal Mountains

❿ *8 mi south of Moab via U.S. 191.*

Although Moab is best known for its slickrock desert, it's also the gateway to the second-highest mountain range in the state—the 12,000-foot La Sal Mountains. Long a favorite stomping ground of locals, the often snowcapped peaks have been discovered by out-of-towners as a welcome retreat from the summer heat. You can picnic in a meadow or take one of many alpine hikes in this largely undiscovered area.

On Old Airport Road (a left turnoff from U.S. 191) 8 mi south of Moab, the 62-mi **La Sal Mountain Loop** climbs over the laccolithic mountain range, affording some great vistas of the valley. The road enters La Sal Division of the Manti–La Sal National Forest just as the dominant red rock cliffs east of Moab begin to alternate with sagebrush and juniper flats. Passing through the cool heights of La Sal Mountains, the loop winds north through red rock country to Castle Valley and an intersection with Route 128. The road is paved, except for a couple of gravel sections, but it does have steep switchbacks, and it does become snow-packed in the winter. Check with the National Forest Service before embarking on winter driving on this road. ⊠ *U.S. 191, 8 mi south of Moab* ☎ *435/259–7155 or 435/637–2817* ⊕ *www.fs.fed.us/r4/mantilasal* ⊙ *Year-round.*

� **Hole 'n the Rock** is a 14-room, 5,000-square-foot home carved into a solid rock wall. It would be just another funky roadside attraction if it didn't represent 20 years of toil for Albert and Gladys Christensen. ⊠ *12 mi south of Moab on U.S. 191* ☎ *435/686–2250* ☞ *$2.50* ⊙ *June–Sept., daily 8–8; Oct.–May, daily 9–5.*

The giant roadside **Wilson Arch** makes a great photo stop. In Moab you can still find old photos of an airplane flying through this arch. No one has tried the stunt lately, probably because it's now illegal. ⊠ *22 mi south of Moab on U.S. 191.*

⎧ off the
beaten
path ⎭ **CANYON RIMS RECREATION AREA –** With a few hours to spare, you can enjoy two remarkable canyon country vistas. Turn off U.S. 191 at a point centered between Moab and Monticello (about 27 mi south of Moab and 26 mi north of Monticello), and the paved Needles Overlook Road runs 22 mi west to Needles Overlook, which takes in the southern end of Canyonlands National Park. Less than 20 mi farther on a good, graded road is the Anticline Overlook, which encompasses the Colorado River, Dead Horse Point, and other locales to the north.

Sports & the Outdoors

Once snow flies, portions of La Sal Mountain Loop road are impassable, but a well-maintained hut-to-hut system, operated by **Tag-A-Long Expeditions** (⊠ 452 N. Main St., Moab ☎ 435/259–8946 or 800/453–3292 ⊕ www.tagalong.com) makes this a wonderful place for cross-country skiing for those of moderate to expert ability. Since roads at the top of the mountain are impassable to cars in winter, you drive to the ski trail's parking lot, and then Tag-A-Long snowcats drop you and your supplies off at one of the two huts for $65. Lodging in the huts is $30 per person per night. Should you require subsequent snowcat transport, it's an additional $150 per day. At the end of your expedition, you can ski back to the mountain-top trailhead and parking lot, where you get your own vehicle for the ride back to town. Marked routes link the three huts.

Where to Stay

$–$$ 🖫 **Mt. Peale Resort.** This outlying guest ranch is at the foothills of the snowcapped La Sal Mountains. The inn features five cozy rooms with homey decor, and the four cabins each have three bedrooms. A hot tub will feel great after a day of snowshoeing (you can rent snowshoes) or cross-country skiing, and if your muscles still need a little help, an on-site massage therapist will do the trick. Hearty breakfasts of multigrain waffles, fruit, and yogurt will start your day in a healthy way. ⊠ *1415 East Hwy. 46, Old La Sal, 84530* ☎ *435/259–5505* 🖷 *435/259–8879* ⊕ *www.mtpeale.com* 🖙 *5 rooms, 4 cabins* ⚇ *Kitchens, hot tub, massage, no room phones, some room TVs, some in-room VCRs* ▤ *AE, D, MC, V* ⦿❙ *BP.*

Canyonlands National Park

Island in the Sky 32 mi southwest of Moab via U.S. 191 and Rte. 313; Needles District 76 mi southwest of Moab via U.S. 191 and Rte. 211.

The saying "you can't get there from here" was coined in response to landscape such as that found in Canyonlands National Park. Thousands of miles of canyons have been cut into the Earth by the Green and Colorado rivers making overland travel difficult, if not impossible. Encompassing some 500 square mi of rugged desert terrain, Canyonlands National Park is naturally divided by the Colorado and Green rivers into three distinct land districts and the river district. Although the Needles and Maze districts are accessible from points farther south and west, the Island in the Sky District is reached directly from Moab. Unless you have several days, you will likely have to choose between the Island in the Sky District or the Needles District—and they are distinctly different in character. Beyond the well-traveled Island in the Sky and Needles districts, only the wildest visitors walk in the footsteps of Butch Cassidy in the Maze District, for it is accessible only by four-wheel-drive vehicles. Other adventurers tackle the rivers of Canyonlands, which are

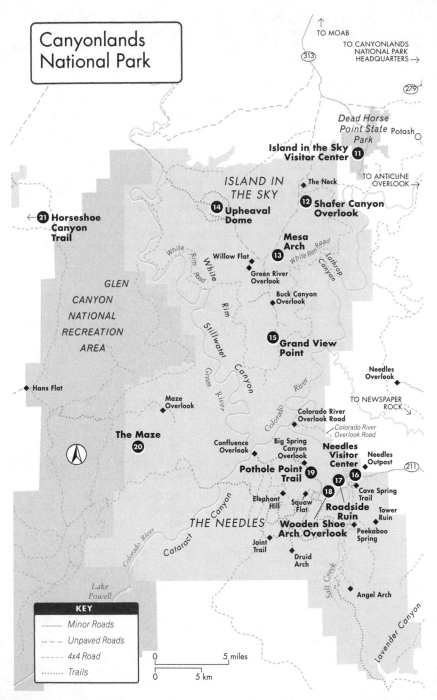

Canyonlands National Park

TO MOAB

TO CANYONLANDS
NATIONAL PARK
HEADQUARTERS →

313

279

*Dead Horse
Point State
Park* Potash

**Island in the Sky
Visitor Center** 11

*ISLAND IN
THE SKY*

The Neck

TO ANTICLINE
OVERLOOK →

14 **Upheaval
Dome**

12 **Shafer Canyon
Overlook**

← 21 **Horseshoe
Canyon
Trail**

**Mesa
Arch**

13

White Rim Road

*GLEN
CANYON
NATIONAL
RECREATION
AREA*

White

Rim

Road

Willow Flat

Green River
Overlook

*Lathrop
Canyon*

White

Rim

Buck Canyon
Overlook

15 **Grand View
Point**

Stillwater

Canyon

Green River

Needles
Overlook

♦ Hans Flat

Maze
Overlook

Colorado

River

TO NEWSPAPER
ROCK →

The Maze

20

Colorado River
Overlook Road

*Colorado River
Overlook Road*

Confluence
Overlook

Big Spring
Canyon Overlook

**Needles
Visitor
Center**

Needles
Outpost

211

**Pothole Point
Trail** 19

16

17

Cave Spring
Trail

Elephant
Hill

Squaw
Flat

18 **Roadside
Ruin**

Tower
Ruin

THE NEEDLES

Cataract

Canyon

**Wooden Shoe
Arch Overlook**

Peekaboo
Spring

Colorado River

Joint
Trail

Druid
Arch

Salt Creek

*Lake
Powell*

Angel Arch

Lavender Canyon

KEY	
——	*Minor Roads*
– – –	*Unpaved Roads*
·····	*4x4 Road*
·······	*Trails*

0   5 miles
0   5 km

as untamed and undammed as when John Wesley Powell explored them in the mid-1800s.

Exploring Canyonlands National Park

a good tour

Be prepared for your trip to Canyonlands because there are no services, including gas or food, inside the large park. The Maze is more than 100 mi from Moab, and roads in this part of the park—suitable only for rugged, high-clearance, four-wheel-drive vehicles—wind for hundreds of miles through the canyons. Within the parks, safety and courtesy mandate that you always park only in designated pull-outs or parking areas.

If you have one day, a good place to start is the Island in the Sky District at the **Island in the Sky Visitor Center ⓫**, where you can watch the orientation film and look at the park exhibits before heading out for more exploration. Make your first stop along the main park road at **Shafer Canyon Overlook ⓬**. A short walk takes you out on a finger of land and gives you views over both sides into the canyon. Drive next to **Mesa Arch ⓭**, where you should grab your camera and a bottle of water for the short hike to the arch perched on the edge of a cliff. Then head to the parking lot for **Upheaval Dome ⓮**. Hike to the first viewpoint, and if you have more energy and a little sense of adventure, continue to the second. You'll probably still have the time and will power to drive to **Grand View Point ⓯** and stroll along the edge of the rim to see how many landmarks you can spot in the distance.

If you have two days, spend your first day as above and then bed down in Moab for the night. The next morning make the 76-mi drive to the southern portion of the park, the Needles District. On the way into the Needles area, stop and visit **Newspaper Rock.** Enjoy the classic western views of mountains, cattle ranches, and sagebrush flats until you reach the **Needles Visitor Center ⓰**. A stop here will orient you, and then you can head out into the park, making your first stop at **Roadside Ruin ⓱**. This is a short, 20-minute walk from the main park road. A few miles farther down the road is the **Wooden Shoe Arch Overlook ⓲**, which is well signposted. A few miles beyond that is the trailhead for the **Pothole Point Trail ⓳**, an easy hike with dramatic views. Don't miss Cave Springs Trail, which takes you down to an old cowboy camp. It's a slightly more difficult hike than the others, with some ladders to negotiate, but is one of the highlights of hiking in the park.

If you have three days, after exploring the sites above, camp at the Squaw Flat Campground and get up the next morning to hike the Joint Trail. This popular hike is part of a loop system that allows you to make your hike as long or short as you like. You'll find yourself hiking through narrow cracks in rock walls. It's the closest thing you can get to a slot canyon without going deep into the backcountry.

With more than three days, the truly adventurous can visit **The Maze ⓴**, the park's most remote section. You must have a four-wheel-drive vehicle and a permit from the National Park Service. An alternative is to hire a local outfitter to take you on an overnight expedition into the Maze District. Another isolated section of the park is the **Horseshoe Canyon**

Trail ㉑, where the highlight of the moderately strenuous hike is one of the best rock art panels in North America.

What to See

ISLAND IN THE
SKY
From any of the park overlooks at the Island in the Sky District, you can see for miles—sometimes as far as the San Juan Mountains in Colorado—and look down thousands of feet to canyon floors. Chocolate-brown canyons are capped by white rock and deep red monuments rise nearby.

⑮ **Grand View Point.** From here you can take in spectacular views of the meandering Colorado and Green rivers, the sandstone pinnacles of the Needles District far to the south, and the labyrinths of the Maze District to the southwest. ⊠ *Island in the Sky Rd., 12 mi from park entrance.*

⑪ **Island in the Sky Visitor Center.** When you arrive in the park, stop in at the visitor center to watch the 15-minute orientation film and browse the books, maps, and postcards. If it's wildflower season, take time to look through the exhibit identifying desert flowers with which you might not be familiar. ⊠ *Past park entrance on Island in the Sky Rd.* ☏ *435/259–4712* ☉ *Daily 8–4:30; extended hrs Apr.–Oct.*

⑬ **Mesa Arch.** This arch, a favorite among photographers, is reached by hiking a ¼-mi trail. The arch frames the canyons that stretch to the horizon as far as the eye can see. Spires and castles rise out of the desert. Peer off the edge of rock beneath the arch and you're looking down about 1,000 feet. A number of scenic overlooks, each of which is precariously perched at land's end, are accessed by 20 mi of paved road. ⊠ *Island in the Sky Rd., 6 mi south of park entrance.*

⑫ **Shafer Canyon Overlook.** From this overlook, you gaze down upon the twisted Shafer Trail—an early 1900s cattle route that was later upgraded for high-clearance vehicles. ⊠ *Main Park Rd., across road from Island in the Sky Visitor Center.*

⑭ **Upheaval Dome.** A detour here introduces you to a whole new world of mystery as you gaze upon this colorful crater, which geologists have speculated may be the site of a meteor crash. ⊠ *Upheaval Dome Rd., 11 mi from park entrance.*

THE NEEDLES
DISTRICT
One of America's premier hiking areas, the Needles District is a popular destination for backpackers. It's also home to a large concentration of Ancestral Puebloan (formerly known as the Navajo word "Anasazi") dwellings and rock art. In this area of Canyonlands you are driving and walking among the needles and buttes, rather than looking out over them as you do in the Island in the Sky. Pink, orange, and red rock is layered with white rock and stand in spires and pinnacles around grassy meadows. Extravagantly red mesas and buttes interrupt the horizon, looking like a picture postcard of the old West.

⑯ **Needles Visitor Center.** This gorgeous building that blends into the landscape is worth seeing, even if you don't need the books, trail maps, or other information available inside. ⊠ *Needles District Rd., less than 1 mi from park entrance* ☏ *435/259–4711* ☉ *Daily 8–4:30; extended hrs Apr.–Oct.*

⑲ Pothole Point Trail. This is an especially good stop after a rainstorm, which fills the potholes with water. Stop to study the communities of tiny creatures, including fairy shrimp, that thrive in the slickrock hollows. You'll discover dramatic views of the Needles and Six Shooter Peak, too. The easy ⁶⁄₁₀-mi round-trip walk takes about 45 minutes. There's no shade, so wear a hat. ⊠ *Needles District Rd., about 9 mi from park entrance.*

⑰ Roadside Ruin. For a look at an Ancestral Puebloan granary, hop out of your car and take a 20-minute walk to this easy-to-reach ruin. There's only one short climb up over some slickrock. The views of the deep red mesas that surround the park are another reason to make this stop. ⊠ *Needles District Rd., less than 1 mi from park entrance.*

⑱ Wooden Shoe Arch Overlook. Stop at this overlook to see if you can find the tiny window in the rock that looks very much like a wooden shoe with a turned up toe. You won't have to find it on your own; there's a marker on the park road. ⊠ *Needles District Rd., about 5 mi from park entrance.*

off the beaten path

NEWSPAPER ROCK – Although not within the confines of Canyonlands National Park itself, Newspaper Rock is an easy stop along Route 211, on the way into or out of the Needles District. Beginning 2,000 years ago, inhabitants of this region began etching cryptic images on a large rock face. In the centuries following, subsequent chapters of an undecipherable history were added, resulting in an impressive collection of petroglyphs that archaeologists cite as one of the most comprehensive in the Southwest. You'll find an interpretive trail and small campground at the rock, all kept up by the Bureau of Land Management. ⊠ *12 mi west of U.S. 191 on Rte. 211* ☎ *435/587–2141 Bureau of Land Management Monticello office.*

THE MAZE DISTRICT
⑳ Of the three districts within Canyonlands National Park, the Maze is by far the most remote. A scrambled collection of sandstone canyons, the Maze is one of the most appropriately named features in southern Utah. For the truly hard-core off-road enthusiast, the Maze offers ample adrenaline-inducing drives. Just to get to Hans Flat Ranger Station, the entrance to the Maze, you must drive 46 mi on a signed but unimproved dirt road that is sometimes impassable to two-wheel-drive vehicles. Stop at the station for permits, books, and maps before you strike out into the wilderness. The Maze is not generally a destination for a day trip, so you'll have to purchase an overnight backcountry permit for $30. At the station there's a pit toilet, but no water, food, or services of any kind. Past Hans Flat, you'll need a high-clearance, four-wheel-drive vehicle to access the Maze. ⊠ *46 mi east of Rte. 24; 21 mi south and east of Y-junction and Horseshoe Canyon kiosk on dirt Rd.* ☎ *435/259–2652 Maze Ranger Station* ⊙ *Daily 8–4:30.*

HORSESHOE CANYON UNIT
㉑
Fodor'sChoice
★
Horseshoe Canyon Trail. Plan carefully if you want to hike in Horseshoe Canyon. This isolated annex of Canyonlands National Park is a bumpy ride on a washboarded dirt road followed by a 6½-mi round-trip hike. Your destination is the Great Gallery, considered by some to be the most significant rock art panel in North America. The hike is moderately stren-

uous, with a steep 750-foot drop into the canyon and a corresponding climb out on the return trip. Allow at least six hours for the trip and take a gallon of water per person. There's no camping allowed in the canyon, although you can camp on top near the parking lot. From April through October, you can join a park ranger for a guided hike of Horseshoe Canyon, which is offered weekends at 9 AM. Walks depart from the West Rim parking lot, which is on a dirt road that may be impassable to two-wheel-drive vehicles in bad weather. ⊠ *32 mi east of Rte. 24, Maze* ☎ *435/259–2652 Maze Ranger Station.*

Sports & the Outdoors

In Canyonlands you need a permit for overnight backpacking, four-wheel-drive camping, mountain-bike camping, four-wheel-drive day use in Horse and Lavender canyons (Needles District), and river trips. Contact the park headquarters for further information.

BICYCLING The only cycling in Canyonlands National Park is on existing roads. There's little vehicular traffic so you might enjoy a tour along the main Needles District Road, which is also fairly flat. More traffic and lots of hills and curves make the main Island in the Sky Road a little more hazardous. Opt instead for the unpaved roads in either district, but understand that you are sharing the road with four-wheel-drive vehicles, and you may have to eat some dust from time to time. Many outfitters in Moab offer guided trips or support vehicles for a safe pedal tour of the park. You can also rent bikes while in town. *See* ⇨ Four-Wheeling, *below* for more routes. *See* ⇨ Mountain Biking *in* Moab, *above,* for outfitters.

White Rim Road. Mountain bikers all over the world like to brag that they've ridden the 112 mi through the Island in the Sky district. The trail's fame is well-deserved: it traverses steep roads, broken rock, and ledges as well as long stretches that wind through the canyons and look down onto others. There's always a good chance you'll see bighorn sheep here, too. Permits are not required for day use, but if you're biking White Rim without an outfitter you'll need careful planning and backcountry reservations—make them as far in advance as possible. Note that there is no water on this route. White Rim Road starts at the end of Shafer Trail near Musselman Arch. ⊠ *Off Island in the Sky Rd., about 1 mi from entrance, then about 11 mi on Shafer Trail; or off Potash Rd. [Rte. 279] at Jug Handle Arch turnoff about 18 mi from U.S. 191, then about 5 mi on Shafer Trail.*

FOUR-WHEELING Nearly 200 mi of challenging backcountry roads lead to campsites, trailheads, and natural and cultural features in Canyonlands. All of the roads require high-clearance, four-wheel-drive vehicles, and many are inappropriate for inexperienced drivers. Especially before you tackle the Maze, be sure that your four-wheel-drive skills are well honed and that you are capable of making basic road and vehicle repairs. Carry at least one full-size spare tire, extra gas, extra water, a shovel, a high-lift jack, and—October through April—chains for all four tires. Double-check to see that your vehicle is in top-notch condition, because you definitely don't want to break down in the interior of the park: towing expenses can exceed $1,000. For overnight four-wheeling trips you must purchase a $30 permit, which you can reserve in advance by contacting Canyonlands National Park reservations. Cyclists share all roads, so be aware and cautious of their presence. Vehicular traffic traveling uphill has the right-of-way. It's best to check at the visitor center for current road conditions before taking off into the backcountry. *See* ⇨ Four-Wheeling *in Moab, above* for outfitters.

Colorado River Overlook Road. For a "short" four-wheel-drive experience, you might try this route. The first half of this road is fairly easy. The second half, however, deteriorates rapidly, with a few large rocks and stair-step drops in the last 1½ mi. Many people prefer to walk the last part of the road to the overlook, which has no guard rails, and gives you wonderful views of the Colorado River. The road is about 11 mi round-trip and takes about five hours to drive. ⊠ *Near Needles visitor center.*

Elephant Hill. This steep road in the Needles District is such an intimidating route that many people get out and walk while experienced drivers tackle the steep grades, loose rock, and stair-step drops. To negotiate some of the tight turns you have to back up on steep cliffs. Beyond the elephant's hump, the road remains equally challenging. From Elephant Hill trailhead to Devil's Kitchen it's 3½ mi; from the trailhead to the Confluence Overlook, a popular destination, it's a 16-mi round-trip and requires at least eight hours. ⊠ *Off Needles Rd., 7 mi from park entrance.*

Flint Trail. This is the most used road in the Maze District, but don't let that fool you into thinking it's smooth sailing. It's very technical, with 2 mi of switchbacks that drop down the side of a cliff face. From Hans Flat to the end of the road at the Doll House it's 41 mi, a drive that takes about seven hours one-way. From Hans Flat to the Maze Overlook it's 34 mi. At the journey's end, you will find not only a wonderful view of the Maze but also a trail of sorts that runs to the bottom. ⊠ *The Maze.*

Horse Canyon–Peekaboo Trails. Know what you're doing if you venture onto these trails. This route traverses a protected canyon up Salt Creek Wash to ancient Native American rock art and ruin sites. The two roads travel along the canyon bottom, where deep sand, deep water, and quicksand are common. The first stretch, Peekaboo Trail, leads to Peekaboo Spring, where vehicle campsites are near some great rock art. Beyond that, Horse Canyon Trail passes several arches and Tower Ruin, one of the park's best-preserved pieces of ancient architecture. Take binoculars to get a good view of it. It is 5½ mi from the trailhead to Tower Ruin. Past Tower Ruin, you can travel only about 3 mi more before you encounter a boulder that has to be driven over, causing your vehicle to tip and leave its paint on the opposite wall. You must purchase a $5 permit to make the Horse Canyon–Peekaboo drive; only 10 private vehicles are allowed into the area each day. ⊠ *Cave Springs Rd., through gate at end, 1 mi from Needles entrance.*

Lavender Canyon. You won't hear much about this road because only eight private vehicles are allowed into this area each day. You'll be able to see many arches and archaeological sites from this rarely used road, which follows a canyon bottom where you may encounter deep sand,

CANYONLANDS HIKING CHART

	Grade	Miles (one way)	Elevation Gain	Open Info	Shuttle Access	Toilet/Restroom	Hiking Level	Trail Conditions
Aztec Butte Trail	Level/incline	1 mile	225 ft	Year-round			Beginner	Maintained
Cave Spring Trail	Level with rocky, uneven surfaces, some rocky climbs, some ladders	0.3 miles	N/A	Year-round			Beginner	Maintained
Grand View Point Trail	Level	1 mile	No elevation change	Year-round		Y (Trailhead)	Beginner	Maintained, partially paved
Joint Trail	Level	5.5 miles	No elevation change			Y (Trailhead)	Intermediate/Advanced	Maintained
Slickrock Trail	Level/Inclines/Uneven surface	1.2 miles	N/A	Year-round			Beginner/Intermediate	Maintained, rock surface
Upheaval Dome Overlook Trail	Steep	.5 miles	50 ft	Year-round		Y (Trailhead)	Intermediate	Maintained
Whale Rock Trail	Steep	.5 miles	100 ft	Year-round			Intermediate	Maintained

deep water, and quicksand in addition to two major creek crossings with steep banks. Allow all day for the 40-mi round-trip. The park requires drivers to obtain a $5 permit for day use; there's no vehicle camping allowed in this canyon. Do not enter if it has been raining or if rain threatens. ⊠ *Off Rte. 211, outside Needles entrance.*

HIKING With relatively few visitors each year, Canyonlands National Park is an excellent place to get out and hike. There's no better place to saturate yourself in the intoxicating colors, smells, and textures of the desert. Many of the trails are long, rolling routes over slickrock and sand in landscapes dotted with juniper, pinyon, and sagebrush. Canyonlands is known as a backpacking park, and many trails require a full day or more, but you will also find a dozen or more short trails to explore on day trips. You need a permit for overnight backpacking; contact Canyonlands National Park reservations.

Aztec Butte Trail. Chances are good you'll enjoy a hike here in solitude. This Island in the Sky trail begins level, then climbs up a steep slope of slickrock. The highlight of the 2-mi round-trip hike is the chance to see ancestral Puebloan granaries. ⊠ *Upheaval Dome Rd., about 6 mi from Island in the Sky entrance.*

★ ☺ **Cave Spring Trail.** To visit a unique historic cowboy camp, see some prehistoric Native American petroglyphs, and enjoy great views along the way, take time to hike this fairly easy trail. About half of the trail is in shade, as it meanders under overhangs. Slanted, bumpy slickrock make this hike more difficult than others, and two ladders, which are easy to navigate, make the ⁶⁄₁₀-mi round-trip walk even more of an adventure. Allow about 45 minutes. ⊠ *Cave Springs Rd., 2⁶⁄₁₀ mi from Needles entrance.*

Grand View Point Trail. Everyone should explore this popular trail. The trail itself is fairly level and not too challenging, but you'll have some of the grandest views in the world. The trail is 2 mi round-trip and meanders along the rim overlooking the vast canyons. Most people just stop at the overlook and drive on, so the trail is not as crowded as you might think. ⊠ *Island in the Sky Rd., 12 mi from park entrance.*

Joint Trail. This well-traveled path is a good summer hike. Part of the Chesler Park Loop, this popular trail follows a series of deep, narrow fractures in the rock. A shady spot in summer, it will give you good views of the Needles formations for which the district is named. The loop travels briefly along a four-wheel-drive road and is 11 mi round-trip; allow at least five hours to complete the hike. ⊠ *Elephant Hill Trailhead, off Needles District Rd., 7 mi from park entrance.*

Slickrock Trail. If you find yourself on this trail in summer, make sure you're wearing a hat, because you won't find any shade along the 2⁴⁄₁₀-mi round-trip trek across slickrock. This is one of the few frontcountry sites where you might see bighorn sheep. ⊠ *Needles District Rd., about 10 mi from park entrance.*

Upheaval Dome Trail. Decide for yourself whether Upheaval Dome is an eroded salt dome or a meteorite crash. It's worth the steep hike to see this formation. ⊠ *Upheaval Dome Rd., 11 mi from Island in the Sky entrance.*

★ ☺ **Whale Rock Trail.** If you've been hankering to walk across some of that pavement-smooth stuff they call slickrock, hike this route. This 1-mi round-trip adventure, complete with handrails to help you make the tough 100-foot climb, takes you to the very top of the whale's back. Once you get there, you are rewarded with great views of Upheaval Dome and Trail Canyon. ⊠ *Upheaval Dome Rd., 11 mi from Island in the Sky entrance.*

RIVER EXPEDITIONS The Colorado River is at the very heart of Canyonlands National Park, and seeing the park from a boat on the river is a treat you won't soon forget. Traveling with one of Moab's many outfitters who offer guided trips through the park via the river saves you the hassle of getting the required reservations and permit from the park service.*See* ⇨ River Expeditions *in* Moab, *above* for outfitters.

Most people enjoy the long stretches of **flatwater rafting** by riding with an outfitter in a large, stable jet boat. The pace is relaxing and the views truly unforgettable. Self-guided canoe trips are popular on the Green River, but you must obtain a permit from the park headquarters in advance.

Some of the best **white-water rafting** in the United States is on the stretch of the Colorado River between the Maze and the Needles District; this part of the river rivals the Grand Canyon for adrenaline-pumping rapids. The canyon cuts through the belly of Canyonlands, where you can see this amazing wilderness area in its most pristine form. The water calms a bit in summer but still offers enough thrills for most people. Outfitters will take you for the ride of your life in this wild canyon, where the river drops more steeply than anywhere else on the Colorado (in ¾ mi, the river drops 39 feet). You can join an expedition lasting anywhere from one to six days. Experts who want to travel on their own need to purchase a permit well in advance.

ROCK CLIMBING Canyonlands and many of the surrounding areas draw climbers from all over the world. Permits are not required, but because of the sensitive archaeological nature of the park, it's imperative that you stop at the visitor center to pick up regulations pertaining to the park's cultural resources. Popular climbing routes include Moses and Zeus Towers in Taylor Canyon, and Monster Tower and Washerwoman Tower on the White Rim Road. Like most routes in Canyonlands, these climbs are for experienced climbers only.

Where to Camp

Permits are required for backcountry camping. Contact the park headquarters for reservations and information on the permit system.

★ ⚠ **Squaw Flat Campground.** Squaw Flat may well be the best campground in the national park system. The sites are spread out in two different areas, giving each site almost unparalleled privacy. Each site has a rock wall at its back, and shade trees. The sites are filled on a first-come, first-served basis. ♿ *Flush toilets, drinking water, fire pits, picnic tables*

25 sites ⊠ Needles District Rd., about 5 mi from park entrance ☎ 435/259–7164 ▦ $10.

🔥 **Willow Flat Campground.** From this little campground on a mesa top, you can walk to spectacular views of the Green River. Most sites have a bit of shade from juniper trees. To get to Willow Flat you have to travel down a rough, washboarded road with tight and tricky turns. Since the drive is so difficult and only two sites are really suitable for RVs, RVers might prefer another campground. It's filled on a first-come, first-served basis only. ♿ *Pit toilets, drinking water, fire pits, picnic tables ⚑ 12 sites ⊠ Off Island in the Sky Rd., about 9 mi from park entrance ☎ 435/259–4712 ▦ $5.*

Shopping
Needles Visitor Center Bookstore (⊠ Needles District Rd., about 2 mi from park entrance ☎ 435/259–4711, 435/259–6003 to order books) sells high-quality books, maps, posters, postcards, videos, and all sorts of guidebooks to Canyonlands at this great little store operated by Canyonlands Natural History Association.

Canyonlands National Parks Essentials

ADMISSION
Admission to the park is $10 per vehicle and $5 per person on foot, motorcycle, or bicycle, good for seven days. Your Canyonlands pass is good for all the park's districts. There's no entrance fee to the Maze District of Canyonlands.

EMERGENCIES
In the event of an emergency, call 911, report to a visitor center, or contact a park ranger. The nearest hospital is in Moab.

TOURS & CLASSES
Both the Island in the Sky and Needles districts have good education programs. The Grand View Point Geology Talk will introduce you to the geology that created Canyonlands. The talks are generally offered twice-daily between April and October; check at the Island in the Sky visitor centers for times and locations. For kids interested in learning more about Canyonlands National Park, you can stop at either park visitor center and ask for the free Junior Ranger booklet. Designed for children ages 6 to 12, it's full of activities, word games, drawings, and educational material about the park and the wildlife. Kids can earn a Junior Ranger badge by completing the booklet, attending a ranger program or watching the park slide program—and one more environment-friendly task—gathering a bag of litter or taking in 20 aluminum cans to be recycled. Rangers at the Needles District created Discovery Packs. The pack contains many useful items including binoculars, a hand lens, a naturalist guide, and a notebook. Before you set out for the day, stop by the Needles visitor center and ask for one. A small fee and deposit are required.

VISITOR INFORMATION
🚩 **Canyonlands National Park** Park Headquarters ⊠ 2282 W. Resource Blvd., Moab 84532 ☎ 435/719–2313, 435/259–4351 Backcountry Reservation Office ⊕ www.nps.gov/cany.

TRAIL OF THE ANCIENTS

As you head toward Monticello, you are not only entering Mormon Country and the Four Corners Region of the United States, but approaching what is known as the "Trail of the Ancients." Route 95 is designated as such because it's rich with ancient Indian dwellings. Deep in the canyons of this area are petroglyphs, pictographs, and artifacts of the Ancestral Puebloan peoples. Enjoy looking but never touch, remove, or vandalize these historic sites or their artifacts; it's a federal offense to do so.

Monticello

㉒ *53 mi south of Moab via U.S. 191.*

Monticello, the seat of San Juan County, is a mostly Mormon community. This quiet town has seen some growth in recent years, mostly in the form of new motels made necessary by a steady stream of tourists venturing south from Moab, but it still offers very few dining or shopping opportunities. Nevertheless, with several inexpensive lodging choices, it's a more convenient alternative to Moab for those visiting the Needles District of Canyonlands National Park. At 7,000 feet, Monticello provides a cool respite from the summer heat of the desert, and it's at the doorstep of the Abajo Mountains. The highest point in the range, 11,360-foot Abajo Peak, is accessed by a road that branches off the graded, 22-mi Blue Mountain Loop (Forest Service Road 105, which begins in Monticello).

The Abajo Loop Scenic Backway (also known as Route 285 or Forest Road 079) climbs to 9,000 feet through the mountains between Monticello and Blanding. This route skirts the base of Abajo Peak and traverses 30 mi of mountainous terrain. The single-lane graded gravel or dirt road is rough and rocky. High clearance and stiff suspension are recommended. The route is impassable in winter and after rain storms. Allow at least three hours to drive this difficult but beautiful drive. Before starting out on any trip into this rugged wilderness area, contact the **Manti–La Sal National Forest** (☎ 435/587–3235) to inquire about road conditions and to get further information about trails.

Blanding

㉓ *25 mi south of Monticello via U.S. 191.*

Pioneers started settling along the base of the Abajo and Henry mountains near Blanding in 1897. Some of the stone buildings they raised still stand, and the town has a number of excellent museums that document the past. Thousands of ancient Pueblo ruins are scattered across the surrounding mesa top. You can't buy alcohol in this solidly Mormon town, and that includes even beer in grocery or convenience stores. Stock up in Monticello, 20 mi north on U.S. 191.

Stretch your legs while you learn about southeastern Utah in the **Blanding Visitor Center.** Maps, guidebooks, and regional books are for sale here, and it's staffed by locals who really know the area. You'll see it right on the highway. ⊠ *12 N. Grayson Pkwy.* ☎ *435/678–3662* ☉ *Apr.–Sept., Mon.–Sat. 8–8; Oct.–Mar., Mon.–Sat. 8–6.*

One of the nation's foremost museums dedicated to the Ancestral Puebloan Indians is at **Edge of the Cedars State Park.** Displays of pots, baskets, spear points, and the only known metal implements from the Anasazi era in Utah are in the museum. The stabilized remains of an ancient pueblo and its ceremonial kiva dominate the park, one of six clusters of ruins within the boundaries. ⊠ *660 W. 400 North St.* ☎ *435/ 678–2238* ⊕ *www.stateparks.utah.gov* ⊠ *$5 per vehicle* ☉ *May–Sept., daily 8–8; Oct.–Apr., daily 9–5.*

🅲 Road-weary travelers, especially children, will enjoy a stop at the **Dinosaur Museum,** the private collection of a family of working paleontologists. Skeletons, fossil logs, and footprints from all over the world are all on display. Hallways hold a collection of movie posters featuring Godzilla and other dinosaurlike monsters dating back to the 1930s. ⊠ *754 S. 200 West St.* ☎ *435/678–3454* ⊠ *$2* ☉ *Apr.–Oct., Mon.–Sat. 9–5.*

off the beaten path

HOVENWEEP NATIONAL MONUMENT – For anyone with an abiding interest in the ancient Anasazi Indians, now called Ancestral Puebloans, a visit to this archaeological site is a must. Along a remote stretch of the Utah–Colorado border southeast of Blanding, Hovenweep features several unusual tower structures that may have been used for making astronomical observations. A ½-mi walking tour, or a more rigorous 1½-mi hike into the canyon, allows you to see the ancient dwellings. A 32-site campground is available for overnighters in tents or small vehicles. ⊠ *28 mi east of U.S. 191 on Rte. 262* ☎ *970/562–4282* ⊕ *www.nps.gov/hove* ⊠ *$6* ☉ *Daily 8 AM–sunset.*

Bluff

㉔ *25 mi south of Blanding via U.S. 191.*

Bluff, settled in 1880, is one of southeastern Utah's oldest towns. Mormon pioneers built a ranching empire that made the town at one time the richest per capita in the state. Although this early period of affluence has passed, several historic Victorian-style homes remain and can be seen on a short walking tour of the town. Pick up the free brochure "Historic Bluff by Bicycle and on Foot" at any business in town, and then take a walk through the era it describes. Most of the original homes from the 1880 town-site of Bluff City are part of the Bluff Historic District. In a dozen or so blocks are 42 historic structures, most built between about 1890 and 1905. On a windswept hill above town, gravestones bear the names of many of the town's first families.

Bluff is something of a supply point for residents of the Navajo Indian Nation, the largest Native American reservation, which lies just beyond the San Juan River. Bluff is a quiet place that has deliberately avoided the development that many nearby towns pursued. The San Juan River corridor and nearby canyons are rich with Native American rock art, dwellings, and other archaeological sites. In September you can see traditional Ute ceremonial dances at the **Bear Dance** (☎ 435/678–3397), sponsored by the White Mesa Ute Council in a three-day celebration held Labor Day weekend.Hot-air balloon enthusiasts gather for the **Bluff International Balloon Festival** (☎ 435/672–2303) each January. Colorful balloons take to the skies over the San Juan River and nearby Valley of the Gods.

Three miles west of Bluff, the **Sand Island Recreation Site** has a large panel of Ancestral Puebloan rock art. The panel includes several large images of Kokopelli, the mischief maker from Pueblo Indian lore. ⊠ *About 3 mi west of Bluff on U.S. 191* ☎ *435/587–1500 Monticello BLM office.*

off the beaten path

FOUR CORNERS MONUMENT – This marker represents the only place in the country where four states—Utah, Arizona, New Mexico, and Colorado—meet. Administered by the Navajo Nation, Four Corners offers not only a geography lesson but also a great opportunity to buy Native American jewelry and other traditional crafts directly from Navajo artisans. Bring cash, as credit cards and checks may not be accepted, particularly when buying from roadside displays or other impromptu marketplaces. To reach the monument, head south from Bluff on U.S. 191 for about 35 mi, to its junction with U.S. 160. (The U.S. 191–U.S. 160 junction is south of the Utah–Arizona border in the Navajo Nation.) Drive east on U.S. 160 for about 30 mi. At this point, U.S. 160 curves north to the monument site.

Sports & the Outdoors

RIVER EXPEDITIONS
While somewhat calmer than the Colorado, the San Juan River offers some truly exceptional scenery and abundant opportunities to visit archaeological sites. It can be run in two sections: from Bluff to Mexican Hat, and from Mexican Hat to Lake Powell. Near Bluff (1½ mi south on U.S. 191), the Sand Island Recreation Site is the launch site for most river trips. You'll find a primitive campground there. Permits from the Bureau of Land Management are required for floating on the San Juan River. For permits, contact the **Bureau of Land Management, Monticello Field Office** (🖰 San Juan Resource Area, Box 7, Monticello 84535 ☎ 435/587–1544).

Wild River Expeditions (⊠ 101 Main St. ☎ 435/672–2244 or 800/422–7654 ⊕ www.riversandruins.com) can take you out on the San Juan River on one- to eight-day float trips. This reliable outfitter is known for educational trips, which emphasize the geology, natural history, and archaeological wonders of the San Juan and its canyons.

Where to Stay & Eat

$–$$ ✕ **Cow Canyon Trading Post.** This tiny but absolutely charming restaurant next to a classic trading post serves three dinner entrées daily. Meals are creative and diverse with a touch of ethnic flair. There's usually a grilled meat with plenty of fresh vegetables, and you can order beer or wine with your meal. ⊠ *Intersection of U.S. 191 and Rte. 163* ☎ *435/672–2208* ▭ *AE, MC, V* ☉ *Closed Nov.–Mar. No lunch.*

¢–$ ⌂ **Desert Rose Inn and Cabins.** Bluff's largest motel is truly a rose in the
Fodor'sChoice desert. It's an attractive log-cabin–style structure with a front porch that
★ gives it a nostalgic touch, and all rooms are spacious and clean with un-
commonly large bathrooms. The cabins have small refrigerators and microwaves. ⊠ *701 W. U.S. 191, 84512* ☎ *435/672–2303 or 888/475–
7673* 🖷 *435/672–2217* ⊕ *www.desertroseinn.com* ⟿ *30 rooms, 6
cabins* ♺ *Some microwaves, some refrigerators, cable TV, in-room data
ports, laundry facilities* ▤ *AE, D, MC, V.*

¢ ⌂ **Recapture Lodge.** Known for its friendliness, this motel can sometimes
offer its guests guided tours into the surrounding canyon country. The
plain, clean rooms come at good prices. This simple lodging option is
a regional favorite, so call ahead for reservations. ⊠ *U.S. 191, Box 309,
84512* ☎ *435/672–2281* 🖷 *435/672–2284* ⊕ *www.bluffutah.org/
recapturelodge/* ⟿ *28 rooms* ♺ *Some kitchenettes, pool, hot tub, laundry facilities* ▤ *AE, D, MC, V.*

Shopping
Comb Ridge Trading Post (⊠ 680 S. U.S. 191 ☎ 435/672–2415) is an absolute gem of a trading post right on the highway. Here you will find
arts and crafts by local Navajo artisans as well as a few well-chosen collectibles.

en route | A red fairyland of slender spires and buttes, the **Valley of the Gods** is
a smaller version of Monument Valley. Approximately 12 mi west of
Bluff, you can take a pretty private drive through this relatively
unvisited area on the 17-mi long Forest Road 242, which winds
through the area and brings you back to Route 163 after depositing
you on Route 261.

Mexican Hat
㉕ *20 mi south of Bluff via U.S. 163.*

Tiny Mexican Hat lies on the north bank of the San Juan River. Named
for a nearby rock formation, which you can't miss on the way into town,
Mexican Hat is a jumping-off point for visiting two geological wonders:
Utah's Goosenecks and Arizona's Monument Valley. Magnificent Monument Valley, stretching to the south into Arizona, is home to many generations of Navajo farmers but is most recognizable from old Westerns.

From the overlook in **Goosenecks State Park** (⊠ Rte. 316, off Rte. 261,
10 mi northwest of Mexican Hat) you can peer down upon what geologists claim is the best example of an "entrenched meander" in the world.
The river's serpentine course resembles the necks of geese in spectacular 1,000-foot-deep chasms. Although the Goosenecks of the San Juan
River is a state park, no facilities other than pit toilets are provided, and
no fee is charged.

The soaring red buttes, eroded mesas, deep canyons, and naturally
sculpted rock formations of **Monument Valley Navajo Tribal Park** are an
easy 21 mi drive south of Mexican Hat on U.S. 163 across Navajo land.
Monument Valley is a small part of the nearly 16-million acre Navajo

CloseUp
WHERE THE WEST WAS FILMED

WERE IT NOT FOR HOLLYWOOD—*with a little help from Harry Goulding—Monument Valley might have remained a quiet, hidden enclave of the Navajo Nation. Goulding urged John Ford to help bring the beauty of Monument Valley to the attention of the America public. Ford began in 1938 with his classic movie Stagecoach, and the film notoriety never ended. Ford subsequently filmed My Darling Clementine, War Party, and She Wore a Yellow Ribbon during the 1940s. Then came Billy the Kid, Kit Carson, Fort Apache, How the West Was Won, The Living Desert, The Searchers, and Cheyenne Autumn. And those were just the John Ford Westerns.*

The area is as popular a film location today as it was in the 1940s and '50s, when Americans (and Hollywood) were just learning about it. Monument Valley is frequently seen as a backdrop for automobile and other commercials. Dozens more films have been shot in the area,

including a few classics (and nonclassics): 2001: A Space Odyssey, Easy Rider, The Moviemakers, National Lampoon's Vacation, Back to the Future Part III, Forrest Gump, Pontiac Moon, Waiting to Exhale, and Windtalkers. While many people associate Monument Valley with filmmaking or as a home to the Navajo Nation, others cannot think about the area without remembering Harry Goulding and his wife Mike, who established the trading post there in 1923. The Gouldings offered crucial trading services to the Navajos for more than half a century. Today, Goulding's Trading Post is on the National Register of Historic Places and still provides lodging, meals, and other services to tourists who visit the area.

Reservation and is sacred to the Navajo Nation, or Diné (pronounced din-*eh*, which means "the people"), as they refer to themselves. For generations, the Navajo have grown crops and herded sheep in Monument Valley, considered to be one of the most scenic and mesmerizing destinations in the Navajo Nation. Director John Ford made this amazing land of buttes, towering rock formations, and mesas popular when he filmed *Stagecoach* here in 1938. The 30,000-acre Monument Valley Navajo Tribal Park lies within Monument Valley. A 17-mi self-guided driving tour on a dirt road (there's only one road, so you can't get lost) passes the memorable **Mittens** and **Totem Pole** formations, among others. Drive slowly, and be sure to walk (15 minutes round-trip) from North Window around the end of Cly Butte for the views. The park has a 99-site campground, which closes from early October through April. Be sure to call ahead for road conditions in winter. The Monument Valley **visitor center** holds a small crafts shop and exhibits devoted to ancient and modern Native American history. Most of the independent guided tours here use enclosed vans, charge about $20 for 2½ hours, and will usually approach you in the parking lot; you can find about a dozen approved Navajo Native American guides in the center. They will escort you to places that you are not allowed to visit on your own. Bring plenty of extra film and batteries to capture this surreal landscape that constantly changes with the rising and setting sun. ⊠ *Visitor center, off U.S. 163, 21 mi south of Mexican Hat, Monument Valley* ⌖ *Box 2520, Window Rock 86515* ☎ *435/727–3353 park visitor center, 928/871–6647 Navajo Parks & Recreation Dept.* ⊕ *www.navajonationparks.org* ⬚ *$3* ☾ *Visitor center May–Sept., daily 7–7; Oct.–Apr., daily 8–5.*

MOKI DUGWAY – Route 261 takes you to the Moki Dugway, a road that was bulldozed out of a cliff during the uranium boom. It's been improved since it was originally built, but its steep grade and tight switchbacks still provide thrills sufficient for most drivers. From the top of the cliff you're rewarded with outrageous views south over the Navajo Reservation with Monument Valley visible over 20 mi away. This drive is not recommended for vehicles over 20 feet in length. ⊠ *Rte. 261, 9 mi north of Rte. 163.*

MULEY POINT OVERLOOK – Five miles beyond the Moki Dugway turnoff on Route 263 brings you to the Muley Point Overlook, which has a panoramic view of the Goosenecks of the San Juan River and Monument Valley. It's also 1,000 feet higher in elevation than the Goosenecks overlook further south.

Where to Stay & Eat

$$$ ✕⊡ **Goulding's Lodge.** With spectacular views of Monument Valley from each room's private balcony, this motel often serves as headquarters for film crews. The lodge has handsome stucco buildings and all the rooms have balconies, coffeemakers, and hair dryers. The on-premises Stagecoach restaurant ($–$$$) serves the area favorite, a Navajo taco, or you can eat traditional American entrées; breakfasts are particularly good. Goulding's also conducts custom-guided tours of Monument Valley and provides Navajo guides into the backcountry. The lodge is 2 mi off U.S. 163, at the Monument Valley Tribal Park turnoff. ⊠ *Off U.S. 163, about 25 mi southwest of Mexican Hat, Box 360001, Monument Valley 84536* ☎ *435/727–3231* 🖷 *435/727–3344* ⊕ *www.gouldings.com* ⬚ *77 rooms* ⚱ *Restaurant, grocery, cable TV, in-room VCRs, pool, shop, laundry facilities, travel services* ▭ *AE, D, DC, MC, V.*

¢–$ ✕⊡ **San Juan Inn & Trading Post.** This spot is a well-known take-out point for white-water runners on the San Juan, a river that vacationing sleuths will recognize as the setting of many of Tony Hillerman's Jim Chee mystery novels. The motel's Southwestern-style, rustic rooms overlooking the river at Mexican Hat are clean and well maintained. Diners can watch the river flow by at the Old Bridge Bar & Grill ($–$$), which serves great grilled steak and juicy hamburgers. Fresh trout and inexpensive Navajo dishes add variety to the menu. ⊠ *U.S. 163* ⌖ *Box 310276, 84531* ☎ *435/683–2220* 🖷 *435/683–2210* ⊕ *www.sanjuaninn.net* ⬚ *39 rooms* ⚱ *Restaurant, grocery, gym, hot tub, laundry facilities, meeting room* ▭ *AE, D, DC, MC, V.*

Nightlife & the Arts

If you find yourself at Goulding's Lodge in the evening, take in the **Earth Spirit Show,** a sound-and-sight show produced by photographer

Ric Ergenbright. Admission to this show is free if you have purchased a Goulding's guided trip through Monument Valley; otherwise, tickets are $2.

Shopping

You can't leave Monument Valley without stopping at the historic **Goulding's Trading Post** (⊠ Off U.S. 163, about 25 mi southwest of Mexican Hat, Monument Valley ☎ 435/727–3231). The store started in a tent in 1923 and the rest, as they say, is history. The trading post has a reputation for selling only authentic Native American art.

Natural Bridges National Monument

26 *33 mi north of Mexican Hat via Rtes. 261 and 275; 38 mi west of Blanding via Rtes. 95 and 275.*

Nowhere but in Natural Bridges National Monument are three large river-carved bridges found so close together. But when Elliot McClure, an early visitor, drove through the park in 1931, using the term "road" to describe the route into the Natural Bridges area was a generous term. It's said that his car literally fell apart on the journey: first his headlights fell off. Next, his doors dropped off. Finally, his bumpers worked loose, and the radiator broke away. Today a trip to see the three stone bridges is far less hazardous. All roads are paved, and a scenic 9-mi drive takes you to stops that overlook Sipapu, Owachomo, and Kachina bridges. Sipapu is the second-largest natural bridge in the world. Kachina is the most massive in the park. It was named for pictographs near its base that resemble katsina dolls. At 106-feet high and 9-feet thick, Owachomo Bridge is the smallest of the three. You'll need an hour or two to drive to overlooks of the natural bridges and remains of an Ancestral Puebloan structure, but if you have more time, you can also hike to each of the bridges on the uncrowded trails that are fragrant with the smell of sage. Sipapu and Kachina are fairly strenuous, with steep trails dropping into the canyon. Owachomo is an easy walk. The scientists among you should be sure to stop by the monument's array of solar panels, once the largest in the world; the solar energy helps keep Natural Bridges National Monument clean and quiet. ⊠ *Rte. 275, off Rte. 95* ☎ *435/692–1234* ⊕ *www.nps.gov/nabr* 🎫 *$6 per vehicle* ⊙ *Daily 7 AM–sunset.*

Lake Powell

27 *50 mi west of Natural Bridges National Monument (to Hall's Crossing) via Rte. 276*

Lake Powell, 185 mi long with 2,000 mi of shoreline—longer than America's Pacific coast—is the heart of the huge 1,255,400-acre Glen Canyon National Recreation Area. Created by the barrier of Glen Canyon Dam—a 710-foot wall of concrete in the Colorado River—Lake Powell took 17 years to fill. The second-largest man-made lake in the nation, Lake Powell extends through terrain so rugged it was the last major area of the United States to be mapped. It's ringed by red cliffs that twist off into 96 major canyons and countless inlets (most accessible only by boat) with huge, red-sandstone buttes randomly jutting from the sapphire waters. You could spend 30 years exploring the lake and still not experience everything there is to see. The Sierra Club has started a movement to drain the lake to restore water-filled Glen Canyon, which some believe was more spectacular than the Grand Canyon, but the lake is likely to be around for years to come, regardless of the final outcome of this plan.

The most popular thing to do at Lake Powell is rent a houseboat and chug leisurely across the lake, exploring coves and inlets. You'll have plenty of company, however, since thousands of people visit the lake during spring, summer, and fall. Fast motorboats, Jet Skis, and sailboats all share the lake. It's a popular spot for bass fishing, but you'll need a Utah fishing license from one of the marinas. Remember also that the lake extends into Arizona and if your voyage takes you across the state line, you'll need a fishing license that covers the southern end of the lake. Unless you love crowds and parties, it's best to avoid visiting during Memorial Day or Labor Day weekends. Because of drought conditions in the West, the level of water in Lake Powell has dropped significantly leading to the closure of boat ramps and marinas. It is important to check with the National Park Service for current water levels, closures, and other weather-related conditions.

Guided day tours are available for those who don't want to rent a boat. A popular full-day or half-day excursion sets out from the Bullfrog and Hall's Crossing marinas to **Rainbow Bridge,** the largest natural bridge in the world, and this 290-foot-high, 275-foot-wide span is a breathtaking sight. The main National Park Service visitor center is at Bullfrog Marina; there's a gas station, campground, general store, and boat docks at the marina. ⊠ *Bullfrog visitor center, Rte. 276* ☎ *435/684–7400* ⊕ *www.nps.gov/glca* ⊡ *Free* ☉ *Apr.–Oct., daily 8–5; Mar., open intermittently depending on weather.*

Hall's Crossing Marina is the eastern terminus of the **Lake Powell Ferry.** You and your car can float across a 3-mi stretch of the lake to the Bullfrog Basin Marina, from which it's an hour's drive north to rejoin Route 95. Ferries run seven days a week and depart on the even hour from Hall's Crossing and on the odd hour from Bullfrog. ⊠ *Hall's Crossing Marina, Rte. 276* ☎ *435/684–7000* ⊡ *$16 per car* ☉ *Mid-May–mid-Sept., daily 8–7; mid-Sept.–Oct. and mid-Apr.–mid-May, daily 8–5; Nov.–mid-Apr., daily 8–3.*

Sports & the Outdoors

Boating and fishing are the major sports at Lake Powell. Conveniently, all powerboat rentals and tours are conducted by the same company, a division of Aramark called **Lake Powell Resorts & Marinas** (⊠ Bullfrog Marina ✉ Box 56909, Phoenix 85079 ☎ 800/528–6154 ⊕ www. lakepowell.com). Daylong tours go to Rainbow Bridge, and there's also a Canyon Explorer tour that goes into some of the more interesting canyons. The company also rents houseboats, which are a popular option on Lake Powell.

Where to Stay

$–$$ ⊞ **Defiance House Lodge.** At the Bullfrog marina, this cliff-top lodge has comfortable and clean rooms, but the real draw is the view. An on-site restaurant also serves three meals a day. Families can take advantage of the three-bedroom units with full kitchens. ⌂ *Bullfrog Marina, Box 4055, Lake Powell 84533* ☎ *435/684–2233 or 800/528–6154* 🖷 *435/684– 3114* ⊕ *www.lakepowell.com* ⇨ *48 rooms, 8 suites* ⚭ *Restaurant, cable TV, boating, marina* ☰ *AE, D, MC, V.*

Hanksville

❷❽ *95 mi northwest of Natural Bridges National Monument via Rte. 95.*

In its early years, Hanksville was the closest settlement to Robbers Roost country, a hangout for Butch Cassidy and his crew of outlaws, the Wild Bunch. Today it's a good place to gas up and grab a burger before continuing north on Route 95.

All of the landscape in this part of the country is strange and surreal, but **Goblin Valley State Park** takes the cake as the weirdest of all. As the name implies, the area is filled with hundreds of gnomelike rock formations. Colored in a dramatic orange hue, the goblins especially delight children. Short, easy trails wind through the goblins, and there's a small, but dusty, campground with modern restrooms and showers. ✉ *Rte. 24, 12 mi north of Hanksville* ☎ *435/564–3633* ⊕ *www. stateparks.utah.gov* 🖾 *$4 per vehicle* ☉ *Daily 8–sunset.*

Where to Eat

¢ ✗ **Stan's Burger Shack.** This is the traditional pit stop along the route between Lake Powell and Capitol Reef. Great burgers, fries, and shakes—and the only homemade onion rings you'll find for miles and miles—can fill your belly. ✉ *140 S. Rte. 95* ☎ *435/542–3330* ☰ *AE, D, MC, V.*

SOUTHEASTERN UTAH A TO Z

To research prices, get advice from other travelers, and book travel arrangements, visit www.fodors.com.

AIR TRAVEL

The nearest large airport to southeastern Utah is Walker Field Airport in Grand Junction, Colorado, 110 mi from Moab. It's served by America West, Sky West, and United Express. Great Lakes Aviation, codeshare partners with United Airlines and Frontier Airlines, offers air service from Phoenix and Denver into Moab's Canyonlands Air Field. 🛪 **Canyonlands Air Field** ✉ 1 Airport Rd., Moab ☎ 435/259-0566. **Walker Field Airport** ✉ Grand Junction, CO ☎ 970/244-9100.

BUS TRAVEL

The only bus service in this part of Utah goes to Green River. 🛪 **Greyhound Lines** ☎ 801/355-9579 or 800/231-2222 ⊕ www.greyhound.com.

CAR RENTAL

Avis and Budget have outlets at Walker Field Airport in Grand Junction, Colorado. Thrifty has an outlet in Moab.

⊠ Avis ⊠ Walker Field, Grand Junction, CO ☎ 970/244-9170 ⊕ www.avis.com. **Budget** ⊠ Walker Field, Grand Junction, CO ☎ 970/244-9155 ⊕ www.budget.com. **Thrifty** ⊠ 1 Airport Rd., Moab ☎ 435/259-7317 ⊕ www.thrifty.com.

CAR TRAVEL

To reach southeastern Utah from Salt Lake City, take I–15 to U.S. 6 and then U.S. 191 south. Take I–70 or U.S. 491 from Colorado and the east. Take U.S. 191 from either Wyoming or Arizona. Most roads are well-maintained two-lane highways. Be sure your car is in good working order, as there are long stretches of empty road between towns, and keep the gas tank topped off.

⊠ Utah Highway Patrol ☎ 435/965-4684 ⊕ www.highwaypatrol.utah.gov. **Utah State Road Conditions** ☎ 511 toll-free within Utah.

EMERGENCIES

⊠ Ambulance or Police Emergencies ☎ 911.
⊠ 24-Hour Medical Care Allen Memorial Hospital ⊠ 719 W. 4th North St., Moab ☎ 435/259-7191. **Blanding Medical Center** ⊠ 930 N. 400 West St., Blanding ☎ 435/678-3434. **Green River Medical Center** ⊠ 305 W. Main St., Green River ☎ 435/564-3434. **San Juan County Hospital** ⊠ 364 W. 1st North St., Monticello ☎ 435/587-2116.

LODGING

Some of the best values in Moab are condominiums. Moab Lodging and Central Reservations, a very professional firm, handles reservations for these units and dozens of other motels, condos, and B&Bs in all price ranges in southeastern Utah.

⊠ Moab Lodging and Central Reservations ☎ 435/259-5125, 800/505-5343, or 800/748-4386 ⊠ 435/259-6079 ⊕ www.moabutahlodging.com.

CAMPING Camping opportunities are abundant and gloriously beautiful throughout southeastern Utah. The area around Moab not only offers camping within the nearby national parks, but up and down the Colorado River corridor. Green River State Park is a favorite shady campground on the banks of the Green River. Lake Powell offers miles of shoreline as well as developed campgrounds. For cooler climes in the summer months, try La Sal Mountains near Moab. There are 342 sites at 18 different Bureau of Land Management campgrounds near Arches and Canyonlands national parks. Most of these are in the Moab area, near Arches and Canyonlands' Island in the Sky District, along Route 128's Colorado River corridor, on Kane Creek Road, and on Sand Flats Road. All sites are primitive and, except for Wind Whistle and Hatch Point, have no water. Campsites are available only on a first-come, first-served basis. The BLM's Moab Field Office can give you a complete listing of campsites in the area. The Moab Information Center has information on Bureau of Land Management, National Forest Service, and National Park Service campgrounds in nearby areas. The Moab or Monticello Ranger District offices of the Manti–La Sal National

Forest can give you information on Forest Service campgrounds in their respective areas.

🔳 **Bureau of Land Management Moab Office** ☎ 435/259-6111 ⊕ www.blm.gov. **Manti-La Sal National Forest** ☎ 435/259-7155 Moab Ranger District, 435/587-2041 Monticello Ranger District ⊕ www.fs.fed.us/r4/mantilasal. **Moab Information Center** ☎ 435/259-8825 ⊕ www.discovermoab.com.

MEDIA

NEWSPAPERS & MAGAZINES Newspapers and magazines in southeastern Utah are published weekly or monthly. The *Times-Independent* gives folks in Moab news on a weekly basis. *Moab Happenings* is a great tool for visitors to the area; it includes a calender of events and options for activities, shopping, restaurants and other necessities for travelers. The *San Juan Record* is the local newspaper for lands south of Moab.

TELEVISION & RADIO Moab's Community Radio Station, KZMU (89.7 FM), will give you a variety of music and community information while you travel in the Moab area. For country music on your travels throughout southeastern Utah, select Canyon Country Radio, KCYN (97.1 FM).

TOURS

Another dramatic way to see southeastern Utah is by air. Trips are available throughout the area including flights over Lake Powell.

🔳 **Slickrock Air Guides** ⓓ Box 901, Moab 84532 ☎ 435/259-6216 ⊕ www. slickrockairguides.com.

TRAIN TRAVEL

The only train service in southeastern Utah is to Green River via Amtrak.

🔳 **Amtrak** ☎ 800/872-7245 ⊕ www.amtrak.com.

VISITOR INFORMATION

🔳 **Arches National Park** ✉ N. U.S. 191, Moab 84532 ☎ 435/719-2299 or 435/259-2200 ⊕ www.nps.gov/arch. **Blanding Chamber of Commerce** ⓓ Box 792, Blanding 84511 ☎ 435/678-2791 or 800/574-4386 ⊕ www.blandingutah.org. **Blanding Visitor Center** ✉ 12 N. Grayson, Blanding 84511 ☎ 435/678-3662 ⊕ www.blanding.net. **BLM Grand Resource Area** ⓓ Box M, Moab 84532 ☎ 435/259-8193 ⊕ www.ut.blm.gov. **Business Owners of Bluff** ⊕ www.bluffutah.org. **Canyonlands National Park** ✉ 2282 W. Resource Blvd., Moab 84532 ☎ 435/719-2313, 435/259-4351 Backcountry Reservation Office ⊕ www.nps.gov/cany. **Grand County Travel Council** ✉ 125 E. Center St., Moab 84532 ☎ 435/259-1370, 435/259-8825, or 800/635-6622 ⊕ www.discovermoab.com. **Green River Information Center** ✉ 885 E. Main St., Green River 84525 ☎ 435/564-3427. **San Juan County Visitor Services** ✉ 117 S. Main St., Box 490, Monticello 84535 ☎ 435/587-3235 or 800/574-4386 ⊕ www.southeastutah.com.

INDEX

NOTES

NOTES

NOTES

NOTES

NOTES

NOTES

NOTES

NOTES

NOTES

ABOUT OUR WRITERS

Writer and photojournalist **John Blodgett** moved to Utah in 1996. He's explored almost every corner of the Beehive State but has a particular passion for the south. It was in these silent canyons and wide-open lands of sage brush and juniper that John discovered a new muse. He also became a much better skier schussing Utah's famous powder. He has written for *Utah Business, Digital IQ, Salt Lake Magazine, Utah Homes & Garden, Salt Lake City Weekly,* and *Catalyst*; and is a former magazine editor, newspaper reporter, and photographer. He updated the Salt Lake City, Smart Travel Tips, and the Bryce and Zion chapters for this book.

Freelance writer **Kelley J. P. Lindberg,** who wrote the Eastern Utah chapter, moved to the state two decades ago and promptly fell under the spell of its mountains, deserts, rivers, and canyons. She travels extensively, but is most at home where the Utah wind carves rock into cathedrals. She loves writing about Utah and has written extensively for *Salt Lake Magazine, Utah Outdoors, Utah Business,* and other regional and national magazines. She's also the best-selling author of a dozen books about software.

Janet Lowe began exploring the Southwest in 1985 and relocated to Moab a few years later to head up the publications and operations department for the Canyonlands Natural History Association. Now a full-time writer, she has published two books on Arches and Canyonlands national parks as well as *Into the Mystery: A Driving Guide to Moab Area Rock Art.* In 2003, she completed the *Arches Audio Tour,* a driving tour of Arches National Park. Her essays appeared for six years in *Moab Happenings,* and she has written for the Moab newspaper, the *Times-Independent,* for which she won a Utah Press Association award for feature-writing in 2003. A frequent contributor to Fodor's, she has explored Utah and its national parks for more than a decade. More of her essays will appear in the 2006 book, *The Natural Superiority of Mules.*

Dana Doherty Menlove and **Mark Menlove** have been exploring Utah most of their lives, in recent years with their two young children Asa and Eliza. A contributing writer to *Park City Magazine,* Dana also works as a freelance editor. Mark's writing has been syndicated in the High Country News series *Writers on the Range* and appears in several anthologies.